EPHESIANS

THE ANCHOR BIBLE is a fresh approach to the world's greatest classic. Its object is to make the Bible accessible to the modern reader; its method is to arrive at the meaning of biblical literature through exact translation and extended exposition, and to reconstruct the ancient setting of the biblical story, as well as the circumstances of its transcription and the characteristics of its transcribers.

THE ANCHOR BIBLE is a project of international and interfaith scope: Protestant, Catholic, and Jewish scholars from many countries contribute individual volumes. The project is not sponsored by any ecclesiastical organization and is not intended to reflect any particular theological doctrine. Prepared under our joint supervision, THE ANCHOR BIBLE is an effort to make available all the significant historical and linguistic knowledge which bears on the interpretation of the biblical record.

THE ANCHOR BIBLE is aimed at the general reader with no special formal training in biblical studies; yet, it is written with the most exacting standards of scholarship, reflecting the highest technical accomplishment.

This project marks the beginning of a new era of co-operation among scholars in biblical research, thus forming a common body of knowledge to be shared by all.

William Foxwell Albright
David Noel Freedman
GENERAL EDITORS

Following the death of senior editor W. F. Albright, The Anchor Bible Editorial Board was established to advise and assist David Noel Freedman in his continuing capacity as general editor. The three members of the Editorial Board are among the contributors to the Anchor Bible. They have been associated with the series for a number of years and are familiar with its methods and objectives. Each is a distinguished authority in his area of specialization, and in concert with the others, will provide counsel and judgment as the series continues.

EDITORIAL BOARD

Frank M. Cross   Old Testament
Raymond E. Brown   New Testament
Jonas C. Greenfield   Apocrypha

EPHESIANS

Translation and
Commentary on Chapters 4–6
by

MARKUS BARTH

1974

DOUBLEDAY & COMPANY, INC.

GARDEN CITY, NEW YORK

Lyrics from *Camelot* on p. 701, fn. 360:
Copyright © 1960 by Alan Jay Lerner and Frederick Loewe. Used by permission of Chappell & Co., Inc.

ISBN: 0-385-08037-9
Library of Congress Catalog Card Number 72–79373
Copyright © 1974 by Doubleday & Company, Inc.
Printed in the United States of America
First Edition

CONTENTS

PRINCIPAL ABBREVIATIONS

I VERSIONS OF THE BIBLE

ASV	The American Standard Version, 1901
JB	The Jerusalem Bible. New York: Doubleday, 1966
KJ	The King James, or Authorized Version of 1611
LXX	The Septuagint, ed. E. Rahlfs. Stuttgart: Württembergische Bibelgesellschaft, 1935
MT	Masoretic (Hebrew or Aramaic) Text of the Old Testament
NEB	The New English Bible. Oxford University Press / Cambridge University Press, 1970
NTTEV	Good News for Modern Man: The New Testament in Today's English Version. New York: American Bible Society, 1960
Pesh.	The Peshitta, a fourth- or fifth-century Syriac version of the Old and New Testaments
RSV	The Revised Standard Version, 1946, 1952
RV	The Revised Version, 1881
SegB	Segond Bible, rev. ed. Geneva: Maison de la Bible, 1964
Symm.	Symmachus' version of the Old Testament, in Greek, late second century A.D.
Theod.	Theodotion's version of the Old Testament, in Greek, second century A.D.
Vulg.	The Vulgate, Jerome's Latin translation of the Bible, late fourth century A.D.
ZB	Zürcher Bibel, Zurich: Zwingli-Verlag, 1935

Note: When in the RSV and other versions the numbering of verses differs (e.g. by one digit) from that of the Greek New Testament text, the numbers of Nestle's Greek text are used.

II SERIES, JOURNALS, AND FREQUENTLY QUOTED MONOGRAPHS

AB	The Anchor Bible. New York: Doubleday, 1964–
AER	American Ecclesiastical Review. Washington
AFAW	Annalen der finnischen Akademie der Wissenschaften. Helsinki
AnBib	Analecta Biblica. Rome: Pontifical Biblical Institute
ANET	*Ancient Near Eastern Texts Relating to the Old Testament,* ed. J. B. Pritchard. 2d ed. Princeton University Press, 1955

ANS   Auslegung neutestamentlicher Schriften. Zurich: EVZ
ARW   Archiv für Religionswissenschaft. Leipzig and Freiburg
ASNU   Acta Seminarii Neotestamentici Upsaliensis. Lund: Gleerup
ATANT   Abhandlungen zur Theologie des Alten und Neuen Testa-
            ments. Zurich: Zwingli
BBB   Bonner Biblische Beiträge. Bonn: Hanstein
BDF   F. W. Blass and A. Debrunner, tr. and rev. of 9th–10th Ger-
            man ed. by R. W. Funk, *A Greek Grammar of the New
            Testament and Other Early Christian Literature.* University
            of Chicago Press, 1961. References to sections
BEvTh   Beiträge zur evangelischen Theologie. Munich: Kaiser
BHTh   Beiträge zur historischen Theologie. Tübingen: Mohr
BhZAW   Beihefte zur Zeitschrift für die alttestamentliche Wissenschaft.
            Giessen (1896–1934) and Berlin: Töpelmann, 1936–
BhZNW   Beihefte zur Zeitschrift für die neutestamentliche Wissenschaft
            und die Kunde der älteren Kirche. Giessen (1923–34) and
            Berlin: Töpelmann, 1936–
BiRes   Papers of the Chicago Society of Biblical Research. Amster-
            dam: North-Holland Publishing Co., 1956–
BiST   Biblical Studies. London: SPCK
BiTod   The Bible Today. Collegeville, Minnesota
BJRL   The Bulletin of the John Rylands Library. Manchester
BWANT   Beiträge zur Wissenschaft vom Alten und Neuen Testament.
            Stuttgart: Kohlhammer
BZ   Biblische Zeitschrift. Paderborn
CAK   *Christus, das All und die Kirche,* by F. Mussner, Trierer
            Theologische Studien 5. Trier: Paulinus-Verlag, 1955, repr.
            1968
CBQ   The Catholic Biblical Quarterly. Washington
CD   Covenant of Damascus
Christus   *Christus und die Kirche im Epheserbrief,* by H. Schlier, BHTh
            6, 1930, repr. 1966
ConcTM   Concordia Theological Monthly. St. Louis, Missouri
CNT   Commentaire du Nouveau Testament. Neuchâtel / Paris:
            Delachaux
ConNT   Coniectanea Neotestamentica. Lund: Gleerup
CRCO   *Corpus Reformatorum, Calvini Opera.* Brunswick:
            Schwetschke, 1863–1900, repr. New York: Johnson, 1964.
            References to columns
CTh   Cahiers Theologiques. Neuchâtel / Paris: Delachaux
CV   Communio Viatorum. Prague
DB   *Dictionnaire de la Bible,* ed. F. Vigoroux, 5 vols., Paris:
            Letouzy, 1895–1912; suppl. vols., ed. F. Pirot, 7 vols. to
            date, 1928–
DFKP   *Die Form der katalogischen Paränese,* by E. Kamlah, WUNT
            7, 1964

EBP   *Ephesians, Baptism and Pentecost,* by J. C. Kirby. McGill
           University Press, 1968
EcuR   Ecumenical Review. Geneva
EE   *The Epistle to the Ephesians: Its Authorship, Origin and Pur-
           pose,* by C. L. Mitton. Oxford: Clarendon Press, 1951
ÉHPR   Études d'Histoire et de Philosophie Religieuses. Paris
EJ   *Encyclopaedia Judaica,* 10 vols. (A–L). Berlin: Eschkol,
           1928–34
EJb   Eranos Jahrbuch. Zurich
ERE   *Encyclopedia of Religion and Ethics,* ed. J. Hastings, 13 vols.
           New York: Scribner's, 1908–27
ET   Expository Times. Aberdeen / Edinburgh
ETL   Ephemerides Theologicae Lovanienses. Louvain: Gembloux
EuG   *Der Epheserbrief und die Gnosis,* by P. Pokorný. Berlin:
           Evangelische Verlagsanstalt, 1965
EvTh   Evangelische Theologie. Munich
FBK   P. Feine, J. Behm, and W. G. Kümmel. *Introduction to the
           New Testament.* Nashville: Abingdon, 1965
First Peter *The First Epistle of St. Peter,* by E. G. Selwyn. London:
           Macmillan, 1947
FRLANT   Forschungen zur Religion und Literatur des Alten und Neuen
           Testaments. Göttingen: Vandenhoeck
GeistLeb   Geist und Leben. Würzburg
GMG   *Der Gott "Mensch" in der Gnosis,* by H.-M. Schenke. Göt-
           tingen: Vandenhoeck, 1962
GNT   *The Greek New Testament,* eds. K. Aland, M. Black, B. M.
           Metzger, A. Wikgren. Stuttgart: American Bible Society,
           1966
HbNT   *Handbuch zum Neuen Testament,* 21 vols. Tübingen: Mohr,
           1911 ff.
HCNT   *Hand-Commentar zum Neuen Testament,* ed. H. J. Holtz-
           mann, 4 vols. Freiburg: Mohr, 1889–91
HDB   *Hastings Dictionary of the Bible,* eds. F. C. Grant and H. H.
           Rowley. Rev. ed. New York: Scribner's, 1963
HE   *Historia Ecclesiastica,* by Eusebius of Caesarea
HMyRel   *Die hellenistischen Mysterienreligionen,* by R. Reitzenstein,
           3d ed. Leipzig: Teubner, 1927
HR   History of Religions. Chicago
HSNT   *Die Heilige Schrift Neuen Testaments,* by J. C. K. von
           Hofmann. 11 vols. Nördlingen: Beck, 1868–86
HTR   Harvard Theological Review. Cambridge, Massachusetts
HUCA   Hebrew Union College Annual. Cincinnati
Hymnen   *Frühchristliche Hymnen,* by G. Schille. Berlin: Evangelische
           Verlagsanstalt, 1965
IB   *The Interpreter's Bible,* 12 vols. Nashville: Abingdon, 1951–
           57
ICC   *International Critical Commentary.* Edinburgh: Clark, 1899–

IDB	*The Interpreter's Dictionary of the Bible,* 4 vols. Nashville: Abingdon, 1962
IKZ	Internationale kirchliche Zeitschrift. Bern
ITQ	Irish Theological Quarterly. Maynooth
JBL	Journal of Biblical Literature. Philadelphia and Missoula
JbLW	Jahrbuch für Liturgiewissenschaft. Münster: Aschendorff
JE	*Jewish Encyclopedia,* 12 vols. New York / London: Funk & Wagnalls, 1901–6
JES	Journal of Ecumenical Studies. Pittsburgh and Philadelphia
JJS	Journal of Jewish Studies. Manchester
JNES	Journal of Near Eastern Studies. Chicago
JQR	Jewish Quarterly Review. London / Philadelphia
JR	Journal of Religion. Chicago
JSS	Journal of Semitic Studies. Manchester
JThC	Journal for Theology and the Church. New York: Harper
JTS	Journal of Theological Studies. London
KEKNT	*Kritisch-exegetischer Kommentar über das Neue Testament,* ed. H. A. W. Meyer, 16 vols. Göttingen: Vandenhoeck, 1832–
KT	Kleine Texte, ed. H. Lietzmann. Berlin: De Gruyter
KTH	Kirchlich Theologische Hefte. Munich
LSLex	H. G. Liddell and R. Scott, *A Greek-English Lexicon* (1843), 9th ed. Oxford: Clarendon Press, 1940, repr. 1953
LUA	Lunds Universitets Arsskrift. Lund: Gleerup
LuthW	Lutheran World. Geneva
MNTC	The Moffat New Testament Commentary, 17 vols. New York: Harper, 1928–50
Nestle	*Novum Testamentum Graece,* 25th ed., eds. E. Nestle and K. Aland. Stuttgart: Württembergische Bibelanstalt, 1963
NovT	Novum Testamentum. Leiden
NRT	Nouvelle Revue Théologique. Louvain
NTA	New Testament Abstracts. Weston, Massachusetts
NTAbh	Neutestamentliche Abhandlungen. Münster: Aschendorff
NTD	Das Neue Testament Deutsch, 12 vols. Göttingen: Vandenhoeck, 1932–
NTF	Neutestamentliche Forschungen. Gütersloh: Bertelsmann
NTS	New Testament Studies. Cambridge
OTTh	*Old Testament Theology,* by G. von Rad. 2 vols. New York: Harper, 1962, 1965
Pauly-Wissowa	*Real-Enzyklopädie der classischen Altertumswissenschaft,* ed. A. Pauly (1839 ff.), rev. G. von Wissowa et al. (1894 ff.), 1st series, 24 vols., 1894–1963; 2d series, 9 vols., 1914–67; 12 suppl. vols., 1903–70. Stuttgart: Metzler
PG	Patrologia Graeca, ed. J.-P. Migne. Paris: Migne. References to columns
PL	Patrologia Latina, ed. J.-P. Migne. Paris: Migne. References to columns

PRE   *Realencyklopädie für protestantische Theologie und Kirche,* 18
             vols. Leipzig: Hinrichs, 1877–88
PRJ   *Paul and Rabbinic Judaism,* by W. D. Davies. London:
             SPCK, 1955
PSM   *Paul and the Salvation of Mankind,* by J. Munck. Richmond,
             Virginia: Knox, 1959
1Q   Dead Sea scrolls from the first cave
1QGen Apocr. Qumran Genesis Apocryphon
1QH   Qumran Hodayoth (Hymns of Thanksgiving)
1QM   Qumran Milḥama (War Scroll)
1QpHab   Qumran Pesher on Habakkuk
1QS   Qumran Sereq (Manual of Discipline)
1QSb   Qumran Benedictions
1QTest   Qumran Testimonia
1Q27   Qumran Book of Mysteries
4Q   Documents from the fourth cave, etc.
QuNT   *Qumran und das Neue Testament,* by H. Braun. 2 vols.
             Tübingen: Mohr, 1966
RAC   Reallexikon für Antike und Christentum, ed. J. Hoops, 7 vols.
             to date. Stuttgart: Hiersemann, 1924–
RB   Revue Biblique. Paris
RecB   Recherches Bibliques. Louvain: Desclée
RelgS   *Die religionsgeschichtliche Schule,* I, by C. Colpe, FRLANT
             78, 1961
RGG   *Religion in Geschichte und Gegenwart,* 3d ed., 6 vols. Tü-
             bingen: Mohr, 1957–62. References to columns
RHPR   Revue d'Histoire et de Philosophie Religieuses. Strassbourg
RivBib   Rivista Biblica. Brescia.
RQum   Revue de Qumrân. Paris.
RSPR   Revue des Sciences Philosophiques et Religieuses. Paris
RSR   Recherches de science religieuse. Paris
SaNT   *The Scrolls and the New Testament,* ed. K. Stendahl. New
             York: Harper, 1957
SbHA   Sitzungsberichte der Heidelberger Akademie der Wissen-
             schaften. Heidelburg
SBM   Stuttgarter biblische Monographien. Stuttgart: Katholisches
             Bibelwerk
SbPA   Sitzungsberichte der Preussischen Akademie der Wissen-
             schaften, Berlin
SBT   Studies in Biblical Theology. London: SCM, and Naperville:
             Allenson
SBU   Symbolae Biblicae Upsalienses. Supplement Litteratur, Svensk
             Exegetisk Arsbok, Lund: Gleerup
ScEccl   Sciences Ecclésiastiques. Montreal
ScotJT   Scottish Journal of Theology. Edinburgh
SNT   *Die Schriften des Neuen Testaments,* 2 vols., ed. J. Weiss,
             2d ed. Göttingen: Vandenhoeck, 1907, 1908

SNVA	Skrifter utgitt ar Det Norske Videnskaps-Akademie. Oslo
ST	Studia Theologica. Lund
StB	H. L. Strack and P. Billerbeck, *Kommentar zum Neuen Testament aus Talmud und Midrasch,* 6 vols. Munich: Beck, 1922–61
STK	Svensk Teologisk Kvartalskrift. Lund
SUNT	Studien zur Umwelt des Neuen Testaments. Göttingen: Vandenhoeck
TB	Theologische Blätter. Leipzig and Bonn
TF	Theologische Forschung. Hamburg: Reiche
ThNT	*Theology of the New Testament,* by R. Bultmann. 2 vols. New York: Harper, 1951, 1955
TLZ	Theologische Literaturzeitung. Halle and Berlin
TQ	Theologische Quartalschrift. Munich, Freiburg, Tübingen
TSK	Theologische Studien und Kritiken. Hamburg, Gotha, Leipzig, Berlin
TT	Theology Today. Princeton
TTK	Tidsskrift for Teologi og Kirke. Oslo
TTS	Trierer theologische Studien. Trier
TTZ	Trierer theologische Zeitschrift. Trier
TU	Texte und Untersuchungen. Berlin: Akademie-Verlag
TWNT	*Theologisches Wörterbuch zum Neuen Testament,* eds. G. Kittel and G. Friedrich, 8 vols. to date. Stuttgart: Kohlhammer, 1932–
TWNTE	*Theological Dictionary of the New Testament* (same work as above but tr. into English by G. W. Bromiley, 7 vols. to date). Grand Rapids: Eerdmans, 1964–
TZ	Theologische Zeitschrift. Basel
Unity	*The Unity of the Church in the New Testament,* by S. Hanson. Uppsala: Almqvist, 1946
VD	Verbum Domini. Rome
VigChr	Vigiliae Christianae. Amsterdam
VT	Vetus Testamentum. Leiden
VTS	Vetus Testamentum Supplements. Leiden: Brill
WA	Weimarer Ausgabe of Luther's Works. Leipzig and Cologne: Böhlau, 1883–
WAATNT	Wissenschaftliche Abhandlungen zum Alten Testament und Neuen Testament. Neukirchen
WBLex	Walter Bauer, *A Greek-English Lexicon of the New Testament and Other Early Christian Literature.* Tr. from the rev. Germ. ed. by W. F. Arndt and F. W. Gingrich, Chicago University Press, 1957
WMANT	Wissenschaftliche Monographien zum Alten und Neuen Testament. Neukirchen
WoDie	Wort und Dienst, Jahrbuch der Theologischen Schule. Bethel bei Bielefeld

WUNT	Wissenschaftliche Untersuchungen zum Neuen Testament. Tübingen: Mohr
WZKM	Wiener Zeitschrift für die Kunde des Morgenlandes. Vienna
WZUH	Wissenschaftliche Zeitschrift der Universität. Halle
ZAW	Zeitschrift für die alttestamentliche Wissenschaft. Giessen and Berlin
ZEE	Zeitschrift für evangelische Ethik. Gütersloh
ZKT	Zeitschrift für katholische Theologie. Innsbruck
ZNW	Zeitschrift für die neutestamentliche Wissenschaft und die Kunde der älteren Kirche. Giessen and Berlin
ZRG	Zeitschrift für Religions- und Geistesgeschichte. Erlangen
ZST	Zeitschrift für systematische Theologie. Gütersloh
ZTK	Zeitschrift für Theologie und Kirche. Tübingen

Note: Titles of ancient Greek, Hellenistic, Latin, and Talmudic writings are abbreviated usually after the pattern used in LSLex, TWNT, StB, or the Loeb editions.

III OTHER ABBREVIATIONS

AT	Altes Testament, Ancien Testament (OT)
Bab	Babylonian
Bh	Beiheft (Supplement)
C.E.	Christian Era (=A.D., after Christ)
ch.	chapter
diss.	Unpublished doctoral dissertation
Fs	Festschrift (anniversary volume, in honor of, etc.)
Hb	Handbuch (handbook, manual)
lit.	Literal, word-by-word translation which appears to render the Greek exactly but may not express its meaning
MS, MSS	Manuscript, manuscripts
N.F.	Neue Folge (New Series)
N.S.	New Series, nouvelle série
NT	New Testament, Neues Testament, Nouveau Testament
OT	Old Testament
par.	and parallel passages (e.g. in Matthew or Luke)
qu.	question
(ref.)	by reference only, original text not consulted
repr.	reprint(ed)
var. lect.	*varia lectio* (variant reading of some Greek NT manuscripts)

Note: For works cited by author's name only throughout both volumes, see Bibliography I, Commentaries and Special Studies, at the back of either volume. If not found there, they will be found in the bibliography to the section in which the reference occurs. Sectional Bibliographies 1–16 appear at the back of volume 34, Sectional Bibliographies 17–22 at the back of volume 34A.

TRANSLATION OF EPHESIANS

1 [1] From Paul who by God's decision is apostle of the Messiah Jesus, to the saints (in Ephesus) who are faithful to the Messiah Jesus. [2] Grace and peace to you from God our Father and the Lord Jesus Christ.

[3] Blessed is God the Father of our Lord Jesus Christ. He has blessed us in Christ with the full spiritual blessing of the heavens. [4] As [we confess]
> Before the foundation of the world he has chosen us in Christ
> to live by love [standing] holy and blameless before him.
[5] He has predesignated us through Jesus Christ to become his children
> according to his favorable decision
[6] so that the glory of his grace be praised
> which in his beloved son he has poured out upon us.
[7] Through [the shedding of] his blood
> we possess freedom in him, forgiveness of our lapses.
Such are the riches of his grace
> [8] which in all wisdom and prudence he has lavished upon us.
[9] He has made known to us the secret of his decision
> —for he has set his favor first upon Christ
[10] that he should administer the days of fulfillment—
"All things are to be comprehended under one head, the Messiah,
> Those in heaven and upon earth—under him!"

[11] As resolved by him who carries out all things after his will and decision, we [Jews] were first designated and appropriated in the Messiah. [12] We, the first to set our hope upon the Messiah, were to become a praise of God's glory. [13] You [Gentiles] too are [included] in him. For you have heard the true word, the message that saves you. And after you came to faith you, too, have been sealed with his seal, the promised Holy Spirit.

> [14] He is the guarantee of what we shall inherit
> [to vouch] for the liberation of God's own people,
> to the praise of his glory.

[15] Therefore, after hearing of the faithfulness [shown] among you to the Lord Jesus and (of the love) toward all the saints, I, for my part, [16] never cease to give thanks for you. When mentioning you in my prayers [17] [I ask] that the God of our Lord Jesus Christ, the all-glorious Father, give you the Spirit of wisdom and revelation so that you may know him [18] [. I ask] that he illumine the

eyes of your hearts so that you may become aware of the hope to which he is calling you, what glorious riches are to be inherited among the saints, 19 and how exceedingly great is his power over us believers. For that mighty strength is at work 20 which God has exerted in the Messiah when

> He has raised him from the dead.
> He has enthroned him at his right hand in the heavens
> 21 above every government and authority,
> power and dominion, and any title bestowed,
> not only in this age but also in the age to come.
> 22 He put everything under his feet
> and appointed him, the head over all, to be head of the church.
> 23 She is his body, full of him
> who fills all things totally.

2 1 You [Gentiles], especially, dead as you were in your lapses and sins . . . 2 in the past your steps were bound by them [. You were] following [the inspiration of] this world-age, the ruler of the atmosphere, that spirit which is now at work among the rebellious men. 3 In the past all of us [Jews], too, followed these ways. In our own fleshly passions, we did whatever our flesh and our thoughts decided. As much as the rest of mankind we were by nature under the wrath [of God]. 4 But

> God who is rich in mercy
> —for he loves us with all his love—
> 5 just because we were dead in our lapses
> has made us alive together with the Messiah.
> By grace you are saved!
> 6 For he has in the Messiah Jesus
> raised and enthroned us together in the heavens.
> 7 In order to prove throughout the ages to come,
> through the goodness [shown] to us in the Messiah Jesus,
> how infinitely rich in his grace.
> 8 By grace you are saved, through faith!

This [was] not out of your own doing—it is a gift of God— 9 not [as a reward] for works lest anyone boast about himself. For

> 10 God himself has made us what we are.
> In the Messiah Jesus we are created
> for those good works which God has provided
> as our way of life.

11 Remember, then, that in the past [and] in the realm of flesh you, the Gentiles—called The Uncircumcision by those who call themselves The Circumcision, that handmade operation in the realm of flesh . . . 12 [Remember] that at that time you were apart from the Messiah, excluded from the citizenship of Israel, strangers to the convenants based upon promise. In this world you were bare of hope and without God. 13 But now you are [included] in the

realm of the Messiah Jesus. Through the blood of the Messiah you who in the past stood far off have been brought near. 14 For [we confess]

> He is in person the peace between us.
> He has made both [Gentiles and Jews] into one.
> For he has broken down the dividing wall,
> in his flesh [he has wiped out all] enmity.
> 15 He has abolished the law [, that is, only] the
> commandments [expressed] in statutes.
> [This was] to make peace by creating in his person
> a single new man out of the two,
> 16 and to reconcile both to God
> through the cross in one single body.
> In his own person he has killed the enmity.
> 17 Indeed when he came he proclaimed good news:
> "Peace to you who are far and peace to those near!"
> 18 Through him and in one single Spirit
> the two [of us] have free access to the Father.

19 Accordingly you are no longer strangers and sojourners, but you are fellow citizens with the saints and members of the household of God. 20 You are built upon the foundation of the apostles and prophets, the keystone being the Messiah Jesus himself. 21 The whole construction, fitted together in him, grows in the Lord into a holy temple. 22 In him you, too, are being built together so as to be a dwelling of God in the Spirit.

3   1 For this reason I, Paul, the prisoner of the Messiah Jesus for the sake of you Gentiles . . . 2 surely you have heard that I was given God's grace in order to administer it to you. 3 As I have briefly written above, the secret was made known to me by revelation. 4 Correspondingly, by reading [this] you are able to perceive how I understand the secret of the Messiah.

> 5 In other generations it was not made known
> to the Sons of Men
> as it is now revealed through the Spirit
> to his holy apostles and prophets:

6 In the Messiah Jesus [and] through the gospel, the Gentiles are joint heirs, members in the same body, fellow beneficiaries in all that is promised. 7 Through the gift of God's grace which was given me—for his power is at work—I was made a servant of the gospel. 8 I, who am less than the least of all saints, was given the special grace to announce to the Gentiles the good news of the unfathomable riches of the Messiah 9 and to make all men see how the secret is administered [by the Messiah] that was hidden from the ages in God the creator of all things: 10 The manifold wisdom of God is now to be made known through the church to the governments and authorities in the heavens. 11 This is the design concerning the ages which God has carried out in the Messiah Jesus, our Lord. 12 In him and because of his faithfulness, confidently we make use of our free access [to God]. 13 Therefore I ask [God] that you do not lose heart over the tribulations I suffer for you. For they are your glorification.

14 For this reason I bow my knees before the Father 15 from whom each family in heaven and on earth receives its name: 16 Rich as he is in glory may he grant that through his Spirit you be fortified with power [to grow] toward the Inner Man 17 [i.e.] that through faith the Messiah may dwell in your hearts. Stand firm on the root and foundation of love. 18 May you be strong enough to grasp together with all the saints what is the breadth, the length, the height, the depth, 19 and to know the love of Christ though it surpasses knowledge. May you become so perfect as to attain to the full perfection of God.

20 To him who by the power exerted in us
is able to outdo superabundantly
all that we ask or imagine—
21 Glory to him in the church and in the Messiah Jesus
from generation to generation,
for ever and ever! Amen.

4 1 Therefore I beseech you, prisoner in the Lord['s service] as I am, to conduct yourselves as men worthy of the vocation to which you were called. 2 Be altogether humble and gentle. Patiently bear one another in love. 3 Take pains to maintain the unity of the Spirit through the bond of peace.

4 One body and one Spirit,

just as there is one hope to which you have been called.

5 One Lord, one faith, one baptism,
6 one God who is Father of all,
he is over all, through all, and in all.

7 The gift of the Messiah is the measure after which grace was given to each of us. 8 Therefore he says,

"When he ascended to the height
he captured a catch of prisoners,
he gave gifts to men."

9 What else does the term "he ascended" imply except that he also descended down to the earth? 10 He who descended is the one who ascended far above all heavens in order to fill all things.

11 He is the one who appointed
these to be apostles and those to be prophets,
some to be evangelists and others to be teaching shepherds
12 to equip the saints for the work of service
for building the Messiah's body
13 until we all come to meet
the unifying faith and knowledge of the Son of God,
the Perfect Man,
the perfection of the Messiah who is the standard of manhood.

14 No longer are we to be babes, tossed by waves and whirled about by every doctrinal gust, [and caught] in the trickery of men who are experts in deceitful scheming. 15 Rather by speaking the truth in love we shall grow in every way toward him who is the head, the Messiah. 16 He is at work fitting and joining the whole body together. He provides sustenance to it through every contact according to the needs of each single part. He enables the body to make its own growth so that it builds itself up in love.

17 Now in the Lord['s name] I say and insist upon the following: No longer conduct yourselves as do the Gentiles in the futility of their mind. 18 Intellectually they are blacked out. Because of their inherent refusal to know [God] and of the petrifaction of their hearts, they are excluded from the life of God. 19 In their insensitive state they have given themselves over to debauchery in order to do all filthy things and still ask for more. 20 But you have not become students of the Messiah this way—21 assuming you have ever listened to him and been taught in his school. Just as [the instruction] is,

Truth in Jesus!
22 You strip off what fits your former behavior,
the Old Man rotting in deceitful desires.
23 Instead you become new in mind and spirit
24 and put on the New Man created after God['s image]
in true righteousness and piety.

25 Therefore put away the lie. Every one shall speak the truth to his neighbor for we are members of one body. 26 If you are angry yet do not sin. The sun must not set on your temper. 27 And do not give an opportunity to the devil. 28 The thief shall no longer go on stealing. To the contrary, he shall work hard and honestly with his own hands so that he may have something to share with the needy. 29 No foul talk whatsoever shall pass your lips but [say] what is right for meeting a need constructively so that it will do good to the listeners. 30 And do not grieve the Holy Spirit of God [for he is the seal] with which you have been marked for the day of liberation. 31 Every kind of bitterness, passion, anger, shouting, cursing shall be taken away from you, together with any [other sort of] malice. 32 Be good to one another. Be warm-hearted. Forgive one another just as God has forgiven you in Christ.

5 1 Therefore, as [God's] beloved children be imitators of God 2 and walk in [the way of] love, just as [we confess]

The Messiah has loved us
and has given himself for us
as an offering and sacrifice
whose fragrance is pleasing to God.

3 Yet as is fitting for saints, fornication and filth of any kind, or greed must not even be mentioned among you, 4 neither shameless, silly, ribald talk. These

things are improper. Instead, [let there be] thanksgiving! [5] For you had better keep this in mind: No fornicating, filthy, or greedy man, that is, no one who worships an idol, has an inheritance in the kingdom of God's Messiah. [6] Let no one deceive you with shallow words. It is because of these things that the wrath of God comes upon the rebellious. [7] Therefore do not associate with them. [8] For in the past you were darkness, but now in Christ you are light. Conduct yourselves as children of light [9] for the fruit of light consists of everything that is good, righteous, and true. [10] Find out by experience what is pleasing to the Lord [11] and have nothing to do with those fruitless deeds done in darkness. Much more disprove them [by your conduct] [12] for it is shameful even to mention the things that happen in secret. [13] [Only] by the light are all reprobate things revealed. [14] All that is revealed is light. Therefore he says,

> "Awake you sleeper,
>   rise from the dead,
>   the Messiah will shine upon you!"

[15] In sum, watch carefully how you conduct yourselves—not as fools, but as wise men. [16] Redeem the time for these days are evil. [17] Therefore do not be senseless but [learn to] comprehend what is the will of the Lord. [18] In particular do not get drunk with wine—that is profligacy—but be filled with the Spirit. [19] Talk to one another in psalms and hymns and spiritual songs. Sing and play to the Lord from your heart. [20] In the name of our Lord Jesus Christ give thanks always and for everything to God the Father.

[21] Because you fear Christ subordinate yourselves to one another—[22] [e.g.] wives to your husbands—as to the Lord. [23] For [only] in the same way that the Messiah is the head of the church

> —he, the savior of his body—

is the husband the head of his wife. [24] The difference notwithstanding, just as the church subordinates herself [only] to the Messiah, so wives to your husbands—in everything. [25] Husbands, love your wives, just as [we confess]

> The Messiah has loved the church
>   and has given himself for her
> [26] to make her holy by [his] word
>   and clean by the bath in water,
> [27] to present to himself the church resplendent
>   free from spot or wrinkle or any such thing
>   so that she be holy and blameless.

[28] In the same manner also husbands owe it [to God and man] to love their wives for they are their bodies. In loving his wife a man loves himself. [29] For no one ever hates his own flesh, but he provides and cares for it—just as the Messiah for the church, [30] because we are the members of his body. [31] "For this reason

> A man will leave his father and mother
> And be joined to his wife,
> And the two will become one flesh."

32 This [passage] has an eminent secret meaning: I, for one, interpret it [as relating] to Christ and the church. 33 In any case one by one, each one of you must love his wife as himself, and the wife . . . may she fear her husband.

6 1 Children, obey your parents because of the Lord; for this is right.

2 "Honor your father and mother"

—this is a basic commandment and contains a promise—

> 3 "in order that is shall be well with you
> and you may live long in the land."

4 And fathers, do not provoke the wrath of your children, but bring them up the way the Lord disciplines and corrects [you].

5 Slaves, obey your earthly lords with fear and trembling, as whole-heartedly as [you obey] the Messiah. 6 Do not imitate people who seek to please men by putting on a show, but do God's will from the bottom of your heart, as slaves of Christ. 7 Render your service with fervor—as [a service] to the Lord, not to men. 8 Be aware that the same good which a man performs—be he slave or free—this he will receive from the Lord. 9 And lords, act the same way toward them. Stop using threats. Be aware that in heaven the same Lord is [ruling] over them and over you: he who fosters no favoritism.

10 For the remaining time become strong in the Lord, that is, by the strength of his power. 11 Put on God's [splendid] armor in order to be able to stand firm against the schemes of the devil. 12 For we are wrestling not with blood and flesh, but with the governments, with the authorities, with the overlords of this dark world, with the spiritual hosts of evil in the heavens. 13 Therefore take up God's [splendid] armor so that you are able to put up resistance on the darkest day, to carry out everything, and to stand firm.
14 Stand firm now

> "Girded with truth around your waist,
> clad with righteousness for a cuirass,"

15 steadfast because the gospel of peace is strapped under your feet. 16 With all [this equipment] take up faith as the shield with which you will be able to quench the fire-missiles of the evil one. 17 Take salvation as your helmet and the sword provided by the Spirit, that is, the word of God.
18 In the Spirit pray at all times through every kind of prayer and petition. To this end stay awake in persevering intercession for all the saints, 19 especially for me [. Pray] that the word may be given to me to open my lips and in high spirits to make the secret known [by proclaiming] the gospel. 20 For this

cause I am an ambassador in chains [. Pray] that I may become frank and bold in my proclamation. For this I must be.

21 In order that you, too, may have knowledge about me and the state of my affairs . . . Tychicus, our dear brother and faithful servant in the Lord, will make known to you all [matters of this kind]. 22 For this very purpose I have sent him to you, that you may know of our situation and that he reassure your hearts.

23 Peace to the brothers, love, and, above all, faith from God the Father and the Lord Jesus Christ. 24 Grace with all who love our Lord Jesus Christ, in eternity.

EPHESIANS 4-6
TRANSLATION WITH
NOTES AND COMMENTS

VIII   THE CONSTITUTION
OF THE CHURCH
(4:1–16)

4 ¹ Therefore I beseech you, prisoner in the Lord['s service] as I am, to conduct yourselves as men worthy of the vocation to which you were called. ² Be altogether humble and gentle. Patiently bear one another in love. ³ Take pains to maintain the unity of the Spirit through the bond of peace.

⁴ One body and one Spirit,
just as there is one hope to which you have been called.

⁵ One Lord, one faith, one baptism,

⁶ one God who is Father of all,
he is over all, through all, and in all.

⁷ The gift of the Messiah is the measure after which grace was given to each one of us. ⁸ Therefore he says,

"When he ascended to the height
he captured a catch of prisoners,
he gave gifts to men."

⁹ What else does the term "he ascended" imply except that he also descended down to the earth? ¹⁰ He who descended is the one who ascended far above all heavens in order to fill all things.

¹¹ He is the one who appointed
these to be apostles and those to be prophets,
some to be evangelists and others to be teaching shepherds
¹² to equip the saints for the work of service
for building the Messiah's body
¹³ until we all come to meet
the unifying faith and knowledge of the Son of God,
the Perfect Man,
the perfection of the Messiah who is the standard of manhood.

¹⁴ No longer are we to be babes, tossed by waves and whirled about by every doctrinal gust, [and caught] in the trickery of men who are experts in deceitful scheming. ¹⁵ Rather by speaking the truth in love we shall grow in every way toward him who is the head, the Messiah.

16 He is at work fitting and joining the whole body together. He provides sustenance to it through every contact according to the needs of each single part. He enables the body to make its own growth so that it builds itself up in love.

NOTES

4:1. *Therefore I beseech you.* When the conjunction "therefore" is used, at the beginning of a second, hortatory part of Pauline Epistles,[1] it bears great weight; it emphasizes the logical dependence of ethical advice upon the preceding doctrinal statements. During the past decades it was often and vigorously stated that Paul's imperatives are dependent upon his indicatives; his *didache* (teaching) is determined by his *kerygma* (proclamation); all things ethical are subject to the gospel and faith. Moral indoctrination therefore appears to be derived from dogmatic doctrine.[2] However, the content of Eph 1–3 is doxological rather than dogmatic. The direct connection of the ethical chapters 4–6 with the praise of God rather than with a doctrine of God is a specific feature of Ephesians. The verb translated by "I beseech" can also be rendered by "I exhort," "I encourage," "I comfort," "I warn." While it includes a direct request (customarily expressed in Papyri epistles by the verb "I ask," *erōtaō*), the word preferred by Paul signifies a will of the writer that is at the same time warm, personal, and urgent. Its sense is stronger than that of the English verb "I exhort."[3]

prisoner in the Lord['s service] as I am. Lit. "I, the prisoner in the Lord." This formulation resembles the opening of the preceding chapter,[4] but is distinguished from it by two features. (a) Instead of "Messiah Jesus" the title "Lord" is used. (b) Instead of calling himself a prisoner "of" the Messiah, the apostle denotes himself a prisoner "in" the Lord. The words "in the Lord" are used by Paul preferably in ethical contexts and suggest, therefore, the paraphrastic version, "in the Lord's service."[5] The apostle is not pleading for compassion, but wants to point out the price he is paying—that is, perhaps, his specific right to be heard and heeded.[6]

---

[1] Thess 4:1; Rom 12:1; Col 3:5 (or 2:6?).

[2] See COMMENT II for a discussion of the relationship between proclamation and exhortation.

[3] The verb used by Paul (*parakaleō*) occurs also in Papyri, e.g. Berlin Pap. 164; 814; Oxford Pap. 292, and is combined with the more frequent *erōtaō*, e.g. in Oxford Pap. 294. Paul employs both verbs as though they were synonyms in I Thess 4:1; Philip 4:2–3. In I Thess 2:12 the escalation from *parakalō* to *paramytheomai* to *martyromai* ("admonish"–"encourage"–"charge") is found. See C. J. Bjerkelund, *Parakalō, Form, Funktion und Sinn der parakalō-Sätze in den paulinischen Briefen*, Universitets Oslo, 1967, for parallels in inscriptions and non-biblical letters. The character and undertone of the *parakalō* clause is friendly rather than authoritative. See also H. Schlier, "Vom Wesen der apostolischen Ermahnung," in *Die Zeit der Kirche* (Freiburg: Herder, 1956), pp. 74–89; O. Schmitz and G. Stählin, TWNTE, V, 773–99. Abbott suggests the translation, "I beseech."

[4] The words, "prisoner of the Messiah Jesus" have been commented upon in a NOTE on 3:1 and in COMMENT III C on 3:1–13.

[5] See COMMENT I on 1:1–2 for the various forms and meanings of the "in Christ" formula. In Rom 16:3, 8, 9 terms such as "cooperator in Christ", "beloved in the Lord" correspond to the "prisoner in the Lord" of Eph 4:1.

[6] Cf. Theodoret. Calvin comments on this verse: Paul's chains adorn him with an authority higher than that deployed by a king's pomp. Thomas Aquinas refers to the obligations under which Paul's imprisonment puts the saints and refers to II Cor 1:6. The key to the effect of suffering is found in Eph 3:13: "the tribulations I suffer for you . . . are your glorification." *See* COMMENT III C on 3:1–13.

to conduct yourselves as men worthy of the vocation to which you were called. As shown in the NOTES on 2:2 and 10, in Pauline letters the Greek verb "to walk" (in our version, "to conduct oneself") suggests something different from a casual promenade: it means to follow a prescribed way in a fixed order, comparable to the march of Israel under God's guidance in the wilderness.[7] "Be imitators of God" (5:1)! The noun and the character of "calling" have been discussed briefly in a NOTE on 1:18. In 4:1 an appointment to a position of honor is described by the same noun. The version "vocation" gives an indication of the honorary place and function with which God has entrusted the saints. See COMMENT II for a discussion of the *noblesse* created by God and of its implications.

2. *Be altogether humble and gentle. Patiently bear.* The Greek original contains the three nouns, "humility," "gentleness," "patience." Lit. "with all humility and gentleness, with patience." The same trio of good attitudes is enlarged to a quintet in Col 3:12 where compassion and goodness are given the leading roles, or to a nonet in Gal 5:22–23 where love, joy, and peace are in the lead. The relatively brief list in Eph 4:2 will be increased by three additional members in 4:32 . The accumulation of nouns or adjectives describing worthy conduct, and the corresponding catalogue of vices, was one of several means used in Paul's time for ethical instruction.[8] Since an English version containing a simple enumeration would be even less attractive than the original Greek, separate sentences containing adjectives and adverbs have been fashioned in our translation. The imperative mood of the added verb "be" and of the word "bear" is suggested by the dominating term "I beseech you" and by the special character of the Greek participle "bearing."[9] Perhaps verse 4:2 contains three rather than two admonitions: (*a*) be humble and gentle; (*b*) be patient; (c) bear. Even so, the sense of the whole is not changed. The peculiarly un-Greek character of the commandments contained in 4:2 will be discussed in COMMENT III.

bear one another in love. The "love" mentioned here is probably the brotherly love among the saints which bears testimony to God's and Christ's love.[10] Elsewhere Paul calls "love of the neighbor" the sum of God's commandments.[11] He attributes to this love the dominant place among all attitudes and deeds that are characteristic of the saints. "Love . . . is the bond of perfection" (Col 3:14).[12] The gracious election of the Jewish and Gentile neighbor is the presupposition, the unshakable ground, and the undying source of the saints' mutual love. The love that rules among them is the necessary and indispensable result of God's care for them. It is the essence of the "good works" created for them, and the ground on which they are to walk (cf. 5:2; 2:10). The terms "love" and "bearing one another" (cf. Gal 6:2) interpret each other mutually. If to love includes bearing one's neighbor, then love is not just an emotion or ideal

---

[7] In Gal 5:25; 6:16; Philip 3:16; Rom 4:12 a verb meaning, "to march in line," "to hold the line" (*stoicheō*), is used by Paul. Twice he mentions a "canon" which the saints are to follow.

[8] See COMMENT VIII on 4:17–32 for a discussion of the lists of vices and virtues.

[9] See NOTE 23 on 3:17 for the imperative interpretation of participles in ethical contexts.

[10] The latter is emphatically mentioned in 1:4, 6; 2:4; 3:19; 5:2, 25; 6:23.

[11] Gal 5:14; Rom 13:8–10.

[12] Mutual love of the saints is often mentioned in Ephesians, see 1:15 var. lect.; 3:17; 4:15–16; 5:2, 25, 28, 33; 6:24.

of the individual soul; rather the personalities of specific neighbors and personal relations actually existing among the saints become the field and material of love. According to this passage there is no love except in relation to specific neighbors.[13] Love is not a disposition of the soul which can be perfect in itself, without being given and shaped in ever new concrete encounters. It is always specific, always costly, always a miraculous event.

3. *Take pains.* It is hardly possible to render exactly the urgency contained in the underlying Greek verb. Not only haste and passion, but a full effort of the whole man is meant, involving his will, sentiment, reason, physical strength, and total attitude. The imperative mood of the participle found in the Greek text excludes passivity, quietism, a wait-and-see attitude, or a diligence tempered by all deliberate speed. Yours is the initiative! Do it now! Mean it! *You* are to do it! I mean it!—such are the overtones in verse 3. Those given the "vocation" to walk worthily (4:1) appear to be urged to race ahead, to meet a deadline, or to receive a prize.[14] Still, an overinterpretation pressing too hard on individual perfection is discouraged by the following:

to maintain the unity of the Spirit. That upon which the full energy of the saints is to be bent is already given and present. It has to be "maintained" rather than "attained." While "perfection" is still beyond their grasp (4:13; Philip 3:12), "unity" is described here as a power that already embraces all of them. "Keep what you have lest someone take your crown" (Rev 3:11). Since a gift given in the saints' possession[15] is presupposed, it is probable that in the translation "spirit" (*pneuma*) must be capitalized. Three things argue against assuming that reference is made to the human spirit:[16] (a) The spirit of community which is experienced in the congregation is not as stable and sure a presupposition as the "Holy Spirit of God" with whom the saints are "sealed" and who must not be grieved (1:13–14; 4:30). (b) Paul would speak of the "spirit of unity," cf. the "spirit of wisdom" (1:17), not of the "unity of the Spirit," if he had in mind an anthropological counterpart to the Holy Spirit (cf. Rom 8:16). (c) The confession "one Spirit . . . one Lord . . . one God who is Father" which follows in vss. 4–6 appears to explain the unity mentioned in 4:3. The unity of the church rests upon the oneness of God rather than upon some common enthusiasm in the community of the church.[17] In the NT the term translated by "unity" occurs but twice, in Eph 4:3 and 13. The special way in which the noun "unity" and the numeral "one" (vss. 4–6) eventually interpret one another will be discussed in COMMENT IV B.

the bond of peace. The term translated by "bond" can have a technical or metaphorical meaning. In the first case it denotes what keeps together a house, a garment, or different members of the physical body: the wooden

[13] See the NOTE on the words "all the saints" in 1:15 for a discussion of the restriction of love to church members.
[14] Cf. II Tim 4:9, 21. In Philip 3:12–14 the term *diōko*, "to pursue," "to press on," expresses the same idea.
[15] Comparable to the "forgiveness" and "free access" mentioned in 1:7; 3:12.
[16] E.g., Anselm, Calvin, de Wette, G. Estius, Gaugler believed that the corporate spirit of the church was meant.
[17] E. Stauffer, TWNTE, II, 440, sees in 4:4–6 a description of the "central guarantees of unity." Robinson and Schlier emphasize that in 4:3 the Holy Spirit is meant.

beams, the fastenings, or the ligaments. In the second case it signifies for classical Greek writers that which preserves the unity of a city, e.g. loyalty or the law.[18] Among Pythagoreans the term means that capital or master virtue which holds all virtues together. In Col 3:14 "love" is called the "bond of perfection." In each case a beneficial bond rather than a fetter is meant.[19]

4–6. These three verses contain a confession or hymn. However, because of its style and the second person address, "you," vs. 4b seems out of harmony with vss. 4–6.[20] The arrangement of the various creedal parts and elements of these verses, some key terms used for making the confession, an important variant reading, finally the relevance of the confession within 4:1–16 will be discussed in COMMENT IV. The title "Lord" and the absence of any polytheistic notion in the juxtaposition of the "Lord" (Jesus Christ) and God (the "Father") have been discussed in COMMENT II on 1:1–2.

4b. *just as there is one hope to which you have been called.* Lit. "just as you have been called in one hope of your vocation." "Hope" signifies here, as in 1:18, the substance of hope rather than just the psychic disposition of "hopefulness."[21] The vocation extended and granted to Jews and Gentiles is in effect a marching order and a goal presented to them. It is, as it were, something "objective" that calls for subjective realization. The common goal is the reason for the appeal to unity (cf. 4:13). The unity of the church is according to vss. 4b and 13 not constituted by something underneath or inside the church or her several members. Rather it is eschatological: the reason for the church's hope for unity, and for her commitment to unity, is "deposited in heaven" (Col 1:5). Not the attainment to unity, but the guarantee of that attainment is, in the best interest of the church, preserved at a place "out of this world."

5. *One Lord, one faith, one baptism.* The three Greek nouns combined in this exclamation are masculine, feminine, and neuter respectively. With each, the form of the Greek numeral "one" is appropriately changed. The flamboyant ring of the corresponding sequence (*heis, miā, hen*) cannot be reproduced in English. See COMMENT IV B.

6. . . . *of all* . . . *over all, through all, and in all.* See COMMENT V B on 1:15–23 and COMMENT IV C hereafter for a discussion of the cosmic implication of the term "all." In what follows, God's universal rule and presence is exemplified by a description of his care for the church.

7. *The gift of the Messiah is the measure.* It is probable that the Messiah is himself the gift and that Rom 8:32 is a parallel: *"He [God] who did not spare his own Son but gave him up for us all, will he not also give all things?"* (RSV). The JB version makes the parallel even more striking: ". . . we may be certain, after such a gift, that he [God] will not refuse anything he can give." The logic of this inference is persuasive. The epistle to the Ephesians itself argues, as it were downward from God to Christ to man: "in his beloved son God poured out upon us . . . his grace" (1:6). Al-

---

[18] For references see LSLex and WBLex, arts. *syndesmos.*
[19] Unlike Isa 58:6, 9; Acts 8:23.
[20] Cf. the prose words inserted in hymnic contexts in 1:11–13; 2:8.
[21] Thomas Aquinas: *res sperata.*

lusions to the riches of God have been made.[22] God himself is the giver of all good things (cf. James 1:17). The many gifts received by men are an outflow of the one great gift of God: "We have different gifts of grace according to the grace given to us" (Rom 12:6). The Gospels of John and Luke make it as clear as does Paul, e.g. in Rom 5 and 8, that the coming of the Spirit upon men is dependent upon the death of Christ and connected with his resurrection.[23] In I Cor 12:18, 28 Paul affirms that according to his good pleasure God himself institutes the members of the body, that is, the ministers and ministries in the church. Therefore in Eph 4:7 the Messiah himself may be denoted as God's gift. In this case he, the great gift, is disclosed in the various gifts received by the church. However, the following verses clearly designate Jesus Christ as the donor. In 1:10; 2:14–17 the Messiah's own activity is pointed out. In harmony with God who freely distributes his riches (1:8), the Messiah's action is characterized by generosity. After a reference to the Messiah's "unfathomable riches" was made in 3:8, it is now shown how he has opened the doors of his storehouse. He distributes nothing less than "grace" and thereby proves to be the plenipotent "administrator" (1:10) of that grace which according to 1:6, 8; 3:2, 7 etc. God himself bestows.

grace was given to each one of us. Three elements of this statement are equally important: (a) The saints experience God's good will, power, and presence by receiving grace; (b) the grace given is neither a pillow for sleeping nor a comfortable warm feeling, but a ministry; it is a privilege implying responsibility and action;[24] (c) this gift is given to each one of the saints, not solely to an inner circle of office-holders inside the church. According to 4:7 "each Christian" participates in grace "as a charismatic."[25] Cf. I Cor 12:7: "To each is given the manifestation of the Spirit for the common good." In Eph 1:17–18 the inspiration of all church members was equally emphasized.[26] In the light of 4:7 a sharp distinction between clergy and laity in the church[27] is inappropriate.

8–10. These verses interrupt the context with an OT quotation and its exegesis. The interruption might appear superfluous, i.e. vs. 7 could be followed immediately by vss. 11 ff.—except for two things: (a) The OT text and its interpretation expose the meaning of the term "the Messiah's gift"; they show why at this point Christ (rather than God, I Cor 12:18 ff.) is described as the giver of the several ministries. (b) The words cited and the comments added to them, especially vs. 10, prepare the way for vs. 12, i.e. toward an appreciation of the cosmic relevance of the gifts given to the church.

8. *Therefore he says.* The quotation formula "he says" is found in several Pauline or other NT writings, and introduces a citation from the Bible of

---

[22] 1:7–8; 2:4, 7; 3:16.
[23] John 7:39; 16:7; 20:22; Luke 24:49; Acts 1:4; 2:33; cf. Hegermann, *Schöpfungsmittler*, p. 155.
[24] See 3:2, 7; 4:11–12; Robinson p. 95.
[25] E. Käsemann, RGG, II, 518. Schlier, p. 191, contests this conclusion. He seeks to discern a "circle" within the church consisting only of those Christians to whom grace is given. His reasons for making this limitation are not convincing. In addition to the clear wording of Eph 4:7, I Cor 12:7, and Eph 4:12 also speak distinctly against the restriction. See below, esp. COMMENT VI.
[26] See COMMENT III on Eph 1:15–23.
[27] Which is declared the prime and basic sacrament of the church, e.g. by O. Semmelroth, *Die Kirche als Ursakrament,* Frankfurt: Knecht, 1953.

Israel.[28] This formula was preferred by the rabbis, Philo, and the early Fathers to the words, "it is written."[29] It is characterized by the absence of a legalistic and polemical undertone.[30] The formula "he says" is an urgent invitation to listen attentively—rather than an expression of bellicose argument. At this point the intention of adducing "proof" from the Scripture appears to be absent from Paul's mind. Who is to be listened to? The translation of the citation formula by "it says" is certainly not impossible. The Bible may be introduced as itself speaking.[31] However, sometimes Paul equates the voice of Scripture with God's own voice; on other occasions he states plainly that the law, David, or Isaiah are heard,[32] and once he makes Israel("?") the biblical spokesman.[33] Heb 2:6 uses a formula which grants the greatest freedom in defining the scriptural speaker: "In giving his testimony somebody said somewhere." The weight and persuasiveness of a given statement rather than the authority of a specific speaker or book are placed on the scales whenever the vague formula "he says" occurs. Bengel goes beyond the wording of Eph 4:8 in affirming that "David, even more, God himself" is introduced as testifying.

"When he ascended . . . he gave gifts to men." The peculiar text of Ps 68:18 used by Paul, and the even more surprising interpretation and application of the Psalm text, will be discussed in COMMENT V.

he captured a catch of prisoners. The *antanaklasis,* "to capture a catch," which our translation seeks to reproduce in English, is found in the LXX,[34] and in additional passages of the Hebrew OT.[35] It corresponds to the phrases, "to bless with blessing," "to love with love" (1:3; 2:4), and must not be

---

[28] Cf. 5:14; Gal 3:16; I Cor 6:16; II Cor 6:2; Rom 15:10; James 4:6; Heb 1:6; 2:12, etc.; the passive or a tense of the past (it is said, he has spoken, etc.) can be used as equivalents. More distinct formulations refer to the testifying, swearing, revealing, blaming, conversing, commanding, promising words contained in the Scriptures; see e.g. Heb 2:6; 10:15; 12:5, 20, 26. Cf. I Peter 2:6; Acts 23:15 var. lect.: "it contains." The Pauline and other passages mentioned make it unlikely that Paul meant to quote in 4:8 (as indeed he does in 5:14) a hymn or perhaps a Targum, rather than a Scripture text.

[29] The latter occurs in Hebrews only once, in 10:7, but prevails in the Pauline and Johannine writings (except Revelation), and in Matthew and Luke. For more evidence see G. Schrenk, TWNTE, I, 746–49; M. Barth, *Conversation with the Bible* (New York: Holt, 1964), pp. 209–13.

[30] The act of writing down a book and depositing a book in a shrine appears as part of a covenant ceremony in Exod 24:4, 12; 34:27; Josh 24:26; I Sam 10:25; Deut 17:18; 31:9; Jer 31:33; Neh 9:38. The book is according to Deut 31:24–27 a "witness" against a rebellious people. A lawyer or scribe will pound upon the letter or a book. Consequently in the course of lively arguments, OT scribes, Paul, Matthew, Luke, and John refer to that which "is written," see e.g. LXX I Chron 15:15; II Chron 30:5; Matt 4:1–10; cf. Gal 1:20; 6:11; Acts 15:23 ff.; I John 2:12–14. In Greece the phrase, "it is written," can be traced no further than to the fifth century B.C. Plato *epistulae* VII 341–42, 344; cf. *Phaedrus* 274 ff, decried the writing of books because they "exposed to unseemly and degrading treatment . . . the highest and first truths of nature." In II Cor 3:6; Rom 2:29; 7:6 Paul makes critical statements on the "oldness" of the law and the "killing" power of "the letter." Luther, e.g. in WA, V, 537; X, 1:1, 625 ff., made a sharp distinction between the living voice of NT preaching and the written words of the OT. Calvin, *Institutes*, I, 7:1, saw the authority of the Bible in the fact that "God's own voices were heard in it" as "flowing from heaven." Thus there is a use for the Bible which is distinct from apologetics. But see B. Lindars, *New Testament Apologetic*, Philadelphia: Westminster, 1962.

[31] This is made explicit, e.g. in Gal 4:30; Rom 4:3; 9:17; 10:11; 11:2; I Tim 5:18; John 7:38, 42; 19:37.

[32] E.g. Gal 3:22 compared with Rom 11:32; cf. Rom 9:25, 27; Gal 4:21; Rom 3:19; 4:6; 11:18–29. A theory describing the technicality of inspiration and a dogma of the Scripture's inerrancy should not be derived from a harmonization of such passages; see T. K. Abbott.

[33] Rom 4:9.

[34] Ps 67:19; Judg 5:12; II Chron 28:5, 11; Esther 1:1c; I Macc 9:72. In Job 1:15; II Chron 6:36 the cognate accusative, "captivity," is replaced by the participle of the verb; the formulation, to "capture [by] capturing," is the result.

[35] Num 21:1; II Chron 28:17.

interpreted as "captivity is captive led."[36] A suggestion that those captured
had previously made others their prisoners (cf. Gen 14:11-16) is not contained in the Hebrew and Greek idioms. Who are the ones caught? The
Synoptic Gospels speak of men possessed by evil "spirits," and Ephesians
refers to the attacks made by "spirits" upon men (6:11-13), but neither
the Gospels nor this epistle contain anything to indicate that the souls of
men are "prisoners" of hostile forces. According to Eph 4:8 those made
prisoners are probably the principalities, powers, aeons. Therefore this verse
does not reflect the Orphic, Platonic, or Gnostic notions of the imprisonment of the soul (e.g. by watchmen or demonic powers). See COMMENT V
for a more detailed discussion of the captor and the captives. The imagery
of the victorious warrior will recur in 6:10 ff., in the context of a description of the splendid armor of God. There and here the *Christus victor* theme can
be recognized on which G. Aulen has elaborated.

9. *What else does the term "he ascended" imply. . . ?* Lit. "what is the 'he
ascended'?" With these words Paul introduces a Midrash, i.e. a subtle form
of Scripture interpretation current among Jewish scholars of his time.[37]
While Philo and many rabbis often engaged in allegorical interpretation and
while Paul occasionally imitates their procedure,[38] the apostle's comments on
Ps 68:18[19] follow a literalist, not allegorical, method. Paul may intend to refute a rabbinic interpretation of this psalm.[39] Passages such as Gal 3:16; Heb
7:1-3, combine allegorical and literal interpretation.

he also descended. In John 3:13 ascent and descent are connected in a
strikingly similar manner. Which document has literary priority? Ephesians
might be dependent upon John, or John upon Ephesians, or both upon a common third source or tradition. Do the references to a "descent" and "ascent" reflect the influence of the Gnostic myths of the soul's fall and imprisonment, and of the redeemer who comes to her rescue by being himself
redeemed?[40] There is no need at this point to repeat earlier general arguments against a Gnosticizing interpretation of Ephesians. Certainly the
"model" of a descent followed by an ascent is also represented in the lives
of the OT righteous ones, e.g. of Joseph, Moses, David, the Suffering
Servant: through utter humiliation all of them attained highest glory.[41]
While it is certain that Gnostics liked to quote Ephesians in support of their
beliefs[42] and liked to manipulate OT texts, there is as yet no evidence available that they preceded Ephesians in such an interpretation of Ps 68 as
is given in Eph 4:9. Several interpreters understand the author of Ephesians

[36] As in an English hymn.
[37] See the literature mentioned in fn. 132 of the Introduction. KJ, RV, ASV, RSV put the vss.
9-10 into parenthetical marks.
[38] E.g. in Eph 5:31-32; Gal 4:21-31; I Cor 9:9-10.
[39] See COMMENT V B C.
[40] So, e.g. Jonas, *Gnostic Religion*, pp. 24 ff., with reference to *Corp. Herm.* I 12-19; C. Maurer,
EvTh 11 (1951-52), 171; Pokorný, EuG, p. 77.
[41] This alternative to the Gnosticizing interpretation of Philip 2:6-11, of Johannine passages, such
as John 3:13; 17:5, and of other texts, has been demonstrated, e.g., by J. Jeremias, TWNTE, V, 677-
717; E. Schweizer, *Lordship and Discipleship*, SBT 28 (1960), pp. 22-76. The humiliation-exaltation
pattern is clearly discernible in Ps 8 and the stories about David in I and II Samuel. It also appears
in Isa 53; Wisd Sol 2 and 5; Mark 8:31; Luke 14:11; 24:26, 46; I Tim 3:16. Cf. Thomas Aquinas'
comments on Eph 4:10.
[42] For references see fn. 148 of the Introduction.

as saying that the descent of Christ "follows" his ascent.[43] According to them the verb "he descended" denotes the advent of the transfigured and exalted Christ among his own, instead of describing Christ's descent out of his pre-existence into human flesh, to the death on the cross, or (possibly) to hell (cf. Philip 2:6–8). His glorious advent follows his humiliation and death; it is accompanied by the bestowal of rich "gifts." This interpretation can certainly prevent a misunderstanding of Eph 4:7 ff. The exalted Lord must not be compared to an absentee landlord who, as it were by remote control, shows concern for his people. When Christ gives gifts, he gives himself and presents himself. Despite the beauty and truth of this exposition, its corroboration by texts such as Matt 28:20; Gal 2:20 notwithstanding, it is not supported by the wording of 4:8–10: these verses place much more stress upon the ascent than upon the descent. The powerful omnipresence of the Messiah is ascribed to his exaltation above all heavens and to the gifts he has given. Acts 2:33 says the same in different words: "Being exalted at the right hand of God, and having received from the Father the promise of the Holy Spirit, he has poured out this which you see and hear." Not until 4:13 will the final appearance of the Son of God in his perfection be mentioned.

down to the earth. The Greek text speaks of a descent to, literally, "the lower parts of the earth."[44] It is unlikely that either a subterranean "hell" (understood as the power-sphere of sin, death, the devil, and the evil spirits) or Sheol (the Pit, the residence of the dead) is meant and that, therefore, 4:9 is a *locus classicus* attesting to Christ's "descent to hell," *ad inferos.*[45] At least six things speak against this widely held view: (a) Though in the LXX a terminology resembling that of Eph 4:9 is employed to describe Sheol,[46] the vocabulary used in Eph 4:9 is not exactly that of the LXX. (b) According to Eph 2:2; 6:12 (also 3:15?) the evil spirit and his hosts are located in heavenly places, not under "the earth." (c) Following Ephesians, the victory of Christ over these powers was attained by his exaltation (1:19–21; 4:8), not by his descent.[47] (d) A descent to hell would be a second step following the descent from heaven to earth; the earth would be its starting point. A descent in two steps would hardly correspond to the single ascent into heaven mentioned in

[43] E.g. von Soden; G. B. Caird, "The Descent of the Messiah in Ephesians 4:7–11," in *Studia Evangelica*, II, ed. F. L. Cross, TU 87 (1964), 535–45; JB in a note; Abbott with reference to the "coming" of Christ mentioned in 2:17; John 14:23. The opinion of these scholars has antecedents: a variant reading of 4:9, found in the Codex Vaticanus, the MSS of the Koine Group, the Syro-Curetonianus, the Latin versions, has "he *first* descended." This variant does not just give superfluous stress to the obvious; it may have been intended to rebut an understanding such as von Soden's, etc., which placed the ascent before the descent. Westcott, Dibelius, Gaugler, and most extensively W. Bieder, *Die Vorstellung von der Höllenfahrt Jesu Christi,* ATANT 19 (1949), pp. 81 ff., argue against von Soden.

[44] The noun "parts," is omitted by a respectable group of MSS and versions. The omission of the noun does not yield a different sense.

[45] Among the commentators who understand this verse to proclaim the descent into hell are Tertullian; Irenaeus *epideixis* 83; Chrysostom; Theodoret; Oecumenius; Victorinus; Ambrosiaster; Jerome; Pelagius; Thomas Aquinas; Bengel; Estius; Hofmann; Westcott; Robinson, pp. 96, 180; Bousset, *Kyrios*, pp. 30–31, F. W. Beare, IB, X, 689. See E. Haupt, *Die Gefangenschaftsbriefe* (Göttingen: Vandenhoeck, 1899), pp. 141–50 for details of the history of interpretation.

[46] In Gen 44:29; Pss 62[63]:10; 138[139]:15; Ezek 32:18, 24; cf. Barn. x 5, "Sheol," the *deepest* places of the earth, or "the depth of the earth," are mentioned as the place of death and/or destruction.

[47] In Col 2:14–15 this victory is ascribed to the cross, rather than to an event following the crucifixion.

4:8, 10. (e) Parallels to Eph 4:8-10, such as John 3:13; 17:5, discourage the thought of hell. (f) A reference to a conquest of (the realm of) the dead would be completely alien to the context of 4:9.[48] Instead, the term "the lower parts of the earth" is probably equivalent to "the low region of the earth" or "the earth down here." Rather than other parts of the earth, "all the heavens . . . above" are the high regions with which the "earth down here" is compared.[49] Therefore, the descent of Christ mentioned in 4:9 denotes his incarnation and, most likely, his crucifixion.[50]

10. *He who descended is the one who ascended.* The Greek text stresses not the sameness of the person who descended and ascended, but the continuation and crowning of the Messiah's humiliation by his exaltation.[51] A theology of incarnation or of the cross which would neglect the triumph and powerful presence of Christ is excluded by this verse. In 4:13 the future and final meeting with Christ will be mentioned.

far above all heavens. Compare the use of the emphatic form of "above" (*hyperanō*) in 1:21 and the discussion of the plural "heavens" in COMMENT III on 1:3-14. While in the epistle to the Hebrews the term "going through the heavens" uses the metaphor of a priest stepping into the innermost sanctuary,[52] Eph 4:10 employs the imagery of a king (cf. 1:20-23) who by visiting all parts of his realm establishes his rule.[53]

in order to fill all things. The distribution of royal gifts and ministries (4:8, 11) is not a substitute for the Messiah's presence but the mode of his being present.[54] As was shown in COMMENT VI C on 1:15-23, the term "filling" denotes the demonstration of authority and the gift of life and unity. By the act of "filling" the Messiah shows himself to be the "head" in both the political and physiological meanings of this term.[55] The term "all things" includes heaven and earth, principalities and powers, also the church, the body of Christ.[56]

[48] For information on the question whether in I Peter 3:19; 4:6 a bodily descent of Christ into Hades or Hell is proclaimed, see Bo Reicke, *The Disobedient Spirits and Christian Baptism*, ASNU 13, Kopenhagen: Munksgaard, 1946; W. Bieder, ATANT 19 (1949), 96-129; also M. Barth, *Die Taufe ein Sakrament?*, pp. 480-97.

[49] See for this interpretation, e.g. Theodore of Mopsuestia and L. Radermacher, *Neutestamentliche Grammatik*, 2d ed. (Tübingen: Mohr, 1925), pp. 69-70, 225. In BDF, 167 this view is contradicted, but the evidence collected in BDF 263:2, 4 for the meaning of genitives combined with adjectives speaks in favor of Radermacher's judgment.

[50] This interpretation is suggested by Calvin; Bieder, ATANT 19 (1949), 81 ff.; Dibelius in his commentary on Ephesians; cf. Dibelius, *Die Isisweihe bei Apuleius*, SHA Phil.-Hist. Klasse 4 (1917), pp. 44-45; repr. in *Botschaft und Geschichte*, II (Tübingen: Mohr, 1956), 70-71; F. Büchsel, TWNTE, III, 641-42.

[51] The Greek words translated by "he . . . is the one who" cannot mean "he is the same as he who" (against Thomas Aquinas and others), for the absence of the Greek article before *autos* (he) excludes the translation which emphasizes exclusively personal identity. More probably the emphatic words "he is the one who" reveal that in vs. 10 the midrashic argument is left behind and replaced by a hymnodic statement. Cf. 2:14; Col 1:15-20; and section II of the Introduction.

[52] 4:14; cf. 6:19-20; 7:26; 10:20.

[53] See, e.g. I Kings 18:5-6; Robinson, 96. E. Käsemann, RGG, II, 518, speaks about the role of the cosmocrator which is seized by Christ.

[54] Abbott.

[55] Jer 23:24; Wisd Sol 1:7; Philo *de somn.* II 221; *Ascension of Isaiah* xi 22 ff.; Eph 1:22-23; cf. 1:10; see also Chrysostom; Calvin; Gaugler; and COMMENT VI A B on 1:15-23.

[56] See COMMENT V B on 1:15-23. Schlier, p. 194, believes that the "fullness" is already present among the faithful, i.e., in the church, and is given its cosmic extension only through the church. But in Eph 1:10 Christ rather than the church is designated as God's plenipotentiary in the world, and vss. 1:22-23 show as much as 4:10 that not only the world but also the church is still being filled by God, cf. 3:19. A statement such as Col. 2:9, saying that the church is already completely filled, is not found in Ephesians. According to this epistle the church's function is not imperial but is restricted to serving God's revelation (2:7; 3:10).

11. This verse may contain hymnic or other traditional material. The solemn phrase with which it begins, "he is the one who"; the catalogue of the members of a group;[57] the un-Pauline vocabulary used to describe the last two or three ministries listed in vs. 11, the lack of a reference to Paul's own special office[58]—each of these elements can indicate a quotation made by the author. But it is also possible that he coined formulations that would sound specifically grave and binding.

He is the one who appointed. Lit. ". . . who gave." See I Cor 12:18, 28; Acts 20:28, and the first NOTE on Eph 1:22 for the translation "he appointed." This version is not meant to exclude the gift-character of the men and titles listed in 4:11. According to vss. 7–8 they are "given" as "gifts," but in vs. 11 Paul shows that this "gift" is distinct from an occasional token of God's and Christ's good will that may be received, consumed, and soon forgotten. By his gift the exalted Christ establishes an order and gives the church a constitution. Gift and institution, or charisma and office, are not mutually exclusive alternatives; they are combined and inseparable. The ministries exerted in the church are, as it were, immediately given from above. Christ gives the church the officers she needs, not vice versa. The church described in Ephesians has a distinctly hierarchical, actually a monarchic structure. Her constitution is distinguished with utmost brevity and clarity from the list of unilaterally dependent or mutually competing church offices to be found in Canon Law or other books of Church Order. God appoints Christ to be the head over church and world (1:10, 20–23); the exalted Christ will fill all, and he appoints ministers to the church (4:8–11). That is all! There are no references to bishops, general secretaries, district superintendents and the like, and no utterances on the authority of higher ministers over a "minor" clergy or over their ordination. What the Pastoral Epistles say on such issues differs from the crisp contents of Eph 4. In Ephesians neither the democratic process of electing officers, nor the aristocratic method of co-option, nor even a ritual of ordination are mentioned. One thing only is clearly stated: Christ himself appoints the special officers.[59] He who despises their ministry would condemn God and reject his gift.[60]

these . . . those . . . some . . . others. The Greek text uses the same article in the sense of a pronoun four times, but the changes offered in this translation prevent monotony. Five things require special notice. (a) The substance of Christ's gift is in this text not called "[spiritual] gifts" (*charismata*), but considered as a unit: the one "grace" given corresponds to the one gift of the Messiah. This gift is the same and has the same measure for "each one of us" (4:7). By providing for all saints equally, God constitutes the unity of the church. No one member possesses anything that is not given

---

[57] Cf. 1:21 and fn. 50 to that verse.

[58] Compare the lists of I Cor 12:28 ff.; Rom 12:6 ff., and Paul's insistence upon the specific relevance of his own election and appointment, Gal 1:10–24; 2:1–10; I Cor 15:5–10; Eph 3:8, etc.

[59] In I Cor 12:7–11; Acts 20:28 "the Spirit"; in I Cor 12:18–31 "God" is named the originator of the various spiritual gifts. In Rom 12:3–7, similarly, the gifts given through *God's* grace are identified with the several ministries carried out in the congregation. The absence from Eph 4:7, 11 of an explicit reference to the inspiration by the Holy Spirit is counterbalanced by the statement on the immediate and ongoing inspiration of all the saints (1:17–18). The inspiration of all saints is also presupposed, e.g. in Gal 3:2–5; I Cor 14; Acts 10–11.

[60] Calvin especially laid emphasis on this consequence.

to the whole body of Christ. It is impossible for any group inside the church to claim an extra gift from the exalted Messiah.[61] (b) The one Messianic gift of one grace is unfolded in diverse ministries. Their diversity prevents dull uniformity. The unity of the church is true and flourishes when the common origin and function of several ministries are gratefully recognized. Christ himself gives the church a diversity of services. (c) Instead of impersonal services, particular servants are listed.[62] The gift of the exalted Christ to the church consists, according to Ephesians, of persons.[63] Unless the church respects the men and women given her, she does not revere her head, Christ.[64] (d) All the ministers listed[65] are persons who fulfill their service by speaking: they are "Ministers of the Word." This does not exclude the view that at the time when Ephesians was written other services were regularly carried out upon God's appointment, in the name and power of Christ, and through inspiration of the Spirit. There were the ministries of elders, bishops, deacons, miracle-doers, and the agents of mercy.[66] However, in 4:11 unquestionable priority is attributed not only to "apostles and prophets" (cf. 2:20; 3:5) but also to "evangelists" and "teachers," i.e. to four functions. (The parallel passage I Cor 12:28–30 lists three that are ahead of all others.) If the "shepherds" mentioned in Eph 4:11 in fact fulfill an additional (fifth) basic ministry, their work must somehow be in line with that of the fellow servants mentioned previously. It is most likely that all of them have to speak, i.e. are "Ministers of the Word." The reference to faith and knowledge (4:13); the opposite role of heretical teaching (4:14); the emphasis which

[61] Westcott, p. 169.

[62] I Cor 12:28–30 lists first the (personal) triad "apostles," "prophets," "teachers," and then diverse (non-personalized) spiritual gifts including administration. In Rom 12:6 ff. only *charismata* ("gifts of grace") are explicitly mentioned, not charismatics (inspired persons). Ephesians stands in direct contrast to Romans: in Eph 4:11, cf. 2:20; 3:5, only persons are listed, not impersonal ministries. Because I Cor 12 combines what is typical of Romans and Ephesians respectively, Ephesians need not be deutero-Pauline. Analogous variations of diction are found in the catalogues of vices and virtues: in Gal 5:18–23; Rom 13:13; Col 3:5, 8, 12; Rev 22:15, gifts and attitudes are listed; in I Cor 5:9–11; 6:9–10; Rev 21:8; Matt 5:3–12 the corresponding persons are described. E. Kamlah, DFKP, pp. 1–3, does not consider these differences sufficiently important to treat them as clues to diverse types of exhortation. The same may *mutatis mutandis* be said, despite A. Harnack's opposite opinion (see, e.g. *The Expansion of Christianity* [New York: Putnam's, 1905], pp. 1–24) of the catalogues of ministers and ministries.

[63] Westcott, 171.

[64] According to John 17:6, 11 Jesus Christ honored the Father in an analogous way: he recognized, accepted, and protected the persons the Father *had given* to the Son. Following the Gospels, only men were called to the circle of the first "twelve" disciples. However, according to I Corinthians women were among those who "prophesied" and led prayer during the church's public worship (11:5, 13; 14:31). The "silence" which Paul enjoined upon them, and the head cover (a kerchief or veil?) which he required them to wear during their participation in the assemblies for worship (I Cor 11:5, 13; 14:34–35) expressed two concerns: preventing interruptions of the worship service by questions that were out of order and could easily be answered elsewhere, and avoiding what he considered the danger and indecency resulting if married women denied or disguised their marital status when they prayed or prophesied in public. In the (deutero-Pauline) First Epistle to Timothy (2:12) women are excluded only from the teaching ministry. In Eph 4:11 nouns of the masculine gender prevail among the titles of all the special ministers given by Christ to the church, yet the grammatical forms of these titles no more exclude the special ministries of good, wise, and eloquent women (such as Elisabeth, Mary, and Anna [Luke 1–2] or Phoebe, Priscilla, Lois, and Eunice [Rom 16:1–5; II Tim 1:5]) than the masculine adjective "saints" (*agioi*) excludes women from full membership in the communion of the saints. See E. Kähler, *Die Frau in den paulinischen Briefen* (Zurich: Gotthelf, 1960), pp. 76–83, 100–1, and COMMENTS II and V C on 5:21–33.

[65] With the possible exception of the "shepherds"—if they are primarily administrators. But see below the NOTE on the "teaching shepherds."

[66] The Pauline passages just mentioned do not belittle them, cf. Philip 1:1; Gal 3:5; Acts 20:28; I Peter 5:2. In James 3:1 overeagerness for the teaching ministry is rebuked; in I Peter 3:1–2 the testimony given "without word" is highly praised. However, Heb 5:11–14 contains a reprimand of the saints because they have not yet attained to the maturity of "teachers."

was earlier laid on the "word of truth"[67] and the "proclamation of peace" (2:17); finally the primacy given in the hortatory section to the fight against "the lie" (4:25), and the emphatic prohibition of "foul talk" (4:29)—all these accents make it probable that only preaching, teaching, and counseling servants of Christ are enumerated in 4:11 (cf. 2:20).[68] (e) All the titles enumerated, except "prophets," are descriptive of secular occupations. Impressive OT titles such as king, priest, scribe, as well as more modest ones such as Levite are bypassed. COMMENT VI will further consider the "secularization" and "democratization" which is apparent in the choice of the church officials' titles.[69]

apostles and . . . prophets. In COMMENT VI C on 2:11–22 it was shown that in 2:20 and 3:5 "apostles" were meant in the narrower sense of the term, i.e. Christ's delegates who went abroad as authorized preachers.[70] At the same point the difference between OT and NT "prophets" was discussed (cf. I Cor 14 and Rom 1:2). NT prophets did not claim to have stood in God's council; some, as the seer John on Patmos, may have been given visions, but not all of them claimed them. A political or cultic role was possible but not indispensable for them. Their special charisma appears not only to have been in making predictions of the immediate future—as in the case of Agabus (Acts 11:28)—but above all in applying the gospel to specific contemporary circumstances.[71] In 4:11 it is assumed that the church at all times needs the witness of "apostles" and "prophets." The author of this epistle did not anticipate that the inspired and enthusiastic ministry was to be absorbed by, and "disappear" into, offices and officers bare of the Holy Spirit and resentful of any reference to spiritual things. Eph 4 does not contain the faintest hint that the charismatic character of all church ministries was restricted to a certain period of church history and was later to die out.[72]

evangelists. Eph 4:11 provides the only mention in the Pauline writings of the specific ministry of an "evangelist," but in II Tim 4:5 a bishop is exhorted to "do an evangelist's work." It is unlikely that in Ephesians this title

---

[67] 1:13; 4:15?, 25, 29, 31; 5:3–4, 12.

[68] Calvin concludes: the church lives from the gospel. The priority given to the ministry of proclamation is also recognized, e.g. by E. Käsemann, RGG, II, 518, and Hegermann, *Schöpfungsmittler,*" pp. 155–56. Robinson, however, assumes that administrators (who according to Acts and I, II Timothy were at work in Ephesus) are not mentioned for one reason only: theirs was a purely local ministry, whereas Eph 4:11 enumerates offices in the church universal, cf. Harnack, *Expansion.* The reference to "shepherds," i.e. to a distinctly local ministry, reveals how brittle Robinson's argument is at this point.

[69] In I Clem 40:5 an opposite tendency is visible: the OT distinction between clergy and laity is considered binding for a corresponding division of ranks inside the church.

[70] Compare II Cor 8:23; Philip 2:25; Rom 16:7 with I Cor 9:1; Gal 1:1, 12. See also *Did.* xi ff.; Lightfoot, *Galatians,* pp. 95 ff. Abbott, J. Huby, Gaugler opt for the wider, Schlier for the narrower sense of "apostles" in Eph 4:16.

[71] See, e.g. Calvin. Bengel puts emphasis upon the opening of the NT prophets' eyes for the future. A main distinction of the NT prophets from their OT predecessors may be seen in the fact that they speak in the name of the risen Lord rather than of Yahweh.

[72] See Robinson, p. 98. In *Did.* xv 1–2 it is explicitly affirmed that bishops and deacons have taken over the ministry of prophets and teachers—apparently in reaction against suspect migrating teachers and false apostles and prophets, see xi–xiii. Calvin taught that "apostles," "prophets," "evangelists" were given only to the primitive church, but that in later times the gospel would be preached solely by pastors and doctors. Thus he sought to refute the Roman Catholic doctrine regarding the transition of apostolic authority to the bishops and the pope. Gaugler, however, mentions Catherine of Siena, Luther, and Bengel as prophets given by God to the church after the end of the NT times. Abbott simply identifies prophets with preachers. Since Ephesians distinctly presupposes that living apostles and prophets are essential to the church's life, the list of 4:11 speaks in favor of an early date of this epistle. Dibelius, on the other hand, believes that Ephesians breaks up the untouchable triad of apostles-prophets-teachers (I Cor 12:28) and thereby reveals its post-apostolic origin.

meant, as it did in later times, the writer of a gospel;[73] rather "evangelists" were missionaries who brought the gospel into new regions—perhaps into the Lykos valley which included the cities of Colossai, Laodicea, and Hierapolis; such "evangelists" may also have converted those "Ephesians" who were not personally known to Paul. Although the extension of their work was probably narrower than that of the "apostles," their work resembled and continued that of the apostles.[74] It is unlikely that their testimony pointed primarily to the past in contrast to that of the prophets which allegedly looked toward the future. Their very name "evangelist" underlines the fact that the church accepted the gospel preached by them as a manifestation of Christ's own proclamation of peace (cf. 2:17).[75]

teaching shepherds. Lit. "teachers and shepherds." Our translation takes a one-sided decision in an age-old issue. According to the Greek wording the teachers and shepherds belong closer together than e.g. apostles and prophets, or prophets and evangelists. The pronominal article, *tous men, tous de,* repeated four times before the ministries previously listed, is missing before "teachers." The conjunction *kai* which is found between "shepherds" and "teachers" does not always mean "and"; it may also mean "that is" or "in particular." Since in Eph 4:11d the conjunction is not followed by the pronominal article, it is probable that it designates "shepherds" and "teachers" as one common group which complements the other three groups of "the apostles," "the prophets," and "the evangelists."[76] Still, the wording chosen is so ambiguous that it is difficult to decide the exact character of the fourth group. Does it unite two lesser groups, i.e. "teachers" and "shepherds," or is it composed of one ministry only, that is, of teaching shepherds, or of shepherding teachers?[77] While sometimes in the NT "teachers" and "shepherds" (or the equivalent of shepherds) are mentioned separately, and at other occasions the titles "bishop" and "elder" occur, all these functions probably belong together.[78] In I Tim 3:2 and Titus 1:9 it is stipulated that

---

[73] D. Hadidian, *"Tous de euaggelistas* in Eph 4:11," CBQ 28 (1966), 317–21, refers to Eusebius HE III 37:2–3; v 10:2, and to a remark in W. M. L. de Wette's *Einleitung* of 1858, in order to establish this meaning. But the NT use of the words, "to evangelize," "the gospel," and the designation of the deacon Philip as an "evangelist" (Acts 21:8; cf. II Tim 4:5) do not support his suggestion.

[74] Schlier; Gaugler; Eusebius HE v 10.

[75] With Calvin, against Bengel.

[76] Some modern commentators (e.g. Westcott, Robinson, Abbott, Dibelius) see in the shepherds and teachers (un-inspired and un-inspiring?) occupants of a *local* ministry while the inspired ministries of apostles, prophets, evangelists are considered functions fulfilled in the church *universal.* Texts such as I Cor 12:28 and Acts 13:1–3 do not exactly bear out this distinction. *Did.* XI 1–2 speaks of wandering teachers, but XIII 1–2 (also XV 1–2) presupposes that some (the better) of the prophets and teachers settle down. If in Eph 4:11 shepherds and teachers are the same persons, their office should be considered strictly local.

[77] According to Theophylact, Calvin, Robinson, Schlier, the work of shepherds is distinct from that of teachers. But Jerome, Bengel, and others assume that the shepherd and teaching ministry is one and the same.

[78] Repeatedly the nouns "shepherd," "bishop," "elder" and the verbs expressing the function of the first two, appear to be synonyms: in I Peter 5:1–2 "elders" are authorized to "tend the flock of God" (a variant reading adds, "by caring for them," *episkopountes*); Christ is called "shepherd and bishop of our souls," I Peter 2:25. The "elders" assembled in Miletus are to "take heed . . . of the flock, in which the Holy Spirit appointed you bishops to tend the church of God," Acts 20:28. Originally, e.g. in the OT legends of David's origin and the promises given to Israel of a Messiah, the title "shepherd" and the verb "tending" described the office of a monarchic ruler. In Ezek 34 the shepherd to be raised is contrasted to the many evil shepherds of Israel; cf. Jer 2:8; 3:15; 23:1–6; LXX Isa 63:11, etc. Correspondingly, in the NT Jesus Christ is called the "good" or the "great shepherd," John 10; I Peter 2:25; 5:4; Heb 13:20; Rev 2:27; 12:5; 19:15; Christ entrusts to Peter the care of his flock, John 21:16–17. But in I Thess 5:12; Rom 12:8 a multiplicity of "officials," in I Cor 12:28

"a bishop must be . . . an apt teacher . . . able to give instruction in sound doctrine." The inclusion of teachers and administrators, or, of teaching and administration, among God's, Christ's or the Spirit's gifts (I Cor 12:28–29; Rom 13:6–8; Eph 4:7–11) shows that the authority of "shepherds" or "teachers" was ascribed to a *charisma* (lit. "a gift graciously given," or "a favor granted") just as much as that of "apostles" and "prophets." Certainly the "shepherds" who were also called "bishops" had to fulfill many other useful functions besides teaching; Eph 4:11 does not pretend to enumerate all authorized services rendered in, to, and by a living church and congregation, see vs. 12. But the company in which the "shepherds" are mentioned here suggests that their teaching work alone is directly related to the risen Christ's rule over the church.[79] According to this passage only teaching bishops belong in the constitution of the church. Thomas Aquinas goes so far as to declare, "The administration of temporalities does not belong to bishops." Our translation "teaching shepherds" seeks to do justice to the stress laid upon the teaching capacity of a bishop, but it leaves open the possibility that at Paul's time some bishops considered other tasks their first responsibility, e.g. the administrative functions mentioned in I Cor 12 and Rom 12.

12. *to equip the saints.* Lit. "for the equipment" (RSV). The Greek noun *katartismos* occurs only here in the NT. It is derived from a verb that means "to reconcile" (e.g. political parties), "to set bones" (in surgery), or more generally "to restore," "to prepare," "to create."[80] The noun describes the dynamic *act* by which persons or things are properly conditioned;[81] it does not mean an "instrument" or "armament."[82] The statements about "God's [splendid] armor" (6:10–17) and the use of imagery from the sports arena (I Cor 9:24–27) would suggest that the "conditioning" of the saints takes place in a battle or in a competition. But Eph 4:12 itself provides a clarification in other terms: by the men appointed by Christ (vs. 11) the saints are being prepared for another specific task.

for the work of service. In contemporary non-biblical and LXX Greek, the noun *diakonia* denoted service of every kind. Originally the verb "to serve" meant serving at the table.[83] In the NT a wide range of services is covered by

---

of "administrations," in Philip 1:1 of "bishops," in Heb 13:7, 17, 24 of "leaders," in Acts 11:30; 14:23, etc.; James 5:14 of "elders" is mentioned. A monarchic episcopate is not attested earlier than in the Pastoral Epistles. Those called "shepherds" in Eph 4:11 are probably not different from elders. "Teachers" are separately mentioned in I Cor 12:28–29; Acts 13:1; cf. James 3:1; Heb 5:12. If I Tim 2:7; II Tim 1:11 contain authentic Pauline elements, Paul called himself, "a teacher of the Gentiles." The Qumran community had among its officers a *mebaqqēr* or *pāqīd* who possessed fiscal and teaching authority; see 1QS vi 11–12, 19–20; CD ix 18–19; xiii 6–11, 16; xiv 8–13 etc. The Jerusalem church and other early Christian congregations apparently adopted this form of ministry.

[79] Schlier's divergent opinion is contradicted, e.g. by a Note of JB on 4:11: "Paul limits his list to charismas that relate to teaching and which are the only ones that apply in this context, vv. 13–15." In turn, the Vatican II "Dogmatic Constitution on the Church" (*Lumen gentium* III, arts. 25–27) declares that the "teaching office" of the bishops is pre-eminent but that bishops also exert the ministries of "sanctifying" and "governing."

[80] Cf. LXX Pss 8:3; 39:7; cf. Heb 11:3; 13:21; I Peter 5:10; Matt 4:21; 21:16; Mark 1:19; Luke 6:40; I Thess 3:10; Gal 6:1; I Cor 1:10; II Cor 13:9.

[81] I.e., according to LSLex, 910, the training or discipline; following Calvin, the constitution.

[82] The robe with which the saints are equipped is the "new man" (4:24); the weaponry they receive are faith, knowledge, the word, the gospel, righteousness (6:14–17); the ground to walk on is the good works provided by God (2:10). In 4:12 such instruments are not mentioned, only the appropriate training of men is in mind.

[83] This is still evident in Mark 1:13; Luke 10:40; 17:8; 22:26–27; Acts 6:1–2.

this word, e.g. the mutual assistance of church members in secular daily matters and the apostolic "service of the word" fulfilled for the benefit of believers and unbelievers.[84] In COMMENT VI the question will be discussed of whether or not a comma ought to be set before (and perhaps after) the words "for the work of service." If it is inserted, then a first purpose, the equipping of (all) the saints, is sharply distinguished from a second aim: the provision made for special ministers inside the church. The "building of the body" may then form a third goal, or it may explain the scope either of the first or the second purpose, or of both. In 4:12-13 the occurrence of no fewer than six teleological clauses (formulations indicating an intention or goal) is surprising; here the church is described exclusively from the perspective of her destiny and hope. See COMMENTS VII on 2:11-22 and VII at the end of this section.

for building the Messiah's body. The mixture of metaphors comes to the point of surpassing the freedom occasionally taken by Greek writers. To the diverse images of training and serving are now added those of building and of a body. The latter two are here, and again in 4:16, combined and intermingled. Conflation of metaphors is not necessarily tantamount to confusion of incongruous thoughts and things; rather it may indicate the insufficiency of any one figure of speech to convey the intended message exactly. Diverse metaphors can be mutually corrective, and they are complementary in this verse. If Paul had used only one image in 4:12 and had spoken, e.g. of the "growth," not the "building," of the body, nothing more would be expressed than a further development of an organism according to the laws of internal cellular processes. The term "building" however, implies that (as it were from the outside) stones, blocks, beams, joints, and finally a keystone must be added. A building under construction cannot grow except by substantial additions which it receives rather than produces itself. On the other hand, the building metaphor alone might depict the church as a mechanical composite and would neglect the gift of life, will, and personality which according to Eph 2:1-6, 16 are essential to the church.[85] The term "body of the Messiah"[86] is as surprising in the Greek text as in its English version. At all other analogous places the Pauline Epistles mention the body "of Christ" (*Christou* without article). In 4:12 the article is found before *Christou.* It is possible that before Paul's letters were written, Jewish-Christian circles under the influence of the speculations about Adam[87] had begun to speak of the body of the Messiah in a metaphorical sense.[88] Most likely vs. 12 is, *in toto* or in part, a quote from a pre-Pauline hymn.

13. *until we all come to meet the unifying faith and knowledge of the*

---

[84] I Cor 16:15-18; Eph 6:21-22; Acts 1:17, 25; Rom 11:13. In Heb 1:14 the angels are defined as "ministering spirits sent out for the benefit of those who are to inherit salvation."

[85] In Gnostic writings metaphors are equally mixed. E.g. the prime man (*Anthrōpos*) is being "built," see Schlier, *Christus*, pp. 27 ff., for references. In Jewish apocalyptic literature, a building's cubic form can denote perfection, see COMMENT VI on 3:14-21. However, these "parallels" do not prove that Eph 4:12-13 reproduces either one of the respective notions.

[86] But cf. I Cor 12:12, "Just as the body . . . so also the Messiah."

[87] See Comment VI B C on 1:15-23 for evidence, esp. R. Jewett, *Paul's Anthropological Terms*, pp. 239-45, 250, 457.

[88] J. J. Meuzelaar, *Der Leib des Messias* [*sic!*], p. 57, asserts that whenever reference is made to the body of Christ, "directly or indirectly the article is added to the name of Christ" so that "the Jewish idea of the Messiah becomes visible" (German: *hindurchleuchtet*).

Son of God, the Perfect Man, the perfection of the Messiah who is the standard of manhood. The vocabulary used in this verse is rather strange to Paul and seems to support the arguments of those who question the authenticity of Ephesians. However, once again this reasoning alone is not sufficient for a final verdict. Vs. 13 looks very much like a hymnic or confessional fragment which was inserted by an editor or copyist of Ephesians, or was added by Paul himself—just as he had used many other liturgical pieces. Or should Paul have borrowed prose terminology from an unknown source, e.g. from mystic circles or Mystery Religions?[89] It is also possible that in this verse the apostle expresses thoughts which he did not publicize in other letters. Presently available tools and criteria of research do not permit a decision. The grave problems of translating and explaining the various words and parts of 4:13 are so intertwined that they defy a brief treatment in this NOTE. See COMMENT VII for all questions of details, coherence, parallels, and possible meanings. At this place only one striking fact must be mentioned: the term *anēr* used here to denote the perfect "man" does not mean "mankind" (as Greek *anthrōpos* and Hebrew *'adām* often do) but "adult man" in contradistinction to a woman and a child.

14–16. In the Greek original these three verses form the second half of one long sentence running from vss. 11–16. This sentence was introduced by the independent clause in vss. 11–12 saying that in order to equip the church for its public ministry Christ has installed distinct ministers. The first dependent clause (vs. 13) has restated the intention of Christ's action and at the same time described the goal toward which the servant church is moving. The second dependent statement, i.e. vss. 14–16, leads back from the glimpse at eschatological fulfillment to the daily exigencies of the migrating church. Except for the final part of vs. 16, the subject matter of vss. 14–16 is more closely related to vss. 11–12 than to vs. 13. Therefore, it may be asked whether vs. 13 with its "eschatological outlook" possesses only the limited weight of a parenthesis? More likely vss. 14–16 confirm the eschatology of vs. 13. They show how at the present time the final event determines the members, the movement, the shape of the wandering people of God. Grammar and syntax provide no answer to the question of how vss. 14–16 are coordinate with, subordinate to, or illustrative of vs. 13. But it is plain that in vss. 14–16 events are described that take place while the church is en route to meet her Lord.

14. *No longer are we to be babes.* Sometimes the Greek word *nēpios*, translated as "babes," is free from a polemical undertone. It may mean very young children or legal minors (see e.g. Gal 4:1–3). But there are passages in which a value judgment is included; then it signifies those who are infantile and stupid.[90] The last meaning is presupposed in Eph 4:14: the imperfection, the immaturity of children is mentioned here in opposition to the perfection of the Perfect Man as described in vs. 13.[91] In other passages of Ephesians

---

[89] Dibelius assumes that in this passage mystic language is taken up but reinterpreted and employed in an ecclesiastic sense.

[90] Cf. I Cor 3:1–2; 13:11; 14:20; Rom 2:20; Heb 5:12–13; G. Bertram, TWNTE, IV, 912–23; W. Grundmann, "*Nēpios* in der urchristlichen Paränese," NTS 5 (1959), 188–205; S. Légasse, "La révélation aux *nēpioi*," RB 67 (1960), 321–48.

[91] Many commentators have seen in vs. 14 a proof that the saints' rather than Christ's adulthood and perfection are described in vs. 13, cf. COMMENT VII C. Indeed in I Cor 3:1 and Heb 5:13–14 those perfect are distinguished from those as yet infantile. But H. Greeven (in M. Dibelius) and

the words "no longer" point to a status or behavior of Gentiles preceding their inclusion in the people of God.[92] Does the exhortation "No longer . . ." in 4:14 insist upon the break with a Gentile past? If this is assumed, then the verse contains a description of pagan life, conduct, beliefs, and it duplicates other passages in Ephesians that serve the same purpose.[93] In that case pagan religion and conduct would be characterized as an infantile state of development, to be overcome by a religion of maturity. Yet for several reasons it is more likely that heretical Christian teachings are meant. Verse 14 interrupts the generally peaceful tone of Ephesians, cf. 2:8-9; 5:5, 11. Almost all other Pauline letters, including Colossians, contain strong polemic outbursts against opponents of Paul and distorters of the gospel. The adversaries so rebuked lived inside the Christian church rather than among unbaptized Gentiles; they were not all of pagan origin but also included Jews (cf. Gal 2:14 and II Cor 11:22). The polemic of Eph 4:14 is in line with the unquestioned Pauline Epistles—except for two facts. (a) Anti-heretical polemic occupies only minimal space. (b) There is no hint that Paul's authority was challenged by Christian or pseudo-Christian opponents. Both features are not sufficient reasons to question Paul's authorship. Either the old Paul was milder, or the specific situation of those addressed made it superfluous to refute errors by more than a general expression of misgivings. If Colossians was written before Ephesians and was known to the "Ephesians," the extensive anti-heretical middle part of Colossians needed no duplication. None of these arguments is decisive, but each would help to explain the peculiarities of Eph 4:14. An exact reconstruction of the beliefs and practices of the heretics decried in this verse is impossible, just as in the case of other Pauline letters, including Galatians, II Corinthians, Philippians and the Pastoral Epistles.[94]

tossed by waves and whirled about by every doctrinal gust. Ps. 107:23-27 contains a vivid description of the impression made by the sea raging upon people who were not traditional seafarers. Men acquainted with the sea know even better the deadly power of wind and waves; they are all the more grateful for the presence of a possible savior or means of salvation.[95] In Isa 57:20-21 the wicked are compared to the raging sea; they are the opposite of those "far and near" to whom "peace" is announced (Isa 57:19; Eph 2:13, 17). In most diverse places in the NT, similar imagery is used to describe erring and misleading teachers and movements inside the church.[96] The storm metaphors are

---

Schlier are right in affirming that in Eph 4:13-14 the contrast is between babes and the perfect man himself, not between babyish and perfect saints. In the interpretation of these verses the identity of the "perfect man" ought not to be determined after the measure of silly infants. Rather one "perfect man" makes apparent the immaturity of many babes.

[92] See 2:19; 4:17, 28: cf. the references to the past in 2:2-3 (including Jews), 11-13; 5:8. As in Acts 17:21 Athens is called the city where the teaching of ever new things was most highly esteemed, also in Eph 4:14 the ever changing deceitful teachings might be identified with pagan, perhaps Greek, wisdom.

[93] See esp. Eph 2:1-2, 11-13; 4:17-19; Rom 1:18-32; cf. COMMENT II on 4:17-32.

[94] Cf. Matt 7:15; 24:11-12 par.; Acts 20:28-30; Rev 2:14-15, etc. The attempt made by W. Schmithals to discover Gnosticism behind most heretical trends has been mentioned before. Rev 2:2 mentions "false apostles" who were unmasked at Ephesus. The term "apostle" can indicate a Jewish and/or Gnostic background of the heretics. More subtle are the procedure and results of D. Georgi, *Der Gegner des Paulus im Zweiten Korintherbrief*, Neukirchen: Neukirchener Verlag, 1964: he distinguishes between Jewish-Hellenistic apologetical and Gnostic trends.

[95] Matt 8:24-25 par.; Ps 107:28-29; Jonah 1; Acts 27, etc.

[96] Besides Eph 4:14 see James 1:6; Heb 13:9; Jude 12. According to Josephus *ant.* IX 239, Nahum called Nineveh "a troubled pool of water."

obviously a trait of anti-heretical polemics that was not originally Pauline.[97] The opposite of the heretics' blatant lack of stability and reliability is called "faith" in the NT.[98] Whose faith? In the Gospels and in James the faith of the Christians is to meet the storms of the sea and of heresy, but in COMMENT VII it will be argued in detail that Ephesians places the accent at a different place: the "faith and knowledge of God's Son" (4:13) is the rock on which the gusts and waves of heresy break, rather than the orthodox and unshakable faith of the believers. In no case is heresy considered or treated as a form of faith. Heresy is identified with unbelief and wickedness.

[. . . caught] in the trickery of men who are experts in deceitful scheming. Lit. "in the cheating of men, in cleverness for the scheming of error." Only two of the five nouns occurring in this overloaded phrase have an inherent evil meaning. (a) The word translated by "trickery" is derived from a word denoting the dice used by players: it means wicked dice-playing.[99] (b) The noun "error" (rendered in our translation for stylistic reasons by "deceitful") needs no explanation. The other three nouns rarely have an evil connotation. There are few cases in the Bible in which the term "men" is used in a depreciatory sense.[100] In Eph 4 man-made doctrines stand in opposition to the Messiah's peace proclamation (2:17), his school (4:20–21), and his authorized ministers' testimony (1:13; 4:11). The word rendered by "scheming" (methodeia, from which "method" is derived) has not yet been traced in pre-NT Greek. But the corresponding verb, "to treat by rule," "to use cunning," "to defraud" (methodeuō), occurs in the LXX (II Kings [II Sam] 19:28) and in non-biblical Greek as well.[101] In Eph 6:11 the noun is used to denote the devil's procedure, and in the text of Pap. 46 Eph 6:12 to describe the principalities' way of operation. It is not found in any other NT book or in the Apostolic Fathers. While the noun translated by "experts" (lit. "in cleverness," "in shrewdness") most frequently has a good sense in the LXX,[102] among classical Greek writers and in the NT its meaning is always bad.[103] In Eph 4:14 cleverness or shrewdness is either the sphere in, or the instrument by which, the heretics pursue their ends.[104] In either case, the phrase "in love" (4:15–16) is directly opposed to the heretical stance and method. Linguistic reasons make it probable that, correspondingly, "deceitful scheming" stands in contrast to the "equipping of the saints" (vs. 12). The heretical teachers are bluntly accused of bad intentions. All the more do unstable and immature saints need teachers who can lead them out of error and toward solid knowledge of the truth.[105]

15. by speaking the truth in love. The Greek verb used at this point

---

[97] Schlier's reference to "each windy . . . ravishing modern doctrine" is homiletical rather than informative regarding the origin of Paul's metaphors.

[98] The root of the corresponding Hebrew noun 'emūnah is, as was earlier stated, the verb "to be firm."

[99] Intentional fraud is probably meant (cf. Epictetus dissertationes II xix 28; StB, III, 599; Dibelius)—rather than "the proneness of the human heart to wander from the truth," as Beare, IB, X, 694, assumes.

[100] E.g. in Isa 31:3; Ezek 28:9; Jer 10:14; Col 2:8, 22; Matt 15:9 quoting Isa 29:13. In I Tim 4:1 false teaching is ascribed to demons rather than to men.

[101] Cf. Ignatius Phil. vii 1.

[102] See the use of the abstract noun and of the corresponding adjective in Prov 1:4; 8:5; 13:1, 16, etc.; but in Josh 9:4 a ruse or fraud is described by it.

[103] It is the method of the serpent, II Cor 11:3; see also 4:2; 12:16; I Cor 3:19; cf. Job 5:12; Luke 20:23.

[104] The latter is the opinion, e.g. of Abbott, KJ, RSV, NEB.

[105] Cf. Gaugler, pp. 180–81.

(*alētheuō*) may mean "to cherish," "to maintain," "to say," "to do," "to live the truth."[106] In the context of Eph 4:15 the testimony given by speech plays an outstanding role as the references to the confession, the ministers of the Word, true and false teaching, and lying show. In Gal 4:16 Paul uses the verb *alētheuō* in the narrow sense of "saying the truth" or "preaching the gospel." There is no evidence that he knew the meanings "to cherish" or "to do the truth." Therefore, it is advisable to understand Eph 4:15a as an allusion to verbal testimony.[107] The passage calls for the right confession, and it urges the whole church and all its members to be a confessing church.[108] Most interpreters agree that the term "in love" is not a redundant duplication of the reference to "love" in vs. 16:[109] there it qualifies the growth, here "speaking the truth." Orthodox teaching can and must not be promoted at the expense of love. Paul speaks of a confessional stance that is founded on God's love, mutual love, and an edifying missionary zeal (cf. 4:29). The truth entrusted to the congregation is the truth of all-conquering love. Where there is no love, the truth revealed by God is denied. Equally, without "truth" there may well be a "conspiracy" that aims to subjugate men to human "opinions" (Calvin), but no solid unity and community.

we shall grow in every way. Lit. "we shall grow all things." In earlier contexts some philological idiosyncrasies and specific undertones of the verb "to grow" and of the ambiguous meaning of "all things" (this term may mean either "all objects" or "totally") have been discussed.[110] There arguments prevailed in favor of the intransitive understanding of "growing" (opposite to the sense "making to grow") and of the adverbial meaning of "all things." But Eph 4:15 poses the same problems again. If a different interpretation were required here, a revision of former judgments would probably become necessary. Does this verse affirm that the saints are "growing in every way" or that they make all (created) things grow toward Christ? Schlier has chosen the second option: "We cause the totality to grow into Christ . . . In his body . . . Christ draws all things into the *pleroma* . . . The Church as his body, when it relates the world to itself, is simply in process of taking over what truly belongs to it."[111] The ecclesiology ascribed to Ephesians in Schlier's interpretation is distinctly imperialist and triumphalist: "The Church . . . is . . . taking over." The protest of E. Käsemann and other expositors that such a doctrine of the church can not possibly be Pauline appears fully justified.

[106] See the variant reading of the Codex Boernerianus; JB; Abbott; Bultmann, TWNTE, I, 251; cf. the distinctive Johannine teaching on truth, Bultmann, TWNTE, I, 245–46.
[107] Among the texts supporting this interpretation are Eph 4:4–6, 11, 14, 20–21, 25; Gal 4:16; cf. 2:5, 14; II Cor 6:7; 7:14; Col 1:5; I Tim 3:15; II Tim 2:15 etc.; outside the NT, e.g. LXX Gen 42:16; Josephus *vita* 132, 338.
[108] Gaugler.
[109] E.g. Theophylact, Oecumenius, Erasmus, Calvin, Grotius, de Wette, Westcott, Abbott, KJ, RSV, NEB. The opposite view is represented by G. C. Harless and Meyer.
[110] See the last NOTE on 2:21; COMMENT VII 2 on 2:11–22; fn. 63 to 1:15–23; COMMENT V B on 1:15–23.
[111] TWNTE, III, 681; see also Schlier, pp. 190, 205–6. Three philological arguments are available in favor of Schlier's translation and exegesis. (a) In classical Greek, as well as in I Cor 3:6–7; II Cor 9:10; Herm. *vis.* III 4:1; see also BDF, 101; WBLex, 121, the meaning of "to grow" is transitive, as in English, growing vegetables. Eph 4:15 may belong to that minority of NT passages in which the classical meaning is retained. (b) While outside of Colossians and Ephesians the term "all things" occasionally possesses adverbial meaning, in these epistles it seems always to denote the universe. (c) Eph 4:15 would duplicate vss. 12–13 and 16 if it treated the church's growth.

Abbott offers a milder version of Schlier's opinion. He understands the passage to describe the growth of individual persons not yet belonging to the church. While indeed 2:7 and 3:10 have shown that in Ephesians the church has a missionary and cosmic role, Schlier's triumphalistic interpretation is subject to serious doubts.[112] It contradicts the servant function of the church (4:12, etc.)[113] Eph 4:15 speaks most likely of the growth of the church members "as a confessing and loving church."[114] Since elsewhere in Ephesians and Colossians the verb "to grow" is always used in its intransitive sense, the same must be true of Eph 4:15. Only if there were no viable alternative to Schlier's interpretation would it be necessary to consider this verse an exception. Our translation shows that there is another choice.

toward him who is the head, the Messiah. While the ancient natural scientists' doctrines of head and body, viz. of the relationship of the brain and the nerves afforded some parallels to the notion of growth "from" the head,[115] the idea of a growth "toward" the head is not supported by physiology contemporary with Paul. At the same time, neither OT nor Orphic nor Gnostic utterances on the "head" provide an unambiguous explication of the diction used in 4:15. Perhaps the building imagery used in 2:20–22 for describing the church's growth toward the keystone is transferred in 4:15 to metaphors belonging to the head-body complex; or the pilgrims' movement toward the coming Christ (4:13) is transformed into the image of "growth toward" a goal. Robinson rightly observes that in 4:15–16 a "struggle of language" takes place, a struggle caused by the fact that Paul was about to work out the novel conception of unity among men depending on Christ. It is unlikely that the apostle speaks of individuals—as if each of them could "grow" up to a self-consciousness, maturity, perfection of his own. Paul portrays people who "learn more and more to live as a part of a great whole."[116]

In harmony with numerous variant readings that add the article to *Christos,* the last word of vs. 15 is translated by "the Messiah" rather than by "Christ." But it is also possible that despite the frequent other references in Ephesians to the "Messiah," at this place the author of the epistle used "Christ" as a proper name.

16. In the original language the diction and syntax of this verse are "rather incomprehensible."[117] A word-by-word translation of the whole clause would be totally obscure. Characteristic of the almost impenetrable dimness spread over 4:16 are the following elements:

a) The vocabulary used here belongs to at least three different realms. Building metaphors, the body-head analogy, and the bridegroom-bride simile (the terms "sustenance" and "love" belong in the latter) can be distinguished.

b) The architectural, physiological, and sociological terms are joined together in a happy, if puzzling, whirl. Several verbs and nouns fit more than

112 (a) God rather than the church gives growth, I Cor 3:6–7; II Cor 9:10; (b) In Eph 1:23 as well as in 4:16 "all things" may be mentioned in the adverbial sense. (c) Repetitions frequently occur in Ephesians.
113 See COMMENT IV on 3:1–13.
114 Gaugler.
115 See the physiological theories collected above in COMMENT VI A B on 1:15–23.
116 Robinson, pp. 102–3; see also Abbott.
117 Schlier, p. 208; cf. Robinson, p. 107. Conzelmann, p. 78 speaks of "a confusing pell-mell of hints . . . unperspicuous."

one imagery; one variant reading omits the seemingly superfluous reference to the fact that somebody or something is "at work"; another replaces the mechanical term "part" by the physiological concept, "member."[118] A palpable reason for the conflation of the several images was mentioned earlier: no single image appeared strong or clear enough to make all the points the author had in mind.[119] The origin of the mixture need not be sought in Gnosticism. As early as in the Genesis (Yahwist) account of the creation of Eve, (1) architectural, (2) physiological, and (3) marital elements are intertwined. According to Gen 2:22, God (1) built (2) the rib which he had taken from man (3) into a woman, according to the JB version which closely follows the Hebrew original. In Eph 5:31 Paul will use a quote from the same OT context.

c) The clarity of the Greek syntax of vs. 16 (i.e. of the relative clause terminating the complex Greek sentence which began in vs. 11) leaves much to be desired. (1) The first two words, lit. "from whom," may be connected with any one of several parts or words of this verse, or with all of them together. (2) The Greek text fails to make clear who supplies a provision and what is actually supplied; also obscure is whose "energy" is alluded to. (3) There is a lack of beauty, though not of meaning, in the words which literally rendered say "The body . . . makes the growth of the body . . . for the upbuilding of itself in love." (4) While those interpreters are to be followed who consider the term "the whole body" the grammatical subject of the whole clause,[120] the logical or material subject is not the body, but the head. The Messiah is the one "from whom" all things originate.

d) Despite the obscurity of several individual words and the whole syntax, substantial components of the author's intention can be clearly seen. All of them share a character of subtle dialectical affirmations. (1) It is Christ, the head, alone "from whom" the body derives unity, nourishment, growth—but Christ's monarchy and monopoly do not exclude but rather create the activity of a church engaged in "its own" growth and upbuilding.[121] (2) All that the body is, has, and does is determined by its (passive and active) relationship to the head—but this ("vertical") relationship establishes an essential and indispensable ("horizontal") interrelation among the church members. (3) While Christ provides for the body as a whole and makes it a unity, and while the body grows as a unit—no individual growth is mentioned here—the distinct personality of each church member is not wiped out but rather established by Christ's rulership and the church's community. What Christ is, does, and gives, is appropriate "to the needs" (lit. "to the measure") "of each single part." If the only things affirmed in Eph 4:16 were Christ's own activity, Christ's rule over all Christians, Christ's relationship to the community, then this verse would have been phrased more clearly in Greek and could be more easily interpreted in a modern language. But in this verse there are several accents, not just one: the church's and each member's responsive

---

[118] J. Horst, TWNTE, IV, 566, n. 81, admits that "part" is the better reading, but in the same breath he asserts that "part" "undoubtedly has here the sense of 'member'." Abbott considers "part" more suitable because of its more general meaning.

[119] See the last NOTE on 4:12.

[120] E.g. Haupt, Dibelius, Schlier.

[121] Cf. K. Barth, Church Dogmatics, IV 2 (1958), 634.

activity is not only recognized or tolerated but receives an emphasis of its own: "The body makes its own growth so that it builds itself up in love."

Our translation is motivated by the intention, but also burdened with the risk, of making the English version more perspicuous than the Greek original. The legitimacy of this motive and the necessity of this risk are subject to serious question, but a few things said clearly may be better than many presented ambiguously.

As stated, in the Greek the whole of vs. 16 forms a relative clause. This dependent clause is in our version recast into the form of three independent sentences. The first of these aims to elucidate what 4:16 says about Christ's unique place and work in regard to the whole church—a function which is also (but with less emphasis) pointed out by the second and third statements. The primary goal of the second sentence is to express Christ's special concern for each church member. The weight of the third sentence lies upon the responsibility and activity of the church as a community. (1) "He is at work fitting and joining the whole body together." (2) "He provides sustenance to it through every contact according to the needs of each single part." (3) "He enables the body to make its own growth so that it builds itself up in love."

He is at work. Lit. "from whom . . . according to inner operation." Since elsewhere in Ephesians energy (*energeia*) is always ascribed to God acting in Christ,[122] it is probable that Eph 4:16 refers to the divine work going on in the church for her benefit, rather than to an operation performed by the church or her members. The parallel Col 2:19 supports this interpretation, but several modern translations of 4:16 ascribe the *energeia* to the joints or parts of the body.[123]

fitting and joining the whole body together. Lit. "the whole body being fitted and kept together." In the second NOTE on 2:21 it was shown which technical meaning the verb "fit together" might have possessed among masons.[124] The second verb, translated by "joining together," is considered by Schlier an exact synonym, but Bengel and G. H. Whitaker have elaborated upon a distinctive meaning.[125] The difference between fitting and joining together has been considered analogous to that between regulation and consolidation, position and movement, or the members' relationship to the head and to fellow members. Since the parallel Col 2:19 contains the second verb only, Colossians may emphasize the unity with the head while Ephesians underlines both the vertical and the horizontal relationship of the saints.[126]

He provides sustenance to it through every contact. Lit. "from whom . . . through every contact of supply." The meaning of the two nouns and of their connection in a genitive construction require elucidation. The terms *epichorēgiā* ("supply," or "provision," or "sustenance") and *haphē* (translated here by "contact") are connected in a curious way. While the text states clearly that through every contact of supply something essential happens to

[122] 1:11, 19; 3:7, 20; cf. the devil's operation in 2:2.
[123] E.g. RSV, Phillips, NEB, JB, NTTEV. See Percy, pp. 413–14, for an interpretation of the parallel line in Col 2:19.
[124] The verb does not occur in Greek writings antedating Ephesians.
[125] G. H. Whitaker, *"Synarmologoumenon kai symbibazomenon,"* JTS 31 (1929–30), 48–49.
[126] So, e.g. Lightfoot, p. 266; Beare, IB, X, 695; Dibelius, p. 83.

the body, it is not equally patent how the instruments used by the head fulfill their function.

The Greek composite noun, *epi-chorēgiā* (in Col 2:19 the corresponding verb, *epi-chorēgeō*) denotes supply(ing) of a special kind. The simple Greek verb and noun, *chorēgeō* and *chorēgiā* mean (to make) payment for the cost of bringing out a chorus at a public festival. Eventually they signify making provisions for an army or expedition. The composite form of the verb which is found in Colossians appears outside the Bible, e.g. in papyri. There it is used as a technical term describing the provision of food, clothing, etc., which a husband is obliged (by marriage contract) to make for his wife.[127] Without employing the technical term, in Eph 5:29 Paul ascribes to Christ the head and to each husband the same responsibility: the "body" of Christ (the church) and the "flesh" of a husband (his wife) are "provided and cared for" by their head. Paul understood the abundant gift of the Spirit and the ample dispensation of seed and bread by God as an act of such providing.[128] In Eph 4:16 it is affirmed that the body receives from the head what nourishment, life, and direction it needs.[129]

By what means or through which channel does the sustenance flow from the head to the body? The text answers: through every *haphē*. The noun used at this point can have several meanings:

a) If one of the several definitions ascribed to Hippocrates is followed, it means the fibrous tissues connecting the body's bones, i.e. the ligaments.[130] Paul may indeed intend to say that upon orders from the head, the several parts of the body are held together by bonds. But in Col 2:19 "ligaments" are separately mentioned in the company of *haphai*. Therefore it is improbable that in Eph 4 *haphē* means ligament.

b) The Old Latin and Syriac, as well as the modern versions mentioned in fn. 123, and the majority of recent expositors take the noun to mean "joints." They think either of such joints of the body as elbows and knees, or of connecting parts, pivots, hinges, etc., of a building, or of both. If Eph 4:16 actually contains an emphatic reference to the function of the joints, then according to this verse some, not all, members of the church, e.g. those enumerated in vs. 11, hold and keep the church together. If this is the case, they are "mediators of grace" possessing a very special "measure of grace."[131] But there is no solid philological evidence that in Paul's time *haphē* ever meant "joint."[132] As long as this is not documented, Eph 4:16 cannot be used to demonstrate that Paul considered certain church members as joints, while the remaining members he identified as bones or muscles that are dependent upon the joints. When in I Cor 12 the body-member image is drawn out in detail, joints are not mentioned

---

[127] In Sir 25:22 the verb occurs in the list of things which a wife ought to provide for her husband.

[128] Gal 3:5; Philip 1:19; II Cor 9:10; cf. II Peter 1:5, 11.

[129] While Robinson, p. 104, rejects this interpretation, Benoit, "Corps, tête," pp. 26–27, and Gaugler, p. 183, support it.

[130] In Galen's *Lexicon*. At another place, Galen asserts that Hippocrates used it to describe a bundle of muscles; cf. Lightfoot, p. 265, for the reference.

[131] As Schlier, p. 208, suggests.

[132] In LSLex 288, only Eph 4:16 and Col 2:19 are quoted for the alleged sense "ligaments." See also WBLex 124. It appears that these lexicographers saw no reason to credit Hippocrates or another pre-Pauline author with this use of the noun.

at all. While no Pauline text speaks of a special charisma given to joints, all relevant parallels of Eph 4 affirm that each member has a charisma.[133] Each saint is a charismatic and serves all other members as an agent or instrument of Christ, the head, and of God's grace.

c) Chrysostom and Theodoret understood *haphē* to mean "sense" or "sensation." But Lightfoot's judgment on this understanding cannot be questioned: "This sense of *haphē* is wholly unsupported."[134]

d) The etymology of *haphē* suggests the translation, "touch," "contact," or "grip." According to Aristotle's knowledge of matters physiological, the parts of the body grow because there is an energy working in the body which enables its members to find connection (or coherence, *symphysis*) by their mutual touch or contact.[135] Indeed, contact is essential for the support, unity, and life of a body, just as a building cannot be stable unless the adjacent surfaces of its parts are linked together. This fact appears to be alluded to in the imagery of Eph 4:16. Most likely the apostle intends to say that in their mutual dependence and communication all church members are chosen tools of the head for communicating nourishment, vitality, unity, solidity to the body (or building) as a whole. The weakest member or part is in this case as essential to the life and unity of the whole as the strongest.[136]

The connection of the two terms, *epichorēgiā* and *haphē*, in the genitive construction, lit. "contact of supply," appears to permit several interpretations: the Greek genitive "of supply" may mean, e.g. that the contacts (or, the joints, according to other translations) "receive" supply (from the head, perhaps for their own benefit), that they "give" the necessary supply (to the body), or, that they themselves "are" the supply. However, in the context of Eph 4:16 only one paraphrase appears appropriate: every contact serves for supply. While this interpretation appears to be nearest the Greek original,[137] in our translation it has been replaced by the even freer version "He provides sustenance to it through every contact."

according to the needs of each single part. Lit. "to the measure of. . . ." This specification counteracts a possible misunderstanding: the church is not treated by her head as a collective of mutually exchangeable individuals who are as equal as drops in a bucket of water or grains of sand in a pile. Certainly all church members benefit from the "measure of the Messiah's gift," and all of them are gauged by the same "standard of manhood," Christ (4:7, 13); yet they are so cared for by the head that each one receives exactly and specifically what he needs.[138] All want forgiveness and are given forgiveness of sins, life from the dead, the seal of the Spirit, the administration of grace through the fellow saints. All move forward toward the final meeting with the "Perfect Man."[139] But since everyone is called to contribute his own share to the servant work and in the growth of the church (4:12),

133 Rom 12; I Cor 12.
134 Lightfoot, p. 265.
135 Aristotle *metaphysica* IV 1014B 20–21. Cf. Lightfoot, pp. 264–66. Abbott; C. Bruston, "Le sense de APHE dans la Bible," *Revue des études grècques* 24 (1911), 77–82 (ref.).
136 Cf. I Cor 12:22–23; 14:16.
137 J. Eadie, for example, avoids taking a position among the viable alternatives: he speaks of "every joint of the supply." Certainly this literal translation fails to make clear sense.
138 Conzelmann, p. 79, alludes to the adage *Suum cuique.*
139 1:7, 14; 2:14; 4:11, 13, 32.

each is also provided with a specific charisma. By giving many and diverse gifts to the saints, Christ himself distinguishes the community of the saints from a uniformed corps. It is he who gives each individual saint the right and the equipment to be, to live, and to act as a distinct person. Every saint is to make his own contribution to the mission and unity of the church.

He enables the body to make its own growth. Lit. "from him . . . the body makes the body's growth." While ancient doctors called the brain the supreme power or acropolis of the body, and compared the nervous system to a tree growing out of the brain,[140] they did not call the head the source of the body's growth. By speaking in 4:15–16 of a growth to and from the head, and of nourishment and life provided by the head, Paul went beyond the imagery provided by contemporary natural science. If there be any precedent at all to his diction, then the OT description of the royal head, the Messiah, as the breath of our nostrils (Lam 4:20) has led Paul beyond the limits of the physiological analogy. While praising the head as the source of life and growth, Paul emphasizes also the responsibility, freedom, and activity entrusted by the head to the body. The head's energy does not remain external, it conveys vitality to the body: the body "is to make its own growth."[141] Certainly the church lives exclusively by receiving Christ's gifts (4:7). She is no more than an instrument by which Christ himself makes God's wisdom known to the powers (3:10). But this recipient of Christ's gifts and this instrument of Christ is given "life" (2:5–6). The saints are to be active servants (4:12). The church is a personal partner (5:25 ff.) rather than an impersonal outgrowth or extension of Christ.[142]

so that it builds itself up in love. Lit. "for the upbuilding of itself. . . ." Once again the church is described under the aspect of her destiny.[143] She is still being built, but is as yet far from being a completed house of God. While in 2:20–22 God himself is the builder and in 4:12 God *or* the saints may be the constructors, 4:16 speaks of the self-edification of the church. Thus the responsibility, partnership, and activity of the servant church are proclaimed. Her commission is limited: she is to build herself. Indeed she cannot build Christ, the kingdom, or a better world. On the foundation laid by God

---

[140] See the quotations from Hippocrates and Galen collected in COMMENT VI A 3 on 1:15–23.

[141] Instead of the periphrastic form "to make growth," in Col 2:19 the simple verb "to grow" is used, and the words "with God's growth" are added. "God's growth" is the growth given by God, I Cor 3:6–7; II Cor 9:10. Similar periphrases of verbs are found in Rom 1:9; Eph 1:16; Philip 1:4; Acts 25:17; 27:18; Luke 5:33; I Tim 2:1; see WBLex, 689. While the meanings of the periphrases may in most cases be identified with those of the single verbs, in Eph 4:16 the formulation "to make growth" is accentuated by the addition of "its own" (lit. "the body's growth") and by the following inculcation, "building itself." No room whatsoever is left for belittling the body's own activity and responsibility under the dominion of Christ, the head.

[142] At this point two earlier observations may be repeated: according to Ephesians growth is ascribed only to the body, never to the head. The head fills the body (and all things), but the church and the universe do not fill up or make complete the Messiah. Schlier's assumption (see, e.g. *Christus,* p. 38) that in Eph 4:16 Christ is not only the head of the body, but head *and* body at the same time, includes the notion that Christ grows when the church grows. Indeed, John 3:30 speaks of a growth of Christ, but there the Pauline head-body imagery is not employed. In his commentary on Ephesians (p. 209) Schlier suggests that a Gnostic concept underlies the formulation used in Eph 4:16: the notion of a cosmic man who grows and/or is being built. This would mean that Eph 4:16 originally described Christ's and the universe's growth rather than the church's life and order. But there are no Gnostic or Gnosticizing documents from a period antedating Ephesians (even if this epistle is considered deutero-Pauline) that would clearly support Schlier's assumptions and conclusions.

[143] Just as in 1:14; 2:20–22; 4:12–13.

she lays stone beside stone or stone upon stone by collecting, adapting, and joining many men together. She gathers, prepares and supports people who have been far off but in whose midst God will dwell. To repeat an earlier formulation, she is to be a lighthouse in a dark world (5:8; Philip 2:15). Which plan is the church to follow during her construction? The text answers "in love." The reference to "love" is not in keeping with the building imagery and belongs to the realm of social behavior, especially of the bridegroom-bride relationship. Just as in I Corinthians a paean on love was inserted between two chapters describing the life of the body and the edification of the church (see I Cor 12–14), so also in Eph 4:16 "love" is denoted as the ground, the sphere, the instrument of the church's existence. This love has at least three dimensions: it is the love of God and Christ for man, man's reciprocal love of God and Christ, and the mutual love of the saints. A church in which this manifold love is at work will not occupy herself with the erection of a Tower of Babel and an empire vying for world dominion. Rather the structure erected will have the character of a building useful for rendering a service to many people. It will resemble, e.g. a pilgrim's inn or a halfway house. It will have gates that are open day and night for all who wish to enter (cf. Rev 21:25; 22:14). The mystery of this building is both contained and revealed in God's promise to dwell in it (2:22). Without the rule of love, the church is not built but dispersed (Calvin).

COMMENTS I–VIII on 4:1–16

I Structure and Summary

Though the word "church" is not used in Eph 4:1–16, this whole passage deals with its life, order, and purpose.[144] In the form of imperatives and of confessional, exegetical, narrative, eschatological, and polemical statements, the constitution of the church is described under diverse aspects.

In the preamble, vs. 1, the imprisoned Paul makes a pathetic appeal in which he introduces all the exhortations to follow with the headline, "Walk as men worthy of your vocation." In the first section, vss. 2–3, the chosen saints are admonished to live humbly, to bear one another, and to preserve unity. Here ecclesiology and ethics are so completely identified that they can neither be separated nor distinguished. In the second, vss. 4–6, the contents and the fact of the church's confession are called to mind to demonstrate how essential is oneness to the very being and life of the church. She can only live as confessing church. In the third, vss. 7–12, it is shown, by means of a comment upon a Psalm text, that the exalted Christ himself gives the church diverse gifts. Each of her members benefits from the gift given from above.

---

[144] Calvin sums up 4:1–16 by speaking of "the rule which Christ established in order to build his church." Literature dealing with the Pauline concept of the church was listed in BIBLIOGRAPHY 12. Monographs and essays treating specifically the church in Ephesians include: H. Schlier and V. Warnach, *Die Kirche im Epheserbrief*, Münster: Aschendorff, 1949; R. Schnackenburg, "Gestalt und Wesen der Kirche nach dem Epheserbrief," *Catholica* 15 (Münster, 1961), 104–20 (ref.); M. Barth, "The Church According to the Epistle to the Ephesians," in *Ecumenical Dialogue at Cornell University*, September 1960–September 1962 (New York: Ithaca, 1962), pp. 7–49; P. Benoit, "L'unité de l'église selon l'épître aux Éphésiens," AnBib 17–18, I (1963), 57–77.

In order that the "one" ministry entrusted to all the saints be fulfilled, "several" specific ministers are given by Christ to the church. They proclaim the Messianic peace, the salvation of those near and far. The church who listens and submits to the word spoken by the ambassadors of Christ is engaged in a public ministry. She is a servant of Christ in the world. In the last section, vss. 13-16, the church is promised that she will meet her Lord face to face. She seeks no other perfection than that contained in, and brought by, Jesus Christ. As long as she is still on the way to that point, she is to beware of heresy, to grow toward Christ and from him—enjoying and manifesting the provision he is making for her life, her unity, and the needs of each one of her members.

Instead of four, only two subdivisions of 4:1-16 may be distinguished: (a) the admonition for unity (vss. 1-6); (b) the diversity of gifts (vss. 7-16).[145] The contraction and expansion (systole and diastole) of the heart would then be an analogy to the movement from unity to diversity made in 4:1-16. However, since in almost all of these sixteen verses unity and diversity are equally emphasized, no one group of verses ought to be understood as discussing only or primarily either oneness or multiformity.

The author speaks mostly in general terms of the universal church rather than of a local congregation. Still, there are many traits that make his message concrete for local churches and his exhortations and promises relevant to daily exigencies. The apostle appears to face the danger inherent in a quest for personal salvation and perfection—if that quest is pursued at the expense of submission to Christ, of the unity of the congregation, of love as the guiding star.[146] Paul knows the breadth and length of mouthed confessions, and wants the Christians to make more than oral affirmations. He seems to be aware of disrespect for authority in the church, and counters by describing Jesus Christ as an omnipotent king who appoints in person some ministers to be respected by all his servants. At the same time he offers no security to saints seeking to dodge any responsibility of their own. No one among the saints can say he is not equipped or has nothing to contribute, for everyone is given a gift and an appointment. Tersely Paul denounces heretical teaching. Finally he runs through a whole gallery of images to demonstrate the source, the means, and the way of the church's growth.

Exhortation and confession, unity with Christ and unity among the saints, communal growth and the gifts given to individuals, the final goal and the way in which progress is made—all these elements are combined in pairs, coordinated, and arranged in order. Their diversity and their unity give this passage richness, depth, dynamic and dialectic power, an incisive but also a very complex character. Ethics, ecclesiology, and eschatology, these seemingly so diverse and unrelated theological disciplines, are here so intimately combined and melted into one whole that it is practically impossible to discern where one begins and the other ends. Still, in COMMENTS III, VI and VII, some

---

[145] Schlier, and others.

[146] Gnostics of the second century and individualists of all times cannot be held innocent of the attitude refuted by Ephesians. But this letter offers a precedent for meeting the indicated danger, rather than explicit polemics against the Gnostic temptation, despite Pokorný's opinion to the contrary (EuG, esp. pp. 126 ff).

inquiry will be made into the distinctive witness of Eph 4:1–16 regarding each of these three fields of proclamation and doctrine.

II   Proclamation, Exhortation, and Vocation

According to many interpretations of Ephesians, vs. 4:1 marks the beginning of the second main part of this epistle.[147] A solemn transition from proclamation (in the case of Ephesians: of hymnic praise) to exhortation, from indicative to imperative statements, from *kerygma* to *didache*, from gospel to law, from dogmatics to ethics—this topical shift has been observed in the external structure of several Pauline Epistles, and also in many individual Pauline affirmations. This sequence and procedure appear essential to Paul's teaching.[148] Before God demands anything of man he gives grace and salvation. When new life, obedience, discipline, and suffering are described, a consequence of justification by grace rather than a precondition or corollary of salvation are in mind. Works of obedience are the fruit of the Spirit, not merits establishing a claim upon God or righteousness. Earlier it was shown why in Pauline doctrine the "good works" expected from the saints by no means fall under the judgment pronounced over the "works of law."[149]

Only in Ephesians is the transition to exhortation made by means of a reference to a specific feature of Paul's own life, i.e. his captivity.[150] This allusion appears to have a double purpose: it makes the following admonitions specifically personal and urgent, and it reminds the readers of the price paid for discipleship.[151] Still, in Eph 4 as well as in the Pauline parallels, it is not Paul but God himself who extends the call and makes the appointment for the specific conduct which makes the suffering for Christ's sake bearable.

A key concept in this context is the term "calling." What is the essence and effect of God's call?[152] Election and calling ("vocation") are sometimes mentioned side by side; are they therefore separate decisions and actions of

[147] See section IX of the Introduction where an alternative is proposed. The resumption of the subject matter of 3:1 (i.e. of the reference to Paul's captivity) in 4:1 may well be a signal showing that the second major part of Ephesians has actually begun with ch. 3 and is continued in ch. 4.

[148] Rom 6 describes the basis of ethics; that chapter follows upon the kerygmatic section Rom 3:21 – 5:21. The special ethics enfolded in Rom 12 ff are connected with the preceding doctrinal chapters Rom 1–11 by the transition formula: "Therefore I beseech you, brethren, because of the mercies of God . . ." Cf. Col 2:6, "As therefore you have received the Messiah Jesus, the Lord, so walk in him"; 2:20 and 3:5, "If you have died with Christ . . . put to death what is earthly"; 3:1, "If therefore you have been raised with Christ, seek what is above"; Gal 5:25, 29, "If we live by the Spirit, let us also walk by the Spirit . . . The fruit of the Spirit is love, joy, peace . . ."; I Cor 5:7, "Cleanse out the old leaven as you are unleavened." Similarly Rom 6:11–13, 17, 19, etc. See the literature on Pauline ethics listed in BIBLIOGRAPHY 17. The particular function which baptism may have in mediating between indicative and imperative is being discussed with radically divergent results. Compare e.g. Schlier's position in his commentaries on Galatians and on Ephesians with von Soden's findings in his essay, "Sakrament und Ethik bei Paulus," in Fs Rudolf Otto, ed. H. Frick (Gotha: Klotz, 1931), pp. 1–40; repr. in *Urchristentum und Geschichte*, I (Tübingen: Mohr, 1951), 239–75; G. Bornkamm, "Taufe und neues Leben bei Paulus," in *Das Ende des Gesetzes* (München: Kaiser, 1952), pp. 35–50. A convenient summary of the recent discussion is found in K. Kertelge, *Rechtfertigung bei Paulus* (Münster: Aschendorff, 1967), pp. 228–63. A radical criticism of the relative consensus of these and other authors has been announced by V. P. Furnish, *Theology and Ethics*, p. 68: "The Pauline letters cannot be neatly divided into doctrinal and ethical sections at all, and . . . the distinction between 'kerygma' and 'didache,' at least when applied to Paul, is more misleading than helpful."

[149] See COMMENT VI B C on 2:1–10.

[150] It recalls the didactic use which Plato, and perhaps Socrates himself, made of Socrates' imprisonment.

[151] Not only in I, II Thessalonians, Philippians, II Corinthians, cf. Matt 24, Revelation, but also in Eph 5:16; 6:12, 20, suffering is an essential element of obedience.

[152] Cf. the third NOTE on 1:18 and the literature mentioned there.

God?[153] Both presuppose that God's specific favor is directed toward a people or person. Both include the revelation of God's decision. Both involve the appointment to, and the equipment for, a task to be fulfilled among other peoples or persons.[154] Those called possess no worthiness of their own. They are deemed worthy by God despite their inherent lack of nobility (I Cor 1:26–29). Through the "calling" they become "saints" (Rom 1:7).[155]

In biblical diction the noun "calling" or "vocation" is never used in the plural. Paul knows of but one calling. It is the same for all the saints—however diverse the spiritual gifts with which they are equipped.[156] God's call entrusts man with a high status and a correspondingly high responsibility and task. "One hope" (rather than diverse hopes to be relied on, or several ways to be followed) is the scope of the one call extended to all saints (4:4).

The nature and effect of calling may be compared with the bestowal of a title or a patent of nobility. Those made God's own people and servants (1:14 etc.) are equivalent knights of God. According to Paul[157] they are bound to a specific code of honor and conduct.[158] In II Peter 1:10 the saints are urged to "make firm" their "vocation and election." Eph 4:1 appeals to their honor: the apostle expects and bids his readers to "conduct themselves as men worthy of God's vocation." Parallel texts speak of that which is "worthy of God, of the Lord," or "of the gospel."[159]

The direct and immediate orientation of all conduct to the specific call of God, that is, to God himself who calls into obedience, is a decisive mark of distinction between Paul's ethical teaching and a moral instruction based upon the elaboration of virtues. Paul uses the term "virtue" but once: in Philip 4:8 he recommends serious pondering of everything virtuous. However, he does not call his ethical lists "catalogues of virtues" or ". . . of vices," as some of his interpreters do. Indeed, this nomenclature is misleading. In both Greek

[153] On the basis of passages such as Matt 22:14; Rom 8:30; II Peter 1:10, Reformed theologians have sometimes sharply distinguished between eternal predestination and (effectual) calling through the preaching of the gospel, see A. Heppe, *Reformed Dogmatics* (London: Allen, 1950), chs. VIII and XX.
[154] This is emphatically pointed out, e.g. in the statements by Paul himself and Luke concerning the apostle's election and vocation: Gal 1:15–16; Rom 1:1, 5; Act 9:15; 22:14–15; 26:16–18.
[155] Other Pauline specifications of "calling" are the following: it occurs "through the gospel," "in one hope," "in Christ," "in grace," II Thess 2:14; Eph 4:4; cf. 1:18; Col 3:15; Gal 1:6. It is a holy calling, both from above and upward, Philip 3:14; cf. Heb 3:1. It sets those called in a forward movement "toward" God's "kingdom and glory," "salvation," "eternal life," "freedom," "peace," I Thess 2:12; II Thess 2:13–14; I Tim 6:12; Gal 5:13; I Cor 7:15; Col 3:15.
[156] Man's professional occupation or social status is never denoted as (result of) God's calling. Rather man is met by God's call whatever his status or work may be (I Cor 7:17–24). The one text that seems to prove the opposite, i.e. Rom 1:1, *"Paul . . . called [to be an] apostle,"* is too ambiguous to establish a doctrine of diverse God-given "vocations." Rather it shows, in harmony with Eph 4:7–12; cf. I Cor 12:28–30, that God's calling is always effective and is manifested in the form of diverse charismas.
[157] Following, e.g. Matt 5:13–16, 46–48; 20:25–27, also according to Jesus' teaching.
[158] Robinson's interpretation (p. 90) can be summed up by the adage *"Noblesse oblige."* W. Jaeger, *Paideia*, 3 vols., 4th ed. (Berlin: de Gruyter, 1959), esp. I, 23 ff., 259 ff.; III, 145 ff. (Engl. tr. *Paideia*, 3 vols., New York: Oxford University Press, 1939–44) discusses the original connection between nobility and virtue among the Greeks, and some early attempts at codifying what was required of a nobleman. D. Daube, in commenting upon the participles with imperative function in rabbinical and NT texts (see fn. 23 to 3:14–21), speaks of an *élite* code that is described with overtones of enthusiasm. An "aristocratic" understanding of God's calling appears not to be strange to Paul's and his readers' thought. If the *saints* were considered to be still in a miserable and low position, the first imperative would probably be, lift up your head! But the first demands of Paul are an invitation to "humility and gentleness"—attitudes which specifically fit the strong and mighty, or may be more easily forgotten by them than by others. See also fn. 172.
[159] I Thess 2:12; III John 6; Col 1:10; Philip 1:27; see also I Clem 21:1; Polycarp v 2.

philosophy and popular opinion, virtues are entities, principles, values, if not deities that exist of their own right. They are ascribed a rank (a) between the levels of the deity and of man or (b) beside (or above) the gods, or they are believed to reside (c) in the human mind or (d) in a selected class of people.[160] Paul, however, does not intend to speak of independent or absolute values. Neither does he propagate ideas or ideals that underlie the universe or are inherent in its structure, in reason, in man's nature, in the *polis* (the political community), or in the rights and privileges of a class of noblemen. He speaks of the will of God that is to be done by all those saved from death, justified, and sanctified. The distinctive history between God and man, i.e. the personal covenant relationship, is decisive in the apostle's argument.

He speaks of "works" to be done or of "fruits" to be borne (Gal 5:22; Col 1:10, etc.) instead of praising abstract virtues. In an earlier context of Ephesians, Paul has mentioned "the good works provided by God as our way of life" (Eph 2:10). These same works are described in chapters 4–6. Their opposites are "the works" or "decisions of the flesh" (Gal 5:19–21; Eph 2:3). Rather than pronouncing a set of laws and imposing certain injunctions,[161] he reminds the Ephesians of what is fitting for the saints. In a friendly but urgent tone he tells them which are the right things to do, and what is improper (5:3–4; 6:1). "Royal princes are treated by their educators not with the stick but with an appeal to their rank and standing."[162] Paul's appeal to worthy conduct is distinct not only from sweeping or apodictic commandments, but also from trite, condescending or blandishing epistolary forms of requesting or suggesting a certain course of action.[163] In repeating the appeal to the ("high," Philip 3:14) vocation of the saints in Eph 4:4, Paul reassures the saints of their exaltation to a high "hope."

In short, the way in which Paul introduces his exhortations shows that he *honors* his readers by expecting of them a specific conduct. His very imperatives imply a privilege the saints can enjoy, not a burden they ought to bear. If Paul had used forms softer than imperatives and less affirmative than participles, he would manifest insecurity in regard to the saints' nobility. But when he honors them by expecting that they will follow the highest call, God's own will, then he preaches good news, the very gospel—even in the form of ethical imperatives! In the OT, imperatives (or imperfect forms, e.g. in the Ten Commandments) are addressed to the people already freed from captivity and slavery; they mark them as God's chosen, special property. Equally the Pauline admonitions document the freedom of the saints to do God's will. Imperatives can be a means of preaching the gospel.

---

[160] See J. Klein, art. *Tugend* in RGG, VI, 1080–85, for a sketch of the development of Greek and medieval concepts of virtue and of the distinctive Pauline testimony. Even among Greek thinkers there was no unanimity regarding the place of the virtues. E.g. according to Aristotle, god was above them, but according to Stoic teaching he who follows the virtues follows the gods; see H. D. Betz, *Nachfolge und Nachahmung*, BHTh 37 (1967), pp. 120–23.

[161] In some cases he does not consider himself sufficiently authorized to give such orders: I Cor 7:6, 25; II Cor 8:8; while on other occasions he gives very blunt commands: I Thess 4:2, 11; II Thess 3:4, 6, 10, 12, etc.

[162] E. F. Ströter, *Die Herrlichkeit des Leibes Christi* (repr. Gümligen: Siloah, 1952), p. 92. When Paul once, and only in passing, threatens with a "stick," he is nevertheless unwilling to perform the task assigned to the lowest type of Greek pedagogue (I Cor 4:21).

[163] Cf., e.g. the formulae "you would do well" and "you did well," as found in secular papyri epistles; also in Philip 4:14; III John 6; see also Acts 10:33.

There are precedents for preaching good news in this form. The advice and commands given in the Wisdom books (supposedly by King Solomon himself!) to princes and sons of the wealthy make them aware of their privileges. These noble young men are to see the world and to stand before kings; they have money to spend and wine to drink. When eventually Wisdom was popularized and each Israelite applied to himself the counsels originally addressed to an elite only, the awareness was not lost that good counsel was beneficial rather than compulsory. The practical, witty, joyful, easily memorized admonition given in the Wisdom style is certainly distinct from those parts and elements of the rabbinic *halacha* that have a legalistic character. A good father or an experienced old friend has the final word, rather than a punctilious scholar, an imposing teacher, or a sharp lawyer.

Though the substitution of participles for imperatives, which is often found in Pauline ethical passages, has no precedent in Wisdom literature and no parallels in the (rabbinical) book *Pirke Aboth,* the apostle retained or revived the character, diction, and contents of admonition given by Wisdom teachers. C. H. Dodd, E. Selwyn, and others sought to explain the NT paraclesis (exhortation) basically upon the background of Jewish ethical, i.e. halachic teaching.[164] More recent work done in elucidating the origin and character of the Wisdom tradition and its influence upon Paul makes a correction necessary.[165] The kerygmatic passages and utterances of the Pauline letters are not related to their ethical counterparts as *haggada* is to *halacha* (narrative to ethical/legal discussion) in rabbinical writings, or as Gospel is to Law in the understanding of many Lutheran theologians.[166] Paul's proclamation resembles the praising narration of God's mighty acts found in the OT historical books and Psalms, and in the NT Gospels and Acts. This narration includes the call to worship and obedience. Paul's exhortation, in turn, is analogous to the wise men's response to the election of Israel.

Thus both the indicatives and the imperatives of the Pauline Epistles contain nothing but good news, the sheer pure gospel.[167] His readers and listeners

---

[164] Dodd, *The Apostolic Preaching and Its Development;* Selwyn, *First Peter.* Above, in the COMMENTS on the *wall* and the *statutes* in 2:14–15, some characteristic features of the "fence" built around the Law by the *halacha* have been described. If in 4:1 ff. Paul were setting out to replace the Jewish *halacha* by an equivalent moral and legal Christian instruction, he would belie what he has asserted in 2:14–15, i.e. the breaking down of the legal *wall.*

[165] See BIBLIOGRAPHY 8, COMMENT X on 1:3–14, and COMMENT VIII on 4:16–32.

[166] In the Gospels and in the NT letters, the good news is not only "preached" but also "taught," in contrast to Dodd's systematization, and correspondingly ethical demands are not only "taught" but also "proclaimed"; see e.g. Mark 1:21–22, 27; Rom 6:17; 16:17; Col 1:28; I Tim 4:11. According to Acts 5:42 the apostles "taught and proclaimed the Messiah Jesus" at the same time. The sequence of the two verbs used in this verse does not prove that the proclamation of a law always preceded the announcement of good news. The speeches summarized in Acts move, on the contrary, from proclamation of the gospel to exhortation. Especially C. J. Bjerkelund, *Parakalō,* and Furnish, *Theology and Ethics in Paul,* suggest a reinterpretation of the Pauline indicatives and imperatives. Furnish discusses Dodd's position on pp. 106–11; in chapters III, IV he elucidates the integral role of ethics in Paul's preaching. "God's claim is regarded by the apostle as a constitutive part of God's gift," pp. 224–25.

[167] As in Paul's writings, so also in the sayings of Jesus (e.g. Mark 1:15) an important distinction between indicative and imperative is made: "The time is fulfilled, and the kingdom of God is at hand; repent, and believe in the gospel." But elements of the Wisdom style of teaching, including imperatives, are much more dominant in Jesus' teaching. Almost the whole of the Sermon on the Mount and most parables teach the good news by presenting examples for conduct, and also by the use of clear-cut imperatives. The one who announces a new order of life and trusts that his listeners will live up to it, may well be a better understood and more successful preacher of God's kingship than a man harping on past historic events only. Like the Sermon on the Mount the epistle of James is written in Wisdom style, and contains only a few pronouncements of the prophetic type.

are confronted with two forms of gospel proclamation, rather than with a gospel limited, if not partially revoked, by a legalistic appendix.

The recovery of ethics as an evangelical discipline is a necessary task to which the Pauline exhortations may make an important contribution. The "way of the Lord" pointed out by the social and moral teachings of Paul is not a corollary to redemption but is comparable to Israel's procession out of Egypt and through the wilderness; it is itself the way of salvation, life, and freedom. On this way God's saving will is carried out.

A close look at the details of Pauline ethics will discover that the structure, the intention, and the individual parts of Paul's admonition are invariably informed and determined by the grace which the apostle proclaims and to which he subjects himself and others. Christ is the key, the touchstone, the scope of all. Proclamation of Christ is made even when imperatives abound. It is beyond dispute that Pauline ethics are based upon, and implicitly contained in, his Christology and soteriology. Even if Paul had written nothing at all about ethical questions, imaginative interpreters might still have derived the Pauline ethics by inference from the Pauline *kerygma*. But it can also be shown that his ethical utterances contain the whole gospel. They attest to it sometimes explicitly, as shown in Ephesians, e.g. by references to the saints as members of one body (4:25; cf. 5:30); to the light they have become (5:4–9); to God's forgiveness (4:32); to Christ's love and sacrifice (5:2, 25–27); to the Messiah's rule at God's right hand (5:5). Specifically Christian elements inhere also in statements that do not make explicit mention of Christ, as will become apparent in the next COMMENT and in the exposition of 4:22 ff. The many kerygmatic elements characteristic of Paul's exhortation are more perspicuous for many readers than the strict logic of his creedal affirmations. Equally Matthew's composition of the Sermon on the Mount may have done more for the proclamation of Christ and for faith in him than dogmatic formulations such as the Apostle's Creed. There is no reason to belittle the relevance of Paul's ethical teaching in the light of the apostle's statements on justification by grace alone. The emphatic practical exhortation in Ephesians matches that of the other Pauline Epistles.[168]

When it is recognized how radically evangelical Wisdom ethics differ from both the Greek systems of virtue and the casuistic legalism of some Jewish halachic materials, the light of Paul's exhortation will shine brightly.

III   Six Constituents of Common Life

Just as elsewhere in Paul's epistles nouns or adjectives describing good and bad works are collected to form lists of varying lengths,[169] so Eph 4:2–3 contains a list of attitudes that fit the conduct of the saints. In each case the apostle appears convinced that the individual terms used are lucid enough, and their combination sufficiently exhaustive or exemplary, to move the saints to voluntary obedience. While modern ethical instruction relies to a lesser

[168] Beside Bjerkelund, Furnish, and Merk, D. E. H. Whiteley, *The Theology of St. Paul* (Philadelphia: Fortress, 1964), esp. pp. 205 ff., and R. N. Longenecker, *Paul Apostle of Liberty* (New York: Harper, 1964), esp. pp. 181 ff., seek most urgently to do justice to the indivisibility of proclamation and exhortation.

[169] The passages are listed below in COMMENT VIII on 4:17–32. Cf. above, fn. 62.

degree on abstract nouns and lists, Paul took over a form of instruction wide-spread in his period. Parallels to, and presumable origins of, his method will be mentioned later.[170]

Paul did not endorse only one model of exhortation in form of a catalogue. At least four can be discerned: (a) the short listings made in Eph 4:2-3, also 4:32, stand somewhere in the middle between (b) the rather dry catalogue describing the fruit of the Spirit in Gal 5:22, and (c) the hymnic praise of love in I Cor 13. Yet another type will be found in (d) the so-called *Haus-Tafel* (table of household duties) of Eph 5:21 – 6:9. At this point only the nouns placed by Paul at the head of his admonition in Eph 4:1 ff. are to be discussed.

The word he uses for "humbleness" (*tapeinophrosyne*) has the bad connotation in pre-Christian and later Greek writing of lacking self-respect. It expresses the temper of a crouching slave.[171] Paul, however, does not degrade humbleness. On the ground of Jesus Christ's example (Philip 2:3-11), the NT points out that humility distinguishes the saints from people who "think highly of themselves."[172]

"Gentleness" (or "meekness," *praytes*) is no more a virtue commonly recommended among the Greeks than humbleness. But the corresponding Hebrew adjective (*anaw*: "lowly," "humble," "pious") provides the NT writers with a tradition of the positive evaluation of meekness. In the Bible a gentle or meek person has no one else to turn to except God or a faithful king. Incapable or unwilling as he is to establish himself by his own might and right, he accepts humiliation from his neighbor without bitterness. The adjectives "lowly" and "poor" (*anaw* and *ani*) are often conflated in the Hebrew OT writings.[173] After the time of the exile the whole of Israel called herself "poor" or "lowly"; perhaps before that period, perhaps later only, special groups and individuals inside Israel described themselves by these terms.[174] Moses was called the meekest man on earth (Num 12:3). Thus an honorable

---

[170] See COMMENT VIII on 4:16-32 for the literature on ethical lists and a discussion of the possible origins and meaning of exhortation in the form of catalogues.

[171] See, e.g. Josephus *bell*. IV 494; Epictetus *diss*. I IX 10; III XXIV 56; Plutarch *de Alexandri fortuna aut virtute* II 336E; *praecepta coniugialia* II 139B; other texts are collected by W. Grundmann in TWNT, VIII, 2–5. But sometimes in the LXX, e.g. in Isa 57:15, and always in the NT and other early Christian literature, the noun and its cognates are used in a good sense.

[172] See also Col 3:12; I Peter 2:21; 5:5; Acts 20:19; Rom 12:16; LXX Ps 130[131]:1–2; John 13:4, 14–15. In *I Clement* humility is an ever recurring topic; see 2:1; 13:1, 3; 16:1, 17; 30:3, 8; 38:2. In his interpretation of Eph 4:2 Chrysostom taught that humbleness presupposed a man's consciousness of being something great. Abbott followed this interpretation. It corresponds to the "nobility" of the saints mentioned in the preceding COMMENT. But any notion of condescension ought to be excluded, see I Clem 38:2: "Let him who is humble-minded not testify to his own humility" (tr. by K. Lake in Loeb Classical Library).

[173] L. Koehler-W. Baumgartner, *Lexicon in Veteris Testamenti Libros*, II (Leiden: Brill, 1953), 720. See also the literature listed in the next fn.

[174] Isa 29:19; 41:17; 49:13; 54:11; 61:1; Pss 9:18; 10:17; 22:26; 34:2; 37:11; 76:9; 86:1–2; 147:6; 149:4; Zech 9:9; *Ps Sol* 1:4 ff.; 5:2; 10:6 etc.; 1QH v 13–14, 16, 18, 21; XVIII 14; 1QM XI 9, 13; XIII 14; 4QPs 37; Matt 5:3–5; James 2:2 ff.; 5:1–6; H. Birkeland, ANI *and* ANAW *in den Psalmen*, Oslo: Dybwad, 1933; F. M. Cross, *The Ancient Library of Qumran* (Garden City: Doubleday, 1958), pp. 61–62, 183–84. "Gentleness" is the opposite of "coming with a stick" in I Cor 4:21. The term occurs in association with forgiveness in Col 3:12–13 and describes the proper mode of mutual correction in II Tim 2:25, or the right attitude to all men in Titus 3:2. R. C. Trench in his *Synonyms of the New Testament* (London: Macmillan, 1880), p. 153, presents David's response to the intemperate cursing of Shimei (II Sam 16:11) as an example of true gentleness. In discussing the silence of the Suffering Servant, W. F. Albright, *From the Stone Age to Christianity* (Baltimore: Johns Hopkins Press, 1940), p. 254, points to the Egyptian and Mesopotamian background of the high esteem in which meekness and silence are held.

ring was sometimes heard in both attributes, "meek" and "poor," even before the NT was written.

The noun *makrothymiā* rendered in the translation given above by the adverb "patiently" signifies either steadfastness or forbearance.[175] In Eph 4:2 the second, i.e. the social attitude is meant, as shown by the following words, "bear one another in love." Chrysostom's etymological interpretation, "have a wide and big soul," is beautiful. However, in the definition and scope of forbearance belongs not only the soul of the individual saint but also his (burdensome) neighbor—and even more is this true of "love":

"Love" is described often and in many ways in the NT. Both in extensive passages and in crisp formulations it is praised above all other attitudes and actions.[176] When in Gal 6:2 and I Cor 9:21 Paul mentions the "law of the Messiah" he probably means the same as the epistle of James with its allusions to the "perfect law of freedom" or the "royal law" (see James 1:25; 2:8, 12). This law is the sum of the OT commandments and their fulfillment: "Love your neighbor as yourself" (Rom 13:9; Gal 5:14; James 2:8). Faith in Christ is in no way opposed to the law given by God on Mount Sinai, but it "works out in love" (Gal 5:6) and it attests that "Christ is the fulfillment of the law" (Rom 10:4; cf. Matt 5:17–20; Rom 8:4).

Four elements are outstanding in the brief formulation of Eph 4:2, "Bear one another in love."

1) The man to be loved is one of the saints: bear "one another." In OT terminology he is the "brother" or "neighbor" included in the election and covenant of God, but also the resident alien whatever his race, status, culture (Lev 19:18, 33–34). According to Ephesians he is a child of God, a fellow citizen in God's city, a fellow worshiper in God's temple. Only in the earliest Pauline Epistle is this restriction broken through: in I Thess 3:12 the apostle expresses the confidence that the Lord will abundantly provide the saints with "love of one another and of all men," and in I Thess 5:14–15 he admonishes them to demonstrate "forbearance toward all men." According to all other Pauline texts dealing with "love," only the saints are to be "loved."[177] Persons who are not "brothers" or "neighbors" have the right to receive a different testimony: they are to be honored, obeyed, respected, etc. When Christians have to deal with them they are expected to do everything that is right and decent and to avoid whatever is unseemly. Evil is never to be repaid by evil.[178] Love, however, is reserved for the brethren: "Love one another with brotherly affection" (Rom 12:10).[179] Still, twice in the NT personal enemies and the persecutors of the church are included among the neighbors to be loved (Rom 12:14–21; Matt 5:43–48).

[175] For the first sense see James 5:10; Heb 6:12. The second meaning prevails where the opposite of a quick temper is meant, see Prov 15:18; James 1:19–20. Cf. the warnings of human irascibility and wrath, Rom 12:19; Eph 4:26, 31; Col 3:8.

[176] E.g. Luke 10:25–37; I Cor 13; Col 3:14; Rom 13:8–10; Gal 5:6, 14. Access to the enormous literature on "love" in the NT is given by C. Spicq, *Agape dans le Nouveau Testament*, 3 vols. Paris: Gabalda, 1958–59. For the following compare also J. Ratzinger, *The Open Circle*, New York: Sheed & Ward, 1966.

[177] If Eph 5:21 ff. is conflated with I Cor 7:14, unbelieving partners in marriage and the children of Christians are also included among the saints.

[178] Rom 13:1–7, 12–13; Philip 4:8; Eph 5:3–4; 6:1; I Peter 2:12; 3:13 ff., etc.

[179] The same distinction is found in I Peter 2:17: "Honor all, love the brotherhood, . . . honor the king."

2) The fellow saint who has the right to be loved is one with whom a Christian is in "contact."[180] A distant and unknown person may be honored, supported, feared, but in none of his epistles except his first does Paul ever demand that he be loved. Love would be totally impersonal and maybe cheap if shown to people never met, or to those only dimly known, for whose specific burdens responsibility cannot be assumed. Love presupposes unity and diversity, i.e. awareness of differentiations between man and man, saint and saint— even in the community of "one faith," in "one body," under "one God and Father" (Eph 4:4–6). The fellow saint who is to be loved is not just an *alter ego;* he may, but he need not necessarily, be a soul brother, a virtual twin, or a dear friend. Rather he has his own origin, history, character, behavior. Life with him and confrontation with him may be encumbered by marks of his sin against God, and may be enriched by the grace given to him by God. But there are also clashes of character, of decisions, attitudes, and actions that cannot be traced back to his sin and weakness, or to his endowment with grace and a special task. In daily life each encounter can lead to tensions, misunderstandings, conflicts of opinion, and disputes in which one saint feels superior and more in the right than his neighbor. Personal conflicts are more acrimonious inside a community than among outsiders, or in the relation of insiders to outsiders. The commandment of love aims at love for those fellow saints who are a problem and cause trouble for the others. This love is neither cheap nor natural.

3) The fellow man to be loved is potentially or actually a burden—or else Paul would not speak of "bearing" him "in love." According to 4:2 the brother is himself a burden; Gal 6:2 may indicate that he "labors and is heavy laden":[181] "Bear one another's burden." In either case Paul expects that fellow Christians will take up the load of others. It is unlikely that the words "in love" intend to say that love of the neighbor might or should incidentally lead to and include such "bearing." Rather mutual love consists of this acceptance of one's neighbor, including the load on his shoulder. Paul never explains what he means by this "burden." Perhaps his own "weakness" which the Corinthians have to bear, and the disorder of the Corinthians or the fickleness of the Galatians which he in turn must cope with, are examples of the meaning of "burden" and "bearing." The mutual love of the saints resembles the love shown by God because it is unselfish; it does not calculate or expect any gain for one who loves; it is forgiving, outgoing, self-de-livering.[182] But it is also distinct from God's love of man. Human love cannot bear and take away sin and weakness, nor can it cause rebirth, res-urrection, sanctification, or unification. A Christian's love accepts him who

---

[180] See the fourth NOTE on 4:16.

[181] Cf. Matt 11:28; Num 11:11–15.

[182] 4:32; 5:25. In Luke 10:37 the "neighbor" to be "loved" is to every reader's surprise identified not with the poor man in the ditch but with the Samaritan "who showed mercy": the interpretation of the parable makes it clear that the love of him who represents Christ the savior precedes responding love. However, in Matt 5:45–48 Jesus shows that he asks for more than love of "those who love you" as it is found among Gentiles. Equally Paul can fully recognize love received from men. He does so when he thanks God for the existence of a congregation or when he writes about his "beloved" cooperators. But he does not forget that those loved or to be loved may behave less than lovingly toward him and one another, and that they have to be borne with unending patience.

is accepted; it attests to a forgiveness and renewal previously secured. To use the imagery of John 13:10 and 15, it can do no more than wash the feet of a fellow Christian who has first been totally bathed by God through Jesus Christ (cf. Eph 4:32; 5:1–2).

4) A conclusion can be drawn from the foregoing three points: "Love" needs the neighbor and is dependent upon him. The neighbor—even the one who is a burden and whose character and behavior prove cumbersome—is much more than just an occasion or test of love. He is its very material. Love is not an abstract substance or mood that can be present in a man's heart even when there are no others in sight and no confrontations are taking place. It does not exist in a vacuum, *in abstracto,* in detachment from involvement in other men's lives. Rather it is a question of being surprised by a neighbor, accepting him, going out to him, and seeking solidarity and unity just with him even if this should mean temporary neglect of, or estrangement from, others. Such love is an event that takes place exclusively when one meets and lives with specific men, women, children, old people, relatives, and strangers. Love is always love of this or that person, love here and now, love shown under ever new conditions in ever original forms. Where there is love, there this and that person in his uniqueness is "borne" and fully accepted. Therefore "love" should not be defined as a virtue of the soul, not even as the highest virtue. It is an ever new miracle which has to happen again and again —just as the filling with the Spirit spoken of in the book of Acts was an ever new experience given whenever there was need of a spirited testimony. In Rom 5:5 the gift of love is identified with the gift of the Spirit, and in Gal 5:22 love is listed as the first "fruit of the Spirit." Specific features of the love between bridegroom and bride, or husband and wife, will be discussed in COMMENT V A on Eph 5:21–33.

For an interpretation of the term "unity," see section B of the next COMMENT. The "unity" mentioned in Eph 4:3 reaches further than the unity of the church, i.e. the union enjoyed by church members. The next and final key term occurring in this subsection of 4:1–16 will show this clearly.

The "peace" of which Ephesians speaks[183] is co-extensive with God's love, but it is wider than the limited range of human love.[184] For the "peace" made by Christ at the price of his blood includes "those who are far" (2:13–17), and not only "neighbors" and "brothers." According to Eph 2 this "peace" keeps the Jews and the Gentiles together in the church, but also—as other Pauline passages show—the strong and the weak, the outstanding and the ignored, the male and the female, the rich and the poor members of the church. And it does still more than just that: "peace" is the gift and work of God which overarches humbleness, gentleness, love among brethren; it reaches far beyond the church. In Col 3:14 the same comprehensive function (*syndesmos*) is ascribed to "love"

---

[183] See the discussion of this term at the end of COMMENT II on 1:1–2, in the first NOTE on 2:14, and in the COMMENTS IV, V, VI on 2:11–22.

[184] Schlier, pp. 180–81, probably over-emphasizes the fact that the ethical part of Ephesians begins with comments on church unity rather than the saints' relation to God or to fellow man. Schlier neglects the missionary character of the church and its unity. Equally JB appears to narrow down the meaning of Eph 4:1 ff. when in a note it stresses above all the threats to church unity offered by arguments between Christians (vss. 1–3), by the diversity of service (vss. 7–11), by unorthodox teaching (vss. 14–15).

as to "peace" in Ephesians; but in contrast to Ephesians, "peace" is in Colossians understood to be extended not only beyond the church but also beyond all mankind: it includes the cosmos. "He reconciled all things by making peace" (Col 1:20). At any rate, in both Ephesians and Colossians the unity of the church is not an end itself but a necessary sign manifesting the will and work of God that transcends the church. The saints and their mutual love are a sign and a servant of God's purpose for all the world.

The imperatives found in Eph 4:2-3 have a common denominator. Paul beseeches each of the saints to yield to his fellow man and to be content with a subordinate place. He sums up his advice elsewhere: "Everybody is to be self-effacing. Always consider the other person to be better than yourself . . . As to honoring a man, honor one another more than yourself . . . Be subject to one another."[185] The opposite would be the attempt to be "holier than thou"; to excel in gnosis (religious insight and perfection) above supposedly inferior Christians; to boast of oneself; to subject one's neighbor to arbitrarily selected elements of one's own religious tradition or preference; or to refuse responsibility for others and to concentrate upon one's private salvation.[186] "Love" reigns where the troubles or bliss of a neighbor weigh more heavily than one's own peace of mind and redemption. Paul gives an example of such love when he solemnly states: "My grief is great and the pain in my heart is incessant. I could wish that I myself were accursed and cut off from Christ for the sake of my brethren. . . . The wish of my heart and my prayer to God is for them, for their salvation" (Rom 9:2-3; 10:1). Only the man who deems himself lower than his most burdensome brother and offers his life in service to others proves his love in action. "Freedom for the other" is the form and content of the piety proclaimed by Paul.[187]

IV   The Creed

It is debatable whether Eph 4:4-6 is one single Creed or should be considered a composite of several originally independent creedal statements.[188] The last part praising the oneness of God and his rule over all (vs. 6) has Jewish and Gentile pre-Christian parallels and may contain copied formulations.[189] However, the first two parts praising the Spirit and Christ are not supported by similar analogies. The combination of all three parts is distinctly Christian. But it is unlikely that at an unknown occasion, for an unknown situation, an author other than the writer of Ephesians should have composed the whole of vss. 4:4-6 as a unit, for the structure and subject matter of

[185] Philip 2:3 JB; Rom 12:10; Eph 5:21.
[186] Galatians, I Corinthians, Philippians, and Colossians reveal that Paul's mission work was seriously threatened by corresponding attitudes.
[187] Cf. Schlier, p 184, and Calvin on 4:4.
[188] For the origin, wording, and development of early creedal formulae, etc., see e.g. O. Cullman, *The Earliest Christian Confessions* (London: Lutterworth, 1949), esp. pp. 20, 51, and J. N. D. Kelly, *Early Christian Creeds*, 2d ed. (London: Longmans, 1960), esp. pp. 25-26.
[189] Cf. the "Shema Israel" of Deut 6:4-6 and its reflection in Zech 14:9; Josephus *c. Ap.* II 193; Philo *spec. leg.* I 67; II Bar 48:24. In Gen 1-2 etc. and in the *Sib. Oracles,* Fragm. I and III, the oneness of God is related to the totality of creation. For non-Jewish parallels see the literature mentioned in fn. 158 to 1:15-23; also M. Dibelius, "Die Christianisierung einer hellenistischen Formel," in *Neue Jahrbücher für das klassische Altertum* 35 (1915), 224 ff.; repr. in *Botschaft und Geschichte,* II (Tübingen: Mohr, 1956), 14-29; E. Peterson, *Heis Theos* (Göttingen: Vandenhoeck, 1926), esp. 141-48, 254-56; Beare, IB, X, 686-87; R. R. Williams, "Logic versus Experience in the Order of Creedal Formulae," NTS 1 (1954-55), 42-44.

these verses so perfectly fit the substance and instruction of this one letter that the author of Ephesians himself should be considered the compiler. Special exegetical problems are posed (a) by the sequence of creedal elements; (b) by the meaning or meanings of key terms (such as "one" and "all"); and (c) by a variant reading of vs. 6.

A   The Sequence of the Articles of Faith

In Eph 4:4–6 the number "one" is used seven times, and the word "all" occurs four times. These figures probably have a symbolic sense, just as in the book of Revelation where the literal meaning of a number is symbolic, not mathematical. In so ancient a hymn as Ps 29 seven successive descriptions of the "voice of the Lord" praise God's universal power and majesty. As Eph 4:6 shows, the preceding hymnic verses intend to lead up to just this praise.

However, in the course of NT exegesis and church history, the trinitarian structure and contents of Eph 4:4–6 have received much greater attention. Here the sequence of the confessional elements collected in the Apostolic, Nicene, and later Christian Creeds is anticipated in reverse order: first the Spirit is praised, then Christ, then the Father.[190] Each part of the confession is unfolded in a triad of about equal length: "body-Spirit-hope"; "Lord-faith-baptism"; "God the Father of all" is called the Father "over, through, and in all." All nouns are preceded by the emphatic numeral "one." The sequence used may express the intention to lead from the reality of the church to her head, Christ, and from him to the origin of all, God. Does the apostle thereby express a preference for an inductive approach based on human experience, as opposed to the method of abstract reasoning, i.e. deductions made from a basic principle?[191] J. Coutts[192] suggests another explanation: the author of Ephesians works backward on what he has laid out in Eph 1–3; he takes up concepts used earlier by himself, rather than a confession previously formulated by others. In either case the confessional verses serve the purpose of summing up what the readers of Ephesians already know. That which is confessed by the apostle, his readers, and (in one or another form) all Christians, is the basis for the exhortation in chapters 4–6. Because the work of the Spirit is palpable in the existence and confession of the church, there is a "unity" which need not be artificially constructed or produced but is worthy of being "maintained" (4:3). It is already given.[193] At this point the author is interested not in the fabrication or existence of an invisible unity but in the factual manifestation and enjoyment of oneness. In 4:13, however, a unity will be discussed that is not yet present among men in its fullness.

It is surprising that in 4:4 the "body" is mentioned before the Spirit. Are not later creeds of the church more wise and reverent in having the Spirit precede the church? Is the church placed above the Spirit in Ephesians just

---

[190] The same sequence has again been supported in recent years, e.g. by H. P. van Dusen, *Spirit, Son, and Father,* New York: Scribner's, 1958.

[191] E.g. Robinson, p. 93; R. R. Williams, NTS 1 (1954–55), 44, give affirmative answers.

[192] In the essays, mentioned earlier; see NTS 3 (1956–57), 127; 4 (1957–58), 202–3. He refers specifically to 1:1–2, 13, 18; 2:16–18.

[193] Abbott; Schlier, etc.

as ecclesiology allegedly displaces Christology? If the communal spirit of the believers were meant,[194] rather than the Holy Spirit, there would be no issue. But in earlier passages of Ephesians the author has again and again praised the Holy Spirit in conjunction with the Father and the Son. Therefore, it is unlikely that he would deviate from the previous pattern at the very moment when a comprehensive confession is pronounced. The Holy Spirit must be meant in vs. 4. In turn the words "one body" do not at this point denote the church exclusively as a social structure (in the sense of I Cor 12:14–27 where Christ was not called her head). Rather the term "body" here as before and later in Ephesians refers to the church as Christ's own self-manifestation.[195] Therefore, Christ's own presence, revelation, and promise among the saints inform the first triad of the confession of 4:4–6. From the one "body" of Christ the apostle proceeds fo the "Spirit's" work, and in the prose addition (vs. 4b) he concludes this part of the confession by praising the "hope" that determines the way of the saints. Compare the sequence, "one body/one Spirit" in 2:16–18. Christology rather than ecclesiology precedes pneumatology. See also 4:21c and 30.

B One God and One Church

The word "one" is a numeral, but it signifies more than a mere number.[196] When used in the context of the revelation and confession of God, the formula "One God!" goes beyond an affirmation of monotheistic belief; it expresses more than God's jealousy of other gods and a rebuttal of the pagans' polytheism —though the NT is no less concerned with these issues than Moses and the prophets:

1) In the OT the unique quality of God (which gives substance to God's numerical singleness) is included in the confession "One God" (Deut 6:4–6); "Who is like thee?" (Exod 15:11). Compare the etymological meaning of the name "Micah," "Who is like Yahweh?"

2) The identity of God with himself, i.e. his faithfulness to himself, is meant by the term "one." The prophetic narrators of Israel's history took pains to show that the same God appeared to Moses who had appeared to Abraham. Several prophets insisted that God would prove to be for the generation of their time what he was and still is, as the creator of heaven and earth and as the redeemer of Israel from Egypt. Always he carries out what he has promised, and he is faithful to his covenants previously made.

3) The oneness of God implies his omnipotence and sufficiency: his dominion extends equally over nature and history, heaven and earth, fields and stables, heavenly and earthly hosts, Israel and Judah, the chosen people and the nations.

4) Correspondingly, his oneness establishes his right and power to lay claim upon body, soul, and spirit, upon the past, the present, the future, and upon the private and social life of man.

5) In the NT, the Christians' confession "One God!" counteracts eventual Jewish accusations of apostasy from the service of the only true God, as

---

[194] As de Wette assumed.
[195] See COMMENT VI B 6 on 1:15–23.
[196] See WBLex, 229–31.

confessed in the words of Deut 6:4–6. Equally later (heretical) Gentile-Christian advances against the Jewish and Christian Creed may be anticipated, e.g. the Gnostic-dualistic idea that an evil creator-god ought to be distinguished from the good Father of Jesus Christ, the redeemer. The NT holds the line of Second Isaiah: God the creator and God the redeemer are one and the same.

6) Finally, in Ephesians the purpose and implication of the confession "One God" is this: God makes the decision, has the power, and performs the deed of making "one new man" out of a mankind divided in hostility. In this epistle God's oneness is directly, i.e. causatively, dynamically, effectively, but also epistemologically, related to the unity of the church. Because God is one, his people are one and are to live on the basis and in recognition of unity.[197] Similarly in OT and Jewish writings the oneness of God is the ontic and noetic presupposition of statements about the oneness of the temple, the law, or the people of God.[198]

Thus the oneness or unity of God is distinct from the uniqueness which an individual person or a specific thing may possess among other persons or things. God's oneness stands apart because of its creative, dynamic, multiform, and comprehensive character; it may be compared to Holiness. Holiness is not a dormant quality of God, but it is God's power and will to sanctify sinners and to be present in the sanctuary chosen by him. Equally, God's oneness includes God's will and power to unite and his success in reconciling those hostile to him and to each other.[199] This oneness is not only an attitude of God the Father: the one Spirit mentioned in 4:4 effects a "unity . . . through the bond of peace" (4:3), and the "one Lord" (4:5) is the same who "made" and "is our

---

[197] The same connection is established in I Cor 12:4–7 and John 17:20–21; see Schlier, p. 189. In the first part of his essay, AnBib 17–18, I (1963), 57–77, Benoit declares that in Ephesians Paul combines the message of Romans and Colossians by elaborating on reconciliation. The unity of the church is based upon the reconciling death of Christ, the new Adam. The reconciliation through the cross is manifested by the unity of Jews and Gentiles (i.e. the church, the body of Christ) and will triumph in the parousia of the Lord. On pp. 66 ff. Benoit describes in vivid terms how the obstacles to unity existing in divided hearts, ministries, spirits are overcome. Finally he finds the purpose of unity in the glorification of God. One element seems to be missing in this thoughtful analysis of unity: the connection between the unity of God (the Father, the Lord Jesus Christ, and the Spirit) and the unity of the church as it is pointed out in I Cor 12:4–7 and Eph 4:4–6. Pokorný, EuG, p. 117, uses too weak an expression when he speaks of "parallelizing . . . the two unities," for there is a causal and final connection between them. Upon the oneness and unity of God depends the oneness and unity of the church, and to this the church is called to bear witness. Beare, IB, X, 686, follows Dibelius, p. 78, is contrasting the biblical sequence, Oneness of God—Oneness of the church to the reverse order, Unity of the World—Oneness of God, which is occasionally found in Stoic writings (e.g. Marcus Aurelius Meditations VII 9). Still the picture offered by Stoic teachers is not uniform. E.g. Cleanthes' "Hymn to Zeus" (for a translation see C. K. Barrett, The New Testament Background [London: SPCK, 1956], p. 63) followed the Orphic Fragment 168 (see O. Kern, Orphische Fragmente, I [Berlin: Weidmann, 1922], 201–2) and ascribed ontic priority to Zeus. It has been said of the Stoics in general, e.g. by M. Pohlenz, Die Stoa (Göttingen: Vandenhoeck, 1948), pp. 77, 79, cf. 218, that they considered "the cosmos unique because it is a manifestation of the one deity" (i.e. of Zeus, Reason, the Logos). Still, Stoic proof of the existence of god argued inductively from the unity, rationality, etc. of the world toward the deity, see Wisd Sol 12–13 and Pohlenz, Stoa, p. 95.

[198] See the passages listed in fn. 189. A seventh meaning of the confession "One God" finds expression in Jewish mystical literature, but appears too far removed from Ephesians to deserve serious consideration: there the oneness of God means that God, together with all things contained in himself also embraces evil and nothingness; he who "has no limits" (ēn sōp) fills even the void. Literature on Jewish mysticism was listed in BIBLIOGRAPHY 16 in AB, vol. 34.

[199] Hegermann, Schöpfungsmittler, p. 186, refers to Ignatius to demonstrate that unity meant more than singularity: God's oneness is a "power-sphere" determined by faith and love; into this sphere those have entered to whom God has revealed himself; it determines their life. See esp. Ign. Philad. II 2; IV 1; V 1; VIII 1; IX 1; Eph. IV 2; V 1; XIV 1; Smyrn. XII 2; Magn. VII 1–2. According to Col 1:20 and Eph 4:6; cf. 1:10; 3:10 not only the church but the whole cosmos is exposed to the manifestation and exertion of God's unifying power.

peace" (2:14–15), he, the head above all, the ruler who fills all (1:10, 22–23; 4:10). Thus creative oneness, that is, the power to unify, is attributed to the Spirit and the Son as much as to the Father. In 4:1–6 Paul speaks first of the life of the unified people of God, then of the oneness of the Spirit, Lord, and Father, respectively. As in the confession (vss. 4–6) God's oneness and his creatures' unity are correlated step by step, the author intends to show that historic and social unity on earth is totally dependent upon God's eternal oneness and unity. Unity on earth is the creation, the manifestation, the glorification of the divine. By its very existence the church confesses God's essence to the universe.

At least three features distinguish the confession contained in Eph 4 from purely logical induction, from a philosophical postulate, or from wishful projection or mythologization. All three demonstrate Paul's dynamic rather than static understanding of God's oneness. And all show why for the apostle God's oneness is God's unity, and the means for the unification of mankind.

1) In their confession of the one God, the saints, assembled (in many places, or many occasions) for one worship and engaged in one mission, distinguish between the Spirit, the Lord (Jesus Christ), and the Father. It is not the magnificence and mystery of the number "One" which determine the confession of God. Rather the astonishing manifestation of God the Spirit, Son, and Father makes them cry out; One! Unique! United! Unifying! Faithful! While the saints confess God's uniqueness, faithfulness, omnipotence, etc., they acknowledge variety and multiformity in God himself. He is the living God, not a dead number. God's oneness is the communion of Father, Son, and Spirit; it is the unity of these three: the mystery of the trinity.[200]

2) The statements regarding God's oneness are made in a tone of admonition, supplication, worship. They reflect not the attitude of onlookers but the rapture of enthusiasts. Those uttering the confession are bound by its implications. They speak as the "body" animated by the "Spirit" and appointed to march on the way of "hope." "Faith" and "baptism" tie them to the "Lord." "In all things" and persons they are willing to recognize the dominion, presence, and operation of "God the Father."

3) The people of God understands itself in the light of God. The one God confessed by the one people is a unity in diversity, and reveals his uniqueness in various manifestations. Therefore, the people of God recognize that they are given knowledge and participation in the qualified (divine) oneness which permits diversity in unity and maintains unity in diversity. God's own oneness and manifoldness determine the church's oneness and manifoldness.[201] This people comprehends Jews and Gentiles; many ministries are exerted in its midst and in the course of its world-wide mission; special gifts of grace are given to its diverse members. The church cannot be one except when it attests to its God-given oneness by proving unity in diversity, and when it ventures to respect diversity in unity. Uniformity would be the alternative— a form of death which is recommended neither by I Cor 12, nor by Eph 4, nor by any other of the ecclesiastic passages of the NT.

---

[200] "Because God is three persons in one, he is united. A God of one person could never be united," Gaugler, p. 166.

[201] In I Cor 12:4 ff. a similar reference to the Spirit, Lord, and God stands at the head of a discourse on the unity in diversity, and the diversity in the unity of the congregation.

To sum up, unless God were three in one, no great feat would be accomplished by calling him "One." It might be questioned how and why an absolute unqualified oneness could ever have a claim upon creatures who are many and manifold. Creation by the one God might by definition mean separation from him. A multiplicity of persons could never truly share in God's oneness, be committed by it, confess it—if God had not proven to be the One even in his Plurality, the unity that permits diversity, the power that holds together, brings together, and guarantees community. Without being bound by the Father, Son, and Spirit, the church could never proclaim that God's own unity is the basis, the source, the energy, and the criterion of her own unity and that of her many members and ministries.

The first part of Eph 4 points out this connection. The exhortation contained in the first three verses of this chapter stands on the foundation given in vss. 4–6. Further implications of vss. 4–6 will be spelled out in subsequent verses. For Paul the transition from the confession of God's oneness in 4:4–6 to the discussion of the many gifts, ministries, members given to the church in 4:7–8, 11, 12, 16, etc., is far from a logical *non sequitur*. It is essential to both his doctrine of God and his doctrine of the church.

But still another element of the confessional statement 4:4–6 is to be considered.

C   Particularity and Universality

The second and third verses of the confession, i.e. vss. 5–6, point in seemingly opposite directions. Both use rhetorical devices typical of Hellenistic Greek: vs. 5 contains the three genders of "one" in grammatically precise sequence of masculine, feminine, and neuter;[202] vs. 6 plays with the prepositions "over," "through," "in." Both verses have more than only rhetorical character and relevance: vs. 5 appears to proceed from the sublime to the palpable, that is, from the mighty "Lord" through "faith" to a specific church ritual, "baptism," whereas vs. 6 bursts through all specifications and limitations in order to praise the universal rule and presence of God. These distinctive tendencies *and* their surprising combination become clear only when each of the words "faith," "baptism," and "all" are understood in a very particular way, and when a variant reading of vs. 6 is excluded altogether. The tension between vss. 5 and 6 would appear if, e.g. "baptism" should have a more general sense and the word "all" a more narrow one than they appear to have at first sight. Several details of these two verses require discussion:

4:5. By the word "Lord," no one but Jesus Christ is meant.[203] The terms "faith" and "baptism" are added as "means of communication with the

[202] See the NOTE on vs. 5.

[203] See I Cor 8:6; Philip 2:11; Rom 10:9; Eph 1:2; Acts 2:36, etc. Schlier, pp. 185–89, is convinced that Eph 4:5 (the confession, "One Lord, one faith, one baptism") is the nucleus of 4:4–6. He understands vs. 4a as a Pauline preamble, vs. 4b as a Pauline comment, vs. 6 as a Christian echo phrased in the form of Hellenistic cosmology. The creed 4:4–6 would then contain a response to problems and opportunities created by Paul's mission work. But Kelly, *Early Christian Creeds*, pp. 24 ff., attempts to show in discussion with Cullmann, *Earliest Christian Confessions*, that the early church's need of a substantial baptismal creed (rather than the disputes with paganism provoked by Paul's mission work), called the binitarian or trinitarian confessional formulae into being. If the authenticity of Ephesians and the pre-Pauline origin of the combined confessional statements of 4:4–6 could be demonstrated beyond any doubt, Kelly's position would be justified.

Lord."[204] The sequence, faith-baptism, corresponds to the mission reports (e.g. in Acts 8:12; 16:14–15, 31–33) and to the (spurious) ending of Mark (16:16). In the early church only people who believed were baptized. But could the terms "faith" and "baptism" also mean something else?

Just as "hope" in 4:4 stands for both the substance and attitude of hope, so also "faith" in vs. 5 may mean the object, the doctrine, or the confession of faith. "Faith" can also denote the faithfulness discussed in the context of 2:8; for only in exceptional cases does Paul understand faith as a quasi objective matter.[205] Whether the noun is employed in a more objective or more subjective sense, faith is always a bond that unites not only God and the saints, but also the diverse members of the church and the congregations.[206] If it could be demonstrated that in Eph 4:5 "faith" is used in the objective sense then this verse is a step toward the second-century and later elaborations on a fixed Confession of Faith, the so-called *regula fidei*. Since in this verse "faith" can mean man's faith in God and the Messiah as well, Eph 4:5 does not prove the post-apostolic date of the whole epistle.

The term "one baptism" offers an analogous problem:

1) Is the emphasis on *one* baptism part of the discussions about a second repentance (or a repetition of baptism) which are reflected in Heb 6:4–6; 10:26–27 and played an important role in the debate about the Pauline origin and the canonical rank of Hebrews?[207] These battles reached a peak not earlier than the third century in Rome, during the Novatian controversies: the "Orthodox" church decided that repentance could be renewed but that baptism must not be repeated.[208] However, Ephesians as a whole does not demonstrate that its author faced a denial of Christ and apostasy as did later church leaders in times of general persecution. The problem of readmitting defectors to the church was not on his mind when he wrote this epistle. Therefore it is most unlikely that Eph 4:5 was written in order to establish canon law or church discipline. It cannot be proven that the words "One Baptism" were uttered originally to prohibit anabaptism.

2) Did the author intend to counteract a distinction between baptism with water and baptism with the Spirit? The difference between these two baptisms was emphasized by John the Baptist. It is also upheld by those baptismal narratives in Acts in which the gift of the Spirit either precedes or follows upon baptism in the name of Jesus Christ.[209] But the interpretation of Eph 1:13–14 has shown[210] that Paul did not simply equate the church ritual

[204] Dibelius, p. 80. For an extensive treatment of the instrumental function of "faith" and "baptism," see Kertelge, *Rechtfertigung bei Paulus*, pp. 161–249.
[205] E.g. Gal 1:23. Allusions to a (fixed?) confession of faith are probably made in I Tim 6:12 and Heb 3:1; see Schlier, p. 188.
[206] This meaning is strongly represented by the shorter text of Eph 1:15, and by Rom 1:12.
[207] See, e.g. C. Spicq, *L'épître aux Hébreux*, II (Paris: Gabalda, 1953), 150–54, 167–78; H. Windisch, *Taufe und Sünde* (Tübingen: Mohr, 1908), pp. 294 ff. Early church authors dealing with this issue are Herm. *mand.* IV 3; Irenaeus *adv. haer.* IV 27:2; Tertullian, speaking from the Montanist viewpoint, *de jejunio* 21; *de pudicitia* 20:3–5; the Novatianists according to Epiphanius *adversus haereses* II 59:2.
[208] Ambrose *de poenitentia* II 2; Philastrius of Brescia (ca. 385) *diversarum haereseon liber* 89 (PL, 12, 1201 f). The Synods of Rome (382), Hippo Regius (393), Carthage (397), made former local and personal decisions official and binding for the whole western church.
[209] Mark 1:8 par.; John 1:33; Acts 8:12–17; 10:44–48. Similarly baptism with water "in the name of . . ." may be distinguished from baptism "with Spirit" in I Cor 1:13–17; 12:13; cf. 10:2.
[210] See COMMENT XVI on 1:3–14.

with the gift of the Spirit. If he had intended to do this, he would probably have mentioned baptism in 4:4 (not in 4:5), i.e. in the confessional statements directly related to the Holy Spirit and the essence of the church.

3) Attempts have been made[211] to understand the formula "one baptism" as a comprehensive concept which holds together (a) Jesus' own baptism in the Jordan, (b) his death baptism suffered on, and administered from, the cross,[212] and (c) the church baptism. Or, the spiritual birth of Christ (from a virgin), the pentecostal birth of the church as a whole, and the baptismal birth of each of her members were understood to be included in the term "One Baptism." On the basis of the oneness ascribed to baptism, this sacrament and not the eucharist[213] was declared "The Sacrament of Unity."[214] It is indeed far from impossible that in creedal formulations a given term combines in itself several meanings.[215] Still, the vivid imagination and the unlimited speculative gifts of expositors, as well as the impact of certain theories upon ongoing ecumenical debates, do not prove their access to the biblical author's intention or the understanding of his first readers.

4) A traditional exegesis has the highest probability: Eph 4:5 speaks of a church ritual, i.e. of baptism with water as it was administered on the basis of Jesus' own baptism by John, in obedience to his ordinance, and, in distinction from other ritual washings, accompanied by the proclamation and invocation of Jesus the Messiah (or the Father, Son, and Spirit). After the "Spirit" has been mentioned in vs. 4, and after his creative, animating, unifying power over the "body" has been sufficiently intimated, there is no need for the author to insist again, in vs. 5, that the gift of the Spirit makes the Christians one body (cf. I Cor 12:13). There is no evidence that Paul was acquainted with the wording of Luke 12:50; Mark 10:38–39, which describe Christ's death as a baptism received (and supposedly spent at the same time). No doubt the apostle proclaims elsewhere the intimate relation of baptism to the crucified Christ, and to man's inclusion in Christ's death. But while he twice explains baptism as a "burial with Christ" he never states that "in baptism" or "through baptism" man dies or rises with Christ.[216] Baptism with water in the name of Jesus Christ (or of the trinity) is therefore not the same as baptism by death (Mark 10:38, etc.) or the baptism with the Spirit (Mark 1:8, etc.). Why, then, is "one baptism" mentioned after the reference to the "Lord" and "faith"? Because it is a comprehensive, practical, public, bind-

[211] Esp. by J. A. T. Robinson, "The One Baptism as a Category of NT Soteriology," ScotJT 6 (1953), 257–74; repr. in SBT 34 (1962), 158–75; T. F. Torrance, "Aspects of Baptism in the New Testament," TZ 14 (1958), 241–60. Counter-arguments against J. A. T. Robinson's exegesis of Eph 4:5 have been collected by W. E. Moore, "One Baptism," NTS 10 (1964), 504–16.

[212] O. Cullmann, Baptism in the New Testament, SBT 1 (1950), 19–20 was apparently the first to explain Luke 12:50 and Mark 10:38–39 by the term "general baptism"—a baptism bestowed "in entire independence of the decision of faith and understanding of those who benefit from it."

[213] As, e.g. in I Cor 10:16–17; Ign. Philad. IV 1.

[214] A conclusion was drawn from this that proved most important for modern ecumenical discussions: while many denominations still exclude members of other denominations from participating in their celebration of the Lord's Supper, nevertheless the baptism common to all constitutes and manifests a pre-given and valid unity of all members of the church.

[215] In the Apostolic Creed the term communio sanctorum may signify either "participation in the holy things," or "fellowship of those sanctified." A Qumran inspired exegesis would explain it as "communion with the angels." As earlier stated, Eph 2:13–19 suggests the interpretation "peace between, and common worship of, Gentiles and Jews."

[216] Gal 3:27; I Cor 1:13; Rom 6:3–4; Col 2:11–12. See AB, vol. 34B for the interpretation of en hō in Col 2:12.

ing, joyful confession of that "one faith" in the "one Lord" which is the beginning of conduct in "newness of life"![217] Thus baptism has its own indispensable function and high dignity.[218]

The omission of any reference to the eucharist does not imply a depreciation of the common meal. According to Gal 2:11–14; I Cor 10–11 the Lord's Supper is as vital for church unity as is baptism following I Cor 1:13–17; Gal 3:26–28; Eph 4:5. A reference to the Lord's Supper may have been omitted from Eph 4 either for stylistic reasons (in order to maintain the triadic structure), or because the repeated celebration of the Lord's Supper excluded the eucharistic meals from the company of the confessional elements which share in the attribute "one."[219]

No less important than the contents of Eph 4:5, but equally prone to variant interpretations, is the substance of 4:6.

The confession praising the "one God and Father" has *in toto* a universalistic ring, but in its details moves as it were from the outside to the inside. God is acclaimed as the "One" who is "above," "through," and "in all." Only in Ephesians (and just once in this epistle) does Paul use the phrase "God *in* all." In vs. 7 the anthropological dimension of this surprising statement will be specified and at the same time protected from a pantheistic misinterpretation: "Grace is given to each one of us." Verse 7 urges the question whether by the term "all" only the saints are meant, or (just as at the end of vs. 10) together with them "all things," including the powers?[220] Arguments are available to support either interpretation.

The restrictive exposition is supported by a variant reading which has "in all of us" instead of the ambiguous "in all."[221] The limiting pronoun "of us," in turn, may belong either only to the formula "[God] in all" or to each of the three formulae "[God] over all, through all, in all."[222] If a Stoic "omnipotence formula" really underlies 4:6, the addition of the words "of us" is a mark of pointed "Christianization of a Hellenistic formula."[223] The author of Ephesians would then reveal a somewhat narrow ecclesiastical concern by asserting: the church alone benefits from that permeating presence which,

[217] Rom 6:4. The "putting on of Christ" mentioned in Gal 3:27 points, in the imagery used for the "investiture" of officials or priests, probably to the assumption of a ministry which marks the beginning of a new life. See COMMENT V B and C on 4:17–32.

[218] However, in section IX of the Introduction and in COMMENT XVI on 1:3–14 it was shown that there is no reason to declare the whole of Ephesians a treatise on baptism. Ephesians, this most ecclesiastic and supposedly most "high churchly" among the Pauline Epistles, surprises the reader by mentioning a sacrament but once, in 4:5. In this epistle ecclesiology is certainly not derived from a doctrine of the sacraments.

[219] Abbott suggests that the eucharist was the expression rather than the ground of unity. But I Cor 10:16–17 does not support this distinction. While the reference to baptism in Eph 4 certainly reminds present-day churches and denominations of an act and sign of ecumenical unity that is given and cannot be lost, the omission of any mention of the eucharist does not amount to the permission to continue the scandalous misuse of the Lord's Table for mutual "excommunication."

[220] See COMMENT V B on 1:15–23 for a discussion of the term "all things," and its OT or Stoic background.

[221] As early as the second century this reading is supported by the Latin and Syrian versions, later by the Codices Claramontanus, Boernerianus, finally by the Koine group and a vast number of other MSS. Irenaeus, Chrysostom, Theophylact, Oecumenius built their expositions upon it. Calvin's version is *in omnibus vobis*.

[222] Vulg. connects the pronoun only with "in all"; it understands the first and third "all" of vs. 6 to be masculine, the second, neuter. *Deus . . . qui est super omnes, et per omnia, et in omnibus nobis*. Erasmus considered the first two neuters, the third masculine.

[223] This is the title of the essay by Dibelius (mentioned in fn. 189); pp. 20–22 are especially pertinent to the issue at hand.

according to the philosophers, penetrates and animates the whole world. The narrow interpretation of God's presence is not dependent solely upon the variant reading; even if the variant is explained as an interpreter's gloss and ruled out as inauthentic,[224] it may show interpreters which way to go.[225] As Paul occasionally, e.g. in Rom 5:15, speaks of "many" when modern languages would say "all," the opposite might also hold true.

However, a literal, i.e. wide and universalistic understanding of "all" can also be defended and is not to be ruled out merely on the ground that it would be analogous to Stoic thought. (1) Whenever in Ephesians the full power vested in the Messiah is described, the term "all" means all things rather than just all the saints.[226] It is hardly conceivable that in 4:6 the omnipotence of God the Father should be described in a more timid and restrained way. (2) When in other confessional formulae[227] different prepositions (i.e. "from," "in," "through," "into") are skillfully linked together to qualify God's or Christ's relationship to "all," the word "all" regularly means all things and persons, not just the saints. Whether Eph 4:6 is treated as originally pre-Pauline, as authentically and originally Pauline, or as deutero-Pauline—it is hard to explain why this one confession should fall out of step with the others. (3) Though there are Stoic parallels[228] to the formal connection of the "one God" with the universe of "all" things, and though the play with prepositions has a Hellenistic Greek rather than Hebrew or Aramaic ring, the NT omnipotence confessions are more informed by OT precedents than by Stoic thought. The NT follows the OT by never identifying the One with the All and by strictly avoiding an equivalent to the *hen kai pan* ("the one is the all," "the all is the one") formula of philosophers and magicians. Paul takes up OT statements about God who "fills heaven and earth," about God's glory of which the temple and all the lands are "full,"[229] and about the power given to the Messiah not only over his people, but over hostile powers and the realm of nature as well (Pss 2; 8; 12; 110 etc.). (4) The arguments in favor of a universalistic interpretation of 4:6 are clinched by 3:14–15: God is Father of those crying "Abba,"—but not only of them. In a wider sense of the term "father," he is the Father also of "each family in heaven and upon earth."

A weighty conclusion can be drawn from the universalistic character of vs. 6: while Eph 4:4–6 probably is a Pauline rephrasing of traditional confessions and stresses the immediate and inseparable connection between God's oneness and the church's unity, at the same time these verses affirm that God, his power, his love, and his work transcend the confines of the church. In basing her confession of her own unity upon the confession of God's unity, the confessing church is forced to look and think beyond her own horizon. While she is

---

[224] This is indeed necessary, if current criteria of textual criticism are applied. In GNT the variant is not even mentioned! A. Harnack, *Marcion*, 2d ed. (Leipzig: Hinrichs, 1924), p. 128x, calls the addition a Marcionite element which in Gnostic fashion distinguishes the loving Father of Christ and of the Christians from the incompetent creator of all things.

[225] The great majority of the commentaries consulted, including Dibelius, decide for the restrictive exegesis. The opposite position is taken e.g. by J. A. Robinson, pp. 93–94. He labels the possessive pronoun, "of us," a "timid gloss"; cf. Abbott.

[226] 1:10, 22–23; 3:9.

[227] I Cor 8:6; Rom 11:36; Col 1:16.

[228] Orphic and Magic texts offer precedents or analogies.

[229] See COMMENT VI C on 1:15–23.

indeed an exponent of a unity secured, proclaimed, and established by God himself, she is not the end of God's way and power. In consequence, "the unity of the church" is not the only or the supreme topic treated in 4:1–16, or in the whole of Ephesians. This epistle looks beyond the church and does not suffocate in ecclesiology; it proclaims that God's kingdom is greater than the church. See COMMENT VIII.

V   The Interpretation of Psalm 68

The form in which Ps 68:18[230] is quoted and the manner in which it is interpreted in Eph 4:8–10 pose serious problems.[231] The author of Ephesians is guilty of willful distortion of the Scriptures[232]—unless it can be shown that his interpretation makes sense in terms of the use and understanding of the psalm contemporary with him. A description of the precedents, environment, and meaning of Paul's interpretation is therefore necessary.

A   The Text

RSV Ps 68:18: "Thou didst ascend to the high mount, leading captives in thy train, and receiving gifts among men, even among the rebellious . . ." The JB version, ". . . you have taken men as tribute, yes, taken rebels," may be tenable on grammatical grounds, but is not supported by the parallel statement in vs. 29 of the same psalm: "Kings bear gifts to thee."[233] The LXX gives at the outset a fitting Greek version, but when it comes to rendering the statements on men (in the MT, "man") and on the rebellious, the meaning of the Greek text is obscure. Only the Sinaitic MS of the LXX offers some clarification regarding the recipient of the gifts, but it contains a surprising change of the subject: "he ascended . . . you took gifts to men."

Paul's citation of this verse deviates twice from the Hebrew text and the majority of the LXX texts: (1) Instead of the second person, "Thou didst ascend . . . ," the third person "he ascended . . ." is used. (2) Instead of mentioning the receipt of tribute from defeated foes or blandishing admirers, Paul mentions the "giving of gifts" and uses the image of a potentate distributing booty or positions of honor.[234] To these variations of the text must be added two interpretative steps taken by Paul which appear to contradict the wording

---

[230] In RSV. In the Hebrew Bible the number is 68:19; in the LXX and Vulg. 67:19.

[231] Among the special discussions of the pressing issues are the following: J. Grill, Der 68. Psalm, Tübingen: Laupp, 1883; E. Nestle, "Zum Zitat in Eph 4:8," ZNW 4 (1903), 344–45; StB, III, 596–98; W. Bieder, Die Vorstellung von der Höllenfahrt Jesu Christi, ATANT 19 (1949), 81–90; J. Cambier, "La signification Christologique d'Éph, 4, 7–10," NTS 9 (1963), 262–75; G. B. Caird, "The Descent of the Messiah in Ephesians 4:7–11," in Studia Evangelica, II, ed. by F. L. Cross, TU 87 (1964), 535–45.

[232] Theodore of Mopsuestia, p. 166, apparently intends to counteract such a criticism of Paul. He assumes that the apostle "does not use the [psalm] testimony as a prophetic dictum, but just as we often make use of Scripture testimonies in liturgical allusions." C. Ellicott, A Critical and Grammatical Commentary on St. Paul's Epistle to the Ephesians, Boston: Draper, 1867 (ref.), attributes to the inspired apostle the liberty of changing the language slightly. He is scolded on behalf of this view by Abbott who believes that such freedom would "open the door to the wildest freaks of interpretation." Calvin defends Paul's exegetical integrity by pointing out the theological depth of the apostle's exposition: "God seems to sleep while the church is in dire need; but when he stands up her victory is assured; thus God himself suffers humiliation before he demonstrates his power." Calvin admits, however, that Paul may not only quote from but also add words of his own to the Scripture text.

[233] See M. Dahood's translation in Psalms II, AB, vol. 17, p. 132, and his NOTE on "Kings," p. 149.

[234] Ps 68:12–13 supports this exegesis: these verses describe the division of the spoils by the women who stayed among the sheepfolds. See also Judg 5:30 where the distributed spoil includes "a maiden or two for every man."

and literal meaning of the psalm. (3) Jesus Christ's ascent to the heavenly throne is praised (cf. 1:20), instead of God's ascent from Sinai to Zion (Ps 68:17). (4) The ascent acclaimed in this passage is said to presuppose an earlier "descent" (Eph 4:9). How could Paul make these four drastic changes?

B   The Background of Paul's Interpretation

Modern research has come to divergent results regarding the origin and meaning of Ps 68. H. Gunkel refused to see historical references in this psalm and classified it among the eschatological psalms that were composed under the influence of prophetic eschatological teaching. The hymn promised God's entry as a victorious king in the midst of fettered enemies.[235] S. Mowinckel was unwilling to accept the alternative, "Either historical or eschatological," and called Ps 68 a cultic or public "victory thanksgiving psalm" which used the form of divine enthronement festivals and the myths connected with it to praise a historical event. He called the psalm "very old" and spoke of the time of Saul or Ishbaal.[236] H. Schmidt explains the psalm as a sort of hymn book for the enthronement and new year festival. He believes that it is composed of a series of independent short songs. Because of the expected return of God to Zion, he assumes a date following upon correlated deutero-Isaiah prophecies. But the assumed post-exilic composition of the psalm is for him less important than the omnipresent imagery of a pre-exilic festival. W. F. Albright offers a variant of Schmidt's interpretation: Ps 68 is a catalogue of about thirty first lines of lyric songs that were composed (or adapted from Canaanite originals) between the thirteenth and tenth centuries B.C.[237] The date of the psalm for A. Weiser is somewhere in the monarchic period. Albright suggests the tenth century, and H.-J. Kraus returns to the time of King Saul, i.e. the eleventh century B.C. While accepting Mowinckel's cultical interpretation, Weiser and Kraus attempt to show that history and eschatology cannot be ruled out either. The remembrance of a past event is the basis for expecting a new advent of the Lord and new help from his side.[238] Dahood, finally, is specifically impressed by those elements that antedate the conquest of the land by Israel and make it possible that the psalm was composed even before the days of King Saul. He stresses two facts: Zion is never explicitly mentioned, and Mount Sinai and the Bashan Mountain (i.e. Hermon) are the ones competing with each other—rather than Hermon with Zion.[239] Especially because of vs. 24 no modern interpreter leaves any doubt that in Ps 68 God's own victorious appearance is described.

---

[235] Die Psalmen, 5th ed. (Göttingen: Vandenhoeck, 1968), pp. 283–85; idem, Einleitung in die Psalmen, (Göttingen: Vandenhoeck, 1933), pp. 79–80. Cf. the description of the foes' fate in Pss 110:1–2; 149:8–9; II Cor 2:14; Philip 2:10; Col 2:15. The Song of Deborah (Judg 5) contains many parallels. It describes a historic battle, and Ps 68 may do the same, despite Gunkel's exclusion of a historic element. Still a third alternative exists: Ps 68 may intend to sum up the whole of Israel's history from Egypt to the days of Ezekiel.

[236] Psalmenstudien, 6 vols. (Kristiania: Dybwad, 1921–24, repr. Amsterdam: Schippers, 1961), II, 10 ff., 68, 141, 332; IV, 10; VI, 31. As parallels for the mythical elements are mentioned Exod 15; Pss 124; 129. The allusion to the king from Benjamin in Ps 68:27 proves the early origin of the psalm—assuming that the mention of Judah and Jerusalem in vss. 27–29 is an interpolation.

[237] H. Schmidt, Die Psalmen, Handbuch zum Alten Testament 15 (1934), 127–31; W. F. Albright, "A Catalogue of Early Hebrew Lyric Poems (Ps. 68)," HUCA 23, I (1950–51), 1–40, esp. 7–10.

[238] Weiser, Die Psalmen, II, Das Alte Testament Deutsch 15 (1950), 313–21; Kraus, Psalmen, I, Biblischer Kommentar Altes Testament 15:1 (1961), 466–77.

[239] Psalms II, pp. 139, 143. See also Albright's discussion of this issue, in HUCA 23, I (1950–51), 24.

However early or late the present form of this psalm may be, the events remembered and the ideas expressed played a great role in the early days of the monarchy, and in later periods of Israel's history. When an earthly king's enthronement was celebrated, hymns were sung that described God's kingship (as opposed to El's?), God's advent, and God's manifestation. Processions and other cultic acts gave dramatic expression to the faith confessed. When David entered Jerusalem, the throne of God, the ark, came into the city. Mowinckel in particular insisted (against Gunkel and others) that the content and forms to the praises of God's procession and enthronement were not derived from political ceremonies. Rather he was convinced of the opposite. The songs composed for the enthronement of an earthly king and the prophecies announcing a righteous and saving Messiah, reproduced the pattern of psalms composed in honor of the heavenly king.[240] It is possible that OT prophets and psalmists transferred upon the present or future Son of David an amazing amount of attributes, attitudes, actions, blessings that originally were, and essentially remained, God's own. For example, the saving righteousness (*tzedeq, tzᵉdaqah*) of God was to be represented by the righteousness of the king shown toward the poor and needy, and by his victory over external enemies. The omnipotence of God was to be manifested by the blessing which the king was expected to guarantee to the field and the stable.[241] The psalms confessing "God has become king" (e.g. 93; 96–99; Isa 52:7–12) fit an enthronement festival of Yahweh as well as the inauguration of a Davidic king, or an annual (or hept-annual?) celebration of his enthronement. Since the earthly king was received as God's plenipotentiary and vice-regent, enthusiastic admirers could call him "God" and his throne "God's throne."[242]

As earlier shown in the discussion of Jesus' title "Lord," NT writers felt even freer than their OT predecessors to interpret the psalms singing of God's kingship as descriptions of God's rule through his Anointed One. When Paul takes Ps 68 to describe Jesus Christ's rulership, he simply extends a pattern already prepared in the hymns used at enthronement festivals of God or of a descendant of David. And he moved inside a Christian tradition which is exemplified by the use of Ps 102:25–27 in Heb 1:10–11. W. Bieder assumes that the Christological exploitation of the psalms was a matter of course among the readers of Ephesians.[243] A similar, though more militant, interpretation of Ps 68 is found in the Qumran literature. Motifs taken from Judg 5:12; Num 10:35; Gen 49:8 and Ps 68:18 are woven together in 1QM XII 10–18, cf. XIX 2–4: "Arise, O warrior! Take thy captives, thou man of glory, and reap the spoil, O valiant. . . ."[244]

[240] *Psalmenstudien*, II, 14–15; idem, *He that Cometh* (New York: Abingdon, 1956), p. 95: "Yahweh . . . the divine archetype of kingship," cf. 143, etc. While Mowinckel through his Psalm studies contributed to the formation of the exaggerated claims raised by representatives of the Scandinavian School on behalf of the "divine kingship" of Israel's kings, he added in his later work necessary safeguards against all too blunt an identification of Israelite with Canaanite, Babylonian, or Egyptian king ideology.

[241] See, e.g. Ps 72, and Mowinckel, *He that Cometh*, pp. 31, 45, 67–69, 89, 92.

[242] Ps 45:6–7 in literal translation; see also the Chronicle verses listed in fn. 139 to Eph 2:1–10. Several interpreters of Ps 45 such as Dahood, *Psalms I*, AB, vol. 16, transl. of and NOTE on Ps 45:7 reject this exposition. But the LXX text of Ps 44:7–8 and Heb 1:8–9 show that it was known and accepted in NT times.

[243] ATANT 19 (1949), p. 82 n. 312.

[244] It is more likely that God himself is addressed in this battle song than that it praises Jonathan Maccabeus, despite M. Treves, "The Date of the War of the Sons of Light," VT 8 (1958), 419–24. The quoted translation is from T. H. Gaster, *The Dead Sea Scrolls* (Garden City, N.Y.: Doubleday Anchor, 1956), p. 297.

But there are still other features in the history of interpretation that left an imprint upon Paul. It is amazing that the Ethiopian, Sahidic, Bohairic, several of the Arabic and the printed Syriac versions[245] of Ps 68 translate the Hebrew verb "you received" by "you gave" or "he gave."[246] Perhaps Justin Martyr quoted for Trypho's benefit not from Ephesians but from a Jewish source when he cited "he gave gifts."[247] Did there exist a quasi-official version of Ps 68 (perhaps a Targum) which was available to Paul, Justin, and the authors of the primary and secondary versions just mentioned? Or did Paul give his own translation of the psalm and arrive at the same result independently? Questions such as these cannot be answered at present. Certainly there is a possibility that the author of Ephesians was not a lonely distorter of Scriptures but belonged in the company of *bona fide* co-interpreters. It is possible that the interpretation of Ps 68 given in Eph 4 is to some extent dependent upon instruction received by Paul before or after his conversion. P. Billerbeck has shown that rabbinical exegesis was open to a very specific understanding of the psalm. There is a Targum on Ps 68 in which Moses is identified as the one who ascended on high. The words "you received gifts" are paraphrased by "You have learned the words of the Tora, you gave them as gifts to the sons of men."[248] If this or a similiar Targum was known to Paul from his studies or from temple or synagogue worship, then he made a daring step: he applied to Jesus Christ what had been understood to relate to Moses, and he put the spiritual gifts given now, at the end time, in the place attributed by his teachers to the Law given on Mount Sinai.[249]

Other rabbinical interpretations probably of a much later date than the Targum just mentioned contribute still more color to the interpretation of Ps 68. Retaining Moses as the one who ascended, and the gift he received as a trust to be passed on to the people, they connect the "reception" of the Law with the "ascent," and the "giving" of the Law with Moses' subsequent descent from Mount Sinai.[250]

---

[245] Which are collated by J. Grill, *Der 68. Psalm*, pp. 31, 134–35, etc.; but see the warning added by E. Nestle, ZNW 4 (1903), 345 against overestimation of the reading "to give."

[246] These seemingly free versions need not be opposite to the literal meaning of the Hebrew or Greek verb, "to take," "to receive." For e.g. in Gen 15:9; 18:5; 27:13; Exod 25:3; Lev 24:2; I[III] Kings 17:10–11, the verb (mostly combined with a reference to a person and in imperative form) means "to take in order to give" (or "to pass on"). Before Meyer, Schlier, and others, Calvin thought of this possibility to vindicate Paul's rendition of the psalm text.

[247] *Dial.* 39.

[248] StB, III, 596–98. J. A. T. Robinson "The Body," SBT 5 (1952), 180, and J. Cambier refer to elements of the same exegetical tradition. Rashi (ca. 1100) also gives a paraphrase which combines the "taking" of the gift from angels with the "giving" of the received good to the people.

[249] The same shifts of interpretation, regarding the giver and his gift, are made in the Pentecost narrative (Acts 2). Beare, IB, X, 689, assumes that Ps 68 "was traditionally associated" with the post-Old Testament Jewish meaning of Pentecost, i.e. with the celebration of the giving of the Law. Indeed, if it could be demonstrated, (a) that as early as in Paul's time the Jewish Pentecost had ceased to be an agricultural feast and had become—just as all other great festivals—a celebration of a specific historical event, and (b) that at the same time Ps 68 was used to glorify Moses and the Law—then several puzzles of Eph 4:8–10 might be considered solved. Both presuppositions are not yet fulfilled. However, recent research in Qumran materials indicates that literary evidence is forthcoming to demonstrate "that Pentecost was devoted largely to the reading of the Law and the celebration of the Sinai event" (according to information received from D. N. Freedman).

[250] While Moses ascended to Mount Sinai and *subsequently* descended from it (Exod 19:3 f), the variant reading "first he descended" (see fn. 43 above) emphasizes that Christ's descent *preceded* his ascent. If the tradition contained in the later Targums goes back to Paul's time, and if it was known to Paul, then it is possible that Paul sought to meet it head-on. He might have felt that he had the same right to add a descent *before* the ascent mentioned in the psalm, as rabbis

The Hebrew term *bāādām* (lit. "in man," rendered in RSV by "among men") is explained in several ways: (1) for the benefit of Israel, in contrast to the nations who refused to accept the Law; (2) because of the Great Man, that is, because of Abraham's merit; or (3) in relation to man, without any specification. The Jewish interpreters agree in considering the communication of the law a gift—rather than an act of selling or buying for a price.

That which was "led captive" is again variously interpreted: (1) "angels of the upper world" were questioning (with the words of Ps 8:4-8: "What is man . . .") the dignity of Moses to receive the great gift, but were silenced; (2) Moses had to wrestle with angels and overcome them as did Jacob; (3) the (pre-existent!) Law was once locked up in God's heart and was now brought forth from its captivity.[251] In each case it is made clear that no man except Moses was ever given such power.

Certainly the literary fixation of such interpretations of Ps 68 occurred much later than any of the early or late dates ascribed to Ephesians. In view of this, it is not impossible that the Jewish expositions contain a reaction against the exegesis offered in Eph 4:8-10. It is more likely, however, that the author of Ephesians was acquainted with a Targum and other antecedents of Talmud and midrash, and that the psalm exposition of Eph 4:8-10 takes up and corrects contemporary exegesis. Even if a person other than Paul wrote Ephesians, it is probable that he not only had rabbinic schooling but also was so concerned with some of its tenets and influence that he placed a correction before his Gentile-born readers.[252]

C   Paul's Exposition

The elements from the history of interpretation of Ps 68 presented above show that Paul did not invent a new hermeneutics. Rather he continued on a way laid out in the OT use of enthronement psalms, and followed with surprising results by rabbinical teachers. Without detriment to its substance and quality Paul's interpretation can be called a midrash.[253] The apostle used the psalm to show that the exalted Christ is the source of the spiritual gifts. The same connection between Christology and Pneumatology is manifest in the Gospel of John,[254] and in the Pentecost narrative and sermon of Acts 2. At the same time and by the same token the divine origin and guarantee of diversity in unity are demonstrated. The monarchy of God is proclaimed as it is established (1) by the enthronement of God's Anointed One; (2) by the power he is given over Israel, over the nations, over other inimical powers, and over all things; (3) finally by the generosity and loyalty shown to the poor and needy through the outpouring of abundant blessing. As shown in the second NOTE on 4:11, in

---

claimed when they made references to a *subsequent* descent. Paul would thus intend to say, "While in the end, Moses was down here with the people, Jesus Christ is now up on high." Again, it is not certain whether Paul really intended to develop such contrasts.

[251] The last interpretation would correspond to the meaning which the term the "revealed secret" has in Ephesians; see COMMENT XI on 1:3-14.

[252] The Epistle of Barnabas and Justin Martyr's *Dialogue* bristle with similar arguments: in antithesis to a Jewish exegesis a Scripture "gnosis" was being developed, for the benefit of Gentiles. A comparison of the methods employed and results achieved cannot be made at this place.

[253] Dibelius; Gaugler; J. Cambier.

[254] John 7:39; 14:16, 26; 15:26; 16:7-15; 20:22.

Ephesians the gift given by the Messiah consists of the persons given to the church.

Paul gives at least three answers to the question, Why does the one God create differences, and yet is victorious over all past or future divisions among his creatures, between mankind, or in the people of God? (1) The "grace [of God] given by the Messiah" (4:7) is a synonym for the "Holy Spirit" with which all the saints are "sealed" (1:13–14; 4:30). In harmony with 4:4–6 and I Cor 12:4–7 Paul refers to the trinity of God as the archetype of unity in diversity. (2) Much emphasis is placed upon the way of the Messiah: Jesus Christ establishes God's gracious dominion by his personal presence, first at the low, then at the high places. Even when the incarnate seems to be an absent Lord after his return to heaven, he proves to be continually present by and in the many gifts given to all the saints, by the special ministers he appoints to engage them in the common ministry, and by continually permeating "all things" with his power (4:7–12). (3) The way of the Messiah includes not only his confrontation with inimical powers but also their defeat: "He captured a catch of prisoners" (4:8). The identity of these prisoners has been explained in various ways.[255] Irenaeus' interpretation[256] makes the best sense: Paul has in mind those principalities and powers that are hostile to God and man and seek to divide them.[257] Eph 4:7 ff. may corroborate and explicate the statements made earlier in Ephesians regarding Christ's dominion over all things and powers, see 1:10, 20–23.

Every element of the psalm interpreted in 4:8 is related to the whole of the epistle and its message. If because of its rabbinical traits the mode of Paul's interpretation appears strange to modern readers, yet it is skilled and appropriate to the situation in which the apostle lived. Hermeneutics cannot be timeless as long as it serves actual proclamation and does not attempt to form an abstract philosophical system. The concrete testimony to Christ and to unity in diversity which Paul intended to give made it natural, if not necessary, that he use the tools and methods available to him and his contemporaries.

VI The Church without Laymen and Priests

In earlier parts of Ephesians many basic descriptions of the church were given. She is the people of God created by the reconciliation of Jews and Gentiles. She is the body of Christ and in Eph 5 will be described as his bride. She is the communion of those saved, forgiven, resurrected from death, and made holy. It is her nature to worship God and to be God's missionary to the world. She is the temple of God in the process of construction and a signal of the new creation that affects all men, powers, and things. God the Father, the Son, and the Spirit create her, rule her, are present in her. This is documented to both the church and the powers, through the testimony given by the apostles

---

[255] Chrysostom spoke of Satan, sin and death; Bousset, *Kyrios*, p. 30, of "the demonic hosts of Hades"; Gnosticizing and other interpreters, of the souls captive in the realm of matter and finiteness, or of the saints liberated from bondage. The first of these interpretations disregards the fact that in Ephesians sin and death are not personalized; the second, that a descent of Christ into Hades (as was shown in the last NOTE on 4:9) is not suggested in this epistle; the third, that "the notion of imprisoned souls is absent from Ephesians" (Bieder, ATANT 19 [1949], 83).

[256] *Epid.* 83.

[257] See COMMENTS V on 1:15–23 and IV on 2:11–22.

and prophets regarding the revealed secret of God. It is recognized when the church listens to the voice of the Scriptures and of the living witnesses; when she believes in, and makes her confession to, the one God; and when her conduct corresponds to her high calling.

All these and other descriptions of the church make plain that the church is established and given its order by God. She is neither only an "institution from above" nor only a "gathered people."[258] Rather she is that peaceful gathering of former children *and* strangers *and* enemies upon which God has decided from eternity, which he carries out through Christ and the Spirit, and which he still leads to completion and perfection. The church's very essence and existence can be described by reference to the order she is given. Since this order is an instruction for those elected to reach a given goal, it must not be considered an end in itself. The order of the church is an instrument serving a given purpose. The means and the end are given by God; therefore, they cannot be separated. But origin and purpose are greater than the means; the order must not be treated as an absolute.

Eph 4:11–13 is a *locus classicus* pointing out the coherence of the church's origin, order, and destiny. Certain ministries are given by Christ (vs. 11) in order that the church fulfill her present task (vs. 12), and, at the end, reach the goal set for her (vs. 13). While the problems of vs. 13 will be discussed in the next COMMENT, those posed by vss. 11–12 are to be considered here. In following the teleological accent set by vs. 13, the treatment of the purpose described in vs. 12 will precede the description of the means mentioned in vs. 11.

In the clause, "to equip the saints for the work of service for building the Messiah's body" (4:12), three elements can be distinguished: (1) the equipment of the saints; (2) the servant work; (3) the construction of Christ's body. These three concepts may denote three distinct purposes—or they may be a triple definition of the one purpose that determines the "gift" of the ministries mentioned in vss. 7, 8 and 11. The wording of the Greek text of vs. 12 does not permit a decision. Different, though practically synonymous, prepositions stand before the first two.[259] This can, but need not, mean that distinct purposes are suggested: first, the equipping of all the saints, and second, the enabling of certain special ministers to do the servant work of building.

If a comma is put between the first two concepts,[260] no doubt is left that the gift of the ministries has a double object: all the saints benefit from it, but only

---

[258] At this point not even a brief report can be given on the perennial Catholic-Protestant, High Church-Low Church disputes; on the nineteenth-century controversy between A. Harnack and R. Sohm; on more recent revivals of the issue, e.g. by K. E. Kirk, *The Apostolic Ministry*, London: Hodder & Stoughton, 1946, on one side; E. Brunner, *The Misunderstanding of the Church*, Philadelphia: Westminster, 1953, on the other side. Comprehensive accounts of the trends before 1930 are given by O. Linton, *Das Problem der Urkirche in der neueren Forschung*, Uppsala: Almquist, 1932, repr. Frankfurt: Minerva, 1957; later periods are covered by F. M. Braun, *Neues Licht auf die Kirche*, Einsiedeln: Johannes-Verlag, 1946; E. Schweizer, *Gemeinde und Gemeindeordnung im Neuen Testament*, ATANT 35 (1959). J. H. Elliot, *The Elect and the Holy*, NovT Supplement 12, Leiden: Brill, 1966, offers a thorough exegesis of 1 Peter 2:4–10 in which many of the issues treated in this COMMENT and scores of pertinent books and articles are discussed.

[259] *Pros* before "equipment"; *eis* before "work of service" (also before "building" and the three parallel lines of vs. 13). In our translation, the differentiation is reflected by the distinction between "to [equip]" and "for [the work of service]," but not in the version given of vs. 13.

[260] The earliest preserved Bible MSS contain no punctuation marks. But, e.g. in the Textus Receptus edition in Oxford (1873), and in many versions, in some editions of KJ, in all prints of RV, ASV, RSV, etc., a comma is placed after "saints."

select ministers carry out the work of building the body.[261] This interpretation has an aristocratic, that is, a clerical and ecclesiastical flavor; it distinguishes the (mass of the) "saints" from the (superior class of the) officers of the church. A clergy is now distinct from the laity, to whom the privilege and burden of carrying out the prescribed construction work are exclusively assigned. Certainly the needs of the laymen saints are cared for: they receive salvation, eternal life, ethical instructions through the saving word, the seal of the sacraments, the doctrinal decisions, the disciplinary measures administered by the officers. Yet two implications of this interpretation are inescapable: (1) the laymen are ultimately only beneficiaries, and (2) the benefits of the clergy's work remain inside the church—though people and power outside the church may witness the clergy's successes and failures.

The meaning of 4:12 is entirely different when the nouns preceded by different prepositions describe[262] one and the same purpose of the ministries mentioned in vs. 11, and when no comma is placed between the first two parts of vs. 12. Then the ministries of vs. 11 are given to the church in order that "the saints" become "equipped" to carry out "the work of service," even "the building." Earlier and later passages in Ephesians show that the "good works" to be done by the church and her members can be summed up in this way: this community makes known or lets shine the light of God's goodness, wisdom, gospel to the powers of this world.[263] Eph 4:12 may indeed underline the fact that the "saints" are not a part of the church but all her members, without excluding any one of them. All the saints (and among them, each saint) are enabled by the four or five types of servants enumerated in 4:11 to fulfill the ministry given to them, so that the whole church is taken into Christ's service and given missionary substance, purpose, and structure.[264] This interpretation challenges both the aristocratic-clerical and the triumphalistic-ecclesiastical exposition of 4:11–12. It unmasks them as arbitrary distortions of the text.[265] Are, therefore, the existence and function of a clergy simply dispensable? Indeed, the traditional distinction between clergy and laity does not belong in the church. Rather, the whole church, the community of all the saints together, is the clergy appointed by God for a ministry to and for the world. This way two widespread opinions are refuted: the assumption that the bulk of the church members are reduced to the rank of mere consumers of spiritual gifts, and the notion that the church as a whole must strive primarily for a "build-up" which benefits only herself. As an alternative the following message is conveyed: the dignity and usefulness of the special ministries given to the church are as great or as small as their effectiveness in making every church

---

[261] This interpretation of vs. 12 is found, e.g. in Chrysostom, Theophylact, Oecumenius, Thomas Aquinas, Calvin, Bengel, Dibelius, Schlier, also in R. Asting, *Die Heiligkeit im Urchristentum,* (Göttingen: Vandenhoeck, 1930), pp. 177–81.

[262] Just as e.g. in Rom 15:2.

[263] Esp. 2:7, 10; 3:9–10; 5:8; 6:15, 19; cf. Matt 5:14–16; Philip 2:15; 1 Peter 2:9, 12.

[264] In COMMENTS X on 1:3–14 and VI B 6 on 1:15–23 the missionary dimension of the terms "knowledge" and "body" was demonstrated. See also COMMENTS V on 2:1–10, II and IV on 3:1–13.

[265] No comma is set after saints by Vulg.; Westcott-Hort; R. F. Weymouth; Nestle; Phillips; NEB; JB; WBLex, 419. It is noteworthy that Haupt, Robinson, Gaugler have anticipated the exposition of vs. 12 which since about 1940 has been promoted esp. by the work of D. T. Niles and the World Council of Churches' Departments of the Laity and of Evangelism. See also J. A. Mackay, *God's Order,* pp. 149–53.

member, including the smallest and most despised, an evangelist in his own home and environment.

A decision between the two interpretations mentioned cannot be made by quibbling about such trifles as the change of prepositions or the appropriateness of a comma. Rather the whole context and all the parallels of 4:12 provide at least four reasons in favor of the second interpretation:

1) The "grace" given to the saints according to 4:7 is certainly the same grace of the same God as the ministerial grace given to Paul of which he speaks in 3:2, 7; cf. Rom 1:5. This grace does not terminate and die in the recipient, but makes him an active servant. Paul states that God's grace has not come in vain but has made him work (I Cor 15:10). A similar connection between grace and servant work is also established in 4:7, 12; cf. Philip 2:12–13. The term "to equip" (lit. "for equipment") corresponds to this essence and meaning of "grace". In the first NOTE on Eph 4:12 it was shown that the Greek noun *katartismos,* ("equipment"), denotes preparation for a job rather than an object than can be possesed or handled.

2) In 4:7 "each" one of the saints i.e. all saints, not only apostles, prophets, evangelists, teaching shepherds are called recipients of grace from on high. In verse 4:13 "we all" is the subject of the sentence, and 4:16 mentions the contribution made by "each single part" of the body, to the growth and building-up of the whole body. The fourth NOTE on the same verse sought to demonstrate that Paul does not attribute to some specific members of the body (e.g. to supposed "joints") a role essentially distinct from that of all members or parts. His interest is focussed upon the mutual contact of all members, not upon special members that reserve for themselves the function of joints.

3) I Cor 12 describes the unity of the body and the diverse functions of its members as much as Eph 4. Absent from that chapter are such Ephesian terms as "body of Christ," "Christ the head," "growth," "building"; the local rather than the universal church order is described. Yet these facts do not exclude the presence of striking parallels to Eph 4. Especially in I Cor 12:7, 18 the "manifestation of the Spirit given to each" saint "for the common good" and the divine appointment of "each member" of the body are as vigorously stressed as in Ephesians. Neither in I Corinthians nor in Ephesians are higher and lower, official and non-official, active and primarily receptive (or passive) church members distinguished as different ranks. On the contrary, in I Cor 12:22–23 the weakest members of the church are declared the most important: "Those organs of the body which seem to be more frail than others are indispensable, and those parts of the body which we regard as less honorable are treated with special honor. To our unseemly parts is given a more than ordinary seemliness" (NEB).

4) There is but one calling or vocation valid in the church: the call of God into his kingdom.[266] One and the same spiritual armor is available to all the saints (6:10–17). Under no circumstances can the persons given to the church as special officers claim or retain any part of the warrior's equipment as belonging to themselves alone. For God has promised and provided the training and the necessary arms to all the saints. Special officers do not form a class,

---

[266] See the third NOTE on 4:1 and COMMENT II.

rank, or caste in the church. They are enlisted and installed for the purpose of "equipping" (all) the saints.

In summary, the task of the special ministers mentioned in Eph 4:11 is to be servants in that ministry which is entrusted to the whole church. Their place is not above but below the great number of saints who are not adorned by resounding titles. Every one of the special ministers is a *servus servorum Dei*.[267] He is a "pastor" of God's flock, who understands himself as a minister to ministers.

In turn, the task of the whole church and of every saint is to carry out a work of service for the praise of God and the benefit of all who need it. There are needy people inside the church—the "lonely men at the top" may well belong among them. There are even more people in want outside the church. According to Matt 10:39, the church can find life only by losing her life in the service entrusted to her. She fulfills her task by following the way of her master (Mark 10:35–45). Divers books of the NT show that all "clerical" titles available from Israel's history and literature have been conferred upon Jesus Christ and comprehended in him. If after Christ's coming and under his rulership any legitimate clergymen are left in the world, then all saints and the whole church are these clergymen of God, installed for the benefit of those as yet unaware of the Messianic peace.

Indeed, nothing that today is considered a prerequisite quality of a pastor or priest of the church remains unmentioned in Ephesians—but all of it serves as a description of every saint. Clergymen are expected to speak the truth, to confess their "faith" openly and to live up to it, to have the "seal" of authority, to be properly "called" and "walk worthy of their vocation," to be men of "hope" filled with the right "spirit," to take a firm "stand," to demonstrate mutual "love," to be faithful in "prayer" and "intercession."[268] According to Ephesians each saint and all the saints are equipped to walk this way, not only some among them.

However, do not all those saints who are not apostles, prophets, evangelists, etc., lack one essential element, ordination?[269] The ordination of Jesus Christ to his ministry was his baptism (Mark 1:9–11). It is possible that the term "one baptism" in 4:5 includes this reminder: all the saints have received the same ordination and made the same pledge to fulfill their share in the ministry entrusted to the church. As previously observed, in Gal 3:27 the effect of baptism is described in a way reminiscent of the investiture of a high priest or the inauguration of a Roman official. The ordination mentioned in I Tim 4:14; 6:12; II Tim 1:6 may well refer to the confession and laying-on-of-hands connected with baptism rather than to an antecedent of a bishop's consecration.[270] In short, it is probable that in the NT baptism included that character and meaning which in later times were attributed to the ordination of special

---

[267] Not even the high claims made by Paul in Gal 1:6–10 permit any of them to claim infallibility or universal jurisdiction.

[268] 1:13–15, 18; 4:1–3, 15; 6:10–18, etc.

[269] As mentioned, e.g. in Acts 6:6; 13:1–3, and perhaps presupposed in the Pastoral Epistles. Ordination seems to distinguish special ministers from the laity.

[270] See, e.g. Bultmann, ThNT, I, 134; J. N. D. Kelly, *A Commentary on the Pastoral Epistles* (London: Black, 1963), pp. 141–47. It is, however, possible that early forms of special ordination borrowed as heavily from baptismal imagery and liturgy as, e.g. the Benedictine consecration ritual.

ministers. Baptism in the biblical sense of the term is ordination for participation in the church's ministry.

It appears that this understanding of Eph 4:12 contradicts the contents of 2:18 and the interpretation given above.[271] There it was said that compared with Christ, The Priest, all Christians are laymen. Now the very term "laymen" has proved inappropriate to the understanding of Ephesians. However, the contradiction is not absolute. What is proper in distinguishing the Christians from Christ is not equally proper in comparing one Christian with another. The findings based upon 2:18 are qualified and ultimately strengthened by 4:12. The latter text avers that in the monarchy of the king and priest Christ, there are only citizens of equal rank, not people of higher and lower orders, forming distinct classes; so they are all laymen. But Christ wants, trusts, and equips all members of God's people to be active servants. Therefore they are all given a priestly function. The grace given to "each one" extols and enables every saint to carry out what pertains "to the glory of God's grace" (1:6, 14).

The resulting democratic character of the church does not obliterate the roles which specific servants must and may play within the church. Christ himself "appointed these to be apostles and those to be prophets, some to be evangelists and others to be teaching shepherds" (4:11).[272] In distinction from I Cor 12:28–30; Rom 12:7–13; I Peter 4:10–11, only "Ministers of the Word" are mentioned at this point. Any indication is absent that administrators of the sacraments, presbyters (or "priests"), organizers, or representatives and agents of unity and continuity possess a dignity and function equal to the teachers and preachers of the Word. In COMMENT XVI on 1:3–14 it was observed that while Ephesians belongs among the most ecclesiastical of the NT letters, this epistle fails explicitly to attribute to baptism and the eucharist that central position which they occasionally attained in later ecclesiology. The OT distinction between the priests and the people, or between the Levites and the other tribes, is absent. Since according to Ephesians 2:15–18 Christ is the Priest whose service and sacrifice are extolled, the church described here is certainly not without a priest. Other passages of Ephesians that come close to I Peter 2:9, that is, foremost Eph 2:20–22, show that the church as a whole fulfills a priestly office—or at least the function of a temple in the world. When the church intercedes for all men and proclaims peace she acts as Christ's spokesman or ambassador. But a multiplicity of individual priests serving inside the church is as little envisaged in Eph 4 as is an anonymous consuming mass of laymen. Rather the church consists exclusively of responsible, active, well-equipped saints and servants. The epistle to the Hebrews points out the way in which the royal high priest Jesus Christ fulfills his ministry. Heb 8:13 especially uses very strong language for saying that his coming and work reduce all other priestly personnel and institutions: this verse speaks of the "obsolete," "senile" and "vanishing" character of the former order.

However, is not the church without "priests" and "sacraments" (in the sense attributed to these terms during two thousand years of church history) condemned to be a church without mystery? Since he is convinced that the one

271 See COMMENT VI B on 2:11–22.
272 See the NOTES on 4:11 for clarification of the individual terms.

"secret" has been and is being revealed, and that it determines essence and existence, doctrine and worship of the church, the author of Ephesians sees (except in 5:32) no need to speak of additional "mysteries."[273] In the epistle to the Colossians the mystery of Christ is set in opposition to a cult and doctrine that tend to dissolve the one mystery into a series of doctrinal, liturgical, ceremonial or other mysteries.

According to 4:14 the church order described in 4:11–13 is opposed to threatening disorder. The confession of the one God (4:4–6) stands in contrast to "doctrinal gusts"; the "truth spoken in love" (4:15) to "deceitful scheming"; the "Perfect Man" (4:13) to the behavior of "babes"; the "apostles, prophets, evangelists," etc. instituted by Christ (4:11) to the "trickery" originating from "men." The special ministers serve in the construction of the body of Christ—a task which includes confounding heretical teaching, worship, and conduct.

How do these ministers fulfill their function? Common to all titles listed in 4:11 is the fact mentioned earlier that they describe men who have something to say. These men work primarily by speaking. Their specific "ministry of the Word" is distinct from glorified verbosity, loquacity, gossiping (as described in I Cor 14). "Apostles, prophets, teachers," etc., listen before they talk (Rom 10:14–18; cf. Matt 10:27; 13:16–17), learn and are sent before they teach (Gal 1:12, 15–16), think before they pronounce, care for being understood rather than impose themselves upon people in need of edifying speech (Eph 4:29). They are motivated by love of their neighbor rather than by the desire to show off a superior intelligence or status of their own (I Cor 13:1–2; 14:3–11, etc.). They speak only when and because they have a most urgent message to convey. This message is called the "word of truth" or "the gospel."[274]

Eph 4:11–12 is not the only passage in Pauline letters which shows the indispensability of preaching, teaching, (directive) counseling by ministers of the gospel. In I Cor 12:28–30 the service done by persons who have something to say is mentioned before the ministry fulfilled by other means and men is described. In Rom 12:6–13 and in the greeting list of Rom 16, persons serving in the ministry of the Word are mentioned among individuals who render a ministry by other means. In all cases the one ministry rendered by the church to God and in the world (Eph 4:12), and the manifold services which the church members render to one another and to men near and far from them, are dependent upon and related to the ministry of the gospel. Where there is no hearing there will be no obeying. Where there is no word of salvation, encouragement, direction, judgment—in short, without proclamation of the Messianic peace—there is no community of saints and no mission. The enumeration of servants who act primarily by speaking does not exclude or devaluate the witness given by other saints through other means.[275] Still, following Ephesians

---

[273] Such mysteries may be called sacraments. They have been combined with various perplexing doctrinal or organizational elements, e.g. the doctrine and techniques of mystic union with Christ; the complementary function of clergy and laity; the representation of church tradition and unity that was attributed to the person or office of the pope or the bishops rather than to Jesus Christ alone. For the *mystērion* mentioned in 5:32 see the first NOTE on that verse and COMMENT VI B on 5:21–33.

[274] See 1:13; 4:20–21; 6:17; Rom 1:16–17, etc.

[275] Examples from the spheres of social, educational, economic life will be given in Eph 4:25–32; 5:21 ff.

"salvation" cannot be effected or communicated merely by providing "soap, soup, and slate," that is, health service, food, and education, to all those in need. This epistle emphasizes above all the necessity of hearing, believing, and spreading "the message that saves you" (1:13; 6:17–20).

At the beginning of this COMMENT it was stated that the church here described is instituted and gathered at the same time. Through Jesus Christ God has effected and instituted that gathering of Jews and Gentiles that is called the church. False alternatives such as "Either institutional—or gathered," and the corresponding insoluble disputes can be avoided when on the ground of Eph 4 the church is understood as a confessing church or as a church of the Word.

The next COMMENT will discuss the question whether Paul ascribes to this concept of the church an inherent perfection.

VII Meeting the Perfect Man

Eph 4:13 has been translated "until we all come to meet the unifying faith and knowledge of the Son of God, the Perfect Man, the perfection of the Messiah who is the standard of manhood." Each element of this verse (the origin, form, meaning, and function of the individual terms and their composition within this unit) is equally puzzling. Most likely we are dealing with a part of a hymn, as the somewhat ponderous diction, the confessional character, the three parallel utterances about Christ (the "Son of God," the "Perfect Man," the "Messiah's perfection") suggest. Since some of the key terms used here are not found elsewhere in Pauline letters this verse may be of pre-Pauline or post-Pauline origin. In writing Ephesians, or in revising a draft of the letter, Paul himself may have inserted vs. 13 between vss. 12 and 14. It is either one among many elements, or it is the very core and climax of 4:7–16, or it is a parenthesis without much relevance for understanding the context. However, vs. 13 may also be a deliberate, a wise, or a misleading interpolation made by a later editor or copyist. While the prehistory of this verse in tradition and literature is unknown, its contents deserve careful attention. Many things are ambiguous:

First, the Greek verb *kantantaō*, here translated by "come to meet," sounds more heavy and loaded, if not pompous, than our version indicates. The choice of this verb by the author requires an investigation. Next, the concept "unifying faith and knowledge" may in the original text either be an attribute of the "Son of God" or a future possession of *all* the saints, or both. Finally, the identity of the one who is called the "Perfect Man" is not clear at first sight. The abstract nouns, here translated by "perfection," "standard," "manhood," may be understood in different ways. All these issues will now be discussed.

A A Solemn Meeting

Etymologically the verb *katantaō* denotes a downhill movement. The Greeks used it to describe such events as the arrival at a given point, an attack upon the enemy, the deeding of property. Twice in II Maccabees and eight times in Acts, the verb signifies "arriving at a certain place."[276] In metaphoric senses

---

[276] LSLex, 903; II Macc 4:21, 44; Acts 16:1; 18:19, etc.

it occurs both inside and outside the Bible.[277] In I Cor 14:36 it means definitely, "to come to," "to reach," "to meet a person." In all cases movement is presupposed:[278] a person or thing moves or is transported toward an individual, a group, a substance, or a place. The goal of the movement is predetermined and/or highly desirable.

Eph 4:13 speaks of a movement in which all saints participate. They are depicted as people moving on a road toward a certain goal. As yet the church lacks fulfillment: she is dependent on that to which she is to come.[279] The Greek text is phrased so as to leave no doubt: one day the goal will be reached![280] The migrating people of God do not face an unknown future.

What is the destination? Three terms are used to describe it—terms that appear to interpret one another mutually. In literal translation they are: (1) "the oneness of faith and knowledge of God's Son"; (2) "the Perfect Man"; (3) "the measure of the stature of the Messiah's fullness." In the Greek text the definite article is used only before the first of these three designations of the goal. This need not demonstrate that the second and third descriptions of the goal are more general or vague, meaning, e.g. "a perfect man," "any perfect man," or "any given measure." Rather all three definitions of the end point are specific. Each contains a reference to a person: "God's Son," "the man," "the Messiah." But each also adds a qualification of the person named: "Oneness of faith and knowledge" is related to the "Son of God," "perfect" is the quality of the "man," "the stature of fullness" is connected with the "Messiah." When the key person in question is met, the situation of the welcomers is changed. Thus meeting a specific man *and* the acquisition of a high status are indissolubly connected. They are simultaneous and inseparable. Without that man— no perfection! How is perfection found? Only by meeting that man!

The Greek verb *katantaō* ("come to meet') contains a key for understanding the casual connection between the person met and the perfect quality acquired at the moment of meeting. The verb is sometimes used to describe the movement of a festival procession that is under way in solemn fashion for a solemn purpose. Those partaking in the cortege go out to meet a very important party bringing them bliss, joy, security, and peace. At least two forms and occasions of such processions were known to Paul, and probably to the readers of

---

[277] In LXX II Kings[II Sam] 3:29; II Macc 4:24; 6:14; Philip 3:11; Acts 26:6–7; I Cor 10:11 it signifies the following: to fall upon the head of a person; to reach the full measure of sins; to secure for oneself the high priesthood; to attain to the substance of hope; to reach the resurrection of the dead; to be confronted with the end of the world. For examples of non-biblical use see the references given by LSLex, WBLex, TWNTE, I and III, arts. *antaō, apantaō, apantēsis, katantaō, hypantaō, hypantēsis, synantaō.* The prepositions *apo, kata, syn* were combined with the verb *antaō* sometimes without giving it a different meaning. Often the composite verbs and nouns appear to have been used interchangeably, as is illustrated, e.g. by the variant reading of I Thess 4:17; cf. E. Peterson, "Die Einholung des Kyrios," ZST 7 (1929–30), 682–702, esp. 693.

[278] See O. Michel, TWNTE, III, 623–25. Schlier, pp. 201–3, avers that in Eph 4:13 "faith and knowledge" are described as a movement, i.e. as ontological events (rather than epistemological happenings only). The context, esp. 2:21; 4:15–16, suggests that the events taking place on the way to attaining, and the process of growing are simultaneous. According to Percy, p. 321, growth not in numbers but in the depths and heights of understanding are in the foreground here as much as, e.g. in 3:18–19; 4:15–16; Col 1:6, 10. But since the building of the temple or of the body (2:21; 4:12), does not exclude the insertion of new stones, external growth must not be excluded.

[279] Or ". . . to grow" (2:20–21; 4:15–16); cf. Calvin.

[280] The political event is clearly alluded to in I Thess 4:15–17 and amply documented by Peterson, the mere eventuality or possibility of an attainment is meant. The conjunction *an* is *not* used in Eph 4:13. The subjunctive of the verb "to come to meet" which follows the particle "until" is called by BDF, 383:2, a "prospective subjunctive possessing a certain relation to the final subjunctive."

Ephesians as well: the oriental ritual of receiving a king who approaches the city, and the related custom of a bridal party's exodus from town or village to meet the bridegroom.[281] In Eph 4:13 the royal titles "Son of God" and "Messiah" suit well the theory that Paul uses political-ceremonial imagery here; indeed Ps 68 (which was quoted in Eph 4:8) describes a royal procession. However, the possibility that allusion is made to the other, non-political, ritual also has support from the context. The term "perfect man," the comparison of the Christ-church relationship with the bond between bridegroom and bride (or husband and wife) in 5:22-33, perhaps also the garment imagery of 4:22-24, may indicate that the verb "come to meet" refers to the marriage custom.[282] In this case the "perfect man" is he whom a teenaged girl hopes (or used to hope) to meet some day: a partner whose reality would surpass her vague expectations of a Prince Charming and whose love would fulfill her highest dreams of happiness. See the last part of this COMMENT.

A choice between a literary association either with political or with marriage rituals need not be made. For in Ps 45, in the Song of Songs, also in the marriage and enthronement rites of most diverse cultures, political and marriage imageries are intertwined. The king is bridegroom as, e.g. the ritual of the *hieros gamos* (holy marriage; see COMMENT VII A B on 5:21-33) shows, and the bridegroom is king of the day. A Prince Charming can be the symbol of a nation's yearning for peace, prosperity, happiness, a town's paragon of strength and joy, a girl's dream and aspiration. The "Perfect Man" is the one who fulfills all these requirements. He deserves to be capitalized no less than an Emperor. The OT speaks of him: "You are the fairest of the sons of man" (Ps 45:2). "You were the signet of perfection, full of wisdom, and perfect in beauty" (Ezek 28:12).

Certainly the origin and meaning of the concept Perfect Man may also be sought in supposedly loftier realms than those of enthronement and marriage ceremonies, that is, e.g. in Gnosticism. In part C of this COMMENT such possibilities will be examined. But as long as the term "come to meet" is under review, the secular, festival, joyous connotation of the imagery and diction used in Eph 4:13 must count as an argument in its own right.

The festival procession toward a potentate or bridegroom implies not only the movement of a town's gentlemen and plebes, or of the wedding guests toward the bridegroom, but also the motion and progress of the important personality toward those expecting him. His majesty the prince or bridegroom is himself approaching those who are on their way to meet him. In I Cor 10:11; 14:36 the same verb as is used in Eph 4:13 denotes the movement of the endtime and of the word of God toward mankind! In Eph 4:13 the movement of the "Perfect Man" toward "all the saints" is not explicitly mentioned, but the ceremonies associated with the verb "come to meet" include *his* forthcoming arrival. Other NT passages demonstrate that the "coming of the Lord" is fun-

---

[281] The political event is clearly alluded to in I Thess 4:15-17 and amply documented by Petersen, ZST 7 (1929-30), 682 ff; cf. Schille, *Hymnen*, p. 144; for the marriage ritual see the Parable of the Ten Virgins (Matt 25:1-13) and the commentaries on that passage; also StB, I, 500-518; II, 398-99. Passages in which Chrysostom, Theodoret, John of Damascus, and Theophylact either refer only to the political imagery contained in the verb *apantaō* (or, *hypantaō*) or combine it with a reference to the bridal imagery are quoted by Petersen, pp. 700-1.

[282] Cf. Rev 19:7-8; Matt 22:11-14; also I Thess 4:17?

damental to the life, faith, confession, worship of the church. The saints pray, "*maranatha*, [our] Lord come!" (I Cor 16:22; Rev 22:20). The hoped-for coming of Jesus Christ is usually called his "parousia" (I Thess 4:15–17; Matt 24:27, etc.).[283]

In conclusion, just as a king or bridegroom, by his advent and through his meeting with those expecting him, fulfills the hope and changes the status of many, so according to Eph 4:13 does the Son of God, the Perfect Man, the Messiah. He makes his people participants in his perfection and riches. All that is his becomes theirs. The transformation of the many, effected by the meeting with the Man, is in this case distinct from a gradual improvement. It resembles a sudden change comparable to the effect of forgiveness and sanctification.[284]

Still, hasty conclusions ought not to be drawn from the imagery suggested by the verb "come to meet." Only if other key elements of Eph 4:13 support the interpretation just offered can a firm exegetical decision be made, and radical theological and ecclesiological inferences become necessary. In the following, all that is tenuous in the exposition proposed so far will be subjected to several tests.

B   One Faith and Knowledge

Eph 4:13a contains the phrase "the unifying faith and knowledge of the Son of God," lit. "the oneness of the faith and knowledge of the Son of God." In COMMENT IV B on 4:1–16, reasons have been given for the interpretation of the attribute "one" and the noun "unity" as a participle, "unifying." Oneness (*henotēs*) in Ephesians is a dynamic, comprehensive force rather than a static entity existing in splendid isolation and lacking any contact with, or influence upon, its environment. Therefore, the "oneness" or "unity" mentioned in 4:13a offers no novel problems. Still, the genitive connection made in this verse among "oneness," "faith," "knowledge," and "the Son of God" requires discussion.

Two unlikely interpretations can easily be eliminated:

1) Does 4:13a promise a future reconciliation of faith with knowledge, an attainable identity of belief and reason, or peace between the alleged or actual opponents religion and science? This is improbable, for the context is not concerned with this epistemological problem. Elsewhere when Paul mentions the "future of belief," i.e. the culmination and final form of man's perception and comprehension of God and his secrets, he speaks of "seeing" the Lord. Sight rather than faith on the part of those who are with the Lord is the *eschatological* fulfillment of man's relation to his creator and redeemer in the NT.[285]

---

[283] F.-J. Steinmetz, "Parusie-Erwartung im Epheserbrief? Ein Vergleich," *Biblica* 50 (1969), 328–36; idem, *Protologische Heilszuversicht*, (Frankfort: Knecht, 1968), pp. 113 ff, shares the view of the majority of commentators on Ephesians, that the traditional *parousia* expectation found in Paul's major epistles is absent from Ephesians. He considers the concepts of head, fullness, filling, growth, a theological equivalent or substitute—without noticing that most likely Christ's advent (the *parousia*) and the concept *plērōma* are combined in Eph 4:13, without absorption of the first by the second.

[284] Bultmann, ThNT, I, 268–69, describes the transition from man's "situation under the Law to the situation under grace" as "not, indeed, a continuity of development as understood within the Greek-idealistic picture of man" but as "a break." The concept *perfect* will be extensively discussed below in Part C of this COMMENT.

[285] I Cor 13:12; II Cor 3:18; 5:7; Col 3:4; Heb 11:1; Mark 9:1; 13:26; 14:62; I John 3:2; Rev 1:7, etc.

Eph 4:13, however, speaks of that recognition or "knowledge" which consists of "faith" and is identified with it.[286]

2) Or does 4:13a reveal Paul's interest in a final, unshakable, and infallible formula of faith, e.g. in a common creed saying "Jesus [is] the Son of God," that ought to replace all differences among various Christological confessions?[287] Such a unified formula of faith (regula fidei) would then deserve the title "orthodox faith" and would form a radiant final alternative to the heretical teaching, scheming, and floundering described in the following verse, 4:14. The day envisaged in 4:13 would above all be the day of triumph over heretics, for heresy would yield for good to one perfect and true, solid and sensible faith and obedience. The disunity of the church's confession at his time might indeed have made Paul as eager for a final solution to the problem of a proper confession of faith, as it has churchmen of later periods. But since the description of the heretics given in 4:14 is too vague and general to suggest that Paul is thinking of predecessors to the Ebionite, Monarchianist, Docetic, or Gnostic Christologies, the notion of an "orthodox" Christological formula must not be imposed upon vs 13.[288] At any rate, orthodox formulations prove little or nothing; the apostle may have been aware that some people (following the precedent set by Satan and by demons according to Matt 4:3, 6; 8:29; cf. James 2:19, or by hypocrites, Matt 7:22; 25:44) used a confessional formula which was adopted by the early church, and yet lived in error and disorder. By "faith and knowledge" something greater and less ambiguous must be meant than a creed, however orthodox. If the apostle had considered the words "Son of God"[289] as the final answer to the question of how Jesus Christ should be confessed, then he would hardly have limited the use of this formula to this single passage in Ephesians. Since he never speaks of a desirable uniformity and an ultimately fixed orthodox confession, the second interpretation offered of "oneness of faith and knowledge" is also to be ruled out.

The literal translation, "unity of faith and knowledge," is inappropriate and misleading because it suggests either of the two interpretations just discussed. Something more important than a new means of human apprehension or a uniform mode of confession becomes apparent when the grammar of 4:13a is carefully observed. It is possible to paraphrase the pertinent words by speaking of faith "in" the Son and knowledge "comprehending" the Son; current translations of 4:13 are based upon this assumption. But the Greek text can be translated equally well as a reference to the faith held "by" the Son of God, and to the knowledge which he possesses. The descriptions of the goal which follow speak of the one who is to be met and the quality he will convey, that is,

[286] Cf. John 6:69; Eph 3:19, and COMMENT X on 1:3-14. But Abbott and Gaugler argue that the difference between "faith" and "knowledge" will be overcome in the future.
[287] In the NT such differences exist, e.g. between the confession "Jesus is Lord" (I Cor 12:3; Philip 2:11); the trinitarian formulations found in II Cor 13:13; Matt 28:19; the ecumenical collection of Christ-titles in John 1:35-51; and the titles of Christ used in Revelation.
[288] Haupt and Percy, p. 320, belittle the relevance of 4:14 for understanding 4:13.
[289] An approach to the extended literature and discussion on this concept is opened by the articles in Theological Wordbooks. Among the most recent treatises see O. Cullmann, Christology (Philadelphia: Westminster, 1959), pp. 270-305; F. Hahn, The Titles of Christ in Christology (New York/Cleveland: World, 1967), pp. 279-346; R. Fuller, The Foundation of New Testament Christology (New York: Scribner, 1965), pp. 114-15, 164-67, 192-96, 231-32; B. Tsakonas, "A Comparative Study of the Term Son of God in St. Paul," Theologia 44 (Athens, 1966), 1-52.

the "Perfect Man" and the "perfection of the Messiah" (4:13b–c). Since vs. 13a is a poetic parallel to vs. 13b–c, it is feasible to see in 13a, as much as in 13b–c, a description of the Son of God's perfection, i.e. of "his own faith and knowledge."

To be specific, 4:13 appears to describe Christ's "faithfulness" to God and his "knowledge" of the bride.[290] This need not exclude the recognition that he is also designated as faithful to his people and as full of the knowledge of God. Eph 4:13a asserts, then, first that only the Son of God lives in total, integral, and comprehensive relationship to both God and man; and, second, that this intimate relationship is not only the source, the means, and the scope of the saints' perfection but will actually be made their own. The unity with God and man in which the Son lives will become their unity. While in 4:3 this "unity" (or "oneness") is a gift of God already given, in 4:13 it is a goal still to be attained.[291] Both verses speak of that which is already true and real in Christ. Realized and futurist eschatology are interlocked in the same dialectic as was described in COMMENT IX on 1:3–14.

According to 4:13 Jesus Christ's "faith" in God and his "knowledge" of his own people are not merely a matter of the past. Rather the church, on the way to meet her bridegroom and head, is and remains dependent on his everlasting faithfulness and personal engagement. Certainly the church herself has also to grow in faith and love and knowledge (Col 1:4–6, 9–10), but Eph 4:13 insists that the unity and peace of Jews and Gentiles who go out to meet their Lord depends completely on the faith of God's Son himself. The same is true of the solidity of their faith, of the substance of their hope, and of their ability to withstand attacks from outside, to face errors from inside, and to fulfill their mission. The church described in Eph 4:13 leaves to Christ the honor of being perfect and making her perfect; she knows that his maturity alone is the victorious counterpart of her infantile diseases, errors, and squabbles.

These observations lead immediately to the last and most serious problem of Eph 4:13, the essence or identity of the Perfect Man.

C   The Perfect Man

Both the adjective "perfect" and the noun "man" permit a variety of interpretations. The adjective may possess either the meaning it has in Greek thought and diction, or a sense determined by Hebrew precedents, or a combination of both. Only if all such interpretations fail can we consider the possibility that the author of Ephesians has introduced a new meaning of the term, cf. 1:10. The noun "man" may denote either an individual or corporate man created and living on earth,[292] or it may signify "the heavenly man," Christ himself, and/or something equivalent to the Gnostic god "Man."[293]

---

[290] Cf. the literature on the "faith of Christ" mentioned in fn. 85 to Eph 2:8. The noun "knowledge," in turn, may have a meaning influenced by the sexual sense of the verb "to know" (Gen 4:1, etc.). Christ's attitude to God and to man is at the same time distinguished and held together, e.g. in Heb 2:17. However, Meuzelaar, *Der Leib der Messiah*, p. 131, offers references showing that the object of both, the faith and the knowledge of the Messiah, is God.

[291] Robinson, p. 100.

[292] For examples of the collective meaning of "man" see, e.g. Eph 2:15; Gal 2:16a; Rom 5:12–21; according to ancient interpreters also the term "Son of Man" belongs here. The names of scholars supporting varieties of this assumption will be given later.

[293] I Cor 15:21–22, 45–49; Schenke, GMG. Schlier's and his followers' interpretation is based upon this equation. See also Jeremias, TWNTE, I, 364–66.

All expositions of Eph 4:13 are determined (1) by the meaning chosen for "perfect" and for "man," (2) by the translation chosen for vs. 13c, and (3) by the combination of their choices made. The implications of meeting the "Perfect Man" appear to be spelled out in the words "the perfection of the Messiah who is the standard of manhood." A decision regarding the identity of the "perfect man" requires that account be taken of the quality and effect of the Messiah as described in vs. 13c. The last part of vs. 13 will therefore be scrutinized before the constituent elements of the formula "Perfect Man" are studied in detail.

As earlier observed, if vs. 13c is rendered by "the measure of the stature of the fullness of the Messiah" a clear sense is not conveyed. A translation is preferable which brings to light at least one important (and if possible, the essential) element of this passage. The words "Perfect Man" (vs. 13b), describe primarily what the Man in question is in himself. Verse 13c adds what this man is to others, or, according to some interpreters, what others contribute to him. The active or passive meanings of *plērōma*, and the subjective or objective character of the genitive "of the Messiah," have led to diverse understandings of vs. 13c: Greek grammar allows the interpretation either of the Messiah who does the filling, or of the Messiah who is being filled.[294] But our earlier discussion of the use of *plērōma* in Ephesians and Colossians has yielded two results which are probably decisive for the exegesis of 4:13: (1) The OT background of the term indicates a filling which flows from the higher and benefits the lower, i.e. which moves from God to his temple or all the lands, or from man and the living creatures to the earth—never vice-versa. (2) The meaning of "filling" is not only quantitative, but includes a personal and qualitative element, i.e. personal presence and perfection. Therefore "perfection" is the translation of *plērōma* that best fits the text and context of 3:19 and 4:13c.

In 4:13 the term *plērōma* is connected with *hēlikiā* (lit. "stature," in our translation "manhood"). This noun may well be a synonym or serve for an explication of "fullness," viz. of "perfection." The Greek word may mean at least three things: (1) the span of life or the age of a person; (2) the size or bodily stature; (3) the full, ripe age, i.e. the maturity or manhood as opposed to the status of babes.[295] The translation "manhood" was chosen because it fits well the preceding term "Perfect Man," and contrasts equally well with the "baby"-hood denounced in the following verse. The three qualifications or attributes of the "Son," the "Man," the "Messiah" in 4:13 do not necessarily refer to three different things that are to be achieved by the saints. Rather the one goal and

---

[294] For details see the NOTE on 1:23 and COMMENT VI C on 1:15–23. For the following see esp. Meuzelaar, *Der Leib des Messias*, pp. 130–42.

[295] The temporal sense is present in Luke 2:52 and perhaps in 12:25; Matt 6:27 (see RSV and NEB including the Notes), but it does not make sense in Eph 4:13, despite H. Almquist, *Plutarch und das Neue Testament*, ASNU 15 (1946), 114. The second, spatial, meaning is presupposed in Luke 19:3 and is considered, together with the temporal understanding, the key to Eph 4:13 by J. Schneider, TWNTE, II, 942–43; Vielhauer, *Oikodome*, p. 137; Hanson, *Unity*, pp. 159–60; Percy p. 321; Dibelius, p. 82; Feuillet, *Christ Sagesse*, pp. 318–19, n. 2; B. Rigaux, "Revelation des mystères et perfection," NTS 4 (1958), 351. Schlier is of the same opinion: he argues that the local sense of the verb, "to come to meet" and the noun "fullness" determine the (local!) meaning of *hēlikiā;* he quotes Od. Sol. XXXVI 5 in support of this interpretation—a passage according to which the Spirit makes the believer as tall as the Highest! The third sense (i.e. maturity or perfection) is found in John 9:21, 23. Abbott and Gaugler recommend it for the interpretation of Eph 4:13. The combination of this term with "fullness" reveals that both nouns may have been considered synonyms.

future enrichment of the saints appear to be described by three synonymous terms.[296] No faith and knowledge are desirable other than the faith and knowledge of God's Son. No man is perfect as is the Man who will be met. There is no standard of perfect manhood—except the Messiah alone.

The whole of 4:13 asserts one thing in three steps: Jesus Christ is in person the perfection of the saints. A similar summation of many possible and actual formulations is found in 2:14: "He is in person the peace between us." Cf. Jer 23:6: "The Lord our righteousness"; I Cor 1:30: God made Jesus Christ "our wisdom, our righteousness and sanctification and redemption." Eph 4:13 appears to add to 2:14 the appropriate eschatological dimension; on the day of their savior's coming and their meeting with him, the saints will be conformed to his glory; cf. Philip 3:20–21; Rom 8:24–25, 29–30.

If, however,[297] a quantitative understanding of plērōma (fullness, perfection) and "stature" is preferred to the interpretation given here, Eph 4:13 is not a parallel to the confession of 2:14. Eph 4:13 may affirm that Christ is not complete or full before the time when all the saints have acceded to him or have been incorporated in him. In this case 4:13 includes a hint of that numerical growth of the church which is so strongly emphasized in Acts. But only one among the several (late!) meanings of plērōma in Gnosticism supports the notion that the deity is filled up, completed, restored, or perfected when the spirits of men enter or return into unity with the formerly split and deprived All-Father, the One-and-All. Not a single passage in Ephesians or Colossians speaks unambiguously of an implementation of Christ by men, or of a growth of Christ himself. In the whole Bible the process of filling, perfecting, and making oneself present heads in the opposite direction. A translation of vs. 13c which suggests quantitative or qualitative increase of Christ by the addition of men is therefore not acceptable. More useful is J. C. K. von Hofmann's interpretation; at the end of time the church will not be a miserable old man. Indeed, she is to be the jubilant partner of the coming Messiah, resplendent in his glory, cf. 5:27. He makes her perfect and full, rather than she him.

So much for the interpretation of vs. 13c. But what can be said about the meaning of vs. 13b, i.e. of the term, the "Perfect Man"?

Several times in the NT the adjective "perfect" denotes the age and status of man as opposed to the immaturity of children.[298] The contrasting pair, perfect-immature (teleios-nēpios), the idea of progress, and the equation of perfection and maturity are typical of Greek thought and diction, as Greek pedagogical theory and practice show.[299] The Greeks spoke of an intermediate stage between a child and a mature person, that is, the age of the adolescent (ephēbos). It is not impossible that the parts of the Bible written in Greek presuppose an equal tripartition of mankind into babes, adolescents, and mature persons, and share in the pedagogical concern devoted to a gradual transformation of

[296] Despite Abbott's opposite opinion.
[297] E.g. with Robinson and Schlier.
[298] See I Cor 3:1; 14:20; Heb 5:13–14.
[299] W. Jaeger, Paideia, 3 vols., New York: Oxford University Press, 1939–44, points out how essential is the idea of education to all Greek thought. A technical term for "making progress" in education was prokoptō. Luke uses this term in describing the child Jesus, Luke 2:52. However, in Gal 1:14; II Tim 2:16; 3:9, 13, the same verb is used with biting irony.

children toward the perfection of mature persons.[300] While Aristotle occasionally attributed perfection to every fully expert doctor, musician, or thief, Zeno and the Stoics followed those Platonic and Aristotelian passages that identified perfection with a supreme ethical status: perfection is present where there is freedom from inner conflicts and where the virtues are fully possessed and exerted.[301]

Entirely different is the biblical meaning of "perfect" (and of the corresponding noun and verb), when the context is determined by Hebrew thought and practice. Then the opposite of "perfect" (tāmīm, šālem) is not a child's immaturity but man's status as conditioned either by physiological processes or by sin. The essence of perfection is determined by the right relationship to the Holy One, God. Perfect is he who is clean and holy. The cultus rather than a process of education is the means of leaving behind what is unclean and profane. The Qumran writings agree with the majority of pertinent OT passages when they use "perfect" in a cultic sense. According to the OT and strictly Hebrew thought an intermediate level, or successive transitory steps between holy and unholy, are non-existent. There is only the choice between them, no midway house.[302] Perfection shares in the either/or character of pregnancy: no one can be a little perfect or increasingly perfect. And yet a transition from impurity to perfection is possible. The holy God proves his power to sanctify by appearing in person or by using the priest, the sacrifice, the sanctuary to sanctify those who are unclean. The epistle to the Hebrews elaborates upon this. Jesus Christ is called the one who is made perfect and who makes others perfect. In Hebrews the term "making perfect" is synonymous with "sanctifying."[303]

[300] Clement of Rome, the Apologists, esp. Clement of Alexandria and Origen, finally the Cappadocians appear convinced that interpenetration of Greek and Christian elements rather than their mutual exclusion determine the purpose and form the contents of Christian theology. In W. Jaeger's brief monograph, Early Christianity and Greek Paideia (Cambridge: Harvard University Press, 1961), pp. 39, 63–68, interpenetration is declared characteristic of the relationship between Christianity and Greek culture. Calvin embarked on the same line of thought when he explained Eph 4:14 by saying, "The life of the believers . . . resembles adolescence"; he accused the papacy of keeping people in an infantile state.

[301] Aristotle metaph. v 16 1021B; ethica magna II 3 1200A; Plato leg. II 653 ff. For more references see P. C. du Plessis, Teleios, The Idea of Perfection in the New Testament (Kampen: Kok, 1959), esp. pp. 45–94; G. Delling, TWNT, VIII, 68–88, esp. 78. See also H. Windisch, Der Hebräerbrief, HbNT 14, 2d ed. (1931), 44–46; J. T. Forestall, "Christian Perfection and Gnosis in Philippians 3:7–14," CBQ 18 (1956), 123–36; A. Wikgren, "Patterns of Perfection in the Epistle to the Hebrews" NTS 6 (1959), 157–67; G. Barth, in G. Bornkamm, G. Barth, H. J. Held, Tradition and Interpretation in Matthew (Philadelphia: Westminster, 1963), pp. 95–105, esp. 97–99. H. K. La Rondelle, Perfection and Perfectionism, Andrews University Monograph 3, 1971, attempts to point out the difference between non-Christian, philosophical concepts of perfection and the biblical meaning which he calls "strictly sui generis, with its own credentials" (p. 28). He observes that "perfection is primarily qualified by the cultus," and he depicts it with good reason as a consequence rather than a prerequisite of election (p. 100). On pp. 183–99 he discusses extensively "the cultic qualification of the apostolic ethics of perfection and holiness." However, the NT "cultus" which he has in mind consists of baptism (see esp. pp. 193–97) rather than of Jesus Christ's perfect sacrifice, and Eph 4:13 is explained as referring to the perfection of the body of Christ, the church, rather than to the coming Bridegroom's own perfection.

[302] Philo does not break out of the Hebrew pattern when (e.g. in de plantatione 66; de virt. 217) he makes rhetorical use of the comparative and superlative of the adjective "perfect." But he follows a Greek idea when (in de agricultura 165) he distinguishes between men who are beginners, who make progress, and who are perfect.

[303] Heb 2:10; 5:9; 7:11, 19, 28; 9:9; 10:1, 14; 12:23. The same cultic meaning of "perfect" is presupposed in Rom 12:2 and probably in John 19:30. Since the Greek terms "perfection" and "making perfect" are also used in magical literature and in the description of the rites of the Mystery Religions, the NT's cultic use of perfection terminology could have been appreciated by some of its readers; see Delling, TWNT, VIII, 70, lines 1–13. It is, however, not certain whether in the Fourth Gospel Jesus' last word "It is finished" (John 19:30) was understood to denote his death as a "mystery" in the sense of the Mystery rites. John 4:34 supports the opinion of G. Dalman (Jesus-

It is most likely that in Eph 4:13 the Hebrew rather than the Greek meaning of "perfect" prevails. Perfection is not described as an ideal, but as the reality to be met when a certain "man" is found. The church reaches perfection when she meets with the bridegroom and king. His perfection becomes hers not because he is contagious, but because his death has the essence of a sacrifice and his ministry is fullfilled in the full power of a priest (2:13–17; cf. John 17:19). Though she is constantly moving forward and comes nearer to him,[304] the church is not at the same time gradually improving. In Heb 3 – 6; 10:19 – 13:22, deadly dangers to be met on the road by God's migrating people are clearly pointed out. The exhortation given in Eph 4–6 attests to the same threats: the church is and remains imperfect—notwithstanding her holiness (1:4; 5:27) —until suddenly, one day, the time of building, moving, waiting, hoping is over, and her hope and joy are fulfilled. On that day the perfection of the king and bridegroom will become hers. The promise that God or the Messiah, is "our righteousness" (Jer 23:6; I Cor 1:30) will then be proven true.

A study of the meanings attributed to the term "man" in 3:13 will serve as a final check on all conclusions reached so far. Why should it be necessary to capitalize the "Perfect Man" and to identify him with the Son of God and the Messiah? The mere fact that in the context of Ps 45:2–4 and Ezek 28:12 a king may be assigned divine titles and called "the fairest of the sons of man" and "a signet of perfection . . . perfect in beauty" supports the equation. Still, it does not demonstrate that in Eph 4, Jesus Christ alone is meant by the title "Perfect Man." Several alternatives have been proposed:

1) One group of commentators assumes that in Eph 4:13 each individual Christian is urged to grow up and to become a "perfect man."[305] To the (many!) babes mentioned in 4:14 would then correspond a community composed of grown-up, mature, "perfect" saints. By this exposition Christ's role as the standard of manhood and as the object of faith and knowledge need not be excluded or belittled. But the accent lies on personal growth—as indeed in 3:16–19 Paul has shown his concern for the personal life of faith. Yet this individualistic interpretation of 4:13 has been met by strong opposition.

2) A second school of interpretation[306] relies upon the contribution made by the context toward understanding 4:13. According to 2:21; 4:15–16 it is the church rather than every individual saint that is "growing." Following 5:26–27, the church as a body is made glorious and spotless—not her single members each for himself. Therefore the "perfect man" of 4:13 may be a synonym of the "new man" mentioned in 2:15, that is, the bride described in 5:25–32. Just as in Qumran[307] so also in Ephesians perfection may be the

Jeschua [Leipzig: Hinrichs, 1922], pp. 190–96) that Jesus died as a worker who has completed his assignment. John 17:19 suggests that the completed work consists of Christ's own and his disciples' "sanctification in truth."

[304] According to 2:20–22, though she is continually being built up, expecting the insertion of the keystone.

[305] Calvin; Percy, p. 322; Masson, p. 194; Rigaux, NTS 4 (1957), 251, n. 2, also 257; Marxsen, Introduction, p. 194. The texts quoted in support of their view include Col 1:28; 4:12; I Cor 2:6; James 1:4; also the Gnostic Naassene Sermon and the Gospel of Truth contain passages speaking of perfect individuals.

[306] Represented, e.g. by von Harless, p. 380; Lightfoot, p. 329; Abbott, p. 120; Dibelius, p. 82; A. Wikenhauser, Die Kirche als der mystische Leib, 2d ed. (Münster: Aschendorff, 1940), pp. 182–84; Benoit, "Corps," 42; Feuillet, Christ Sagesse, pp. 285, 318–19, n. 2.

[307] For references see Rigaux, NTS 4 (1958), 237–42; du Plessis, Teleios, p. 108.

end of a way on which all the elect walk together—a destination which they can only reach as a community. In this case, a perfect church is the goal of the church's migration. The communal perfection, in turn, by no means excludes the final holiness of each of her members.[308] Indeed, since 4:13 makes explicit reference to all of us ("we all") who are to attain to the perfect man, the collective interpretation of this verse is more appropriate than its individualistic counterpart. Yet why should Paul speak of a perfect "man" if in reality he means a perfect *bride?* While in Eph 2:15 he used the Greek term denoting "man" in general (*anthrōpos*[309]), in 4:13 he chose the noun *anēr* which distinguishes a male adult from a woman or child! And why should he declare the bride or church the end of the way on which the saints move forward, when elsewhere, e.g. in 1:22–23 and 3:19, he has stated clearly that Jesus Christ is greater than the church? Obviously Ephesians was not written to prove that the church is an end in herself. Even in 5:27 when the future splendor of the church is mentioned, the text speaks of a "resplendence" produced by the Messiah and for the Messiah, not of an intrinsic and autonomous perfection of the bride.

3) A period characterized by attempts to explain the concept of perfection from the background of Mystery Religions had barely reached its apex when Gnostic "parallels" to Eph 4:13 were introduced as the key to its riddles.[310] The "Perfect Man" mentioned in this verse is now considered a reflection, or more specifically a demythologized, Hellenistic-Christian reproduction, of the Prime Man, or Adam, or Highest God, or Thought of Life, of whom the Naassene Sermon, the Mithras Liturgy, Mandean texts, and Mani's Psalm Book speak.[311] Schlier finds three parallel doctrines in Ephesians and Gnosticism: (a) the perfect man is being constructed out of the ascending souls; (b) the perfect man also exists independently of the souls, in the heavenly places; (c) the perfect man himself effects the building of his body. Thus a certain "identity" of the Redeemer and the redeemed is established at the same time that the superiority of the head over the body is proclaimed.[312] Translated into ecclesiastical language, for Schlier the Gnostic parallels demonstrate that Christ is depicted not only as the head "of" the body but also as both head "and" body combined—so that in a certain sense the church is Christ.[313]

---

[308] Michel, TWNTE, III, 624.

[309] This term includes women and it describes humans in contrast to animals, spirits, plants.

[310] This movement was spearheaded by R. Reitzenstein, HMyRel, pp. 177 ff, 388 ff, but it was opposed by e.g. H. H. A. Kennedy, *St. Paul and the Mystery Religions* (London/New York: Hodder and Stoughton, 1913), pp. 130–35; C. A. A. Scott, *Christianity According to St. Paul* (Cambridge University Press, 1927); G. Wagner, *Pauline Baptism and Pagan Mysteries*. London: Oliver, 1967. A Gnosticizing interpretation of *teleios*, ("perfect"), is suggested, e.g. by Dibelius in his interpretation of Philip 3:12–16 (in HbNT), and Schmithals, *Gnosticism in Corinth*, pp. 80–86; cf. 166–218.

[311] See beside Hippol. *ref. haer.* v 7:7; 8:13 ff., the texts quoted by Schenke, GMG, pp. 6–15; Schlier, *Christus*, pp. 27–34; Reitzenstein, HMyRel, pp. 279–82; Bultmann, ThNT, II, 151–52; Jonas, *Gnostic Religion*, p. 235. Percy, p. 321, n. 78; Mussner, CAK, pp. 61–64, 153–72; Cerfaux, *Théologie de l'église*, pp. 317–18, are among those who refuse to acknowledge Gnostic influence upon this verse. According to Porkorný, EuG, e.g. p. 78, the author of Ephesians corrects Gnostic tenets; instead of pronouncing the essential identity of the true Gnostics with the Redeemer deity, he urges the saints to grow toward the Savior.

[312] *Christus*, pp. 29–30.

[313] See, e.g. Schlier, p. 202, "Being the body of Christ . . . we become, together with the head, the *totus Christus.*" Schlier admits that a "totally different" *Sachverhalt* (fact of the case) characterizes Ephesians and Gnosticism respectively. In the Gnostic individualistic doctrine of redemption the redeemer's fate and man's redemption are simply identified; the redeemer appears to be no more and nothing else than what the redeemed are. Ephesians, however, maintains that

As has been mentioned in the interpretation of 1:22–23, Christ is considered incomplete (not yet "fulfilled") until the saints fill up what is missing. The saints' perfection (by their incorporation in Christ) is in this case simultaneous and congruous with Christ's own perfection. The same Gnostic analogies would also be useful for refuting a synergistic, as it were meritorious, understanding of the saints' contribution to the construction of the "whole Christ": the Perfect Man is and remains head over the body. In the process leading to his own and the church's perfection, he retains not only the initiative but also the functions of rulership and of the source of life.

Thus Schlier has made a substantial contribution to the capitalized spelling of "Perfect Man," but above all to equating this "Man" with Jesus Christ himself. However, as mentioned in the Introduction and in several COMMENTS, (1) the date of the Gnostic sources adduced by Schlier is far too late to allow them a direct influence upon the contents and diction, e.g. of Eph 4:13; (2) the use which Schlier makes of diverse Gnostic sources lacks discrimination; (3) the combination of the various creation, fall, separation, redemption, body myths into one full-grown Redeemed Redeemer myth was probably the work of Mani. Gnostic sources speak of a perfect or primeval (bisexual, viz. androgynous) *anthrōpos,* not of an *anēr.* The way in which Schlier understands the "Perfect Man" of Eph 4:13 is actually so replete with essential corrections of and deviations from Gnostic notions that not a single feature of the alleged "parallels" is fully convincing.

But what about Schlier's theological conclusions? It is surprising that scholars who do not share in Schlier's methodology come to essentially identical results.[314] Thus the detour taken through Gnostic jungles cannot be considered a necessary or indispensable way to reach Schlier's conclusions. On the contrary, the detour gives no more than a pseudo-historical backing to an interpretation that is opposed to the intention of Eph 4:13: it concentrates attention on an event taking place during the church's pilgrimage, i.e. the complementation of Christ, but it fails to elaborate on the unique event happening at the end of the way, the meeting with Jesus Christ. The miracle of the eschatological transformation is displaced by the process and progress of pious convictions, sacramental incorporation, churchly activities, or numerical growth.

4) Since none of the briefly sketched interpretations of "man" is convincing, a fourth alternative deserves consideration. The mention of the "Son of God" and the "Messiah" in the parallel lines that precede and follow the term "Perfect Man" in 4:13b, the meaning and *Sitz im Leben* of the verb *katantaō,*

Christ is a person of his own right. Still, Schlier assumes that Gnostic notions provided Paul with the "possibility" of communicating to his readers "the fact of the church . . . in an illustrative manner." He has in mind specifically the intimations pertaining to the *essential* unity of the church with the head, and to the church's *existential* "growth toward the head." Thus in Schlier's commentary Gnosticism serves a useful double purpose: it accentuates both the difference *and* the connection of the church's metaphysical status and the communal existence of its members.

[314] That Christ is not only the head, but both head *and* body, and that he is therefore *totus Christus,* even the "perfect man," only when all the saints are united with him—this is also affirmed in the exegesis of as diverse scholars as Robinson, p. 100; F. Prat, *Theologie* I, 356; K. Barth, *Church Dogmatics,* IV 2 (1958), 623–25, cf. 60, 657–60; JB n. j on 4:13. The concept *totus Christus* was apparently first used in the sense mentioned by Augustine *enarr. in Pss.* XVII 51; XC 2:1 (PL 36, 154; 37, 1159).

and the biblical sense of the adjective "perfect"—all these facts suggest that the (male!) "Perfect Man" is none other than Jesus Christ himself. The moment of meeting is the day of his parousia, according to the undisputed Pauline letters, the epistle to the Hebrews, the Synoptic Gospels, and the book of Revelation. In stating that "all" the saints are on the way to meet the coming Lord, Eph 4:13 and its context affirm as clearly as other NT books, especially Hebrews, that the church is a procession of pilgrims (or a migrating people) that is well equipped to march forward in order, and to endure the hardships of the way bravely and joyfully, in anticipation of the moment when she meets her loving and beloved triumphant Lord and will be transformed by his glory (cf. Col 3:4; I John 3:2; Eph 5:27).

In summary, Eph 4:13 does not only belong to the other futuristic-eschatological passages of the epistle,[315] but crowns them with an explicit reference to the parousia. The words of Philip 4:5 (and of Col 3:1-4, if Colossians is considered an authentic epistle) show that even in his later years Paul had not given up the conviction that "the Lord is near" (NEB; "very near" JB). If Eph 4:13 equally refers to the parousia, one of the reasons is eliminated for which Ephesians was ascribed a date no earlier than those late decades of the first century in which the hope for the imminent parousia (the *Naherwartung*) had faded away.

VIII   Beyond the Church

In the first COMMENT on 4:1-16 it was said that each subdivision of this passage deals with the church. Indeed Ephesians says more about the church than do large parts of other NT writings, and the first half of Eph 4 is more directly devoted to a description of the church's existence and order than any other section of Ephesians. Nevertheless Paul is far from suggesting a self-contained and boisterous church or doctrine of the church.

The first three verses (4:1-3) contain not only the urgent advice that the saints be humble, united, and strong in mutual love; but they also mention the peace which according to 2:13-17 was made for "those far." Vss. 4-6 combine distinctly Christian creedal elements, although some formulations may have reminded the Gentile-born readers of Ephesians of a Stoic creed. The creed of the church, however traditionally or originally formulated, speaks of a oneness which exerts a unifying force beyond the community of the saints. The "calling" is still going out. The "one body" is still growing. The "one baptism" is still a declaration—a confession of that sin which plagues the church and her members together with all non-believers. The Father's government "over all" and "through all," also his presence "in all," cannot possibly be restricted to those believing in him at the present time. In the next subsection, vss. 7-10, the distribution of various gifts by the exalted Christ is mentioned as proof

---

[315] Other eschatological, in some cases apocalyptical, formulations and statements are found in Eph 1:14, 21c; 2:20; 4:10, 15-16, 30; 5:27; 6:9, 13, 18. Bultmann (ThNT, II, 175) acknowledges that in Ephesians (and Colossians) "the basic . . . meaning of the between-situation is grasped; for the determination of the present by the future is grasped." But Bultmann believes that "the nearness of the parousia is not discussed," and he observes most boldly that in Ephesians, "in contrast to all Pauline epistles, and even to Col 3:4, any mention of the parousia is lacking." In turn, F.-J. Steinmetz (Biblica 50 [1969], 334, 366) is willing to concede the silence of Ephesians regarding the parousia, but assumes that the utterances on the "head" and the "fullness" are a "transformation" and serve as an "equivalent of the Jewish-traditional parousia expectation."

that "all things" are being filled by Christ. The special ministers given to the church according to vs. 11 have not only the function of communicating riches to the church; rather their charge is to train all the saints for their ministry in the midst of all mankind, to prepare them for meeting the Lord, and to protect them from childish and deceitful behavior (vss. 12–14). The glory of the "Perfect Man" is to be found by the saints, but the present church cannot claim any glory for herself. "Perfection" is a gift to be handed out at the Last Day; it is not yet possessed (vs. 13). In vss. 14–15, finally, the accent is set upon the "growth" of the church. The people of God cannot live without their "head." Continuous change and renewal in the hope of being conformed to him who is greater than the church—this is the mark of the living body of Christ.

Eph 4:1–16 describes a humble and loving church who is responsive to her present task and eager to reach her goal. Such a church will not consider herself an empire-builder. She will not pretend that she possesses, masters, and administers the Lord and his gifts. She will be meek before the Lord and modest before unbelievers. She has a promise to trust, a way in which to go, a commitment to fulfill, and an energy given to her, which are not her own. The church is as much as, but no more than, a happy migrating people moving forward to the day of redemption. She is a hard-working community of servants who accept their call into God's witness stand for the sake of the whole creation.

Having her eyes directed upon the Lord and enduring the hardships found on her way, this church can, as much as Israel according to Ps 123, endure the "contempt of the proud." But under no circumstances will she glorify herself at the expense of God. The work in which she is engaged is still unfinished. It is still to be proved anew that she really is God's people and does God's will. According to the constitution of the church her origin and purpose lie beyond herself. She is neither her own master nor her own end. That which is beyond the church establishes her essence. Beyond the church are God himself and all the men, the ages, the creatures whom the church is to serve.

The following verses of Ephesians will admonish the church and her members to live a life neither similar to, nor in competition with, the life of other communities and individuals.

IX THE NEW AGAINST THE OLD
(4:17–32)

4 17 Now in the Lord['s name] I say and insist upon the following:
No longer conduct yourselves as do the Gentiles in the futility of their
mind. 18 Intellectually they are blacked out. Because of their inherent
refusal to know [God] and of the petrifaction of their hearts, they are
excluded from the life of God. 19 In their insensitive state they have
given themselves over to debauchery in order to do all filthy things
and still ask for more. 20 But you have not become students of the
Messiah this way — 21 assuming you have ever listened to him and
been taught in his school. Just as [the instruction] is,
> Truth in Jesus!
> 22 You strip off what fits your former behavior,
> the Old Man rotting in deceitful desires.
> 23 Instead you become new in mind and spirit
> 24 and put on the New Man created after God['s image]
> in true righteousness and piety.

25 Therefore put away the lie. Every one shall speak the truth to
his neighbor for we are members of one body. 26 If you are angry yet
do not sin. The sun must not set on your temper. 27 And do not give
an opportunity to the devil. 28 The thief shall no longer go on stealing. To the contrary, he shall work hard and honestly with his own
hands so that he may have something to share with the needy. 29 No
foul talk whatsoever shall pass your lips but [say] what is right for
meeting a need constructively so that it will do good to the listeners.
30 And do not grieve the Holy Spirit of God [for he is the seal] with
which you have been marked for the day of liberation. 31 Every kind
of bitterness, passion, anger, shouting, cursing shall be taken away from
you, together with any [other sort of] malice. 32 Be good to one another. Be warm-hearted. Forgive one another just as God has forgiven you in Christ.

NOTES

4:17. *Now in the Lord['s name] I say and insist upon the following.*
Here finally is the admonition which probably was on Paul's mind and should
have followed immediately when he dictated or wrote 3:1, 13–14; 4:1. Each
time he seemed to prepare for a new section but was sidetracked by some
other consideration. The two verbs, "I say and insist," are reminiscent of a
similiar combination of terms in I Thess 2:12.[1] There an escalation of introductory verbs is found. In Ephesians the stepping up of the entreaty's intensity has a more complicated form: first (in 3:1) the apostle points out that
he is a "prisoner of the Messiah for the sake of you Gentiles"; then (in 3:13–
14) he "asks" that they may not falter over his afflictions; then (in 4:1) he
"beseeches" them as a prisoner in the Lord's service, and now (in 4:17) he
first uses the simple verb "I say" and then interprets it by the strong term "I
insist upon." The latter Greek verb (*martyromai*) means originally "I call to
witness"; then also "I affirm," or "I protest with finality." Paul speaks with an
unmistakable tone of authority.[2] In order to explain this tone, he adds, lit. "in
the Lord." In 3:2–12 a description was given of his special relationship to
Christ's revelation and of his own and the church's commission. Now, the
formula "in the Lord" recalls that relationship and function. Paul speaks as an
"ambassador of Christ" and warns his readers: "God is giving exhortation
through us" (II Cor 5:20).

No longer conduct yourselves as do the Gentiles. The Greek has the infinitive
rather than the imperative of the verb. The former is occasionally used in the
sense of the latter.[3] A weakly attested variant reading has, as do the "other"
Gentiles—as if to make clear that not all Gentiles are alike after some of
them have become Christians. However, the text is clear enough without the addition of "other": though the saints of Gentile origin represent all those who
have been "far" (2:13, 17) and are urged to remember their origin (2:11–12),
they have neither the right nor any reason to uphold the life-patterns of those
not yet raised from death in sins and not yet sealed by the Holy Spirit. The
new day which has already dawned includes no permission to turn the clock
backwards and relive once more the preceding night (5:8). For what lies
behind the Ephesians amounts to an "exercise in futility."

in the futility of their mind. The very strong noun "futility" implies emptiness,
idleness, vanity, foolishness, purposelessness, and frustration. With one single
word Paul describes the majority of the inhabitants of the Greco-Roman
empire, including the shapers and beneficiaries of its magnificent cultural
elements, as aiming with silly methods at a meaningless goal! The charge of
"pursuing empty phantoms" which, according to Jer 2:5 (NEB), God raised
against Israel, is made by Paul against the nations.[4] See COMMENT II for

---

[1] "Like a father his children so we exhort and encourage and charge each of you to conduct
yourselves worthily of God," I Thess 2:11–12; cf. 4:1.
[2] Calvin; Abbott, p. 128.
[3] See e.g. Acts 15:23, etc.; Luke 9:3; Rom 12:15; Philip 3:16; BDF, 389.
[4] Schlier, pp. 211–12, offers a rhetorical interpretation of this charge by writing, *Eitel denkend
selbst eitel alles vereitelt* [should probably be: *alles vereitelnd*], *wird und ist der ganze Mensch*

the resemblance of Paul's statements to contemporary Jewish propaganda literature, and for their vital differences.

18. *Intellectually they are blacked out.* Lit. "darkened in their understanding." The opposite is the "illumination of the eyes of the heart" mentioned in 1:18;[5] cf. the connection between the "creation of light" and the process of "knowledge" (II Cor 3:18; 4:6). When knowledge is identified with light and ignorance with darkness, then the previously mentioned ontological dimension of the mind's activity is made apparent. Just as knowledge means participation in life and obedience to God, so ignorance equals the inability to live, to grow, to act sensibly. The perfect participle, "blacked out" (lit. "darkened")[6] has the meaning of an adjective.[7] The Greek participle *ontes* ("being") which is added to the perfect participle "blacked out" for good measure, emphasizes the present status rather than the moment or mode of its origin. In the interpretation of 1:10 it was shown that summing up "under one head" does not necessarily mean "to restore a former order or unity."[8] Neither does the perfect participle "excluded," lit. "alienated" (2:12, 4:18) presuppose an original unity of Gentiles and Jews, or of Gentiles and God. Equally, the verb to "become new" (4:23) cannot be pressed into meaning "to reestablish an original state of affairs." Ephesians speaks of new "creation" (2:10, 15) and of a "new man" (4:24) rather than of reconditioning or repairing a damaged creature. Before Jesus Christ's coming and work effected the great change, the Gentiles were "not my people . . . not shown mercy" (I Peter 2:10; cf. Rim 9:25). In the parallel passage (Rom 1:21–23), aorist tenses are used to describe the fall of the Gentiles into futility, darkness, foolishness—and yet no previous state of wisdom and obedience is implied.

Because of . . . The complex structure of the one Greek sentence in 4:17–19 makes it impossible to state whether merely the "refusal to know," or this refusal in combination with the petrifaction of their hearts, is the reason either for the "conduct in futility" or for the "intellectual blackout," or for the "exclusion from God's life," or for all three. The translation given is determined by the quest for clarity and readability.

their inherent refusal to know [God]. The Greek noun *agnoia,* here translated by "refusal to know," usually denotes ignorance, lack of knowledge. Indeed, in most cases where they occur in Greek literature, the noun and the corresponding verb *agnoeō* possess this sense. Inability to comprehend and see the light then are meant. Even in the Bible a legal excuse, or at least a plea for mitigating circumstances, can be implied when ignorance is mentioned.[9] But just as in biblical terminology "knowledge" transcends a merely intellectual

---

eitel . . . Er vereitelt . . . sich und seine Welt, i.e. "In thinking vainly, by being vain and making everything vain, the whole man becomes and is vain . . . He makes vain . . . himself and his world."

[5] See COMMENTS III on 1:15–23 and IV on 5:1–20.

[6] Unlike in Josephus *ant.* IX 67, where it means the blinding of men who were formerly able to see.

[7] This view is supported, e.g. by Abbott against the opposite opinion of Bengel and von Harless. Schlier sees in the beginning of vs. 19 a reason for speaking of the loss of man's original relationship with God, i.e. of an event rather than of a status.

[8] See fn. 95 to 1:10.

[9] E.g. Acts 3:17; 13:27; 17:30; 23:5; Luke 23:34; I Tim 1:13.

process or possession, and means existential acknowledgment and recognition (that is, honor, obedience, acceptance shown to a partner),[10] so also ignorance is frequently a stance of the total man that includes his emotion, will, and action. Not to know the Lord is as much as to ignore him. While indeed in the OT, Israel is accused of ignoring her Lord, in the NT also Gentiles are declared guilty of this sin.[11] "Ignorance . . . in a religious sense, almost is equal to sin."[12] It amounts to "suppressing the truth by unrighteousness" in flagrant repudiation of God's revelation, and to "considering the knowledge of God unfit"; in short, it is an inexcusable and ungrateful attitude (Rom 1:18–23), a deliberate commission rather than an incidental omission or lack. Two parallels, Rom 1:19–21 and I Thess 4:5, suggest that in the translation of Eph 4:18 the object ("God") must be added to the text.[13] The English pronounced adjective "their inherent" has been chosen to render the somewhat clumsy but emphatic Greek words *tēn ousān en autois*, lit. "the one being in them." There is no cause to put the blame upon external, circumstantial reasons for what has its origin and seat in man himself. Even the (evil) "spirit working" in man (2:2) is no excuse.

and of the petrifaction of their hearts. It is not certain whether the conjunction "and" must be added before the noun "petrifaction" in the translation. In the Greek wording "petrifaction" may be the cause or effect of the "refusal to know," rather than only the accompaniment of the latter. A discussion of the term "heart" was given in the third NOTE on 3:17. The noun translated by "petrifaction" (*pōrōsis*) is as surprising in Greek as in this translation. When this noun or the underlying verb recurs elsewhere, editors or copyists felt free to substitute the better known word "blindness" (*pērōsis*).[14] The early versions of the NT and a strong tradition among the commentators, represented e.g. by Thomas Aquinas, followed their example. Indeed, Paul speaks not only of the "hardening" of Israel (Rom 11:7, 25), but also of their being "blinded" (II Cor 3:14). But while the noun and the adjective derived from the Greek verb *pēroō*, "to maim," include the meaning blindness, blind, the noun *pōrōsis* (which is contained in the better MSS of Eph 4:18) points in an entirely different direction. It is derived from *pōros*, meaning marble, tufa, stalactite, or in medical terminology callous, insensitive skin or bone tissue. Only this meaning corresponds to the "insensitiveness" mentioned in 4:19.[15] While in pagan moral exhortations it is not customary to mention an

[10] See COMMENT X on 1:3–14.
[11] Isa 1:3; Jer 8:7; LXX Dan 4:34; 6:5, 23; Sir 23:3; 28:7; Rom 10:3; I Peter 1:14; perhaps also Acts 17:23, 30 ("The Ignored God"?). See esp. Hosea 4:6, "My people are destroyed for lack of knowledge; because you have rejected knowledge, I reject you." Here distinctly *lack* of knowledge is identified with *rejection* of knowledge.
[12] WBLex, 11. Schlier, p. 212, points out that the reference to ignorance is *not* meant to serve as an excuse.
[13] Calvin states explicitly that only blindness in regard to God's kingdom is meant. He concedes that in other matters men are able to see, to discern, and to decide. And he goes far beyond the text of Eph 4:18 and parallels when he affirms that "little sparks" (*scintillae*) of knowledge are left to natural man by which he is able to be aware of the existence of some god and of the need to serve him. See his commentary on Eph 4:17–19 and his *Institutes*, I, 3:1. Bengel, however, in commenting on Eph 4:17, calls the absence of the recognition of God the root of all error. Indeed, just as 4:18–19 proceeds without reservation from theological to moral deviation, so does Rom 1:18–32.
[14] Mark 3:5; 8:17; John 12:40; Rom 11:25.
[15] See Robinson, pp. 264–74 for an extended argument, and the discussion between Archbishop Fisher of Lambeth, Bishop Colville of Culross, B. Lindars, C. H. Dodd, in *Theology* 69 (1966), 25–26, 121, 171, 223–24, which appears to suggest that *pōrōsis* in Eph 4:18 is to be *translated* by

"obdurate" heart, the Manual of Discipline refers to stubbornness, certainly because of the Qumran community's acquaintance with the Hebrew OT.[16] The decision to translate with "petrifaction" or hardening makes it no longer possible to ascribe hardness of heart only to Jews, and to excuse Gentiles by regarding them as merely lacking (in-)sight. In Eph 4:18 the *Gentile*-born Christians are warned of obduracy!

excluded from the life of God. See the second NOTE on 2:12 and the second on 4:18 for the translation "excluded." The concept "life of God" is puzzling.[17] It can hardly mean a godly life or conduct, for the Greek word here employed for "life" (*zōē*, not *bios*) does not mean curriculum or conduct. Neither can life of God mean the living God, though the LXX uses many different phrases for describing God as living; for the terminology of Eph 4:18 is not found in the LXX. Eph 2:1-5 (i.e. the reference to the spiritual death of man from which he is saved only by resurrection) makes it probable that "the life" mentioned in 4:18 is an equivalent to what elsewhere, e.g. in Rom 3; 6; 8; Gal 3, is called "righteousness" and what in Ephesians is called "salvation" or "peace." Earlier, in 2:12, Paul described the Gentiles as people who formerly lived without God's help and outside his election and mercy. The term "life of God" is in 4:18 a circumscription of that life and light which according to John 1:4 is in God, and which following John 17:3 is experienced where there is knowledge of God and of his Anointed One. In Rom 8:2, 10 the Spirit is identified with this life.

19. *In their insensitive state.* The rare metaphor (*apēlgēkotes,* lit. "having given up feeling") is replaced in a few MSS and some early versions by the verb "having given up hope" (*apēlpikotes*). This variant reading recalls the statements made about Israel's hope in 1:11 and the Gentiles' bareness of hope in 2:12. Compare the hopelessness mentioned in Job 7:16; Jer 18:12. The rarer verb is probably authentic. Some interpreters[18] understood "insensitivity" to mean the Gentiles' want of fear of judgment and their lack of any pangs of conscience which would prevent or restrict the completion of sinful actions.

they have given themselves . . . in order to do. Just as in this verse so also in Rom 1:18-32 the commission of evil deeds and the captivity in wickedness are described as a result of rejecting knowledge of God. But the transition from cause to effect seems to be described in different ways: Rom 1:24, 26, 28 states that God delivered the idolatrous to shameful and fatal behavior. The imagery is that of a judge delivering a man found guilty to execution.[19] According to Eph 4:19, however, the guilty fools deliver themselves to the immoral practices that in 2:1-5 are called "lapses" and "sins," and that cause or indicate man's

---

"hardness," but to be *interpreted* by "blindness"! Bengel wants to endorse both meanings. Dodd's uncompromising version, "grown hard as stone" (NEB), is to be preferred to any compromise solution, cf. Abbott. Certainly, blindness of the heart is included in petrifaction. But the forced discussions of e.g. Calvin on the extent and limitation of "blindness" (see fn. 13) are not to the point. When Paul describes Jews exclusively by this term in II Cor 3:14, he shows that he was not concerned with the problem of "natural theology."

[16] See Jer 3:17; 7:24; 9:14, etc.; Ps 81:12; 1QS I 6; II 114; v 4; Braun, QuNT, I, 218-19. The LXX does not employ the noun *pōrōsis.* The verb "to be petrified" occurs in one MS of LXX Job 17:7, but is displaced elsewhere by a version suggested by the context, i.e. by "blinded."

[17] Cf. the various interpretations offered by Calvin (regeneration; *fruitio vitae Dei*); Abbott ("life of God in man," see Gal 2:20); Dibelius ("communion with God").

[18] As Calvin and Gaugler.

[19] Cf. Matt 27:26 par.; Rom 4:25; I Cor 5:5; Acts 7:42; I Tim 1:20.

death while he still imagines himself alive. The substitution of self-deliverance
for deliverance by God cannot be considered an un-Pauline trait. Paul himself
speaks in undisputed letters now of Christ's deliverance by God, now of Christ's
self-deliverance.[20] Ephesians implicitly calls God the builder of the temple,
yet at the same time the body of Christ is said to build itself.[21] An analogous
interchange occurs in the use of the passive and the middle of the verb, to
baptize.[22] Similarly, in II Cor 5:18–20, reconciliation is described as a deed
performed by God alone and also as an event for which men are responsible.

   debauchery . . . all filthy things and still ask for more. Lit. "lasciviousness
. . . each sort of impurity in greed." The combination of the three nouns "lasciviousness," "impurity," and "greed" will be discussed in COMMENT II (b).
What is the meaning of these terms and what alternatives exist for translating
4:19? Because the last word offers more problems than the first two, it will be
examined first: the Greek noun *pleonexiā* (greediness, avarice) occurs in
association with *philargyriā* (love of money)[23] but need not have the same
meaning. It has been understood as a synonym of *ametria* (lack of moderation,
indulgence in excess, insatiability). Not only Greek ethical thinkers such as
Plato, Aristotle, and the Stoics, but also the Bible[24] and Christian authors
affirm the principle of measure and moderation.[25] In Eph 4:19 the formula
en pleonexiā ("in greed") apparently describes the atmosphere in which all
other wicked works are carried out. However, in 5:3, 5 the same noun is used
to denote a vice that stands beside others. See below, fn. 137 for parallel
passages indicating that the formulae "in" greed or "with" greed might substitute for "and" greed. Our translation of 4:19 "and still ask for more," leaves
open the relationship of *pleonexiā* to the other vices, but does not exclude a
more specific understanding of the noun, e.g. in the sense of selfishness,[26] or
love of money. The impurity of any sort mentioned in the same verse (in our
version, "all filthy things") includes but is not restricted to sexual disorder and
perverse actions committed alone, with persons of the same or the other sex, by
incest, or with animals. In the OT prostitution, fornication, and related behavior are prohibited not primarily on moral grounds but rather because of their
association with pagan sanctuaries and fertility rites. A passage from the
Covenant of Damascus (IV 17–18), perhaps also 1QS IV 9–11, combines impurity with desecration of the sanctuary. The Artemis temple of Ephesus and
other shrines of Paul's time were famous because of the opportunities they
offered to those who identified sex and religion. In the eyes of a Jewish writer
such as Paul, impurity and fornication are always expressive of a religious
attitude; they are never judged as "only" carnal excesses or moral turpitude.
Consequently, even such people are subject to the charge of impurity whose
sexual behavior may be faultless. When their talk, their eating and drinking
habits, their personal and social behavior reveal enslavement to idolatry, then

[20] Cf. Rom 4:25; 8:32 with Gal 2:20 and 1:4.
[21] Cf. 2:21 with 4:16 (and 4:12).
[22] Cf. I Cor 1:13 with I Cor 10:2; or Acts 2:38; 8:16 with Acts 22:16.
[23] So, e.g. Polycarp *Phil.* II 2; however, in XI 2, only avarice, in VI 1 only love of money are
mentioned.
[24] E.g. LXX Hab 2:9; II Peter 2:12–15.
[25] The Greek adage *mēden agan* ("nothing beyond measure") is favorably reflected by Christian authors, such as Chrysostom, Theodoret, Thomas Aquinas, Calvin.
[26] Robinson; Abbott; E. F. Scott.

they are treated as impure. See COMMENT II (b) for references. The noun rendered by "debauchery" (*aselgeia*) means in Greek lewdness, outrageous lasciviousness, licentiousness. Again, this concept alludes to sexual depravity but is not limited to it.[27] A notion of violence is present. The noun describes the conscious neglect of measures and limits, the refusal to follow any distinct way or order. Each of the three nouns combined in 4:19 is comprehensive in character and denotes man's total determination by vice. There is no remedy against the dominion of such deeds, least of all in any patchwork procedure. Rather, as vss. 22-24 will make clear, a totally "new man" has to replace the "old man" characterized by those vices. The difference between the "old" and the "new" is like that between "death" and "life" (2:1-5), or between "light" and "darkness" (5:8). Half-way houses between impurity and saintliness are as much out of question as between idolatry and worship of Yahweh.

20-21. *you have . . . become students of the Messiah . . . you have . . . listened to him and been taught in his school.* Lit. "you learned the Messiah . . . you heard him and were taught in him." In COMMENT III three surprising formulations found in the Greek original will be discussed. In seeming tension with the *suddenness* of the change from Old Man to New that is discussed in COMMENT VII C to 4:1-16 and in COMMENT V C to this section, Paul speaks in 4:20-21 of a *process* of learning, hearing, teaching. Previously in Ephesians, specific emphasis was placed upon "the word" that was being proclaimed.[28] Now intimations are given regarding the students' hearing and learning that correspond to the teachers' speaking. While the Greek text does not explicitly mention a "school" or call the saints "students," the vocabulary and contents of 4:20-21 evoke the image of a school. In commenting on 4:17, Calvin summed up 4:20-21 by speaking of the "teaching received in Christ's school." See COMMENT III for the reasons why Calvin's nomenclature was used for our translation of these verses.

21. *assuming.* There is no ironic undertone in this term.[29] Paul uses a restrictive conjunction (*ei ge,* lit. "if at all") because he does not know the readers personally and has not been present when the gospel was preached to them. In the case of the "Ephesians" he cannot, as he does in I Thess 4:1, remind the recipients of the present letter of the oral preaching, teaching, counseling from which "you received [instruction] *from us* how you ought to conduct yourselves and please God." His intention is to appeal to the Ephesians' thorough acquaintance with the gospel, gained through evangelists other than Paul himself. Instead of calling their awareness into question, he expresses his trust in an instruction not imparted by himself. Obviously he does not claim a monopoly of truth for himself alone or for a "school of Paul."[30]

Just as [the instruction] is. In the second part of COMMENT III the addition of the bracketed words to the original text will be explained. The conjunction

---

[27] See Wisd Sol 14:26; III Macc 2:26; Gal 5:19; II Cor 12:21; Rom 13:13; I Peter 4:3; Mark 7:22; II Peter 2:2, 7, 18; Jude 4; see Schlier, p. 214.
[28] See esp. 1:13; 2:17, 20; 3:5, 6; 4:11.
[29] See the first NOTE on 3:2.
[30] Cf. I Cor 1:13-17; 3:4-9; Philip 1:15-18. Gal 1:6-9 far from proves the opposite, for this passage emphasizes the oneness of the gospel rather than an exclusive right of Paul to its proclamation.

"just as" is here (unlike Col 3:13; Eph 5:24; etc.) not followed by "so also"; therefore it does not introduce a comparison but rather a quotation.[31] The Greek text (lit. "just as is truth in Jesus") is so ambiguous and surprising in its context, and so unique in a Pauline letter, that it appears most necessary and reasonable to label it an interpolation.[32] It is indeed possible that a marginal gloss added by some reader was at one stage of the tradition inserted into the main text. However, though the temptation is strong to use such a theory for "solving" (or dodging) the problems posed by vs. 21c, the interpolation theory is not fail-safe. There are no MSS that omit the difficult words. It appears more likely that the words "just as is" are an ellipsis: a participle (e.g. attested, affirmed, or said) has been omitted and a quotation follows, beginning with the exclamation "Truth in Jesus!" and ending with vs. 24. Certainly the conjunction "therefore" at the opening of vs. 25 shows as much as similar conjunctions do in 1:15; 2:11, 19; 4:15 that the end of the quotation has been reached, and that the author resumes his own formulation and train of thought. The presence of a quotation in 4:21c–24 is made even more probable by the occurrence of the term "truth"[33] both at the beginning and end of these verses —a feature which is typical of so-called ring-compositions—and by the parallel thoughts, lines, stanzas that are characteristic of Hebrew poetry. Finally the surprising occurrence of the single name "Jesus" may indicate Paul's use of traditional material.[34]

Truth in Jesus! If a quotation begins at this point, then these words form a headline corresponding to 2:14a: "He is in person the peace." See COMMENT IV for a selection among the proposed interpretations.

22–24. *You strip off . . . you become new . . . and put on.* The Greek text has three infinitives. The first of them, in vs. 22, is in the aorist tense and denotes a once and for all, definite, concluding action: the stripping off is to be done at once, and for good and all. The second infinitive is in the present tense: the "renewal" is to be perpetual and cannot be concluded in one act. The third is in the aorist tense again, just like the two participles in Col 3:9–10: a resolute, final step of "putting on" is envisaged.[35] But the triple use of infinitives is somewhat strange. Would not three imperatives be much clearer? Three explanations deserve consideration: (a) The infinitives are dependent upon the verb "taught" in vs. 21. Then the Greek text is to be rendered, "You have been taught to put off . . . , to become new . . . , to put on . . ."[36] (b) The infinitives are equivalent to imperatives and express the commands: "Strip off! Be-

[31] See 1:4; (4:25?) 5:2, 25 for parallels of this function of "just as."

[32] Dibelius calls vs. 21c *eingeschoben* (inserted, interpolated).

[33] The article is missing in the first occurrence of "truth," and there is evidence for its omission in the second instance as well, if we may rely on certain variant readings. The absence of the article before key terms was shown to be characteristic of hymnic or confessional diction (cf. the Introduction, section II).

[34] Schmithals, *Gnosticism in Corinth*, pp. 130–32, draws attention to a puzzling feature of the Pauline writings, but neglects the evidence of Gal 6:17; II Cor 4:5–6, 10–11, when he asserts, "When Paul coins original formulations, he never calls this God-man, Jesus." See COMMENT IV for a discussion. Dibelius, p. 87, assumes that in Eph 4:25 ff. (but not yet in 4:21c–24) traditional materials have been reproduced. But if catalogues of commandments can indeed have an origin antedating the writing of the Pauline epistles, so can confessional formulae or basic elements of instruction.

[35] Abbott, p. 138.

[36] Phillips; Dibelius.

come new! Put on!"[37] (c) The infinitives are dependent on "truth" and make explicit both the substance and effect of truth. Then vss. 21 ff. say as much as, "The truth in Jesus is this: to take off, etc."[38] Our translation does not exclude an imperative sense but seeks to retain the ring of a happy announcement which includes an appeal. Compare "you are being built . . . the body builds itself" (2:22; 4:16).[39] The metaphors "strip off" and "put on" will be discussed in COMMENT V B. The role of the verb "become new," which in 4:23 may play an important role between the clothing metaphors of vss. 22 and 24 (but not in the parallel Col 3:9–10), will be considered in the NOTE on vs. 23.

22. *what fits your former behavior.* In the Greek text, these words are the poetic parallel of the formulation, "created after God" (vs. 24), lit. "according to the former behavior" and "created according to God." In both cases an attempt is made by an apposition to explain the essence and main characteristic of the "Old" and the "New Man" respectively. Since the undisputed Pauline letters do not use exactly the same terminology for instruction in ethics, it is more likely that Paul took up an existing tradition than that he was the first to speak of these two Men in ethical contexts. He (or an unknown teacher or preacher before him) may have unconsciously used older conceptual, if not mythical, material. Whichever alternative is chosen, it is obvious that he felt the need to clarify his terminology. The interpretory remarks added in Col 3:9–10 and Eph 4:22 and 24 to the terms "Old" and "New Man" show that these titles either were not in common use in Asia Minor or were not necessarily understood in just one sense. It is impossible to solve all the problems by proclaiming that these terms occurred in a pre-Pauline baptismal liturgy in which they also were interpreted in an ethical sense. In Rom 6:1–2 and 6, a reference to "remaining" and "living in sin" precedes mention of the "Old Man." In Col 2:11 only the "body of flesh," in I Peter 3:21 only the "filth of flesh" are mentioned in connection with reference to baptism—but (unlike the reference to the "body of sin" in Rom 6:6) not in connection with the term "Old Man." If a widespread, fixed baptismal liturgy had existed containing the terms "Old" and "New Man," then probably either of these terms would very frequently occur when baptism is mentioned in the NT, or they would be

---

[37] E.g. the Greek oral and written greeting, Rejoice! (*chairein*), has the form of an infinitive but the meaning of an imperative. In Rom 12:9–15; Luke 9:3; Acts 23:23–24; Titus 2:1–10, explicit imperatives and/or imperative participles (see the last NOTE on 3:17) are followed by infinitives that possess the distinct character of commands; see D. Daube in Selwyn, *First Peter*, p. 480. C. F. D. Moule, *An Idiom-Book of New Testament Greek*, 2d ed. (Cambridge University Press, 1963), pp. 126–27, doubts whether Semitic style, that is, the Hebrew infinitive absolute, influenced this use of the Greek infinitive. For as early as in Homer the infinitive with imperative sense is found. A fair number of MSS, also several early and later translators and commentators of Eph 4:22–24, agree in understanding the infinitives as imperatives, see, e.g. the reading of vss. 23–24 in Papyrus 46, the Latin and the Greek versions, and the pointed JB and NTTEV translations, "You must . . ."

[38] Compare the analogous formulations "faith . . . hope to be saved," Acts 14:9; 27:20; "hope to have a share," I Cor 9:10; "desire to come," Rom 15:23; "time to give birth, power to tread, opportunity to betray," Luke 1:57; 10:19; 22:6. While in these examples the article is used before the Greek infinitives, passages such as I Cor 9:4–6; Rom 13:11; Heb 13:10; I Peter 4:17; John 1:12; 10:18 reveal that after abstract nouns that are connected with the verbs, "to be, to give, to have, to take," etc., the article may or may not be omitted. Cf. also, "A mouth to speak," Rev 13:5. See BDF, 393:3, 5–6; 400:1–2. The syntax of Eph 4:22–24 may well be that of an accusative with infinitive. Therefore it need not be labeled (with BDF, 406:2) "not at all clear."

[39] Following D. Daube, "Haustafeln," in *The New Testament and Rabbinic Judaism* (London: Athlone, 1956), p. 94, it is possible to find an analogous diction in English statements such as, "A boy scout helps anyone in need." Such an indicative contains an appeal that is stronger than a blunt imperative.

left unexplained at least in several of the cases where they are found. It is certain that Ephesians and Colossians use both terms without explicit mention of baptism in the context, and that both epistles combine a brief explanation in the form of keywords (Eph 4:22, 24; Col 3:9–10) with a more detailed description in catalogue form of what is to be put off and on (Eph 4:25–31; Col 3:8, 12–17). In Comment V B, C the function of baptism will be discussed in more detail. The Greek noun *anastrophē*, translated by "behavior," is attested as denoting human conduct since the time of the later parts of the LXX.[40] In undisputed Pauline epistles the word occurs only in Gal 1:13, but it is a favorite of I Peter, see, e.g. 1:18 "the futile behavior inherited from the fathers." Modified by proper adjectives, this noun can also signify good behavior.[41] Biblical writers prefer to speak in terms of "walking on a way" rather than to depict features or define virtues of a better world (see the first NOTE on 2:2; cf. 2:10).

the Old Man. See the first NOTE on 4:24 for the translation "Man," (as opposed to "nature") and COMMENT V A.

rotting in deceitful desires. Lit. "perishing according to the desires of deceit." Following a pattern observed elsewhere (e.g. in 2:2–3), a short narration takes the place of defining the "Old Man" with adjectives or other means.[42] Criteria for adjudicating the Old Man's essence and conduct are these: the means employed and the effect achieved by him (Calvin). Because of the vanity of the things he desires, the Old Man is effete (see the NOTE on "futility" in 4:17). The strong term "rotting" is a more adequate translation of the underlying Greek present participle *phtheiromenon* than any other term that might express compassion or suggest that the mode of the Old Man's perdition is as yet invisible. Verse 4:22 asserts that the end of the evil way is already at hand and experienced: a realized eschatology of evil is deployed. Every trait of the Old Man's behavior is putrid, crumbling, or inflated like rotting waste or cadavers, stinking, ripe for being disposed of and forgotten. The error or "deceptiveness" of the Old Man's desires[43] corresponds in negative terms to the role attributed to "truth" in 4:15, 21, 24. Paul points out in Rom 7:11; cf. 6:23, that "sin cheats" man in every way.[44] A detailed description of the "bondage to decay" (Rom 8:21) to which "each man" is subject under the wrath of God, is given in Rom 1:20–32.

23. *you become new.* In the summary NOTE on vss. 22–24 it was stated that the present tense is used only in vs. 23, describing perpetual and ever repeated renewal. II Cor 4:16 speaks of a "day by day" or "every day" renewal of the "inner man." The concept of "renewal" occurs elsewhere in the NT;[45] in Eph 4:24, however, a verb is used which etymologically seems to emphasize the temporal rather than the qualitative element of change.[46] But because of the parallel (Col 3:10) it is most unlikely that in Eph 4:24 a renewal

---

[40] Tobit 4:14; II Macc 6:23; also in inscriptions.
[41] E.g. I Tim 4:12; I Peter 3:1, 2, 16; II Peter 3:11.
[42] Cf. the reference to the evil "spirit now at work" (2:2).
[43] Not necessarily all men's or every desire! See fn. 111 to 2:1–10.
[44] See also II Thess 2:10; II Cor 11:3; Heb 3:13; Matt 13:22.
[45] The noun in Rom 12:2 and Titus 3:5; the verb in Col 3:10 and Heb 6:6.
[46] *Ananeoō*, instead of the usual *anakainoō, anakainizō, anakainōsis.* See COMMENT VI A 2 on 2:11–22, esp. fn. 235, for the distinction between *neos* and *kainos*.

is meant that does not affect the total quality of man. The original difference between the two Greek concepts of "newness" was not always in the mind of a speaker or of his hearers. Since the expected and commanded newness is unprecedented, it is not advisable to overemphasize the preposition *ana* in the Greek verb (*ana-neoō*). While in other cases[47] this preposition may indicate the restoration to a former state of affairs, the preceding parts of Ephesians do not suggest that the same is true of Eph 4:23-24. It was shown earlier that the terms "comprehend under one head" (1:10), "alienate" (2:12; 4:18), "black out" (4:18) did not necessarily imply a (Gnostic!) doctrine of original unity in a world of light. The version "become new" is preferred to the weaker "be renewed." An absolute novelty[48] and nothing less than new creation is in mind. Much more than rejuvenation[49] or a restoration of the first Adam and his status will be brought about by the eschatological innovation. With good reason JB speaks of a "spiritual revolution." The "futile minds" of 4:17 need rebirth rather than repair. The "newness of life" mentioned in Rom 6:4 is unheard-of news!

in mind and spirit. Lit. "by the spirit of your mind." The translation offered here is that of NEB. There seem to exist many reasons for capitalizing the noun "spirit" and treating it as a reference to the "Holy Spirit of God" who is mentioned in 4:30. Among these reasons are: (a) The absence of the preposition "in" (or "by") in analogy to 1:13;[50] (b) the Pauline distinction between spirit (Spirit?) and mind (I Cor 14:14) or between (God's) Spirit and the (human) spirit (Rom 8:16);[51] (c) the attribution of "newness," "regeneration," "rebirth" to the Spirit in other NT passages[52] and the corresponding conviction that man's spirit and mind are too corrupt to be a means of eschatological renewal.[53] If at this point, however, Paul had intended to say that the Spirit must exert its creative and guiding rule over the human mind, he would probably have qualified the word "spirit" with unmistakable epithets (as he does in 1:13; 4:30) and not have spoken of (lit.) "the spirit of your mind." Rather he uses the words "spirit" and "mind" practically as synonyms (Dibelius) for describing man's innermost being. It is the core, the heart, the soul of man (called in the terminology of some Greeks and of II Cor 4:16 the "inner man")[54] that require total and ongoing renewal, cf. Rom 12:2: "Be transformed by the renewal of your mind." In substance Eph 4:23 unfolds the meaning of the terms *metanoia* and *metanoeō* ("repentance," "repent") which occur often

---

[47] E.g. when classical writers employ the term "to renew."

[48] Cf. Abbott.

[49] C. Jordan, in his striking *Cotton Patch Version of Paul's Epistles* (New York: Association Press, 1968), p. 110, uses "rejuvenate."

[50] Papyrus 49, the Codex Vaticanus, Minuscule 33, and a few other MSS insert the preposition "in" and show in their own way that they thought of the Spirit. The use of the preposition is appropriate to the mention of the Holy Spirit: unlike water the Spirit is not a mere instrument but an agent, see, e.g. Matt 3:11; John 1:33. However, the Vatican Codex omits the preposition before the reference to the Spirit in Mark 1:8. Since, equally, in Eph 1:13 a simple instrumental dative is used for describing the Spirit's work, the same might be true of 4:23 also.

[51] But, e.g. in I Cor 2:10-15, 16 Spirit and mind (of Christ!) are used as synonyms.

[52] Rom 7:6; II Cor 3:6; Titus 3:5; John 3:5; 4:14. See also the Qumran doctrine on essence and effect of the Holy Spirit, 1QS III-IV. H. Mueller, "The Ideal Man as portrayed by the Talmud and St. Paul," CBQ 28 (1966), 278-91, states that the contrast between Talmud and Paul culminates in the fact that the first relies on the power of the law, the second on the fulfillment brought by the Spirit.

[53] Eph 4:17; Rom 1:21, 28, etc.

[54] But not in Rom 7:22 or Eph 3:16; see COMMENT IV on 3:14-21.

in the Synoptic Gospels, Acts, and Revelation but rarely in Pauline writings.[55] Renewal means much more than reform, reorientation, or reactivation.[56] Since spirit and mind exert a dominating and steering function, a renewed "spirit and mind" mean no less than a total change of the total man. His internal and external capacities and actions are equally affected. The whole man with his very best concerns, highest abilities, and deepest exigencies is subject to "revolution" and new beginning. In vs. 23 the means used by God for effecting this change are not mentioned. However, the next verse reveals that the instrument of renewal is not taken from some untapped or unspoiled resources inside man; rather it is given to him from outside. Its name is the "New Man." In Stoic anthropology the "mind" of natural man (a part and exponent of the Logos-Zeus who permeates the world) guarantees man's capacity of being reasonable and virtuous. In Ephesians the "New Man" created in God's likeness, and a new event, the clothing with the New Man, are the presupposition and means of human conduct in true righteousness and piety.

24. *and put on the New Man.* In COMMENT VI A 2 on 2:11-22 some reasons were given for retaining the literal version "New Man" rather than substituting an explanatory translation such as "new nature" (RSV) or "new self" (JB). In the same COMMENT and in the first NOTE on 4:23 the term "new" has been discussed. Just as the "one new man" (2:15) is a partner of Christ and "the inner man" (3:16) is Christ himself dwelling in the hearts of the saints, so the "New Man" of 4:24 is a person, not a thing; the head or ruler over man, not man's struggling better self. Since the New Man is called "created" (by God), Paul makes an allusion to the creation story, or to his hope of new creation, or to both. Paul's anthropology is based upon ever new relationships between persons; the relation of man to impersonal things such as law, righteousness, and newness is not forgotten but is subordinated to the events, attitudes, and actions that result from the rule of this or that person over man. See COMMENT V A for an attempt to identify the "New Man." The metaphor "put on" possesses a rich background in the history of religions, in magical practice, in mystic thought, and in some rituals. In COMMENT V B the possible relevance of parallels to 4:24 will be considered.

created after God['s image]. The addition to the Greek text of the word "image" can be justified by a reference to Gen 1:27 and Col 3:10, i.e. to those passages which explicitly state that Adam or the "New Man" was created after the "image" of the creator.[57] Among others Abbott and JB reject this supplementation; they suggest that Eph 4:24 be translated "created according to God's will" or "created in God's way." But their versions amount to a tautology. To whom else but God should the power, will and way, of creation be attributed?[58] The character and consequence of God's act are predicated in an amazing way when a creature is called a bearer or reflection of God's image.

[55] Rom 2:4; II Cor 7:9-10; 12:21; II Tim 2:25.

[56] Calvin. The potential seen by Bultmann in the diverse faculties of "man prior to the revelation of faith" (see for details COMMENT IV B on 3:14-21) is to be subsumed under those constitutive human traits that are in need of new creation.

[57] Monographs on the concept "image," e.g. J. Jervell, *Imago Dei,* FRLANT 76, N.F. 58, 1960, will be named in the context of the explanation of Col 1:15. In Col 1 Jesus Christ is called the "first-born of all creation" and the "image of the invisible God."

[58] Eph 2:10; 3:9 and uncounted OT and NT texts make clear that the creator carries out his creative work in his own manner according to his own plan.

The aorist tense of the Greek participle "created" makes it unlikely that at
this point an ongoing act of creation is meant. The accent lies upon the pre-
existence of the one New Man—a preexistence that is comparable to that of
Wisdom and of good works.[59] One New Man is created for the sake of all
men. What the saints are continually to "put on" is new for them and makes
them new, but it is not a novelty with God. While God has already created
the one who makes them new, and while the "truth" of their renewal is
already present "in Jesus" (4:21), the saints still need be "transformed into the
likeness" of the New Man (II Cor 3:18). "Just as we have borne the image of
the earthly man, we shall also bear the image of the heavenly" (I Cor 15:49).
Regarding the question whether the "createdness" of the New Man excludes
his identity with the Son of God who preexists in eternity, see COMMENT V.

in true righteousness and piety. Lit. "in righteousness and piety of truth."
A few variant readings juxtapose "truth"; they read "in righteousness and
piety and truth." But in most MSS the genitive "of truth" qualifies the nouns
"righteousness" and "piety." The majority contain a sharper contrast to the
"deceitfulness" of the Old Man's desires (4:22), the "deceitful scheming"
of the heretics (4:14), and the cheating serpent (II Cor 11:3) and sin (Rom
7:11).[60] The Old Man may make whatever claims he pleases, but he cannot
claim to possess, or to live in, true righteousness and piety. In Philip 4:8
the saints are admonished to "ponder all that is true, honorable, just," etc.;
Eph 4 admonishes them to be selective. Similarly the Johannine adjective
"true" (alēthinos) has a polemic undertone; it urges the readers to discriminate
between false claims and the revelation (or truth) given in Jesus Christ.[61] The
nouns translated by "righteousness and piety" and their cognate adjectives
denote in classical Greek the right attitudes toward men and the gods respectively.[62] However, not all Greek writers always upheld the distinction
just mentioned. Neither can the OT or the Pauline concept of "righteousness"
be limited to man's correct social attitude. Either of the two terms could denote "a summary of human virtue."[63] Thus it is all the more astonishing that
"righteousness," which in the undisputed Pauline letters is a powerful act of
mercy and a gift of God (Rom 1:17; 3:21 ff., etc.),[64] appears to occur in Ephesians in the sense of man's right attitude.[65] Does this fact demonstrate the non-
Pauline origin of Ephesians, or can the epistle's authenticity be upheld only at
the price of assuming that Paul either forgot or sidestepped the heart of his
earlier message? Several passages in the undisputed letters show that even there
Paul felt free to use the words "righteousness" and "righteous" in an ethical

[59] See Prov 3:19–20; 8:22 ff.; Eph 2:10, and COMMENTS V and X on 1:3–14, also VI C on
2:1–10. Cf. Gaugler, pp. 184–90.
[60] Chrysostom emphasizes the opposition of truth in Eph 4:24 to the falsehood mentioned
earlier.
[61] See John 1:9; 4:23, 37; 6:32, etc., and C. Maurer, Ignatius von Antiochien und das Johan-
nesevangelium, ATANT 18 (1949), 46–50.
[62] E.g. Plato Gorgias 507B; Euthyphro 12A, 15B; Philo de Abr. 37 (208). See also I Thess 2:10;
Luke 1:75; Titus 1:8; I Clem. 48:4. In Rom 1:18 the opposites of righteousness and piety, that is
"godlessness and unrighteousness," are mentioned explicitly, though in reverse order. Calvin understood "rectitude" to refer to the second, "sanctity" to the first tablet of the law.
[63] Abbott, p. 139. See Plato Gorgias 507B for a Greek passage pronouncing the mutual coinherence of the two virtues; cf. also "meet and proper" in Polybius xx 10:7.
[64] See, e.g. E. Käsemann, "God's Righteousness in Paul," JThC 1 (1965), 100–10; P. Stuhlmacher, Gerechtigkeit Gottes bei Paulus, 1965.
[65] See also 5:9; 6:14; cf. the adjective in 6:1.

sense.[66] Since in Ephesians the noun "peace" holds the place which elsewhere in Pauline writings is attributed to "righteousness,"[67] the shift in wording is obvious: in this letter "righteousness" is mentioned *only* in ethical contexts. But a change of doctrine or a contradiction to genuine Pauline teaching is not necessarily connected with this usage of the term; see COMMENT III B on 6:10–20. As repeatedly stated, Paul was not bound to the same vocabulary or to one exclusive sense of a given word.

25. *Therefore.* In the second NOTE on vs. 21 it was shown that a quotation and the return to the author's own formulation are frequently indicated by the conjunction "therefore." If, however, all the verses 21c–24 are an interpolation, then the conjunction would connect vss. 25 ff. directly with the statement about the school of the Messiah (vss. 20–21b), as if to say: because you have received proper instruction, let your actions bear testimony to your knowledge of God, just as your former Gentile conduct was the result of a perverted mind (vss. 17–19). It is more likely that the verses 21c–24 were always an essential element of Ephesians. For example, the resumption of the noun "truth" from 4:21, 24 in 4:25 indicates that vs. 25 was originally composed as an interpretation and application of the quote contained in vss. 21c–24.[68]

put away the lie. Every one shall speak the truth to his neighbor. The Greek verb translated by "put away" is the same as the one occurring in vs. 22, where it was translated by "strip off." In what follows Paul presents examples to show what specific deeds and attitudes are rejected when the "Old Man" is cast away.[69] In Col 3:8 "all" vices (several of which are mentioned by name), in Eph 4:25 specifically "the lie," are to be discarded like a worn-out, useless dress. The position of "lie" at the head of other evil deeds is a fitting antithesis to the stress laid on "truth" in the preceding three verses. In Col 3:9 "lying" is the main characteristic of life under the sway of the Old Man. The words "rotting in deceitful desires" are in Eph 4:22 used to describe the same life. Thus the whole former existence of the saints is defined as a lie, or as living a lie; if the existentialists' terminology has any validity as a tool for interpreting Paul, then this is the place to speak of "inauthentic existence." But while secular existentialism considers inauthenticity a deviation from each individual man's potential, Paul measures man's existence against the "truth in Jesus" or the "true word," i.e. the Gospel, and their social effect, i.e. the fact that "we are members of one body." "Falsehood is unnatural: it is disloyalty to Christ

---

[66] II Cor 6:7, 14; 9:10; Rom 6:13, 16, 18–20; Philip 1:7; 4:8, etc.

[67] Dibelius, p. 87; in Rom 14:17 "righteousness, peace and joy in the Holy Spirit" appear to be almost synonymous.

[68] Dibelius, p. 87, and Schlier, p. 223 (cf. W. Schrage, *Die konkreten Einzelgebote in der paulinischen Paränese* [Gütersloh: Mohn; 1961], pp. 187–271, regarding similar passages in undisputed Pauline epistles) state emphatically that 4:25 ff. contains materials from the storehouse of Jewish, Hellenistic, and Christian exhortation. However, it is not necessary to conclude that therefore the borrowed material contradicts Pauline ethics or is strange to it. The author of Ephesians may well have selected and so arranged traditional elements that they serve the points which he specifically wanted to make. J. Gnilka, "Paränetische Traditionen im Epheserbriefe," in *Mélanges Bibliques*, Fs B. Rigaux, eds. A. Descamps and A. de Halleux (Gembloux: Duculot, 1970), pp. 397–410, esp. 403–4, mention as evidence of such a tradition e.g. Zech 8:16–17; Ps 4:5; *Test. Dan* I 3; II 1, 4; III 5–6; IV 6–7; V 1; VI 8; *Test. Naphtali* III 1; VIII 4, 6; *Test. Asher* III 2; *Test. Issachar* V 3; VII 5; *Test. Zebulun* VI 5–6; 1QS V 25–VI 1; VII; X 22; CD V 11–12; James 1:19; 4:7. In the pastoral Epistles, Ignatius, and Hermas are found abundant additional examples of the same tradition.

[69] Robinson, p. 111, expresses joy over these illustrations because they show "how practical he [Paul] is in all his mysticism."

in Whom we all are. In a healthy body the eye cannot deceive the hand."[70] He is a liar who speaks, acts, and lives as though no one had come and made peace by "creating one new man" (2:14–18). And he "speaks the truth in love" who acts as a man responsible for the growth of a community "toward Christ" and "from him" (4:15–16). "Truth" in this sense is narrower and more specific than the same term used in the setting of a juridical inquiry, a historiographer's research, a natural scientist's quest for facts, or a philosopher's meditation about the ground of being or the possibility of knowledge.[71] On the other hand, in Eph 4:25 "truth" has a much wider meaning than in the spheres mentioned. The command to "speak the truth" includes and expresses the responsibility to be a witness to revelation, to follow Christ who gave his life for saving sinners, to show unselfish love, and to build up the fellow man to his own best.[72] The Hebrew concept of "truth" (*'emet*, cf. *'emunah;* the LXX translates this word often by "truth" or by "faithfulness," once by "righteousness") underlies and specifies the meaning of Eph 4:25: the wording of the commandment, "speak the truth . . . ," is almost the same as that found in LXX Zech 8:16. In Qumran, in the Fourth Gospel, and in some Greek philosophical and later Gnostic writings, the term "truth" is tinged by eschatological and dualistic elements respectively.

for we are members of one body. This is a surprising, but also a simple motivation for speaking the truth. It is surprising because it does not look specifically theological and seems to lack a reference to Jesus Christ and his work. It is almost platitudinous to undergird a social ethical admonition by an appeal to tribal solidarity. Should these words be considered an interpolation because they appear superfluous or misplaced? There is no reason to treat them as spurious, for they are found in all MSS, and all individual prohibitions and commands in 4:25–32 are followed by a reason for their observance. On the other hand, the motivation given for "speaking the truth" is as simple as that found in the related Zechariah passage, but it is different. In Zechariah the argument against untrue and divisive judgments, against evil devices fostered in the heart and false oaths pronounced openly, is this: "For all these things I hate, says the Lord." This motivation is theological and refers to God's will, emotion, authority. The exhortation of Eph 4:21c ff. began with a Christological headline ("Truth in Jesus!"), but the ethical argument in 4:25 appears to be sociological only. The Greek text does not even mention the body (of Christ) but speaks, in literal translation, of "members of one another" as though,

---

[70] Westcott, p. 73.

[71] Eph 4:25 does not, for example, oblige the saints of later times to betray the presence of a hidden Jew to an inquiring *Gestapo* agent who is hired to deliver the fugitive to organized mass murder. In Zech 8:16–17 an authentic comment on the command to "speak the truth" is given: it means to render "in your gates judgments that are true and make for peace, to devise no evil" in one's "heart against another," and "not to love a false oath." In Eph 4:25 as much as in Zech 8 and in one of the Ten Commandments (Exod 20:16) a limitation is obvious: the "neighbor" is entitled to hear the "truth," and the "neighbor" is protected from "false testimony" and a wicked verdict based on lies. See J. J. Stamm and M. E. Andrew, *The Ten Commandments in Recent Research*, SBT, 2d ser., 2 (1967), 107–10, for other specifications.

[72] For this reason, Eph 4:25 does not permit or bid the saints to "tell one another off" though they may often feel inclined to spell out to one another's face what they really think. Because the testimony to Christ (that is, the "gospel" or the edifying word that "does good" to the hearer and "saves" him, 1:13; 4:15, 29) is the essence of the truth to be spoken, the command "speak the truth" includes a missionary charge for the benison of all "those far" who have been brought near by Christ. For the following see G. Quell and R. Bultmann, TWNTE, I, 232–51.

e.g. the hand were a member of the eyes. Still, Eph 4:25 means by members obviously "fellow-members" in the one body whose head is Christ (1:22–23; 3:6; etc.). It is possible that the lack of precision in the Greek formulation reveals a hand other than Paul's, i.e. the presence of a hidden quotation from a pre-Pauline formulation.[73] Otherwise it ought to be assumed that at this place (as in I Cor 12:12–27; Rom 12:5) Paul himself used the metaphor "member," without connecting it with the idea of Christ the head. Nevertheless an exclusively sociological understanding of 4:25b[74] is discouraged by 4:15–16 and 5:30, for in these verses the statements about "members" are linked up with references to Christ "the head" and the church "his body." The Messiah Jesus was mentioned in 4:20–21, probably also in 4:24.[75] Thus the Christological argument was so obvious that it did not need repetition in 4:25. An appeal to self-consciousness, if not to élite-consciousness,[76] is perceptible in the exhortation, "Members [of Christ's body] do not lie!" In all they say to one another they bear testimony to the revealed secret, that is, the unity and peace created by Jesus Christ. While common and mutual membership is a valid motive for all exhortations that follow, Paul will give other equally urgent reasons in vss. 27–32. The issues related to motivation will be more fully discussed in COMMENT VI.

26. *If you are angry yet do not sin.* Lit. "be angry and sin not." The LXX version of Ps 4:4 is worded the same way and sounds like a proverb. But the original Hebrew psalm[77] contains the (corrupt?) reading "stand in awe [or, tremble; or, be worried]—and sin not." H. Gunkel calls the first of these two imperatives "a mocking concession." The OT and NT contain rare additional examples of this "concessive imperative."[78] In most cases a factual permission is granted by this imperative, but an explicit command is not contained in it.[79] Eph 4:26 concedes that righteous anger is aroused by injustice. Among the saints who are "God's imitators" (5:1) such anger cannot be excluded any more than in God himself (Rom 1:18; 2:5, 8; 5:9) or in the Messiah (Mark 3:5, etc.). "Wrath against a brother" draws judgment upon the angry man (Matt 5:22; cf. Gen 45:24), but "indignation on behalf of others is one of the common bonds by which society is held together."[80]

The sun must not set on your temper. In other words, "The day of your

[73] P. Carrington, *The Primitive Christian Catechism* (Cambridge University Press, 1940), p. 75; Dibelius, p. 91; Schlier, p. 223, think of a catechism for neophytes (newly converted Christians), but Gaugler, p. 193, argues against this theory: at all times Christians are and remain neophytes. The commandment not to lie is not only appropriate to the needs of *new* members of the congregation.
[74] As it would be based upon the argument, e.g. "we are a team and under any circumstances must live up to the *esprit de corps.*"
[75] See the interpretation of the term "New Man" in COMMENT V A.
[76] See 4:1–3, esp. COMMENT II on 4:1–16.
[77] According to H. Gunkel, *Die Psalmen*, 5th ed. (Göttingen: Vandenhoeck, 1968), p. 16, Ps 4 is a psalm of confidence. Following H.-J. Kraus, *Psalmen*, I, Biblischer Kommentar zum Alten Testament 15:1 (1961), 34, it is a petition for God's legal assistance in a lawsuit; M. Dahood, *Psalms I* (AB, Vol. 16), p. 23, calls it a prayer for rain.
[78] Eccles 11:9; II Cor 12:16; esp. John 2:19, "Destroy this temple, and in three days I shall raise it up." See BDF, 387:1–2.
[79] Thomas Aquinas affirms, "He does not command it [anger] but permits it"; wrath directed against one's own sin is good; Christ is the sun which sets a limit to this self-punishment; wrath against a neighbor's sin cannot be avoided, cf. Num 25:11; I Kings 19:10; the sun of reason must not be clouded over by it. Bengel, "Wrath is neither commanded nor fully prohibited; occasionally it has the power of a medicine but it must be treated with greatest care." Cf. Aristotle *eth. Nic.* IV 5 1125–1126.
[80] Eadie, p. 258, quoted by Abbott, p. 140, and Robinson, p. 112.

anger should be the day of your reconciliation."[81] According to Deuteronomy, the sunset is the time limit for several actions: goods taken as a pawn from a poor man have to be returned, a hired hand's wages have to be paid out, the body of a man who has been impaled must be buried. Following Plutarch[82] the Pythagoreans applied the same rule to outbursts of anger. The noun translated by "temper" (*parorgismos*) occurs only here in the NT. It has not yet been traced in secular Greek literature written before NT times, but it is found, e.g. in LXX Jer 21:5; III Kings 15:30; cf. 16:33. The corresponding verb is frequently used in the LXX and occurs also in Eph 6:4; Col 3:21 var. lect. A violent irritation is meant, expressed either by hiding oneself from others or by flaming looks, harmful words, inconsiderate actions, that is, something distinctly less permanent than deep-rooted wrath, anger, or hostility. God's own wrath is limited in the same way:[83] "In overflowing wrath for a moment I hid my face from you, but with everlasting love I will have compassion on you" (Isa 54:8). When "space is given" to the "wrath of God" then man's desire to justify or avenge himself by his own unrestricted and unlimited wrath is cut short (Rom 12:19).[84] A less theological but still passionate warning against wrath is found in the Testaments of the XII Patriarchs:[85] "Anger is blindness and does not suffer one to see the face of any man with truth" (Test. Dan II 2). Though in this statement the meaning of the term "truth" may not be as qualified as in Eph 4:21, 24–25, the contrast between living in truth and exploding in anger is shown as distinctly as in Eph 4.

27. *And do not give an opportunity to the devil.* Lit. "and give no place. . . ." Here and elsewhere the Greek noun *topos* ("place") is used in a metaphorical sense, i.e. for denoting either an opportunity or an office.[86] The word *diabolos,* translated by "devil," was originally an adjective but eventually became a noun denoting a slanderous, unfriendly, hostile person. The LXX employs it to describe Satan, mostly in his function as an adversary or prosecutor in court, but sometimes also in his capacity as a seducer or executor. No unified doctrine on Satan exists in the OT or in later Jewish texts.[87] Since Hebrew *śāṭān* describes in I Kings 11:14, 23, 25 an earthly adversary of Solomon or Israel, also in Eph 4:27 the adjectival noun *diabolos* may denote a human slanderer or calumniator.[88] However, Paul may also mean the one who

---

[81] G. Estius, as cited by Abbott, p. 141, with the remark, "for the new day began at sunset." Idiomatic references to the sunset are found, e.g. in Deut 21:23; 24:13, 15; Josh 8:29; 10:27.

[82] *De amicitia fratrum* 488BC.

[83] See, e.g. Hosea 2:21–23; Lam 3:31–36; Ps 103:9; Exod 20:5–6.

[84] Calvin enumerates the following three faults of wrath and the corresponding antidotes: (a) Small things are the cause of man's anger–but God's glory alone has to be sought. (b) Human wrath trespasses all limits—but God uses the sun to make man aware of the necessary limitation. (c) In our anger we impose our own fault upon fellow man—but God makes us realize our own failure and teaches us to put the blame upon the (impersonal) fault rather than upon the person of the neighbor.

[85] In *Test. Dan* I 3; III 6; IV 6; V 1; VI 8 wrath and anger are treated as inseparable.

[86] Rom 12:19, "Give an opportunity [lit. give space; RSV: leave it] to the wrath [of God]." In Wisd Sol 12:10; Heb 12:17; I Clem 7:5; Prayer of Manasseh 8, the *opportunity* for repentance; in Sir 19:17 a *chance* for the law of the Most High, are mentioned. The meaning "office" (or works to be done, job) is discernible in Rom 15:23 and Acts 1:25; I Clem 40:5; Ign. *Smyrn.* VI 1.

[87] See Job 1–2; Zech 3:1–3; I Chron 21:1, etc.; StB, I, 136–49; W. Foerster and G. von Rad, TWNTE, II, 72–79; see also COMMENT II on 2:1–10.

[88] The noun was understood in this sense, e.g. by the Syriac versions, Erasmus, Luther, and the adjective describes mischievous men in II Tim 3:3; Titus 2:3. Sir 4:5 gives to the wise the counsel not to turn away from a beggar lest the beggar have an *opportunity* to utter a curse.

resides in the air of the heavens (2:2; 6:11–12) and is often referred to as the (capitalized) Devil in English. In several of his undisputed letters he makes references to a super-human person called Satan, Destroyer, Beliar.[89] The term "devil" is used only in exceptional cases in Pauline literature, i.e. in Eph 4:27 and 6:11, also in the epistles to Timothy, as the name of the arch-enemy, Satan.[90] This fact has been pointed out by scholars who question the Pauline authenticity of Ephesians, but it is not more conclusive than other linguistic idiosyncrasies of Ephesians. Whoever admits that Paul incorporates in his exhortations traditional material has also to accept the possibility that Paul himself endorsed, together with earlier elements of exhortation, a name for Satan which was strange to his own diction.[91] At any rate it is more likely that 4:27 speaks of the personal devil than of a human calumniator. For in 6:11 the same term designates the monarchic arch-opponent, and in 4:30 it is shown that "not grieving the Holy Spirit" is the opposite of yielding space "to that spirit which is now at work among the rebellious" (2:2). The warning of 4:26–27 can be summed up this way: the Devil will take possession of your heart if your wrath endures.[92]

28. *The thief shall no longer go on stealing.* The translation of the Greek present participle (*ho kleptōn;* lit. "the stealing one") by "thief" is not universally accepted.[93] But if only some improvised shoplifting, or the occasional appropriation of a master's or client's property by a slave, laborer or craftsman were in mind, the aorist rather than the present participle would be used.[94] However uncomplimentary it is for saints to realize that the apostle reckons with thieves in their midst, Paul fights the opinion that theft in any form may be sanctified if the thief is a member of the congregation. Because of the subsequent admonition which encourages honest manual labor, it is probable that Paul includes in the term "thief" those who make money without working; who get rich at the expense of slaves or employees; who by artificial price-fixing take advantage of those in need; or who cheat the community of the saints after the pattern of Ananias and Sapphira (Acts 5:1–11). Their way of making a living is according to the apostle's message no less opposed to the order of God's people than is a successful career in burglary, larceny, embezzlement or bank-robbery. In either case thievery may be or become a profession. Every saint engaged in such conduct before his incorporation into God's people and his reconciliation with God is told "no longer" to follow his former trade. The new aeon which has dawned with the Messiah's advent leaves room for many occupations—but not for all. In the OT, prostitution, soothsaying, necromancy are prohibited to members of God's people. Because of their connection with pagan sanctuaries and their competition with the worship of Yahweh these professions were considered a sin against God, and

[89] See the references given in fn. 28 to Eph 2:1–11 and COMMENT III on the same section.
[90] In the NT the title "devil" occurs in the Synoptic Gospels, in Acts, in Heb 2:14; James 4:7; I Peter 5:8; I John 3:8, 10; Jude 9, and five times in Revelation.
[91] In the Introduction, on the last pages of section II, it was shown that references, e.g. to the "blood" of Christ or to "forgiveness," demonstrate the same fact, even within kerygmatic parts of Paul's epistles.
[92] Calvin.
[93] See, e.g. Vulg. Similarly, Bengel argues, "Stealing is perhaps less hard than the noun thief (*kleptēs*)."
[94] Abbott suggests a compromise solution: the author forbids actions halfway between occasional and professional thievery.

therefore also against fellow men.[95] In Rom 2:21–22 stealing and robbing the temple are mentioned in close succession; in some epistles insatiable greed is identified with idolatry.[96] But in vs. 28 the reason offered for the prohibition of theft is not weighted down with strictly theological arguments (as occur in 4:21c, 30, 32; 5:1–2). The motivation is social or sociological, as the next words show.

To the contrary, he shall work hard and honestly with his own hands. Lit. "He shall tire himself out by working with his own hands the good." There are seven readings in existence which vary the sequence of the words, working with his own hands the good. They give emphasis to "his own hands" or to "the good," or else they omit either "his own" or "his own hands" or "the good."[97] Some of the variants appear to fight verbosity. Since, e.g. a man cannot use hands other than his own for tiring himself out, the words "his own" appear superfluous. Alexandrian scholars seem intent on reducing the praise of manual labor; their reading affirms that (all) labor in the pursuit of the good is all right even if it is not manual.[98] The text reproduced in our translation deserves preference to all variants[99]—not despite but rather because of its inherent problematic features; difficult features would have been eliminated or smoothed out rather than interpolated by later copyists.[100] It can easily be explained why Paul laid emphasis on manual labor. Most rabbis of his as well as of later times made their living in some civic profession, preferably as artisans. Paul himself was a tent-maker (Acts 18:3); others earned what they needed as a hired hand, a nail-smith, a miller, a scribe, a money-changer, a cattle-trader, a barber, etc. Some rabbis spent one third of the day meditating on the Torah, another in prayer, the last working in their trade.[101] Since the examples listed include some occupations that are performed mainly by desk work, there is no reason to suspect that the "hand"-work mentioned in Eph 4:28 has so narrow a sense as to exclude labor done in offices or libraries. To "work hard with his own hands" may in vernacular English simply mean to work with the sweat of one's brow. But not only a rabbinical and Pharisaical tradition is reflected in the command to "work." According to Mark 3:1–6 Jesus himself healed in a synagogue a man's "withered hand," and thereby "saved life" (Mark 3:4) and restored a man's ability to earn his livelihood. In I, II Thessalonians Paul points out that the nearness of the end is no reason to be lazy. A charming utterance illustrates the apostle's stance and doctrine:

---

[95] Lev 19:29; 20:23–25; Deut 18:9–14; 23:17, etc. However, the story of Judah and Tamar (Gen 38) appears to demonstrate that at certain periods of Israel's history strictly commercial prostitution was tolerated. While, save for a few exceptions such as Rahab of Jericho, persons stamped by an idolatrous and immoral profession were not granted access to God's house and people (see, e.g. II Sam 5:8; Deut 23:1, 17), Ephesians proclaims their admission to the community of the saints and God's temple (2:11–22; 3:5). Later it will be shown that not even in 5:5 is their inclusion retroactively negated. Yet the continuation of former pagan practices is no more tolerated in Ephesians than in the OT.

[96] I Cor 5:10–11; Col 3:5; Eph 5:5.

[97] The variants are conveniently listed in GNT. For the history of the Latin texts see *Vetus Latina* 24:1, ed. Erzabtei Beuron (Freiburg: Herder, n.d.), p. 196.

[98] Clement and Origen.

[99] It is supported by the first hand of Codex Sinaiticus, Codices Alexandrinus, Claramontanus, Boernerianus, by several Italic versions, the Clementine Vulg., Pesh., most Latin and some Greek fathers, though not by Papyri 46 and 49, Codex Vaticanus, and Minuscule 33.

[100] However, it is also possible that the adjective "own" was inserted by a later hand because of the parallel I Cor 4:12, and/or that the term "the good" was borrowed from Gal 6:10; see Abbott, p. 142.

[101] StB, II, 10–11, 745–47.

"If I knew that tomorrow the world should perish, I would still plant a little apple tree today in my back-yard."[102] The advantage, that is, the "good" of such work (cf. vs. 29c) is spelled out by Paul in the following line:

so that he may have something to share with the needy. Abbott calls this motivation "striking and characteristic" but utters his own objection in the name of "the law of nature." He is convinced that according to natural law the prime object of work is the working man's own subsistence and the support of his family. Indeed, in other epistles Paul gives various reasons why man must work and why human labor is not "in vain."[103] It is "commanded"; it is a "fitting" behavior according to the opinion of "those outside"; it makes men independent of support from fellow men (I Thess 4:10-11; cf. I Cor 4:12). Further, there is the threat, "If anyone will not work, let him not eat," and the exhortation, "Do your work quietly and eat the bread you have earned." Not to work is "disorderly conduct"—though laziness may be covered up by "busybodiness" (II Thess 3:10-12). Strikingly absent are any references to work as a deployment of creativeness, productiveness, dominion over nature, or as a means for empire-building or world-improvement. Equally missing are direct denunciations of slave labor and descriptions of work as a curse. In its positive evaluation of "hard work," 4:28 resembles the jubilant, though not the playful tone of Ps 104:22-23, 14-15, "When the sun rises . . . man goes forth to his work . . . that he may bring forth food from the earth and wine to gladden the heart of man" (cf. Ps 90:10, 17). In Eph 4:28 the opportunity to help the needy fellow man is the rationale for working, not self-satisfaction. What a man may gain for himself is certainly not excluded, but it is incidental to the motive here given: labor is necessary in order that the needy may live! In turn, liberal giving of the yields of one's labor is not recommended as a meritorious act deserving a reward or covering sins; it is rather a recognition of God's immeasurably rich gift (cf. Gal 2:6-10; II Cor 8-9).[104] When Paul recommends to the Corinthians and Romans the collection for the "saints," that is, for "the poor among the saints at Jerusalem" (Rom 15:26), he uses a great variety of theological, Christological, personal, and common sense arguments to demonstrate the necessity and effect of the planned gift.[105] However, in 4:28 only one reason is mentioned for working and giving,

---

[102] This dictum has been ascribed to Luther but is an apocryphon. It may stem from a grenadier of Frederick II of Prussia.

[103] Gal 2:2; I Cor 15:10, 58; Philip 2:16.

[104] The passages collected in StB, IV, 537-45, 562-65, show that some Jewish scholars esteemed almsgiving and other works done out of love higher than the fulfillment of other commandments of the Torah and the bringing of sacrifices: works of love make God man's debtor and make man resemble God; they save the life of others and bring the evil impulse under control; they earn a reward in this world and the coming one; they atone for sin including former theft; they are intercessors before God and establish peace between God and Israel. Other Jewish teachers come closer to Paul's message in Ephesians when they affirm that man was created for one purpose only, to do acts of mercy. They affirm that man does God's work and fills the world with God's love by being merciful from the depth of his heart. Eph 4:28 far from supports the business practice of "making up for unlawful taking by dutiful giving" to foundations and charities. The blood of Christ (1:7; 2:13, not a payment in cash, I Peter 1:18-19) is the means for wiping out the past.

[105] In I Cor 16:1.4; II Cor 8-9; Rom 15:25-28 he calls the collection a "[gift of] grace," an "[act of] thanksgiving," a "service," a "largesse": it supplies the need of the saints and overflows in God's praise, II Cor 9:12-13. It is good not only before God but also in the judgment of men, II Cor 8:21. It imitates Christ and fellow Christians who by becoming poor made many rich; it creates equality between the churches, and resembles an exchange of fleshly for spiritual gifts, II Cor 8:2, 9, 13-15; Rom 15:27. It is at the same time a harvest of God from seed sown by him, and a seed sown by the saints that will lead to a rich harvest for them, II Cor 9:6, 8-10; cf.

and the obligation of support is (unlike love, 1:15; 4:2) not restricted to the "brethren" or "neighbors" among the saints: the "needy" (whoever he may be!) is to be the beneficiary of the saint's labor! This universality of concern is characteristic of Ephesians. In 4:25c common membership was the reason for speaking the truth. Both here and there the social argument stands in the foreground. According to 4:28 in all matters related to work, responsibility for the poor is to be the primary consideration, rather than productivity for its own sake, not to speak of personal profit.[106]

29. *No foul talk whatsoever shall pass your lips.* The adjective "foul" can designate anything that is rotten, putrid, filthy, and therefore, unsound or bad. In the NT the term is used to describe bad trees, foul fruit, rotten fish.[107] Paul's metaphoric application of the term to a certain sort of talk or voice has scarcely any parallels in Greek writings. But it has a positive counterpart in the reference to "salted" (i.e. well-seasoned and well-preserved) speech in Col 4:6. In Eph 4:28, each "good" word is the alternative to "foul" talk. The formulation "pass your lips" (lit. "go out from your mouth") resembles Hebrew diction (Lev 5:4; I Sam 2:3) and the Homeric idiom "to escape from the hedge of the teeth." The nearest equivalents are found in the LXX.[108] Just as in James 3:10-12 (cf. Matt 15:11), so here the mouth is considered a spouting source. In biblical anthropology the mouth is representative of the whole body and reveals the whole man. The "fruit of the lips," i.e. man's speech, reveals the quality of the tree. Bad language and foul talk defile the whole man and manifest his corruption.[109]

but [say] what is right for meeting a need constructively. Lit. "but if there be a good [word] for the upbuilding of the need." The noun rendered by "need" (*chreiā*) has many meanings. It may denote not only want, poverty, or a request, but also (military) service, business, function, intimacy, or a rhetorical device, a pregnant sentence or maxim.[110] Many of these secondary meanings would give a good sense to the interpretation of Eph 4:29, but since in the preceding verse the same word clearly described the poverty of a fellow man,

---

Philip 4:17; Gal 6:7-8. It expresses the voluntariness of the donors; it justifies the apostle's expectations; and it puts the contributors on the same level with other donors, II Cor 8:1-2, 8, 10, 22-24; 9:3-5, 7. In some aspects this collection is an analogy of the temple tax collected among Jews for Jerusalem, cf. I Chron 29:2-9. But it resembles much more the bringing of the Gentiles' riches to Zion of which the prophets had spoken, Isa 2:2-4; 60:5-14; Micah 4:1-3; Hag 2:7-9; Zech 14:14. See Munck, PSM, ch. x; and D. Georgi, *Die Geschichte der Kollekte des Paulus für Jerusalem*, TF 38 (1965), esp. pp. 28, 30, 72-73, 85.

[106] If Sir 4:5 (i.e. the advice to be liberal to the poor lest he "curse you") is considered a key to Eph 4:27, then *diabolos* means a fellow man who brings dishonor and damage to the man who fails to be liberal. In this case, vs. 27 rather than vs. 28c contains the motive for hard and honest work: work—or else your fellow man will revile you! However, formal considerations militate against an interpretation which would replace the indicated social concern with the interest of the individual saints: Eph 4:25-32 possesses a stereotyped structure. Five times a point is made in the sequence, prohibition—command—motive, see vss. 25, 26-27, 28, 29-30, 31-32. This structure is neglected or destroyed when vs. 27 is associated with the issue of work *vs.* theft, rather than with the preceding statements on anger.

[107] LSLex, 1583; Matt 7:17-18; 12:33; 13:48; Luke 6:43.

[108] "Come out from the mouth" (i.e. to promise): Num 32:24 in lit. translation; "come out through the mouth": Deut 8:3; Matt 4:4; "come out through the lips": Jer 17:16. Perhaps a common (Phoenician?) tradition explains the similarity of the Hebrew and Greek expressions.

[109] See esp. Isa 57:18; Matt 12:33-34; Isa 6:5, 7; Dan 10:16; Zeph 3:9; James 3:1-12; Heb 13:15. Yet in some instances biblical writers allude to a contrast between the confession of the lips and the state of the heart: Isa 29:13; Ps 78:36-37; Matt 15:8.

[110] The plural of the noun is used by several Greek writers as the title of a Collection of Famous Sayings, see LSLex, 2002-3.

it is unlikely that the author used it here in a much more sophisticated sense. Verse 29 does not speak of a need that has to be built up;[111] for the genitive *tēs chreiās* (lit. "of the need") is[112] a genitive of substance or quality rather than an objective genitive. The "need" consists of a lack of upbuilding.[113] Constructive work has to be done, and in all conversations the choice of language and subject matter has to be such that edification takes place. Obviously no room is left for empty chatter or for remarks that serve no other purpose than to detract from a person's honor. Who are the prime objects and beneficiaries of the upbuilding done by constructive speech? If in 4:29 pre-Pauline material is used,[114] the whole congregation may be meant, or any individual in the church or outside the congregation. It is not known whether the material itself which Paul has perhaps endorsed was more specific than its quoted form in Ephesians. If the rest of Ephesians is consulted for an answer, the church is in mind—for only the church, not the world or pious individuals, is the object of building in this epistle. On the other hand, in undisputed Pauline letters, "building" (the verb and noun) refers to both the church's and the individual's upbuilding.[115] Since in 4:25 ff. the author of Ephesians reveals an almost casuistic interest in the behavior of each saint and his relation to other persons, it is probable that in 4:29 he discusses the role of words exchanged between individuals, not the purpose of public preaching. His concern for Christ the head, the community of the body, the worldwide mission of the church is misinterpreted when he is understood to permit the neglect of this and that fellow man's specific personal woes, sorrows, needs. The apostle is far from sacrificing the unique occasions and specific exigencies of daily life to a general over-all purpose;[116] see, e.g. Rom 14:1: "When a man is weak in faith, accept him warmly, without starting an argument." According to Paul everyday conversation is the fitting place for what in German is called *Seelsorge* (care or cure of souls). The opposite to constructive talk is described, e.g. in II Tim 2:14: "Disputes" are "good for nothing" because they "subvert the hearers." Equally "lies," the outbursts of "anger, shouting," as mentioned in Eph 4:25, 26, 31, are among the destructive antonyms.

so that it will do good to the listeners. Lit. "so that it gives grace to those hearing." The minimal and maximal interpretations of the Greek term *didōmi charin* ("to give grace," here translated by "to do good"), describe the limits within which various expositions of 4:29c move: (a) Chrysostom, followed by Theodoret, understood Paul as calling for a charming mode of speech that would give pleasure to the audience and make the listeners grateful to the speaker. Indeed, Eccles 10:12 asserts, "The words of the mouth of a wise man

---

111 Abbott's translation "improvement of the occasion" is probably misleading.

112 Unlike the genitive "[upbuilding] of the body," in 4:12.

113 Dibelius, p. 88; cf. Schlier, p. 226; Spicq, *Theologie morale*, II, 525 n. 4.

114 The diction found in 4:25 ff. is distinct from that of most other parts of Ephesians for its bluntness. Hardly any trace of liturgical pomp or repetition is present. Ethical tradition is seldom hymnic in character.

115 See Eph 2:20–22; 4:12, 16; I Thess 5:11; I Cor 3:9; 8:1, 10; 10:23; 14:3–5, 12, 17, 26.

116 Gaugler, p. 195. A variant reading (the first hand in Codex Claramontanus; Codex Boernerianus [G]; also Vetus Itala and the Clementine Vulg.) replaces the noun "need" by "faith." This variant solves many problems: if faith is to be built up, the vexing alternative, Individual or Communal Construction, disappears. But the variant reading is spurious not only because of its rather weak attestation but even more because it is obviously an attempt to replace an apparent lack of clarity by a simplifying version.

are grace," and Luke 4:22 reports, "All spoke well of him [Jesus] and wondered at the gracious words that proceeded from his mouth" (cf. Col 4:6).[117] Chrysostom's own rhetoric was a great mixture of depth, flamboyancy, and mellowness. The pearls from his mouth drew well-deserved applause. However, it is not certain whether in Eph 4:29 the noun "grace" (*charis*) really means— as it often does in classical Greek—no more than "charm." In Pauline diction the gift of gracious speech would be called a *charisma* rather than a *charis*. Also this graciousness would be described as a gift given to the speaker rather than "to the listener." It is unlikely that Paul, whose own rhetorical power was not beyond reproach,[118] should have expected all the saints to become Chrysostoms. (b) Instead of referring to distinguished oratory, the term "grace" in 4:29 may point to God's grace and power, and therefore may have the same meaning here as in the phrase "to give grace" (3:2, 7).[119] The grace to be given to all hearers is particularly the gift of "hearing" and "believing"; cf. 1:13: "You have heard the true word . . . And after you came to faith you, too, have been sealed."[120] Eph 4:29 may charge the saints to converse with their fellow men in such a way that their words become a vehicle and demonstration of the very grace of God. Indeed, several NT authors ascribe such power to words spoken by Christians: the peace greeting uttered by Christ's messengers brings peace to a house; the words of forgiveness they pronounce mean no less than God's own forgiveness; the gospel proclaimed by Paul and others is "God's" own "power of salvation."[121] Therefore, 4:29 can be understood to say that dialogue is a sacrament.[122] This verse is then specifically remarkable for three reasons. (1) In congruence with the elevation of the "ministry of the word"[123] it attributes to speech above all (and, perhaps, exclusively) the power to communicate God's grace. (2) It opposes clericalism, for *all* saints (not solely some special officers among them) are urged to administer the "sacrament of the word." (3) It fights a narrow and egotistic ecclesiasticism because the identity of the hearers is not specified: not only the fellow saints are beneficiaries to the grace conveyed by the testimony of the saints. The exegetical criteria available today are not sufficient for definitely excluding either of these expositions. Whereas the first interpretation appears to lay too much stress on aesthetics, the second comes close to magical notions regarding the transforming power of the right formula properly intoned. Unless subsequent statements of Ephesians contribute toward solving the puzzle of 4:29c, no single convincing exposition is as yet available.

30. *And do not grieve the Holy Spirit of God [for he is the seal] with which*

---

[117] Compare the role of grace in e.g. Exod 3:21; Luke 2:52; 6:32-33—though in these verses the reference to "grace" is not related to gracious "words."

[118] II Cor 10:10; I Cor 2:1, 4, 13; II Peter 3:15-16.

[119] See, e.g. Thomas Aquinas; Scott; Schlier; Gaugler.

[120] The close relation among the words "preaching," "hearing," and "obeying" is also illustrated by Gal 3:2, 5; Rom 1:5, 16.

[121] Matt 10:13; 16:19; 18:18; John 20:23; Rom 1:16.

[122] The meaning of this proposition can either be determined by the Reformation teaching on the character and power of "preaching the word" (see e.g. *Confessio Augustana* V, and *Second Helvetic Confession* I) or by the more general sense of "sacrament of dialogue" in M. Buber's thought. Cf. Bengel, *Magna vis in colloquiis piis.* Schlier, p. 226, speaks of "spending grace"; C. Spicq, *Théologie morale,* II, 525, of "communicating a grace"; Gaugler, p. 96 calls speech a "supernatural power, a mediator of grace." In modern, late-Heideggerian, terminology the self-communication of true being through the speech-event (*Sprachereignis*) may mean something analogous.

[123] See the exposition of 1:13; 2:20; 4:11 in the NOTES and COMMENTS.

you have been marked for the day of liberation. Lit. ". . . by which you have been sealed . . ." The literary peculiarities, the character, and the substance of this verse, especially the meaning of "grieving the Spirit," will be discussed in COMMENT VII. Earlier it was shown why, despite a strong trend among commentators, Eph 4:30 ought not to be understood as a reference to baptism.[124] In 4:13 the author of Ephesians has given a description of "the day of liberation" and of the transformation it involves (cf. 1:14).[125]

31–32. *Every kind of bitterness, passion, anger . . . shall be taken away from you . . . Be good . . . Be warm-hearted. Forgive . . . just as God. . . .* This summary admonition differs from the exhortations in the preceding verses. No longer are specific actions and attitudes treated individually, following the pattern (a) prohibition of wicked behavior, (b) commandment of proper action, (c) motivation for obedience. Instead, two brief catalogues of opposite actions are presented,[126] characteristic of the Old and the New Man respectively, and one short and striking motive is added, God's forgiveness. The introduction of the motivation by "just as" and the phrase, "God has forgiven you in Christ" (the latter occurs nowhere else in Pauline epistles) may reveal an allusion to a liturgical or catechetical formula.[127]

31. *bitterness, passion, anger, shouting, cursing. . . .* The arrangement of these terms is climactic. The catalogue moves from a hidden state of the heart to public disgrace caused by words. Just as in previous passages so here too the role of spoken words is paid primary attention. In one of Philo's writings "bitterness" is the first item in a similar catalogue of vices; Aristotle described "bitterness" as the attitude that creates a lasting wrath, hard to reconcile, and sustaining anger for a long time. "Passion" is that excitement which according to Stoic teaching indicates that an outburst of "anger" or fury is at hand; it is to be totally shunned by the wise man.[128] In Acts 19:28; 23:19 (cf. Luke 23:23), "shouting" is characteristic of a mob or assembly that covers up the lack of sober arguments by its loudness. But the verb and noun are also used to denote prophetic speech, intensive prayer, or the expression of pain.[129] In many cultures lifting the voice to the level of shouting has a magical meaning, and the next term used by Paul indicates that he, too, associated with shouting the throwing of a spell over one's fellow men: "cursing" (*blasphēmiā,* lit. "blasphemy") means a violent form of slandering or reviling, including the use of ominous and dirty words. In both non-biblical and biblical literature, God or man, or both, may be the object of such cursing.[130] This does not, however, prove that Eph 4:32 speaks of "blasphemy against God and man."[131] Other ethical lists contain the same term and show

[124] See COMMENT XVI on 1:3–14. The opposite opinion is represented, e.g. by Thomas Aquinas and Schlier.

[125] See esp. COMMENT VII on 4:1–16.

[126] See COMMENT VIII for a discussion of the origin, parallels, and meaning of such lists.

[127] In Col 3:13, however, the traces of pre-Pauline diction have practically vanished: "just as" is matched by "so also"; "the Lord" rather than "God in Christ" is the subject of forgiveness. See the third NOTE on 4:32 regarding the Pauline origin of the verb used for "forgiving."

[128] Philo *de ebr.* 223; Aristotle *eth. Nic.* IV 5 1126A; among the Stoics, see, e.g. Diogenes Laertius *de clarorum philosophorum vitis* VII 114.

[129] Luke 1:42; John 1:15; 7:28, etc.; Heb 5:7; Rev 14:18; 21:4.

[130] Biblical examples for *blasphēmiā* directed against God are LXX Ezek 35:12; Dan (Theod.) 3:96; Mark 2:7; 3:29; 14:64; John 10:33, 36; Rom 2:24; James 2:7; Jude 8, 10; Rev 13:5–6.

[131] Despite Gaugler's and others' opinion to the contrary. See Abbott, p. 144.

that sometimes *blasphēmiā* is directed exclusively against men.[132] This term may have been chosen in order to show that one's fellow man is under God's protection: he who reviles his brother by using profane speech shouts obscenities against God.

shall be taken away from you. In the first three petitions of the Lord's Prayer (Matt 6:9–10) the same form of the imperative ("shall" with a passive verb) combines two meanings. E.g. in the first petition God is asked to sanctify his name by his own power, and at the same time he is implored to make men sanctify his name. Equally in Eph 4:31 the taking away (*arthētō*) of all malice from man certainly cannot be effected by man's Herculean effort alone. While God must do it himself, man is called upon not to resist the lifting away of "malice" but to set all his energy upon "stripping off" what belongs to the "Old Man" (4:22, 25). In Johannine literature the verb "to take away" (*airō*) is used in a double sense. E.g. in John 1:29 and I John 3:5 it signifies both the carrying and the removing of sin or sins. The OT formula *nāśā ᶜāwōn* has the same double meaning. However, in Eph 4:31 "taking away" has only the second of these senses, as the words "from you" and the parallel term "strip off" in 4:22, 25 demonstrate. The opposite of having all evil "taken away" from one's shoulders would be "to bear one's guilt."[133] While according to 4:3; Gal 6:2, the saints are to bear the fellow saints and their burdens, bitterness and other forms of malice are by no means humanly bearable or tolerable. They must disappear. The evangelical character of Paul's ethics is plain: it is good news to hear that all malice can and shall be shaken off because it is being "taken away" by God. The imperative "be taken away from you" contains the indicative of the following verse, "God has in Christ forgiven you."[134] In I Cor 5:2, 13 Paul uses the verb "take away" to describe the removal of an evildoer from the congregation (cf. Deut 17:7; 19:19, etc.). In Col 2:14 the same term is a parallel to the "wiping out" of the IOU or bond that was held against the saints. "Live as people who are forgiven!"—this is the sum of Eph 4:31–32.

together with any [other sort of] malice. The attempt has been made[135] to define malice as a sixth vice beside the five previously listed, e.g. as "meanness of mind" or "plotting wicked deeds" which stands in contrast to humaneness, equity, and charitable thoughts and plans. The Shepherd of Hermas[136] describes in detail how the presence of ill temper, silliness, etc., creates an overcrowding in man which compels the "delicate" (i.e. the Holy) Spirit to depart. Indeed, the preposition "with" (*syn*, in our translation "together with," cf. *meta* in 6:23) may have the sense of the conjunction "and."[137] However, it is more likely that "malice" is a summary concept which includes the five kinds

---

[132] Mark 7:22; I Cor 4:13; Col 3:8; I Tim 1:13; 6:4; II Tim 3:2; Titus 3:2.

[133] Synonyms for "bearing sin(s)" are found, e.g. in Exod 28:43; Lev 5:1; 19:8; Isa 53:4, 11; for "taking away iniquity" and guilt by making atonement in Exod 10:7; 34:7; Micah 7:8; LXX I Kings[I Sam] 15:25.

[134] Instead of the phrase, "carrying away iniquity," e.g. in LXX Gen 50:17; Ps 84:3[85:2] a terminology is used that expresses "forgiveness."

[135] E.g. by Calvin; cf. also A. Vögtle, *Die Tugend- und Lasterkataloge im Neuen Testament,* NTAbh 16 (1936), 124 and 214.

[136] *Mand.* v 2:4–7.

[137] This is the case in the Semitic use of "with," e.g. in 1QS iv 7, 8. In enumerations, the preposition "in" is used in a similar sense; see Eph 4:19; 5:26; 6:24; 1QS iv 13, etc., following K. G. Kuhn, NTS 7 (1960–61), 537.

of wickedness mentioned before. The end of 4:31 is in this case equivalent to Greek *ktl* (*kai ta loipa*) and English "and so on" or "etc." A similar generalizing summary is found in 1:21, where after listing by name four different groups or dimensions of the "powers" a summary reference is made to "any title bestowed" beside those mentioned. This way of terminating a list is more than a literary device to exhibit the author's unexhausted resources and prevent the reader's boredom. It acknowledges incompleteness, the sample character of the specific things mentioned by name, and, above all, the absence of any belief that the evil powers can be banned or at least controlled by the sheer pronouncement of all the proper titles or definitions. On the other hand, the apostle is aware that the very "mention" of vicious forms of behavior is a threat to the congregation (5:3–4). Therefore he gives examples only, and does not pretend to have canvassed and eventually covered the whole realm of evil.

32. *Be good to one another.* It is possible that goodness, warmheartedness, and forgiveness are alternatives to bitterness, passion, and anger respectively. "Goodness" (*chrēstotēs,* derived from the adjective good, *chrēstos,* 4:32) is in Titus 3:4 an attribute of God. In writing Eph 4:32; 5:1, Paul presupposes that God himself is the model of "goodness" for in the context he admonishes the saints to be followers of God, "Be imitators of God" (5:1)! C. Spicq calls the goodness of the saints "an epiphany of God's *chrēstotēs.*"[138] In Luke 6:35 God is praised as the one who is "good to the ungrateful and evildoers." The translation "kind," instead of "good," is found, e.g. in RSV and Phillips. But since "kind" may possess a connotation of condescendence or softness, it is less appropriate than a term that describes a firm and reliable attitude.

Be warm-hearted. Etymologically the Greek adjective (*eusplagchnos,* here interpreted by an imperative because of the preceding command, "Be . . .") characterizes a person "having healthy bowels," or "having a firm, stout heart."[139] This term is not found in the LXX, but it occurs in the apocryphal Prayer of Manasseh (7), the *Testaments of Zebulon* (IX 7) and *of Simeon* (IV 4), and in I Peter 3:8, as well as in the Magic Papyri; in these writings it means "compassionate," "tender-hearted." The underlying anthropology is common to Hebrews and Greeks: the bowels or kidneys are considered the seat of emotion and intention.[140] In the main languages of Europe, this role is attributed to the "heart." See COMMENT VI for a discussion of the trio "hands, lips, heart" in Eph 4:28, 29, 32.

Forgive one another. The Greek verb *charizomai,* used here and in the parallel Col 3:13, is distinct from the verb *aphiēmi* (cf. the noun *aphēsis*) which is employed in the Gospels and Acts whenever these books speak of "forgiveness."[141] *Charizomai* means originally "to grant a favor," "to give cheerfully." In this sense it occurs several times in the latest books of the LXX and in the NT.[142] Vulg. and Erasmus have interpreted Eph 4:32 correspondingly. But in

[138] *Théologie morale,* II, 800–1.
[139] These meanings are found in the writings of Hippocrates and Euripides, respectively.
[140] Col 3:12 expresses the same notion when it speaks of (lit.) "bowels of compassion," that is, bowels moved by compassion.
[141] Mark 1:4; 2:7, 9; 3:28–29; Matt 6:12, 14; 18:21, 35; 26:28; Acts 2:38; 8:22, etc.
[142] Luke 7:21; Acts 3:14; equally in the majority of cases in the uncontested Pauline letters, e.g. Gal 3:18; I Cor 2:12; Rom 8:32, etc. Cf. the "pouring out" and "lavishing" of grace mentioned in Eph 1:6–8.

Col 2:13 and in unquestioned Pauline texts[143] the verb means unequivocally "to pardon." It is therefore safe to assume that in Eph 4:32 it has this meaning. The Greek pronoun rendered by "one another" is different from the one used at the beginning of this verse (*heautois*, not *eis allēlous*). Did Paul wish to show that what the saints do to one another they actually do to themselves?[144] The change of pronouns is rather to be explained as a rhetorical device to avoid monotony.[145] Just like 1:15 and 4:2 also 4:32 reveals a certain restriction of love, or in this case of forgiveness. Forgiveness is a form and manifestation of the love that rules or is to rule inside the circle of the saints. This does not make the command to forgive any easier to fulfill. On the contrary, the misdeed or failure of a well-known and trusted brother hurts more, and is forgiven and forgotten with more difficulty, than the behavior of a Genghis Khan, Nero, or Attila. No man can really forgive a man whom he does not personally know. How often are the saints to "forgive one another," cf. Matt 18:21? Paul uses an aorist form to describe God's forgiveness, for God's forgiveness was granted once and for all, the sin against the Spirit notwithstanding.[146] Yet in the imperative part of 4:32 the present tense indicates that forgiveness among the saints is to be ever new.[147]

just as. While in the parallel (Col 3:13) the term "just as" is matched by the following "so also," Eph 4:32 contains more than a mere comparison between God's and man's forgiveness: the source and norm of mutual forgiveness is made explicit. Since elsewhere in Ephesians the same conjunction, "just as," introduces a quotation, it is possible that here too a citation from a hymn or confession is announced in the briefest possible form.[148]

God has forgiven you in Christ. A group of MSS and early fathers contain the variant reading ". . . has forgiven us."[149] This variant crudely interrupts two long series of second person plural forms ("you") found in the context, but it is so well attested that it may represent an original (pre-Pauline?) text which contained the "we"-form of the diction typical of early hymns. "We" recurs in 5:2. Still, the reading "you" may be preferable, for just as the preceding verses alluded in the form of direct address ("you . . .") to traditional ethical teachings, so the end of 4:32 appears to continue the admonition in the same didactic rather than hymnic style. The relation between God, Christ, and the Christians is expressed in terms similar to II Cor 5:19, "In Christ God was reconciling the world to himself." Paul does not substitute Christ for God or deny that "God alone can forgive sins" (Mark 2:7; Matt 6:12, 14–15). In

---

[143] II Cor 2:7, 10; 12:13; see also Josephus *ant.* vi 144.
[144] Abbott mentions this interpretation of Origen and others, and he rejects it.
[145] A similar change is made, e.g. in Col 3:13 and I Peter 4:8–10.
[146] See COMMENT VII below.
[147] Matt 18:22; cf. Gen 4:24. The idiomatic expression "to forgive" or "to avenge seventy-seven [or seven times seventy] times," not only "seven times," means unlimited, not only generous forgiveness, viz. or revenge. In homiletical terms, the symbolic number seventy-seven may be paraphrased by "every day of the week throughout a man's life." When in Matt 6:12 the aorist is used twice to describe God's *and* man's forgiveness, the ever new granting of forgiveness is not excluded. However, there the accent is not set upon repetition or continuity, but upon granting forgiveness here and now.
[148] 1:4; 4:21; 5:2, 25. The conjunction "therefore" (5:1; cf. 2:19; 4:1) would then signal the end of the quote and the return to Paul's own formulations.
[149] Papyrus 49; Codex Vaticanus; Greek text of Codex Claramontanus, etc. For full documentation see GNT, p. 674. It is noteworthy, however, that sometimes the same codices that in 4:32 replace "you" by "we" substitute "you" for "we" in 5:2. In our translation the text-critical decisions made by E. Nestle and GNT for 4:32 and 5:2 have been followed.

2:13–18 the apostle has described Jesus Christ as sacrifice and priest at the same time. Through the sacrifice of the Messiah God granted that forgiveness which according to Heb 7–10 (cf. Rom 3:21–26) was foreshadowed by the sacrificial institutions of Israel.[150] Thus the exhortation in Eph 4:25–32 ends with a summary of the message that "saves" (1:13); the people who were dead in sins and raised by sheer grace, that is, those who are forgiven, are called and equipped to be witnesses to God's grace in their behavior toward one another. These sinners are sanctified. Through them God will publicly manifest his own goodness and wisdom (2:7; 3:10).

COMMENTS I–VIII on 4:17–32

I Structure and Summary

The whole of Eph 4 is a manifesto declaring the inseparability of ecclesiology and ethics: both are founded upon the coming and the proclamation of Jesus Christ. While the first half puts more stress on the order, purpose, and life of the church as a whole, the second part (vss. 17–32) emphasizes above all those things that constitute the conduct and motivation of each single saint. But the two sections are not exclusive: ecclesiology is ethics, and ethics is ecclesiology.

The subdivisions of the second half of Eph 4 are easily distinguished. Section A (vss. 17–19) offers a piercing study of, and a penetrating warning about, the Ephesians' former pagan conduct. Section B (vss. 20–21b) calls to mind the school in which the saints have learned ways better than those of the Gentiles. The total of their instruction is presented, probably in pre-Pauline terms, in section C (vss. 21c–24): have done with subservience to the Old Man, let the New Man take over; then you will be totally renewed! Subdivisions B and C show how the break-away from the abysmal wickedness described in section A was and is effected: it is a transformation characterized by intellectual, moral, and existential events. In the last section, D (vss. 25–32), examples are given that illustrate the change from old to new. Almost each one of verses 25–32, or each group of two, contains the same sequence of an interdiction of the old conduct, an exhortation to the new way of life, and a strong motivation. References to the mouth, the hands, the heart of the saints show that the whole mind and each part of the body of those who are members of the one body of Christ are claimed and enabled to serve the Lord. When Paul draws up a list of exemplary evil and good works, he does not shy away from the borderlines of casuistry.

While the condemnation of pagan conduct echoes 2:11–12 and Rom 1:18–32, the emphasis placed upon instruction resembles Eph 1:13, 17–18 and e.g. Rom 6:7; 16:17. Also, the image of a robe that is to be put off or on, and the reference to an "Old" and a "New Man," have some parallels in uncontested Pauline letters (see COMMENT V). In Eph 4:22–24 the clothing image and the Old/New Man metaphor are combined in a way that has a close analogy only in Col 3:9–10. Detailed exhortations are found in all Pauline

---

[150] See 5:2 and COMMENT V on 2:11–22 for the understanding of Christ's death as a sacrifice.

letters. Neither their form, nor their substance, nor the addition of motivations was invented by Paul; the author of Ephesians was acquainted with the traditional ways of teaching ethics. However, while ethical instruction among Greeks and Jews, and sometimes among Christians, too, is often tainted by intellectualistic, dualistic, moralistic, or legalistic features, the apostle gives the traditional material a distinctly theological basis and an evangelical ring. The truth of "Jesus," the presence of the "Spirit," and the forgiveness of "God" granted in Christ form the backbone of the ethical calls (see Eph 4:21, 30, 32). The relationship of the saints as members of one body, the exclusion of any legal claim of the devil upon the saints, the right of the needy to receive support, the opportunity to help one's fellow man by good works, to address him with true and constructive words and to meet him with goodness (vss. 25, 27, 28, 29, 32)—these social acts of response to the work and presence of Christ, the Spirit, and God are the foundation of Paul's exhortation. A reference to personal rewards is not made. God and the grace granted to one's neighbor are the basis of the ethics unfolded in this passage.

Each of the subdivisions in 4:17-32 presents a specific exegetical problem. The issues are now to be discussed in the order of their appearance.

II   The Indictment of the Gentiles

The strong words used in Eph 4:17-19 to describe and denounce the Gentiles' way of life take up elements of Jewish apologetics. Similar terminology occurs again in Christian apologetic writings.[151] It seems surprising that the man who is an apostle *for* the Gentiles should engage in a wholesale denunciation of their thought and conduct. Why does he not make an exception either for certain cultural values or exceptionally virtuous personalities, or at least for certain good elements or a potential that might inhere in all mankind?[152] Three observations may contribute to understanding his harsh words.

a) The core of the Gentiles' error and futility is their idolatry; the epitome of all vanity and futility is the idol. He who "goes after" false gods "becomes worthless" himself (Jer 2:5) and can demonstrate nothing else but futility (III Macc 6:11).[153] This is true not only of the pagans; the condemnation of the Gentiles' idolatry is matched, and perhaps overshadowed, by the condemnation of Israel whenever this people has chosen false gods and served them. According to Rom 1:18-23 the "wrath of God" is kindled against "every man" who "suppresses truth" and "righteousness" by neglecting or distorting the plain manifestation and the distinctly offered knowledge of God. Nothing in Rom 1 indicates that only the Gentiles are meant; rather the biblical passages to which

---

[151] See, e.g. Wisd Sol 12-15; 18:10-19; *Aristeas* 140, 277, etc.; *Sib. Or.* III 220-35; IV 1 ff.; V 219 ff.; Rom 1:18-32; *Diogn.* II; Moore, *Judaism*, II, 385; StB, IV, 1250-51, Index under "Nichtisraeliten"; the *Derek Eretz* literature discussed in G. Klein, *Der älteste christliche Katechismus* (Berlin: Reimer, 1909), 137 ff.; Davies, PRJ, 132 ff. See also W. Sanday and A. C. Headlam, *The Epistle to the Romans,* ICC, 5th ed. (Edinburgh: Clark, 1958), pp. 49-52; O. Kuss, *Der Römerbrief* I, 2d ed. (Regensburg: Pustet, 1963), 34-42; P. Dalbert, *Die Theologie der hellenistisch-jüdischen Missions-Literatur,* TF 4, 1954.

[152] The question whether in Rom 2:14-15 some unregenerate Gentiles are exempted from condemnation cannot be discussed in this context. Exegetical arguments supporting the rejection of "a Christian theory of natural law" are collected, e.g. by F. Flückiger, "Die Werke des Gesetzes bei den Heiden," TZ 8 (1952), 17-42; and M. Barth, "Natural Law in the Teachings of St. Paul," in *Church-State Relationships in Ecumenical Perspective,* ed. E. Smith (Pittsburgh: Duquesne, 1966), pp. 113-51.

[153] See also Jer 8:19; LXX Esther 4:17 par.; Acts 14:15, etc.

Rom 1:23 alludes originally condemn Israel's deviation.[154] Because of their willful "refusal to know God" which closely resembles Israel's similar refusal, the Gentiles are indicted in the NT.[155] Sometimes Jews and Gentiles together are called ignorant, or it is pointed out that there is no distinction between them—though the Jews sin against the law, the Gentiles sin without possessing the law.[156] Since Ephesians is directed only to pagan-born Christians, the epistle speaks solely of the Gentiles' sin and futility. Earlier and elsewhere, e.g. in 2:3; Rom 2:17 ff., Paul spoke of the trespasses and sins of the Jews, thus showing the solidarity of Jews and Gentiles. Never did he make accusations against the Jews for the purpose of supporting Gentile prejudices. Gentiles are given no reason to feel superior to Jews. By looking at themselves and their own sin, not by looking at the Jews and condemning them, Gentiles realize what sin is.[157] Jew and Gentile—each has to sweep before his own house and to bear his own burden (Eph 2:2–3).

b) The scandalous conduct resulting from idolatry is described by the three Greek nouns "lasciviousness," "impurity," and "greed." They are rendered in our translation of 4:19 by "debauchery," "filthy things," and "still ask for more." These attitudes and actions are mentioned again in the same sequence in 5:3, 5, but there the term "fornication" is substituted for "debauchery." "Robbers" instead of "practitioners of impurity" occurs in a similar triad in I Cor 5:10–11.[158] On one occasion these evil works are described as (natural?) results of the depravity of the mind; another time they are shown to be God's punishment upon men who misuse their intelligence to fabricate and venerate idols. More often the causal connection between idolatry and evil works is not made explicit, but evil works are mentioned in association with idol-worship, or simply identified with idolatry itself.[159] In their tirades against Israel the

---

[154] Jer 2:11; Deut 4:15–19; Ps 106:19–22; Wisd Sol 12:24.

[155] Rom 10:3; Acts 3:17; 13:27; Eph 4:18c, etc.; cf. Acts 17:30 (also 17:23?). See also OT texts such as Isa 1:3; Jer 8:7.

[156] I Cor 2:8?; Luke 23:24; Gal 2:15; Rom 2:12; 3:22–23.

[157] The Augustinian opinion (found e.g. in enarr. in Pss. LVII[LVI] 7 that the Jews exemplify to all the world the rebellion, confusion, and blindness of man (see also K. Barth, Church Dogmatics, II 2 [Edinburgh: Clark, 1957], 198), is not supported by the testimony of Eph 4:17–19; 2:11–12; Rom 1:18–32.

[158] See also the catalogues of vices in Mark 7:21–22; Rom 1:29; I Clem. 35:5; Barn. XX 1; Did. v 1. Only in the last two of these texts is "idolatry" listed among other vices. The absence of an explicit reference to "idolatry" from several lists of vices demonstrates that the original source of these catalogues cannot be located exclusively in Jewish catechetical instruction for converts from paganism. Cf. Test. Levi XIV 5–8. In CD IV 17–18 "fornication," "wealth," "desecration of the sanctuary" are mentioned in succession, and Jews are warned against committing these sins. On the other hand, following Acts 7:41–43, Stephen quoted Amos in order to demonstrate to Jewish listeners that because of their idolatrous actions God had delivered the children of Israel to idolatry (sic!). R. H. Charles, Apocrypha and Pseudepigrapha, II (Oxford: Clarendon, 1913), 809; W. D. Davies, "Paul and the Dead Sea Scrolls: Flesh and Spirit," in SaNT, p. 174; S. Wibbing, Die Tugend- und Lasterkataloge im Neuen Testament, BhZNW 25 (1959), 112, believe that the enumeration of "lasciviousness," "impurity," "greed" in Eph 4:19; 5:3, 5 demonstrates the dependence of Ephesians on a Qumran tradition. But in CD IV the arrangement of the three wicked attitudes and corresponding actions is different; the defilement of the Jerusalem temple is the heart of impurity; and trespasses of the leader of the community against the vow of celibacy and of all community members against the avowed monogamy and poverty may be in mind. The impurity mentioned in Ephesians is hardly to be identified with the desecration of the Jerusalem temple, and the noun pleonexiā, translated by "and still ask for more," is not necessarily a description of the wealth prohibited by the statutes of Qumran.

[159] Cf. Eph 4:18–19 and Rom 1:24–29 with Eph 5:3, 5; Col 3:5; I Cor 5:10–11; 6:9–10. In Test. Judah XIX 1, "love of money"; in Test. Reub. IV 6 "fornication" is said to "lead to" idolatry. Polycarp Phil. XI 2 warns, "If any man does not abstain from avarice he will be defiled by idolatry." But according to Wisd Sol 14:12, 14 "the idea of making idols was the beginning of fornication," or ". . . the beginning and cause and end of every evil." Thus the causal connection between idolatry and moral depravity is described in multiple ways. Theodoret explained the bond

classic prophets of the OT as well as Deuteronomy and the Deuteronomic redactors of Israel's historic traditions attacked the cultic prostitution which was typical of Canaanite sanctuaries and threatened to invade Israel's worship. While there is no doubt that Paul warned of idolatry in the course of his missionary work to the Gentiles (see e.g. I Thess 1:9), Ephesians gives an example of the same warning addressed to Christians. Here the accusation is aimed at those designated to form God's house, not at those outside God's people. Occasionally Paul affirms that his intention is anything but to "condemn those outside": he wants no more than to keep God's house clean (see I Cor 5:6-13 and Eph 5:3-5). "Cleanse out the old leaven" (I Cor 5:7).

c) In 4:17-19 special emphasis is laid upon the connection between cogitation and conduct, resolve and actual behavior. Paul allows for no subterfuges and excuses that may be sought in the alleged tragic conflict between soul and body, theory and practice, or willing and doing.[160] "Futility of the mind" is the human condition in which the Gentiles "do their thing"; at the same time it is also the motivation behind their conduct and the result of their behavior. Stress is not placed just upon the baseness of the Gentiles' mentality, nor upon deficient theory which involves inept practice. Rather Paul emphasizes the complete harmony between the Gentiles' mind and action. The whole man is under judgment, including the best he presumes to possess: his reason, his mind, his intelligence, his will, his emotion. In Eph 4:22 this man in his totality is called the "Old Man": neither his alleged noble thoughts nor his voluntary or involuntary achievements count for anything. He cannot be repaired but is to be relinquished, thrown off in favor of the totally "New Man" (vss. 22, 24). The reference made in 4:23 to the "renewal in mind and spirit" makes no exception; it corresponds to the determining role ascribed to the "mind" in 4:17. Even that which is deemed best in man has to become completely new. When the LXX occasionally, and NT authors frequently, rendered the Hebrew verb and the corresponding nouns "turning around," "turning back" (shub, shubah, etc.), by, "repent" (meta-noeō, lit. "re-think") and "repentance,"[161] they do not intend to limit repentance to a merely intellectual act. Rather they chose a terminology which would inform Greek hearers and readers that the whole

---

between avarice and idolatry by referring to Matt 6:24: Love of money is worship of the god Mammon. The silversmith Demetrius of Ephesus may be described by Luke as an example of this connection (Acts 19:24 ff.). However, there are no explicit rabbinic parallels to the equation avarice-idolatry, according to StB, II, 606-7.

[160] In Rom 7:14-23 a conflict between will and performance, the law of God and the flesh, the inner man and the members of the body is described at length and in moving terms. Classic Greek philosophers as well as Gnostics have portrayed similar tensions. Every honest man's experience bears testimony to it. When Paul concludes his discourse by crying out, "Wretched man that I am" (Rom 7:24), he seems to join in the self-pitying lamentation to which existentialists of all ages are prone. Yet he does not use the tension between will and performance as an excuse. Nor does he presume that without God, without God's law, and without the work and "law" of the Spirit, man's own nature (e.g. his being soul and body at the same time) guarantees his engagement in the holy struggle of the Spirit against the flesh. Even if Rom 2:15 described natural man's struggle (but see the literature mentioned in fn. 152) it still would not speak of the struggle of the mind against the body. Rather the text mentions accusations and excuses exchanged between man's different thoughts: "Their conflicting thoughts accuse or perhaps excuse them."

[161] E.g. Jer 8:6; 38[31]:19; Matt 3:2; 4:17; Acts 2:38. In Acts 3:19; 26:20 the two Greek verbs "repent" ("re-think") and "turn back" are used in combination: they interpret one another mutually.

man needs and is granted renewal.[162] They wanted to say that in the light of the greatness of God's gift, even man's greatest possessions, capacities, and performances, including those of the cultured Greeks and the uncounted "noble savages," lose their glory; they "fall short of the glory of God" (Rom 1:23). To repeat an earlier observation, Paul makes the same judgment in regard to Jewish pride and heritage (see II Cor 3:10; Rom 3:3; 9:31–10:3; Philip 3:8). The Jews are as much under God's wrath as are the Gentiles (Eph 2:3).

Thus the indictment of the Gentiles in Eph 4 presents at least three prophetic features: (a) It is made in the name of God who is jealous of false gods and has decided to save not only the Jews but also the Gentiles from futile religion and conduct. Thus the gracious judgment of God is proclaimed, but not as a result of sociological or cultural analysis. (b) Rather than proclaiming a judgment over "those outside" (I Cor 5:12–13)—who according to Eph 2:13, 17 are no longer "far off"!—Paul impugns and warns the saints inside the church. (c) The denunciation of all those subject to futility is not an end in itself. Just as the formulation "dead in lapses and sins" was a post-resurrection statement rather than a *post-mortem*,[163] so the retrospective description of the Gentiles' status and way in 2:11–12; 4:17–19 stands under the caption, "No more." It does not provide a program or example for further elaborations: "Leave the dead to bury their dead" (Matt 8:22).

III   The School of the Messiah

The Greek original of Eph 4:20–21 contains no less than three surprising forms of diction. Individually considered, each of them may be no more than a sample of an extraordinary use of language; the NT, especially the book of Revelation but also the undisputed Pauline epistles, contains a great number of such examples. Still, taken together the three baffling expressions found in Eph 4:20–21 may well bear testimony to a specific idea: the image of a Messianic school. Allusions to a certain school, or to various Christian schools, have been discovered in other NT contexts.[164]

a) Eph 4:20 says in literal translation, "You have learned the Messiah." The phrase "to learn a person" is found nowhere else in the Greek Bible, and so far it has not been traced in any pre-biblical Greek document. "Learning the Messiah" probably means more than merely learning of his existence or learning to know his doctrines. While other texts affirm that Jesus Christ is "preached,"[165] "known," "received," or "believed,"[166] Eph 4:20 affirms that the same Christ is also the subject matter of "learning." In Rom 6:17 a

---

[162] In COMMENT IV C on 3:14–21 it was observed that in Eph 3:16 the term "inner man" probably does not denote the human "mind"; only in Rom 7:22–23 is the "inner man" identified with the "mind" of (regenerate!) man.

[163] See COMMENT III on 2:1–10.

[164] See, e.g. James 3:1; Heb 5:12; Matt 23:1–12. According to B. Gerhardson, *Memory and Manuscript*, ASNU 22, 1961, Jesus gave halachic instruction to his disciples—much as a rabbi of Jesus' time might have done; a palpable result of this instruction consisted first of notebooks written by the disciples, then of a collection of such notes which took the form of Gospel accounts, finally of the canonization of the four Gospels. Among others M. Smith, "A Comparison of Early Christian and Early Rabbinic Tradition," JBL 82 (1963), 169–76, has subjected this theory to strong criticism. See also Gerhardson's rejoinder, *Tradition and Transmission in Early Christianity*, ConNT 20, 1964. Other scholars have spoken of a school of Matthew, of John, of Paul, respectively.

[165] Acts 5:42; Gal 1:16; I Cor 1:23; II Cor 1:19; Philip 1:15.

[166] Philip 4:9; I Cor 15:1–2, 11; Eph 1:13. Cf. Abbott, pp. 134–35; Schlier, p. 216.

surprising formulation is used, "You have been delivered to the type of doctrine"; the essence of that "type" is Christ himself, according to Eph 4:20.

b) Similarly the phrase, lit. "to hear him" (in our translation of 4:20, "you have listened to him") implies more than mere "hearing of him" or "hearing about him." Paul cannot have called the Ephesians (who during Jesus' lifetime lived neither in Galilee nor in Jerusalem nor anywhere near the sites of Jesus' earthly ministry) eye and ear witnesses of Jesus. Nor were they present either during the forty post-resurrection days mentioned in Acts 1:3, or during the visions and auditions experienced by Paul according to Acts and II Cor 12:1–4; Gal 2:2, etc. Thus it is all the more surprising that the saints in Asia Minor are described as people who have "listened" to the Messiah. The wording of Eph 4:20 makes sense when it is assumed (as indeed is the case, e.g. in II Cor 13:3) that "Christ" himself "speaks in" those proclaiming him. Their proclamation of peace (Eph 1:2; 6:23) is ultimately his own proclamation (2:17). See Luke 10:16, "He who hears you hears me."[167]

c) The phrase, lit. "you were taught in him" (vs. 21b), recalls the wide variety of meanings inherent in the formula "in Christ" (see COMMENT I on 1:1–2). If the diction of 4:21 is Semitic, the words "in Christ" may be equivalent to "by Christ"; in this case, Christ is understood as the teacher. Again, Christ may also be the subject matter of teaching; the beginning of vs. 20 would then be duplicated by the statement "Truth [is] in Jesus" (vs. 21b).[168] Still, it is more likely that the words "in him" describe Christ as the foundation upon, the sphere within, or the administration under which teaching and learning have taken place. Since the place where instruction is given is usually called a "school," and since the beneficiaries of planned and careful instruction are called "students," these two terms have been used in our translation of 4:20–21.

The linguistic idiosyncrasies just mentioned lead to the necessary conclusion that the author of Ephesians intended to present Christ as a message and a teacher, a lesson and a school at the same time.[169] In the Messiah school the medium and the message are not only inseparable but completely identified: here, indeed, "the medium is the message." Why and when can a school effect as great a change as the liberation from the futile Gentile way? The answer of 4:20–21 is this: when Jesus Christ is the headmaster, the teaching matter, the method, the curriculum, and the academy, then the gift of new life takes the place of a diploma.

An alternative to this ("academic") interpretation of the perplexing diction of 4:20–21 is offered by Dibelius. He refers to the *Odes of Solomon*[170] and attempts to demonstrate that in Eph 4 the words "teaching," "hearing," "learning" possess a "mystical sense" which, however, was "generalized." Still, the evidence adduced by Dibelius is too far-fetched to be convincing. Why should the mists of mysticism substitute for the sober thoughts and solid learning that befit

---

[167] Gal 1:6–9, 16 would contain an impossible claim of apostolic infallibility, if these utterances were not based upon the promised presence of Christ in the gospel proclamation of his servants. See COMMENT XV on 1:3–14.

[168] In good Greek the accusative case or an infinitive would be proper, just as in English, "I was taught calculus, or . . . to calculate" (never, "I was taught in calculus"; but compare, "I was instructed," "I received an education in mathematics").

[169] Cf. Robinson, p. 106. Schlier, p. 222, asserts that "Christ and his lesson" stand between paganism and the saints.

[170] VII 4 ff; see Dibelius, p. 86.

a school?[171] Paul trusted the effect of the apostolic ministry carried out "in the flesh" (Gal 2:20) more than the influence of "angels" (Gal 1:8) or cultic visions (Col 2:18). Though there were many witnesses of the resurrected Christ besides himself (I Cor 15:4–8), he did not suggest that the visions and revelations given to him (II Cor 12:1–4) were common experience to all believers.

Precedents for the role ascribed by Paul to schooling are found not only in Greek philosophical academies, but also in early and later rabbinic schools and in the disciplined study pursued among the Covenanters at Khirbet Qumran. In the OT, e.g. in Deut 18:22, Israel is given the privilege of receiving specific instruction: while the nations are "listening to soothsayers and diviners," God's people are promised a prophet who speaks in the name of God and is to be heeded. In Eph 4:17–24 Jesus the Messiah is the teacher or prophet who overcomes and prevents the catastrophes met along the way of the nations. The Messiah school is the alternative to perversion and futility operating in, and produced by, idolatry. Not that this school offers emotions rather than sober reasoning, or mystic experience instead of arguments! Rather here ignorance is replaced by knowledge. The refusal to know God is overcome by the joy of acknowledging God and giving him glory in mind and deed. Following Col 3:10 "knowledge" is the essence of that renewal which distinguishes the "Old Man" from the "New."[172] Such knowledge or wisdom could not be claimed as a monopoly by the "School of Matthew," or by a Pauline or Johannine School— if such schools existed at all. Whenever Christians are called students they are designated as "disciples" of Jesus Christ (Matt 23:7–11, etc.). They speak of the Spirit's teaching rather than of human wisdom, and they will not rely on the hallowed names of famous men.[173]

The context provides a means for double-checking the school imagery of Eph 4:20–21. Provided that vss. 21c–24 contain a quotation or an allusion to a text formulated before the writing of Ephesians,[174] the question is appropriate: what sort of material is cited here? The sequence, first a Christological affirmation ("Truth in Jesus") then three exhortations ("strip off . . . become new . . . put on"), is very different from the content and structure of the hymns or confessional pieces that have been used in earlier parts of Ephesians. The "we"-style is replaced by the address "you" (see also 5:14); infinitives take the place of indicatives, of aorist participles, and of relative clauses. The title line "Truth in Jesus" and the affirmation "the New Man [is] created after God's image" reflect the confessional tone and contents of a hymn, but may well belong in a different context.

Which genre is recognizable? In the quotation the verbs "stripping off" and "putting on" form one dominant pair. The same two metaphors are also found elsewhere in the NT, especially in ethical instruction.[175] In consequence, it is probable that the quoted text (if it was one piece rather than a composite of several elements) was originally part of early Christian catechetical teaching in

---

[171] Merits and problems of explaining Paul as a reconstructed mystic or reinterpreter of mystic terms have been examined in COMMENT IV A on 3:14–21.

[172] Cf. Eph 1:17–18; II Cor 3:18; 4:6, etc.

[173] I Cor 1:12–13; 2:13; 3:1–9.

[174] See the second NOTE on 4:21.

[175] I Thess 5:8; Rom 13:12, 14; Col 3:8, 12; Eph 4:25; 6:11–17; I Peter 2:1; 3:21; James 1:21; Heb 12:1.

the field of ethics.[176] The addition of the words "the instruction" in our translation is justifiable only on the basis of this assumption. No doubt the "stripping
off" and "putting on" imagery is so widespread in the NT that Paul cannot
have been its inventor; it is also unlikely that he should have totally ignored its
use by other people.

However, a more precise specification regarding the origin, character, and
function of the text underlying Eph 4:21c–24 cannot be made. (a) Though the
Gospels clearly show that Jesus' relationship to his disciples included the
teacher-student relationship after the rabbinical pattern, it is not certain
whether after his death and resurrection real Christian schools existed with
regular class meetings and textbooks (or catechisms) for instructing prospective
converts or newly baptized persons. At least no evidence is as yet attainable
when a date in the early sixties is ascribed to Ephesians. Therefore it is still
possible that the allusions made in Eph 4 to a school and to students are purely
metaphorical. (b) It is not certain whether a written form of a catechism can
be presupposed, or whether such a catechism existed only in oral forms that
were eventually fixed in writing. Nor can it be decided whether the embryonic
catechism was composed only for pagan converts. The usage of the clothing
metaphor in James 1:21; Heb 12:1 speaks against this assumption, but Eph 4:
17–19 testifies in its favor. (c) It cannot be firmly stipulated that a baptismal
setting is the only or the best frame for the words quoted in Eph 4:22–24.[177]
The one NT passage (Gal 3:27) in which the metaphor "put on" is directly associated with a reference to baptism supports this assumption. Indeed, ritual
clothing with new or white garments eventually belonged to the rite of baptism.
But this ceremonial clothing is safely attested in post-NT times only, and the
Gal 3 text is too isolated to demonstrate a general spread of the clothing ritual.
Thus there is insufficient evidence for restricting the clothing imagery to a sac-
ramental setting and meaning.

Paul appears to endorse a schoolman's conception of turning from ignorance
to wisdom, from old life to new. Does he believe that virtue can be taught and
that no more than enlightenment is necessary to do away with the essence and
existence, the mind and behavior of the Old Man? If there were no references
to the Messiah who in personal union is the teacher as well as the subject matter taught, and if there were no indications regarding the miraculous new creation of a totally new man, the apostle might be accused of putting too much
trust in an educational process, especially in learning by the communication of
knowledge. In actuality, Eph 4:19–24 can hardly be equated with a *magna
charta* of Christian education. A reference to *paideiā* ("education") is blatantly
absent. When in Gal 3:24–25 the term (literally) "pedagogue" occurs (RSV
translates, "custodian"; NEB, "tutor"; Phillips, "governess"), it is applied to the
law. There all emphasis is laid upon the transitory and subordinate, rather than
saving or life-giving role of the law in Israel's history. In Eph 4:20–21 a much
stronger accent is placed on Christ the teacher and the subject matter of learn-

---

[176] See A. Seeberg, *Der Katechismus der Urchristenheit*, Leipzig: Deichert, 1903; Carrington,
The Primitive Christian Catechism; Selwin, *First Peter*, pp. 393–406; Davies, PRJ, pp. 122–30.
[177] "The readers are reminded of their baptismal instruction," Conzelmann, p. 80. Abbott, p. 131,
may be right when he says that the put-off-on imagery is so frequently used among Greek
writers that there is no need to restrict it to baptismal catechesis.

ing than upon enlightenment and the students' progress. Being raised in the cultured cities of the Hellenistic world, the readers of Ephesians may have held that education alone was strong enough to dispel darkness and overcome evil.[178] Paul, in turn, had experienced both the potential and the limits of rabbinical schooling.[179] In Eph 4:20–21 the apostle transplants neither Hellenistic nor rabbinic, not to speak of Qumranite, notions of education upon the church. Rather the Jewish-born missionary of Jesus Christ reminds his Gentile-born readers of a school unique in kind, bearing the name of the Messiah Jesus.

The Fourth Gospel speaks (in metaphoric form, with a polemic undertone, and in favor of a "high" Christology) of Jesus the vine and of the pruning of the branches, of Jesus the shepherd and his task of uniting, of Jesus the way and of the disciples who follow him. In Eph 4 a similar inroad is made into contemporary secular and religious use of key terms: Jesus Christ is proclaimed as the only teacher, the sole teaching, the exclusive pedagogy, the one great opportunity for the creation of a new man who is free from the corruption of the old.

IV   Truth in Jesus

In Pauline writings, the use of the name "Jesus" alone is relatively rare.[180] This name appears to have its most regular place in the confessions of Jesus' Lordship and in passages speaking of his resurrection.[181] The phrase "Truth in Jesus" cannot be ascribed to either one of these. It has a Johannine ring, though it does not follow the pattern of such self-proclamations as "I am the way and the truth and the light" (John 14:6). Among the viable meanings of the acclamation "Truth in Jesus!" are the following:[182]

a) The Son of God is The Truth, i.e. he answers the question, "What is truth?" (John 18:38) by being in person the full revelation of God, the totality of God's will and promise, and the sum of the fulfillment of all that is hoped for and commanded. Perhaps his "deity" is stressed above all (cf. Matt 11:25–30), including his pre-existence and eternal glory. Indeed, the Fourth Gospel depicts him as the "revealer" of all that was hidden in God: it reports that he called himself "the truth."[183] The canonical Gospels agree in recording that at the beginning of certain statements Jesus Christ used a formula unparalleled among Jewish teachers, that is, "Amen" or "Amen, Amen" (Matt 5:18; John 1:51, etc.). Paul may allude to this peculiarity of Jesus' speech when he calls Jesus Christ the epitome of both God's promises and man's "Amen" (II Cor 1:20). A variant of the same interpretation affirms that the Son of God is totally different from all men because he "does the truth" (cf. John 3:21). He is faithful and

---

[178] See the description of Greek culture given by W. Jaeger, *Paideia* I–III, New York: Oxford University Press, 1938–44.

[179] Gal 1:13–14; Philip 3:4–11; Acts 22:3.

[180] Much more numerous are the designations "Jesus Christ," "Christ," "the Messiah," "the Messiah Jesus," "the Lord," etc.

[181] I Thess 4:2, 14; I Cor 12:3; II Cor 1:14; 4:5, 10, 11, 14; 11:4; Philip 2:10, 19; Rom 8:11; Col 3:17. In these passages Paul is probably taking up formulations used in churches not founded by himself. In Gal 6:17; II Cor 4:5b, 10–11, however, the apostle uses "Jesus" in phrases that appear to be coined by himself. W. Schmithals' divergent opinion was mentioned in fn. 34; cf. below, fn. 187.

[182] Various meanings of "truth" are systematically discussed, e.g. by Bultmann, TWNTE, I, 24–47. Westcott, pp. 70–71, present excerpts from a spirited correspondence between himself and F. J. A. Hort about the text and meaning of Eph 4:21c.

[183] 1:18; 14:6, 9, etc.; R. Bultmann, *The Gospel of John*, Philadelphia: Westminster, 1971, *passim*; idem ThNT, II, 33–69.

obedient to God—not only as an example but much more as a mediator and savior of all mankind who have "suppressed the truth in unrighteousness."[184] Jesus Christ is then the saving truth to be trusted in faith and followed in obedience. He is the presence of power and the radiance of truth in the midst of the world. Upon him depends all search for truth in reflection and conduct. But another exposition or accentuation requires equal attention.

b) The incarnation is the core of the gospel. Eph 4:21a may speak against the notion that the saints confess solely the total difference of the *Logos* (Word), Son, or Wisdom of God from man, that is, his deity or otherworldliness. What then is the criterion of orthodox doctrine and sound moral conduct if it does not consist solely in the affirmation of Christ's deity? The alternative to a "revealer" who excels by his difference from all men is the Word, Wisdom, Will of God which became "incarnate" and lives and dies among men as the "offspring of Abraham" and "David" (Gal 3:16; Rom 1:3). This incarnate one has a name that is also the name of other men, i.e. Jesus. The confession "Truth in Jesus" lays stress upon the man of Nazareth rather than on the Son's preexistence and otherness. Pauline writings emphasize that the Son sent by God was a Jew according to the flesh, born of a woman and put under the law, incorporate in the same "flesh of sin" that makes every man "weak," but obedient and faithful to God and his law where all others were disobedient, obedient even to the death on the cross, and finally vindicated by his exaltation.[185] The Gospels and Acts lay equal stress on his birth, his teaching, his healings, his suffering, his death, and his resurrection. The Messiah of whom the OT and the NT speak is distinct from a metaphysical being and from a timeless hope or process. Nowhere else but in history, in the flesh, in his death, is God present, active, and fully revealed (John 1:14).[186] Since Gnostic teachers fostered the opposite opinion, Eph 4:21c has been considered an anti-Gnostic creedal formulation, coined to counteract a separation of "the Christ" from the historical, crucified "Jesus." Rather than "a Gnostic Christ-idea," *Jesus* Christ is confessed and obeyed by the saints.[187] Thus in Eph 4, instead of the well-known and fre-

---

[184] Rom 1:18.

[185] Rom 4:25; 5:19; 8:3-4; 9:5; Gal 4:4; Philip 2:8-11; I Corr 1:23; 2:2; I Tim 3:16; cf. Heb 2:16-17; 5:7-9; 7:14; 10:5-10; I Peter 2:21-24; 3:18.

[186] According to Schmithals, *Gnosticism in Corinth*, pp. 124-32; idem, "Zwei gnostische Glossen im Zweiten Korintherbrief," EvTh 18 (1958), 552-73, esp. 552-64; cf. the revised edition of this essay in *Gnosticism in Corinth*, pp. 202-25, esp. 202-15, the Gnostics in Corinth went so far as to "curse Jesus" (I Cor 12:3). An interpolation in II Corinthians, that is, the words, "Even so we once regarded Christ from a human point of view [lit. according to the flesh], we regard him thus no longer" (II Cor 5:16), is supposed to give Paul's own teaching Gnosticizing character. But B. A. Pearson, "Did the Gnostics Curse Jesus?" JBL 86 (1967), 301-5, has shown how weakly founded the first assumption is. For the theory that II Cor 5:16 is interpolated, is supported by no textual evidence and disregards several less artificial ways of interpreting that verse, see e.g. J. Cambier, "Connaissance charnelle et spirituelle du Christ dans II Cor 5:16," in *Littérature et théologie paulinennes*, ed. A. Descamps (Louvain: Desclée de Brouwer, 1960), pp. 72-92. H. Koester, "Gnomai diaphorai," HTR 58 (1965), 279-318, esp. 287; idem, "Häretiker im Urchristentum als theologisches Problem," in *Zeit und Geschichte*, Fs. R. Bultmann, ed. E. Dinkler (Tübingen: Mohr, (1964), pp. 61-76, esp. 70-71 carefully discusses some of the problems involved. See also E. Käsemann, "Blind Alleys in the 'Jesus of History' Controversy," in *New Testament Questions of Today* (Philadelphia: Fortress, 1969), pp. 23-65.

[187] Schlier, p. 217; against this view, see Dibelius, p. 86. Without referring to Gnosticism and anti-Gnostic polemics, von Soden and Abbott converge upon an interpretation that corresponds to the anti-Gnostic exposition. The first considers "the Messiah" (or Christ, vs. 20) the subject of the sentence; since Christ is "truth in Jesus" (vs. 21c and nowhere else!), belief in Christ alone is not sufficient. Christ will be recognized in "Jesus": this happens by a life in truth. Abbott's argument runs parallel: in Christian instruction all teaching on *hope* was centered in (the idea of) "the Messiah," but questions of obedience were solved by reference to the historical person bearing the name "Jesus."

quent NT affirmation "Jesus is the Messiah,"[188] the confession, "The Logos is Jesus," viz., "The Logos [or, Christ] became incarnate in the flesh of Jesus [of Nazareth]," would be vigorously upheld, cf. John 1:14; I John 4:2. Still, there are other possibilities.

c) All that "Jesus" taught during his ministry on earth is also the essence of the church's proclamation and doctrine if the church's testimony is to be "true." There can be no ecclesiastical preaching and exhorting unless it is the same as Jesus'. The basic identity of both is an absolute necessity; the body cannot contradict the head or improve upon it. "Orthodoxy" is not only a requirement binding on the church, it is also a fact: whenever the church has been true to her Lord she has in fact always and everywhere fought distortions of Jesus' teaching and sought to obey and preach obedience to the Word incarnate.[189] If this be the meaning of the confession "Truth in Jesus," then the words contained in Eph 4:22–24 may be introduced by vs. 21c as quasi-authentic words of Jesus, or at least as an authentic summary of Jesus' own preaching. Eph 4:21 would then anticipate not only the second-century and later disputes between the orthodox fathers and their Gnostic adversaries, but also the nineteenth- and twentieth-century struggle over the historical Jesus and his relevance for faith and conduct. Perhaps this verse justifies the writing of Gospels such as those of Matthew and John, if not of an apocryphal Gospel like that of Thomas. Matthew and John reproduce an abundance of sayings and discourses, and Thomas nothing but the teachings of Jesus.[190] In addition, Eph 4:21c–24 may corroborate the evidence given by the NT passages that quote words of Jesus as the foundation of ethical instruction.[191]

d) In Eph 4:21c the noun "truth" can denote an ethical attitude, that is, a conduct true and faithful to Jesus, a walking in his footsteps. In 1:1, 15 the author of Ephesians used the terms "faithful" and "faith" to describe the saints' total relationship and attitude to Jesus Christ and to one another. Faith includes love and obedience, as the variant readings of 1:15 and Rom 1:5 show. Correspondingly the phrase "Truth in Jesus" may include trusting in Jesus, fol-

---

[188] So, e.g. Matt 16:16; John 20:31; Acts 9:22.

[189] According to A. Harnack, *What is Christianity* (New York: Putnam, 1901), p. 55, Jesus' own teaching had its center in three topics: the Kingdom of God and its coming; God the Father and the infinite value of the human soul; the higher righteousness and commandment of love. But a great chasm began to separate the church's teaching from Jesus': inspired by Paul, the church substituted the (metaphysical and speculative) doctrine of the Son. Harnack's intention was to call the church back from a high Christology to the simple teachings of Jesus. M. Kähler, *The So-Called Historical Jesus and the Historic, Biblical Christ*, Philadelphia: Fortress, 1964 (German original 1892), and R. Bultmann, *Jesus and the Word*, New York: Scribner's, 1934 (German original 1925) have strongly rebutted Harnack's analysis and conclusion. They argued that the historical Jesus (as reconstructed by historians) is not a subject-matter of faith. Rather the faith of the church depends upon the post-Easter proclamation of the exalted Lord. "The message of [the historical] Jesus is a presupposition for the theology of the New Testament rather than a part of that theology itself" (Bultmann, ThNT, I, 3). Following the summation of more recent research as presented, e.g. by J. M. Robinson, *A New Quest of the Historical Jesus*, SBT 25 (1959), esp. 46–47, 76–78, the church's proclamation of Christ is not totally devoid of a basis in Jesus' own preaching: a historian equipped with, and reliant upon, an existentialist view of history can demonstrate that there are authentic words of Jesus which call for the recovery of authentic existence by the encounter with Jesus and a specific attitude to him. Certainly the church, by preaching the resurrected Christ, urged this encounter with Jesus. Thus the church did not basically change, but rather took up and carried out the intent and content of Jesus' own teaching.

[190] See A. Guillaumont, H.-Ch. Puech, et al., *The Gospel According to Thomas*, Leiden: Brill, 1959, for the text; and R. McL. Wilson, *Studies in the Gospel of Thomas*, London: Mowbray, 1960, for a commentary.

[191] E.g. I Thess 4:15; I Cor 7:10; 11:23–25; Acts 20:35; Rev 2–3.

lowing after Jesus, confessing Jesus. Truth is in this case not only something to be said, accepted, known, and believed,[192] but also that which is to be "done" (John 3:21). The double action of "stripping off" and "putting on" (vss. 22, 24) is then decisively qualified by vs. 21c. This double action is true to Jesus or performed in Jesus when it is interpreted as a synonym of "dying and rising with Christ," of "suffering and being glorified with him," or in short, of being "conformed to his image."[193]

Though it is not impossible, it is hardly conceivable that all of these interpretations and perhaps more were intended by the unknown person or congregation who first formed the phrase "Truth in Jesus," or by the author of Ephesians, in taking up this formulation and inserting it into his epistle. There is no single literary meaning for these three words which would permit some of the suggested interpretations to be rejected as allegorical or merely homiletical. Yet a selection among the proposed alternatives should be made; some of them are more likely to be true to the author's mind than others.

Most suspect are the second and third expositions, for they impose problems upon the text of Ephesians which did not become urgent before the time either of fully developed heretical Gnosticism, or of nineteenth-century historical research. The knowledge available regarding the spiritual movements which shook the Asiatic churches during the second half of the first century A.D. is so scanty that it fails to provide a firm foundation of exegesis. To use Ephesians as primary evidence for early forms of second-century and later heresies, or of the distinction between a Jesus of history and a Christ of faith, is a dubious procedure as long as other interpretations offer a minimum of good sense. The first exposition (Johannine or incarnational) and the fourth (ethical) are nearer the historical setting of Ephesians and need not be considered mutually exclusive. The "wisdom," "word" or "truth" which, according to the Fourth Gospel, to some Synoptic sayings, to Hebrews, to Paul and other NT books, is incarnate in Jesus, is also the wisdom, word, and truth of right conduct. When in John 1, Matt 11, Hebrews, Colossians, and Revelation use is made of Wisdom tradition, the highest Christology and direct ethical appeal are combined.

Because features of the Wisdom tradition are the most helpful in explaining the mysterious vs. 4:21c, it may be surmised that the whole quotation contained in 4:21-24 had its origin, place, and function among wise men, and is used by Paul to express the conviction that the saints ought to conduct themselves "not as fools but as wise men" (5:15). If vss. 20-21 hint at a school at all, then vss. 21c-24 explain why so great an effect can be attributed to this school: Jesus Christ, the truth incarnate, is the reason and instrument for turning away from the futility of the Gentiles and beginning a new life. The academy in question is then a School of Wisdom in which the wisdom incarnate in Jesus Christ is proven to be the light of life and the guide of the perplexed.

V   From the Old Man to the New

The observations made so far regarding the form and content of Eph 4:22-24 leave at least three burning questions open: Who is meant by "the

---

[192] Eph 1:13; 4:15, 25.
[193] See e.g. Rom 6:1-11; 8:17, 29; Philip 3:10-11, 21; II Corinthians *passim*.

Old" and "the New Man"? What is the sense of the metaphors "to strip off" and "to put on"? What information is available on the manner and time of change from the old to the new?

A   Two Representative Persons

Many attempts have been made to explain the meaning of the terms "Old Man" and "New Man."[194] Expositors who retain the personal noun "man" in their translation remain closer to the Greek text than those who render *anthrōpos* with a term describing an impersonal or abstract substance such as "nature," "life," "being," "humanity" or "self." Bengel insists that a *concretum*, not an *abstractum*, is meant. However, the more literal interpreters pay a price for their faithfulness to the Greek original, in that they fail to give any immediate help for understanding the substance or identity of the "Old" and the "New Man." The commentators' ways lead in several directions:

1) One group assumes that every man has to jettison his old self—indeed Rom 6:6 speaks of "your old man"—and has to don his own, individual, new selfhood. Both events are attributed to personal regeneration, cf. John 1:13; 3:5. Dibelius is convinced that the words "old" and "new man" are "mystical terms given an ethical slant."[195] The capitalized spelling of "Old Man" and "New Man" is in this case as appropriate and meaningful as is the occasional capitalization of Nature or Self in English. A total change of man's whole personality, not of some particulars only, is meant.[196]

2) A collective interpretation is proposed whenever "Old Man" is considered a name given to sinful humanity as a whole (the *massa perditionis*) and "New Man" is understood (just as in 2:15) as a title of the church, that is, as a beginning and result of new creation. In this case both "the old" and "the new" men are corporate personalities. For several reasons each of them may be called a "man." (a) The two ways of life and the two groups of men adhering to them may be raised to the level of quasi-mythical figures.[197] (b) "Old" and "new" may be personified just as elsewhere in Pauline writings the "flesh," the "law," "sin," and the "Scriptures" are personified—without any implication that they might possess the rank of (supposedly mythical) angelic or demonic powers (Rom 7–8; Gal 3, etc.). (c) The diction of Eph 4:22, 24 may be neither mythical nor anti-mythical, but simply poetic, perhaps tinged by a touch of humor: how could you cling to that "old man"? Look how lovable the "new" one is! Since in Eph 2:15 the "new man" created by Christ and in Christ is a social event and has social character, the terms "Old" and "New Man" can certainly designate a community in 4:22, 24. Equally, the man who according to II Cor 5:1–10 is now a stranger on earth, living in a hand-made domicile and hoping

---

[194] RSV translates: "old, new nature"; JB: "old, new self"; Phillips: "the old way of living, the new life"; J. Jeremias, TWNTE, I, 365: "sinful, renewed being." Literature on the "Old" and the "New Man," and on Adam and Christ, is listed in BIBLIOGRAPHY 18. The relevance of the doctrine of the New Man for the Eastern Church is briefly demonstrated by D. Ritschl, *Memory and Hope* (New York: Macmillan, 1967), pp. 96–100.

[195] In commenting on Col 3:10 (in HbNT, 12, 3d ed. [1953], p. 42) M. Dibelius proposes a mystical understanding of the terms "put off," "put on" just as in his commentary on Eph 4:20–21 he suggests a mystical meaning of "learning," etc.

[196] So, e.g. Robinson and Abbott. Dibelius, HbNT, 12 (1953), suggests that the imperative "Become Christians!" sums up the contents of 4:22–24.

[197] Corresponding, e.g. to contemporary references to "the French," "the Whitey," "the Negro."

to be "clothed over" with a heavenly domicile, is perhaps the community of the saints rather than only each individual member.[198]

3) A third group of interpreters goes beyond both the individualistic and the collective understanding of the two Men. This group splits into three subdivisions: (a) exegetes who, following the Medieval and Reformation tradition, take no account of non-Christian "parallels" to the doctrine of the two Men; (b) expositors who make the most of the possible influence of pagan materials upon the NT;[199] (c) commentators who counter the alleged impact of pagan materials by collecting and utilizing Jewish intimations regarding the "first Adam" and the confrontation of this Adam by an equally or even more important "second Adam."[200] The latter maintain that Adam is meant by the title "Old Man" and Jesus Christ by "New Man."[201] According to them, in Ephesians as much as in Rom 5 and I Cor 15, Adam and Christ are considered representatives of the whole human race.[202] They are related to one another like the old aeon to the new (Gal 1:4); like the flesh to the Spirit (Gal 5:16-25; Rom 7-8); like the two spirits who are at the same time cosmic, anthropological, and moral powers (1QS III-IV); or, perhaps, even like Belial to Christ (II Cor 6:15). Each of the two Adams is a ruler: each fulfills the function of a head and is related to the Many represented by him as the head is related to the body.[203] Every man bears the image of one or the other in I Cor 15:49. "Stripping off the Old Man" amounts therefore to deposing and exiling a wicked ruler,[204] and "putting on the New Man" means hailing and following

---

[198] But compare the individualistic and cosmic complementation of II Cor 5 by I Cor 15:35-55, esp. vs. 53.

[199] Schmithals, *Gnosticism in Corinth*, represents the Gnosticizing interpreters of the NT. Most members of this school discover or reconstruct as often as feasible the pattern of the Redeemed Redeemer myth.

[200] Key elements in the arguments of Davies, Barrett, Scroggs (*The Last Adam*), and esp. of Scandinavian interpreters are: the corporate personality concept underlying the biblical and later references to Israel's patriarchs, to the king, or to servant of the Lord; Philo's doctrine on the creation of two men (one earthly, one spiritual) *leg. all.* I 31-42, 53-55; II 4; *de opificio mundi* 134; apocalyptic and rabbinic references to the first Adam, IV Ezra 3:21; 4:30-32; 7:116-31; II Bar 54:15-19. Mention of a "last" or "higher" Adam occurs again in much later Jewish literature, that is in cabbalistic materials of the Middle Ages; see StB, III, 477-79. More ancient apocryphal glorifications of the sinlessness of the first Adam, and identifications of Adam with Christ are found in Slavonic (II) Enoch 30-31; Ps.-Clem. *hom.* I 45, 47; II 52; *recognitions* III 52. There is also the rabbinic notion of Adam as the treasure-house containing the souls of later men. Indeed, Jewish mythological or poetic ideas regarding the role of Adam may demonstrate the non-Gnostic origin of Paul's teaching on the two men, the first and the last Adam (Rom 5:12-21; I Cor 15:21 ff., 45 ff.). But for some scholars the Philonic and later texts mentioned prove the presence of a Gnostic mythological thought pattern even in Jewish literature. Perhaps a reference to the Canaanite king ideology as expressed in Ezek 28 (and reflected or rejected in Ps 8:4; Dan 7:13?) ought to be added to the Jewish texts just mentioned.

[201] The Christological understanding of the term "New Man" is supported by Gal 3:27 and Rom 13:14 (these two passages speak of "putting on [the Lord Jesus] Christ") and by Diognetus (II) who refers to "the dispensation of the new man Jesus Christ." Yet the attribute "created" of the "New Man" (Eph 4:24; cf. Col 3:10) appears to contradict this interpretation; cf. Robinson, p. 109. Nevertheless Paul may have used this attribute to describe Jesus Christ: he was not engaged in fighting the Arian heresy. Compare the adoptionist sound of Luke 3:22 in the reading of the Western text; Acts 2:36; Rom 1:3-4, and the use made of Prov 8 ("Wisdom," the first creature of God) in NT "high-Christological" passages such as John 1:1 ff.; Col 1:15 ff.; Heb 1:3; Matt 11:25-30.

[202] So Thomas Aquinas, Calvin, and others; among recent interpreters, e.g. Hanson, *Unity*, p. 78; J. Behm, TWNTE, III, 449; Benoit, AnBib 17-18, I (1963), 6-64; D. M. Stanley, "Paul's Interest in the Early Chapters of Genesis," AnBib 17-18, I (1963), 250. Kamlah, DFKP, p. 37. Robinson, p. 109, believes that the individualistic interpretation can be reconciled with the Christological.

[203] See COMMENT VI A 1 and B 3 on 1:15-23 for the derivation of the head-body metaphor from OT and later Jewish notions. Perhaps the "body of sin," "of death," "of flesh" mentioned in Rom 6:6; 7:24; Col 3:11 is to be understood as an "anti-body" corresponding to the "body of Christ."

[204] Cf. Col 2:15: "[Christ] has stripped the principalities and powers."

the good king given by God. Both events are illustrated by the prophet-inspired revolutions that repeatedly shook Samaria and Jerusalem.

These three major interpretations need not be mutually exclusive. But since the last includes the former two and gives them proper edge and depth, it is to be given preference. Every time the singular of the noun "man" occurs in Ephesians, the "man" mentioned has a specific relation to Christ. The "perfect man" (4:13) as well as the "inner man" (3:16–17) is Christ himself. The "single new man" (2:15) is his partner, created by and in Christ.[205] Therefore in 4:24 the "New Man" is most likely Christ himself, understood as the head, the epitome, the reality, the standard, the representative of the new "creation" (2:10; II Cor 5:17; Gal 6:15).[206] As soon as it is recognized that Christ is the real, true "Man for all men," or "Man for the new season," the identity of his counterpart is no longer a puzzle: the "Old Man" is Adam, the anti-type of Christ (Rom 5:12–21; I Cor 15:21–28, 45–55).

This understanding implies that Eph 4:22–24 is an equivalent to, though a new way of phrasing, the Pauline doctrine of sin and justification. If in other letters the apostle wrote that those who have been caught in sin and death are justified "in Christ" (Gal 2:17, etc.), the imagery used in Eph 4 points out that those invested with the characteristics of Adam's fall and death are to be clothed with the life and righteousness that are Christ's. The same thought is expressed, without use of the clothing metaphors, in the triumphant indicatives of Eph 2:1–6: because of the love of God those "dead in sins" are raised together "with the Messiah," "in the Messiah."

It is not only in Ephesians (4:22, 24, 25; 6:11–17) that clothing imagery is used. The same vocabulary serves also in undisputed Pauline letters to describe this radical change.[207] Just like old wineskins, so the old cloth is to be completely discarded, for the new cannot be used to cover the old.[208] But one exception is noteworthy: in the Corinthian letters an event or act of "clothing over" is mentioned which shows that the new garment can be understood as a second robe covering the dilapidated first.[209] This image illustrates the connection between the old and the new existence of man: the sinner himself, the man caught by death, is justified and glorified—he and no one else! In Eph 2 and 4 less emphasis is laid upon the single identity of the person formerly wearing the old and now given the new robe—but it is still presupposed. Those "stripping off the Old" are the same who also "put on the New Man." Yet the accent here lies upon the "grace" by which alone man "is saved" (2:5, 8) and upon the ensuing radical change of life and conduct. According to 4:22–24 there is no way whatsoever to improve, repair, reform, or in any other sense to preserve and continue sinful man. A totally other person has to take over:

---

[205] See COMMENTS VI A 2 on 2:11–22; IV C on 3:14–21; VII B on 4:1–16.

[206] In the exposition of 2:10 (cf. II Cor 5:17; Gal 6:15; James 1:18) it was shown that unlike the sequence of creative acts in the first creation (Gen 1–2) in the new creation man's total renewal precedes that of all other creatures.

[207] See I Thess 5:8; Gal 3:27; esp. Rom 13:12, 14.

[208] Col 2:11, 15; 3:9–10, 12; cf. Mark 2:22.

[209] I Cor 15:53–54; II Cor 5:2–4; cf. Rev 6:9–11, R. Bultmann's utterances about "historical continuity" of the old and new "existence" (ThNT, I, 268–69) appear to be appropriate to these texts. An alternative to Schmithals' Gnosticizing interpretation of II Cor 5:1–10 (Gnosticism in Corinth, pp. 259–75) has been offered by C. Demke, "Zur Auslegung von 2. Korinther 5, 1–10," EvTh 29 (1969), 589–602.

Christ. He is the "New Man" who is given full control. He is to be "put on." If any doctrine of man's salvation can be more radical than the doctrine of justification unfolded in Paul's undisputed letters, then it is the doctrine of the "Old and New Man" in Ephesians and the Colossian parallels to Ephesians.

This impression can be tested, and perhaps corroborated, by a study of the verbs "to strip off," "to put on," "to be renewed."

B Stripping, Clothing, and Renewal

In COMMENT III it was shown that in the early church there may have existed a "type of teaching" (Rom 6:7) which included the clothing metaphors in ethical contexts, and which was either quoted or alluded to in Eph 4:22–24; Col 3:8–10, 12. The combination of these metaphors with the concepts, "first" and "last Adam," and with the idea of new creation (perhaps also with baptism: see section C of this COMMENT) creates an equivalent to a doctrine of rebirth.[210] Biological imagery is employed to describe "rebirth," e.g. in John 3:3–5. Juridical expressions play a large role in the Pauline proclamation of "justification." In Eph 4:22, 24 clothing imagery takes the place of other metaphorical forms of speech. Are the clothing metaphors intended to make a specific point, or to clarify something that might otherwise be obscure?

When 4:22–24 is separated from all biblical and non-biblical parallels and explained as an isolated unit, the two verbs "strip off" and "put on" appear to denote an external action which is complemented by an internal event, the renewal mentioned in vs. 23. The clothing metaphors may reveal that the internal event has also an external dimension—just as the "futility" of the Gentiles' (inner) "mind" works out in (external) impure deeds according to vss. 17–19. The change effected by renewal within one person is then explained as a change essentially related to persons outside himself, i.e. to those called the "Old" and the "New Man." Freed from the strange yoke of the "Old Man," the saint receives, obeys, and wears the colors of the "New Man" (cf. Rom 6:12–23; I Cor 15:49). The clothing metaphors may indicate that the change of "mind" will be visible and palpable. On the other hand, vs. 23 may add a reminder not contained in the parallel Col 3:9–10: the outer redressing is meaningless without a complete inner renewal; both the vine and the skins have to be new (Mark 2:22). Form and content, existence and essence are inseparable when new life is under discussion.

However, even if the diction of Eph 4:22–24 intimates the dialectical relationship between external and internal, the imagery employed for the dismissal of the "Old" and the acceptance of the "New Man" probably intends much more. The metaphorical use of the terms, "put off," "put on," reflects a belief and conviction spread throughout all cultures and religions: "Clothes make the man." Garments and the act of changing a garment are effective symbols. Clothes serve for protection, ornament, and augmentation of power.[211] Whether in relation to a deity or to the human community, they signify man's

---

[210] Davies, PRJ, pp. 119–27.

[211] In English the terms "invest" and "divest" have almost completely lost their original palpable meanings. For brief surveys on the role of garments in religion see G. van der Leeuw, *Religion in Essence and Manifestation* (Gloucester: Smith, 1967), pp. 309–11, 373–74, and dictionary articles on *Kleidung* (clothes), etc. such as RGG, III, 1646–48, and *Gewand* in the Index of Reitzenstein, HMyRel.

second, or rather his real, self. A man's power extends to his garb, and the power of a specific robe is communicated to its wearer. Transfer of clothes, including weapons, means more then fraternization, it is an exchange of personalities and the transmission of power. When the coat of a high official or priest is torn, energy is lost, deprivation takes place, grief is expressed, or the high position is jeopardized. Going naked or in sackcloth and ashes is a means and expression of repentance, asceticism, and self-denial. The transition into another community or age group, office or status, is not only indicated but also affected by the throwing off or destruction of the old cloth and the "investiture" with a white (e.g. baptismal) shirt, a *toga virilis,* a marriage gown, a uniform or *livrée,* an apron, a priest's or magician's stole, or a monastic garb.

The OT and NT show traces of almost all known features of garment and clothing symbolism.[212] The version "strip off" (4:22), is more in line with biblical precedents than the more tame translation "put off," or the cruder "take off." "Stripping off" suggests a violent effort which includes the abandonment, perhaps also the destruction of the old garment. There is nothing to be saved. A connotation of repentance and self-denial is not to be excluded. Correspondingly the garment which is to be "put on" (vs. 24) is something new, festive, and joyous. Investment with the new robe implies the conveyance of a new status and office; it makes the bearer a member of a given community and involves public responsibility. In 6:10–11 the terms "to become strong" and "to put on" are mutually interpretative.

Two elements found in various religions are bypassed in Eph 4:22–24 and perhaps—whether by intent or inadvertently—repudiated:[213]

1) Absent from Ephesians is the notion that the body is the soul's clothing,[214] i.e. its prison or tomb. This idea entails that no more is necessary for gaining new and true life than to divest one's true self, the soul or the spirit, of the material and mortal body, or to subdue the body by rigorous mental or physical ascetic practice. Following vs. 23, neither the spirit nor the mind of man can simply ascend to heaven. Rather they need renewal as badly as the body. In II Cor 5:2–4; I Cor 15:35–55 Paul expresses the hope that of all things the mortal body will be clothed over and glorified. Discarding the body and saving a "naked" soul are out of the question. Total man shall live and be new.

2) Excluded also is the idea that the whole cosmos is God's garment. However, an allusion to it is found in Ps 104:1–2.[215]

Thus neither an individualistic nor a cosmological interpretation nor a com-

---

[212] Gen 3:21; 9:23; 37:3, 23; Exod 28; Lev 16:4, etc.; I Sam 4:12; 15:27–28; 17:38–39; 18:3–4; 24:5, 6; II Sam 10:4; I Kings 19:13, II Kings 2:8, 12–14; Isa 3:22; Ezek 16:8; Ps 22:19; Matt 22:11–12; 26:65; 27:31, 35; Luke 8:27; 15:22; John 13:4, 12; II Cor 5:2–4; Rev 3:4–5; 4:4; 6:11, etc. Such stories as that of the Gibeonites' ruse (Josh 9:4–13) and idioms such as "wolves in sheepskins" (Matt 7:15) show that clothes do not always confer upon a man, or reveal, his real identity. However, a passage such as Zech 3:3–5 is more typical: the garments of the high priest reveal the state in which he finds himself. Filthy garments reflect his status as a prisoner under indictment, whereas the new clean garments which are put upon him show him to be innocent of charges and vindicated by God.

[213] The first is present in Orphism and Plato, also in Buddhist, Christian, and Islamic mysticism; the second in combination with the first, e.g. in magical and Gnostic texts.

[214] Among Jewish writers, e.g. Philo *de fuga et invent.* 110, represents this view.

[215] Philo *de fuga et invent.* 110. The Gnostic idea that the universe is the body of the Aion-god, was expressed by calling the world the deity's garment. Obviously it is impossible to connect the clothing imagery of Eph 4 with a cosmic meaning.

bination of both as found in Gnostic and magical systems, are keys for explaining Eph 4. The clothing imagery may remind one of magical notions, and it is also used in mystic thought and practice. But Eph 4:22–24 suggests neither a magical transformation, nor a mystic loss of personality, nor a cheap escape from captivity. "Become new in mind and spirit" (vs. 23) : these words not only point out the inner, invisible locus and mode of change, but they also prevent a magical understanding of the clothing formula. Clear and rational rethinking, reorientation, and renewal are called for. Man is by no means to "get out" either of his body or of his mind—he is to become new "in mind and spirit." A renewed mind and a newly dressed body, in short, man's total self is claimed for the service of God. "Present your bodies as a living sacrifice . . . be transformed by the renewal of your mind that you may find out by experience what is the will of God" (Rom 12:1–2).[216]

In summary, the clothing metaphors in Eph 4:22 and 24 and the call for renewal in 4:23 interpret one another mutually. The verbs "strip off," "put on," and "become new" convey the good news that now the time, the means, the power, the reality of total change are at hand. If there was an "Old Man"—and he was real enough—see how he "rots" (vs. 22b)! A "New Man" has appeared and with him come "true righteousness and piety" (vs. 24). God's creative power attacks, overwhelms, "renews" man in the center of his being, "in his mind and spirit" (vs. 23).[217] This power is not a blind force which operates much as a mythical figure, outside and above man. The author speaks in a prophetic tone of that which man is and needs, and what he is being given and is to do: man is neither a lazy spectator to a cosmic drama, nor a mere object or tool of some destiny. With his insight, emotion, will, and decision he participates in the confrontation of the old by the new. He is a partner in the dramatic struggle. He cannot help taking sides and cooperating. The Greek infinitives "to strip off," "to put on," "to become renewed" possess not only imperative force, but also affirm an event and have the character of radiant indicatives.

It is this which distinguishes the message conveyed by clothing metaphors from the preaching about justification and rebirth; the clothing imagery is less susceptible to an interpretation ascribing to man a completely passive role. It challenges him clearly to say "No" here, and "Yes" there, and to live out his decision. While the proclamation of rebirth and justification includes an appeal to distinct ethical behavior, the doctrine of discarding the "Old" and accepting the "New" Man is thoroughly ethical. It is safely founded upon the conviction that "the old has passed away, the new has come. All this is from God" (II Cor 5:17–18). The ethical form of the gospel preached in Eph 4 may be chosen to reveal that in making all things new, "God the creator of all" (Eph 3:9) does not disdain to engage man's mind, decision, and action. By God's grace man is freed to participate in God's rejection of and victory over evil, and in all the good that God elected to do and to bestow. In being "made new" by God, man is also equipped to choose renewal. Equally man's reconciliation by God's grace

---

[216] In Colossians a renewal of the mind is not mentioned. In that epistle the subtle polemical allusion to Greek notions, the dialectic internal-external, the invitation to sobriety and the anti-magical warning seem to be lacking. But Col 3:10 gives an emphasis to "knowledge" which may well substitute for the points made more explicitly in Romans and Ephesians.

[217] See 1:17–21; 2:2; 3:10; 6:10–17 for statements on the conflict of God's power with other powers.

is inseparable from God's confidence and command that man "be reconciled" (II Cor 5:18–20).

Since Eph 4:22–24 urges an actual and concrete change of historical man, the question to be raised now is whether this passage also contains information on the means or the time of change.

C   The Moment of Change

The verb "to put on" is used by Paul in several contexts. Three groups of statements can be discerned.[218] (1) The change of clothing occurs in baptism.[219] (2) The new clothes are put on in ever new acts of ethical decision and action.[220] (3) The bestowal of a new garment is a final (eschatological) event that takes place not earlier than after man's death, i.e. on the Last Day.[221]

The same tri-partition can be made with the various synonyms of "putting on," that is with the NT references to being "renewed," "raised with Christ," "conformed" or "transformed" according to his image.[222] Neither the parallel NT passages nor the vocabulary used in Eph 4:22–24 reveals unambiguously which of the three moments of change is meant in Eph 4. The Christological understanding of the "New Man" as proposed in section A of this COMMENT provides no clear answer. Christ is the clothing put on in baptism, *and* in daily ethical conduct, *and* also on the Last Day.[223] Still, the Pauline letters contain a negative and a positive clue for ascribing a time to the disrobing and dressing mentioned in 4:22, 24:

1) Paul never explicitly mentions a cloth made of fiber or any other material. It is purely conjectural to assume that not only in Gal 3:27, but by each and every employment of the term "to put on" he alluded to the clothing of actors, cultic enthusiasts, or novices—an act which in some religious rites signified deification.[224] The apostle may have used the clothing metaphors without any

---

[218] With Schlier, p. 118.

[219] Gal 3:27: "All those of you who have been baptized in [the name of, I Cor 1:13] Christ have put on Christ." Kamlah, DFKP, pp. 35–38, follows P. Carrington, Selwyn, Davies, Dibelius and others in considering the references to "putting on" examples of baptismal diction. Kirby, EBP, p. 159, endorses this interpretation; he lists Eph 4:22–24 among the "Indirect References to Baptism" in Ephesians.

[220] I Thess 5:8; Rom 13:12, 14; Col 3:9–10, 12; Eph 6:11, 14. Davies, PRJ, pp. 119 ff, represents those scholars who explain NT ethical codes as traces of a catechism composed for persons baptized or to be baptized. An ethical interpretation of baptism, or, rather, a baptismal interpretation of ethics, is suggested by N. Gäumann, *Taufe and Ethik*, BEvTh 47, but a sacramentalism which swallows up ethics is opposed and confronted with an alternative by K. Barth, *Church Dogmatics*, IV 4 (1969).

[221] I Cor 15:53–55; II Cor 5:2–4; cf. Rev 6:11.

[222] See I Cor 15:44–52; II Cor 3:18; 4:16; Rom 6:4–5, 8, 11; 8:17, 30; Philip 3:10–11, 20–21.

[223] Gal 3:27; Rom 13:14; I Cor 15:49.

[224] E.g. animal skins, masks, veils, or symbols of the sun have been donned for processions, dances, or other ceremonies on festival days. Occasions for such clothing were magical performances, Mystery Cults (esp. the Isis Cult), and Gnostic rites. White dresses have been used in the church's second-century and later baptismal practice. It is debatable whether in some or in all of these rituals a substantial identity of man with the deity, an enthusiastic identification, a dramatic representation, and/or the beginning of a new life in the deity's service, was to be established. Most likely the symbolic action of clothing possessed widely different, perhaps partly contradictory, meanings. See Plutarch *Iside et Osiride* III 352B; Apuleius *metamorphoses* XI 21–24; F. J. Dölger, *Ichthys*, I (Rome: Spithöver, 1910), 115 ff; Reitzenstein, HMyRel., esp. p. 314; J. Leipoldt, *Die urchristliche Taufe im Lichte der Religionsgeschichte* (Leipzig: Dörffling, 1928), pp. 6–61; M. Dibelius, *Die Isisweihe bei Apuleius*, SbHA 4, 1917; repr. in *Botschaft und Geschichte*, II (Tübingen: Mohr, 1956), 30–79; Pokorný, EuG, pp. 118–19; H. D. Betz, *Nachfolge und Nachahmung Jesu Christi im Neuen Testament*, BHTh 37 (1967), 64–65. The baptismal interpretation of the clothing metaphor has been forcefully challenged, e.g. by G. Wagner, *Pauline Baptism and Pagan Mysteries* (London: Oliver, 1967), esp. pp. 113–14, 273. See also COMMENTS XVI on 1:3–14 and IV F on 5:21–33.

thought of a specific moment during church ritual.[225] Not even the statement "As many of you as were baptized into Christ have put on Christ" (Gal 3:27) offers sure evidence to the contrary. Neither Ephesians nor any other canonical epistle offers unambiguous evidence of the belief that baptism is the miracle by which (through God's grace and institution, rather than mechanically or *ex opere operato*) the devil, the old Adam, or the filth of the flesh are disposed of, and by which at once resurrection and new life are attained. On the contrary, in I Peter 3:21 the idea of removal of the "dirty flesh" (or "fleshly dirt") by baptism, and in II Tim 2:18 the presumption that resurrection (through baptism?) is safely possessed, are explicitly negated. In I Cor 10:1–13 Paul fights the superstition that any baptism, ancient or recent, can or will protect from temptation, sin, and death. While in Rom 6:4–5 he affirms that baptism is oriented toward "resurrection" with Christ and a conduct in "newness of life," he does not claim that all is perfected and achieved in a single ritual, i.e. "through baptism."[226] Indeed Eph 4:22–24 is a piece of instruction well suited to the preparation for, or the liturgy of, baptism. But its usefulness for a given service does not necessarily demonstrate the original *Sitz im Leben*. As yet there is no evidence that the exhortation to "strip off," to "be renewed," or to "put on" is in substance to be identified with the command and promise, "Be baptized and you shall be new men!"

2) In distinctly ethical contexts the garment to be "put on" consists of (good) works or of (spiritual) armaments.[227] In turn, an event of the eschaton, the Last Day, is described whenever the "spiritual body" or an equivalent term is employed to denote the metaphorical robe.[228] Ethical exhortations are found immediately before and after the parallel Ephesian and Colossian utterances on the stripping off of the "Old" and the putting on of the "New Man." They require an end to vicious attitudes and an appropriation of good deeds. An ethical interpretation of Eph 4:22–24 is strongly suggested by the Ephesian context of, and the Colossian parallel to, these verses.[229] It may be granted that if vss. 22–24 are a quotation, the reference to the two Men (the first and the last Adam) and the imagery of putting off and putting on, origi-

---

[225] Similarly the term "burying" in Rom 6:4; Col 2:12 does not demonstrate that in Rome baptism had always the form of total immersion and was understood (after the pattern of a sailor's funeral on the high seas) as a burial in water. No more does the metaphor used in I Cor 12:13, "you were made to drink of one Spirit" (or "you were watered with one Spirit," cf. I Cor 3:6) necessarily contain an allusion to a ritual drinking of baptismal water.

[226] That which happens "through baptism" has the character of a "burial with Christ" according to Rom 6:4—though it need not have its form. Paul describes baptism in this way because he considers it an event that occurs *between* the dying with Christ and the resurrection with Christ. Baptism is received by those who have been made participants in Christ's death, that is, who have been "crucified with him" on the cross (Gal 2:19; 6:14; II Cor 5:14). They are therefore dead in a "death like his." But they rely upon their future participation in his resurrection (Rom 6:5). The sudden occurrence of the perfect tense in the first half of this verse contrasts with the aorist tense of the words, "we were baptized . . . we were buried" (vss. 3–4). Baptism confirms a death that has already occurred, but it is not an act of killing or dying. Further, it attests to the hope for resurrection, but it does not raise from death. However, does Col 2:12 assert that resurrection with Christ happens "in baptism"? In the exposition of this verse it will be shown why the crucial words *en autō* (that may mean either "in Christ" or "in baptism") have to be understood as referring to Christ. "In Christ" (rather than "in baptism") the saints have already been raised with Christ, as Eph 2:6 distinctly affirms.

[227] I Thess 5:8; Rom 13:12; Col 3:12; Eph 4:24; 6:11, 14–17.

[228] I Cor 15:53–54; II Cor 5:2–4.

[229] Col 3:8, 12 form a frame around Col 3:9–10; the verb, "put off" (Eph 4:22), is resumed in Eph 4:25.

nally served as dogmatic and eschatological instruction. This instruction may or may not have been connected with baptismal teaching and liturgy. But in their present location the verses are given and possess a preeminently ethical ring.

The date of the change expected in Eph 4:22–24 is therefore every hour of man's life. The author certainly does not exclude the memory of baptism and the hope of the final day. His mention of the "seal of the Spirit" in 1:13–14 and 4:30 includes a reminder of a past and a future event, but the intention and meaning of his references to that seal are not exhausted by memory and hope. In 4:22–24 as much as in 1:14; 4:30, the central concern is neither with a sacramental (re-)enactment of the past nor with the perfect fulfillment in the future; in focus are the present and ever-new decision and action of the saints. In 4:22–24 Paul speaks of the daily struggle against the shackles of the "Old Man" and of the uninterrupted groping for the "New."[230] He is confident that now the "sealing with the Spirit" will prove effective.

Even in the present evil days (5:16; 6:13) the saints need not abandon themselves to despair, to nostalgic glances at the past, or to world-negating hopes for a golden future. The time in which God effects and accepts the most radical personal change and renewal is now! The urgent ethical appeal contained in 4:22–24 forcefully demonstrates that "now is the acceptable time . . . now is the day of salvation" (II Cor 6:2). Realized, present eschatology is far from unethical. It is both the world-political and the psychological basis of true ethics. Because this is taught in the "School of the Messiah," that school was described as the means by which pagan-born saints have been separated from their "hopeless" past.

After the general outline of ethics has been given in 4:17–24, vss. 25–32 offer special exhortations. The special ethic is, in turn, undergirded by particular reasoning.

VI   Motives for Members

As stated previously, 4:25–32 contains a series of units that exhibit a recurrent pattern, even the sequence: prohibition-commandment-motivation. While this passage is most likely a composite of traditional materials, the elements brought together form something better than a potpourri. The way they are selected and arranged reveals a skillful collector and competent counselor, a deep thinker and artistic editor.[231] Here the distinct substance of the several admonitions need not be discussed again (see the NOTES), but two dimensions of the exhortations require attention: (a) the motivation given for

---

[230] Cf. Philip 3:12–14. Luther's words about the daily drowning of the old Adam and the daily resurrection of the new (*Ninety-five Theses*, and *Smaller Catechism*, Baptism 4) as well as Calvin's description of a Christian's life under the aspect of mortification and resurrection with Christ (*Institutio*, III 6–10) correspond exactly to the intent of Eph 4:22–24.

[231] See fn. 68. Schlier, pp. 223 ff. has emphasized more than others the selection, the corrections, and the additions that must probably be ascribed to Paul and that distinguish Eph 4:25 – 6:9 from Jewish and Hellenistic, but also from early Christian ethical tradition. Schlier discerns the following divisions and subdivisions: I. Personal Ethics: 4:25 – 5:21: (a) love: 4:25 – 5:2; (b) light: 5:3–14; (c) "sober drunkenness" (*sic*) in the cult: 5:15–21; II. Social Ethics: 5:22 – 6:9 with three subdivisions regarding (a) husbands, (b) parents, (c) masters. The relationship between faith and action in the undisputed Pauline letters and the problem of ethical motivation is the main topic of O. Merk, *Handeln aus Glauben: Die Motivierungen der paulinischen Ethik*, Marburg: Elwert, 1968; cf. V. P. Furnish, *Theology and Ethics in Paul*, Nashville: Abingdon, 1968. The role of motivations that seem not directly derived from the gospel and faith, is discussed by R. J. Augsten, *Natural Motivation in the Pauline Epistles*, University of Notre Dame Press, 1966.

specific attitudes and actions; (b) all statements regarding the mode in which the saints are expected to follow these commands.

According to this passage, all ethics are social: the first motive mentioned is "We are members of one body" (lit. "of one another"; 4:25c, cf. Rom 12:5). The same ethic is spiritual: "grieving the Spirit," who has taken hold of the saints and guarantees their election and freedom, must be avoided at all costs (4:30; see the next COMMENT). Finally the ethic of this passage is directly related to physical life. Several members of man's physical body are enumerated, and all are drafted for service: the "hands" (vs. 28), the "mouth" (vs. 29; in our translation, "the lips"), the "entrails" (vs. 32; cf. Col 3:12; in our translation, "the heart") are explicitly mentioned. Therefore the exhortation of 4:25 ff. may be called an "ethic of the body." The locus of renewal and the instrument of obedience are not to be restricted to a hidden spirituality, but they also involve the physical existence of man. Just as in Hebrew anthropology each member is not only a part of the body but much more man's total self in a specific function, so each member of Christ's body is exhorted to act as an exponent of the whole.[232] In Eph 4:25-32 the statements on the social body, i.e. the church, are most intimately related to the statements made about the physical body of each saint. The destination for service of the holy members of the "body" of Christ includes the responsibility for proper use of their physical members, and vice versa. Cf. I Cor 3:16-17; 6:15-19: each church member's physical body, and the whole body of the community of the saints, are "the temple of the Holy Spirit of God" himself.[233]

If sinners, formerly as "dead in sins" as the Ephesian saints, can be resuscitated and "saved" for doing "good works" (2:1-10), then certainly "lips" that were blaspheming, a "hand" expert in stealing, and a "heart" full of bitterness or meanness can also be renewed to proper use. The salvation of the "saints" and their "enthronement in heaven" would lack reality and totality if it could not be described in terms of new life conveyed to their hands and lips and hearts. If they are now a praise of God's glory at all (1:6, 12, 14), then they must be enabled "with hearts and hands and voices" to give thanks to God. How deep salvation reaches, and how total its effect is, becomes even clearer in Eph 4:25 ff. than in 2:5-10.

Ethics makes the gospel concrete. The Ephesians are told by the apostle that there is no reason to despair of speech and labor, of thought and decision; for in the name of the Lord it is asserted that your dirty tongue, your crafty hands, your hard and violent heart (that is, precisely you, the egotists), can and shall do what befits a "member of one body." You and no one else are to take care of the "needs" of others; you are to "build them up"; you are to perform that which is "good" for many. Since you are no longer under the rule of the "Devil," he has no right and you must not give him "opportunity" to use you for

---

[232] Cf. K. Graystone, "The Significance of the Word 'Hand' in the New Testament," in *Mélanges Bibliques*, Fs B. Rigaux, eds. A. Descamps and A. de Halleaux (Gembloux: Duculot, 1970), pp. 479-87, esp. p. 482.

[233] For similar reasons Schlier, p. 224, states, "Christian existence is the critical eschatological discovery and recovery (*Erschliessung*) of natural existence." Nearer the thought of Ephesians would be a reference to the creation of true humanity by resurrection and salvation. R. Bohren, *Das Problem der Kirchenzucht im Neuen Testament*, Zürich: EVZ, 1951, has attempted to show the connection between physical, moral, and church discipline.

your own and your neighbor's destruction (vss. 25, 27, 28, 29). The examples
given regarding misuse and proper use of the body's members are thoroughly
evangelical.

The same is true of the motivations attached in 4:25–32 to the prohibitions
and commandments.[234] They are in succession: (a) the right of one's neighbor
to be treated as a fellow member in Christ's body; (b) the prevention of any
interference by the Devil; (c) the privilege granted to the needy: he is to experience charity; (d) the power of words to edify and to do good; (e) the pain
inflicted upon the Spirit by liars, angry men, thieves, insulting speakers;[235]
(f) the forgiveness granted by God in Christ. A seventh motive is added in
5:1–2: the Messiah loved the saints so much that he gave his life for them.
Unlike passages such as I Cor 9:3–4 or II Cor 8–9 where Paul mixes motivations for ethical conduct, derived from the Bible or from Christ's coming,
with common sense or natural motivations, the apostle (or the source or
sources used by him?) proffers in Eph 4:25 ff. only motivations founded in the
gospel and faith.

While in substance and form the first four motives sound surprisingly secular, the last three refer directly to the Spirit, to God, and to the Messiah.
Any allusion to personal satisfaction by good works or to a reward for good
behavior is absent. The motivation for leading a life worthy of God's vocation
is sociological and theological rather than egotistic, individualistic, psychological, or perfectionist.

The motive listed under (e) stands out from the others, and requires special
consideration.

VII   The Sin against the Spirit

For several reasons the sentence, "Do not grieve the Holy Spirit of God
[for he is the seal] with which you have been marked for the day of liberation" (4:30), is a stray element in the context of 4:25–32.

a) The negative imperative "do not grieve" has a grammatical form distinct
from the longer forms used in vss. 28, 29, 31 (lit. "shall not steal," "shall not
go out," "shall be lifted"). Only the prohibition "do not sin" (vs. 26), and some
of the positive commands in vss. 25, 26, 32, replace the heavy formulation
"shall . . ." by the blunt and short imperative.

b) While the prohibition against grieving the Spirit is underlined by a motive,
that is, by a reminder of the eschatological-missionary function and power of
the Spirit,[236] a complementary positive command is missing. All other prohibitions in 4:17–32 are matched by an explicit command. Verse 30 resembles the
majority of the Ten Commandments which have only prohibitive, not prescrip-
tive, character.

---

[234] The addition of positive commands (as alternatives to the forbidden actions and attitudes)
distinguishes the exhortation of Eph 4:25 ff., from most of the Ten Commandments. On the other
hand, three topics discussed in 4:25 ff. resemble the references to lying, theft, and coveting in the last
three Commandments. Finally, the reasoning with motivations corresponds to a Deuteronomic feature. For example in Deut 5:12–15 the Sabbath commandment (Exod 20:8–11) is buttressed by the
reminder that Israel was but is no more a servant in Egypt, just as in Eph 4:32 mutual forgiveness
is based on forgiveness received from God.

[235] Verse 30 may, however, not offer a motivation. This verse can be considered a commandment
of its own. See the next COMMENT.

[236] See the last pages of COMMENT XVI on 1:1–14.

c) The evil deeds mentioned in 4:25 ff. resemble the acts and attitudes prohibited in the so-called Second Tablet of the Ten Commandments. The words "Do not grieve the Holy Spirit of God" speak of a sin against God. They fit among the deeds forbidden in the First Tablet and are perhaps used as a summary of its substance.

d) The motive "[for he is the seal] with which you have been marked" has in Greek the syntactical form of a relative clause (lit. "with whom you have been sealed"). Similar relative clauses with proclamatory contents are more often found in hymnic compositions than in hortatory contexts.[237] Indeed, not only the pleonastic formulation "the Holy Spirit of God," but also the pathetic verb "to grieve," may indicate that vs. 30 was originally part of a liturgical confession. The great repentance-liturgy of Isa 63:10 contains the words, "They rebelled and grieved[238] his Holy Spirit, therefore he turned to be their enemy and himself fought against them." A reference to (the marking for) the day of "liberation" was previously made in Eph 1:14, in a distinctly hymnic text.

Observations such as these can corroborate the theory that Eph 4:17–32 contains collected and re-edited pre-Pauline materials. However, the distinctive features of 4:30 are of greater than only formal or traditio-historical interest. By citing or alluding to a supposedly well-known line of prayer or confession, the author of Ephesians may wish to set forth the basis and motive for all ethics rather than to utter just one more special prohibition. The predominantly social reasoning of vss. 25–29 is here crowned by an explicit theological motivation. Previously an appeal had been made to the "truth in Jesus"—this was and is fundamental (4:21). A reminder of "God's" gift of "forgiveness" is found in vs. 32. In 5:1–2 "imitation of God" and "love of the Messiah" will be mentioned as the criteria of conduct. Verse 30 adds a reference to the "Holy Spirit of God."

Why is a good relationship to this Spirit a motive for good conduct? Schlier points out that in 4:30 the "Spirit of joy" is in the mind of the author: "All Christian existence is entering a joyful being."[239] It is this Spirit, this existence in joy, which must not be "grieved." No saint can take the risk of introducing sadness into the realm of joy created and guaranteed by God (cf. Heb 13:17). Just as an OT prophetic voice (Isa 63:10) had affirmed that God himself is hurt and becomes his people's enemy when his Holy Spirit is grieved, now the trinitarian elements among the motives collected in Eph 4 show that God's majesty is offended by disobedience to the Spirit. Not an inferior part of God or an incidental mode of his self-manifestation, but God himself, God in essence, truth, action, manifestation, effect, is repudiated whenever the saints hurt their fellow men. Though an explicit reference to "grieving" the Father is not found in 4:30, this text comes near an affirmation of patripassionism (the preaching of a suffering God). The God proclaimed in Ephesians is not an unmoved mover.

Eph 4:30 may possess outstanding importance for the whole context. This verse not only contains a motivation for the immediately preceding prohibition

---

[237] See the Introduction, section II.
[238] So MT; in the LXX, "they embittered."
[239] On p. 227 of his commentary on Ephesians, Schlier refers to I Thess 1:6; Gal 5:22; II Cor 2:2–7; Rom 14:17; Heb 12:11; John 16:20.

and command, but also pertains to all other warnings and exhortations.[240] To the ever-repeated admonitions regarding speech[241] corresponds the elevated role assigned to the Spirit. The Spirit is most directly related to prophetic speech, i.e. to a use of the lips for bearing testimony to God.[242] In 6:17 the "sword provided by the Spirit" is called the "word of God." The Spirit who makes men attest to the truth is put to shame when the saints "lie" to one another and utter "foul talk." But the Spirit rejoices when the lips of God's children pronounce and confirm the "good, constructive" word which is the Spirit's instrument, product, and trademark for "meeting" man's "need" (vs. 29) and "glorifying God's grace" (1:14).

Two features distinguish Eph 4:30 from seemingly parallel teachings found in the environment of the NT:

a) According to the teaching of Qumran, the holy spirit of the saints (rather than the Spirit of God) is contaminated by an evil tongue.[243] This spirit is a creature of God.[244] Paul would not deny that God is most angry with those defiling the "spirit of meekness" or "wisdom" (Gal 6:1; Eph 1:17) which God creates in man or gives to him. Yet in Ephesians the apostle speaks of an immediate and total affliction of God himself by those who utter lies, angry curses, and filth.

b) According to the Shepherd of Hermas, grief (lypē) is a sister of double-mindedness and bitterness.[245] This grief sits "in the heart . . . of mournful man" and is "more evil than all the spirits." It plagues those who "only have faith" but never really "inquire concerning the truth" because they are "mixed up with business and riches and heathen friendships." Such grief "wears out" and "oppresses [lit. grieves] the Holy Spirit which dwells in you" and makes it impossible that a man's "intercession ascends in purity to the altar." While it is admitted that grief in the form of "repentance . . . seems to bring salvation" and indeed "saves us," yet the final exhortations are, "Put away from yourself grief. . . . Purify yourself from this wicked grief, and you shall live to God. . . . For the Spirit of God which is given to this flesh endures neither grief nor oppression. . . . Put on, therefore, joyfulness, which always has favor with God and is acceptable to him, and flourish in it; for every joyful man . . . despises grief." Indeed, Paul himself on one occasion discusses "grief" in a way which reveals his sensitivity to its impact upon individuals (see II Cor 7:8–12). In this passage he distinguishes "grief according to God" from "worldly grief." But Eph 4:30 is misinterpreted when Hermas' psychological and individualistic categories are imposed upon it or elicited from it. This text speaks of God's own suffering. "In all their afflictions he was afflicted" (Isa 63:9).[246]

[240] Most of the motives listed in 4:25–32 can be called pertinent to each negative and positive command.

[241] See vss. 25(–27?), 29; "shouting" and "cursing" are mentioned in vs. 31. Other references to the importance of words are found in 1:13; 2:20; 4:11, 15; 5:3; 6:9, 15, 19.

[242] Joel 2:28–29; cf. the apocryphal Martyrdom of Isaiah I 7; Matt 10:20; Luke 4:18; Acts 1:8; 2:4, 17; I Cor 14; Rev 2:7; 19:10; 22; B. Yoma 9b; Davies, PRJ, p. 215, etc. See COMMENT XVI on 1:3–14.

[243] CD v 11–12; vii 3–4.

[244] The same is said of the spirit of darkness, 1QS III 25 – IV 26.

[245] Mand. x 1–3. The following quotes are from K. Lake's translation in The Apostolic Fathers, II, Loeb Classical Library, pp. 110–17.

[246] The quoted RSV version of Isa 63:9 is subject to serious criticism but expresses the suffering of God under the burden of Israel's sin, to which other passages also bear testimony. Bengel's (cf. Thomas Aquinas) interpretation of Eph 4:30 looks like a combination of the doctrines of

On the other hand, Paul makes clear that when the Spirit is hurt—the one who gives the saints all they have, who assures them of all they know, who is the creative power by which God makes all things new—then it is not just God who suffers. Then not only the present and future victory of God is belied, but also the saints' own share in "the tree of life and the holy city" is diminished (cf. Rev 22:19); God's loss involves theirs. Eph 4:30 contains, despite its resplendent beauty and moving theopassionism, an unmistakable threat which is reminiscent of the Synoptic words about the "sin against the Holy Spirit" (Mark 3:28–30 par.). Who would want to die the death of Ananias and Sapphira described in a legend in Acts? According to Acts 5:3, 9 the death of this couple was the result of a test to which they subjected the Holy Spirit. The fact that they were living as liars (instead of "putting away the lie," Eph 4:25) proved fatal. "Grieving the Holy Spirit" may well be a synonym of "sinning against the Spirit"; nothing but death can be its consequence.

Eph 4:30 ends with a reaffirmation of the scope of God's work, the "liberation of his people" (cf. 1:14). Here the anticipation of the end-time and the fulfillment of all hope by the presence and work of the Spirit are proclaimed.[247] In 4:25, 27, 28, 29 the basic motives for obedience consist of realities and opportunities of the present. In 4:32 a past event is mentioned, the effect of which is now enjoyed: the "forgiveness" of sin procured by Christ's blood (1:7). Verse 30, finally, refers to liberation to be brought in on a future day and to its documentation by the Spirit's presence and operation, here and now. The saints are "marked for" and by their destiny—which is freedom. It is their privilege and calling to shine in the light that is to go up over all, and to bring peace and freedom to all.

One other element of Eph 4 requires special attention.

VIII   Exhortation by Catalogue

Eph 4:2–3, 19 contain brief and unobtrusive lists of attitudes that are characteristic of saints and pagans respectively: humility, gentleness, patience, love, unity are pitted against debauchery, impurity, greed. In English an exhortation by the enumeration of "Do's" and "Don'ts" leaves a moralistic and legalistic impression, but that was hardly the intention of the author of Ephesians. Therefore our translation of 4:2–3, 19 has hidden a casuistic monotony which is offensive to the reader. In no English version of vss. 31–32, however, can the presence of straight moral lists be covered up: bitterness, anger, passion, shouting, cursing must yield to goodness, compassion, forgiveness. In the Greek text the latter three attitudes are described by adjectives and a participle, but an enumeration is as clearly evident as when nouns are used.

Lists of ethical prohibitions and commands are frequently found in the

---

Qumran and Hermas. He explains Eph 4:30 with the words, "The Holy Spirit is not grieved in himself, but [only] in us; for His serene testimony is being disturbed." Probably the notion of an essentially unmovable God underlies this exposition. The OT bristles with passages speaking of God's anger or grief.

[247] See the last NOTE on 1:14, and COMMENTS IX and XVI on 1:3–14 for a discussion of the relation of the future to the present and of the Spirit's function as guarantor.

NT.[248] Among scholars today they are labeled "catalogical parenesis." In earlier nomenclature they were "catalogues of vices and virtues."[249] Frequently they are attributed to a more or less fixed catechetical form of instruction prepared for people who were about to become Christians or who had just been baptized, i.e. for novices and neophytes. In COMMENTS II and III on 4:1–16 it was shown that the aristocratic or moral-philosophical term "virtue" is an inappropriate designation for the "good works" or attitudes which, according to the fatherly advice of the apostle, correspond to the (new) "creation" (Eph 2:10) and the "will" (Rom 12:2) of the living God. Also it is unlikely that Paul simply quotes part of an early Christian catechism anywhere in his epistles—without changing the wording, the arrangement, or the stress. The variety of good deeds and attitudes mentioned by the apostle,[250] their frequently changing arrangement, the leading or the concluding role of love, the omission of any reference to love in Eph 4:32, the absence of a system distinguishing cardinal and subordinate virtues, and the admitted incompleteness of the lists[251]—elements and features such as these demonstrate that Paul far from slavishly follows a given pattern or collection of written or memorized materials.

Still, there are precedents for the Pauline enumerations of good and evil deeds, and an understanding of Paul can only gain from a comparison of his exhortation with ethical instruction given before or at his time. Parallels are found in the OT, in classic Greek philosophy, in Persian religion, in Stoic teaching, in popular orators' effusions, in Philo's philosophy of religion, in Qumran writings, in rabbinical *halachah*, in Jewish liturgies, and in Christian forms of instruction.[252] While scholarly research, as exemplified by the works mentioned in BIBLIOGRAPHY 19, is still moving to and fro between various extremes, the tentative results of at least one of the latest books, that by Kamlah, will be summarized here:

Two types of "the form of catalogical parenesis" can be distinguished in the NT. One type registers good and evil deeds, adding a threat of destruction and a promise of blessing respectively. The other enumerates vices and acts of righteousness, and supplements the two catalogues by the exhortation to "strip off" allegiance to evil and to "put on" loyalty to the good. The origin of such

[248] See Gal 5:16–26, esp. 19–23; I Cor 5:9–11; 6:9–10; II Cor 6:14 – 7:1; Rom 1:19–32; 13:12–14; Col 3:5–17; I Tim 1:9–10; 3:2–12; II Tim 3:2–5, 16–17, etc.; Rev 21:7–8; 22:14–15; Matt 5:3–12; 19:2–30; also I Clem. 62:2, etc.

[249] See BIBLIOGRAPHY 19. Among the names there listed, Klein and Weidinger pioneered in drawing attention to the Jewish and/or Hellenistic origin of the catalogical passages in Pauline exhortation, and B. S. Easton, P. Carrington, and A. M. Hunter followed in their tracks, adding Christian traditions. The more recent books elaborate on specific aspects of the problem: Vögtle scans the pagan-Hellenistic world; Wibbing believes that Jewish, especially Qumran, texts such as 1QS III 13 – IV 26 underlie the ethics of the NT epistles; Kamlah adds references to Iranian and to apocalyptic dualistic sources.

[250] E.g. "humbleness," "gentleness," "love," 4:2–3; "faith," "hope," "love," I Cor 13; Eph 1:15, 18, etc.

[251] See e.g. the words "together with any [other sort of] malice" (4:31).

[252] E.g. H. Lietzmann, in his interpretation of Rom 1 (HbNT 8, 4th ed. [1933], 35–36, 132–33), refers to the following Jewish, Greek and Latin texts: Exod 20 – 23:19; 33:14–26; Lev 19; Deut 27: 15–26; Hosea 4:1–2; Wisd Sol 12:3 ff.; 14:22 ff.; IV Macc 1 – 3; *Test. Levi* XVII; Philo *de sacrificiis Abelis et Caini* 20 – 22, 32 etc.; Plato *Gorg.* 525A; Diogenes Laertius VII 110–14; Cicero *Tusculanum* IV 5:9 ff.; Ps.-Aristotle *de virtutibus et vitiis* II 1249, etc. While the Stoics engaged more passionately than other thinkers in listing virtuous and vicious attributes and actions, traces of a similar concern and method are also found in as diverse settings as the Hermetic Literature and early medieval Jewish confessions used on the Day of Atonement, see Lietzmann, HbNT 8, 36. NT parallels have been listed in fn. 248.

lists can be traced in Iranian sources, in the ethical writings of Plato and Aristotle, in Stoicism, in Wisdom Literature, in Qumran, and in Philo. Similar lists occur in Jewish apocryphal writings including the *derek 'eretz* booklets, and in the Jewish and Christian doctrine of the Two Ways. Kamlah concludes that Judaism became for early Christianity the mediator of an originally Iranian, mythological (sometimes astrological), world-view which presupposed the existence of two opposite spirits. These spirits were understood to operate in man and to vie for dominion over him. Jewish thinkers far from endorsed this scheme of thought without making substantial changes: they fitted the (mythical) dualistic elements into their monotheistic belief in the creator. For this purpose they converted the two opposed cosmic spirits into "angels," "ways," or "impulses." Paul went even farther in demythologizing this inherited material. He transposed the mythical-dualistic imagery (esp. in Gal 5:17) into the concept of two subsequent aeons and two correlative modes of being. In his teaching there is no room for two deities, inasmuch as creaturely existence and God-given new existence form the basic pair of contrasts.

Kamlah concentrates upon baptism as the occasion for both the admonition given in catalogue form and the imagery of putting off vices and putting on Christ (or, the armor of God and the "actions typical of the righteous"). While Stoics describe the ideal of the individual wise man in their lists, Paul uses catalogues to show the holiness of the congregation. The holiness conveyed to the Christians in baptism prevents the church from imitating pagan conduct. Holiness is the essence of the (non-mythological) concept of the "New man," the true Adam, and the body of Christ. The description of that holiness by catalogical exhortations is fully in line with the eschatological character of the proclamation of Christ.

Not all of Kamlah's findings are incontestable, but his research offers an essential contribution to an understanding of 4:22–32. It is a common feature of the longer and shorter NT ethical lists that they confront the reader not with a dualistic (mythological) world-view but with a radical (ethical) call to faith and decision.[253] Instead of offering a description of successive steps to be taken on the path leading from a lower to a higher form of existence,[254] they reflect the tension between sin and holiness, between Adam and Christ. In focus is the historical and eschatological dethronement of the former by the latter,[255] rather than an unresolved and timeless tension between two ontic realms and their reflection in anthropology and morality. There is no hint of double predestination or of a limitation which would condemn or permit one part of mankind or one dimension of human existence to remain under the power of evil. Those that have been "far" have been "brought near" and are to receive knowledge of God (1:17–18; 2:13; 3:10). All evil attitudes and actions "shall be taken away" (4:31). People who were "dead in sins" and ruled by the evil "spirit" (2:1–2) shall be "good"; because they are "forgiven" they can forgive (4:32).

Paul's teaching is distinguished from fatalism by the emphasis placed upon

[253] In recent decades it has often been repeated that in the NT an ontic dualism is replaced or reinterpreted by a dualism of ethical decision.

[254] See COMMENT VII A C on 4:1–16.

[255] Rom 5:12–21; I Cor 15:21 ff., 45 ff.

man's responsibility. In stripping off the "Old Man" and putting on the "New," man throws off malice and chooses the good. If there is yet an absolute destiny reflected in Paul's ethical teaching then it is this: in Christ the same man who was dead in sins is to live a new life. The very same man who has heard God's saving word and awakening call is enabled to respond by active faith, love, and hope. For this reason Pauline ethics are a proper form of proclaiming the "justification of the godless" (Rom 4:5). Whether Paul composes or edits lists, he uses them as instruments to preach the concreteness and incisiveness of salvation.

X LIGHT OVER DARKNESS
(5:1–20)

5 ¹ Therefore, as [God's] beloved children be imitators of God ² and walk in [the way of] love, just as [we confess]

The Messiah has loved us
and has given himself for us
as an offering and sacrifice,
whose fragrance is pleasing to God.

³ Yet as is fitting for saints, fornication and filth of any kind, or greed must not even be mentioned among you, ⁴ neither shameless, silly, ribald talk. These things are improper. Instead, [let there be] thanksgiving! ⁵ For you had better keep this in mind: No fornicating, filthy, or greedy man, that is, no man who worships an idol, has an inheritance in the kingdom of God's Messiah. ⁶ Let no one deceive you with shallow words. It is because of these things that the wrath of God comes upon the rebellious. ⁷ Therefore do not associate with them. ⁸ For in the past you were darkness, but now in Christ you are light. Conduct yourselves as children of light ⁹ for the fruit of light consists of everything that is good, righteous, and true. ¹⁰ Find out by experience what is pleasing to the Lord ¹¹ and have nothing to do with those fruitless deeds done in darkness. Much more disprove them [by your conduct] ¹² for it is shameful even to mention the things that happen in secret. ¹³ [Only] by the light are all reprobate things revealed. ¹⁴ All that is revealed is light. Therefore he says,

"Awake you sleeper,
rise from the dead,
the Messiah will shine upon you!"

¹⁵ In sum, watch carefully how you conduct yourselves—not as fools but as wise men. ¹⁶ Redeem the time for these days are evil. ¹⁷ Therefore do not be senseless but [learn to] comprehend what is the will of the Lord. ¹⁸ In particular do not get drunk with wine—that is profligacy—but be filled with the Spirit. ¹⁹ Talk to one another in psalms and hymns and spiritual songs. Sing and play to the Lord

from your heart. 20 In the name of our Lord Jesus Christ give thanks
always and for everything to God the Father.

NOTES

5:1. *Therefore.* Sometimes the conjunctions *oun, dio, dioti* are used in Ephesians (also in disputed Pauline Epistles and in classical Greek) to introduce a logical conclusion or presupposition. However, in Pauline writings and elsewhere the same words can also indicate the beginning of a new paragraph which after a quotation either returns to the author's own formulations or contains another block of traditional material.[1] Lexicographical evidence and Pauline concordances do not permit a decision whether *oun* separates Eph 5:1–2 from the preceding (traditional) admonitions,[2] or designates these two verses as their continuation and climax.[3] Still, one difference is striking: in 5:1–2 the command and its motivation are not preceded by a corresponding prohibition—as was regularly the case in 4:25–32. The author has chosen strictly positive terms to sum up the preceding passage and to introduce a new line of thought.[4]

as [God's] beloved children. The addition of the word "God's" is recommended by Pauline parallels that explicitly speak of "God's children" or "sons." Since in 4:14 Paul has warned against babylike conduct, he cannot have a sentimental glorification of childish behavior in mind. But he does point out that only where there is a father and abounding love is the injunction to imitate appropriate. Not just any person, not to speak of an impersonal ideal, is to be followed. Rather he who knows whose child he is will strive to emulate in a way that is free from ridiculous pretension and calculation of expected rewards. Only the people whom Paul has converted himself he calls his own children.[5] When he addresses the Corinthians by this endearing term, he also urges them to "imitate himself" (I Cor 4:14–16). A mountain peasant's child following in his father's footsteps through high snow is a proper illustration of the biblical concept of imitation.[6] The distinction between father and child is by no means obfuscated by the child's acts of imitation.

be imitators of God. The term "imitators of God" is found only here in the Bible,[7] but in both the OT and the NT the command to imitate God has certain

[1] See the Introduction, section II. Compare, e.g. Eph 5:7; 3:13; I Cor 15:9 with Eph 2:11, 19; 4:25; 5:15. Paul uses the conjunction *gar*, lit. "for," in an equally diverse way as is illustrated esp. by Rom 1:16–18 or Eph 5:5, 6, 8, 9, 12, 13.
[2] The present chapter division suggests that with 5:1 a new unit begins. Calvin and Gaugler distinctly understand 5:1–2 as part of the following section of Ephesians.
[3] So e.g. Robinson.
[4] While in Col 2:12–13 the simple reference to God's "forgiveness" is considered sufficient, in Eph 5:1–2 Paul elaborates on the nature of the "forgiveness" granted by "God through Christ" (cf. 4:32): three or four of its constitutive elements are mentioned in quick succession—the Father-child relationship, the imitation of God, the love and the sacrifice of Christ.
[5] See, e.g. Gal 4:19; I Cor 4:14–17; Philem 10; I Tim 1:2; II Tim 1:2; 2:1, etc. In I John two different forms of the noun "child" are used: *teknon* for God's children, 3:1, 2, 10; 5:2; and *teknion* (cf. Gal 4:19) for the author's (spiritual) children, 2:1, 12; 3:7, 18; 4:4; 5:21; cf. *paidion*, 2:14, 18. III John 4 is an exception: there the author speaks of "his" *tekna*.
[6] This image is used by E. Schweizer, *Lordship and Discipleship*, SBT 28 (1960), 11. Thomas Aquinas writes, God "must be imitated insofar as it is possible for us to do so—a son must imitate his father." Cf. Matt 5:45, 48; Luke 6:35–36. According to Robinson, p. 114, "The imitation of God in his mercifulness is the characteristic of sonship."
[7] In the Apostolic Fathers it occurs twice: in Ign. *Trall.* I 2 and in *Philad.* VII 2 where Christ is called an imitator of God. In Ign. *Rom.* VI 3 imitation of the "passion of my God" means imitation of Christ's suffering.

analogies. The OT speaks frequently of "following Yahweh"; it uses this concept as a parallel or synonym of "being brought by Yahweh into the land," or "serving" him, or "walking in his ways."[8] The opposite is "to follow after" idols.[9] The meaning of Eph 5:1 may be revealed by all those OT passages that describe the Lord's holiness, truth, righteousness, mercy, and that promise or command at the same time that holiness, faith, justice, charity are the proper response of God's covenant partner, the chosen people and each of its members, especially the king.[10] The Gospels and I Peter 2:21 speak of "following after Christ"; the Pauline Epistles contain references to the "imitation of Christ" (I Thess 1:6; I Cor 11:1). Other texts refer to "imitation" of the "type" offered by the apostle.[11] H. D. Betz locates the terminology of "following" in Palestinian Judaism (though not in the OT), and the references to "imitation" in Hellenistic Mystery Cults, particularly in the Dionysos cult.[12] Thomas Aquinas, however, held that the OT and Gospel formula, to "follow the Lord," was the key to understanding Eph 5:1. He translated, "Be ye therefore followers of God." The grave problems posed by Greek and Hellenistic derivations of the meaning of "imitators" and their far-reaching consequences for a full interpretation of Eph 5:1 will be discussed in COMMENT II.

2. *walk in [the way of] love.* Lit. "walk in love"; cf. Rom 14:15, "you walk no more according to love." In the first NOTE on Eph 2:2 it was shown why the verb "walk" implies the idea of a way to be followed. Paul calls love "a way" in I Cor 12:31. Since in Eph 5:2 the imperative "walk" occurs in the immediate context of the command, "be imitators," there can be no doubt that imitation can be understood in the sense of the OT and Synoptic term "following after." While in Mystery Religions imitation is not necessarily connected with a specific ethical demand but means the result of a sacramental experience (e.g. rebirth, resurrection, deification, salvation of the soul, release from anxiety), Eph 5:2 shows that the imitation mentioned in 5:1 aims at ethical conduct. Men

[8] Exod 13:21-22 (23:20); 40:34-38; Num 9:15-23; 14:24; 32:11-12; Deut 1:30-33, 36; 13:5; 26:8; Josh 14:8-9, 14; I Sam 12:14; I Kings 11:6; 14:8; 18:21; II Kings 23:3; cf. Isa 40:3-5; 52:12; 57:14; 58:8; Ezek 20:6, 15-16, 18-19, 28, 34-38, 42; Job 23:11; Sir 46:10; Eccles 2:12 (if the original text is translated with Thomas Aquinas, "What is man, I said, that he can follow the king his maker").

[9] Deut 4:3; 6:14; 8:19; Jer 2:5, 8, 25; 7:6, 9, etc.

[10] Hosea 2:19-20; Lev 19:2; 20:7-8; 21:15; 22:9, 16, 32; Matt 5:48; 18:23-35; Luke 6:36, etc. In Jewish writings the term "imitating God" or an equivalent occurs when a reference to the exemplary goodness of God is made, see e.g. *Aristeas* 187-92; 210; 281, etc.; Philo refers to acts of *charizesthai*, "being gracious," in *de virt.* 168; *spec. leg.* IV 73. He attributes this insight to the teaching of a "man of old," that is, perhaps (as Philo *de fuga. et inv.* 63 suggests) to Plato who taught (in *Theaetetus* 176AB) that man could become similar to God "as far as possible" by being "righteous and holy" (*dikaios kai hosios*). Cf. the quote from Thomas Aquinas in fn. 6. A similar thought is expressed in later Jewish Bible interpretation, see Mekhilta Exod 15:2; Sifre Deut 49. According to H. J. Schoeps, *Aus frühchristlicher Zeit* (Tübingen: Mohr, 1950), pp. 288, 290, 301, "imitation in the Jewish sense is founded in the createdness of man in God's image, and finds its perfection in the Messianic future." Another aspect of man's resemblance to God is discussed by Philo in *spec. leg.* II 225; *de decalogo* 51, 120: in producing children parents imitate God's creative power. Obviously Eph 5:1 does not intend to point to any such sort of creativity: not as parents but as "children" the saints shall be "imitators of God." The preceding verse, 4:32, has stated explicitly that *charizesthai*, "forgiving," is the way in which the saints are to follow God's example, cf. Col 3:13.

[11] I Thess 1:6; II Thess 3:7, 9; I Cor 4:16; 11:1; cf. Col 4:12. In the OT, equally it is not only God who is "[to be] followed" but also his servant, esp. the prophet (I Kings 19:19-21; II Kings 2:3 ff.; Isa 8:15-18) and the wise man in his function as a spiritual father (Prov 1:8, 10, 15; 2:1, etc.). To follow after a man not appointed by God leads to a catastrophic end, as is shown by Judg 9. In the Talmud (*passim*) the relationship between a disciple and the rabbi who instructs and guides him is described by the term "to follow," see G. Kittel, TWNTE, I, 213 for references.

[12] In *Nachfolge und Nachahmung*, BHTh 37 (1967), pp. 46 f., 60, 74, 102, 172, 186, Betz opposes the assumption that imitation, wherever it is mentioned in the NT, includes the (Gnostic) notion of deification.

cannot copy the essence of God, e.g. his work as creator or redeemer, or his trinity, but they are called to imitate his love and make progress on the way of love.[13] After the words of 4:32, "forgive . . . as God has forgiven you," have been restated and explained in Eph 5:1-2a, the next line shows what was meant by the formula "in Christ." According to Calvin the imitation of God and of Christ belong together: "As much as we can, we are to return God's good deeds. . . . What we discern in Christ, is our true rule of life."

just as [*we confess*]. The function of "just as" is at this point manifold: it introduces a reason, a comparison, and a quote.[14]

The Messiah has loved us and has given himself for us. These words and the rest of 5:2 appear to be cited from a hymn or confession. For whenever in Pauline writings the offering of Christ is mentioned (with an allusion to Isa 53:6, 12), the tone of diction is raised to a poetic level, and sometimes parallel members distinguish several lines or stanzas from the prose of the context.[15] Among the diverse hymns and confessions used in early churches, some included a reference to Christ's love, to the church (the bride) as the beneficiary, and/or to sin as the power left behind. Compare e.g. Eph 5:2 with 5:25-27. The love of the Messiah is emphatically praised in Rom 8:35, 37; it is often mentioned in the Fourth Gospel, see e.g. 13:1, 34. In John 15:13 the giving of one's life for one's friends is the test and sign of the greatest love. In the Gospel and First Epistle of John the love of the neighbor is as much founded upon God's and Christ's love as in Eph 5:2. The reading, "he has loved us," is supported by the Chester Beatty Papyrus (P 46), a correction found in Codex Sinaiticus, Codex Claramontanus and other majuscules, a respectable group of minuscules spearheaded by Codex Regius (33), and as diversely located fathers as Aphraates, Chrysostom, Jerome. Sometimes Clement of Alexandria and John of Damascus offer the same reading. The next line of vs. 2 also supports it, according to the majority of good MSS; a shift from "you" to "us" or vice versa is most unlikely in closely parallel lines. But the original script of Codex Sinaiticus as well as the Alexandrian and Vatican codices, Pelagius, Augustine, Theophylact read, ". . . love you." If this reading is authentic, Eph 5:2 cannot be called part of a hymn; or it must be called a revised form of a hymnic statement. For, as was shown in the Introduction, section II, the "we"-style, not the proclamatory address "you," is characteristic of a hymn. Together with the first mentioned codices and fathers, the Latin and Syriac versions, and e.g. Dibelius and GNT, but in contrast to Nestle's Greek NT, the reading, "loved us," is probably to be accepted as authentic: the author of Ephesians likes to quote hymns, as Schille has shown, in a form nearer their original wording than is found e.g. in Colossians.

as an offering and sacrifice. Originally, the Hebrew nouns *minhah* and *ōlāh*

---

[13] Thomas Aquinas, Abbott, Gaugler. Schlier states concisely that the imitation of God happens in the imitation of Christ, by a life lived in love.

[14] Dibelius believes that the conjunction "just as" (*kathōs*) introduces a reason. Similarly K. Romaniuk, "De usu particulae KATHOS in epistulis Paulinis," VD 43 (1965), 71-84, has limited himself to discussing the logical role of the conjunction. But he finds that it can also introduce a comparison. Though Schille, in his book *Hymnen,* does not mention 5:2, 25-27 among the redemption hymns quoted by the author of Ephesians, these verses appear to belong to this genre (*Gattung*).

[15] See Eph 5:25; Gal 1:4; 2:20; Rom 4:25; 8:32; I Tim 2:6; Titus 2:14. The verb "deliver" also occurs in I Clem 16 in the frame of a full quotation of Isa 53.

(which underlie the Greek terms *prosphorā* and *thysiā* and are here translated by "offering" and "sacrifice") mean different cultic gifts and actions. The first term could denote e.g. products from the fields and trees which, after deposition at the sanctuary, contributed to sustaining the priests; the second term described animals from the flock or stable which were killed at the holy place and portions of which were burnt upon the altar. In addition, the first could signify a life of obedience, the second a reference to atoning death. Several other types and purposes of sacrifice are also distinguished in the OT.[16] However, as early as the Exile, if not before, a sharp differentiation between bloody and unbloody sacrifices was no longer made. E.g. in Ps 40:6 [LXX 39:7]—a psalm reflecting Jeremiah's experience—"sacrifice" and "offering" are a hendiadys. All offerings and sacrifices mentioned in Ezek 45–46, including cereal gifts, are called "sin-offerings . . . to make atonement." It is probable that the same is true of Eph 5:2, and that the technical meaning of the two terms was forgotten. In Rom 12:1; Philip 4:18 Paul uses the noun "sacrifice" (*thysiā*) for an unbloody sacrifice, in Philip 2:17 for the death of a victim. Even the author of Hebrews, an enthusiastic student of sacrificial matters, did not use *thysiā* in its original narrow sense: "Let us offer a sacrifice [*thysiā*] of praise to God, that is, the fruit of lips . . . Do good and share what you have, for such sacrifices [*thysiai*] are pleasing to God" (Heb 13:15–16). In Heb 10:5–6 the hendiadys of Ps 40:6 is found, together with two other designations of sacrifice used by the same psalm. In Heb 10:10, 14, 18 *prosphorā* (originally an unbloody offering) means a sin offering brought at the expense of life. These examples reveal the complete fusion of the terms "offering" and "sacrifice," or of the notions of unbloody and bloody sacrifices. Two conclusions must be drawn for the interpretation of Eph 5:2. (a) The author designates Jesus Christ's death as an atoning sacrifice offered by the pouring out of blood. Sacrifice is not just a metaphor, but here—as much as in Rom 3 and Hebrew—its essence and fulfillment are declared as present on the cross. The author's theology and soteriology are priestly. (b) The reference to the "love" of the one who was priest and victim at the same time shows that the prophetic, i.e. ethical and metaphorical, meaning of sacrifice was joined with the cultic and priestly understanding. Equally in Heb 9:14; cf. 5:7–9; 10:5–10, the "Spirit" in which Jesus Christ brought his sacrifice, i.e. the obedience of this priest, is pointed out.[17] In summary, the reference to the Messiah's death in Eph 5:2 has a double function. The "cross" (2:16) is a once and for all valid saving event that cannot be du-

[16] *Hatah* and *asham*, *zebah* and *shelem*, see esp. Lev 1–7. For a brief discussion and comparison of early Jewish, Greek and Roman sacrifices and their various forms and meanings, see R. K. Yerkes, *Sacrifices in the Greek and Roman Religions and Early Judaism*, London: Black, 1953. The sacrifices in Israel are described, e.g. by G. B. Gray, *Sacrifice in the Old Testament*, Oxford: Clarendon, 1925; W. O. E. Oesterle, *Sacrifices in Ancient Israel*, New York: Macmillan, 1937; Pedersen, *Israel*, III–IV, 299–375; W. Eichrodt, *Theology of the Old Testament*, I (Philadelphia: Westminster, 1961), pp. 142–72.

[17] Priestly sacrificial concepts are taken up by Paul, e.g. in Eph 1:7; 2:13–16; I Cor 10:16; 11:25; Rom 3:25; 5:9. See also COMMENT V B on 2:11–22. But when Paul refers to Christ's obedience and love (e.g. in Philip 2:8; Rom 5:19; 8:3–4; Gal 2:20) he depicts Christ as fulfilling the prophets' interpretation of God's will, see Micah 6:8, etc. For a more extensive discussion see M. Barth, "Was Christ's Death a Sacrifice?", ScotJT Occasional Papers 9, Edinburgh: Oliver, 1961; idem, *Justification*, Grand Rapids: Eerdmans, 1971. Abbott, pp. 147–48, and Dibelius, p. 89, assume that the combination of love with sacrifice in Eph 5:2 excludes the idea of a "scientific" theological or soteriological doctrine on atonement by sacrifice. Yet just as the classic OT prophets did not denounce sacrifice as such, but insisted upon a sacrifice involving man's heart (so, e.g. Ps 51), so Paul did not preach the Messiah's love without the cost of sacrifice. In Gal 2:20 as much as in Eph 5:2, 25 love and self-offering are combined; "He loved me and gave himself for me."

plicated or imitated, *and* it is an example which is to be followed.[18] Because Christ's love is as unique and inimitable as God the Father's, the Gentile-born Ephesians are brothers, have brothers, and can behave as brothers united in love. Because Christ is the first-born among many brethren (Rom 8:29, etc.), his way, including his death, invites and inspires the saints to follow in his footsteps on the way of love, cf. I Peter 2:21.

whose fragrance is pleasing to God. This translation follows NEB but is slightly at variance with the syntax of the Greek text. More literal is the version, "[an offering and sacrifice] to God for an aromatic odor." The corresponding Hebrew formula *reāh hanniḥoāh* is found about forty times in the Pentateuch.[19] This term seems to express crude anthropomorphism: it suggests the joy experienced in smelling roasted meat. However, it also has a more specific meaning: sacrifice is not understood to be acceptable to God *ex opere operato*, i.e. just because it is properly performed. Though the cereal or animal offered may be valuable to man, its value to God depends on whether God is pleased with the offerer and his gift.[20] Thus sacrifice as such is no more than an offer. Unless God accepts what is offered, it does not fulfill its purpose. Its success depends totally on him to whom it is brought.[21] God is not bribed, his favor is never bought, but a supplication or plea is made to God—just as is also done in prayers of petition or thanks, or in the attempt to lead a life of obedience. When a prayer is heard and fulfilled, it has succeeded. Only when God is pleased by what a man does is the doer of good works righteous. "Offering sacrifices" and doing what "is pleasing to God" could therefore become synonyms, as e.g. LXX Dan 4:37a shows. In Eph 5:2 the accent probably lies on the assertion that the acceptance of Christ's love and sacrifice by God demonstrates the acceptability of human acts of total obedience to God and self-deliverance for others.[22] Passages such as Rom 12:1 and Heb 13:15–16 reveal that exclusively on the ground of Christ's unique atoning sacrifice, spiritual sacrifices can now be offered by many worshippers. These spiritual sacrifices are by no means more cheap than bloody offerings, as Philip 2:17 shows. For even in spiritual sacrifice the life of man is at stake and may have to be laid down. Although large portions of Eph 4:25 ff. were dominated by social moti-

---

[18] In his lecture on Hebrews (1517–18; *Anfänge reformatorischer Bibelauslegung*, II, ed. J. Ficker [Leipzig: Dieterich, 1929], "Glosses," p. 9, "Scholia," pp. 14–15, 23–24, 106; see also WA, XI, 18, lines 18–24), Luther distinguished between two functions of Christ's death, called *sacramentum* and *exemplum*; cf. E. Bizer, "Die Entdeckung des Sakramentes durch Luther," EvTh 17 (1957), 64–90. The distinction between Christ as a *gift to* man and as an *example for* man is found, e.g. in the account of the footwashing in John 13 (compare esp. vss. 8, 10 with vss. 14–15). Betz's book *Nachfolge und Nachahmung* culminates in the statements, "The concept imitation of Christ encompasses the relationship between indicative and imperative which is characteristic of Paul's theology" (p. 170); this concept shows that salvation comes from outside and cannot be repeated or controlled, but lays its claim upon man (pp. 3, 42, 173, 187). Schlier introduces the ambiguous term *Nachvollzug* ("actualization," or "reenactment") into the discussion: "Imitation of God in the Pauline sense is the actualization of the sacrifice of Christ which directs us upon itself" (p. 232).

[19] E.g. Gen 8:21; Exod 29:18, 25, 41; Lev 1:9, 13, 17; 2:2, 9; cf. Ezek 20:41.

[20] Cain's offering as well as the protest of Amos, Hosea and later prophets against a mechanized cultus demonstrate this point.

[21] See G. von Rad's essay on the OT concept *ḥāshab*, "to reckon," "to account for," and its synonyms: "Die Anrechnung des Glaubens zur Gerechtigkeit," TLZ 76 (1951), 129–32; Engl. tr. in G. von Rad, *The Problem of the Hexateuch and Other Essays* (New York: McGraw-Hill, 1966), pp. 125–30. See also the second NOTE on the formula "pleasing to the Lord," in Eph 5:10.

[22] Gal 2:2; I Cor 15:10, 58. The same apostle who passionately fights justification by works affirms bluntly that human labor is not condemned to be useless under all circumstances. See COMMENT VI B C on 2:1–10.

vations, in 4:32; 5:1–2 theological and soteriological arguments express the core of Pauline ethics. It is not the saints who possess or produce a fragrance with which God has to be pleased, and which may also be spread throughout the world. Rather they are "the aroma of Christ [pleasing] to God among those saved and those perishing" (II Cor 2:14–16).[23]

3. *as is fitting for saints.* The occurrence of the term "fitting" in Matt 3:15 does not demonstrate that Matthew or Jesus referred to a written code by which Jesus was bound to be baptized.[24] Equally, the same formula in Eph 5:3; cf. Philem 8, and its opposite in 5:4, are insufficient evidence for stipulating the existence of an early Christian manual of discipline.[25] Rather, the term "fitting" shows that voluntary obedience was expected of the saints to a standard that could not be legistically codified. Those raised to new life, enthroned in heaven, adopted to be children of God, are treated as are princes or noblemen.[26] The question whether Eph 5:3 ff. is, at least in part, to be applied to non-Christians as well, will be discussed in COMMENT III.

fornication and filth of any kind, or greed. Fornication was denounced by Hosea and other prophets. Though in NT times it was considered a vice typical

---

[23] However, in Philip 4:18; Barn. II 10 the imagery of a pleasing odor is used without an explicit reference to Christ or his sacrifice.

[24] M. Pohlenz, *"To Prepon,"* Nachrichten von der Gesellschaft der Wissenschaften in Göttingen, Philol.-Historische Klasse 1933, I (Berlin: Weidmann, 1933), 53–92, gives a sketch of the history of the term "fitting." He shows that this word was first used to describe (a) the beauty of a person that strikes the eye; then (b) the distinct behavior that is suitable and normative for different persons (e.g. men and women, old and young people, free men and slaves); then (c) such a recitation and/or composition of poetic texts as was appropriate to the artist, the subject matter, and the audience; then (d) the harmony and measure characteristic of all arts and all wise behavior. In each case the Greek term allows for differences among various individuals and calls for proper use of the occasion (*kairos*, cf. Eph 5:16!). By doing what is fitting to them men gain rather than lose character and personality. Sometimes the term contains an appeal to the rational and natural, but more often it is stated that only the aesthetical judgment is aware of that which is fitting. A fitting composition and conduct come out of pleasure and create pleasure. In short, the history of this term among the Greeks expresses the consistent belief that the beautiful and the good (*kalon k'agathon*) coincide and come to manifestation in the world of phenomena. Cicero and Horace are among the Latin writers who transferred the term "fitting" from Aristotle and the cynic philosopher Diogenes' disciple Panaitios into Roman culture. They translated it by *aptum, decet, decorum est* ("it is appropriate, decent") or similarly. E.g. in Epictetus *diss.* II 10; 17:31 and Diogenes Laertius VII 108 the original aesthetical and individualizing meaning of *to prepon* appears to disappear, and the term *to kathēkon* (or its plural form) which describes a perfect standard valid for all men is increasingly used as a synonym of *to prepon; cf.* Menander *fragm.* 575. In NT ethical exhortations, forms of *prepō* are found in I Cor 11:13; I Tim 2:10; Titus 2:1. *Kathēkō* never occurs in parenthetical contexts of the NT (unlike I Clem 1:3; 3:4; 41:3), but it is used in two sentences expressing a judgment, i.e. in Rom 1:28 and Acts 22:22. Various forms of the related *anēkō*, that were much used among Stoics, occur in the exhortations of Eph 5:4; Col 3:18; Philem 8. Schlier, TWNTE, III, 437–40, believes that such terms contain an appeal to a concept of "fitting" which was valid among Christians and Gentiles alike. Certainly the term *to dikaion* ("what is right," e.g. Philip 4:8; Eph 6:2; in Sir 10:23 it is a synonym of *kathēkei*) can include a standard that is recognized not only among the "saints."

[25] The Qumran Community possessed such a manual. A forceful attempt to prove that a tradition fixed in writing underlies NT parenthetical passages was made, e.g. by Selwyn, *First Peter,* pp. 365–439. Schlier speaks of a moral code (*Sittenkodex*) but does not insinuate that it existed in writing. Braun, QuNT, I, 219–22, recognizes analogies between Eph 5:3–11 and Qumranite teaching. But he explains them as the result of a dualism which is common to Qumran, Ephesians, and John 8:12; 12:35–36, and does not ascribe them to a direct borrowing by the author of Ephesians from Qumran. The soteriological frame and some particular terms used in Eph 5:3 ff. are so distinct from Qumran thought and diction that a literary dependence of Ephesians on Qumran literature is unlikely.

[26] See COMMENT II on 4:1–16. There the appeal made to that which is "worthy" of those "called" with a "high calling," and the evangelical character of the Pauline imperatives was discussed at some length. Quoting the maxim, *Noblesse oblige,* Robinson calls 5:4 an appeal to "a new Christian *decorum.*" The addition of the words "for saints" to "fitting" demonstrates beyond any doubt that Paul is alluding neither to natural law nor to the voice of a conscience possessed by every man. Rather the apostle speaks of an order recognized among those who are raised from death in sin.

of pagans,[27] Israel, too, was called by Jesus an "adulterous generation" (see Matt 12:39; 16:4; Mark 8:38). In the Bible "fornication" often describes not only the promiscuous behavior of unmarried and married people but each of those sexual activities and relations (including adultery, incest, and homosexuality) that is prohibited in the Pentateuch and discussed in the context of Eph 4:19. When in 5:3 "filth," lit. "impurity," is added to "fornication" then the meaning of the latter appears to be restricted to promiscuity and adultery, whereas filth denotes the wider range of putrid or wild sexual behavior. In his commentary on Ephesians Thomas Aquinas gave "filth" a very specific meaning: he defined it as every sexual act "not ordered toward the generation of offspring." Still, Gen 2:24 as quoted in Eph 5:31, as well as Paul's teaching in I Cor 7:2–11, are far from the assertion that sexual relations between husband and wife have exclusively one purpose.[28] "Insatiability" would be a literal translation of Greek *pleonexiā*, which is here interpreted by "greed." In Eph 4:19 the same term was paraphrased by "still asking for more." Other occurrences of the triad, fornication-filth-greed, and the identification of one or another of its members with idolatry (cf. 5:5), were discussed in COMMENT II on 4:17–32, especially fn. 158.

must not even be mentioned among you. Dibelius (cf. also Schlier) calls this injunction "exaggerated." Dibelius explains this duplication of 4:29–30 by suggesting that in 5:3 ff. another set of traditional material is used. Bengel understands the words to mean: fornication etc. shall not occur among you; then they cannot even be mentioned as facts. Indeed, I Cor 5:1 presupposes publicity of shameful events in the congregation (lit. "they were heard"). However, as Abbott states, the emphatic "not even" (*mēde*) does not create room for such an interpretation. Just as in Rom 1:16–17 the (word of the) Gospel is called a power of salvation, so filthy or "foul talk" (4:29) is considered a power of destruction. To mention foul things by name (*onomazō*, cf. 1:21; 3:15) is as much as to make them present, to initiate their operation, and to accept their control. Evil talk and bad language resemble a magical incantation. Once again the outstanding relevance which is attributed to the spoken word throughout Ephesians becomes apparent.[29]

4. *neither shameless, silly, ribald talk. These things are improper.* Lit. "and shamelessness, silly talk or levity. . . ." The first of the three Greek nouns found in the original text, *aischrotēs*, need not refer only to a way of talking, but may mean "ugliness" or "wickedness."[30] Yet it is probable that this verse adds three vices of the tongue to the three vicious forms of conduct described in vs. 3. *Aischrotēs* can be a synonym of *aischrologiā*.[31] The second noun, *mōrologiā*, means "silly talk." It is rare among classical writers and occurs nowhere else in the LXX and the NT. The Latin has a similar noun: *stultilo-*

---

[27] Eph 4:19; cf. Rom 1:29 var. lect.; I Cor 5:1a, b; 6:13, 15, 18 (7:2?); Col 3:5, etc.; Dibelius; Schlier. In his book, *Die Ehe im Neuen Testament* (Zurich: Zwingli, 1967), pp. 135–49, 197, H. Baltensweiler shows that *porneiā*, here translated by "fornication," may also mean incestual marriage; see esp. I Cor 5:1 and I Thess 4:3–8, and, perhaps, Matt 5:32; 19:9.

[28] The command, "Be fruitful and multiply" (Gen 1:28, cf. Ps 127:2–5) and the Papal encyclical *Humanae Vitae* of Paul VI notwithstanding. See fn. 205 on Eph 5:21–33.

[29] Similarly among the Persians "it was forbidden to say that which was forbidden to do," according to Herodotus I 138.

[30] So e.g. Plato *Gorg.* 525A.

[31] "Obscene speech" is mentioned in the catalogues of Col 3:8 and *Did.* v 1; see WBLex 24, against Abbott.

quium. Bengel defines it as fishing for a laugh, even without salt in one's speech (cf. Mark 9:50; Col 4:6). The last noun, *eutrapeliā,* means among Greek writers "wittiness," "facetiousness," and "pleasantry" in a good sense.[32] A line from Plautus' *miles gloriosus* suggests that Ephesus was especially known for producing facetious orators: "I am a facetious caviller, because I was born in Ephesus, not in Apulia or Animula." The parenthesis, "these things are improper,"[33] seems redundant after the reference to "fitting" in 5:3, but there may be a special reason why it is inserted immediately after *eutrapeliā:* even that manner of speech which is considered humorous and is well-accepted among pagans is radically opposed to the ministry of Christians (Calvin). "Coarse jesting" or "ribaldry" may serve as English translations whenever the noun possesses an evil sense. The two conjunctions "and" "or" (*kai, ē*) which connect the three misuses of the tongue already mentioned are not the same in all MSS. In several codices they are interchanged or one of them occurs twice. The variants may prove that Paul was not understood as speaking of only two things, one of which he described with a hendiadys. Cf. the changes of conjunctions in 5:3, their sameness in 5:5, and the genitive-plus-preposition formulation in 4:19.

Instead, [let there be] thanksgiving. The addition of "let there be" follows Abbott's suggestion. Instead of the telegram style (brachylogy) of the Greek text, a complete sentence is preferable in English. It is not advisable to eliminate the brachylogy by connecting the words, lit. "instead thanksgiving," directly with the verb "[must not be] mentioned" (vs. 3)—as if the author wanted to say, rather thanksgiving shall be mentioned![34] Why is just "thanksgiving" contrasted with ribald behavior and speech, rather than, e.g. love or decency? Interpreters such as Clement of Alexandria, Origen (*Catenae* VI 190), Chrysostom, Jerome (cf. Calvin) demonstrate their exposure to Greek education when they understand *eucharistiā* (here translated by "thanksgiving") to mean speech that is "gratifying," viz. that is pleasant to men. But when the formula (lit.) "giving grace" was discussed in the third NOTE on 4:29, it was shown why this interpretation can be called into question. How then shall "thanksgiving" be interpreted? Nothing is gained by minimizing its importance, e.g. by saying that the term was chosen only because it rhymes with *eutrapeliā.*[35] Rather "thanksgiving" may include a reference to Paul's own thanksgivings in his letters,[36] and may urge the saints to reciprocate in kind. It is still more likely that gratitude is here singled out as the basic structural feature of the Chris-

---

[32] Aristotle (*eth. Nic.* II 7, 13 1108AB; *rhetorica* II 12 1387B) places it in the middle of buffoonery and boorishness, and he describes it as hybris on a leash.

[33] Lit. ". . . were improper." The past (imperfect) tense of *anēkō* corresponds to the English form "ought" (originally, "owed") and does not require translation by a past form of an English verb. See BDF, 358:2.

[34] Indeed, 1QS X 21–24 offers support to this interpretation, because in the *Manual of Discipline* "thanksgiving" is described as the opposite of shameless, deceitful, silly talk. But Philo suggests an understanding that declares gratitude as the alternative to all vicious conduct, not just to evil words. He taught that the entire religious obligation of man was summed up by "thanksgiving" (*eucharistiā*) which is preeminent among the virtues, see *de plant.* 126, 131; since God himself offers thanksgiving within man, gratitude is not a product of man's soul, *leg. all.* I 82. Schlier understands *eucharistiā* as a reference to the eucharist (the Mass), cf. Justin Martyr *apol.* I 65 f., and *Did.* IX 1 – X 6; XIV 1.

[35] B. S. Easton, JBL 5 (1932), 1–12, suggests that rhymes could play a role in the composition of ethical lists.

[36] E.g. Rom 1:8; I Cor 1:4, etc., see COMMENT II on 1:15–23.

tians' ethic; cf. II Cor 4:15; 9:11–12; Philip 4:6. While "love" sums up the substance of all commandments and their fulfillment (Rom 13:9–10; Gal 5:14), references to "thanksgiving" point out the ontological structure of love: love is a joyful "response" to that grace which is always "prevenient." In Rom 1:21 "ingratitude" is mentioned as the analogous form of vicious behavior. More will be said about the fundamental role of "thanksgiving" in the exposition of Col 3:15, 17.

5. *you had better keep this in mind*. Lit. "[you] know understanding." Two synonymous Greek words are combined after the pattern of a Hebraism found in the Greek OT.[37] Whether *iste* (a form of *oida*, "to know") is an indicative or an imperative cannot be decided on grammatical grounds.[38] Just as in the parallel passages (I Cor 6:9–10, 15:50; Gal 5:21) a similar introductory formula introduces a reminder, not new information, so Eph 5:5 reminds its readers of what they ought to remember without outside help. The version "you had better keep this in mind" combines the synonymous Greek verbs into one and reproduces the ambivalence between indicative and imperative which is found in the Greek original. A simplified, most likely secondary, reading of vs. 5a is found in Theodoret and Theophylact, also in the ninth-century codices K and L: "Be understanding" or "know!" (*este ginōskontes*). The stylized, if not stilted, introduction of vs. 5 is followed by a dictum that belongs probably (to use a nomenclature suggested by E. Käsemann) to the genre of "sentences of holy law."[39] The unusual wording of 5:5b makes it probable that Paul quotes a dictum not coined by himself.

No fornicating, filthy, or greedy man, that is, no one who worships an idol. Lit. "Each fornicator . . . [does] not. . . ." See COMMENT II on 4:17–32 for the listing of these three vices, and for their equation with idolatry. The explicatory words, lit. "which (*ho estin*) is an idolator," are linguistically rough. They have been subjected to beautifying operations: some codices read *hos estin*, "[the greedy man] who is . . ."; others that are followed by most Latin versions read "[greed] which is idolatry."[40] Indeed, the parallel Col 3:5 uses good and unambiguous Greek: "greediness which is idolatry." It is possible that in Eph 5:5, just as in the Colossian parallel and in *Test. Judah* xix 1, only the greedy man is equated with an idolater. For if all three types of men were meant, in classical Greek the plural of the relative pronoun (*ha* instead of *ho*) would have been used. In his explanatory remark "that is, no one who worships an idol" (5:5), the author of Ephesians shows that he knows the demands of good grammar. However, it is still possible that the singular *ho* (or its variant

---

[37] Robinson, p. 199, mentions LXX I Kings[Sam] 20:3; Symm. Jer 49[42]:22. The two verbs in question, *oida* and *ginōskō*, are used as synonyms e.g. in LXX Isa 59:8; Esther 4:17d; Sir 34:9–10; also in John 7:27; Rom 7:7 and finally when Matt 16:3 is compared with Luke 12:56 and Matt 7:23 with Matt 25:12.

[38] Cf. the ambiguity of the form *iste* in Heb 12:17; James 1:19; III Macc 3:14. Erasmus, Calvin, Westcott, Robinson, Abbott, Schlier decide for rendering Eph 5:5a by an indicative, "You know full well," or similarly; Vulg., Thomas Aquinas, Bengel, Haupt, Dibelius prefer the imperative translation.

[39] "Sentences of Holy Law in the New Testament," in *New Testament Questions of Today* (Philadelphia: Fortress, 1969), pp. 66–81. Käsemann dates Ephesians in the post-apostolic period and does not mention Eph 5:5 among the examples mentioned for the *genre* of such sentences. He enumerates, however, among other passages I Cor 3:17; 14:38; 15:22; II Cor 9:6; Rom 2:12; Mark 8:38; Matt 16:27; 10:32–33, which are all versions of the *lex talionis*.

[40] Nestle's NT edition mentions only the first variant, GNT neither of the two. Full evidence of the Greek codices and the early Latin versions offering these two (and other) variants is found in the Beuron edition of the *Vetus Latina*, 24:1 (Freiburg: Herder, n.d.), p. 215.

hos) includes all acts previously enumerated. In focus is the evil man, who reveals his sin against God in multi-dimensional evil deeds against men. The man or the men in question cannot be the Gentiles living in the "deadness" that has preceded their resurrection and enthronement with Christ. Otherwise the author of Eph 5:5 or the tradition from which he quotes would have closed the door of God's kingdom to all who were once "dead in sin" and "far" away from God's people. He would contradict not only Eph 2 but also the Jesus logion, "I came not to call the righteous, but sinners" (Mark 2:17), the corresponding church confession, "The Messiah Jesus came into the world to save sinners" (I Tim 1:15), and the Pauline formulation, "He [God] justifies the ungodly" (Rom 4:5). The immoral persons mentioned in Eph 5:3 ff. are members of the congregation, not people outside the Church. See COMMENT III for the relation of this passage to Qumran and to II Cor 6:14 – 7:1; I Cor 5; Matt 18:15–17; Rev 22:14–15.

has an inheritance. "Inheritance" (*klēronomiā*) may either mean the actual possession of a bequest or the title to receive it.[41] In 2:18; 3:12 and especially in 1:7 the verb *echō,* "to have," has a full and weighty meaning: it describes a status, a possession created by gifts or privileges that have been handed out to the saints, not the mere possibility of forgiveness or of gaining access to God. The same is probably true of 5:5. This verse is not a parallel to the Synoptic statements about "entering" the kingdom (Matt 5:20; Mark 10:24–25, etc.). The Synoptic sayings (so-called *logia*) contain a call to repentance which originally was extended to unbaptized Jews, and was later understood as applying also to Gentiles. Eph 5, however, is—except for vs. 14?—addressed to Christians. In question is solely the retention of all that already has been granted, i.e. adoption, resurrection, enthronement, access, freedom. Vs. 5:5 warns the saints, do not disinherit yourselves! A parallel is Rev 2:25; 3:11, "Hold fast what you have" (*ho echete kratēsate; kratei ho echeis*). Neither the repentance of unbelievers, nor—as vss. 11–14 will show—the renewed repentance of church members is excluded by this article of holy law.

the kingdom of God's Messiah. Lit. ". . . of the Messiah and God." Though there are many passages in the OT and NT that reveal the close relationship, viz. inherence, of God's and the Messiah's kingship, the formulation used in Eph 5:5 is unique in the Bible.[42] Little wonder that there exists a series of variant readings which brings the verse in line with other biblical texts.[43] Since only one article and the singular of *basileiā* ("kingship," "kingdom") are used, it is certain that only one reign is meant, and that at this point a succession of two forms of God's kingship is not envisaged.[44] While a futuristic eschatology

---

[41] Abbott, p. 151. Paul uses the parallel expressions, "to inherit" and "to possess inheritance," only in negations (Gal 4:30; 5:21; I Cor 6:9–10; 15:50; Eph 5:5). Elsewhere he has many positive things to say about heirs and inheritance; see the exposition of 1:11 and 14, COMMENT IX on 1:3–14, and esp. the essay of P. L. Hammer in JBL 79 (1960), 267–72.

[42] See, e.g. I Chron 28:5; 29:23; II Chron 9:8 (cf. 13:8); Isa 9:6–7, also COMMENT II on Eph 1:1–2; fn. 138 to 2:1–10. Cf. John 18:36; Luke 1:33; 22:29–30; 23:42; Matt 13:41; 16:28; I Cor 15:24–28; Col 1:12–13; II Peter 1:11; Rev 11:15; 21:22; 22:1, 3.

[43] Chester Beatty Papyrus: "Kingship of God"; Codex Boernerianus and Ambrosiaster: "Kingship of God and the Messiah"; Minuscule 1739 (uncorrected): ". . . of the Messiah of God" (cf. Ps 2:2: "The Lord and his anointed"); Minuscule 1836: ". . . of the Son of God."

[44] O. Cullmann, "The Kingship of Christ and the Church in the New Testament," in *The Early Church* (Philadelphia: Westminster, 1956), pp. 101–37, has shown that there are NT passages, esp. I Cor 15:24–28, in which two phases of kingship are distinguished. Through Christ God rules now, in the period in which God's dominion is still contradicted and belied by opposing forces. But there

is by no means absent from the testimony of Ephesians, in this verse realized eschatology has the upper hand: may the saints beware lest they lose their crown (cf. Rev 3:11). This does not mean that the author simply identifies being in the church with being in the kingdom, and that he thereby implicitly equates the church with "the kingdom" of the Messiah and God.[45] Rather he reaffirms that the community gathered in the church is God's "own people" (1:14); they are "citizens" of his realm and "members" of his house (2:13, 19). For this reason they are the first to be subject to the discipline of the world-wide rule of Christ and God. On grammatical grounds another translation is equally tenable: "the Kingship of the Messiah, that is, of God."[46] If this version is chosen, Eph 5:5 belongs among NT passages such as Heb 1:8 that assert the deity of Christ. Perhaps the author of Ephesians intended to state what was implicit in 1:4, 10. In those verses the closest possible coordination of God the Father and the Messiah was proclaimed, cf. 1:2, "Grace and peace from God our Father and the Lord Jesus Christ." The same point is made in e.g. Col 2:2 where without any transition or limitation the "secret of God" is identified with the "Messiah" (cf. Col 1:27). While the sequence "God the Father–the Lord Jesus Christ," seeks to explain who God is, how he is now revealed, and through whom he is recognized and honored, the reverse order, "Messiah–God" in 5:5 may indicate that to be exposed to Christ and his rule means to be confronted immediately with God's own presence and dominion: the full power of God is placed in the Messiah's hands (cf. 1:10; Col 1:19; Matt 28:18).

6. *Let no one deceive you with shallow words.* The author probably has in mind people who by their promises, doctrines, arguments, counsels, or consolations encouraged the saints to lead a permissive, if not licentious, life in word and deed. Rev 2:14–15, 20 speaks of the example of "Balaam," of the "Nicolaitans" and "Jezebel"; in the epistles of Jude and II Peter similar groups are condemned; in Rom 6:1, 15 (cf. 3:8), Paul refers to people or to a (hypothetical?) doctrine saying, "Let us continue in sin that grace may abound"; and in Galatians, I Corinthians, and Philippians a libertinist movement is included among the heresy or heresies which the apostle attacks. It may be that those speaking "shallow words" were the same men who also boasted of "salvation through works" (Eph 2:8–9) but they may also have belonged to a different group—just as it is possible that in Galatians, Philippians, and Romans Paul battles either against one single front, or is engaged in a two-front war. Most likely the heretics mentioned in Eph 5:6 are the same as those called "experts in deceitful scheming" (4:14). "Doctrinal gusts" are then the frame and content of

will be a day when all opposition will be quashed; then God will be all in all. Correspondingly, Schlier, p. 235, gives the definition, "The reign of Christ is also the reign of God, [that is] the present and the eschatological form of God's reign." The present rulership of Christ is affirmed by the ever-repeated NT references to the Messiah's enthronement at the right hand of God, whenever Ps 110:1 is quoted; also, e.g. in Rev 11:15; 12:10; I Clem. 50:3; Barn. IV 13; VII 11; VIII 5–6; *Mart. Polyc.* XXII 1, 3.

[45] In the parallel passages, I Cor 5 and Matt 18:15–17, the removal of offenders from the church is urged and executed; nothing is said about their concomitant exclusion from the kingdom. To what extent "the keys of the kingdom" promised to Peter in Matt 16:19 include the power to "shut the kingdom of heaven" against men, cf. Matt 23:13, cannot be discussed here.

[46] Bengel; von Harless.

the "shallow words" that are ridiculed in 5:6. Can anything be established regarding the origin and identity of the seducers warned against in these verses? H. Grotius assumed that some of these men were Gentile philosophers, while others were Jews who "promised to all Judaizers, whatever their conduct, a share in the future eon."[47] Meyer identifies them as "unconverted Gentiles."[48] Schlier sees in them representatives of a morally indifferent or libertinistic Gnosticism. Though Abbott's opinion is somewhat vague, it is still to be preferred to others: Eph 5:6 refers to "Christians who made light of sin." Certainly Dibelius states with good reason that the description of the heretics in Ephesians, if compared with Col 2:8, is "remarkably colorless." As was pointed out previously, the specific interest of Ephesians is not in polemics. However, when the author turns to polemical statements, he reveals that the heresy he has in mind contains both doctrinal errors and ethical deviations, and he strikes equally hard against each form of seduction. The "shallow words" are the opposite of the edifying words of grace mentioned in 4:29. The adjective *kenos* may refer to the contents or to the effect. In the first case, the "words" are declared void of substance and truth; in the second, they are denoted as idle, ineffectual, witless, or pretentious.[49] Both meanings are probably present in 5:6. By their fruits the essence of words will be known. To the "foulness" of the words correspond the "fruitless deeds" (5:11).

It is because of these things. Lit. "For because . . ." It is probable, though not entirely sure, that the author is thinking here of works (see vs. 11) rather than words.[50]

the wrath of God comes. Parallels in Ephesians and in other Pauline Epistles show that God's judgment is not only a future threat (as in 6:8–9?), for judgment or "wrath" are already experienced at the present time.[51]

the rebellious. Lit. "the sons of disobedience." Thomas Aquinas translates, "children of despair"—as if to recall the "hopelessness" of the Gentiles mentioned in 2:12; 4:19 var. lect.; cf. 1:12. See the last NOTE on 2:2 for a further discussion. The same title and history that were attributed to the Gentiles in 2:2 are in 5:6 held as a warning before the eyes of the Christians. There is no judgment in store for those who are far from God which does not begin at God's own house (cf. I Peter 4:17; Jer 25:29; Ezek 24:21). But lest fear of punishment become the primary motive of the saints' obedience, the author will turn soon enough, in vs. 8, to a positive description of that which enables the saints to walk in the way of obedience and love.

7. Therefore do not associate with them. Lit., ". . . do not become their participants." Either this verse prohibits any kind of association with erring church members or it excludes only identification with their works and

---

[47] If Grotius is right, perhaps also those stipulating "salvation by works" and "boasting," cf. 2:9, ought to be considered Jews (see however COMMENT VI B on 2:1–10). Just as in the heresy or heresies fought in Galatians, a combination of righteousness by works and moral libertinism would then be typical of the Ephesian heretics.

[48] P. 219. Eph 2:1; 4:17–19 might support this interpretation.

[49] LSLex, 938.

[50] Abbott. In exact Greek, the reference to the "words" mentioned in 5:6a would require *dia toutous*, not *dia tauta*.

[51] Calvin; Abbott. Cf. 2:3; I Cor 5:4–5; 11:29–30; Rom 1:18 ff. Rom 5:9, however, and the Thessalonian Epistles speak of the wrath to come.

words.[52] In the first case, the apostle commands that erring and misbehaving Christians are to be totally ostracized—lest the punishment coming upon them be shared by those found in their company.[53] However, vss. 11–14 will support another interpretation. There it is clearly stated that the saints must not associate with the "deeds done in darkness," not even with gossip about them. Still, they are not freed from responsibility for erring brothers: "Disprove [or, convince] them" (vs. 11)!

8. *For in the past you were darkness, but now in Christ you are light. Conduct yourselves as children of light.* The contrast between "past" and present ("now") is typical of the "realized eschatology" proclaimed in Ephesians.[54] The metaphors of "light" and "darkness" (which often occur in Qumran literature and in the Fourth Gospel) have been used in Eph 1:18 and 4:18. Their meaning and role in Eph 5 will be discussed in COMMENT IV. The logic of Eph 5:8 follows the pattern indicative-imperative.[55] The new being of the saints is manifested in new conduct. Their resurrection from the dead produces good fruit.

9. *for the fruit of light consists of everything that is good, righteous, and true.* Lit. "for the fruit of the light is in every goodness, righteousness, and truth." Bengel suggests the version "consists of. . . ." A strong group of MSS is led by the Chester Beatty Papyrus and reads, "fruit of the Spirit" instead of "fruit of the light." This variant is probably the result of a secondary adaptation to Gal 5:22. It obfuscates the dominant role of "light" in Eph 5:8–14. In vs. 8 the nouns "children" and "light" were used without the article, but in vs. 9 the article is found before both "fruit" and "light."[56] This slight change may have been made for rhetorical reasons; or it may suggest a distinction between the "children of light" who are human beings, and the "fruit of light" which consists of attitudes and works; finally, it may reveal that vs. 9 is not phrased in the author's own style but contains a quotation, e.g. of a non-biblical proverb. The term *karpos*, lit. "fruit," may designate (as much as the noun child) the son or daughter of a couple, and not only the product of a field or tree, as in e.g. Luke 1:42: "Blessed is the fruit of your womb."[57] Metaphorical senses of *karpos* are: result, reward, profit, or gain; but these meanings do not totally obliterate the original biological sense. The reference to "children" in vs. 8, the allusion to "fruitless" works in vs. 11, and the mention of the "secret production of shameful things" in vs. 12 suggest a translation of *karpos* in vs. 9 which carries the overtone of generation rather than of mechanical production. If *karpos* is understood in this sense, then vss. 8–9 credit the "light" with two groups of children: (a) the saints, and (b) all that is good. The pos-

[52] E.g. Theodoret, von Hofmann, and Haupt decide for the first, Abbott for the second interpretation. Gaugler observes that there is "no moral solidarity between the old and the new man." Thomas Aquinas refers to II Cor 6:14–15.

[53] The principle of "guilt by association" is represented in the Bible, e.g. by Deut 17:7; Isa 53:9; Mark 14:67–70par.; I Cor 5:6; II Cor 6:14 – 7:1; cf. also I Enoch 91:4; 94:3–5; 1QS v 1–2, 10–11, and the etymological meaning of "Pharisees," i.e. people who "separate" themselves (from the *ammē haarez,* the *massa perditionis*).

[54] See 2:1 ff., 11 ff.; 3:5; 4:17 ff. and COMMENT IX on 1:3–14.

[55] See COMMENT II on 4:1–16.

[56] Abbott, p. 153 refers to a so-called "rule of Apollonius" which requires that "nouns in regimen" have the article either in both cases or in neither.

[57] See also Gen 30:2; Micah 6:7; Lam 2:20; Ps 132:11; Acts 2:30. Since a classic Greek writer such as Euripides (*Ion* 922) speaks of "fruit of Zeus" it is not necessary to call this employment of the term fruit a Hebraism (against WBLex, 405).

sibility cannot be excluded that the abstract terms goodness, righteousness, truth substitute for adjectives describing good, righteous, true men. The Pauline catalogues of powers, of ministries, and of good and evil deeds enumerate either abstract qualities and functions, or the persons (or personified powers) who are their bearers; or they combine both modes of description without indicating a change of meaning.[58] Therefore, a paraphrase of 5:9 saying, "The offspring of light consists of all men who are good, righteous and true," cannot be ruled out. Indeed, according to Eph 5 the "light" has living, flourishing children— in contrast to the "deeds of darkness" that are barren, even "fruitless" (5:11), and the (lit.) "sons of disobedience" who are under the wrath of God and dead even while they live (5:6; 2:1–3).[59] The composition of the triad goodness- righteousness-truth is reminiscent of I Sam 15:22; Micah 6:6–8, and other prophetic passages in which obedience shown from the depth of the heart is placed above cultic rites and performance. Even closer is the parallel 1QS I 5, a text which sums up the message of Moses and the Prophets by the commandment that the covenant members "keep all works of the good, [that is] do truth, righteousness [=mercy] and justice." Since truth, justice, and loving devotion are also found among the six virtues listed in 1QS v 3–4, it is possible to consider Eph 5:9 a dictum of Jewish, perhaps Qumranite, origin.[60] Yet it may also be that allusion is made to an enumeration of capital virtues that was known to the readers from Greek philosophy, if not from Iranian religious tradition. Just as OT and apocryphal Wisdom Books borrow freely from non- Israelite moral tradition, so Paul's exhortation to live "as wise men" (5:15) may contain elements drawn from non-Christian sources. "Whatever is true, whatever is honorable, whatever is lovely . . . think about these things" (Philip 4:8). In I Clem 62:2 righteousness, truth, and long-suffering are mentioned together, but embedded among other virtues that were respected by honorable pagans. However, the existence of non-Jewish and non-Christian lists of good attitudes does not preclude the possibility that Paul understood goodness, righteousness, and truth in their Hebrew rather than in their Greek sense. In the OT "righteousness" and "truth" often denote a covenant-like behavior toward God and fellow man which reflects God's own loyalty. Seven times in Ecclesiastes "goodness" (*agathōsynē*) means enjoyment, but in LXX II Esd 19:25, 35 [Neh 9:25, 35] it signifies God's "goodness," and in LXX Ps 51:5[52:3] it is used as a term parallel to righteousness (and to speaking the truth).[61] Perhaps "goodness" (*agathōsynē*) in Eph 5:9 is a synonym of the "goodness (*chrēstotēs*) mentioned in 2:7; cf. 4:32.

10. *Find out by experience.* Just as in 3:17; 4:2–3, so here the participle

---

[58] See the catalogues of powers: Rom 8:38–39; 13:6–7; Eph 1:21; of ministries: I Cor 12:4–11; 28–30; Rom 12:3–13; Eph 4:11–12; of so-called vices and virtues: Gal 5:19–23; I Cor 5:9–11; 6:9–10; II Cor 6:14 – 7:1; Rom 1:19–32; 13:12–14; I Tim 1:9–10, etc. In analogy, the "Old" and "New Men" are described by both personal adjectives and abstract nouns that characterize their history, see Eph 4:22, 24; Col 3:9–10.

[59] Modern scientific insights into the biochemical influence of light upon growth and reproduction corresponds to this attribution of productivity to light.

[60] S. Wibbing, *Tugend- und Lasterkataloge im Neuen Testament*, BhZNW 25 (1959), pp. 61–64, 111– 12; K. G. Kuhn, "Die in Palestina gefundenen Texte und das NT," ZThK 47 (1950), 210; and H. Braun, QuNT, I, 222 comment on these parallels.

[61] The Hebrew meanings of the three terms do not support Thomas Aquinas' suggestion that the nouns either express the relationships of a saint (a) to himself, (b) to his neighbor, and (c) to God; or, the attitude of (a) man's heart, (b) man in action, and (c) man's tongue respectively.

dokimazontes has imperative character; it contains the first explanation of "conducting oneself as a child of light" (5:8b). Two further specifications follow: "Have nothing to do . . . ," and "Much more disprove" (5:11). The first command tells the saints to look up to God and to learn from him; the second, to keep aloof from evil works; the third, to fulfill their responsibility toward their brothers. Outside and inside the Greek Bible, the verb *dokimazō* (here translated by "finding out by experience") has at least two meanings: (a) put to the test, examine, check credentials, try to learn; (b) prove by testing, accept as proved, approve, think fit.[62] Reasons for the translation "find out by experience" will be presented in COMMENT V.

what is pleasing to the Lord. Variant readings substitute here and in vs. 17 "God" for "the Lord"—perhaps in an attempt to assimilate these verses to several other NT and OT passages. In the NT the words, "to please the Lord" (or God) or a similar phrase are employed to describe the gracious acceptance of a sacrifice, of a person, or of a deed. When they occur in the LXX they render in most cases the *hitpaël* of *hālak* which in RSV and elsewhere is translated by "to walk with" or "to walk before," and describes a person's pious conduct, or God's pleasure with his ways. The seemingly anthropomorphic idea that God is pleased with a man or his offering is shunned neither by the Greek OT versions nor by the NT, see the earlier remarks on the sacrificial "fragrance" of the sacrifice that is pleasing to God (Eph 5:2).[63] There are also texts which describe man's pleasure in his relationship to God, a fellow man, a plan, or an action.[64] A sharp distinction between the acceptability of sacrifice and of good attitudes is made neither by Paul nor in the epistle to the Hebrews: sacrificial language serves in Philip 4:18; Rom 12:1–2; Heb 13:16, 21 to describe correct ethical conduct. Therefore, the "pleasing" deeds mentioned in Eph 5:10b cannot be separated from the pleasing sacrifice offered by Christ (5:2). Only in living by the effect of Christ's sacrifice and after its pattern can the saints find out and attempt to do "what pleases the Lord." If in 5:10 the term "the Lord" refers to Jesus Christ, then his love shown on the cross is the criterion of gracious acceptance of the saints and their works. Equally, if the variant readings should reproduce a better text, i.e. if by "the Lord" God (the Father) is meant, no other way is envisaged for the saints except to follow in the footsteps of the Son of God. The combined rulership of the Messiah and God (5:5) makes it unthinkable that either a man or a deed can please the Father or the Son alone.

11. *have nothing to do with those fruitless deeds done in darkness.* Lit. ". . . with the fruitless deeds of darkness." The fruitless deeds stand in con-

---

[62] Among the biblical and early post-biblical references for these meanings are the following: (a) Jer 6:27; 9:6[7]; 11:20; 12:3; 17:10; 20:12; Job 34:3; LXX Ps 16[17]:3; 25[26]:2; 65[66]:10; 94[95]:9; 138[139]:1, 23; I Thess 2:4c; 5:21; Gal 6:4; I Cor 11:28; II Cor 13:5; (Rom 12:2?); I Tim 3:10; I John 4:1; I Clem. 42:4; *Did.* XII 1; Herm. *mand.* XI 7; (b) Prov 8:10; 17:3; 27:21; Wisd Sol 1:3; II Macc 4:3; I Thess 2:4a; I Cor 3:13; 16:3; II Cor 8:8, 22; Rom 2:18; 14:22; Philip 1:10; I Peter 1:7; Acts 2:22 var. lect. in Codex D; I Clem. 1:2; *Did.* XI 11; Herm. *vis* IV 3:4. The opposite is "to reject" (Jer 6:30), or "to refuse" (Rom 1:28).

[63] A pleasing "sacrifice" or "fragrance" is mentioned in Aquila, Symm., Theod. Exod 29:18; Symm. Ezek 20:41; Theod. Lev 1:9; Rom 12:1(–2); Philip 4:18; Heb 13:16. Reference is made to a person with whom God is pleased in Gen 5:22, 24; 6:9; 17:1 (Codex Alexandrianus); 24:40; 48:15; Judg 10:16 (Codex Alexandrianus); LXX Ps 55:14[56:13]; 114[116]:9; Wisd Sol 4:10; Sir 44:16; Rom 14:18; Heb 11:5–6; Titus 2:9; cf. I Clem. 62:2. A "deed" is accepted by God according to Wisd Sol 9:10; Rom 12:(1)–2; II Cor 5:9; Col 3:20; Heb 12:28; 13:21.

[64] Gen 39:4 (Codex Alexandrianus); Exod 21:8; LXX Ps 25[26]:3; 34[35]:14.

trast to the "fruit of the Spirit" described in Gal 5:22–23. The author does
not deny that some result is harvested from evil: "rotting" is the effect of deceitful desires (4:22); death is the wages of sin (2:15; Rom 1:32; 5:12; 6:23).
Since such results are not deemed worthy to be called "a fruit," they are
called akarpos, "fruitless," "barren." "What fruit did you get of the things of
which you are now ashamed? The end of these things is death" (Rom 6:21).
Hosea threatened that Ephraim's glory would vanish because there is "no
birth, no pregnancy, no conception"; even if there were "pangs of childbirth,"
yet no baby presented himself "at the mouth of the womb" (9:11; 13:13).
James 1:13–18 contains a complete nativity story of evil, as a counterpart to
the birth of the saints by God the "Father" through the "word of truth." But
James can speak of no better result than Paul; his story, too, ends with the
birth of sin and death.[65] The rhetoric used in the epistle of Jude against
Christians who behave shamefully is flamboyant. The perpetrators of evil deeds
are called "waterless clouds, carried along by winds; fruitless trees in late
autumn, twice dead, uprooted; wild waves of the sea, casting up the foam of
their own shame" (Jude 12–13). In Eph 5:11 the translation "done in darkness"
is suggested by the reference to the hidden places or nocturnal periods that are
preferred for immoral deeds and words. From the metaphorical meaning of
"darkness" in Eph 5:8, etc., the author turns to a specific physical function of
darkness: it is supposed to hide and therefore to protect evil works. The words
"have nothing to do with" illuminate the meaning of "do not associate" in
5:7. Perhaps 5:7 was a fragment of traditional material quoted by Paul, and
therefore was ambiguous: that verse seemed to prohibit all contact with
Christians walking in pagan ways. However, vs. 11 dispels the ambiguity. Here
the apostle interprets the fragment which he had probably quoted earlier, at
the same time limiting and extending its application: while all contact with the
erring brethren is not cut off, the break from their evil works (even when the
brethren are not present) has to be complete.[66] See COMMENT III for specific
features of the church discipline established in this context.

Much more disprove them [by your conduct]. The verb elegchō, here translated "disprove by conduct," occurs again in vs. 13. In pre-biblical Greek,
in the LXX, and in the NT, it has several meanings: (a) to reveal hidden
things;[67] (b) to convict or to convince;[68] (c) to reprove, to correct;[69] (d) to

[65] Jerome comments on Eph 5:11, "Vices find their end and perish in themselves"; cf. Abbott,
p. 154.
[66] NTTEV, however, makes 5:11 an exact duplication of 5:7 by translating, "Have nothing to
do with people who do worthless things."
[67] E.g. I Cor 14:24; John 3:20. On the ground of non-biblical passages, but also of John 3:20–21;
I Cor 14:24–25, Abbott states that the verb is almost a synonym of "to reveal" (phaneroō), as indeed it occurs sometimes in the context of a reference to something previously hidden. Dibelius
makes the direct equation, elegchein means phaneroun, cf. NEB. In their versions of Eph 5:11, 13,
RSV and WBLex, 248 translate the word by "to expose"; NTTEV by "bring out to light," similarly
Calvin. But LSLex, 531; F. Büchsel, TWNTE, II, 473–76; and Spicq, Théologie morale, II, 526
n. 4, show that this meaning of the verb does not do justice to the majority of the NT texts and to the
cognate nouns elegchos, elegxis, elegmos.
[68] E.g. John 8:46; 16:8; Jude 15. Plato Sophista 241E; 259A, and Aristotle Sophistici elenchi IX 170B,
use the term for "disproving" false utterances or axioms. Zeno the Stoic wrote two books under the
title Elegchoi. After his time the verb and the cognate noun were increasingly employed to denote
not only refutation or disproof of theories, but also to describe practical-ethical orientation and
behavior, see, e.g. Epictetus diss. III 9, 13, etc.
[69] Men are called upon to correct one another in, e.g. Lev 19:17; Prov 9:7–8; 10:10; 15:12;
28:23 (according to the Proverbs only a wise man is to be given and will accept correction); Luke
3:19 (cf. Mark 6:18); Matt 18:15; I Tim 5:20; II Tim 4:2; Titus 1:9, 13; 2:15. A correction by

punish, to discipline.[70] It is not always clear which of these four meanings is meant or combined with another in a given biblical passage.[71] Instead of four varying degrees of rebuttal, different ways of exerting censure may be expressed, that is, reprobation (a) by words spoken in privacy, (b) by public scolding, or (c) by conduct.[72] The last mentioned sense of *elegchō* is adopted in Phillips' version, "Let your life show by contrast how dreary and futile these things are." Indeed, the next verse avers that speaking about evil things is "shameful" (rather than constructive in liberating a brother from his sin); and the summary given in 5:15 of 5:3–14 speaks of "conduct." For these reasons it is most likely that as early as vs. 11 a behavior is meant that may correct a brother's erring ways and help him follow a straight path. However, can it be demonstrated that behavior rather than words was considered proper means of correction in early congregations? While according to Gal 2:11–21, for one, Paul himself certainly did not abstain from using sharp words, an explicit warning against trusting only talk is directed to women in I Peter 3:1; "May those disobedient to the word be won without a word by the behavior." This injunction is valid not only for (verbose?) women; following several NT passages all members of the congregation are called upon by their "conduct" and "good works" to invite others to glorify God.[73] In the same way, Eph 5:11 includes a warning against reliance upon oral exposition, discussion, or vituperation in dealing with sin. The light in which the Christians stand, and which they reflect, consists of much more than intellectual enlightenment which

God is mentioned in e.g. Prov 3:11–12; Sir 18:13. The Spirit, or the exalted Christ, corrects according to John 16:8; Rev 3:19. Following Josephus *bell.* VII 330, 447; *ant.* VIII 325; *vita* 255, etc., men or documents expose or convict sinners of a lie. The Qumran Community made it their members' duty to correct a brother on the day of his misbehavior in a spirit of faithfulness, humility, and love: 1QS v 24 – VI 1; IX 17; see K. G. Kuhn, "Der Epheserbrief im Lichte der Qumrantexte," NTS 7 (1960–61), 340–41. Referring to the commands "You shall not hate your brother in your heart, but you shall reason with your neighbor, lest you bear sin because of him" (Lev 19:17) and "Reprove a wise man, and he will love you" (Prov 9:8), several rabbis declared that mutual correction was part of brotherly love and was promised God's blessings; see StB, I, 787–90. Th. Zahn, *Das Evangelium des Johannes*, 5th and 6th ed. (Leipzig/Erlangen: Deichert, 1921), p. 428, n. 42, believes that the verb means "less than to convince but more than to accuse." In referring to Lev 19:17–19; Sir 19:13–17 and NT occurrences, L. J. Lutkemyer, "The Role of the Paraklete," CBQ 8 (1946), 220–29, esp. 221–23, points out that the verb describes that action between friends or brothers, by which one "shows or makes see" the other what may have been wrong, and by which a voluntary insight and self-conviction can be produced. Jesus' attitude toward the Pharisees (John 8:3–9) is quoted as an example. P. Dacquino, "Filii Lucis," VD 36 (1958), 222, defines the mode of argument to be used by the words *declarate vestra recta agendi ratione* ("prove by way of your correct action") the fallacy of the way chosen by the erring brethren. Dacquino's interpretation comes nearest to the meaning of the text of Eph 5, if vs. 11 is understood as part of the context 5:11–14.

[70] Wisd Sol 1:8; Job 5:17; Heb 12:5. In SegB *elegchō* in Eph 5:11, 13 is translated by "punish," "condemn" them. ZB gives the version, "reveal by punishing." In several of the Scripture passages mentioned in the last footnotes "chastising" is used as a synonym of *elegchō*. Gaugler, p. 202, suggests that in Eph 5:11, 13 the verb means more than to expose, namely, "to judge," "to reprimand," "to call from sin to repentance."

[71] LSLex, 531 mentions, in addition, the meanings "to put to shame," "to cross-examine," "to prove." Some of these senses come close to those of *dokimazō* in Eph 5:10.

[72] See I Peter 2:12; Philip 2:15; Matt 5:16.

[73] See I Peter 2:12; Philip 2:15; Matt 5:16. In his interpretation of 5:10 Bengel speaks of the necessity to use "words and deeds." The deeds in question are characterized by "goodness," "righteousness," and "truth" (5:9). Such deeds rather than clever or sharp words of condemnation correspond to the "light" in which the Christians stand (5:8, 14). Schlier observes: "Of course this convincing happens not only through the word . . . it is distinct from mere talking." P. Lippert, *Leben als Zeugnis*, SBM 4, 1968, has made a courageous attempt to gather and emphasize NT passages that describe the apologetic or missionary testimony given by Christians to their environment without word (I Peter 3:1), that is, by a certain conduct or life-style.

they are given and pass on by words. While Ephesians attributes the greatest importance to the spoken word, in many places where fighting immorality is concerned the shining light of Christ himself (5:13-14) and the example given by faithful Christians is trusted more than moralistic effusions, legalistic prescriptions, verbal punishments, acts of excommunication. For this reason the paraphrasing translation was chosen, "disprove [by your conduct]."

12. *it is shameful even to mention the things that happen in secret.* Lit. "to mention the secret things happening by them." The tone of this sentence expresses contempt. The meaning and sound of the Greek word *ginomena* (lit. "happening," "occurring") is similar to *gennōmena* ("begotten, or born"). Notwithstanding the unproductivity of the "deeds of darkness" mentioned in vs. 11, the author acknowledges readily that a vain activity and a senseless productivity are carried on under the cover of darkness. According to Calvin, allusion is made to a proverb, "Night knows no shame" (*nox pudore vacat*). According to vss. 4-5 shameful talk is characteristic of saints who have returned to their former pagan ways and who thereby disinherit themselves of the kingdom. Eph 5:12 takes a surprising and radical turn: even the talk of those who condemn their erring brothers is called shameful. Paul addresses those saints who by loudly condemning other men's sin and shame seek to prove their own purity. Those who glibly discuss and censure evil deeds are declared as guilty as the objects of their scorn. Things done under the cover of darkness must not be dragged into the limelight. It is bad enough that they happen, but their effect can only become worse when they are taken hold of by garrulous tongues and fed on by self-righteous ears.

13. *[Only] by the light are all reprobate things revealed.* Lit. "all that is exposed [or, tested, convicted, punished, disproven] is revealed by the light."[74] It is unlikely that 5:13 contains a tautology or a truism and nothing more. Even if the author of Ephesians takes up proverbial sayings in vss. 12-14a,[75] his thought moves forward. The translation offered here seeks to make this progress visible by adding the word "only" to the Greek text. In Semitic languages, and in Hebraizing Greek, the use of "only" (*monon*, see, e.g. James 2:24) or of an equivalent is often dispensable for indicating exclusivity, whereas in modern occidental languages this is not the case. In the translation of Eph 5:13 the insertion of "only" is as fitting and necessary as in Thomas Aquinas' exposition of I Tim 1:8 and Luther's translation of Rom 3:28: both asserted that Paul meant by "faith" (*pistei*) *sola fide*, i.e. only by faith, by faith alone. The Greek verb *phaneroō*, translated by "are revealed," is not the same as is used in Eph 3:5 (*apokalyptō;* cf. the noun *apokalypsis* in 1:17; 3:3). Both verbs can be used as synonyms to denote the final eschatological unveiling of the secret which was formerly hidden. In that case they describe an event of the end-time in which God reveals himself fully and gives men a share in eternal

---

[74] The diction of Ephesians, as well as that of unquestioned Pauline letters, allows the double connection of a given formula, that is, with the words preceding and following it; see e.g. the function of "in love" in Eph 1:4-5, and of "in Christ" in Gal 2:17. Thus in Eph 5:13 the phrase "by the light" may belong either to the participle "disproved" or to the finite verb, "are revealed," or to both. Therefore, the following versions can also claim to be literal: (a) all things that are tested by the light are revealed; (b) all things tested by light are also revealed by light. *Elegchō* in the sense of "exposing" may be a synonym of revealing; or, if it means "testing," may describe a preparation of revealing.

[75] Calvin observes this of vs. 12, Schlier of vss. 13-14.

life.[76] In the Gospel of John (except in the quote 12:38) and in I John (cf. Rom 16:26) *phaneroō* takes the place of *apokalyptō*. However, sometimes in Pauline letters, including Eph 5:13–14, *phaneroō* signifies not the disclosure of God and his secret, but of man, his plans, and his deeds. Then the revelation occurs either before man or before God himself.[77] Eph 5:13 speaks of a revelation that is taking place here and now. This verse probably announces that the saints, in "conducting themselves as children of light" (5:8) and in fulfilling their responsibility of "disproving" evil deeds, stand in the service of that light which alone is stronger than darkness. The name of the light will be mentioned in 5:14d. COMMENT III will discuss the theological relevance of the seemingly trite observation that light alone combats darkness.

14. *All that is revealed is light.* Cf. the Vulg., SegB, RSV, ZB. The baffling content of this statement has led to most diverse interpretations, some of which are enticing for their simplicity but do not correspond to the grammar and syntax of the Greek text.[78] Certainly the harsh diction and surprising substance of this verse must not be explained away or attenuated.[79] The

[76] Gal 1:16; I Cor 2:10; 3:13; II Cor 2:14; 4:10–11; 5:1–10; Rom 1:17–19; 2:5; 3:21; 16:26; Eph 3:5; Col 1:26; I Tim 3:16; II Tim 1:10; Titus 1:3, etc. See COMMENT II on Eph 3:1–13 regarding the ontological character of *revelation*.
[77] I Cor 4:5; II Cor 3:3; 5:10–11; 7:12; 11:6.
[78] In his exposition, e.g. Calvin makes no less than three debatable grammatical assumptions. When he says, *Lux est . . . quae omnia manifestat* ("it is the light that reveals all"), he reproduces what was shown to be the exact content of the preceding verse, but does not do justice to the particular statement made in vs. 14a. For he presupposes (a) that the sense of *phaneroumenon* is active (though the form is middle or passive); (b) that the "light" is subject of the sentence and *pān to phaneroumenon* belongs to the verb "is," as its predicate; and (c) that *pān* is the object of *phaneroumenon* rather than that it forms, in conjunction with the participle *phaneroumenon*, the subject of the whole sentence. Each of these mutually coinherent assumptions is unwarranted, for the following reasons:
In pre-biblical Greek, in the LXX, in the NT, in the Apostolic Fathers (see LSLex; Hatch and Redpath, *Concordance to the Septuagint*, Oxford: Clarendon Press, 1892; WBLex; E. J. Goodspeed, *Index Patristicus* [1907], repr. Naperville: Allenson, 1960), there is no evidence that middle forms of *phaneroō*, "to reveal," were ever used in the active sense of, e.g. "to reveal in one's interest." Certainly the article (*to*) before *phaneroumenon* may indicate that *pān* means "all" in this verse, not "each"; in 2:21 this clarification was lacking. However, the same article can also fulfill another function which it often has in classical Greek sentences: the noun which is the subject of a statement is supposed to have the article, the predicative noun is to be left without it. Since there is no article before *phōs* ("light"), but there is one before *phaneroumenon*, the "revealing" agency most likely is the subject in this sentence, and "light" is the predicative noun, not vice versa. Finally, the position of *pān* at the beginning of the sentence makes it most improbable that *pān* is the object of the revelation here described.
Abbott follows Calvin in attributing to *phaneroumenon* an active meaning, but he avoids the Reformer's other two steps.
[79] Bengel and J. Eadie lay emphasis upon the present tense of *phaneroumenon* and interpret the particle as meaning, that which "does not escape being manifested," viz. that which "forces to disclose."
Phillips exploits the tentativeness or sheer possibility which may be inherent in the participle: "It is even possible (after all it happened with you!) for light to turn the thing it shines upon into light also."
Others care less about the tense and mood in which the verb *phaneroō* occurs but ascribe special meanings to the verb. For example NEB translates, "Everything that is illuminated is all light." Or the verb "is" is subjected to a paraphrasing interpretation. Then it means, *relationem habet . . . refertur ad* ("it is related to"); see Dacquino VD 36 (1958), 223. Or it is interpreted as "becoming": "anything that is clearly revealed becomes light," see NTTEV; "all that shines up, in the sense of becoming radiant, is light," (see Schlier; cf. JB). Earlier Bengel had suggested that "becoming" and "being" be combined in the interpretation: *fit, et mox est, lux* ("it becomes, and soon is, light").
However, there is no evidence that *phaneroō* ("to reveal") and *phōtizō* ("to illumine," "to enlighten," see Abbott, p. 156) are synonyms or exchangeable, and the qualifications "clearly revealed" or "becoming radiant" (the latter would be *doxazomenon* in Greek, as indeed Schlier intimates by reference to Col 3:4; I John 3:2) are not automatically inherent in *phaneroō*. A truism such as, What is illuminated is bright, was hardly in the mind of the man who added vs. 14a to the two preceding sentences.

Ephesians are told that revelation by the light (vs. 13) produces or manifests light even where nothing else appeared to prevail but darkness and its works. The closest biblical parallels are Ps 139:11–12: "If I say, Let only darkness cover me, and the light about me be night, even the darkness is not dark to thee, the night is bright as the day; for darkness is as light with thee"; John 1:5: "The light shines in the darkness, and the darkness has not overcome it"; and II Cor 4:6: "God who said, Let light shine out of darkness . . . has shone in our hearts to give the light of knowledge of the glory of God in the face of Christ." Even more striking is the parallel of Eph 5:8: those who were "darkness" have become "light." Verse 14a states that this complete change is the effect of revelation, see COMMENT IV. Verse 14b–d will give information about the name, the power, and the procedure of the revealing light.

Therefore he says. The meaning of the widespread quotation formula "he says" was discussed in the first NOTE on 4:8. To the text in 5:14 is attributed authority equal to that of the Psalm cited in 4:8. While the Psalm quote is followed by midrashic expository remarks, the authoritative text mentioned in 5:14 clinches the diverse statements that came before.[80] Here and there it is plain that the author uses hymnic material. The specific contribution of the quote to the context will be described at the beginning of COMMENT IV. The origin, that is, the original form, setting, and function of the hymnic lines have been explained in different ways: (a) The text is a combination of canonical OT passages.[81] (b) The text stems from a Greek or an apocryphal Jewish book.[82] (c) The words contain a saying of Jesus, transmitted through one of his prophetic ministers (Calvin). (d) The text is part of an early Christian hymn composed by an inspired church member.[83] (e) The hymn's form and content are to be explained against the background of pre-Christian, non-Jewish conceptions of cultic mystery and salvation.[84] Not all of these five interpretations

[80] Dibelius, pp. 90–91, assumes that 5:14 is related to 5:8 rather than to 5:13. Actually the quote appears to sum up and interpret all that is said in 5:3 ff.
[81] Thomas Aquinas lists Isa 60:1; 26:19; Prov 6:9; Ps 13:2[12:4]; 27[26]:1; 41:8[40:9]; others mention Deut 33:3; Isa 9:2; 51:9 ff.; Mal 4:2[3:20].
[82] Jerome compares the citation with that of the Aratus verse in Acts 17:28; Epiphanius (*haer.* 42, 2:3) suggests that a prophecy of Elijah is used; the margin of Codex Boernerianus ninth century) mentions a Book of Enoch; Schille, *Hymnen,* pp. 94–101, wavers between a Jewish and a Jewish-influenced pagan background.
[83] In I Cor 14:26 such compositions are mentioned. In Eph 5:18–19; Col 3:16, the saints are encouraged to sing songs for their mutual edification. Luke 1:46–55, 68–74; 2:19–32; I Tim 3:16 offer examples. In the Introduction, section II, it was mentioned that Ephesians bristles with quotations of, or allusions to, such compositions. Origen (in the *Catenae*) and Theodoret (PG 82, 844–45) appear to be the first to suggest that Eph 5:14 quoted (from) a Christian hymn. Most modern interpreters endorse this explanation. Schille, *Hymnen,* pp. 94 ff. refers to I Enoch 94:1 ff.; John 7:37; Rev 22:17; II Cor 5:20–21; Matt 11:28–30, and *Od. Sol.* He designates the type of short exclamation found in Eph 5:14 as an "awakening call," belonging to the *Gattung* of "revelation song" or "revelation-speech" that may in part be traced back to Wisdom Literature. He affirms that Eph 5:14 does not deviate from other uses of such songs when it employs the quote within the frame of a "missionary discourse." Though such songs reveal more missionary concern than does the older Wisdom Literature, their prehistory may be "centuries old," according to the same author. Together with von Soden, Robinson, K. G. Kuhn (NTS 7 [1960–61], 342); Dibelius; Schlier; Gaugler, Marxsen (*Introduction,* p. 195) and others, Schille considers a baptismal liturgy the original *Sitz im Leben* of the text quoted in 5:14. B. Noack, "Das Zitat in Epheser 5, 14," ST 5 (1951), 52–64, believes that the stanza originally described the parousia of Christ, but was then found appropriate for baptismal use. According to some scholars the quote is a part of a longer composition, and its continuation is found in Clement of Alexandria *protrepticus* IX 84:2: ". . . the one born before the morning star" (cf. Ps 110:3; Micah 5:2[1]) "who gives light by his own rays"; see F. J. Dölger, *Sol Salutis,* 2d ed. (Münster; Aschendorff, 1925), pp. 364–410.
[84] R. Reitzenstein, *Das Iranische Erlösungsmysterium* (Bonn: Marcus, 1921), pp. 3, 6, 135–50, offers an Iranian "salvation-pronouncement" as the source; he emphasizes the inseparable connection of enlightenment, resurrection, and deification, but does not connect the origin of Eph 5:14

are mutually exclusive. Early Christian composers (just like the authors of more recent Christian hymns) did incorporate and amalgamate various biblical texts into new units. Apocryphal elements have found reception even in canonized literature, see Luke 11:4a; John 7:38; I Cor 2:9; James 4:5; Jude, 6, 9, 11, 14–15. Indeed, most if not all biblical genres of prose and poetry are far from being original inventions of Hebrews or Christians. Yet the reception of a given form does not exclude originality of content. The assumption that an early Christian hymn is quoted in 5:14 is safer than those more particular theories which pretend that more is established with certainty than can really be known. Inasmuch as the authority of the quoted lines is considered the same as that of the Psalm citation in Eph 4:8, the hymn in Eph 5:14 is a precedent for the formation of an enlarged canon, consisting no longer just of the (OT) Law, Prophets, Writings, and some apocryphal books, but also of distinctly Christian (i.e. NT) materials.

Awake you sleeper. In Greek the imperative *egeire* corresponds to the calls, *age* or *epeige*. These imperatives can be translated by the brief English "Up!" (Abbott). "Sleep" is an eulogism for death, just as "falling asleep" (*koimaomai*) is a metaphorical description of dying. Parallels to these expressions exist inside and outside the Bible;[85] they do not necessarily imply belief in resurrection, but can prepare the way for a proclamation or demonstration of resurrection.[86]

rise from the dead. Lit. "and rise . . ." The normal Greek imperative of the verb "rise" is *anastēthi*, see Acts 12:7. The abbreviated form used in 5:14 (*anastā*) has analogies in the short exclamations, "Step down!" "Step Up!" (*katabā, anabā*, Mark 15:30 var. lect.; Rev 4:1). Those who composed and used the hymn quoted in Eph 5:14 were not primarily interested in Atticistic Greek, but followed trends in the contemporary vernacular.[87] The idea that a dead man, just like a sleeper, is called by a voice or sound, hears it and reacts to it, is also expressed in I Thess 4:16; John 5:25, and in resuscitation stories such as John 11:43; Mark 5:41; Acts 9:40. Certainly the reference to an awakening call or to trumpet blasts does not imply that the dead possess a hearing ear and the ability to obey! Rather the signal is considered capable of

---

with baptism. Jonas, *Gnostic Religion*, pp. 68–69, 80–86, 114 adduces parallels that appear to demonstrate the Gnostic origin of the quote; cf. Bultmann, ThNT, I, 174–75. Pokorný, EuG, pp. 93 ff., 119, agrees with Schille in tracing the form of the hymn back to "missionary Hellenism," see, e.g. *Corp. Herm.* I 27; VII 1. But Dibelius seriously questions the Iranian (and implicitly: the Gnostic) origin. He suggests that parallels found in Mystery Religions, rather than in Isaiah and other Jewish literature, are decisive. In turn, Kuhn, NTS 7 (1960–61), 341–44, rejects a derivation from Gnostic sources, for "Paul interprets the sacramental indicative . . . as an ethical imperative." What in Qumran is attributed to God or to the act of joining the community of the faithful (1QH IV 5–6, 23), is in Ephesians declared to be Christ's gift.

[85] See e.g. Homer *Iliad* XI 241; in XIV 231; XVI 672, 682 the god Sleep is called a brother of Death. Cf. Sophocles *Electra* 509; Callimachus *epigramma* XI 2. Inscriptions take up the poetic diction. In the Bible the metaphors are found in I[III] Kings 2:10; LXX Pss 12:4[13:3]; 87:6[88:5]; Dan 12:2; Sir 46:20; I Thess 4:13–15; 5:10; I Cor 7:39; 11:30; 15:6, 18, 20, 51; Matt 9:24par.; 27:52; John 11:11–13; Acts 7:60; II Peter 3:4. See also Jub. 23:1; 36:18; I Enoch 49:3; 92:3; IV Ezra 7:32; *Pirke Aboth* VI 10.

[86] Cf. R. E. Bailey, "Is 'Sleep' the Proper Biblical Term for the Intermediate State?", ZNW 55 (1964), 161–67, esp. 166. Literature on resurrection was listed in BIBLIOGRAPHY 10. Brief discussions of the resurrection and enthronement (a) of Christ and (b) with Christ were presented in COMMENTS IV on 1:15–23 and III–IV on 2:1–10.

[87] Since the second century A.D. the verb *anistaō* begins to replace *anistēmi*. The imperative *anistā* is anticipated by the *anastā* of Eph 5:14.

creating both. Indeed in the huge majority of the resurrection accounts of
Christ and in passages such as Eph 2:5–6 the dead appear to play a passive
role in their resurrection, but I Thess 4:14; Mark 8:31, etc. (cf. John 10:18)
on one side, and Mark 5:42; 9:9–10; 12:25, etc.; Eph 5:14 on the other, indicate that an action of Christ and of all those being raised follows the creative
awakening call: They stand up. In Eph 6:11, 13–14 further commands are
added to the imperative, "Stand up!": "Stand" and "withstand" in the face of
Satanic attacks!

the Messiah will shine upon you. Lit. "and the Messiah . . ." Unlike John
5:25 where the voice of the Son of God effects the raising, at this point the
means employed by the Messiah are compared to the rays of the rising sun. In
the OT passages mentioned in fn. 81, God's glory or light appearing over
Israel exerted the life-giving power.[88] Ephesians shares with the Fourth Gospel
the identification of "the Messiah" with "the light." It is unlikely that the Greek
conjunction "and" (kai) at the beginning of this line and the future tense of the
verb "shine" must be understood to mean that only after the raising by a call
will the light of the Messiah prove effective. While the conjunction "and" between "Awake" and "rise" seems to indicate that awakening precedes rising, the
same conjunction can also have interpretive power without any implication regarding the sequence of events. The last line of the cited hymn or stanza takes
the place of a more extensive comment on the first two lines, as if to say, "This
(the awakening and rising of the dead) happens not on the ground of man's
own power but because of the radiant Messiah himself." The promised light, the
Messiah, is the presupposition of the imperatives and of obedience. "We are not
illuminated only after we have been raised, but when Christ illuminates us we
rise to new life."[89] The verb "shine upon" (epiphauskō) is rarely used by Greek
writers.[90] Perhaps for this reason several ancient texts and commentators read
for "the Messiah will shine upon you," "you will touch Christ," or "Christ will
touch you" (epipsauseis tou Christou).[91] References to a healing, cleansing, or
raising touch reflect the conviction that divine power (mana) is tangibly communicated.[92] Jerome brands as a silly novelty seeker the man who claimed that
Adam was buried on Calvary and brought to life again as he was touched by
Christ's body. Certainly the variant reading of Eph 5:14d is so weakly attested
that it does not deserve much attention. Nevertheless, taken as an attempt at
interpretation, it contains a particle of truth: the Messiah shining upon the dead
communicates something of his essence to those illuminated. In his light they

---

[88] According e.g. to Ps 104:29–30; John 6:63; Rom 8:11, the "Spirit" is God's agent of resurrection. Rom 6:4; Acts 5:31 attributed the same function to "the glory" of God. The various agents
mentioned in the Bible are not mutually exclusive. All of them affirm that only God can give life.

[89] Calvin. In our translation the substitution of a comma for the Greek conjunction kai (in vs.
14c, d) was made in order to avoid the misunderstanding fought by Calvin. Verse 14d is not a
superfluous addition or a prophecy of a later event, but contains the cause and means of the foregoing.

[90] It appears to be derived from phaō, "to shine," and is according to LSLex, 670 and WBLex,
304 a synonym of anatellō which describes the shining of the rising sun or moon. In the Bible it
occurs in LXX Job 25:5; 31:26; 41:10 (with the variant reading epiphōskō); cf. phausis (illumination) in Gen 1:15.

[91] So, e.g. the original text of the sixth-century Codex Claramontanus and some Latin versions;
also Jerome, Chrysostom, Victorinus, Paul of Nola. See Robinson, p. 300, and Vetus Latina, 24/1,
ed. Beuron, p. 227.

[92] See, e.g. Isa 6:7; Dan 8:18; Mark 1:41; 5:28–31. Other effects of physical or spiritual contact
are presupposed in John 20:17, 25, 27; I John 1:1–4; Acts 17:27.

become light: even though they had slumbered in the "darkness" of death, "in [the power sphere of] the Lord" they now have become "light" (5:8). The startling statement of 5:14a is confirmed: "All that is revealed is light." More happens in Christ's light than just "illumination of the eyes of the heart" (1:18): the whole man is light (cf. Matt 6:22–23). In substance the enlightenment described here is equivalent to justification of the sinner, creation out of nothing, raising of a dead body, see Rom 4:5, 17–24; II Cor 4:6, and COMMENT IV.

15. *In sum, watch carefully how you conduct yourselves.* Lit. "therefore, look . . . ," cf. I Cor 3:10: "Let each man take care how he builds." As happens frequently in Ephesians, the end of a quote and the resumption of the author's own diction is indicated by a conjunction (in this case, *oun*) that introduces a logical conclusion or a summary. Variant readings offered by some eastern and western texts and commentators shift the position of "carefully" so that the statement reads, "Look how you conduct yourselves carefully."[93] This shift anticipates the following words, "not as fools but as wise men," but it extenuates the urgency of the call to watch out, that is, to examine and criticize oneself.[94] In actuality, vs. 15 resumes the substance of vs. 11 by insisting upon right "conduct." Seven preceding references to "conduct" in Ephesians (*halāchā* in Jewish writings) are crowned by this last occurrence of the verb *peripateō*.[95]

not as fools but as wise men. In COMMENTS X on 1:3–14 and IV on 4:17–32 intimations were made regarding the strong influence of Wisdom teachings upon Ephesians. In 5:15 the author makes explicit that all he has to announce and to urge is summed up in the call of Wisdom and the invitation to follow her. The passing ("unproductive") pleasures found on the way of the flesh are e.g. in Prov 7–9 set in opposition to the joy and stability to which Wisdom leads. In Eph 5:1–20 the same contrasting colors are used. The forbidden fruits look poor in the light of the joy and gratitude generated in God's children. What God gives makes sense; everyone seeking Wisdom will recognize it. As long as in OT research the contents and intent of the Wisdom Books were attributed primarily to the influence of Greek, especially Stoic, teachings, the admonitions of Eph 5:1–20 looked more Greek than Hebrew. However, since the Qumran library was discovered and since biblical Wisdom teaching has been traced back to the days of David and Solomon,[96] it is no longer necessary to consider Eph 5:15 a demonstration of Christian assimilation to Stoic thought. The Wisdom teaching of Ephesians is not Stoic, as an example shows: according to Stoic teaching reason and virtue alone make man wise and free[97]

---

[93] The variant is contained, e.g. in the Greek text of the Codex Claramontanus, in several ninth-century codices, also in minuscules, in some (late) Italic and Syriac versions, in Ambrosiaster, Jerome, Theodoret, Thomas Aquinas. Gaugler gives preference to the variant. Thomas Aquinas finds in the command, "Let your eyes look directly forward" (Prov 4:25), an example of the recommended "circumspect" way of walking! The text used for our translation appears to be older and more genuine; see the Chester Beatty Papyrus, the original script of Codex Sinaiticus, the Codex Vaticanus, among the minuscules esp. Min. 33, also Origen and Chrysostom.

[94] Calvin paraphrases, "When you enlighten others, watch out that you yourselves walk in the light." But Abbott remarks that this interpretation would require the presence of Greek *autoi*.

[95] See Eph 2:2, 10; 4:1, 17 (twice); 5:2, 8.

[96] Literature describing the character of OT Wisdom and its influence upon the NT has been listed in BIBLIOGRAPHY 8. In 1QS IV 24 conduct "in wisdom" (cf. Col 4:5) is contrasted with foolish behavior.

[97] See, esp. M. Pohlenz, *Die Stoa* (Göttingen: Vandenhoeck, 1948), pp. 153–58 for a brief description of the Stoic ideal.

—so much so that he can be compared to a king who is determined by (pure) ideas and subject to no law, being law to himself.[98] But the saints have become "enthroned" by other means, i.e. "with Christ" and "in Christ," see 1:20–23; 2:5–6. Not because of an ideal placed before them, but on the ground of their election, vocation, exaltation by God (1:4 ff.; 2:1 ff.; 4:1 ff.), and because of the forgiveness and unity imparted to them by the crucified Christ (1:7; 2:13 ff.), finally as men sealed and motivated by the Spirit (1:14; 2:18, etc.), they are equipped to "conduct themselves . . . as wise men." Paul's ethic is built upon the "mercies of God" (Rom 12:1), upon "Christonomy" (I Cor 9:21; Gal 6:2), and upon the Spirit's manifestation and guidance (Rom 8; Gal 5), not upon the rule of absolute virtues or the autonomy of the wise. In God's name the saints are admonished to walk wisely.[99]

16. *Redeem the time.* Lit. "Redeeming . . ."; in the last NOTE on 3:17 participles with imperative meaning have been discussed. In 5:19–20 similar participles are found again. Neither the verb "redeem," nor the noun "time" (*kairos*), nor any other text that may be adduced as a parallel of 5:16 offers unambiguous clues for explaining "the obscure expression" (Chrysostom) "redeem the time," which is used here and in Col 4:5.[100] It is not clearly stated whether the time is to be redeemed from the devil (Calvin); from evil men (Bengel); from the depravity characterizing it because of Adam's or each man's own prior sins (Thomas Aquinas prefers the first alternative); or from loss and misuse (Robinson). Should it be assumed that a saint can transform bad days into good ones (Origen; cf. 5:14a)? Or is it suggested that a wise man keep silent in evil times (Amos 5:13), or at least behave "specifically moderately" (Bengel)? Not even the means to be employed or the price to be paid for the redemption of time is mentioned. Only one thing is clear: the transitoriness, deceptiveness, and adversity of the time in which the saints live does not excuse the people of

---

[98] Plato (*politicus, passim;* also, e.g. *resp.* v 473D) and Aristotle (*pol.* III 13 1284A 13; see also 1284B 32 ff.) stand behind the Stoic doctrine.

[99] Col 4:5 adds to the counsel of Eph 5:15 the words "toward those outside," and I Peter 2:12 contains in substance a parallel to the Colossian passage: "Maintain a good conduct among the Gentiles." There are at least two ways to explain the absence of a reference to non-Christians in Eph 5:16: (a) in Eph 5:3 ff. (internal) church discipline is in focus, rather than (external) mission among Gentiles. (b) The author who in 2:13–19 proclaimed that even those "afar" have been drawn "near" is unwilling now to speak of people who are still "far off" or "outside." Even when in I Cor 5:12–13; cf. II Cor 6:14 ff., a sharp distinction between those "outside" and those "inside" is made, the apostle's judgment pertains primarily to the saints. They are, as Eph 5:15 shows, above all to watch themselves. Calvin, however, emphasizes that even in 5:16 not just Christians watch the Christians' behavior; the saints are "as if on the most famous stage, for they live under the eyes of God and the angels." See also I Cor 4:9: "We have become a spectacle to the world, to angels and to men."

[100] Jesus Christ is called "redeemer" of men in Gal 3:13; 4:5; cf. I Cor 6:20; 7:23. The active form of the verb "redeem," if connected with "time," means in LXX and Theod. Dan 2:8 "to gain time." In Eph 5:16 and Col 4:5 the middle form is used, not the active; therefore, Dan 2:8 can hardly solve the puzzle of Eph 5. In contrast to *chronos* (often meaning any time or period) *chairos* can signify a very special, unique, favorable, or critical "time," e.g. the end-time (Gal 6:9), or the present as the moment of fulfillment (II Cor 6:2; Eph 1:10). Theodore of Mopsuestia among the Greek fathers, Gaugler among the modern interpreters, understand Eph 5:16 to speak of discerning and grasping the present opportunity, even the right moment. But the difference between *chronos* and *kairos* is not always observed in the Bible, as a comparison between Eph 1:10 and Gal 4:4 shows. In Rom 3:26; 8:18; 9:9; I Cor 7:29 *kairos* is used—though the more general *chronos* would appear more appropriate; cf. Robinson, pp. 202–3. See also R. M. Rope, "Studies in Pauline Vocabulary: Redeeming the Time," ET 22 (1910–11), 552–54; Büchsel, TWNTE, I, 128. To use one's time wisely, viz. to exploit given opportunities, was considered a feature typical of a wise man among Stoics. Non-biblical parallels to Eph 5:16 do not always use *kairos* in its narrow meaning; see Lysias XIII 84; Plutarch *Sertorius* VI 6; Antoninus VI 26; Stobaeus *eclogae* I 7, 18.

God from using every opportunity and tackling each task they are given. They can use the given time wisely instead of foolishly—though they can by no means redeem either themselves, or their fellow man, or the world by their own works. Time is entrusted to the saints so that they may do good works (Gal 6:10; Eph 2:10; cf. Rom 12:11 var. lect.; cf. Schlier). The opposite of "redeeming the time" is to lose it, according to Bengel. Mark 13:10; Rev 6:11; II Peter 3:9 show that the time left before the parousia is particularly reserved for the spreading of the gospel and the repentance and salvation of men, cf. Eph 6:18–19.

for these days are evil. The logical connection of these words with the preceding imperative may be twofold: either the need for redemption is explained, or—and this is more likely—the logic of this sentence corresponds to that of Gen 8:21: "I will never again curse the ground because of man, for the imagination of man's heart is evil from his youth." In the face of onrushing evil, the saints are all the more called upon and equipped to consider the present period a time of salvation, to take up the good fight, and to carry it out successfully (6:10–17). They are neither a lost nor a doomed generation, but shall "stand" as witnesses to the victory of God's light over darkness. The present days may be called "evil" because of the moral evil abounding in them (cf. Rom 7:14 ff.). Calvin speaks of a "time full of scandals and corruption," especially in view of the external and internal distress it brings upon the saints. According to the Freer Logion (Mark 16:14), the present "aeon of wickedness and unbelief is under Satan." Ephesians does not pass as strong a verdict on the present time span. The realized eschatology preached in this epistle includes a realistic appraisal of the "evil" time of temptation and persecution, but the same eschatology does not permit any judgments or lamentations of a dualistic or fatalistic world view. Verses 6:11, 12, 16 make it probable that forthcoming "evil days" belong to the evil already felt at present. Current sufferings anticipate the final, eschatological tribulations, but both are embraced by the anticipation and ultimate fulfillment of redemption from all evil.[101]

17. *Therefore do not be senseless.* The adjective "senseless" (*aphrōn*) is used by Greek writers to describe an inert object, a statue, or a crazed, frantic, silly or foolish person. In the LXX, the term occurs frequently in Wisdom books, sometimes also in Psalms influenced by Wisdom thought and style. It may describe both the petrification of the heart (cf. 4:19) and the panic-stricken or impulse-ridden activity of a spellbound man (cf. 5:18a; I Cor 12:2). The imperative "Do not become senseless" is a call to sobriety, chastity, and a reasonable, moderate reaction to whatever happens.[102]

[learn to] comprehend what is the will of the Lord. The verb "to comprehend" (*syniēmi;* cf. the noun "understanding," *synesis,* in 3:4) sets a slightly stronger accent upon intellect or intellectual grasp (cf. 3:18–19) than other verbs denoting the act of gaining knowledge (*gignōskō, oida*). Vs. 5:17 demonstrates that despite the emphasis placed upon the practical orientation and

[101] Eschatological days of evil are mentioned, e.g. in II Tim 3:1; II Peter 3:3 (James 5:3?); Matt 24:19–31; *Test. Zebulun* IX 5 ff; *Test. Dan* v 4a. But the idea that "the light, threatened from the side of the flesh and the world, is continually in danger of becoming weak and to be extinguished" (Schlier, p. 243) is not found in any of these passages, least of all in Ephesians.

[102] Rom 12:3; I Peter 4:7; I Tim 2:9, 15; 3:2; II Tim 1:7; Titus 2:4–6, 12 contain comments urging sobriety and reasonableness.

theoretical limitation of knowledge,[103] the author of Ephesians is not anti-intellectual; the saints are encouraged to make use of their reasoning power.[104] In our translation, the words "learn to" were added to the Greek text in order to indicate three things. (a) "Comprehending" includes, or is included in, the learning "by experience" (*dokimazō*) mentioned in 5:10. (b) Comprehension is an ongoing process and always an unfinished business—especially when the "will of the Lord" is its object and total "submission" of the self (5:21) its essence. (c) The man who "understands" (*ho synhiōn*) is silent in the "evil time," according to Amos 5:13. Eph 5:17 may include the advice to learn by listening rather than by speaking too much. While in our version of 1:1, 5, 9, 11; cf. 2:3, the noun *thelēma* was rendered by "decision,"[105] in ethical contexts the more common translation "will" has to be retained. In Christ God carries out his surprising and overwhelming "decision," while the flesh attempted to initiate and counteract God by "decisions" of its own (2:3). But in the framework of exhortation, not only unique resolutions and their consequences but above all the firm and stable "will of the Lord" (var. lect. "of God"[106]) is referred to, a will revealed and to be heeded by words and deeds. Schlier emphasizes that this will of God is in no wise distinct from his decision to save. See COMMENT V for a discussion of the recognition of God's will.

18. *In particular do not get drunk with wine.* The Greek conjunction *kai* which stands at the beginning of this sentence most frequently means "and," but it can also indicate the transition from something general to a particular instance.[107] The sudden reference to drunkenness has been explained in two ways: (a) an acute alcohol problem in the private lives of some of the saints; (b) an attempt by the saints to gain or to increase unity with the divine world by cultic inebriation as practiced in the Dionysos cult and—in post-NT times—in Simonian Gnostic mystery rites.[108] The text of Ephesians contains nothing that would permit a choice between secular and religious alcoholism. Perhaps misuse of alcohol is in itself an attempt to bridge the gap between the secular and the religious. Bacchus festivals have both dimensions. At any rate, a warning against excessive drinking (and eating) appears to belong to the traditional pattern of exhortation—just as drunkenness has a firm place in descriptions of

---

[103] See 1:8; 3:19, and the COMMENTS X on 1:3-14; VI on 3:14-21.

[104] Even in the battle cry of Enlightenment, *Sapere aude,* "Have the courage to make use of your own reason" (cf. I. Kant, *Religion Within the Bounds of Reason Alone*), it is possible to recognize an echo of Eph 5:17. According to Gaugler, "sharp reflection is a necessity" for a saint. Calvin was convinced that "he who exercises himself in the meditation of the Law day and night will easily emerge victorious over all difficulties"; cf. Ps 119. To Thomas Aquinas Eph 5:17 offers an opportunity to engage in a discourse on the superiority of wisdom (which puts things in order) over prudence—and of knowledge of divine things over science dealing with human matters. Wisdom, he says, leads to the beatific vision, prudence to individual action; when the will of God is the guiding principle, man's intellect will be prudent. In COMMENT III on 4:17-32 the alleged "intellectualism" of Ephesians has been extensively discussed.

[105] This translation was explained in the second NOTE on 1:1, its Christological foundation in COMMENT V on 1:3-14.

[106] Cf. 1:1; Rom 12:2.

[107] See, e.g. Mark 1:5; 16:7; Abbott, pp. 160-61.

[108] Different opinions are represented, e.g. by D. M. Stanley ("Carmenque . . . ," CBQ 20 [1958], 175): "Stop getting drunk with wine"; Scott; Abbott (in their commentaries on Ephesians); Pokorný (EuG, p. 120, cf. 91). In I Sam 1:14; Amos 2:8; Isa 28:1, 7-10 and I Cor 11:21; cf. 10:20-22, allusions are made to scandalous "happenings" in the worship of God. A detailed description of inspiration by inebriation in the Dionysos cult and other bacchanalia, and of their neo-Pythagorean and Stoic-diatribal counterparts is found in H. Lewy, *"Sobria Ebrietas,"* BhZNW 9 (1929), 42-72.

evil conduct that were composed before and after the writing of Ephesians. Unlike neo-Pythagorean teachings that call for total abstinence, in Stoic and similar diatribes, and in the Bible, the condemnation of misuse of wine does not preclude a proper use of alcoholic beverage.[109] Again, it is not obvious that Eph 5:1 ff. follows a given pattern.[110] No more than guesses can be made why the warning of vs. 18 was placed in its present context. Maybe under the pressure of evil days (5:16) and as a measure against despair some saints sought oblivion of the dire reality by turning to "spirits"; or in awareness of their exaltation upon "heavenly thrones" and their sure "possession" of heavenly "blessings" (1:3, 7; 2:6), they felt entitled to celebrate their liberty in orgies (cf. I Cor 11:17–21). Following the line of advice given to the King of Massa in Prov 31:1–9, Eph 5:17 appeals to the saints: Behave as people worthy of your royal dignity!

that is profligacy. Lit. "in which is . . ." In Eph 5:3–4 the words "fitting for saints" and "these things are improper" were used to remind the saints that not all kinds of conduct acceptable among Gentiles are appropriate among them. Similarly in 5:18 the comment "that is profligacy" may have much more weight than a marginal note. Since ecstasy and orgies were allowed in the cult of some pagan sanctuaries, it was necessary that a letter addressed to former Gentiles should point out the impropriety of certain cultic forms and their reflection in everyday life. Whenever Israel turned to pagan forms of worship and conduct, e.g. by the adoption or permission of prostitution, the Prophets scolded Israel in the strongest terms. "Profligacy" renders the Greek noun *asōtiā,* which is derived from *saoō* ("to be healthy"); from the latter the verb *sōzō* ("to save") is formed. However, this derivation does not make it necessary to interpret *asōtiā* etymologically in every case, and therefore as the opposite of *sōteriā* ("salvation") in the NT, that is, as "incurability" or "condemnation." Rather the rarely used noun *asōtiā* was sometimes defined by intemperate spending for licentious behavior.[111] In medieval Latin *luxuria* had a similar meaning, i.e. "profligate, lascivious living." Most likely Eph 5:18 intends to

[109] See, e.g. Prov 23:31 (esp. in the LXX); 31:1–9; LXX I Esd 3:18–24; Matt 24:49; Luke 12:45; I Thess 5:7; I Cor 5:11; 6:10; I Tim 3:8; Titus 2:3. Many reasons are given to explain why heavy drinking is pernicious. An idiomatic association of wine with "anger" is made in Rev 14:8, 10; 16:19; 17:2, 6; 18:3, 19:15. "Injustice" toward the poor results from a powerful man's drunkenness: Isa 28:7; Prov 31:5; Wisd Sol 2:7, 10. The unrepenting generation of the Flood and the last generation before the parousia are proverbial victims of "eating and drinking," Matt 24:38. In the story of Noah's drunkenness (after the Flood) the blame is put on Noah's disrespectful son, Ham, not on the father's inebriation, Gen 9:20–27. Moderate use of wine is recommended to Bishop Timothy, I Tim 5:23. Total abstinence was observed by the community of the Rechabites and the Nazirites; it was occasionally connected with a vow to God or an oath: Num 6:2–4; Judg 13:5, 7; 16:17; Jer 35:2 ff.; cf. I Sam 14:24; Matt 26:29; Acts 23:12–14. Paul counsels the "strong" Christians in Rome that for a "weak" brother's sake they should willingly abstain from certain food and drink, Rom 14–15. Thomas Aquinas warns against the excessive consumption of food or drink because it increases carnal desire. On the other hand, wine is praised as a gift of God, protected by God, e.g. in Ps 104:15; Eccles 10:19; Rev 6:6. According to Prov 31:1–9 the mother of Lemuel, King of Massa, recommended that wine be given to the poor in order that they forget their misery, but she forbade her royal son to drink wine lest as a judge he distort justice. The offer of spiced wine to the crucified Jesus, which was rejected (Matt 27:34; Mark 15:23), had probably been made in the spirit of the Queen Mother's advice, see StB, I, 1037–38.

[110] Only in Eph 5:15 ff. the admonition to behave wisely, to redeem the time, or to comprehend God's will is immediately followed (in vs. 18) by the warning against drunkenness. Parallel exhortations in Colossians and Romans are followed by different elements.

[111] E.g. Plato *resp.* VIII 560E; Aristotle *eth. Nic.* II 7 1107B 10 ff.; IV 1 1119B 31 ff. In Jewish-Greek writings the term occurs in Prov 28:7; II Macc 6:4; cf. Prov 7:11; Theod. Isa 28:7; *Test. Judah* XVI 1; Titus 1:6; I Peter 4:4; cf. Luke 15:13. See W. Foerster, TWNTE, I, 506–7.

describe drunkenness as waste which has no place in the life and worship of the saints.

but be filled with the Spirit. Lit. ". . . in the Spirit." To both non-Christians and members of the congregation, the external phenomena of inebriation and inspiration looked so similar that one could be mistaken for the other (see Acts 2:13, 15).[112] Perhaps the Corinthians considered drunkenness a help or means of speaking in tongues (I Cor 11:21), just as the "priests and prophets" indicted in Isa 28:7–10 actually seem to have been drunkards.[113] But it is not certain whether the author of Eph 5:18 was acquainted with the Pentecost report of Acts 2.[114] It has also been questioned whether "Spirit" and "wine" are considered comparable "filling substances."[115] For that in which there is "profligacy" is according to this verse not wine but drunkenness, and it may be that the formula (lit.) "in the Spirit" dominates the verb "be filled" so completely as to give it a metaphorical sense. Therefore 5:18 may mean "be filled" (or "be perfect"[116]) in the spiritual sphere (that is, in a Spirit-directed conduct); see Gal 5:25: "If we live by the Spirit, let us also walk by the Spirit," and Rom 12:11: "Be aglow with the Spirit" (or "let the Spirit be your yeast"; or "Seethe with the Spirit").[117] However, this interpretation and the traditional understanding[118] are not mutually exclusive. Not only is the "fullness of wine" compared with the "fullness of the Spirit," but also the filling materials are contrasted: spirits are neither a guarantee of, nor a substitute for, the Spirit, i.e. "the power of Christ's presence" (Schlier). Still, the radical prohibition against using alcohol to fight spiritual sloth is not meant to suppress or exclude the display of vivid emotions, even of enthusiasm.[119] In the next verse the simplicity of children who again and again reveal their joy in singing appears to be the pattern which the saints are to follow.

19. *Talk to one another in psalms and hymns and spiritual songs.* By quoting, transforming, and composing hymns in the writing of Ephesians, the author of this epistle has given his readers an example of the feasibility, usefulness, and beauty of the directive given here. Early Christian congregations

---

[112] Philo *de ebr.* 146–47, states that "many of the foolish are deceived [by those whose soul is so filled with grace that they rejoice and smile and dance, that even their bodies are flushed and fiery] and suppose that the sober are drunk," cf. I Sam 1:14. H. Lewy, *Sobria Ebrietas*, has shown which sources and streams of religious, philosophical, and mystical thought and practice have flowed together in Philo's writings and which influence has been exerted by the Jewish philosopher's oxymoron "sober drunkenness" upon the Christian fathers of the first four centuries. The pertinent texts in Philo are *de ebr.* 145–53; *de fuga et inv.* 166: 31–32; *leg. all.* I 82–84; III 82; *quod. omnis probus liber sit* 12–13; *op. mundi* 70–71; *de vita Mosis* I 187; *de vita contemplativa* 89.

[113] Every "band of prophets" equipped with harp, tambourine, flute, and lyre created a similar impression (I Sam 10:5, 10–12).

[114] Mitton, EE, p. 205 affirms it, while Dibelius raises doubts about it.

[115] Abbott, pp. 161–62; see also Dibelius, p. 92.

[116] See the end of COMMENT VI C on 1:15–23 and the interpretation of 3:19; 4:13.

[117] The formula "in the Spirit" may correspond to "in Christ." While it occurs also in Eph 2:22; 3:5; 6:18 and in the undisputed Pauline passages I Cor 12:3, 13; Rom 14:17; 15:16, the phrase, "filled by the Spirit," is found nowhere in Pauline writings but often in Luke: see Luke 1:15, 41, 67; Acts 2:4; 4:8, 31; 9:17; 13:9, 52; cf. "full of the Holy Spirit," Luke 4:1; Acts 6:3, 5; 7:55; 11:24. Does this prove the literary dependence of Ephesians upon Acts, and incidentally the non-Pauline origin of Ephesians, as Mitton, EE, p. 206, assumes? This argument neglects the fact that Luke (except in Acts 13:52) uses special verbs to denote "filling," i.e. *pimplēmi* or *plēthō*, rather than the verb *plēroō* found in Ephesians.

[118] The latter is represented, e.g. by Thomas Aquinas, Calvin, and Gaugler.

[119] Robinson, pp. 121–22 refers to Acts 2:43, 46; 5:5, 11, 41; 8:8; 9:31; 16:25. A legitimate self-abandonment to "inspiration" is not prohibited by Paul's fight against wild enthusiasts in Corinth and elsewhere.

were singing, jubilant, exulting assemblies (Acts 2:46–47, etc.).[120] The book of "Odes" found in the LXX after the Psalms (except in the Vatican and Sinaitic codices) was composed for use in Christian churches.[121] Existing collections of older or newer psalms did not exclude but rather promoted the composition of new songs to the Lord: "Each one has a hymn!" (I Cor 14:26). The possible meanings and the distinction of the several nouns denoting a "song" or "hymn," as well as the attribute "spiritual" (which is omitted in several MSS), will be discussed in the interpretation of the parallel to Eph 5:19, i.e. Col 3:16. Unique to Ephesians is the specification that the "singing" be performed "to one another." The precedent of the Therapeutes and Pliny's formulation (see fns. 120, 121) would suggest that antiphonic (and polyphonic) singing is meant. In turn Col 3:16 exhorts the saints to "teach and admonish one another," and Paul insists that vocal utterances in worship must be mutually edifying (I Cor 14:1–19). These passages make it probable that more is meant in Eph 5:19 than the antiphonal choruses observed by Pliny. Just as in 4:2, 32 love and forgiveness are shown by the Christians to "one another," so in 5:19 "singing" is part of the mutual edification of the saints. An intramural rather than a missionary purpose is to be fulfilled by singing. This means not only that its special place is in common worship[122] (not excluding the family), but also that it has to be so qualified that the faith, obedience, love, and joy of fellow Christians are stimulated and increased. The singer's private pleasure alone, not to speak of ancient or modern exhibits, cannot be its primary purpose. Thomas Aquinas taught that "singing" addressed itself to three persons: to God, one's neighbor, and one's self.[123] Calvin stays nearer to the text when he asserts that the saints are not told to "sing unto themselves." As the next verse shows, only the praise of God is to be sung. That praise will serve mutual edification.

Sing and play to the Lord from your heart. Here as in Col 3:16 the reference to the heart is an appeal to the center of man's intellect and will, even to the total man, and not primarily to emotion. Excluded is singing with inaudible voice, or a misty pious feeling without articulation. The verb "play" (*psallō*) which is not found in the Colossian parallel, may in its combination with "sing" (*ādō*) be

---

[120] Pliny the Younger *ep.* X 97 confirms the picture of Acts and the book of Revelation, and he reveals the core of Christology when he describes the purpose of the Christians' cultic assemblies as *carmen Christo quasi Deo dicere secum invicem,* "to sing alternating among themselves a hymn to Christ as to God." F. C. Dölger, *Sol Salutis,* 2d ed. (Münster: Aschendorff, 1925), esp. pp. 103–36, describes the content of early Christian hymns and discusses why and how (in morning hours facing East) prayers were offered to Christ: Jesus Christ was honored as the saving sun of righteousness. D. M. Stanley, CBQ 20 (1958), 173–91, distinguishes three types of Christ hymns in the NT: (a) Enthronement hymns; (b) Servant hymns praising the suffering and the glorification; (c) Son-of-Man hymns. He believes that the liturgical place, e.g. of I Tim 3:16 and Eph 5:14 was in baptism (p. 184).

[121] Despite its insertion into an OT canon, its Christian origin is obvious: besides selections from Exod 15; Deut 32; I Sam 2; Jer 9; Hab 3; Isa 26; Jonah 2; Dan 3, it contains the *Magnificat* and *Benedictus* of Luke 1, in some codices also parts of Isa 5; 38; the Prayer of Manasseh, the *Nunc dimittis,* and an extended form of the *Gloria in excelsis* from Luke 2. Qumran had its book of Hodayoth; the Therapeutes (a Jewish sect described by Philo) sang together in mixed choirs, using choric dances under the leadership of a precentor, see Philo *vita contempl.* 80–89; an unknown Syrian community (in Edessa?) used the *Odes of Solomon.*

[122] Gaugler. Schlier, pp. 246–47, 250 considers "the situation of the cultus" decisive, but Robinson, p. 122, wishes to exclude public worship and finds only in the love-meals (*agapai*) the proper frame of such singing. Abbott puts the whole assumption of the connection of worship and song into question—without giving persuasive reasons.

[123] He referred to Pss 81:2[80:3]; 92:3[91:4]; 96[97]:1; 148:14. The pronoun "to one another" (*heautois*) was understood by him in the sense of "to yourselves." Though I Cor 14:2, 3, 6, 28 speaks of glossolalia directed to God and to one's self, the "singing" mentioned in Eph 5:19 and Col 3:16 is in no sense to be equated with a soliloquizing glossolalia.

part of a hendiadys. In this case it is a synonym of "singing."[124] If, however, the original meaning of *psallō* is in mind, that is, "to pluck or twang a string" (in particular the bowstrings of a musical instrument), then Eph 5:19 encourages the use of fiddles, harps, and other instruments. A decision for or against accompanied singing cannot be made on philological grounds, but precedents in the Jerusalem temple worship and the mention of instruments, e.g. in Ps 150: 3–5, speak in favor of the second interpretation.[125] Another difference between Eph 5:19 and Col 3:16 has been emphasized by W. Bousset: in Ephesians it is "the Lord," in Colossians (except some variant readings) it is "God" who is the object of the congregation's praise. "The cultic significance of the 'Lord' Jesus is in a state of increase" between the time of the writing of the (authentically Pauline) letter to the Colossians and of the (deutero-Pauline) epistle to the Ephesians, according to Bousset.[126] He argues that in a late apostolic passage, that is, in I Tim 3:16, a complete hymn praises Christ alone and that the hymns, viz. the "new songs," addressed to both "God and the lamb" in Rev 5; 14:3; 15:4, anticipate this development. Bousset neglects the great "cultic significance" of the "Lord" Jesus, e.g. in I Cor 1:3; 13:3; 16:22–23. In addition, the phrase "singing to the Lord" may be borrowed from OT or contemporary temple worship, and it may refer to God rather than the Messiah.[127] Certainly among Christians Jesus Christ is included in the praise of God.[128] The next verse confirms this interpretation.

20. *In the name of our Lord Jesus Christ give thanks always and for everything to God the Father.* "Thanksgiving," cf. 5:4, receives strong emphasis in Col 3:15, 17. In the exposition of these Colossian verses various forms of "thanksgiving" (including the "eucharistic") will be discussed, together with the meanings of the formula "in the name of." Both Col 3:17 and Eph 5:20 contain one unique element which is not found in the parallel: Colossians specifies the occasion and means of thanksgiving by speaking of "all that you [the saints] do in word or deed." Ephesians insists upon thanksgiving "for everything" (*hyper pantōn;* lit. "for all things" or "for all men"). Only the Ephesian text is to be discussed here. According to Theodoret, Paul thought of thanksgiving in behalf of other men. Indeed, the intercessory character of Pauline thanksgiving suggests this interpretation: while Paul thanks God for the gift of other people he also offers or sums up the gratitude owed or expressed by

---

[124] The same pair is found in LXX Ps 20:14[21:13]. Among the synonyms of "confessing" compiled in LXX I Chron 16:8–12 are *āsate and hymnēsate* ("sing" and "praise"). In I Cor 14:15 Paul speaks of his "singing (*psallō*) with the spirit and . . . with the mind also." Epictetus *diss.* I 16:21 states proudly, "I am a reasonable man, [therefore] I must praise [*hymneō*] God."

[125] J. Foster, "The Harp at Ephesus," ET 74 (1963), 156, produces the following arguments. (a) A harp mentioned in a letter written from Ephesus, i.e. in I Cor 14:7; (b) a harp occurring in a book related to Ephesus, Rev 5:8; (c) a bishop and a presbytery, said to be as interrelated as a harp and its strings, Ign. *Eph.* IV 1; (d) the harp on the seal of Polycrates, Bishop of Ephesus in A.D. 190, Clement of Alexandria *paed.* III 9. The author concludes from this evidence that Ephesus and the local Christian congregation had an antique musical tradition which included the use of at least one musical instrument.

[126] See his book, *Kyrios*, pp. 234–35. Dibelius, pp. 92–93 follows Bousset's argument.

[127] Equally the phrase "will of the Lord" (Eph 5:17) appears to be interchangeable with "will of God" (6:6; Rom 12:2).

[128] Ign. *Eph.* IV 2 illustrates how in the second century the praise of the Father and the Son could be combined: "Sing with one voice through Jesus to the Father." When in *Eph.* II 2 the same author speaks of "praising Christ," he does not speak of singing, but of a praise offered through orderly conduct and submission to the bishop. At about the same time Pliny the Younger speaks of a "hymn sung to Christ as to God."

others.[129] Therefore it is possible that in 5:20 the church is admonished to take up a priestly function on behalf of all mankind, even of all creatures. However, another exposition is more general: Paul exhorts the saints to accept with manifest gratitude, i.e. with great joy, *all* that they receive and are called to do or to suffer. Under all conditions God is to be praised: Give thanks under all circumstances (*en panti;* I Thess 5:18)! Jerome and Thomas Aquinas insisted that not only felicitous gifts such as health and daily bread, but also "adverse circumstances" ought to be received in this spirit. Chrysostom went so far as to say, "We must thank God even for hell." The interpretations of Jerome and Thomas Aquinas are confirmed by the many NT passages that speak of joyous glorification of God, above all in suffering.[130] According to Calvin the "provision by uncounted benefits of ever new material for joy and thanks" made it necessary for the saints "to continue throughout their whole life the study and exercise of praising God."

COMMENTS I–V on 5:1–20

I Structure and Summary

Eph 5:1–20 has the following five parts. Verses 1–2 call for an imitation of God which consists of walking in the way of the love established by Christ's death. These two verses form either the climax of the preceding section, 4:17–32, or the headline for all that follows in 5:3 ff. In either case they occupy a central position among the admonitions contained in the larger context, 4:17–6:9.

Verses 3–7 pronounce that the congregation is subject to discipline. No compromise is acceptable with modes of speech and conduct that are typical of the pagan past. A threatening and rigorous, almost legalistic, tone prevails in this subsection.

Verses 8–14 put forth the evangelical foundation and character of the sharp statements in vss. 3–7. The victorious power of light is praised. Christ is that light in person. This light has completely changed and will continue to change the saints. Rather than excommunicate deviating brothers, the text recommends such a testimony by conduct as will win over the perpetrators of evil. The saints are daily to learn and to demonstrate by action what is the will and power of the good Lord.

Verses 15–18a insist that even during the present evil days the Day of the Lord is at hand. The reference to love in vss. 1–2 is here complemented by a reference to wisdom. To live from Christ's awakening call (vs. 14b, c) means to make good use of the given time and of one's intellect—not to seek refuge in drowsiness, or courage in the forgetfulness produced by inebriation.

Verses 18–20 sum up the preceding subsections. References to the Spirit, Jesus Christ, God the Father follow upon another. The Christian's life is described as a demonstration of exuberant joy. Inspiration (or enthusiasm)

---

[129] See, e.g. *hyper hymōn* in Philip 1:4; Rom 1:8 var. lect., cf. *peri hymōn* in I Thess 1:2; Rom 1:8. See COMMENT II on 1:15–23 for the Pauline combination of thanksgiving and intercession.
[130] See, e.g. Eph 3:13; Col 1:24; James 1:2–3; I Peter 1:6; 4:12–13; Luke 21:28; Acts 5:41; 16:25.

caused by something better than alcohol makes the congregation resemble a group of singing children who are assembled by Christ and whose gratitude to God the Father overflows.

Thus the stream of thought moves from a praise of love, through stern warning, to the glorification of light and wisdom; it ends in the call to gratitude. This preponderance of adoration motifs is found nowhere else in the NT epistles. A traditional model does not appear to have been used here. But other Ephesian passages, such as the so-called *Haustafeln* (5:21 – 6:9) reflect a pattern that must have antedated this epistle, and even in 5:1–20 the style and content of several individual parts are not original products of the author. What "traditional elements" can be discerned?

In vss. 2 and 18 formulations are taken up from the LXX—though the author does not say that he is quoting.

In vs. 14 an early Christian hymn is cited, introduced as an authority equal in rank to a canonical Psalm (see 4:8). The core of vs. 2 reminds the reader of Gal 2:20 and Eph 5:25; cf. Gal 1:4. The combination of the "love" motif of Deuteronomy[131] with Second Isaiah's concept of "deliverance" may be originally Pauline, but it is more likely that it was present in a Christological hymn used in pre-Pauline congregations. Since in 1:4; 4:21, 32; 5:25 and elsewhere the words "just as" or "just as also" (*kathōs, kathōs kai*) include the function of a quotation formula, the same is probably true of 5:2. In this case vs. 2 contains a quote, just as much as vs. 14.

The apodictic character of 5:5, perhaps also of 5:6b, fits the narrower context of vss. 3–7 well, that is, the enforcement of church discipline. The phrases "kingdom of God's Messiah" and (lit.) "sons of disobedience" are so surprising in a letter ascribed to Paul that they may have to be explained as elements stemming from a special tradition. In the first NOTE on 5:5 it was stated that the tradition in question may have been that of (a collection of?) "sentences of holy law." The content and character of vss. 3–7 closely resemble II Cor 6:14 – 7:1. Both the Corinthian passage and its Ephesian parallel appear to be heavily influenced by the content and style of Qumran community discipline. I Cor 5 contains an example showing how Paul exercised church discipline.

In Eph 5:9, 12, 13, 14a, 16b, 18b general truths are pronounced, mostly in proverbial form. Like the canonical book of Proverbs and the apocryphal Wisdom of Solomon, the Pauline exhortation is spiced by observations that could be made by anyone of sound mind. The ethics of Ephesians do not intend to contradict common sense.[132] Because so many non-Pauline dicta are present in 5:1–20, it is no wonder that *hapax legomena* as well as brief traditional catalogues occur in the same passage.[133]

Verses 8–14 include both traditional and original statements on Christ the

---

[131] See the interpretation of 1:4, above.

[132] In I Cor 9:7–17 four arguments are combined to make one ethical point, i.e. supplying adequate provision to an evangelist: (a) the analogous treatment of a soldier, a peasant, a shepherd; (b) the (allegorical) meaning of a Scripture passage; (c) the suitability of palpable gratitude which corresponds to spiritual labor as harvesting does to sowing; (d) a command of the Lord. The first of these arguments is clearly an appeal to common sense. In Eph 5:9 ff. proverbial affirmations abound. No allegorical use of Scriptures is made before 5:32.

[133] E.g. 5:9 contains the *hapax legomenon*, lit. "fruit of light" and the catalogue, lit. "goodness," "righteousness," "truth"; see also esp. 5:3–5. Marxsen, *Introduction*, p. 195, overemphasizes the catalogical element when he considers the whole of vss. 3–7 a catalogue of vices, and vss. 8–21 a catalogue of virtues.

light, the Christians as light, the power and effect of light. Only Second Isaiah, the Gospel and the First Epistle of John contain similarly rich elaborations on the "light."[134] The author of Ephesians did not discover the metaphorical potential of this keyword; throughout the Bible it occurs in the context of revelation, salvation, and/or ethical exhortation. In Eph 5:1–20, "the figure of light governs the whole passage."[135]

Finally, it need not be demonstrated that the exhortations to behave wisely in evil days (vss. 15–17), to be sober (vs. 18), to sing God's praise (vs. 19) and to live a life of gratitude (vs. 20), take up elements from canonical and non-canonical Wisdom and Psalm books.

An expositor should begin rather than conclude his work with the distinction among such manifold nonbiblical, biblical, kerygmatic, exhortatory, proverbial, or hymnical elements. In order to prevent an interpretation that is no more than a tracing of origins and parallels from triumphing over the biblical author's creative synthesis, the questions must be asked: What did the author do with the materials he used? What did he achieve by melting them into one unit? A close observation of Paul's procedure may allow the intention and effect of Eph 5:1–20 to be discerned:

Paul holds the diverse elements together with an external frame and by internal seams that unify whatever may appear centrifugal. Frame and seams consist mainly of imperatives: "Be imitators of God. . . . You had better keep this in mind. . . . Let no one deceive you. . . . Do not associate with them," etc. The number and urgency of these imperatives, also the section describing church discipline (5:3–7), show that the Pauline admonition must not be taken more lightly than the proclamation of the gospel. His exhortation (parenesis) is as radical and uncompromising as his preaching (*kerygma*). For this apostle, just as, e.g. for John the Baptist, the Sermon on the Mount and the epistle of James, imperatives are an indispensable way of describing God's will. Does this mean that the "easy yoke" of the Savior and the gospel of salvation (Matt 11:30) are complemented by a heavy yoke of ethical demands?

Most of the smaller traditional units contained in 5:1–20 dispel this impression. Traditional formulations signal the fact that more is offered than a mere collection of demands: the sum of God's will is a call to love, an invitation to enjoy the light, an encouragement to be responsible for weak brothers, to behave reasonably, to rejoice and give thanks under all circumstances. In each case it is made clear that God does more than pronounce a law: he has given to mankind the Messiah who loved men to the end; he has proven the power of light by saving Gentiles such as the "Ephesians" from the darkness which held them; he has prepared a way which is more convincing than mere words; Christ's call is still to be heard, his light is still to be seen; reasons and means to rejoice are amply present. Only on the grounds of the indicative statements describing Christ's love, the light's victorious power, the Spirit's presence even on evil days, are the imperatives pronounced. If there were no way to love and no reason to rejoice, the urgent invitations to charity and gratitude would be nonsensical. Since God has founded and still sustains a com-

---

[134] Esp. Isa 60:1–3, 19–20; John 1:4–9; 3:19–21; 12:35–36, 46; I John 1:5, 7; 2:8–10.
[135] Abbott, p. 153.

munity of beloved children, these children are free and can be encouraged to
live up to the bond that unites them and to break into song.

The sum of Paul's intention and achievement may be formulated in two dialectical sentences: (a) His ethical exhortation (parenesis) is based upon the
gospel preached before him; it has no other foundation than the good news of
God's grace that is known and accepted in the church. (b) The grace of God
which is confessed in the congregations is so complete that its effect and manifestation cannot and must not be subdued: total love, strict discipline, full responsibility, wisdom even in adverse circumstances, overflowing gratitude are
of the essence of grace, not mere appendages. The two dialectical elements
can be combined in one sentence: if the aim and result of God's will were
scorned, then the revealed and worshiped God himself, the work of Christ, and
the Spirit would be rejected.

Four of the six major topics of this passage will be treated in the following
COMMENTS: imitation of God, church discipline, the victory of light, the recognition of God's will. The statements related to singing and gratitude will be
reserved for the exposition of Col 3:15–17.

II   Imitation of God

In the last NOTE on 5:1 and the footnotes thereto a suggestion was made regarding the interpretation of the surprising expression, "Be imitators of God."
On the grounds of OT, rabbinic, and other Jewish statements and thought patterns, it was shown that the meaning of "imitating" may be "following." In his
description of the biblical concept of "imitation," W. Michaelis is a strong exponent of this view. He holds that in Pauline writings "following the fatherly will
. . . recognition of authority . . . obedience" exhaust the meaning of "imitating," and that therefore no Greek or Hellenistic notions of "imitation" must be
taken into consideration when explaining Eph 5:1.[136] Indeed it is probable that
OT, rabbinic, and Gospel texts which speak of discipleship (viz. of *akoloutheō*,
"to follow") can to a large extent explain the Pauline statements calling for imitation of Christ, of the apostle, or of both.[137] However, the full weight of the
unique formulation "Be imitators of God" is not adequately recognized when
"God" is considered no more than the first among several persons to be imitated. Of course "imitation of God" may include an anthropomorphic element:
if the principle of "supererogation" is applied to Eph 5:1, then this verse means
that what man owes to servants of God on earth, he owes all the more to God
himself in heaven. But since Ephesians was written in Greek to readers living
in a Hellenistic environment, it remains to be seen whether additional overtones
and/or completely different meanings can be discovered in 5:1.

Recent monographs on the concepts "following" and "imitating" recognize
the problem and come to diverse conclusions, certain common grounds notwithstanding.[138]

A consensus is in sight inasmuch as the Hebrew tradition prefers to speak
of "following God" and "obeying" him—while the idea of "imitating" a god,
the gods, or the divine world is a favorite in Greek thought and much more

[136] TWNTE, IV, 659–674, esp. 667–71.
[137] See fn. 11 to 5:1–20, and its context.
[138] See BIBLIOGRAPHY 20.

broadly developed in the pagan Hellenistic world than in Jewish writings. The Hebrew language has terms such as "walking after," "walking in the ways," but no word for "imitating."[139] Nevertheless, the difference between Hebrew and Greek diction and thought is not absolute and total, for occasionally writers of either cultural tradition appear to move along parallel lines or to borrow from one another. Classical and later Greek writers use the term "to follow god[s]," preferring *hepomai*, but not excluding *akoloutheō*.[140] The LXX uses, though rarely, the verb *mimeomai* and the noun *mimēma* ("to imitate," "imitation").[141] M. Buber endorses the "paradox" that the invisible God himself is to be imitated by man; though man cannot imitate God's "secret" attributes and ways, yet he is created in God's image, he can cleave to the way of God's mercy, grace, long-suffering, faithfulness, and thus aim at a final perfection of the soul. A. Marmorstein follows Buber's understanding of Talmudic, especially haggadic, statements, but he admits that the paradoxical statements of the Talmud were not undisputed and seeks to distinguish carefully between rabbinical teaching on imitation and Hellenizing misinterpretation.[142]

A major disagreement among scholars becomes apparent when the questions are posed: What exactly are the origin and essence of Greek *mimēsis* ("imitation"), and which of the several features of Greek imitation may have influenced Paul?

a) *Mimesis* has cosmological meaning when it describes the relation of the created world to the invisible world, or of man to the whole cosmos or to the deity.[143] The existence of a structural analogy between the lower and the higher world, viz. between the microcosmos (man) and the macrocosmos, can be suggested by employment of the term "imitation."

b) *Mimesis* may denote an ethical relation between man and deity which includes an appeal to man's free will and responsibility.[144]

c) *Mimesis* is sometimes the name given to the work of the artisan, the painter, the poet, or the orator.[145] Each in his own way and with his own tools (the ax, the chisel, the brush, or the pen) creates a reproduction of the original that stands before his mind. Thus the artist may be the paragon of an imitator, and art, including skill, the most perfect imitation.

---

[139] Only by straining the evidence, e.g. of Gen 1:26–27 and Exod 25:8–9, 40; 27:8; Ezek 40 ff.; Heb 8:5 (i.e. texts speaking of man's creation "in the image after the likeness of God," and of the heavenly prototype of the earthly sanctuary) has the notion of imitation been imposed upon pre-Hellenistic parts of the OT.

[140] E.g. Plato *Phaed.* 248A; Epictetus *diss.* I 20:15.

[141] Ps 30:7 (in the Codex Vaticanus *emisēsas* is changed by a corrector to *emimēsas*); Wisd Sol 4:2; 9:8; 15:9; IV Macc 9:23; 13:9. In Josephus *ant.* I 4:19–20, imitating and following (*mimeomai, akatoloutheō,* and *hepomai*) are synonyms; the reward of following/imitating God is a happy life (*eudaimōn bios*). For corresponding references in Philo see fns. 10, 144, 150.

[142] Pp. 106 ff.; H. O. Betz, p. 84–101, gives a summary of the diverse arguments. See also H. J. Schoeps, pp. 286–90

[143] Democritus and Pythagoras prepared the way for the view which is elaborated upon, e.g. by Plato *resp.* x 597–605; *Timaeus* 30–39. The Johannine *logos* doctrine, neo-Platonic and mystical elements were combined in various ways by Athanasius, Cyril of Alexandria, and Maximus Confessor when they formed the concept of *theōsis dia mimēseōs* ("deification by imitation"); see Schoeps, p. 298, for references.

[144] See, e.g. Philo *de virt.* 168, "Moses teaches to imitate God as far as possible," cf. *spec. leg.* IV 73; *leg. all.* I 148. In *de fug. et inv.* 63, this *Jewish* scholar quotes Plato enthusiastically; see *Theaet.* 176AB. It is the king's duty especially to imitate God through kindness and magnanimity, according to the Table Talks contained in *Aristeas* 187–92, 210, 281, etc.

[145] Plato *resp.* x 597 ff. uses as an example the production of a bed by a cabinetmaker and gives only secondary honors to the fine arts. Aristotle *poetica* v 1449AB, pays highest tribute to the poet's work, esp. to tragedies. Among modern writers, E. Auerbach uses the term *mimesis* to describe "the representation of reality in . . . literature."

d) *Mimesis* is the relation of a pupil to his teacher, or rather, of a disciple to his master. It can describe the power of the educational process as well as the goal of education.[146]

e) *Mimesis* occurs in the wearing of masks, in dances, in theater, in the cult. More happens in such performances than make-believe, more also than mere dramatic recollection, representation, re-enactment. The imitator (through him also those watching him, especially the chorus in the tragedies) identifies himself and is identified with the comic or tragic, happy or fateful nature of life, its changes, its challenges. Identification takes place not only with human experiences, necessities, exigencies, but also with the deities of a cosmic order that cause and protect the several phases and incidents of individual and communal life. Imitation may therefore become equated with deification or with the restoration of a lost unity. Aristotle speaks of *catharsis* (purification).[147]

f) *Mimesis* has a lighter and brighter character whenever happiness (*eudaimonia*) is declared the apex of kinship to the gods.[148]

More meanings of Greek *mimesis* could probably be listed, but the several senses discussed may suffice to show that in the Greek-speaking world before and in Paul's time imitation had cosmologic, ethical, artistic, educational, cultic, hedonistic dimensions. Are some of these features mutually exclusive? In the discussion of ethical catalogues[149] the connection between dualistic ontology and ethics was mentioned. The *logos* is sometimes described as bearing two functions: he obediently imitates the ways of the Father, and he shapes visible things after the model of invisible patterns.[150] Thus ethical and technical imitation are combined in the *logos*. Are these two forms of imitation perhaps essentially at variance with the imitation performed in a cultic framework and in ceremonial form? The distinction between the ethical and cultic realms is a feat of western culture; it is exemplified e.g. by the variant readings of the Apostolic Decree in (Acts 15, etc.), by the Scholastic distinction between transitory cultical and permanently valid moral laws of the OT, and by the preference given by J. Wellhausen (also by his philosophical predecessors and exegetical followers) to the ethical religion of the Prophets over the ceremonialism of the Priests. But in so-called primitive religions the differentiation is as

---

[146] See e.g. Xenophon *memorabilia Socratis* I 6:3; the proposition, "Teachers make their disciples copy their teachers" is apparently accepted by Socrates. Plato's relationship to Socrates was that of an imitator in the best sense. Dionysius of Halicarnassus (a first-century B.C. historian and orator) *de Lysia* 11, considered imitation of the gracious style and diction of Lysias the Orator (fifth century B.C.) as the means by which perfect ("Atticistic") use of the Greek language could be restored. M. Pohlenz, "To Prepon" (see fn. 24 to 5:1-20), pp. 64–65 points out that *mimēsis* refers to both, the ideal itself and to the recognition and overcoming of the difference between the original and the copy. According to W. P. DeBoer, pp. 6 ff. the system of Greek education (*paideia*) may lie at the root of various other meanings of *mimesis* (ref.).

[147] M. Eliade, e.g. in *Cosmos and History*, esp. pp. 21–34, has contributed much to elucidate the meaning of cultic acts. E. G. Gulin and J. M. Nielen see in the cultic meaning of *mimesis* the substratum of all other senses. It is regrettable that Aristotle neither in *poet.* 1449A nor in *pol.* VIII 1342 explains exactly what he means by "purification."

[148] Strabo X 9, 467 (quoted in TWNTE, IV, 662–63, n. 5) contains a passage (of the middle Stoic Posidonius?) that combines doing good with being happy. In happiness this geographer of the first century B.C. sees the highest form of imitating god. Joy, celebration, philosophizing, surrender to music—these features of enthusiastic self-delivery into the arms of the deity—are explicitly mentioned. All (except philosophizing?) are reflected in the calls to wisdom, singing, gratitude contained in Eph 5:15–20. Cf. Josephus *ant.* I 4:19–20.

[149] COMMENT VIII on 4:17–32.

[150] E.g. in *de confusione linguarum* 63, Philo combines Platonic and Stoic elements.

little pronounced as among classical Greek writers, for originally the cult, the order of the community, education, art, and virtue belong together: Sophocles' *Antigone* fulfills her *moral* obligation to her dead brother by granting him (a token of) a *ritual* burial. The same coherence of ethical and cultic elements is typical of the OT commandments (see fn. 153 to 2:11–22).

Certainly the Greek term *mimēsis*, even when it occurs in the Hellenistic period, can comprehend and combine many senses. When one is clearly expressed the others need not be totally absent. The same is probably true of Eph 5:1. The Hebraizing equation of an imitator with a follower cannot be excluded; it corresponds to the second and fourth of the six Greek meanings outlined above. But in spite of some acquaintance with the OT (and maybe some rabbinical teachings) which Paul apparently presupposed among his readers, he could not assume that they would automatically translate his Greek words into Hebrew conceptuality. Perhaps he did not even want this to happen.

While the insulated words, "Be imitators of God," permit a great number of interpretations,[151] the immediate context provides criteria and suggestions for uncovering the author's intention and, perhaps, the understanding of his first readers:

a) The references to Christ in the preceding and following verses (4:32 and 5:2) reveal that the imitation of God by man is dependent upon the mediation of a third person. While "following" presupposes no more than two partners who trust each other, e.g. a master instructing a disciple, the imitation of God is based on a preceding event in which a third partner plays a decisive role: "God in Christ has forgiven you," and "the Messiah has loved us and has given himself for us." The imitation of God is not only exemplified but also has a sacramental basis in Jesus Christ's love and death. Thus 5:1 shares with middle-Platonists and Stoics, including Philo, the idea that man cannot immediately imitate God. Yet according to the context of the same verse it is Christ crucified who is the mediator between God and man, not a timeless *logos* principle. In the Bible the concept of "following" Yahweh or Jesus does not always have to do with a cult (exceptions are especially Deut 5–13 and Heb 5–12). But in Eph 5:1 "imitation" is indissolubly connected with references to Christ, the forgiving priest, and to his voluntary sacrifice. "Through him . . . we have free access to the Father" (2:18).

b) If imitation of God means no more than submission to authority by strict obedience, then the allusions made in 5:8–20 to light, wisdom, music, and joy have little to do with the words, "Be imitators of God." But certain elements of Greek culture help to explain why the passage 5:1–20 that begins with the concept of imitation of God ends with references to music and other expressions of joy and happiness. At least three such features can be listed: (1) the idea that the visible world is formed after the pattern of the invisible and reflects in some way the perfection of ideas, pure forms, or the gods; (2)

---

[151] Including flagrant misinterpretations such as, You are able to be and do all that God is and does, for you are a part of the deity; or, You are indeed to become like God, just as the Serpent promised; or, deification is man's true nature. Expositions that flatly contradict Pauline statements need not be considered, even though in the frame of Mystery Cults or Gnostic rites the words used in Eph 5:1 might have one of these meanings.

the conviction that the inspiration of muses or special qualifications enable outstanding men such as artists, actors, soothsayers or priests to recognize and express better than others true being, true life, the nature of existence; 3) the *joie de vivre* (*eudaimōniā*, "happiness") which is believed to be accessible to every wise man. If Eph 5:1-20 is understood as a reflection, qualification, and correction of Greek "imitation," then this part of Ephesians is no longer a haphazard collection of counsels tagged on to the command, "Be imitators of God." Then the many imperatives of 5:3-20 unfold and explain the one, "Be imitators," as if to say: Light is not just opposed to darkness; much more, it is victorious over it; the passing days may be evil, but wise use can be made of them because now is the Lord's day on which he awakens dead men; pleasures such as those found in drunkenness are silly and cheap if compared with the abounding joy and happiness provided by God and expressed to him. *You* are the people qualified to praise God through your existence.

In short, the manifold dimensions and the evangelical character of the words "Be imitators of God" are suppressed or bypassed when the full Greek meaning of *mimesis* is neglected in the interpretation of the Greek term "imitators of God." Just as (according to Luke) Paul in his Areopagus speech told the Athenians who the god was whom they did not know (or rather, whom they had ignored), so in the context of Eph 5:1 the apostle tells pagan-born saints what the term "imitators of God" truly means. The references to the Father-child relationship (5:1), to Christ (4:32, 5:2, 14, 20), and to the Spirit (4:30, 5:19), reveal that Paul does not adapt his idea of God to the internal dynamics of the Greek term imitation, but follows the opposite procedure: he who is to be imitated determines the nature of imitation. The utterances about love and mutual admonition show that instead of individualistic perfectionism a very special social conduct is in Paul's mind. The description of the power of light and the invitation to manifest gratitude enhance the effect of God's work: there is no room for passivity, but ample space for human response, imaginative activity, and public confession. Finally the verses dealing with church discipline (5:3 ff.) dispel the notion that some cultic action or spiritual trance[152] exert a magical power that guarantees a place in God's kingdom under any circumstances.

In the next two COMMENTS, special attention will be given to the *particularistic* utterances about discipline and the *universalistic* statements about light.

III   Church Discipline

Eph 5:3 ff. belongs to those NT passages that not only make a sharp distinction between good and evil deeds but also demand a clear-cut separation between the children of light and of darkness.[153] Like the spiritual leaders of Israel, the Qumran community, and the Jews living in the Diaspora, the apostles and their followers were faced with an evil greater than the wicked ways of life found outside the chosen community. Flagrant sins were committed by people

---

[152] E.g. baptism, participation in the Lord's Supper, or speaking in tongues: I Cor 10:1-13; 11:27-33.

[153] See esp. Gal 1:8-9; 5:16-24; II Cor 6:14 - 7:1; I Cor 5:1-13; 6:9-10; 16:22; Rev 22:14-15, 18-19; Heb 6:4-8; 10:26-27; 12:17; Matt 18:15-18; 16:18-19; John 20:23; I John 5:16-17; cf. *Did* XIV; XV 3.

who were counted among the saints and attended their worship.[154] Since the end of the first century A.D., the measures taken among Jews in regard to erring, falling, relapsing "brothers" culminated in the "synagogue ban." Analogous steps taken among Christians are usually called "church discipline"; they could lead to "excommunication."

In the NT, forms of church discipline cover a wide range. One extreme is Jesus' attitude to the adulterous woman, his prohibition against pronouncing judgment, perhaps also his treatment of Judas the traitor.[155] His words and example are sometimes understood as an absolute prohibition: in no way must Christians imitate either the less or the more stringent forms of the "synagogue ban."[156] The other extreme is represented by casuistic injunctions that distinguish between different sins, that recommend various successive steps (resembling the order followed in synagogue practice) to be taken against offenders, and that include with excommunication from the church the exclusion from God's kingdom.[157] Between the extremes stands Paul. His practice of church discipline includes at least three variants: (a) he pronounces an anathema over those who distort the gospel (Gal 1:8–9); (b) he solemnly delivers ("in the name of the Lord Jesus" in conjunction with "your and my spirit and the power of our Lord Jesus") a fornicator "to Satan in order that the spirit be saved on the day of the Lord" (I Cor 5:4–5); (c) he grants "forgiveness" to an offender (II Cor 2:1–11), and he admonishes the Galatians to meet a fallen brother in a "spirit of meekness" (Gal 6:1).

It is impossible to discuss here the manifold interpretations of the NT texts and the mild or harsh church practices derived from them. It must suffice to state that exegetes, pastors, canon lawyers, and ecclesiastical courts have either sought to understand and reenact the NT teachings on church discipline as a harmonious unit, or have absolutized and rigorously applied only one of the several NT passages and precedents. Thus the supposed institutionalism of Matt 16; 18 and the Pastoral Epistles, the alleged purism of Heb 6; 10; 12; I John, the elastic contextualism of Paul, or the baffling tolerance of John 8 were chosen as models by different Christian communities at different times. The problem of defection during periods of persecution, especially the desire of defectors to rejoin the church; the threat of heresies that distorted the message of Christ; the legalism or libertinism which gained the upper hand over the responsible freedom and the free response shown in ever-new decisions and acts of obedience; the establishment of the church as a state-supported institution and the opposite attempts to form a perfect church; the changing understanding of the essence and nature of the church dictated by repentance, reformation, or mission movements—these and other factors were decisive for various forms of church discipline derived from the Bible.[158] In the follow-

[154] In fn. 69 to Eph 5:11 some OT, Qumran, and rabbinic references were given.
[155] John 8:1–11; Matt 5:22–24; 7:1–5; 26:23–24, 49–50.
[156] See e.g. K. Bornhäuser, Die Bergpredigt (Gütersloh: Bertelsmann, 1923), pp. 69 ff.
[157] I John 5:16–17; Matt 16:18–19; 18:15–18; Heb 6:1–6; 10:26–31; 12:15–17; Rev 22:14–15; cf. 3:16. Especially the Pastoral Epistles describe in some detail the pertinent duties and powers entrusted to a bishop.
[158] The development in the first two centuries is described, e.g. by H. Windisch, Taufe und Sünde, Tübingen: Mohr, 1908. Augustine discusses the issue, e.g. in civ. Dei I 9; sermones 82; Thomas Aquinas in Summa Theologica II II 33; Luther in Formula Missae et Communionis (1523), WA, XII, 205–20; Calvin in Institutio IV 12; idem, de scandalis (1550); the Heidelberg Catechism in

ing discussion, only the special accents contributed by Eph 5:3 ff. to NT church discipline will be presented.

"No fornicating, filthy, or greedy man, that is, no one who worships an idol, has as inheritance in the kingdom of God's Messiah" (5:5). In the second NOTE on this verse it was pointed out that Paul would flatly contradict himself and certain *logia* of Jesus if he meant to exclude from access to the "kingdom" all Gentiles and Jews who had committed such sins. Still, the mere unlikelihood of such a contradiction does not necessarily prove its absence. During some periods at least, Israel excluded eunuchs from admission to the service of God.[159] If Paul was a moral zealot, he could in principle exclude all immoral persons from the church. The Qumran community had no room for any proselytes from the Gentiles (except in CD XIV 4-6?). Paul could have followed this example by keeping at least some Gentiles out of the church. There is indeed evidence that on one occasion a congregation suspected or accused him of calling for a total segregation from certain people. This impression was apparently created by a first letter of Paul to the Corinthians, which contained the Qumran-style passage II Cor 6:14-7:1 and requested unconditional separation of the (children of) "light" from the (children of) "darkness." Rev 22:14-15 presses a similar point: "Outside are the dogs . . . !" However, in his second letter to Corinth (in our canon I Corinthians; see 5:9-13) the apostle Paul answers, "I wrote to you in my letter not to associate with immoral men; not at all meaning the immoral of this world, or the greedy and robbers, or idolaters, since then you would need to go out of this world. But rather I wrote to you not to associate with anyone who bears the name of a brother if he is guilty of immorality. . . . For what have I to do with judging outsiders? Is it not these inside the church whom you are to judge? God judges those outside. Drive out the wicked person from among you." Those "unrighteous" men who according to I Cor 6:9-10[160] will "not inherit the kingdom" are obviously people "who bear the name of a brother," not "outsiders" (I Cor 5:11-12).

Only Christians are warned of the consequences of their own evil conduct, inasmuch as Paul does not summarily condemn the immoral people outside the church. "Let anyone who thinks that he stands take heed lest he fall" (I Cor 10:12). In I Corinthians, Ephesians, and elsewhere in the NT, the

---

Question 85. Among recent writers, R. Bohren, *Das Problem der Kirchenzucht im Neuen Testament,* Zurich: EVZ, 1951, intends to show that the church, in being the bride and body of Christ, is most emphatically charged to prevent carnal-sexual sin in her midst (p. 41). One unified, though not legalistic, concept of church discipline can and must be derived from the NT, according to Bohren. However, Käsemann's essay "Sentences of Holy Law" (see fn. 39) has demonstrated that diverse NT authors and writers reflect a diversity of opinions and practices that defy harmonization: church discipline was originally a charismatic act performed by prophetic figures for the sake of the salvation of the offenders; eventually it became the tool of an organized church that succumbed to legalistic sacred and secular practices which contradict the eschatological self-understanding of the early community. Käsemann's findings supersede the debate between R. Sohm, A. Harnack and their successors regarding the presence or absence of "Law" in the NT church. Käsemann shows that a very specific, even a "holy" law, informed by awareness of the nearness and validity of God's Last Judgment, was proclaimed by early Christian prophets; but he also points out that as early as in the apostolic period this "holy law" was replaced by institutional, be it sacred or profane, legalism. The triumph of legalism, in turn, contributed to the formation of so-called "early Catholicism."

[159] Deut 23:1-2; Isa 56:3-5; cf. Acts 8:27-39.
[160] See also Gal 4:30; 5:21; I Cor 15:50.

sharpest moral indictments and the most clear condemnations are directed against members of the congregation. Not of unconverted pagans but of Christians is it said, "They are waterless springs and mists driven by storm; for them the nether gloom of darkness has been reserved . . . After they have escaped the defilement of the world through knowledge of our Lord and Savior Jesus Christ, they are again entangled in them and overpowered, the last state has become worse for them than the first. For it would have been better for them never to have known the way of righteousness than after knowing it to turn back . . . The dog turns back to his own vomit, and the sow is washed only to wallow in mire" (II Peter 2:17-22; cf. Jude, *passim*). With less picturesque language essentially the same message is conveyed by Matthew: the place of "outer darkness" where there is "weeping and gnashing of teeth" is a threat to "sons of the kingdom" of God, to citizens of "Christ's kingdom," to people caught in the "net," to "servants" appointed by the "Lord," to "virgins" invited to the feast.[161] No equally strong prediction is found regarding those who never have been reached by God's call, included in his flock, given the awareness and hope of God's goodness. If the "outer darkness" can be equated with the place which in common church parlance is called "hell," then the NT epistles quoted and Matthew lead to the conclusion that "hell is for Christians only"—that is, for those saints who betray their faith, belie their name, and dishonor their Lord. "The judgment begins at the house of God" (I Peter 4:17).

While in Gal 1:8-9 and I Cor 16:22 Paul appears to pronounce a final anathema over heretical and licentious Christians, in I Cor 5:5 he affirms that even the sternest disciplinary measure is *for the salvation* of the offender's "spirit." Heb 6:4-8 seems to exclude a second repentance, and Matt 18:17 says nothing about the future of the man counted as a "gentile and tax-collector." Eph 5:3 ff. contains no explicit statement regarding the future of the evil-doer; only the danger of contact with his evil works and the need to restore him or to disprove his conduct are mentioned. However, the goal of brotherly correction exerted in a meek spirit (Gal 6:1) is spelled out in I Cor 14:25: "The secrets of his heart are disclosed; and so, falling on his face, he will worship God and declare that God is really among you." In Paul's epistles the correction of an evil-doer has a positive purpose: the preservation of the holy congregation and the salvation of its weakest member. Ephesians stands out among the Pauline letters for its extensive description of the motivation and mode of church discipline. Responsibility for the erring brother is shown by good conduct and exemplification of the triumph of light—this, rather than the recommendation of casuistic procedures, is the sum of this epistle's doctrine on church discipline.

Several examples of how Ephesians differs from other NT texts describing church discipline can be mentioned by brief reference only. (a) No use is made in Ephesians of the (prophetic and) apostolic prerogative to pronounce an

---

[161] Matt 8:11; 13:41-42, 47-50; 22:13; 25:12. Compare the judgment on Jude, the treacherous *disciple:* "Better if he had never been born," Matt 26:24. However, in the book of Revelation, esp. in 22:15, the "outside" appears to be reserved for those who have never been inside the people of God. Revelation may reflect an apocalyptic-predestinarian dualism. The same certainly cannot be said of Ephesians.

anathema. (b) The whole congregation rather than its bishop or board of elders is declared responsible for the care of the erring brother. (c) A special code of discipline for clerics is not envisaged. (d) Letting the light of Christ shine—this is the only method of brotherly admonition and conviction. This light alone reveals all reprobate things and changes darkness into light (5:13–14). Neither the reading of a law, nor the enumeration of sins committed, nor the vituperative condemnation of the sinner, nor his deliverance to punishment but rather a life led according to the gospel is envisaged here as the means of convincing and winning over a fellow man. "Don't you know that the goodness of God leads you to repentance?" (Rom 2:4). Knowledge, confession, and forgiveness of sin come solely from that light which God lets shine. (e) While Eph 5:7 (and II Cor 6:14 ff.) can be understood to prohibit all contact with the evil-doer, vs. 11 prohibits association and solidarity only with his "works." Eph 5:3–14 makes the same distinction between the man and his evil spirit or evil deed as Jesus did, e.g. in his dealing with the demoniac in the synagogue (Mark 1:21–28) and with the adulterous woman, according to John 8:2–11 (a passage which may not be an authentic part of the original Gospel of John). The sinner is called to leave behind darkness, death, and all the works belonging to them, and to rise as a creature renewed by Christ's light. (f) If a distinction between ethical and doctrinal heresy can be made at all, then Eph 5:3 ff. is primarily concerned with the realm of ethics, while in 4:14 and 2:9 doctrinal concerns are in the foreground.

These features distinguish Ephesians from the injunctions regarding church discipline that are found, e.g. in the Pastoral Epistles. The thesis of E. Käsemann and others, that because of the church order and doctrine reflected in Ephesians this letter typifies the development of "early Catholicism" and the legalistic ecclesiasticism of the post-apostolic period, is not only unsupported but contradicted by the specific contents of 5:3 ff. Indeed, the topic of this passage is church discipline, and the tone of 5:3–7 is stern. But the character of the admonition given here is evangelical, and a premonition of canon law cannot be found in it. The whole context is illuminated by the radiant statements about the conquering light, as will be shown in the next COMMENT.

However, this emphasis upon the evangelical character of church discipline in Eph 5 is not beyond dispute. The accents fall upon entirely different places if a caesura is made after vs. 5 (or after vs. 10), and if vss. 6–14 (viz. 11–14) are understood to speak of the saints' relationship to non-Christians.[162] The following arguments for the caesura deserve consideration. (a) In several NT texts the church is described as a light shining in and for the (dark) environment of "the world," of "those outside."[163] Thus the function of light is not restricted to benefitting only church members. Is Ephesians therefore more narrow than other epistles and the Gospel of Matthew? Ephesians itself urges the church to fulfill its cosmic mission:[164] the creative power of light experienced by the saints (5:8; cf. I Peter 2:9) is declared victorious over all reprobate things. It is

---

[162] Calvin believes that vss. 3–5, 15–20 speak of the Christians' behavior toward believers, vss. 6–14 of their attitude to unbelievers. Schlier, p. 199 speaks in his exegesis of vs. 11 suddenly of "convincing . . . the gentiles" and of "a revelation of the gentiles."
[163] Philip 2:15; Matt 5:14–16; cf. Prov 4:18; I Thess 4:12; Col 4:5; I Peter 2:9, 12, etc.
[164] Esp. in 1:20–23; 2:7; 3:10; 6:15.

praised because it turns into light "all that is revealed" (5:13–14a). (b) The term "the rebellious" (lit. "sons of disobedience") which occurs in 5:6 is in 2:2 used to designate Gentiles dead in sin, not renegade Christians. (c) What is called "fitting for saints" (5:3) does not resemble the exclusive ethic of an elite which cannot be shared by all men of good will and sound sense. Rather it appears to be an expression of God's will for every man, of a life style suitable for all humanity. (d) The lines quoted in 5:14 may well have been taken from a baptismal hymn, praising the effect of light on former non-believers. If this was their original meaning and if they are quoted in their original sense, then the immediately preceding (three or eight) verses may also speak of the conversion of outsiders.

Arguments such as these can be used to form the thesis that only in the first part of Eph 5:3–14 is internal church discipline discussed: its character is rigorous, reminiscent of Qumran and synagogue discipline. But the main emphasis of vss. 13–14 lies then upon the church's mission to the world—a mission which here is described as censuring, convicting, and raising.

Does this exposition represent the intention of 5:3–14 better than the interpretation presented earlier? Hardly! For there is no indication that a transition is made after vs. 5 or 10 from the discussion of intramural issues to the topic of foreign relations. The words of vs. 6 show clearly that the Christians themselves are in danger: "Let no one deceive you!" An appeal to missionary engagement on the part of the congregation will be found in 6:15–20; but in the context of 5:1–20 it would interrupt the treatment of domestic ethical problems which dominates 4:17 – 6:9. Of all people, the Christians are the first who need reminding of the light's irresistible power (and perhaps also of the promise and command connected with their baptism). If the disciplinarian pronouncements of 5:3–5 or 5:3–10 have nothing to do with the victorious message of vss. 13–14, then they describe a church determined by legalistic principles, despite the evangelical indicatives found in vss. 8 and 9. By the same token, if the mission of the saints to the world is described in vss. 6–14 or 11–14, this mission aims at a very strange end: The saints have to test, to prove wrong, and thereby to convict the world. The sum of the matter would then be the following: the church must impose upon all mankind the same law to which she is bound to adhere herself, or more briefly, the church is the divinely appointed police force of the world. Though the task of the church (e.g. in Geneva in the days of Calvin) as well as of so-called Christian nations has sometimes been conceived in such a manner, it is more than doubtful whether such an ecclesiology is true to the message of Ephesians. All that is said in other chapters of this epistle contradicts the dogma that the church is a legal structure which has to impose its moral power upon the world.

For these reasons it cannot be assumed that a new topic is introduced after vs. 5 or 10. The whole passage 5:3–14 describes church discipline as a strictly internal matter, not as a step taken to enable the church to control the world. The "unbeliever" who according to I Cor 14:24–25 is "convicted by all, judged by all," is not an outsider—as his presence in the worshipping community shows. Paul states explicitly, "What have I to do with judging outsiders. Is it not those inside the church whom you are to judge? God judges those outside" (I Cor 5:12-13).

The form of properly "judging" a church member is mutual brotherly exhortation. According to Rom 12:8-9 such exhortation is not everybody's business, but a special gift (charisma) granted by God to some church members more than to others—just as is serving at the table, teaching, consoling, administrating. Except when God himself exercises discipline, or a prophetic man in the Lord's name (as Paul in I Cor 5:3-5), it can never have the character of condemnation or exclusion in a juridical sense.[165]

IV   The Victory of Light

The poetic form, the central position, and the specific content of the words, "Awake you sleeper, rise from the dead, the Messiah will shine upon you," give to Eph 5:14 a prominent role in the context of 5:1-20. All that is said about the imitation of God, church discipline, wise use of one's time, singing, and thanksgiving can be understood as a ramification of the many statements made about the light in vss. 8-14, especially vs. 14.

Within a narrow context, the stanza quoted in vs. 14 fulfills the following functions: (a) It reveals that the author wanted all statements about the light in vss. 8-9, 13-14a to be understood as statements about Christ and his power. (b) It makes clear that the transition and transformation of a man from darkness to light is as overwhelming, complete, and eschatological as is resurrection from death. Enlightenment is resurrection. (c) The combination of the indicative, "The Messiah will shine upon you," with the imperatives "awake" and "rise"[166] shows that resurrection is not a blind fate or a haphazard accident, but contains an appeal to the ear, the will, the action of man, and is to be followed by obedience.[167] (d) The saints are still in need of the same admonition which is also extended to Gentiles in missionary preaching or at the moment of joining the church.[168] The men who are already raised must again and again be raised.[169]

---

[165] I Cor 4:3-4; Rom 2:1-4; 14:3-4; cf. Matt 7:1-5; James 4:11-12.

[166] A similar connection of proclamatory and hortatory statements characterizes vss. 1-2, 8-14a.

[167] Cf. the imperatives, "strip off . . . the Old Man . . . and put on the New Man," which are pronounced upon the basis of the good news, "You . . . [who] were dead in lapses, God has made us alive together with the Messiah" (4:22-24; 2:1-6). Thomas Aquinas explains 5:14 by distinguishing between prevenient and subsequent grace: since we cannot rise from sin by ourselves, this resurrection is grace. But man has to make the decision to cooperate in the act of rising; see also Summa Theol. I ɪɪ 111, 3c. While in his commentary on Ephesians Thomas mentions "meritorious actions that follow . . . from subsequent grace," in Summa Theol. I ɪɪ 111, 2-3, he denies that creative grace implies any merits of man.

[168] As shown above, in the NOTE on "Therefore he says" (5:14), the words cited after the quotation formula may well have originally been a missionary awakening call or part of a baptismal liturgy. While, as was stated, e.g. Calvin and Schlier assumed that originally and in Eph 5 the hymnic lines were addressed to Gentiles, Gaugler, pp. 203, 249, points out that in the present context they are understood to concern Christians. Actually, throughout the ethical part of Ephesians (and other epistles), formulae, confessions, doctrinal and ethical pieces are applied to baptized people that had originally been elements of missionary, catechetical, or baptismal instruction. See, e.g. Rom 13:11-12: "You [the saints] know what hour it is, how it is full time now for you to wake from sleep. . . . The night is far gone, the day is at hand."

[169] The same logic can be observed in Pauline statements on dying to sin, on reconciliation, on spiritual life, see, e.g. Col 2:20; 3:3, 5; II Cor 5:18-20; Gal 5:25. While Ephesians, true to its emphasis on realized eschatology, calls for an instantaneous ever new rising of those already raised with Christ (cf. 2:5-6 with 5:14), in I Cor 15 an analogous point is made by slightly different means: the accent is laid upon the future resurrection of the saints. According to I Cor even those who firmly believe that Jesus Christ has been raised (15:11) but cannot boast of their pos-

These and other points are made in elaboration upon the metaphor "light" and its opposite "darkness." A preliminary discussion of the use of this figure in the NT and Ephesians was presented earlier in this commentary:[170] "light" and "enlightening" are metaphors that describe a noetical and hermeneutical process. By "enlightenment" knowledge is communicated, insight is generated. But this "knowledge" and "perception" are not only an intellectual event, for it is understood to involve salvation and a new way of life. While 1:18 and 4:18, and perhaps the statements made in 4:19–20, are susceptible to an interpretation that overemphasizes the intellectual moment, in 5:8–14 the nature and power of light are unmistakably described in much wider terms:

The caption, "In the past you were darkness, but now in Christ you are light" (5:8), is explained and unfolded in successive steps. Verses 8b–9: the light produces "children of light" and "fruit of light," i.e. it creates men who behave as creatures of light and as witnesses to it. Verses 10–12: life in this light means to learn continuously the will of the Lord and to put to shame the unproductive, hidden works of "darkness." Verses 13–14a: the revelatory power of light is not only informative, but also transformative; by exposing the realm of evil, light overcomes its power and turns into light, creates anew and saves "all" that was captive in darkness. Verses 14b–d (cf. 2:1 ff.): the Messiah himself is this creative, awakening, liberating light; the beneficiaries are men who had been dead in lapses and sins.

This means that in this passage the figure of "light" has at least four dimensions which prohibit a purely noetical or intellectualistic understanding:[171]

a) Light has *ontic* status. It is a power outside and above man. Man lives because of the light and he can enjoy its blessings. It is not a condition brought about by human awareness, but its benefits include the gift of awareness, knowledge, (in-)sight.[172] This light would have to be called a mythical entity if it

---

session of the earnest of the Spirit, their knowledge, etc., are to recognize the as yet future bodily resurrection of the dead (15:12–57). Denial of the latter would abrogate the validity of Christ's resurrection (15:13, 15–16).

[170] See the exposition of 1:18; 2:7; 4:18, and the last parts of COMMENT V on 2:1–10.

[171] Among books that discuss the manifold meanings of light and darkness in such literature as may have influenced Ephesians or was influenced by this epistle, the following are to be mentioned: G. P. Wetter, *Phos*, Leipzig: Harassowitz, 1915; M. Dibelius, *Die Isisweihe bei Apuleius*, SbHA 4, 1917; repr. in *Botschaft und Geschichte*, II (Tübingen; Mohr, 1956), 30–79; R. Reitzenstein, *Das iranische Erlösungsmysterium* (Bonn, Marcus: 1921), esp. pp. 6, 135–50; F. J. Dölger, *Sol Salutis*. More literature will be discussed in fn. 176. *Od Sol* xv reads like a compendium on the meanings (and the sacramental experience?) of light. Attributed to the light are joy in the Lord who is "like the sun," resurrection from darkness through the rays of this light, vision of the holy day, knowledge implying the turning away from "the way of error," redemption and immortality.

[172] The creation of light and the limitation of darkness (viz. of the abyss or chaos) stands at the beginning of the creation of the universe and of man, according to the Priestly account Gen 1. Throughout the Bible God's appearance, his will, his word, his work, sometimes even God himself, are called light. Thus the essence and existence of light are not found in man or determined by his experience. Light is a creative force that precedes and dominates human existence, according to Gen 1:2–5; see also Micah 7:8; Isa 9:2; 60:1–5; Ps 139:11–12; John 1:5–9; 8:12; 12:35, 46; I John 1:5; 2:8, 9, 11; I Cor 4:5; II Cor 4:6; Rev 21:23–27. In his interpretation R. Bultmann, *The Gospel of John* (Oxford: Blackwell, and Philadelphia: Westminster, 1971), p. 41, cf. the context pp. 40–45, contends that "in its original sense" "the light of men" mentioned in John 1:4 is "not an outward phenomenon" but "the brightness itself in which I find myself here and now . . . the illuminated condition of existence, of my own existence." (The original German wording is even more complex than this translation by G. R. Beasley-Murray.) However, the text of John 1:4 states that the light is the life which is "in Him," the eternal *logos*, rather than only in a condition of man. Indeed, the light of the *logos* is not understood as an external phenomenon comparable to the sun or a lamp; yet it is clearly denoted as an event and power coming to man through revelation (and incarnation!) as it were from outside. The ontological and epistemological priority of light and darkness over human experience and self-understanding is also expressed in

meant no more than a certain self-understanding of man, projected upon a metaphysical plane and described in personalistic terms. Occasionally biblical authors make use of mythological forms of diction, but when they describe light as the essence, work, and manifestation of God himself they dispel the notion that it is a mythological figure among others. He who is exposed to light is confronted with the one creative, redemptive, life-giving God—not just with a better self. As a beneficiary of light, man in turn becomes a living proof of its power: "now . . . you are light" (5:8). The ontic superiority of light over man's existence and self-awareness is not denied when man's participation in it is asserted. The same is true of "darkness": it is a power superior to man that manifests itself to and through man. It can hold him captive, it has an ontology of its own, yet its essence can only be described in negative terms. Its very nature is lack of light, absence of order, opposition to life, freedom, and joy. While in the absence of light it seems to wield unlimited power, it is no match for light whenever it comes to a conflict. The darkness "does not overcome it" (John 1:5), for darkness must yield wherever light shines. However devouring and devastating its power may seem (Eph 4:18; 6:12), it is ultimately contemptible.

b) The terms light and darkness possess *ethical* meaning. "Light" and "darkness" represent certain attitudes and deeds, just as do "Spirit" and "flesh" according to the ethical catalogues discussed above. Light and darkness determine conflicting ways of life; therefore they are names for describing good or evil conduct. They call for a radical decision and do not permit neutrality.[173]

c) Light has *existential* meaning. It is not only the giver of life, redemption, reconciliation, joy to man, but also the effect of the gift, that is, vitality, freedom, honor, peace, security, gladness.[174] Light means well-being; again the hedonistic element is present which was shown to be inherent in the Greek concept of imitation. A child of light is more than just a knowledgeable and ethically oriented man: his liberation from all the evil things represented by darkness makes him a happy fellow. It is natural for him to be grateful and to break out in singing. There is more than the obligation that a lighted lamp *must* shine in a dark environment; it will shine—for this is the very nature and power of light.

d) Light fulfills a function in the *cultus* and appears to be an indispensable element of cultic language and liturgical form. In many religions light symbolism determines not only the forms, instruments, and times of worship, but also the substance of holy stories, doctrines, beliefs and customs. Worship of the sun

---

formulae such as, "children of light," "to be in darkness," "to walk in darkness," "deeds done in darkness": Isa 9:2; Ps 82:5; Prov 2:13; 16:15; Eccles 2:14; 5:16; 6:4; Sir 23:18; I Thess 5:5; Eph 5:8–9, 11. In I Peter 2:9 redemption is described by the words, "He called you out of darkness into his marvelous light"; in Col 1:13 by the sentence, "He rescued us from the power of darkness and transplanted us into the kingdom of his beloved Son." Thomas Aquinas states in his exposition of Eph 5:8, "They are not referred to as light in essence but through participation."

[173] The nearest non-biblical parallel to the combination of ontological and ethical statements about light is found in the Qumran literature, see 1QS I 9; II 16; III 3, 13, 24–25, and the "War-Scroll" 1QM *passim*. Luke 16:8 and John 12:36 show as much Qumran influence as II Cor 6:14 – 7:1. The term "children of light" is "unequivocally Qumranite" (not from the OT) according to Braun, QuNT, I, 221. In the OT the Torah, David, Zion, Israel are called a light. Rabbinical applications of the term are listed in StB, I, 236–40.

[174] Amos 5:18, 20; Ps 27:1; Job 22:28. Most outspoken is Esther 8:16–17: "The Jews had light and gladness and joy and honor. . . . There was gladness and joy among the Jews." Cf. Philo's "sober intoxication" which is experienced when the mind reaches out after the intelligible world and sees pure ideas and the Great King himself in a torrent of light (*op. mundi* 70–71).

and homage to its earthly representatives (kings, priests, holy men) are often combined. Astrology is the art of recognizing and utilizing the power of heavenly lights. The extensive use of light symbolism in the language, teachings, and forms of the church's worship during the first four centuries has been described by F. J. Dölger.[175] Allusion to the cultic, and implicitly to the saving, function of light is made whenever the verb "to enlighten" and the noun "illumination" (*phōtizomai, phōtismos*) are employed. Justin Martyr and Clement of Alexandria called the sacrament of baptism "enlightenment." Perhaps they were not the first Christians to do this.[176] We may ask whether all references to light in Eph 5, especially the hymn quoted in vs. 14, contain an allusion to baptism; it certainly cannot be demonstrated that in the NT the verb "to enlighten" and the cognate nouns "light" and "enlightenment" always refer to baptism. Many, perhaps all, ways of communicating and receiving the word of salvation can be meant.[177] In each case light means salvation—a salvation that is not only offered as a possibility but is imparted to and received by the worshipping community. Cultic elements such as preaching, teaching, confessing, repenting, baptizing, singing are demonstrations of the saving effect and success of Christ, the light.

The recognition that outside and inside the Bible the light-darkness imagery has intellectual, ontic, ethical, existential, and cultic dimensions and functions need not lead to the conclusion that these aspects, or some of them, are mutually exclusive. In the interpretation of Eph 5:8–14 especially it is impossible to operate with an either-or,[178] and the same is probably true of the exposition of Philonic, Hermetic, and Mystery Religion texts. One or another aspect of the essence, power, experience, and consequence of light or darkness may receive special emphasis, but just as Wisdom is manifold and yet one[179] so is the meaning of light and of darkness.

Common to all the various accentuations found in the Bible is the radical and total mutual exclusion of light and darkness. Either light rules or darkness does. The human condition is either black or white; there is no grey, no transition or progress from one to another, no middle ground, no mediation, no neutrality. Light and darkness can be mixed as little as Spirit and flesh, life and death, fertility and sterility.

---

[175] *Sol Salutis.*

[176] Justin Martyr *apol.* I 61:12; *dial.* 39:2; 122:1–2; Clement of Alexandria *paed.* I 6:25–27; *protrept.* IX 84; see also *Acts of Thomas* 132; Ps.-Clem. *hom.* VII 8; *Catechism of Trent* II 2, qu. 3–4. It is still uncertain whether Heb 6:4; 10:32 is the earliest evidence of that equation. Ephraem the Syrian's reading of Heb 6:4, points in that direction. Behind the intellectual, sacramental, and mystical meanings of this nomenclature stands a doctrine of revelation, light, enlightenment, imitation as found in Philo (e.g. *quis rerum divinarum heres sit* 263–66; *de praemiis et poenis* 46; *migr. Abr.* 38–39), the Isis Mystery (Apuleius *metamorph.* XI 23), the Mithras Liturgy (Firmicus Maternus *de errore profanarum religionum* II 4), the Hermetic Writings (e.g. *Corp. Herm.* XIII 18–22). See E. R. Goodenough, *By Light Light: The Mystic Gospel of Hellenistic Judaism* (New Haven: Yale University Press, 1935), esp. pp. 146–49, 166–71, 382–86; Dibelius, *Isisweihe*, p. 8; A. Dieterich, *Eine Mithrasliturgie*, 2d ed., Leipzig: Teubner, 1923; G. Wagner, *Pauline Baptism and the Pagan Mysteries* (Edinburgh/London: Oliver, 1967), pp. 61–256.

[177] I Cor 4:5; II Cor 4:4, 6; John 1:9; Luke 2:32; 11:35–36; II Tim 1:10; Acts 26:23; Rev 18:1; 21:23; 22:5; Eph 1:17–18; 3:9.

[178] Dibelius, p. 90, distinguishes between the "purely religious sense" of light in II Cor 4:6 and the "ethical sense" in Eph 5:8 ff. Gaugler, p. 201 observes, "The genuine early Christian image of darkness and light . . . is at this place not related to knowledge but to the status without and within salvation."

[179] See COMMENT X on 1:3–14 and the first NOTE on 3:10.

Does this mean that Paul together with other biblical authors[180] has succumbed to a deterministic, dualistic, if not tragic and Gnostic, world view? This would be the case if the powers of light and darkness were described as maintaining some balance, or if the conflict between them were considered open-ended. Actually, from the first to the last page of the Bible the superiority of light over darkness is proclaimed. Darkness possesses nothing, lacks everything, and can never prevail in conflict with light. Light knows no compromise and depends on no mediation. By its own nature it solves the problem of communication: it expands, it defeats, it makes its opposition disappear.[181] Therefore, Jesus Christ is never called a mediator between light and darkness or the reconciler of the two. He is in Eph 5:14, as much as in the Gospel of John and in Revelation, praised as the victorious light in person.

The puzzling words "All that is revealed is light" (5:14a) proclaim in magnificent brevity the dimension and effect of Christ's victory. These words are, except for the hymn (vs. 14b–d), the climax of the praise of light contained in 5:8 ff. Taken as a whole, 5:14 spells out the reason for the proposition uttered in 5:8. It is shown why only "in Christ" those who were totally identified with "darkness" now simply and in toto are called "light."[182] Indeed, the author of Ephesians no more neglects or underestimates the threat of darkness to the saints and their faith in Christ than do the authors of other biblical books.[183] Yet the reality, presence, and victorious power of the light make him a radiant optimist.

The same faith prevents Paul's teaching from being as devoid of ethical and especially social concerns as were the systems of several Gnostic groups during the second and later centuries.[184] The light of which Paul speaks produces results here and now on earth. If this were not the case, light would resemble a remote idea or future state of happiness. It would be as dead as is a body without the Spirit or faith without works, according to James 2:26. Resurrection would not be preached as an event in history. While in Gal 5:19 Paul had spoken of "fruits of the Spirit," in Gal 5:22 he assigned to the "flesh" no more than "works." In Eph 5 this distinction becomes even sharper: while the "deeds done in darkness" are called "fruitless" (5:10), the "fruit of light consists of everything that is good, righteous, and true" (5:9), and the saints themselves belong to that seed—they are "children of light" (5:8c). By doing what the

---

[180] E.g. the Priestly texts of the OT, the Prophetic books that include apocalyptic material, the Fourth Gospel, Revelation.

[181] Robinson, pp. 118 and 201 writes, "Right produces right; it rights the wrong. Or, as St. Paul prefers to say, light produces light: it lightens darkness. . . . Darkness itself is transformed into light."

[182] In John 12:35–36, also in Matt 5:14–16; I Thess 5:4–5; Rom 13:11–14; Philip 2:15; I Peter 2:9 the same Christological core of the NT teaching on the light is revealed. In their own way the Lukan account of Jesus' nativity, the descriptions of Jesus' transfiguration, and the reports of Paul's conversion point to the same center. Kuhn, NTS 7 (1960–61), 339–40 considers the words "in Christ" (Eph 5:8) as evidence of "Christianization" of a light-darkness tradition which connects Ephesians with Qumran.

[183] See, e.g. Amos 5:18; Matt 8:12; 24:29; Rev 9:2; II Peter 2:17; Eph 6:12.

[184] See esp. Pokorný, EuG, passim, for an elaboration on the contrast between the social-ethical tenor of Ephesians and the escapist individualism of the Gnostic type. Kuhn, NTS 7 (1960–61), 340, affirms that "the contrast light-darkness is totally distinct from Gnostic thought." For the Gnostic dualism of substance (in which the matter forming the divine sphere of light is placed opposite the material forming the lower cosmos) is in Ephesians replaced by the doctrine of two modes of existence, characterized by doing what pleases God, and by performing works of darkness, respectively. The urgent call to test and decide found in 5:10 makes it palpable that the dualism of Ephesians is "ethical, related to decision," according to Kuhn. Reference is made to Micah 6:8 and to 1QS I 5; II 24–25; IV 21; V 3–4.

light produces and by behaving as members of the family of light, they recognize the era and realm in which they live: in the new aeon, in God's and the Messiah's kingdom, or more briefly, "in Christ" (5:8). The same point has been made, though in different phrasing, in 2:10: "In the Messiah we are created for those good works which God has provided as our way of life."

In Eph 5:8 ff. the victory of Christ the light over all darkness and compromises with works of darkness is proclaimed in terms so triumphant and objective that the question must be asked, does Paul consider this victory an automatic event which so determines men that almost nothing is left to subjective recognition, awareness, conscience, decision and action?[185] The next COMMENT will discuss some of the elements in Eph 5:1 ff. that describe the modes of man's subjective involvement in the manifestation and victory of light.

V   The Recognition of God's Will

Eph 5:1–20 bristles with imperatives. If they have a weight of their own alongside the radiant indicatives, then they include an appeal to man's will and do not exclude or condemn human decisions and acts.[186] In the same passage the mighty acts of God are called to mind that were described in Eph 1–2: Christ has died for people dead in sins, Gentiles have been adopted into God's household as children, they have heard the gospel, they have received the Spirit (and baptism), they are members of the community of saints. They are now light—by God's grace alone. However, the ethical admonitions add something which for Paul is as essential as his so-called *kerygma*: God's election, Christ's death, the Spirit's operation, and the experience of preaching, baptism, and gathering do not exhaust or terminate the manifestation and recognition of God's will. There still has to take place an increase in comprehension of the Lord's will (5:10, 17), a radical severance from evil deeds and words (5:3–7, 11–12), and a wise exploitation of the opportunities of the present time. A continuous *aggiornamento* is called for; the church has to correspond to the Day of the Lord that has dawned in the midst of the present evil days (5:14–16).

Thus the saints are given a responsible part in the present and future acknowledgement and execution of God's will. They are not reduced to being its unconscious and unwilling objects or tools. It is not by gloomy submission that they dissociate themselves from darkness. On the contrary, only by their joy, jubilation, and gratitude can they reveal their conformity to God's will, even their "imitation of God" (5:1, 18–20). Either God's will is done from "the bottom of the heart" (6:6), that is, voluntarily, enthusiastically, totally—or it is not done at all. The struggle and victory of light is achieved at the price of the death of Jesus Christ and by the miracle of man's rising with Christ. But God does not win his battle over the dead bodies of men, at the expense of *their* life.

---

[185] If, e.g. the term "fruit of light" (5:9) is understood to imply an *automatic* process of growth or production—as Mark 4:28 appears to affirm—then a deterministic undercurrent must be attributed to Eph 5:8 ff. Such an interpretation would have a parallel in the Qumran teaching on the effect of the two spirits, and in the alleged predestinarian teaching of Eph 1:4 ff. But these possible analogues do not necessarily demonstrate the appropriateness of a deterministic understanding of Eph 5.

[186] Though in I Cor 9:16–19 Paul speaks of a "necessity" that is "laid upon him," he does not consider himself a mechanical tool of his Lord. He is drafted into a service that requires not only suffering in passivity, but active personal obedience, reflection, formation of plans, and embarkation on adventurous journeys.

More than any other epistle Ephesians proclaims the raising to full life of those
who had been dead. When they "stand up," "imitate God," leave behind and
"disprove unproductive deeds of darkness," make "wise" use of the "time"
given to them (5:1, 11, 15, 16), they are engaged in the "holy war" fought by
God for man. They participate in God's fight against darkness and in his victory.[187] While in 6:10 ff. the defensive war of the church against onrushing external powers is described, Eph 5:3 ff. shows that the first battle is to be waged
against the sin found in the church herself.[188]

How do the saints conform to the will and work of God, according to Eph
5:1-20? Four aspects of their response and obedience are outstanding. (a)
Verses 10 and 17 speak of an act involving *intellectual* activity: "Find out (lit.
"test") what is pleasing to the Lord . . . [learn to] comprehend what is the will
of the Lord." (b) Almost every verse contains an allusion to the *social* character of the decisions to be made: as "imitators of God" the saints will show by
their love and respect "all that is fitting for saints" who have citizenship in
God's kingdom; they will care for the erring brothers by "disproving" their evil
deeds; together they will "sing" and "thank" God for all things or persons. In
each of these ways they dissociate themselves from the darkness which held
them captive. (c) Their total conduct, not just certain individual good deeds,
will distinguish the saints from perpetrators of evil works; they bear practical
and palpable testimony to the gift of new life even to all those who were dead
in sins. (d) The character of their testimony is far from bitter, gloomy, or desperate, despite the evil days of the present. It is full of emotion, of a joy that
breaks out in jubilation. The saints form a celebrating community which consists of free men acting voluntarily and gladly.

These four elements show that a man who is engaged in doing God's will is
involved with the totality of his existence. The indissoluble unity of man's intellectual, social, existential, and festival activity distinguishes the obedience of a
Christian from a purely academic, individualistic, psychological, mystical involvement. Paul is not the first to put emphasis on this unity and totality. In
5:15 he makes an appeal to heed the counsels of Wisdom. He ascribes to the
light a power and function as divine, universal, existential, and moral as the
Wisdom teachers had attributed to Wisdom long before his time.

Of special interest is the fact that Paul connects the acts of learning and doing
God's will. Repeatedly his exhortations contain the term *dokimazō*.[189] In the
first NOTE on 5:10 the many meanings of this verb were subsumed under two
groups: (a) to arrange and execute a test; (b) to accept and heed the result of a

---

[187] Cf. 6:10-20; I Thess 5:5-8; Rom 13:11-12. The "good fight of faith" in which a servant of
Christ is engaged, is mentioned in I Tim 6:12; II Tim 4:7; see also Heb 10:32; 12:1, 4; Jude 3,
and the logion of Jesus, "I have not come to bring peace but the sword" (Matt 10:34). The motif
of the "holy war" will be more extensively discussed in the context of Eph 6:10-20, see esp. COM-
MENT II.

[188] The battlefield is Jesus Christ himself, according to the Gethsemane story: Matt 26:36-46; cf.
Heb 5:7-10; Eph 2:16c; the individual believer, according to Rom 7:14-25; Philip 3:10-14; I Cor
9:15-27.

[189] In the version of Eph 5:10 given above this verb was translated by "finding out by experience." Other occurrences of the same verb have been listed in fn. 62. An exhaustive study of the
meaning of this term in Paul's epistles has not yet come to my attention, but some information is
given, e.g. in WBLex, 201; LSLex, 442; W. Grundmann, TWNTE, II, 255-60; Bultmann, ThNT, I,
214-15; II, 223; K. Barth, *Church Dogmatics*, II 2 (1957), 636-41; O. Cullmann, *Salvation in History* (London: SCM, 1967), pp. 333-35.

test. Both senses presuppose that a careful examination is carried out: it is not only man's mind that is engaged in the scrutiny,[190] but also his eyes, his hands and sometimes an instrument. Mastering some simple skill or a whole life's experience may be among the prerequisites. Extensive labor, including many frustrating disappointments, may be its price, great discoveries and rewards its result. Not only can the matters or evidence looked for be discovered, but baffling surprises may be in store. In each case *dokimazō* implies much more than merely an intellectual procedure and achievement; it describes a personal, existential, perhaps critical relationship between him who searches and decides, and the person or object that is scrutinized.

If this meaning of the verb *dokimazō* is accepted, Eph 5:10 and several of its parallels speak of a mode of recognizing and affirming God's will that includes the activity of the intellect, the will, the emotion, the action, the total life of man.[191] Alternatives to discovering and heeding God's will through these means have been sought in mouthing biblical verses or creedal affirmations, in the magnification of minutiae and the development of casuistic systems, in the substitution of ritual performances for obedience from the bottom of the heart.[192] Yet according to Paul "the comprehension of the will of the Lord" (5:17) and the conduct "fitting a saint" and "wise man" (5:3, 15) cannot be found in quotations by inductions or deductions. Rather, a combination of learning and doing is recommended. The maxim "Learning by Doing"[193] may aptly sum up what Paul has in mind. The nearest and most important parallel to Eph 5:10 is probably John 7:17: "When any man's will is to do his [God's] will, he shall learn whether the teaching [of Christ] is from God." Excluded is the notion that a theoretical knowledge of God's authority and will precedes the doing of good works. Only when man's will and action are involved in the process of knowledge will the Lord's authority and his specific will in a given situation be recognized.[194] Eph 5:10, 15–17 calls for this manner of learning the will of God. Though the Bible has no word for the ambiguous English term "experience," it appears that a version which refers to learning by experiment and experience brings to light best what Paul intends to say in 5:10, 17: "Find out by experience what is pleasing to the Lord! . . . Learn to comprehend what is the will of God!"

Indeed, the unique authority of the Bible, the inspired direction of the prophets, the wise counsel of the teachers of the church, the benison of mutual brotherly admonition and of respect for an accepted code of conduct "fitting for

[190] As in the case of the philosophical use of *elegchō*, see fn. 68 above at 5:11.

[191] The "putting to proof" happens "partly by thought, partly by experience," according to Abbott, p. 153. While Bultmann, ThNT, I, 215 rightly finds elements of "will" and "decision" in *dokimazō*, he may restrict the agency of testing too much when he defines it as man's "mind" (*nous*), i.e. his capacity to pass judgments. Cullmann, *Salvation in History*, pp. 333 ff. sees the essence of *dokimazō* in the application of something old or eternal to present history: *dokimazein* takes place when the old law that was fulfilled in Christ is applied to the new situation created by the Christ-event; in his conscience, motivated by love, the Christian sees the unchangeable plan of God (the norms of saving history) converge with the historical contingency of the moment. Gaugler, p. 202, speaks of the "formation of a sense of tact that grows out from the ever new search for faithfulness to God." Because in the NT neither the law nor a strategy of salvation is immediately connected with the application or exploitation of a test, Cullmann's interpretation calls for alternatives.

[192] See, e.g. Matt 4:1–11; 7:21–23; 15:1–20; 23:1–36.

[193] Which is familiar to pedagogues through J. Dewey's philosophy of education.

[194] A statement of Calvin, *Institutio* I 6:2, gives classical expression to this interpretation: *Omnis recta cognitio Dei ab obedientia nascitur* ("All true knowledge of God is born out of obedience.").

saints"—these criteria and tools of recognizing and heeding God's will are not ruled out by the admonition, "learn by doing!"[195] But the accent placed in 5:10 and 17 upon continuous searching shows that the recognition of God's will and pleasure—however this learning was initiated, is sustained, and will be adjudicated—is an event taking place immediately between God and man. Neither fixed definitions nor the voice of conscience are mentioned as intermediaries. It is presumed that the Lord lives and still has ways to make his will known; it is also assumed that he will not let go of his saints but will grant them the wisdom to comprehend his will, together with the courage and endurance to do it. God's revelation is the source, the community of the faithful is the framework, a social stance is the result, joy and gratitude are the mode by which God's will is recognized.

Many features distinguish the ethic of Ephesians from the rigorous moral teaching, the catalogues of virtues, and the notions of conscience developed e.g. by Stoic philosophers.[196] Three distinctive traits are noted below.

a) "Good" is what "pleases the Lord" and what he "wills" each one of his servants to do here and now. But "the good" cannot be defined in an absolute way.[197] In gladly receiving the advice and consolation of the Scriptures and of brethren in faith, each one of the saints is sent on a way to "find out" what is good.

b) "Free" is the man who no longer identifies freedom with a free choice between the possibilities of good and evil. Light and darkness are realities, but realities of mutually exclusive character and of opposite ontological standing. A man who after his redemption from darkness decides in favor of allegiance to the defeated power does not exercise his freedom but negates and forfeits it. A man is free inasmuch as step by step and day by day he makes use of his liberation from captivity in darkness, and does those works that are ripe fruits of light, prepared to be done by the "new man" whom the Lord has created.[198]

c) The Gethsemane prayer (Matt 26:39) and the Lord's Prayer (Matt 6:10) make explicit what is stated only implicitly in Eph 5 (though vss. 19–20 point to it): search for the Lord's will and subjection to it come from prayer and lead to prayer. All reflections, deliberations, and attempts made in the quest for obedience profit from prayer and call for it. Since the prayers of the saints are based upon Jesus Christ's accepted "offering" and are uttered following his example (5:2), they are distinct from the expression of vain guesses and faint hopes. They are the saints' way of confidently approaching, under Christ's leadership and in one Spirit, the throne of the Father (2:18; 3:12).

Other important issues of Eph 5:1–20 will be taken up in the exposition of the parallel passages in Col 3 (AB, vol. 34B).

[195] Eph 4:25, 29; 5:3, 10, 14, 17; 6:2–3 show that all these elements are complementary rather than mutually exclusive.
[196] Cf. COMMENTS II on 4:1–16 (near fn. 160) and VIII on 4:17–32.
[197] D. Bonhoeffer, Ethics, 6th ed. (New York: Macmillan, 1968), p. 38, speaks in the spirit of Eph 5 when he asserts that the ultimate ethical question is not, "What is good?", but "What is the will of God?" "The will of God is not a system of rules which is established from the outset; it is something new and different in each different situation in life, and for this reason a man must ever anew examine what the will of God may be." See also K. Barth's discussion of "The Unique Opportunity" in Church Dogmatics, III 4 (1961), 565–94.
[198] 5:9; 2:10; 4:24.

XI CHRIST'S RULE IN ALL REALMS
(5:21–6:9)

PART ONE   *Husband and Wife*   5:21–33

5 21 Because you fear Christ subordinate yourselves to one another
—22 [e.g.] wives to your husbands—as to the Lord. 23 For [only] in
the same way that the Messiah is the head of the church
    —he, the savior of his body—
is the husband the head of his wife. 24 The difference notwithstanding, just as the church subordinates herself [only] to the Messiah, so
wives to your husbands—in everything. 25 Husbands, love your wives,
just as [we confess],
    The Messiah has loved the church
        and has given himself for her
    26 to make her holy by [his] word
        and clean by the bath in water,
    27 to present to himself the church resplendent
        free from spot or wrinkle or any such thing
        so that she be holy and blameless.
28 In the same manner also husbands owe it [to God and man] to love
their wives for they are their bodies. In loving his wife a man loves
himself. 29 For no one ever hates his own flesh, but he provides and
cares for it—just as the Messiah for the church 30 because we are
members of his body. 31 "For this reason
    A man will leave his father and mother
    And be joined to his wife,
    And the two will become one flesh."
32 This [passage] has an eminent secret meaning: I, for one, interpret
it [as relating] to Christ and the church. 33 In any case, one by one,
each one of you must love his wife as himself, and the wife . . . may
she fear her husband.

NOTES

5:21. *Because you fear Christ.* Lit. "in the fear of Christ."[1] While the ethic taught in Rom 12:1 ff. is motivated by the "mercies of God," the reference to a "fear" evoked by Christ is strange. Never again in the NT is the formula "fear of Christ" found. Probably in order to harmonize 5:21 with OT and NT passages that denote the "fear of God" or "of the Lord" as the basic human attitude, some MSS have substituted either of those readings for the one given. Our translation of *phobos* in vs. 21 with "fear" and of *phobeomai* in vs. 33 with "fearing" is literal and follows the precedent set by the older versions.[2] Most interpreters shun the idea that in man's relationship either to God or his fellow man anything good can be achieved by ethical action motivated in fear. Therefore the Greek of 5:21 and 33 is translated by terms that soften or ignore the notion of terror, horror, panic, trembling, or turning to flight, which is inherent in the Greek noun and verb "fear." Paraphrases are substituted which dull the sharp edge of the Greek text and eliminate the appeal or allusion to the sensation of the "holy."[3] The eschatological element inherent in the term "fear of Christ" forms a bridge between the seemingly irreconcilable statements on marriage found in 5:22–33 and I Cor 7. See COMMENT III for a discussion of the eschatological meaning of this formula.

subordinate yourselves. In the Greek text of Eph 5:18–21 five successive participles are attached to the imperative, "Be filled with Spirit." Do they mean that such "inspiration" is present and manifest where there is conversing with hymns, singing, praying, thanksgiving, and "giving way" (JB) to one another? This is possible but there is also an alternative: in the last NOTE on 3:17 it was shown that participles can possess the power of independent imperatives.[4] For grammatical reasons 5:21 belongs to the preceding verses, but the content of this sentence forms an essential element of the section of Ephesians which follows.[5] Among modern scholars, the list of the pairs of exhortation found in

---

[1] Special literature used for the NOTES and COMMENTS on the section 5:21–33 is listed in BIBLIOGRAPHY 21.

[2] "Fear of the Lord," or "of God," is "the beginning of wisdom": Prov 1:7; 9:10; 15:33; Ps 111:10; Job 28:28. In the NT it is mentioned, e.g. in Rom 3:18; II Cor 7:1; Col 3:22; I Peter 2:17. Cf., e.g. Eph. 5:21 in Vulg., KJ.

[3] E.g. RSV, NEB, NTTEV translate by "reverence" and "respect"; JB by "obedience" and "respect"; SegB by *crainte* and *respecter*. In the LSLex articles on *phobos* and *phobeō*, no reference to the meanings "reverence" or "respect" is made, though some of the passages mentioned there permit the attenuating interpretation; but in the art. *phoberos* the meanings "formidable," "regarded with respect," "awe-inspiring," are listed; see pp. 1946–47. In WBLex, 870–71 the impression is conveyed that "fearing" and "revering," viz. "fright" and "respect," are equally literal translations of the stem *phob*. But if Paul had no more in mind than reverence and respect, he might have chosen the verb *timaō*, "to honor." Cf. Eph 6:2. When in the NT "fearing" is used in a positive sense, it includes "honoring." But as I Peter 2:17 shows, "fearing" is totalitarian, while "honoring" may have its limits: "Fear God, honor the emperor." However, in Rom 13:7 Roman officials are said to deserve both "fear" *and* "honor."

[4] Abbott applies this rule to 5:21. In COMMENT II on 4:1–16 the grounds and relevance of ethical exhortation in indicative and participial form were discussed, the evangelical character and intent of the obedience of the saints called for grammatical forms distinct from blunt imperatives.

[5] So most modern versions of Ephesians; W. Lueken; Abbott with special emphasis; Schlier; Bailey, p. 131, n. 3; K. Barth, III 4, 174–75, and others. But, e.g. NEB, Dibelius, and Gaugler assign to vs. 21 a pivotal position between vss. 18–20 and 22 ff. Again, among others, GNT, SegB, Thomas Aquinas, Weidinger, p. 59, Baltensweiler, p. 219, interpret vs. 21 as belonging only to vss. 18–20. According to Sampley, pp. 106, 116–17, this verse, together with the Christological arguments unfolded in vss. 23 ff., contains a critique of, and "nearly eclipses," the whole traditional *Haustafel.*

5:21 – 6:9 is called a *Haustafel* (Table of Household Duties). Two similar *Haustafeln* are presented in Col 3:18 – 4:1 and I Peter 2:13 – 3:7,[6] but only the Ephesian version opens with a call to mutual subordination. In Eph 5:22 ff., the call for specific subordination of one group to another is indissolubly tied to the mutual order proclaimed in 5:21. Except in some variant readings (see fn. 8), the term "subordinate" is not even repeated in vs. 22. The single imperative of vs. 21 ("subordinate yourselves to one another") anticipates all that Paul is about to say not only to wives, children, and slaves, but also to husbands, fathers, and masters, about the specific respect they owe because of Christ to those with whom they live together either by choice, or by birth, or by historical circumstances. Does this seemingly humiliating command demonstrate that Pauline ethics are basically conservative? Only a study of the meaning of "subordinate" in different contexts and of individual Pauline statements can provide an answer. Certainly the translation "be submissive" is alien to the sense and intent of the verb (*hypotassomai*) used by Paul, as will be shown later. The participles or imperatives calling for subordination may well contain an appeal to free and responsible agents that can only be heeded voluntarily, but never by the elimination or breaking of the human will, not to speak of servile submissiveness. Most likely Paul has in mind a subordination distinct (a) from the "subjection" of the creatures "to futility" (Rom 8:19), (b) from the present and future "subjugation" of principalities and powers to the feet of Christ (I Cor 15:25–27; Eph 1:21–22), and (c) from loss of all power and from exposure to ridicule (Col 2:15). See the NOTES on vss. 22–24 and 33, and especially COMMENT V C.

to one another. How can persons be mutually subject to one another? The reciprocal, if not paradoxical, relationship expressed by these words is not a unique Pauline invention. When discussing the patriarchal relationship between the man of the house and his wife, children, and slaves, Aristotle avers, "In most constitutional states the citizens rule and are ruled by turns," and Plutarch speaks of "the honor accorded by man and wife to each other," or of the unique "respect shown" by the husband "for his wife."[7] In COMMENT V C it will be shown that military groups could "subordinate themselves" (mutually) to other units in battle line-up. Still, the mutual subordination proclaimed by Paul seems to contradict the subsequent and detailed exhortation. Paul seems to enjoin only women, children, and slaves to give way—not their husbands, parents, and masters. A contradiction may be found in vs. 21 not only of the context

---

[6] Early Christian *Haustafeln* are also found in Titus 2:1–10; I Tim 2:8–15; 6:1–2; *Did.* IV 9–11; Barn. XIX 2–12; I Clem 1:3; 21:6–9; Polycarp *Phil* VI 2 – VI 1. In the Anchor commentary on Colossians (vol. 34B, esp. on 3:18 – 4:1), literature devoted to *Haustafeln* will be listed and problems will be discussed which have emerged in the search for their Jewish and/or pagan origins, their eventual "Christianization," and their impact upon the moral teachings and customs of the church. A preliminary reference to the place of the *Haustafeln* among the NT ethical catalogues was made in COMMENT VIII on 4:17–32; there, in fn. 249, the important titles of some recent monographs were named. Below, in the GLOSSES on 6:1–9, some general observations regarding the *Haustafeln* will be drawn together.

[7] Aristotle *pol.* I 1259B; Plutarch *moralia* 143B; 144F. E. Percy, p. 405, calls the term "to one another" "unprecise," or, "lacking essentiality" (*uneigentlich*), and Baltensweiler, p. 219, speaks of a "tension" between vss. 21 and 22 ff. E. Lohmeyer, KEKNT, IX (on Col 3:18 ff.), 155 offers a traditio-historical explanation: Paul had found in Jewish catechetical tradition groups of exhortations that were directed only to women, children, slaves, and that enjoined them to obey those in the superior positions; even before Paul began to write his epistles, these one-sided Jewish *Haustafeln* were complemented by certain counsels addressed to husbands, parents, masters; but Paul fell back on Jewish originals when he gave detailed commands to the weaker groups rather

but also of sound logic and moral order: the call to mutual subordination seems to relativize, if not blur and destroy, any clear notion of authority and subservience. COMMENT V C will show why and how in Pauline teaching mutual subordination is neither self-contradictory nor a call to chaos, but a challenge to the conservative and patriarchal concepts of social order which have often been attributed to Paul or derived from his teaching. The unique message of Ephesians is silenced whenever the dominant position of vs. 21 over the *Haustafel* and the peculiarly startling content of this verse are neglected.

22. [*e.g.*] *wives to your husbands*. Lit. "the wives to their own men." Stylistic and material reasons recommend the addition of "e.g." in the English translation. "E.g." communicates exactly what is indicated by the structure of the Greek sentence: the subordination of wives is an example of the same mutual subordination which is also shown by the husband's love, the children's obedience, the parents' responsibility for their offspring, the slaves' and masters' attitude toward one another. Instead of something equivalent to "[e.g.]," the great majority of MSS add at one place or another in vs. 22 the imperative, "subordinate yourselves," or "shall be subjected." These MSS obfuscate the fact that a wife's subordination to her husband is commanded only within the frame of mutual subordination; they support masculine superiority complexes that are supposedly grounded in Paul's ethics.[8] Still, vs. 22 calls women to subordination. Does Paul thus want to force all women into submission to men? The Greek speaks not of females and males in general, but only of "wives" and their "husbands."[9] Eph 5:22 does not affirm that females (women) are inferior to males (men) and must on all societal and professional occasions take and retain the second rank. Paul discusses only the special relationship between husband and wife.[10] Though the very use of the term "subordinate" reflects the esteem

---

than to the stronger. For example in I Tim 2:8–15 one verse is considered sufficient to describe the duty of a man, but seven verses are devoted to the obligation of women! Sampley, pp. 112–17, 158 believes that despite the qualification of the subordination by fear of Christ and by mutuality among the church members, husbands are in no wise subordinated to their wives.

[8] See GNT for a full listing of the variant readings represented by a considerable number of text families. Though Jerome asserts that in Greek MSS vs. 22 never repeats the verb "subordinate" from vs. 21, only Papyrus 46, the Vatican Code, Theodore and some of Clement of Alexandria's and Origen's readings of vs. 22 buttress his observation. For example the Codices Sinaiticus and Alexandrinus, also Minuscule 33, the ancient primary and secondary versions, Chrysostom and Theodoret repeat "subordinate." GNT attributes a low grade of probability to the shorter reading, and yet recommends it. Erasmus offers a succinct explanation for the origin and spread of the longer version: it aims at clarifying the sense of vs. 22 and it permits the liturgical use of vss. 22 ff. as a separate pericope. Abbott considers the *shorter* reading typical of Paul's style. Since the later addition of the imperative is much more likely than its omission, the shorter text has more claims upon authenticity. In addition, the fact that "subordinate" appears at different places in the variant readings of vs. 22 suggests that it is a secondary addition.

[9] The nouns *gynē* ("wife," "bride") and *anēr* (fortified by *idios*, "own husband") are used, not the adjectives *thēly* and *arsen* ("female" and "male"). For example in LXX Gen 1:27; 2:22–23; Gal 3:28; Matt 5:28, 31–32 one or both of these nouns. viz. adjectives, are used with sharp awareness of their distinct meanings, though commentators often overlook the differentiation.

[10] See Kähler, ZEE 3 (1959), 1, 4; idem, *Die Frau*, pp. 101–2, 253. Just as in 5:33 the wife is told to "fear" her husband, so in I Peter 3:1, 5 "wives" are urged to show "subordination" and "fear" only vis-à-vis their husbands. In Rom 13:1 ff. and I Peter 2:13–17 all Christians receive a similar command pertaining to their relationship to the civil authorities; the same is the case in I Peter 2:18, regarding the slaves' attitude toward their own masters. All these examples (probably including I Peter 2:17: "honor all men") speak of a specific relation between specific persons; in each case the context hints at a corresponding obligation of those in the superior position. However, Gaugler, pp. 207–8, follows the host of those interpreters who discovered in Eph 5:22 a completely "unilateral" subordination of women to men: "The woman must see Christ in the man."

in which women in general were held,[11] actually Paul announces a drastic restriction of women's subordination: it is due only to her husband, just as the husband "owes" marital love only to his wife (vss. 25, 28, 33). This corresponds to his subordination to her (vs. 21) which consists of a love measured after Christ's self-giving love for the church (vss. 25–27, 32–33). Unlike I Peter 3:5–7 and other Greek texts, Paul does not use the verbs "obey" and "serve" as synonyms for the "subordination" expected of wives. He does not stipulate a legislative, juridical, and executive power of the male. Neither does he call women "weaker" than men.[12] Rather he addresses them as persons who are free and able to make their own decision. The solemn address directed to women, "wives" (lit. "the wives"), recognizes that they stand on the same level as their husbands. In Koine Greek and in Semitic languages, the address "the wives" (hai gynaikes) substitutes for the classical Greek, "Oh wives" (ō gynaikes).[13] The restrictive term (lit.) "to your own husbands,"[14] makes the wife's subordination resemble the "yielding" which a senator gladly offers to a fellow senator, but not to any government spokesman or other interlocutor. See COMMENT V C.

as to the Lord. Because the Greek particle hōs (as) has as many different meanings as the English word "as,"[15] there are many ways to interpret the term "as to the Lord." Two methods are outstanding:

a) Thomas Aquinas among the older, and Gaugler among the more recent expositors, suggest that "lord" (kyrios) ought not to be capitalized, and that the article (tō) stands for the possessive pronoun, "your." The sense is then, wives be subject to your husbands because they are your lords. As proof of this interpretation vs. 23 is adduced in which the husband is called "head." I Peter 3:6 serves the same purpose: "Sarah obeyed Abraham, calling him lord." But gram-

---

[11] In older Jewish and Greek traditions, though less in Roman custom at Paul's time. See COMMENT II.

[12] When speaking of children and slaves, but never when speaking of wives, Paul explains subordination by references to "obeying" (Eph 6:1, 5) and "serving" respectively (6:7; cf. Col 3:20, 22); see Bengel; von Allmen, p. 34; Kähler, ZEE 3 (1959), 1 ff. Indeed, Thomas Aquinas, in his interpretation of 5:22, affirms that in a certain way the husband-wife relationship is like that of master and servant, so that "commands" are the appropriate means of governing. In a similar vein Aristotle pol. I 1252B; eth. Nic. x 1180A, and Plato leges III 680B, quoted Homer Odyssey IX 114–15, "Each one gives law to his children and to his wives"; cf. Aristotle pol. I 1259B, "The male is by nature fitter to command than the female." However, the text of Eph 5 does not quote Homer, neither does it simply reproduce and confirm what Plato and Aristotle in their time, and what Thomas Aquinas and a host of theologians in more recent periods have asserted. The term "weaker sex" occurs (only) in RSV I Peter 3:7; it is at home among Greeks and Romans (e.g. Plato resp. v 451E; 455E; 456A, etc.; Tacitus ann. III 33–34), not in Paul's writings. Despite all Paul says about the creation of woman out of man, and about her role in the fall (I Cor 11:3, 7–9; II Cor 11:3; cf. I Tim 2:14), his letters surprise the reader by an overwhelming number of passages which treat man and woman on an egalitarian basis. See especially I Cor 7:2–5, 8–16, 28, 32–34; Gal 3:28; Eph 5:21 and the gratitude expressed to women in the greeting list, Rom 16:1–15.

[13] BDF, 146–47. See also Rom 8:15; Matt 11:26; Luke 8:54; Mark 5:41.

[14] The omission of "own" in our translation is justified by the fact that in Hellenistic Greek "own" (idios) can substitute for the general or possessive pronoun "your" (BDF, 286) and vice versa. In 5:28 "their (heautōn) bodies" stands for their "own" bodies. Idios is also found before "husbands" in I Peter 3:1, 5; Titus 2:5 (cf. 2:9). However, in the closest parallel to Eph 5:22, i.e. Col 3:18, no possessive pronoun is used at all. In I Cor 7:2 heautōn and idios are used as synonymns; in Eph 4:28; I Cor 4:12; I Thess 4:11, idios occurs before the noun "hands" without bearing a special accent. J. Moffatt, Introduction to the Literature of the New Testament (New York: Scribner's, 1925), p. 383, considers the occurrence of idiois in Eph 5:22 a proof that the author of this epistle was familiar with I Peter; Mitton, EE, p. 194 arrives at exactly the opposite conclusion. In actuality, "the uncontrollable possibilities of how parenetic materials were tradited," of which Weidinger speaks in his Haustafeln, afford no criteria to pass judgment on literary dependence one way or another. See also Baltensweiler, pp. 215–17.

[15] See fn. 19.

mar opposes this exegesis: if in Eph 5:22 husbands were given the rights and title of a lord, in Greek as well as in English the text should read, "as to the(ir) lords" (Abbott).

b) If at this point—as in many ethical passages that contain a motivation for a preceding command—the *kyrios* is Jesus Christ, the reference to "the Lord" can qualify the expected subordination in several ways:

1) It can indicate both the urgency and the limit of the wives' subordination. *Hōs* ("as") can have causal force: wives have to yield because "it is fitting in the Lord," as the parallel Col 3:18 states, or "because you fear the Lord," as Eph 5:21 has emphasized. This excludes an obedience due to a mankind which would excel the obedience owed to God (cf. Acts 5:29) or Christ.

2) It can describe the mode, integrity and radicality of subordination. If *hōs* has comparative force, wives are instructed to give way to their husbands with equally unlimited trust and in the same unrestricted manner with which they subject themselves to Christ. Cf. 5:24: "in everything."

3) Motivation and comparison may be welded together as is the case in the subsequent uses of *hōs* or *kathōs* ("as," "just as"). Subordination to Christ and subordination to the husband are then as related and inseparable as are the love of God and the love of man, or, perhaps, as the love of the neighbor and the love of self. Thus to the husband—and if not to him, then to the wife's attitude of subordination—may be attributed a typological, sacramental or eschatological role: he may be designated as the representative of Christ to his wife, and she would thus have access to Christ only through him.[16] In this case her subordination could be compared to the mystery of visiting, feeding, and clothing the poor: "As you have done to one of the least of these my brethren, you did it to me" (Matt 25:40). Then Christ receives homage "together" with the husband, and a woman obeys Christ by obeying her husband.

4) The subordination may pertain to Jesus Christ supremely or exclusively, so much so that the husband is merely an occasion or training ground for a much higher allegiance, or an obstacle or chastisement to be met and overcome in the quest for true subordination. In 6:6–7 Paul appears to recommend even this attitude to slaves, and in Col 3:23 it is explicitly stated that slaves shall do their work "as for the Lord, and not for men." If the negative "not for men" is applied to a woman's subordination, she is to render her "obedience to the husband in intuition of Christ" (Bengel)—however divergent and different her husband's behavior be from Christ's.[17]

The telegram style of the formula "as to the Lord" does not permit a decision in favor of either of these expositions. Yet it is unlikely that Paul intended to be ambiguous and to let each reader choose the exposition he liked best. Only the verses which follow can provide the necessary clarification; vs. 22 cannot be understood without them. So far, two things have become clear: (a) Paul does not call for absolute submissiveness of all women vis-à-vis all men, or for total dependence of wives upon their husbands. He speaks of the selective sub-

---

[16] Luther's dictum that men ought to become a Christ to one another may point in this direction. Eph 1:23 has been understood to aver that the husband is his wife's savior, see below. K. Barth, III 4, 175 observes crisply, "Man is not the Christ of woman" but a "joint heir of the grace of life" (I Peter 3:7).

[17] Different interpretations of Eph 5:22b including those outlined here, are presented in, e.g. Mussner, p. 148; Schlier, p. 253; Gaugler, pp. 207–8; Baltensweiler, p. 221.

ordination of the wife to her husband. (b) The apostle does not refer to nature, to general standards of decency, to the law, or to the fall, as though any one of these or all together contained the ground or motive of his exhortation.[18] Only the Lord Jesus Christ is the source, standard, and motivation of a woman's subordination. This means that he is also its limit and reward. In the following, Paul attempts to show why faith in this Lord calls for subordination above all.

23. *For [only] in the same way that.* A literal translation of this verse would be, "For the man is the head of his wife as also the Messiah [is] head," etc. The literal version creates the impression that the Messiah is an "also ran" in matters of headship, fitting a model that is known and perfect enough without him. However, what is unquestionably true of the context, especially vss. 25–27, is also true of vs. 23, the Messiah is not reduced to the level of a secondary example. Indeed Paul could not have been ignorant of the fact that a majority of married people of his time followed a pattern of behavior which attributed superior responsibility to the husband and an inferior position to the wife; also he must have known that this pattern was considered by many perfectly reasonable and adequate—without being informed by Jesus Christ's love for the church. Does this mean, however, that those married needed no more than some additional (and ultimately superfluous) information and advice? It is clear that in his discussions on other topics Paul does not consider Jesus Christ a confirmation of natural law or general customs. Always, the references made by the apostle to the Messiah and the church contribute more than embellishment, a halo, or a mythological framework to an indisputable status quo. If in other contexts and in the present section Paul succeeds in showing that the Messiah is "head" and loves in a unique manner, then it is probable that also in 5:23 Jesus Christ is the only cause and standard for the saints' conduct. The logical structure of the next verse (5:24) confirms this interpretation. There the church-Christ relationship is the archetype of the wife's subordination, not just its illustration. Two seemingly irrelevant and unambiguous words in vs. 23 are easily misunderstood: *Hōs kai* is simply translated by "as also" in the vast majority of versions and commentaries, but these two words can have much more weight, as their use in the following verses shows. *Hōs* can have a force other than that of announcing a comparison. Just as the English word "as" and the Hebrew *ki* have innumerable senses and can indicate more than one logical connection, so do the Greek *hōs* and its Hellenistic equivalent *kathōs*. They can serve as a conjunction, introducing a dependent clause which provides a reason for the content of the main clause. In the specific case of 5:23, the elliptical Greek diction calls for the insertion of the verb "is" in the translation. Therefore, the words *hōs . . . ho Christos kephalē tēs ekklēsiās* have not only the meaning of the comparison "*as* the Messiah is . . . ," but also the sense "*because* the Messiah is the head of the church."[19] Finally, the added conjunction *kai* may

---

[18] Cf. the different modes of reasoning used in e.g. I Cor 11:6, 13–15; 14:34; II Cor 11:3; I Tim 2:13–14. In COMMENT I the unity and diversity of motivation will be discussed more extensively.

[19] See LSLex, 2038–40; WBLex, 905–7; BDF, esp. 453, for careful discussion of the various senses of *hōs*. The comparative and causative forces are combined, according to Baltensweiler, pp. 221–22, and others. In Eph 4:32; 5:2 the formulae, "as also God," "as also Christ" point distinctly to the temporal, logical, causal priority of God's and Christ's action, not to an incidental illustration proffered by them.

well mean more than "also." Sometimes *kai* serves to emphasize and clarify the terms with which it is connected. While in vs. 24b and in some variants of vs. 28 (each time in an apodosis beginning with "so") *kai* must mean "also," in the three protases beginning with "as" (*hōs* or *kathōs*) and connected with "the Messiah" (vss. 23, 25, 29), it may increase and emphatically point out the force of *hōs* and the uniqueness of the Messiah.[20] Expressed by a paraphrase, the Greek words *hōs kai ho Christos* signify in this case, "exclusively in the way of one single cause and model, even the Messiah." Our translation of vs. 23 follows the linguistic and logical analysis reflected in a few modern versions of Ephesians:[21] "[Only] in the same way that the Messiah . . . !" If this interpretation is not only tenable but necessary, then Christ is not depicted as a supreme example of male superiority over woman. Rather the "husband's" function as "head" is modeled after (and limited by) the measure of Christ's headship. Thus, not an absolute, but only a very qualified role as "head" is attributed to man. I Cor 11:3 makes this explicit by the sequence in which Christ's and the husband's headship are given: the "head of every husband is Christ, the head of a wife is her husband."[22] Similar restrictions were observed in the description of the wife's subordination in vs. 22.

the Messiah is the head of the church.[23] In Eph 1:22–23 Christ was described as the head "over all" who was appointed also and specifically to be "head of the church" (cf. Col 1:15–20). While Christ exerts his headship over principalities and powers by using unequaled (brute) "power" to which both friendly and inimical "powers" are successively subjugated (whether they will or will not; faith, love and hope are not expected of them), he is the head of the church in a distinct fashion (1:19–23). In 4:15–16 the modality of his headship over the church was unfolded: Christ the "head" enables the church to grow; he knits her into a unity; he nourishes her by caring for each member; he gives her strength to build herself up in love. In 1:23 this work of Christ the "head" was called an act of "filling." In 5:29 Paul reminds the readers of the nourishment and loving care the church receives from Christ, in 5:25 (and 5:2) of the price he paid for his love, and in 5:26–27 of the purpose of his action.

he, the savior of his body. In our translation, these words are marked as a parenthesis which complements the Messiah's title "head" with a more specific and extensive description. To use a paraphrase again, the parenthesis says in effect, "He, and he alone, is not only Head but also Savior"; or, "He proves Himself Head by saving"; or, "His work of salvation includes His dominion over the

---

[20] LSLex, 857, section B 5–6; under rubric A III 1–2, examples are given showing that after statements expressing sameness or a comparison, *kai* can substitute for *hōs*. According to WBLex, 94, II 3, in the NT (esp. in Pauline Epistles) *kai* occurs in clauses describing both the prototype and antitype. In Matt 6:10; Luke 6:31 Codex D and Marcion's var. lect.; Acts 7:51; Gal 1:9; I Cor 15:48; Philip 1:20; John 6:57; 13:15, *kai* is used in the place of *hōs* or *houtōs*.

[21] JB, "Since as Christ is the head of the church and saves the whole body, so is the husband . . ." NTTEV, "For the husband has authority over his wife in the same way that Christ has authority . . ." Cf. Phillips.

[22] See K. Barth, III 4, 173 for a non-hierarchical interpretation of this verse, which corresponds to the destruction of claims for male superiority by Eph 5:25–27.

[23] In COMMENT VI A on 1:15–23 the alternatives were listed for explaining the origin and meaning of Christ's designation as the "head." Especially OT, Orphic, Stoic, Gnostic, and medical analogies were examined. Preference over a unilateral explanation (such as Schlier's from Gnostic texts) was given to the assumption that several sources contributed to the specific concept of "head" not only in Ephesians and Colossians but also in I Cor 11:3. E.g. J. Dupont had suggested that Semitic and Stoic elements had been combined; Benoit spoke of Semitic and medical sources.

church."[24] However, this interpretation and its variations have always been and still are challenged by a sizable group of commentators who believe that Christ is not the only one predicated as "savior." They hold that in a subordinate way the husband, too, is the "savior of his wife."[25] If he cannot be savior of her soul or "savior of the world" (John 4:42), yet he can be savior of his wife's body, that is, he can save or protect her from improper personal conduct or from an intolerable yearning or suffering of her body (cf. Gen 3:16). Perhaps the strongest argument for this interpretation can be made by reference to Hosea 3:1–2. The prophet was told by Yahweh to buy "for fifteen shekels of silver and a homer and a bushel-and-a-half of barley" his wife who had de-livered herself to a paramour. God's forgiving love for the harlot Israel is depicted by the actual "redemption" of a woman performed by her earthly husband. The "drama of the victorious bridegroom" in heaven in this case has its counterpart in a dramatic redemptive action performed by a male on earth.[26] The analogies between Eph 5:23–32 and the prophetic description of the bridal or marital Yahweh-Israel relationship are unquestionable; see COMMENT IV A. But there is no evidence that Paul wanted to make the unique events in Hosea's marriage the model for all married couples. Gomer was Hosea's wife even before he had "bought" her again for himself. Not every woman is a Gomer, nor each husband a Hosea. The same applies to Boaz who "redeems" a parcel of land and thereby buys a close relative's widow, according to Levit-ical Law (Ruth 4). However, do the words "savior of the body" perhaps de-scribe what happens in the carnal (sexual) relation between husband and wife[27] or in their total (spiritual, social, and physical) communion? An inter-

[24] See, e.g. Thomas Aquinas; Calvin; Bengel; Haupt; Abbott; Dibelius; Weidinger, p. 60; Schlier; K. Barth, IV 4, 173–75; Mussner, p. 148; Benoit, "Corps, tête" 28; Best, pp. 173–74; G. Fohrer, TWNTE, VII, 1016; Baltensweiler, pp. 222–25.

[25] So, e.g. the Greek fathers Chrysostom, Theophylact, Oecumenius; Calvin (with great hesita-tion); M. Bucer, *Résumé sommaire de la doctrine chrétienne*, German original 1548 (ref.); Robin-son, pp. 124, 205; Scott; J. Huby; L. S. Thornton, *The Common Life of the Body of Christ* (Lon-don: Dacre, 1942), p. 222. Sometimes Tobit 6:18 is quoted in support of this view: "You [as husband] will save her," but with Sampley, pp. 59–60, this statement about a very special case can-not be considered the source and criterion for the interpretation of the general counsel given in Eph 5:23.

[26] Chavasse (p. 104; cf. the context pp. 89–110) and H. Greeven (in Dibelius, p. 93) draw at-tention to Hosea 3, but they do not infer that a heavenly marriage is re-enacted by the marriage of an earthly pair. Though Schlier, pp. 272–78, rejects the application of the words "savior of the body" to earthly husbands, he wants to explain human marriage and its mystery as a *Nachvollzug* ("reenactment," "actualization," "representation") of Christ's love for the pre-existent, the fallen, then redeemed church, see pp. 261–63, 266, 269, 272, 279.

[27] Von Allmen, pp. 29–30. According to W. Meyer, *Der erste Brief an die Korinther* (Zurich: Zwingli, 1947), I, 237, both husband and wife are in their sexual union one another's savior. Kähler, *Die Frau*, p. 206, is certainly justified in repudiating this view. It goes far beyond the unilateral utterance of Eph 5:23. When in I Cor 7:16 Paul envisages the possibility that a wife may *save* her husband and vice versa, he thinks of conversion to faith in Christ, not of the salvation of the body by a carnal event. A seemingly more subtle biblical argument in favor of the above proposition proceeds (in abbreviated form) in the following manner: because of God's curse woman has a carnal desire for man (Gen 3:16). In principle Paul holds that "it is well for man not to touch a woman" (I Cor 7:1). But "because of the temptation to immorality . . . it is better to marry than to be aflame with passion" (I Cor 7:2, 9). As in the OT God's curse included a blessing for the offspring of Eve who was to bruise the serpent's head (Gen 3:15), so in the NT it is confirmed that "woman will be saved through bearing children" (I Tim 2:15). Inasmuch as the husband in his marital relation contributes to his wife's "salvation through mother-hood," he is aptly called her "savior" (Eph 5:23). Augustine's doctrine on marriage, as developed esp. in *de bono coniugali* (PL 40, 373–96), can be recognized behind this argument. Its logical con-clusion is that marriage is an antidote against overflowing carnal desire, and that sexual intercourse is sanctified only when it aims at, or does not prevent, conception. See also fns. 32 and 205. In COMMENT VII B it will be shown that the Augustinian and official Roman Catholic doctrine on marriage is *not* exhausted by the argument just mentioned regarding sexual intercourse.

pretation built upon this assumption is not supported by the wording of vs. 23, the context, or biblical parallels:

a) In the Greek text the two nouns (subjects) "husband" and "Messiah" are followed by the pronoun *autos,* meaning "he" ("himself"). If both preceding nouns were included in this pronoun, the plural *autoi,* "they" ("themselves"), would have been used and the plural "saviors" would have followed. The singular *autos* and the position of the *autos* sentence indicate that only the last-mentioned subject, the Messiah, is called "savior of the body."[28]

b) As 2:14 and 4:11 show, *autos* at the beginning of a descriptive statement introduces a laudatory, perhaps hymnic, utterance. The acclamation, "This is the One who . . . ," or, "He, the . . . ," is characteristic of an "aretalogy" (praise of a hero or of a moral giant's miraculous deeds and virtue).[29] Also the *hapax legomenon* "savior of the body" may reveal that this formulation is not originally Pauline. Finally the seemingly particularistic limitation of Christ's saviorhood to the church corresponds to the "we"-style of many NT hymns.[30] In the early church such hymns were sung to God and Christ, never to a man or husband.

c) The title *"savior"* (*sōtēr*) has a long and colorful history.[31] If 5:23 called each ordinary man or husband "savior" it would be without precedent or par-

---

[28] As in many other cases, so here Abbott's careful linguistic analysis proves its supreme value.

[29] The variant readings of 5:23 in some uncials, and the majority of minuscules attest to a corresponding interpretation. They have, "And (or, Even) He is . . ."

[30] See section II of the Introduction, criteria 2 and 4, for biblical, and E. Peterson, *Heis Theos* (Göttingen: Vandenhoeck, 1926), pp. 183–212, for Hellenistic parallels: "There exists a close connection between acclamation, hymn, and psalm" (p. 203). Baltensweiler, pp. 224–25 ponders, but finally dismisses, the possibility that in 5:23 a liturgical fragment is used. Schille, *Hymnen,* does not even discuss this verse though it meets a sufficient number of his criteria for discerning a hymn, and though the *genre* "Redeemer Hymn" may be an appropriate classification for this fragment. Without considering the hymnic character of *autos,* G. Fohrer, TWNTE, VII, 1016, observes that this word introduces a new thought rather than an interpretation of the term "head." The only mention of Christ the *savior* in undisputed Pauline Epistles is made in Philip 3:20. There this title has the same eschatological ring which in the homologoumena also characterizes the verb "to save" and the noun "salvation." In Eph 2:5, 8 this eschatological flavor seemed less dominant, though it was not completely absent. Regarding the realized eschatology of the whole of Ephesians see COMMENT IX on 1:3–14. In 5:23 futurist eschatology need not be minimized. Just as the reference to the meeting with the coming Christ in 4:13, so verses 5:26 and 27 have a distinctly futurist character. These passages may be the epistle's own interpretation of the otherwise cryptic term "savior of the body."

[31] See LSLex, 1751; Bousset, *Kyrios,* pp. 240–46; W. Staerk, *Soter,* 2 vols., Gütersloh: Bertelsmann, 1933, 1938; Dibelius, *The Pastoral Epistles,* excursus on II Tim 1:10, HbNT 13 (1931), 60–63; O. Cullmann, *Christology* (Philadelphia: Westminster, 1959), pp. 239–45; Schlier, *Christus,* pp. 72–73; W. Foerster and G. Fohrer, TWNTE, VII, 1004–24. In the LXX primarily God himself (e.g. Micah 7:7; Isa 12:2; Deut 32:15; Isa 45:15; 62:11; Wisd Sol 16:7), but in some cases also men such as the Judges (e.g. Judg 3:9, 15; but compare 2:18) are given this title, yet never priests, prophets or kings, i.e. persons who were called *Anointed* (Messiah). Philo, the Jewish Apocrypha, the *Psalms of Solomon,* and the *Sibylline Oracles* use this noun only for God, Josephus only for political rulers. In the *Testaments of the XII* only one passage that uses the term "savior" in application to God (*Test. Joseph* I 6) is free from the suspicion of being a Christian interpolation. Thus in the time of the NT and among Jews, "savior" was not a widely used designation of the Messiah or of any man. But among the Greeks since Aeschylus, both gods and men were called "saviors," and in the Hellenistic period not only the healer-god Asclepius and deities celebrated as life-givers in Mystery Cults, but also philosophers, rulers, and politicians were so named. Occasionally (but not automatically) the hope for the bringer of a golden age was connected with the use of this word, especially in the emperor cult. In the NT, the noun is used of God in Luke 1:47; Jude 25 and six times in the Pastoral Epistles; of Christ, in Luke 2:11; Acts 5:31; 13:23; John 4:42; I John 4:14, also frequently in the Pastoral Epistles and II Peter—and in Philip 3:20 and Eph 5:23. The uneven distribution of the title in the NT and the reluctance of the Apostolic Fathers to use it, make it impossible thus far to ascribe to this title a definite origin or purpose—e.g. polemics against the developing emperor cult in and outside Rome. In Gnostic sources the Heavenly Man can be called or described as "savior." In the Valentinian Gnosis Christ is not only bridegroom but also savior; see Irenaeus *adv. haer.* I 2:4–5; Clement of Alexandria *excerpta ex Theodoto* 35:1 f., as Schlier, *Christus,* p. 72, observes.

allel. A man who wonders why God should remember him at all (Ps 8) and who cannot redeem himself or his brother (Ps 49:7–8) cannot possibly be called "savior" in the immediate context of Eph 5:25–27 where Christ's unique work is described.[32] The title "Redeemer of Israel" is applied neither to Hosea nor to Boaz, but is reserved for Yahweh (Isa 43:14; 48:17). Paul would be suspect, if not guilty, of idolatry if he attributed an analogous title to every married man.

d) The Jewish and medical sources which may have determined Paul's use of the title "head" for Christ never associate "headship" with "saviorship." In the OT the connection is very rare; see COMMENT VI A on 1:15–23. Not earlier than in the Gnosticizing *Odes of Solomon* XVIII 14–15 are the title "head" and the act of "redemption" closely related. Unless Ephesians is considered to have been stamped by a minute detail of Gnostic diction, "head" in 5:23 does not include the meaning "savior." Only in Christ's case are both functions combined in personal union. The beginning of vs. 24 will indeed show that Paul was aware of having stepped beyond the Christ-husband analogy when he called the Messiah "the savior of the body."

If, then, Christ alone is named "savior," the "body" saved can only be his body, i.e. the church (vs. 24). See COMMENT VI B on 1:15–23. In our translation the Greek definite article has therefore been rendered by the possessive pronoun "his." In vss. 28–31, a corresponding use will be made of the term "body"; the wife will be described as "her husband's body," as "one flesh" with him.

is the husband the head of his wife. In their commentaries and monographs, a great number of the modern interpreters of the *Haustafeln* express the opinion that pagan or Jewish standards and lists (or both) underlie the pertinent NT passages. It is assumed that non-Christian materials were eventually "Christianized" more and more.[33] Among the specific elements said to be endorsed by the NT is the notion that man is superior to woman, and that the priority of males must be enforced. While earlier it has been observed that Eph 5:22 ff. speaks of husbands and wives, not of males and females in general, the question remains whether the designation of the husband as "the head of his wife" is not a quote from older or contemporary Jewish, Greek or Latin literature, or at least a reference to an established theory and custom sanctioned in Paul's time? By putting "head" inside quotation marks Phillips certainly conveys this impression. However, no evidence has yet been produced from literary or other sources that anybody near or far from Paul's environment held the opinion, "The husband is his wife's head," and, correspondingly, "The wife is his body"

[32] Additional reasons for rejecting the "theology of marriage" sketched in fn. 27 can now be mentioned: (a) It is arbitrary to connect the term "savior" in 5:23, with the verb "will be saved" in I Tim 2:15 and to draw the conclusion that a man "saves" a woman by making her a mother; Eph 5:23 and I Tim 2:15 do not belong in the same literary unit. (b) The statement, "it is well not to touch a woman" (I Cor 7:1) probably expresses the opinion of the enthusiasts among the Corinthians rather than of Paul, see Orr, 3, pp. 6–8. (c) In I Tim 2:15 not childbirth as such, but a very special education of the children is connected with salvation: "If they [the children] continue in faith and love and holiness, a woman will be *saved*"; cf. Titus 2:4 and Dibelius, *Pastoral Epistles*, p. 30.

[33] Cf. fn. 3. A brief but classic representation of this view is given by M. Dibelius, *An die Kolosser, Epheser, an Philemon*, HbNT, 12 (1953), 48–50: "The Christian parenesis preserved, for the average ethics of the Occident, the moral principles regarding family life which were expressed in Greek popular philosophy and in the Jewish halacha" (p. 49).

(cf. 5:28). To be sure, Aristotle had written, "The rule of the household is a monarchy, for every house is under one head," and he compared the husband-wife relationship to the one-sided relation between soul and body in which the soul (the husband!) must rule, not be ruled.[34] But Aristotle had not called the "man of the house" the "head of his spouse" in so many words. When the Romans called a married woman *domina* or *matrona*; when a sweetheart or wife among Greeks was addressed as *kyriā* ("mistress," "lady"); when, at the latest during the first century A.D., the name *Martha* ("mistress") begins to occur in Syria, the woman in question was certainly not equated with a body that receives life and direction only from the head, i.e. the bridegroom or husband. Unquestionably, patriarchal notions played a dominant (though receding, see COMMENT II) role in the life and literature of the Mediterranean peoples of Paul's period. But the same Dibelius who inspired Weidinger to write his famous work on the *Haustafeln* admits, "We cannot say from where the idea stems that the husband is the woman's head."[35] There is as yet no proof that Paul repeated a generally accepted contemporary opinion, and that he contributed to it no more than a few more or less penetrating Christian phrases. Instead the proposition, "The husband is the head of his wife" must be understood as original with the author of Ephesians. In consequence, it has to be explained by the context of Ephesians in which it is found, and not by contemporary or later prejudices in favor of, or in opposition to, a special responsibility entrusted to the husband for his wife. The logical structure of 5:23 shows that both the fact and modality of a husband's headship is totally determined not only by the double meaning of Hebrew *roš* ("head" and "chief") but above all by the event and mode of Christ's headship. In vss. 25–27 Paul appears to be swept away from the marriage topic by and for the description of headship in terms of Christ's love. Mark 10:42–45 contains a parallel to the surprising definition of headship given in Eph 5: "The Son of Man came not to be served but to serve and to give his life." When a husband understands his manhood and headship in this Christological sense, he will consider it both a privilege and a grave responsibility. Even more than an enlightened monarch in his relation to his subjects, he is then "the first servant" of his wife. In short, a headship qualified, interpreted, and limited by Christ alone is proclaimed, not an un-

---

[34] Aristotle *pol.* I 1255B; 1254AB; cf. Plutarch *moralia* 142E. In commenting upon Eph 5:28–29 Thomas Aquinas uses the soul-body analogy to explain Paul.

[35] Dibelius, p. 93, is supported by Baltensweiler, p. 222, who adds that a derivation from "natural law" is excluded by the fact that in some cultures the matriarchate is considered the "natural" order. Best, p. 178, believes that "headship implies here [in Eph 5:23] not organic unity but the power to rule." But the part of God's curse on the first couple saying that Adam "shall rule over" Eve (Gen 3:16), is not quoted by the apostle who argues about marriage and sex on the basis of Gen 2:24, i.e. of the statement concerning the union in "one flesh" that antedates the fall. The priority of Eve's over Adam's fall is in II Cor 11:3 not exploited for a demonstration of the inferiority of all women. Probably the order of divine worship rather than marriage as such is discussed in I Tim 2:11–15 where Eve's second place in the creation and first in the fall is mentioned; see Kähler, *Die Frau*, pp. 150–61. Statements such as Josephus *c. Ap.* II 201, "The woman, says the Law, is in all things inferior to the man. Let her therefore be submissive," are linguistically and in substance different from Eph 5:22–23. Even the Talmud affirms emphatically that for a man to make a woman his wife takes more, and something else, than to say, "I am your husband, I am your lord"; see Bab. Kiddushin 5b. Plutarch *moralia* 142E; 145C, denounces the husband who treats his wife as a boss (*despotēs*) treats his property (*ktēma*); he urges him to "enter into her feelings and be knit to her through goodwill," to be "a father and a precious-loved mother, yea, and a brother as well to her," to whom she can say, "My dear husband, Nay, but thou art to me guide, philosopher and teacher in all that is most lovely and divine" (*moralia*, II, tr. F. C. Babbitt, Loeb Classical Library [London: Heinemann, 1928], 322–23, 336–39).

limited headship that can be arbitrarily defined and has to be endured. If a colloquialism can help to understand 5:23, then the husband is told always and under all circumstances to "go ahead" by loving his wife and by paying gladly whatever the appropriate price.

24. *The difference notwithstanding.* Lit. "But." The most frequent function of Greek *alla* is to introduce a positive counterpart after a negative clause, or vice versa. The same conjunction can also signal the beginning of a question or objection, or the abrupt end of an argument, or the resumption of an address after a parenthesis.[36] It always indicates a contrast and bears more weight than the weaker *de* ("but", "and", "that is"), not to speak of *kai* ("and"). It must not simply be omitted in the English translation. Neither should it be rendered by "and," "or," "consequently," "and so";[37] for these meanings are alien to *alla.* There are two linguistic and logical alternatives for a translation that is as literal as possible: (a) *Alla* may point out the contrast between "being head" and "subordinating oneself." This is unlikely because the two positions and actions complement rather than contradict one another.[38] (b) The apostle may have had in mind an objection to the preceding statement which he wished to answer. In vs. 33 he uses *plēn* ("in any case") to introduce such an answer. Several authors have pointed out that in vs. 24 Paul intends to warn against a misunderstanding of vs. 23.[39] If some people thought—as indeed the history of interpretation shows (see fns. 19, 28–30)—that in a restricted sense the husband could be his wife's savior and become her Christ, then vs. 24 "demythologizes" both the husband and marriage. In opposition to many a vain man's opinion, the human male is not given a "power of command . . . unlimited."[40] He is not his wife's lord and savior. Wherein lies the difference?

just as the church subordinates herself [only] to the Messiah. There is a difference between brutal subjugation which denies, breaks or obliterates the will of the subjected party, and the way in which Jesus Christ meets and treats sinners in order to save them. There is a corresponding difference between the submissiveness and crouching subservience of a bootlicker who has lost all sense of dignity, and the voluntary acceptance and fulfillment of an appointment that calls for total devotion, imagination, and enthusiasm, as well as for a vital contribution to the common good. These differences will be discussed in COMMENT V C. Examples of how the church subordinates herself to her Lord and Savior by faith and confession, love and unity, hope and testimony, missionary action and ministerial endurance, are spread all over Ephesians. Especially in 4:25 – 5:20 has Paul shown how ("with heart and hands and voices") every member of Christ's body and the whole church continuously seek to learn and do the will of the Lord. In 5:19–20 "singing" was described as a

[36] LSLex, 67–68, sections I–II.
[37] As in RSV, JB, SegB, NTTEV, respectively.
[38] Robinson argues that just as in Gal 4:23, 29; I Cor 12:24; II Cor 3:14; 8:7, so here *alla* fixes the attention upon a special point of immediate interest and lacks contrasting force. But the meaning, "what I really want to say is this," is not sufficiently confirmed by dictionaries. WBLex, 38, sections 3, 5, 6, offers other meanings without a contrasting element: either transition to a new topic, or, strengthening of an imperative, or, a rhetorical escalation ("not only this, but rather"). As long as one of these meanings is suggested for Eph 5:24, the specific meaning of this verse is suppressed rather than reproduced.
[39] Bengel; von Hofmann; Meyer; Dibelius; Best, pp. 173–74. "Notwithstanding the difference" is the rendition suggested by Abbott.
[40] Though Mussner, p. 148, believes that such authority is here established.

primary form, and gratitude as the basic motive for the attitude of the church to her Lord. 5:24 adds to all preceding specifications of the church's place and function the statement, she "subordinates herself [only] to the Messiah." No one else but him can she serve without losing freedom and dignity. She loves to be his maid—otherwise she is not the true church. This authentic summary of the ecclesiology of Ephesians contradicts and excludes once and for all the notion that the term "body of Christ" implies a (mystical) identity of the church with Christ. The church is in no wise Christ himself or an impersonation of Christ. In serving Him who loves her she attests to the unity with him into which she was elevated, but she does not pride herself and boast of being a "quasi second Christ." "The church as Christ's body stands before Christ as some sort of personality of her own."[41]

so wives to your husbands. In vs. 22 the verb "subordinate yourselves" was missing though it was presupposed as dominating both vss. 21 and 22. Equally in 24b the same verb, after being used in 24a, is not repeated. The result of the elliptical diction chosen here and there is this: the author of Ephesians cannot be quoted as the originator or defendant of the flat command, "Wives must subordinate themselves."[42] In this epistle there is no absolute decree enjoining women always to take, or to be bound to, an inferior place. On the contrary, the call to subordination is qualified at least three times: first, by the overarching exhortation which calls for mutual subordination; next, by the unambiguous statement that a woman has to subordinate herself only to her husband (not to men in general);[43] finally, by specifying the wife's subordination in terms of the church's servant function before Christ. In vs. 23 two indicative statements place cause and effect, or model and copy, side by side: "As the Messiah *is* head . . . so the husband *is* the head." It is unlikely, therefore, that the two halves of vs. 24 consist of an indicative, "the church subordinates herself," changing then to an imperative: you wives "must" subordinate yourselves. In vs. 23 husbands were not told that they "must" be heads, but the gospel of Christ, the head, implied that they were heads after the manner of Christ. Equally the wives are not intimidated by a law saying, you must be subject. Rather an evangelical message is extended to them: just as the church is well off in her dependence upon Christ (cf. Mary "at the feet of the Lord"; Luke 10:38–42), so you women are and will be good wives when you give way and yield to your husbands. You need not compete with them or be jealous because of what they do for you. You have the right to receive love and care, as vss. 29, 33 will affirm. Subordination to love? Indeed! Only this and nothing else is preached in Eph 5:21–33. Where there is no love Paul does not expect submission—except in the case of principalities and powers.

in everything. Cf. the command given in Titus 2:9, saying that slaves shall

---

[41] Pius XII, *Mystici Corporis,* 1943, Acta Apostolicae Sedis 35 (1943), p. 218, had asserted that the church is *quasi altera Christi persona.* Schlier, p. 279, makes the quoted assertion—though in the immediate context he contradicts it by calling the church "the incorporation and representation" of Christ himself. Pauline diction permits one to speak of the incorporation of all the *saints* into Christ's body, 3:6; cf. 5:28–30. Johannine diction suggests Christ's incarnation, viz. his incorporation in a human body representing *total* humanity, John 1:14; cf. Heb 2:14–16. But to call the church Christ's incorporation is not warranted by Pauline or Johannine texts.

[42] However, variant readings of vs. 22, also Col 3:18, contain the command in so many words.

[43] The "subordination" to the requirements of a "decent and orderly" worship service (I Cor 14:34, 40) (see Kähler, ZEE 3 [1959], 4) and to the civil authorities (Rom 13:1–7) is required of women as much as of men.

subordinate themselves to their masters "in all things." According to Theodoret, the husband—just as Christ—is to be accepted as legislator (*nomothetōn*).[44] It is unlikely that this is Paul's opinion. Since not one OT ruler or king was permitted to consider himself the source and giver of *tōrā*, but could at best rediscover, read, and pronounce a hitherto hidden law of God,[45] and since all members of God's people were measured by their obedience to the Law, not their legislative creativity, it would take more than the words "in everything" to make every married male member of the NT church the legislator in his home. Other interpreters[46] pointed out that "in everything" cannot mean "absolutely," for however great the responsibility and authority of the husband, his wife has to obey God more than men (Acts 5:29), and she is not constrained to follow her husband when he demands things contrary to God and moral decency.[47] Yet it is improper to explain the words "in everything" by compiling a short or long list of exemptions to prove that "in everything" actually means, "not in everything." Most likely "everything" can be as little arbitrarily defined as, e.g. the term, "omnipotence of God." In the context, especially in 4:25 – 5:20, Paul has given examples of what he means by "everything": the witness given by the thoughts of the heart, the work of the hands, the words of the mouth, the disciplined use of intellect, of time, of liquor, etc.

25. *Husbands, love your wives.* "*Agapāte* [the command to love] points out to the husband the meaning of *hypotassomenoi* [vs. 21, the command to subordinate oneself to one another mutually]" says Dibelius, p. 94. For the first time in Ephesians the term "love" (*agapaō*) includes the erotic relationship and sexual union by which a man and a woman become "one flesh." In the great majority of its occurrences in the Bible, *agapaō* means the attitude and acts of unselfish giving.[48] According to Paul the other-directed, creative, and self-sacrificing character of love does not prevent a husband from loving his wife "as his own body" and therefore "as himself" (vss. 28–29, 33). Paul will not state this, however, until after he describes the love shown by Christ which is the source and standard of the husband's love. In vs. 25a the meaning of "love" is as yet undefined. The imperative "love!" has here the quality of an x in an equation: it evokes curiosity and requires close scrutiny if it is to become more than a cipher or platitude. What will Paul, the "prisoner in the Lord['s service]" (4:1)

[44] Perhaps the quotation from Homer in Aristotle, which was mentioned in fn. 12, inspired this surprising exposition—though Homer used a different and more subtle term (*themisteuei*).

[45] See M. Noth, "The Laws in the Pentateuch," in *The Laws in the Pentateuch and Other Essays*, I, Philadelphia: Westminster, 1961; Edinburgh: Oliver & Boyd, 1966.

[46] E.g. Thomas Aquinas and Gaugler.

[47] On the basis of modern psychological and sociological insights, at least one more limitation ought to be added to these exceptions and limitations: When or inasmuch as a husband is about to destroy the personality and selfhood of his wife, he deserves to be met by her resistance, not her passive submission. For then he has associated himself with the onrushing principalities and powers that can and must be "withstood" by the persons who have "put on" God's "[splendid] armor," viz. the "New Man," 6:10–17; 4:24.

[48] In the LXX, *erōs* occurs only in Prov 7:18; 30:16 in a bad sense; the verb *eraomai*, "to love," "to desire," is found in LXX I Esd 4:24; Esther 2:17; Prov 4:6 in good and bad senses; the noun *erastēs*, "lover," in both senses in Wisd Sol 8:2; 15:6; Hosea 2:7, 9, 10. In the great majority of cases the terms *agapaō* and *agapē* signify God's love, love for God, and brotherly love. But they are also used to denote marital and extramarital sexual union. All NT books avoid *eraomai* and *erōs* completely, though the proper name *Erastos* occurs in Rom 16:23; Acts 19:22; II Tim 4:20. It is possible that at least in one passage, Luke 7:47, *agapaō* has a primarily sexual overtone. See the NOTES on Eph 5:33 and esp. COMMENT V D for a more extensive discussion of *agapē* and *erōs*, and for a critical appraisal of A. Nygren's sharp distinction between the two.

have to contribute to the perennial problem of love, libido and marriage? Will he be able to show, as Calvin believes, that because of "Christ's example" the mutual love of spouses "need not be a vulgar love"?

just as [we confess]. Verses 1:4; 4:21, 32 and 5:2 have shown that *kathōs* ("just as") can be used to introduce a comparison, a causal motive, or a quotation. Several of these meanings can be combined. (a) In vs. 25 *kathōs* has comparative force, as the "so (also)" in vs. 28 shows. (b) It also has causal force. According to 5:2 Christ's death is not only the example but also the sacrament ("sacrifice") of love which creates the "way" and guides the saints on the way of love which they are to follow. Equally in 5:25 the love of the Messiah is more than just a phenomenological parallel to human ways and means of loving. Paul describes it as the ontological ground of the husband's special love for his wife. (c) Finally, *kathōs* has the force of a quotation formula—provided that sufficient grounds exist for considering the following lines a quote from, or allusion to, a traditional confession, a liturgical formula, or a hymn.[49] Features such as the following show that in 5:25–27 traditional material is used:

a) The common occurrence in 5:2, 25 and Gal 2:20 of almost exactly the same words, "He has loved . . . and has given himself for. . . ." Probably Paul cites a clause formed by someone else, or he quotes himself.

b) The combination of three indicatives with three telic affirmations in a parallel structure. Different cola (poetic lines) and different stanzas can be distinguished. They have the Semitic poetic form of "parallel members."[50]

c) The Pauline *hapax legomena*, "he loved the church," "bath in water," "church resplendent," "spot and wrinkle." Most of the *hapax legomena* in Ephesians are found within hymnic passages.

d) The fact that these verses contain a Christological summary that appears to be complete in itself but to overlap the argument at hand.[51]

[49] Until more extensive research in the interconnection and the distinctive marks of NT liturgical confessions, formulae, and hymns has been done, it is impossible to place passages such as 5:2, 23b, 25–27 into one or another *genre*. In L. Cerfaux's chapter on Christological hymns (*Le Christ*, pp. 279–301), also in E. Schweizer, *Lordship and Discipleship*, SBT 28 (1960), these passages are bypassed. Schille (*Hymnen*) does not list Eph 5:25–27 among the *Gattungen* of redemption songs, initiation songs or baptismal-liturgical formulae. But Baltensweiler, p. 226, observes that these verses "bear a strong liturgical stamp," presuppose a (liturgical?) skeleton that was "replenished," and reveal their "origin in the church tradition of the passion narrative" by the (prominent) use of the term, "to give up," "to deliver" (*paredidōmi*); cf. Matt 17:22; 26:2; 27:2, 18, 26–27. Compare the following with the criteria for discerning hymns listed in the Introduction II.

[50] In the Greek text the indicatives "he has loved" and "he has given" are followed by the participle *katharisas* (lit. "having purified"). The three affirmations are complemented by three *hina* (lit. "in order to" or "so that") clauses: purpose and consequence of Christ's action are the sanctification, the splendid presentation, and the holiness and blamelessness of the church. In our translation the final and consecutive clauses are the lines 2, 4, 6 of the six lines that can be divided into two stanzas. It is also possible to distinguish three stanzas consisting of much shorter cola; in this case the *hina* clauses would form the last line of each stanza. Perhaps 5:2 was originally the first strophe of the hymn quoted in 5:25–27. There the effect of Christ's "sacrifice" was to "please God." Here the effect of his love is to create a fitting partner for himself and to allow the church to benefit from his riches. Both times love and sacrifice are combined. Cf. Robinson, p. 125.

[51] E.g. Best, p. 174, observes that the author of Ephesians "is carried away" when he describes Christ's love in greater detail than strictly fits the comparison with the husbands. An equally hymnic Christological excursus is found inside a *Haustafel* in I Peter 2:21–25. The exhortation to servants is buttressed by a comprehensive Christological creed. In Philip 2:1–11 the members of the congregation are urged by the extensive quotation of a Christ hymn to demonstrate unity, humility, unanimity, altruism. Christ is more than just an example: he is the (sacrament and) ground of all that is expected of the saints. All these cases exemplify that Christian ethics in general, and *Haustafeln* in particular, were a means to remember and to proclaim Christ, rather than an occasion to return to legalism or to seek refuge in compromises with Jewish or pagan standards of conduct.

e) The focus of attention upon Christ's work "for the church" as it is expressed by the "we"-form of many hymns.

f) The presence in the substance and phrasing of this passage of OT poetical, perhaps mythological, motifs and, perhaps, the reflection of pagan-mythological elements—though in "de-mythologized" form.[52]

While all these points suggest that Paul used or paraphrased a hymn, formula or confession possibly known to the readers of Ephesians, they cannot serve as a fail-safe demonstration of the use of traditional material. As much as every church member in Corinth, Paul himself could "have a psalm" (i.e. formulate and pronounce it before or during the worship service under the impact of the Spirit), according to I Cor 14:26. But several puzzles contained in Eph 5:25–27 come nearer a solution when the hymn theory is used as a working hypothesis, as the following NOTES will show.

The Messiah has loved the church and has given himself for her. The metaphoric description of the Messiah as a bridegroom and of his people as a bride (which is unprecedented in the OT[53]), the analogy between this Bridegroom's and Bride's union to the marital relationship between man and woman, the special way in which in vs. 25 love and death are connected—topics such as these will be scrutinized in COMMENTS IV and V. At this point attention is to be drawn to the logical structure, the subject, the style of this sentence, and its relation to other literary discussions of marriage.

a) Strictly speaking, vs. 25 contains only one *tertium comparationis* between the pairs that are treated as analogous: the "love" of the male partner for the female. For only the verb "love" is found in both vss. 25a and 25b. Only if the verb "love" were not repeated in 25b would the verbs "give oneself," "make holy," "make clean," "present to oneself" also contain the model for the husband's love. Indeed later, in vss. 31–32, Paul will turn to an allegorical interpretation which leads upward to "Christ and the church" from a statement on human marriage. However, he does not suggest a reverse allegorization in vs. 25, i.e. a descent from Christ's unique acts to the single actions of every husband. As stated earlier, the apostle far from suggests that the husband become a duplicate of Christ and consider himself his wife's "savior," cf. vs. 23.

b) The Messiah in person (cf. 2:14) and he alone is the origin and criterion of marital love. Instead of a love principle, the Prince of Love is set forth; instead of a daemonic power (eros, libido), the Friend is praised who died for his friends; rather than paint a rose-colored cloud, Paul calls to mind specific events in the history of God and man. By benefiting and drawing from the

---

[52] A. M. Dubarle, "L'origine dans l'AT de la notion Paulinienne de l'église corps du Christ," AnBib 17–18, I (1963), 231–40, and others have drawn attention to the anticipation of Eph 5:25–27 in the story of God's love for Jerusalem in Ezek 16. Schlier, pp. 252–80; *Christus*, pp. 60–75, is the strongest exponent of a school of interpreters that finds in Ephesians allusions to, and corrections of, the myth of heavenly pairs (*syzygies*), of an original androgynous man, of a cultic re-enaction called *hieros gamos*, and of the identification of sexual and religious experience. See COMMENT VII A. If it could be demonstrated that an original Christian hymn underlying 5:25–27 had used and assimilated *pagan* materials, then the origin of the hymn ought to be sought in Gentile-Christian ("Hellenistic") communities. However, the possible allusion of the hymn to the Jewish custom of a bridal bath, also the confrontation of Canaanite by Israelite elements, e.g. in Hosea, and the tendency of some Jewish heretical groups toward Gnosticism, suggest even more strongly a Jewish-Christian environment.

[53] See J. Jeremias, TWNTE, IV, 1099–1106; but cf. fn. 253. The Gospels contain hints of this equation: John 3:29; Matt 9:15 par.; 22:1–14 par.; 25:1–13; the book of Revelation presupposes the metaphors: 19:7, 9; 21:2, 9.

fact, mode, intention, and achievement of Christ's love, a husband shall learn what is the essence of love.

c) The essence of love is not described by either a definition or a methodology. Instead of giving technical advice, Paul follows the literary method of poets and novelists: he gives his testimony to true love in the form of an epic which relates how one great lover, Christ, loved his chosen one. The substance of vss. 25–27 is a narrative which can be given the title "The Romance of Christ and the Church."

d) Describing Christ's love as the source, inspiration, criterion, challenge, and promise of marital love, Paul presents an alternative not only to the famous, but also to the infamous love stories connected with names, such as Zeus, Solomon, Paris, Odysseus, Oedipus, Pyramus, Tristan, Don Juan, Abelard. His alternative is also distinct from scientific (philosophical, medical, psychological, sociological), not to speak of commercial, ways of describing, prescribing, or proscribing love.[54] Paul can do no better than tell the unique story of Christ.[55] By letting the Messiah sit on that throne which in some discussions about marriage is attributed to sex, Paul has not denied the power and function of sex, but has placed it together with other easily idolized forces on a level where it may fulfill its function properly.[56]

26. *to make her holy by [his] word and clean by the bath in water.* Lit. "to sanctify her, having purified [her] by the bath of the water by word." In Col 2:12 the parenthetical participle construction, "being buried with him in baptism," interrupts, but also illuminates the preceding and following statements that use finite verb forms.[57] Equally, in Eph 5:26, the words (lit.), "having purified . . . ," appear to be a parenthesis. The term "by word" at the end of the clause may well have the same decisive accent as analogous formulae elsewhere—such as "in love," "in his beloved Son" in 1:4, 6. It is unlikely that the phrase "by word" qualifies exclusively the noun "bath" or the noun "water"

[54] Paul's choice and procedure do not demonstrate or encourage lack of concern for personal and environmental, cultural and accidental factors that influence the common life of a couple. But at this place he does not give counsel in an individual marriage situation; the epistle to Philemon is an example of how Paul would argue in a specific case. Neither does Paul's argument prove that he did not know, but rather ignored or despised what Jewish and Gentile poets, novelists, philosophers, historians, doctors, psychologists, orators, mothers (in-law!), and the simple people's proverbial wisdom before and at his time had taught about sex, eros, love, and marriage. But when he attempts to present Jesus Christ as the gift and giver, the teacher and healer of love, he makes that specific contribution to human knowledge and experience which can be expected of an intelligent Christian: far from being simply overwhelmed and muted by information available and spread elsewhere, he says those basic things which can be learned only in the "School of the Messiah"; see COMMENT III on 4:17–32.

[55] In Hellenistic lower and higher schools, "aretalogies" (accounts of mighty deeds of virtuous men) were used together with treatises on ethics and special moral problems, or were inserted into them for illustrative purposes. In the education of children their use preceded the teaching of abstract virtues from philosophical books. Eph 5:25–27 is an example of what von Rad calls *rühmendes Nacherzählen* ("admiring narration"; see OTTh, I, 111 etc.). In I Cor 13 (the great Pauline hymn on "love") a Wisdom pattern becomes visible: "Love" is personified and described by one verb after another, not by definition through nouns and adjectives. If the reader of I Cor 13 asks who after all is the person who loves in the manner described by this chapter, Eph 5:25–27 provides the answer: Jesus Christ.

[56] The references to the "blood," "flesh," and "body" of Christ in 2:13–16, combined with the Christological interpretation of the Genesis passage speaking of "one flesh" (5:31–32), show that Paul's Christ-centered doctrine of marriage does not mean sheer spiritualization in the sense of "Platonic love" or asceticism. In I Cor 7:2–9, 25–38 Paul discusses the sexual problem in marriage frankly and without devaluating it, cf. I Peter 3:7.

[57] Cf. Eph 3:17: "firm on the root and foundation of love." Such parentheses may one day be declared glosses. But in this commentary the method of excising troublesome verses or words is not followed. As Eph 5:25–27 is hymnic, the parallelism of members confirms the authenticity of vs. 26b.

or both, and that Paul wanted in passing to emphasize that a spoken word must be added to a material element or a physical action in order to make it a sacrament.[58] See COMMENT IV F for a discussion of the question whether 5:26 must be understood as a reference to baptism. Probably the term "by word" qualifies the whole clause and describes the instrument by which the church is "made holy" and/or "clean." The verbs "making holy" and "making clean" have a cultic meaning originally. So often do they denote the same action that the conclusion can be drawn: they are used interchangeably or as a hendiadys. In turn, sanctification by any means and purification by a ritual bath can include the meaning of "setting apart" and "appropriating for service." Calvin speaks of a "segregation for God." All these observations are based not only on OT evidence (as theological wordbooks show) but also on NT parallels. The OT and the Talmud confirm them and offer a key for explaining Eph 5:26.[59] Obviously, purification is more often connected with the

[58] Augustine (tract. in Ioann. 3 LXXX) said ["Subtract] the word, and what is water except water? But when the word comes to the element the sacrament comes into being, and so it is as much as a visible word"; cf. Thomas Aquinas on Eph 5:26. Luther refers to Eph 5:26 in his Smaller Catechism, Bapt. 3: "Water indeed cannot do the job, but the word of God which is in and by the water, and the faith which trusts in this word of God in the water. Without God's word, water is nothing but water and not baptism, with God's word it is a baptism, that is a water of life full of grace." In his interpretation of Eph 5:26 Calvin warns passionately against the idolatry into which Christians fall when they neglect the primary and indispensable role of the word. Following his Institutio (IV 14:4–14), there also must be a faith corresponding to the word of God if a sacrament is to exert its true force. The necessity and usefulness of the sacrament is, in turn, explained by the fact that God is gracious enough to provide crutches to the imbecility of our faith. Man needs and wants to see and to touch something, not only to hear (Institutio IV 14:1, and commentary on Eph 5:26). Among modern interpreters see esp. R. Schnackenburg, Baptism in the Thought of St. Paul (New York: Herder, 1964), pp. 5–7. The JB version is obscure, "washing with water in a form of words."

[59] Examples of the interchangeability of "sanctifying" and "purifying" are Heb 1:3; 2:11; 9:13–14, 22–23; 10:2, 10, 14; 13:12; I Cor 6:11. In Rev 1:5 var. lect. and 7:14 washing is done through the "blood" of Christ. Titus 2:14 speaks of a "purification" of a people "to be God's own people," referring perhaps to Ezek 37:23: "I will cleanse them, and they will be my people," cf. 16:8–9, and to other biblical passages in which transition from the property of one owner into possession of another was marked by a bath. The tebilah ("bathing") mentioned in Exod 19:10 was understood as a precedent of the proselyte baptism which may have become customary as early as the first century A.D., and perhaps also of the (later?) Jewish baptism into slavery, viz. liberty; see Mekh. Exod 19:10; Bab. Yebamoth 45b–47; StB, I, 102 ff.; Moore, Judaism, I, 332 ff ("There is no suggestion that baptism was a real or symbolical purification," p. 334); W. Brandt, Die jüdischen Baptismen, Giessen: Töpelmann, 1910; F. Gavin, The Jewish Antecedents of the Christian Sacraments, London: SPCK, 1928; W. F. Flemington, The New Testament Doctrine of Baptism (London: SPCK, 1948), pp. 3–12. Instead of "appropriation," the term "transition" may also be used. Passing through water can be a rite de passage and indicate the exit from one dominion and the entrance into a new realm and life, as indeed Israel's passages through the Red [Reed?] Sea and the Jordan indicate: Exod 14–15; Josh 3; cf. Isa 43:2. Perhaps the "salvation through water" in Noah's ark belongs in this context, too: Gen 6–8; I Peter 3:20. According to Bab. Kiddushin [henceforth Kidd.] 2ab—this book title means lit. "Sanctifying"—"appropriation" is the biblical term for marriage, and "sanctification" (or "consecration," as still in Jewish marriage rituals) is its rabbinic equivalent. L. Goldschmidt, Der babylonische Talmud, VI (Berlin: Jüdischer Verlag, 1932), 506, n. 15, believes that this change reveals a revision in the concept of marriage: in the Torah it was a matter of civil law; the rabbis elevated it to the level of a religious ceremony. This explanation may be called into question since the sharp distinction between secular and sacred rites is a modern invention rather than a trait of the Bible. At any rate, in the Talmud the term "sanctify" is explained by "setting the wife apart from all the world, just as a sanctified thing," Kidd. 2b. In I Cor 7:14 the same verb is used to describe what husband and wife do to one another mutually. According to the Talmud, the legality of a betrothal or marriage depends to a large extent not only upon the fulfillment of certain conditions regarding money, marriage contract, and intercourse, but also upon that which a bridegroom "says" to his bride in order to make her his wife. In Kidd. 2b–7b, the function of the right word at the right time is extensively discussed, and this tractate comes again and again back to it (see, e.g. 12b–13a; 60a; 65a). Betrothal or marriage is not valid when the man says only "I am your husband, I am your Lord, I am your betrothed," but they are legal and binding in the private and public spheres when he says, "Be betrothed, be married, be my wife . . . Be united with me, be destined for me, be my help, be my received one, be my counterpart, be my rib, be my attached one, be my complement, be my seized one, be taken" (Kidd. 5b, 6a). Thus post-NT rabbinic utterances can contribute much to elucidating what "purification by a bath" and "sanctification by a word" might mean in Eph 5:26. The question remains open whether Paul was really

use of "water" than with a "word" (for the latter, see John 15:3). Nowhere else in the Bible is it associated with "water" and "word" at the same time.[60] SegB and NTTEV connect the "word" with sanctifying and purifying, rather than with the specific mystery of the water-bath alone. In consequence, in our translation the "word" was drawn to "making holy," and the relative independence of the poetic parallel clause, "made clean by a bath of water," was made visible. Sometimes in Hebrew poetry a corresponding arrangement of words is necessary for an intelligent interpretation.[61] The meaning of the nouns "word" and "water," their instrumental function in the process of sanctification and purification, and the addition in our translation of "[his]" before "word" will be discussed in COMMENTS IV E and F. However, a minor and a major grammatical feature have to be pointed out immediately:

a) It is unlikely that the past (aorist) tense of the Greek participle *katharisās* ("having purified") means that purification precedes sanctification.[62] In hymns, participles can substitute for indicatives or are used alternately, see e.g. 2:14–16. The moment of purification is probably the same as that of sanctification.

b) The aorist subjunctives of the verbs "make holy," "present," and the corresponding telic meaning of the participle "making clean" reveal that Paul speaks about one or several future events intended by and resulting from Christ's love. Thomas Aquinas calls sanctification the effect, cleansing the result, and presentation in glory the goal. While romantic love between two people engaged to be married is oriented toward the future, marital love includes retrospective, if not nostalgic, elements.[63] Why does Paul refer only to the bride-bridegroom relationship between Christ and the church, but avoid specifying Christ as a husband and the church as his wife? Most likely his interest is centered in the creative, futurist character of a bridegroom's love. At any rate, the love of the betrothed pair, Christ and the church, is described as the standard for the married life of a man and a woman.[64] This love is so full of hope that it forgets what lies behind: it is telic, not static; imaginative, not pedantic; self-giving, not devouring; creative, not analytical; passionate—in

---

acquainted with forerunners of those rabbinic-legalistic niceties which were put in writing long after his time. For the time being, the rabbinic materials mentioned here appear to be the closest and best way to explain why the terms "sanctify by a word" and "purify by a bath" occur in a romantic song. If Jewish-Christian and Hellenistic-Christian origins can be distinguished at all, then the song describing the Messiah's love should be attributed to a Jewish-Christian milieu. It is all the more astonishing that this song is used as an argument for the Gentile-Christian readers of Ephesians.

[60] See, e.g. Exod 19:10 (washing of garments at the foot of Mount Sinai); Num 5:16–31; 19; 1QS III 4–12 (water of impurity); Ezek 36:25–29; Zech 13:1; cf. Ps 51:2, 7 (God promises, creates, sprinkles purifying water); II Kings 5:10–14 (Naaman the Syrian washing himself in the Jordan); Lev 14:8–9; 15:5–10, 22, etc.; Heb 10:22; Josephus *c. Ap.* I 282 (ritual washings with water); John 2:6 (water jars for Jewish rites of purification); 3:25 (dispute between disciples of John and a Jew over whether John's baptism is a valid means of purification); 13:10 (a word of Jesus about purity on occasion of the foot-washing).

[61] By letter D. N. Freedman has drawn my attention to the fact that among the four lines of, e.g. Lam 3:56 (a) "Hear my call," (b) "Do not close your ear," (c) "For my relief," (d) "To my outcry," the lines (a) and (c), and (b) and (d) belong together.

[62] Robinson, p. 205, and Abbott, p. 168, acknowledge that, logically, "purifying" at this place precedes "sanctifying." But because in I Cor 6:11 the sequence is reversed ("You were washed, you were sanctified, you were justified"), they declare that "the two are coincident."

[63] Jer 2:2 reflects this fact, when Yahweh says to Jerusalem, "I remember the devotion of your youth, your love as a bride, how you followed me in the wilderness . . ." Cf. Ezek 16:6–14. Jeremiah and Ezekiel presuppose the completed marriage between Yahweh and Jerusalem and denounce the infidelity of Yahweh's partner. But compare the promise of a new and everlasting "betrothal" in Hosea 2:19–20.

[64] As Schlier and others observe.

the sense of uplifting—rather than condescending, compassionate (cf. Ezek 16:3-14). Essential to this love is the "vision" which animates it, the continuous act of creation which reveals its power, and the perfection which emanates from it, as will be shown in more detail in COMMENT IV B C.

27. *to present to himself the church resplendent.* The position of the adjective "resplendent" in the Greek text and the article before "church" indicate that "resplendent" has predicative force. It is not a "splendid church" (comparable to an ideal and dreamlike, beautiful and virtuous, wise and rich girl) whom the Messiah finds and makes his own. Rather his love encounters a *tabula rasa*, if not (as in Yahweh's and Hosea's case) a professional or occasional prostitute (cf. the Samaritan woman in John 4:18 and the woman [Mary Magdalene?] described in Luke 7:36-50). This Bridegroom's love is characterized by the will and power to effect a total transformation. He attributes qualities to the bride which she does not possess of her own. In COMMENT IV C the many meanings inherent in the verb "to present" and in the adjective "resplendent" will be discussed extensively. They encompass seemingly trivial elements of OT and Jewish marriage customs at one extreme, and the highest Christological and ecclesiastical implications at the other.

free from spot or wrinkle or any such thing. Lit. "not having. . . ." The Greek noun *spilos* ("spot," also in II Peter 2:13) occurs only in late Greek and appears to have been used as a synonym of the classical *kēlis*. The latter denotes any blot or defilement on e.g. a person or garment, but also the marks of a disreputable disease which was considered divine punishment.[65] In the LXX the noun *spilos* is never used (though the cognate verb occurs once, in Wisd Sol 16:5), and *kēlis* is found only in Wisd Sol 13:14; II Macc 6:25 to designate a stain in untreated wood, viz. a moral blemish. The word *rytis* ("wrinkle") does not appear elsewhere in the LXX and NT. Since its use is also very rare among classic Greeks and Hellenistic writers,[66] it is amazing that Paul knew and used it at all. In which context or *Sitz im Leben* did he find it? The hymnic character of vss. 25-27 and a poetic line such as, "You are beautiful, my dearest, beautiful without a flaw" (Song of Songs 4:7, NEB),[67] suggest that it stems from a romantic song. But the terms "spot" and "wrinkle" may also be borrowed from a medical book, a beautician's parlor, the slang of the gutter, or a disreputable "house." Or the shock produced by the sight of disfiguring congenital marks or the effects of certain diseases (of venereal or leprous character) may have provided the background.[68] Finally, an allusion may

[65] LSLex, 949 and 1628. *Kēlis* can mean both an innocent congenital mark (*naevus*) and the horrible spots and holes produced in the skin by, e.g. syphilis. Whether *spilos* has a narrower or an equally wide range of meaning is debatable.

[66] E.g. Plato *symposion* 190E, 191A; Aristophanes *Plutus* 1051; Plutarch *moralia* 798D.

[67] The Greek text of Song of Songs uses *mōmon* ("blemish"), not *rytis*. At the end of Eph 5:27 the adjective *amōmos* ("blameless") occurs—perhaps in allusion to the line from Song of Songs which has been used in Catholic exegesis to demonstrate the immaculate conception of Mary, but in actuality this verse expresses the "vision of love" (which will be discussed in COMMENT IV B).

[68] Thomas Aquinas followed the Vulg. version when in his interpretation of Eph 5:27 he referred to Job 16:9[8]: "My wrinkles bear testimony against me." These "wrinkles" are the effect of the same disease as is mentioned in Job 2:7: With God's permission, "Satan afflicted Job with loathsome sores from the sole of his foot to the crown of his head." Among the modern versions of Job 16:9, RSV has "He has shrivelled me up," and M. H. Pope (in AB, vol. 15) "All my woe has wizened me." In each of these translations, as also in the very free version of the Hebrew text in LXX (but not in JB and NEB), it is made patent that the "wrinkles," viz. the shrivelling, are the sign of a disease. Correspondingly, the "smiting" of "girl with a scab" is a way by which Yahweh shows his wrath (Isa 3:17).

be made to the unclean and ugly appearance of a newborn baby,[69] or to the effect of a major operation.[70] Spots or wrinkles or both would be present in either case. The wealth of possibilities to choose from, and the absence of any clear indication as to which would be true to Paul's intention and the earliest reader's comprehension, do not permit the easy solution offered by those who stipulate that "spots" and "wrinkles" are mentioned as signs of old age. They believe that the church in Eph 5:27 is described implicitly as "ever young."[71] But that which Christ removes when he sanctifies, purifies, and glorifies his Bride is most likely the effect of neglect, loneliness, and/or sin, not of old age.[72] Rev 12 and Herm. *vis.* I 2:2 describe a woman splendidly dressed who represents the church in mature, i.e. relatively advanced, age. The rejection of childish and immature behavior in Eph 4:13–14 excludes the possibility that 5:27 supports the idolization of youth. The words "or any such thing" correspond to the English "and so on" or "etc." They seem ill-suited to a poetic line, especially in a love song. However, such an abrupt and generalizing end to an enumeration was also found in 1:21 and 4:31.[73] It occurs in liturgies after the enumeration of angels and saints by name, also in confessions of sin and prayers of intercession. For this reason it does not disprove the working hypothesis that 5:25–27 contains hymnic material.

so that she be holy and blameless. Our translation of the preceding clause, "free from . . . ," has obfuscated the rough change of structure present in the Greek text: in the original, the negative participle construction, (lit.) "not having . . . ," is continued by the finite clause (lit.) "but that she be . . ." If the author (or the original hymnist) had subjected himself to laws of stylistic consistency and beauty he would have said, "but possessing holiness and blamelessness." The impression would have been created of a church which already is free of any defiling blemish, and already possesses what makes her suitable to the Bridegroom. This misunderstanding is avoided by the grammatical *tour de force*:[74] The eschatological future of the church is described, even the perfection promised to her, not a present status or possession.[75] The terms "holy and

---

[69] Especially if it is not at once properly cared for, see Ezek 16:4–5.

[70] According to a myth of the creation of male and female out of the original (hermaphrodite) man, new creatures were at first full of wrinkles (*rytides*). Their skin was like leather put over a shoemaker's last before Zeus told Apollo to straighten it out, see Plato *symp.* 190E, 191A. However, e.g. in Plato *resp.* v 452B the adjective *rysos* ("wrinkled") describes the effect of old age.

[71] Schlier, p. 259 produces no philological evidence for his proposition, *"rytis* is the wrinkle as the sign of old age." He refers to Herm. *vis.* III 12:1; 13:1, 4, i.e. those visions in which indeed the church appears "more youthful" than before, that is, "young and beautiful and joyful." But in *vis.* III 13:4 the "recovery of youth" is attributed to repentant individual believers rather than to the church as a community. Even if Hermas hints at a rejuvenation of the church, this idea cannot be proven to underlie Eph 5:27. Though unconscious of the logical consequence, expositors who insist upon the "youthful" appearance of the church in fact denounce signs of a woman's aging as disgraceful and promote the use of artificial means for hiding the tell-tale marks on the skin. Eph 5:27, however, does not insist upon youth at any price.

[72] Sores much worse than just the phenomena of advancing years had to be removed from Oholah and Oholibah (Ezek 23), also from the Jews and Gentiles described in Rom 1–3; cf. Eph 4:17–19.

[73] "Above every government and authority, power and dominion, and any title bestowed . . ." "Every kind of bitterness, passion, anger, shouting, cursing . . . together with any [other sort of] malice."

[74] Space does not permit the demonstration that, e.g. in Gal 2:4–5 and 2:6 the grammatically inconsistent sentence structures (viz. "broken sentences," called *anokolutha*), serve a similar purpose: if Paul had continued the sentences the way he started, he would have asserted something contrary to his intention. See also his self-correction in Rom 1:11–12. For other broken *hina* clauses, see the NOTE on Eph 5:33b.

[75] However, in 1:7; 2:18; 3:12 the verb *echomen* ("we have" or "we possess") was used in positive assertions describing the present time. Cf. COMMENT IX on 1:3–14.

blameless" are also combined in 1:4 and Col 1:22. Their original meanings, especially in relation to the cultus, have been discussed in the NOTE on "saints" in 1:1 and in COMMENT VII on 1:3–14. Since it is most unlikely that in 5:27 the Bride is described in a sacrificial function, the term *amōmos* ("blameless") alludes here not to a sacrifice but to the verse from Song of Songs which was quoted earlier (4:7).[76] *Hagios* ("holy") is probably substituted for *hagnos* ("pure"); cf. II Cor 11:2: "to present you as a pure bride to the husband."[77] However, it is also possible that allusion is made to the term *hagiazo* in vs. 26 as was illustrated through rabbinical texts in fn. 59. In this case, Christ's will and power "to make holy" is complemented by the promise that the Bride will be "holy."

Since the Bridegroom-Bride relationship between Christ and the church is described in all statements of vss. 25–27, not their marriage (see COMMENT IV), there is no single element in the prototype to which an earthly couple's physical intercourse would form the antitype. In consequence, the slightest reference to the procreation of children is also notably absent. This does not mean that Paul intends to bypass the sexual realm in silence (see vs. 31) or to neglect the parents' responsibility for children (see 6:1–4), but it reveals that the love of husband and wife, for which Christ's love is the source and example, is greater than the mysteries of sex and procreation. Only because it is so great and perfect in itself can it also serve as the basis and sphere for physical *henōsis* ("communion") and the generation of children.

28. *In the same manner also husbands owe it [to God and man] to love their wives for they are their bodies.* This translation is at variance with the vast majority of interpretations found in older and more recent versions and commentaries.[78] The seemingly literal rendition, "So the husbands ought to love their wives as [they love also] their own bodies," is ambiguous, inaccurate, and contrary to the intent of the context.[79] The better MSS have *kai* (meaning

---

[76] Von Allmen, p. 28, n. 1. Sampley's arguments to the contrary (p. 139) are not convincing.

[77] Though *hagnos* is originally a cultic term like *hagios*, it has undergone secularization much more completely than *hagios* ever could. It could describe chastity, innocence, moral purity, and a clean conscience. On the other hand, any bodily disfigurements or handicaps that disqualified a priest for priesthood could be used by a husband, if found on his wife, as grounds for divorce, according to Keth. 72b, 75a. Perhaps already at Paul's time a wife was expected to be as *holy* (in the sense of "whole" or healthy) as a priest.

[78] It was, however, chosen on the basis of such precedents and arguments as were proposed by H. Olshausen (*Biblical Commentary on the New Testament*, V [New York: Shelden, 1858], p. 137); Haupt, p. 229 (". . . als die eure Leiber sind"); Abbott, pp. 170–71 (". . . as being their own bodies"); Dibelius, p. 94 (". . . als wäre die Frau des Mannes Leib"); Best, p. 117 (". . . because they are [part of] their own bodies"); Mussner, p. 150, and von Allmen, p. 27 (similarly); K. Barth, III 4, 134 (". . . as those who have become one body with them"); C. Jordan's *Cottonpatch Version of the Bible* (". . . as though she were you").

[79] The versions of Vulg., KJ, SegB, RSV are *ambiguous* because they do not make clear whether the words "as their own bodies" mean that the wives *are* the bodies of the husbands, or are to be loved as much as the husbands love their physical bodies. Outspoken and clear, though *arbitrary*, are the interpretations found in JB, NEB, NTTEV which suggest that man's love of his body is analogous to the expected love for his wife. *Contrary* to the argument of the whole context are all versions which in effect dethrone Christ from his unique position as the source, measure, and judge of marital love, and introduce a second, competing standard, even man's natural self-love. Thomas Aquinas had no qualms in seeing Christological and Natural Law arguments peacefully combined and finally complemented by an appeal to a command of Holy Writ. It may indeed be asked: Does not Paul, by his references (a) to the creation story in vs. 31, and (b) to the effect of fornication, I Cor 6:16, reveal that he conceives the love relationship between a male and a female and its effect as relatively independent of Christ's love for the church? In actuality, both passages answer in the negative: Paul, for one, understands Gen 2:24 as a testimony to Christ and the church (Eph 5:32); and the conduct chastised in I Cor 6:12–20 is sin and perversion, a travesty of the union in one *flesh*, precisely because it is irreconcilable with a saint's *belonging* to Christ.

in this sentence "also" or "too") before "husbands."[80] This *kai* makes unmistakably clear that the word *houtōs* ("so," "in the same manner") at the beginning of vs. 28 points back to the love of Christ described in vss. 25–27, not forward to an egotistic love.[81] Only if *kai* were placed before "bodies" (*somāta*), would this verse clearly affirm that husbands must love their wives, as (or because) they "love also their bodies."[82] Actually the position of *kai* indicates clearly that the husband is compared with Christ, and his love with Christ's (as in vs. 25), not husbandly love with a man's (natural) love of his own body. Paul does not depreciate the husband's love by measuring it with the stick of natural egotism and by subjecting the wife to her husband's untamed selfishness. It is not only the position of *kai* which calls for this conclusion: after a quote (see, e.g. Rom 11:5) *houtōs* has in addition to its comparative meaning a causal one, as if to say, "therefore," or "on the strength of the event or argument just mentioned." Both the questions how and why are answered.[83] In turn, the word *hōs* (lit. "as") before "their bodies" need not introduce a clause which strictly corresponds to a preceding *houtōs* sentence, but can point out a logical conclusion. This is the case in vs. 28. After the cause, quality, and totality of the husband's love has been described by the reference to the glorious, unique, and powerful originator and model, Jesus Christ, the perfect lover (vss. 25–27), the effect of such love upon the beloved is now described. What is a wife in the presence and under the impact of love abounding? She *is* her loving husband's body, "her husband's *alter ego*" (Schlier)— just as the people chosen and loved by Christ are "members of his [Christ's] body" (5:30). Paul will quote in vs. 31 an OT text (Gen 2:24) which confirms this description of the effect of love.[84] Instead of calling the wife her husband's "body," he might equally well have called her his soul,[85] for in the Bible neither

[80] Papyrus 46, the Codices Vaticanus, Alexandrinus, Claramontanus, and Boernerianus, Minuscule 33, the Latin versions. However, Codex Sinaiticus, the MSS of the Antiochian (Koine) group, and the Syro-Palestinian version omit *kai*. The editors of GNT consider the omission of *kai* so improbable that they do not even mention the variant represented by the last-mentioned groups of texts.

[81] *Houtōs* usually points backward—though it can also point forward, as in, e.g. I Cor 3:15; 4:1; Eph 5:33. Abbott observes with good reason that the presence of *kai* in 5:28 forces the interpreter to understand *houtōs* as pointing to vss. 25–27.

[82] Or, "as they first of all love their own bodies." Cf. vs. 25, lit. "just as also Christ has loved the church."

[83] Best, p. 177, and Mussner, p. 150.

[84] Another OT precedent which, however, might not have been susceptible to an interpretation such as that given in 5:32, is found in Job 2:5–9. After Satan had received permission to touch and destroy all of Job's possessions, including his children, he asks for authority to touch also his "bone" and his "flesh." The whole body of Job is covered with loathsome sores—but that is not enough: even his wife turns against him, "Curse God and die." The permission granted for damaging the physical body of Job apparently included permission to turn his wife against him. She was considered his "bone" and his "flesh" as much as his physical body, or rather, as its epitome. Sir 25:26 contains another parallel: A bad woman must be "cut off from" the husband's "flesh" (see the LXX text).

[85] There are OT and NT passages that speak of a union of the soul(s) of different people, and one NT text mentions the oneness of the spirit: according to Gen 34:3 "Shechem's soul was drawn to Dinah" because "he had delight in Jacob's daughter" (vs. 19). "The soul of Jonathan was knit to the soul of David and Jonathan loved him as his own soul" (I Sam 18:1; the words "as his own soul" correspond amazingly to [lit.] "as their own bodies," Eph 5:28). "He who is united to the Lord becomes one spirit with him" (I Cor 6:17). "Those who believed were one heart and one soul" (Acts 4:32). Pedersen, *Israel*, I–II, 265, 285 etc., has shown that in ancient Israel entering a covenant meant to become one flesh, and that oneness of flesh included unity in spirit. According to Josephus *c. Ap.* II 25, in physical intercourse the soul is shared with the partner; this is why an ablution must follow upon intercourse. In all these cases the unity of body *and* soul is presupposed. When there is only unity of bodies, the essence of union is denied, see Ignatius *Pol.* v 1; Bailey, pp. 43–44, 51–53; K. Barth, III 4, 134–35. Von Hattingberg, pp. 301, 310, refers to a German

body nor flesh have a necessarily derogatory meaning. Since in Ephesians and Colossians the church title "body of Christ" is honorific, the description of the wife as the husband's "body," and the invitation to love this "body," mean glorification (cf. vs. 27), not devaluation. The resumption of the Christological argument by Paul in vss. 29b–32 shows clearly that the apostle had nothing else in mind—least of all a husband-wife relationship which would be a parallel to the soul-body relationship postulated by Plato, Aristotle, and the Stoics.[86] The apostle wants to show how creative love is. The loving man and the beloved woman "become one flesh." Only through the event of Christ's love did the Gentiles become members of the same body (3:6). In the same way, only through love do a man and a woman become so intimately one that the husband can call her "his body," and his love for her, love for his body. A man does not bring this body into marriage; outside the union with one woman, he does not know what love for that "body" is; he does not know or possess in himself the power to love as he is entitled to love. Rather this body, this oneness, this love is a gift he receives. He knows of this gift because he knows Christ and his love. He finds the same gift confirmed in marriage. In short, Paul is unable to describe marital love without speaking of Christ's miraculous gift.

owe it [to God and man]. The Greek verb opheilousin has a more specific meaning than the vague English "ought." In secular Greek, opheilō means originally that something has to be paid back to a deity or a man. Combined with an infinitive (as in Eph 5:28) the verb can describe a moral obligation. Among the Greek moral philosophers, general duties that exist by nature or correspond to the supreme virtues are introduced by formulae such as prepon or kathēkon ("it is fitting"). Opheilō and its derivates ("to owe," "debtor," "debt") have in moral treatises a more personal character.[87] In the LXX, the term "owing" is rare; even then it reproduces a Hebrew equivalent only when expressing financial obligation, not the effect of a divine command. But in Philo's writings this concept, and among post-tannaitic rabbis an Aramaic equivalent (hūb), was chosen (most likely because of their legal connotation) to describe man's moral obligation to God, the Law, and sacred customs. The Bible never uses a term corresponding to English "duty" or German Pflicht, for this Prussian-Kantian concept is foreign to its ethics. Paul, however, employs "owing" and its cognates in every one of their various meanings: to describe a financial debt, taxes, and rewards owed;[88] for conduct in accordance with Jewish and Christian standards of decency and law,[89] including those concerning

saying, "In his wife the husband loves his own soul." He understands this to mean that man "makes the soul his highest value" and "puts the female nature above himself as his ideal"—hoping to "be drawn upward through the eternal feminine." Without anticipating the idealistic features of the Germanic (Goethean) yearning, Paul certainly does respect the singular dignity of the wife by calling her the husband's "body."

[86] See the NOTE on "is the husband the head of his wife" in vs. 23. So far only one book has come to my attention which dares to swim against the stream of the traditional scholarly association of Pauline with Aristotelian-Stoicist ethics: N. W. DeWitt, St. Paul and Epicurus, Minneapolis: University of Minnesota Press, 1954. However, this book does not discuss Paul's teaching on marriage.

[87] According to F. Hauck's description of their use among Stoics in TWNTE, V, 560. See also fn. 24 on 5:3.

[88] Philem 18; Rom 13:7; 4:4.   [89] Gal 5:3; I Cor 7:36; 9:10; 11:7, 10; Eph 5:28.

marital and parental obligations,[90] gratitude,[91] and the responsibility for the weak (Rom 15:1).[92] In Rom 13:8 the apostle makes a pun on the financial and moral meanings of the same term "owing": "Owe no one anything, except to love one another." In some cases (as in Eph 5:28) the spiritual ground of the debt is explicitly mentioned: it consists of a deed of God. Elsewhere no cause or motivation is explicitly named.[93] Since the context of Eph 5:28 speaks of the love of Christ and its effect, not of a law or custom, this passage does not prescribe what "ought" to be done for reasons unknown or according to some general standard of decency, but urges an attitude and acts of recognition, gratitude, and public attestation. The love of the husband for his wife is a necessary, voluntary, joyful, and public affirmation of the love of Christ for his body, the church.[94]

In loving his wife a man loves himself. Lit. "He who loves. . . ." P. W. Schmiedel (quoted in Nestle) considered these words an interpolation; Schlier, a parenthetical insertion of proverbial origin.[95] While it is indeed possible that a proverb is taken up that expressed (perhaps in a humorous tone) a pleasant, if not typically male and egotistic, aspect of marriage, this sentence has a special function in the present context: its truth is founded in Christ rather than in nature or common experience, as the following verses will show. The formulation "loves himself" is specifically important for a linguistic, traditio-historical, and logical reason: (a) the pronoun "himself" is used as a synonym of "his own body" (vs. 28a) and of "flesh" (vss. 29, 31).[96] There is obviously no depreciative overtone present when any of these three synonyms are used here. (b) In this verse, and even more in vs. 33 ("love . . . as himself"), Paul may have consciously alluded to Lev 19:18 and 34, "You shall love your neighbor as yourself. . ." "The stranger . . . you shall love him as yourself." The apostle may have known an early form of that rabbinic tradition which

---

[90] I Cor 7:3–5; II Cor 12:14. According to Mekh. Exod 21:10 a husband "owes" his wife food, clothing, and cohabitation. Keth. 47b–48a adds redemption from captivity and a funeral. A standard for the frequency of intercourse was set up according to the professional occupation of the husband: Berak 22a; Keth. 62b; see also StB, III, 368–71. According to Plutarch (*moralia* 769A) Solon had prescribed to the men of Athens a minimum of three times per month. While Victorian language speaks with preference of the marital "duty" of the woman, Paul enfolds in I Cor 7:3–5 the *mutual* indebtedness of husband and wife. In Eph 5:28, however, he speaks—much as the rabbis—only of the debt owed by the husband, probably to God, Christ, the church, and all those entitled to perceive the testimony of the church, rather than to his wife alone.

[91] II Thess 1:3; 2:13; Rom 15:27.

[92] Among non-Pauline epistles, those under the name of John speak of "owing" sanctification, sacrifice of the self, brotherly love, hospitality; see I John 2:6; 3:16; 4:11; III John 8.

[93] Cf. Rom 1:14; 8:12; 15:3, 27 with I Cor 5:10; 9:10; II Cor 12:11.

[94] The missionary character of the marital love described by Paul is emphatically pointed out by Bieder, pp. 60–64; cf. K. Barth, III 4, 224–39. The hiddenness, seclusion, and privacy of a lovers' nest does not exempt marriage from a public function to be fulfilled in human society.

[95] In Prov 31:10–31 not just the virtues of a good wife, but also the "husband's gain" from possessing a good wife are extensively described: ". . . He will have no lack of gain. She does him good . . . Her husband is known in the gates." One of the many rabbis by the name of Eleazar said, "A man not having a wife is no man." Rabbi Tanchum ben Chamilai (ca. A.D. 280) declared, "A man not having a wife lives without joy, without blessing, without kindness." She is created as a helper though sometimes she fails to be a help. But even a bad woman bears her husband children, educates them, and keeps him from sin, Bab. Yeb. 62b–63b. Good fortune and riches are sometimes equated with having a prepared bed and a well behaved wife, Shabbath 25b. The schechina dwells where there are both, a man and a woman, MidrR Gen 17:3. God is praised because he created man male and female, so that there would be a loving pair, Keth. 8a.

[96] E.g. by Bultmann, ThNT, I, 192–203, esp. 196, also 229–30, the interchangeability of body, flesh, self, person is pointed out, but attention is also drawn to those passages in Paul where "flesh" is sharply distinguished from "body." According to, e.g. I Cor 15:50 "flesh" cannot inherit the kingdom of God, but man given a new "body" will enter it. See COMMENTS VI B on 1:15–23 and II on 2:1–10, also fn. 185 to 1:15–23, and fn. 101 below.

perhaps applied Lev 19 to marriage and praised highly the man "who loves his wife as himself and honors her more than himself" (Yebamoth 62b). In COM-MENT V B the "as yourself" formula and its various interpretations will be discussed. (c) In Eph 5:25-33 Paul's thought does not ascend from love of self to love for one's wife, and from there to love of Christ. Rather his logic goes in the opposite direction: from the love shown by Christ (vss. 25-27), he descends to the love shown for the wife, and he ends with the love of the husband for "himself."[97] Natural man's selfish inclination to do himself every favor is not the ground or measure of a husband's love.[98] Rather true love for his wife will not be wasted but will carry its reward in kind. Paul might have quoted Song of Songs 8:10: the beloved woman is to her lover "as one who brings peace." Or he might have paraphrased and applied a saying of Jesus, "He who loses his life" in so loving his wife as Christ loves the church, "will gain it" (Matt 10: 39). Certainly the apostle knows that "love does not seek its own advantage" (or "is not selfish," I Cor 13:5). But he also recognizes the effect of love upon the lover. Just as the Messiah presents "to himself" a perfect bride (Eph 5:27), so the husband will receive by giving. Love is from above. It is grace.

29. *For no one ever hates his own flesh.* Lit. "for no one ever has hated." The aorist tense of the Greek verb *miseō* ("hate") contrasts with the present tense of "provides" and "cares" in the next clause. The discrepancy is easily explained and can be glossed over even in a literal translation: a "gnomic aorist" is used which occurs frequently in generalizing (or proverbial) statements in Greek.[99] Several authors insist that the conjunction "for" links vs. 29 with 28a, not with 28b.[100] Their opinion is valid if vs. 28b is a conjecture or marginal gloss. In that case Paul would have intended to say, "Since as husbands you feed yourselves to the best of your capacities, you may or must include your wives in that process; this will be true love." The banality and absurdity of this thought can hardly be surpassed. If some interpreters believe such was Paul's way of reasoning, their belief speaks against themselves rather than against the apostle. Actually, no MS exists in which vs. 29 follows immediately upon vs. 28a, and it is more natural to relate the word "for" in vs. 29 to 28b than to 28a. In turn, vs. 29a points forward to (and is logically dependent upon) the Christological statements that follow: vss. 29 and 30 are a unit in which "Christ's" love for "his" flesh (i.e. his body, the church) is declared the source and standard of marital love. Man's natural urges and the means employed to still or satisfy them cannot take Christ's place. Abbott's interpretation, as reproduced in the NOTES to vs. 28, leads to the conclusion that the words "his own flesh" denote the husband's wife in vs. 29, not man's stomach, sexual drive, need of a home base, help and comfort, etc. After she was called

---

[97] According to H. Weidinger, p. 62, self-love is "not important" in this context, but only Christ's and the husband's love for their respective partners. The opinion of S. Freud that ego-libido and object-libido are antithetical is contradicted by R. May, pp. 83-84: "When I fall in love I feel *more* valuable and treat myself with more care."

[98] Abbott. The Talmud and Midrash passages quoted in fn. 95 show how, among Jews, love and marriage were attributed to the good will and gift of God. No Jew would dare say that in marriage a man's selfish love is applied to the woman and gloriously justified. While Greeven, *Theologie der Ehe*, p. 78, believes that in Eph 5 Paul wants to describe love as a "natural" thing, it is unlikely that Paul really intended to make nature or self-love the basis of marital love.

[99] BDF, 333:1.

[100] Haupt, p. 129; Best, p. 177.

"his own body" in vs. 28a, she is now called "his own flesh."[101] The transition from "body" to the synonym "flesh" is best explained by the intended use of the Genesis text in 5:31. The quotation from Gen 2:24, including the longer quotation found in variant readings of vs. 30, illustrates only why man and woman are "one flesh" but makes no contribution toward linking self-love and self-care with the husband's love. In the light of Gen 2:(23-)24, Eph 5:29 avers that no one ever hates his wife considering that she is his body and that love of her is love of the self. In the absence of this consideration there was, is, and will be alienation, hostility, hatred—as there also was, is, and will be enmity between Jews and Gentiles when and where Christ's work for peace is belied. But when Christ's care for the church and the union of diverse people in "one body" is the model, then the wife will be esteemed as the husband's "own flesh," and "hating" will have no place. Certainly the "gnomic aorist" emisēsen (lit. "has hated") can indicate that vs. 29a contains a proverb, or a continuation of the proverbial saying found in vs. 28b. In its original form the second (half of the?) proverb probably had nothing to do with the Hebrew concept of "one flesh" and Paul's Christological interpretation of Gen 2:24. But what was and looks like banal common sense is placed by Paul in a very elevated context and used with a purpose that is at variance with the (presumed) original statement.[102]

but he provides and cares for it. Strictly speaking the words "no one" ought here to have been complemented by a new pronoun, e.g. by "but everybody. . . ." When indeed in vs. 33 the opposite of "no one" is explicitly mentioned, Paul uses the words, "one by one, each one of you" (*hymeis hoi kath' hena hekastos*). The specification, "each one of *you*," may reveal that as early as vs. 29a "no one" (and his opposite ["everybody"] in 29b) means not necessarily each male and female on earth, but foremost (or exclusively?) the saints, and among them, the married men (but see below, fn. 113). The origin

---

[101] Abbott, pp. 170–71; Dibelius, p. 95; Best, p. 177. The exchangeability of the terms as mentioned in fn. 96 is evident in, e.g. I Cor 6:15–16; 15:39–40; II Cor 4:10–11; also II Cor 12:7 compared with Gal 6:17.

[102] This exposition makes superfluous the apologetic devices chosen by Thomas Aquinas, Bengel, Haupt and others, to demonstrate that vs. 29a contradicts neither the Bible nor careful observation of individual behavior. They mention a series of potential and actual exceptions to the statement, "No one ever hates his own flesh," and observe that Paul himself battles against his body and flesh (Rom 7:7–25), or, that all Christians, because of the shameful "works of the flesh," have to "crucify the flesh with its passions and desires" (Gal 5:19–21, 24). Since among the Jews the term "flesh" includes the senses, the relatives, or the self of man, the prohibition against hating one's own flesh in Eph 5:29 seems flatly to contradict Luke 14:26—the text according to which Jesus expects that for his sake "father, mother, wife, children, brothers, sisters, even the own soul be hated." In turn, the rich farmer who appears to love his flesh when he finds delight in food and drink, is headed for death (rather than for exemplary husbandry) according to Luke 12:19–21. "He who finds his life will lose it" (Matt. 10:39). Only by denying himself, by prayer and fasting, can a man become a disciple of Jesus and can evil be swept out (Mark 8:34; 9:29). On the basis of Matt 19:12 Origen took drastic steps against his own body. Many ascetics, flagellants, mystics found ways to obey the command of Col 3:5, i.e. to "kill the members" of their bodies, together "with their evil desires." Luther's attitude to his own body which he called a *Madensack* ("bag of maggots") was anything but friendly. Uncounted suicides are motivated by self-hatred. The solutions offered for such contradictions against the wording of Eph 5:29a include the following arguments: (a) In Eph 5:29a Paul describes the normal and natural behavior of man; self-hatred is against nature. (b) The self-love (which is also mentioned in Lev 19:18: "Love your neighbor as yourself") undergoes correction and purification whenever it is confronted with God's command. (c) Not in itself is the flesh hateful, but only by accident, i.e. under the impact of sin. (d) He who corrects his self-love by disciplining his flesh and subjecting it to the Spirit, does not really hate himself but also acts out of a superior love: "For me it is good to adhere to my God" (Ps 73:28). See esp. Thomas Aquinas' commentary on Eph 5 and *Summa Theol.* II ii 25, 4, 7; 26, 13 ad 3. Cf. COMMENT V B.

and meaning of the verbs "providing" and "caring" can be explained in at least four different ways: (a) They describe a father's, mother's, nurse's, etc., care for children.[103] The way in which the Foster Father and Bridegroom Yahweh treats the foundling girl Jerusalem (Ezek 16:1–14) shows which details of caring for the baby, child, and adolescent were repeated when a bride was washed, fed, and dressed up in splendor. (b) The terms "provide" and "care" may allude to a formula of Jewish or to pagan marriage contracts.[104] (c) The terms individually or jointly can have cosmological and political meaning. Sometimes they describe the heavenly All-Father or Head as he cares for his body, the cosmos—or a king who is a benefactor to his subjects.[105] (d) The choice of these terms may have been dictated by him whom Paul proclaims as the archetype of the head-body and husband-wife relationship: Christ who provides sustenance (*epichoregeo*) to the church (Eph 4:16b). Since he nourishes the church by, e.g. the festival "supper" offered at his "table" (I Cor 10:21; 11:20), the verbs "care" and "provide" have been interpreted as alluding to the eucharist.[106] These four interpretations are not mutually exclusive. The first three are supported by earlier statements in Ephesians where the saints were called "children" or "babes" (1:5; 4:14); the bride of Christ (5:25–27); "citizens" in his kingdom and inhabitants of the Father's "house" (2:11–19). The last has supporting parallels in the immediate context only if it can be demonstrated that 5:30–31 speaks of the eucharist,[107] and/or that 5:26 and 32 complement the sacramental meaning of 5:29 by references to the sacraments of baptism and marriage respectively. See COMMENTS IV F, VI C, and VII B for arguments in favor of and against this interpretation.

29–30. *just as the Messiah for the church, because we are the members of his body.* For the third time in this unit (cf. vss. 23 and 25) the words "just as the Messiah"[108] are found in the second half of a statement. Here as much as before they describe the Messiah's action and attitude as the model and cause of the action and attitude expected of each husband, rather than as their mere exemplification. The words "because we are members of his body" resemble 4:25, "for we are members of one body." But while 4:25 recalled those passages in the undisputed Pauline letters that designated the church as a "body" without speaking of Christ the "head,"[109] 5:30 reiterates the doctrine of

[103] In Eph 6:4 the first verb occurs in the sense of "bringing up children"; in I Thess 2:7 Paul uses the second to compare himself with a "nurse taking care of her children." See Best, p. 178, n. 1. Both terms are found nowhere else in the NT, but several times in the LXX.
[104] See fn. 90 for an enumeration of things "owed" by the Jewish husband even when they were not specified in writing. Jewish and pagan marriage contracts contained additional stipulations.
[105] Pertinent passages from, e.g. the Leiden Papyrus v and xii, and from the Acts of Thomas have been collected by Schlier, pp. 260–61, n. 4; *Christus*, pp. 59, 70–71.
[106] See Justin Martyr *apol.* i 66:1; also, e.g. Calvin; Schlier; Baltensweiler, p. 230. In his exegesis of 5:29 Calvin affirms with great passion that the Lord's Supper is a "mystical communication with Christ," in which "his substance is communicated to us" so that "we grow into one body with him," cf. I Cor 10:16–17. Calvin declined to follow those Reformation theologians (e.g. Zwingli) who celebrated the sacraments as a mere "commemoration of Christ's death." Best, p. 178, however, puts the eucharistic interpretation of Eph 5:29 into question. For only the term "provide" (*ektrepho*) can be used for its support, not the verb "care" (*thalpo*).
[107] Theodoret, Theophylact, Calvin and, among more recent interpreters, esp. Olshausen, *Biblical Commentary*, pp. 138–40.
[108] Lit. "just as also," or "just as even," or "just as only the Messiah"; see the first NOTE on vs. 23 for the omission in our translation of Greek *kai*.
[109] Rom 12:5; I Cor 10:17; (11:29?); 12:12 ff.; cf. Eph 4:4. However, I Cor 6:15; 11:3; 12:27 show that forerunners of the Ephesians-Colossians doctrine are present even in the homologoumena. See COMMENT VI B on Eph 1:15–23 and esp. E. Käsemann, *Leib und Leib Christi*, Tübingen: Mohr, 1933.

the body of Christ which is peculiar to Ephesians and Colossians. Christ, the head, is present in the body and manifested by it, as he gives it life, unity, and direction.[110] In 5:30 the emphasis lies on the fact that the church as body is his and no one else's,[111] and therefore enjoys the effect of love described in vs. 28. What is this effect? The lover is so closely united with his beloved that his love of her can be called love of himself. But couldn't this idea have been expressed by the wording, just as the Messiah (provides and cares) for "his body, the church," or for the "church which is his body,"[112] without reference to the (individual) "members"? According to Dibelius, the author alludes to the creation of woman from Adam's "flesh and bones" (cf. 5:30 var. lect.), but Best's (p. 178) suggestion may be more accurate: Paul wanted to assert that what is valid for the church as a whole also benefits "each one" of the saints. Thus nothing is asked of husbands that has not first been realized in the church for the benefit of each saint. "One by one, each one" of them (vs. 33) can perform—not because they must or ought to, but because "they are members of Christ's body." When the question is asked, how did they become such members, the early chapters of Ephesians answer: because and when they were beloved and chosen in Christ, resurrected and enthroned together with him, enlightened and marked by the Spirit, etc. So far no explicit reference has been made to the eucharist in this epistle, though in I Cor 10:16–17 the eucharist's indispensable function in the formation of the "one body" is mentioned. It is, therefore, unlikely that Eph 5:30 suddenly and cryptically alludes to that meal. Lacking is any reference to the eating of, or partaking in, one body, also to the drinking of a cup (cf. I Cor 10:16–17; 11: 24–26); instead of the mention of "flesh and bones" of Christ (as made in the variant reading of 5:30 that is soon to be discussed), only a reference to Christ's flesh "and blood" would have suggested or supported the eucharistic interpretation. Chrysostom, Thomas Aquinas and others have offered an alternative in seeing a reference to the incarnation in vs. 30. But Abbott objects, on the grounds that the variant reading of vs. 30 does not say Christ is "from our flesh." The better text of vs. 30 describes being, not becoming, and speaks of a result of grace, not its means. The complete and solid foundation of all worship is pointed out, not an ever repeatable cultic mystery action (cf. Heb 5–10). Because and just as formerly divided and hostile Jews and Gentiles were united in "one body" (2:16; 3:6; 4:4 etc.), the difference between male and female is no hindrance for husband and wife to be united by love in one body. Thus vs. 30 is the crown and key of the whole argument in vss. 28–29. These three verses do not add a peculiar argument from natural law or human selfishness to the Christological reasoning of vss. 23–27. Certainly 5:30 must not be treated as an

---

[110] Eph 1:22–23; 4:15–16; 5:23. Robinson, p. 126 believes that in vs. 28 Paul has turned away from the argument of *head*ship to the thought of complete oneness. In his attempt to separate these points, Robinson forgets that in 1:10, 22–23; cf. 2:11–22 the function of creating and sustaining unity is attributed precisely to the one *head*.

[111] As Mussner, p. 151 points out.

[112] In Col 1:18 the shorter; in Eph 1:22–23 the slightly longer formulation is used. Bengel believes that in 5:30 "body" means "the body of Christ himself," not the church. Though this distinction was considered in the exegesis of 2:16 and may be decisive for understanding I Cor 12:12, it does not throw light on 5:30.

irrelevant pious gloss, which was added to "Christianize" (Dibelius) a basically Jewish or pagan teaching on marriage.[113]

In a large group of early MSS, Eph 5:30 continues with the words "from his flesh and from his bones."[114] These words are an (inexact) allusion to the "bones" and "flesh" of Adam out of which Eve was made; see Gen 2:21–23. According to current philological criteria of textual criticism, these words must be considered a later addition to the original text.[115] The wealth of contradictory interpretations produced by those who defend authenticity demonstrate that 5:30 var. lect. does more to obfuscate the context than to clarify it. See COMMENT VI A.

31. *For this reason.* Though no quotation formula is used either before or within vs. 31, the whole verse is a quotation from Gen 2:24. Perhaps the reason for omitting a citation formula lies in the fact that the beginning of the Genesis text itself resembles such a formula and fulfills its function.[116] Most likely the quotation was intended to be literally exact and true.[117] Yet it differs in several minor ways from the Greek OT which is presupposed in Jesus' quote from the same text, according to Matt 19:5 and Mark 10:7. It is also different from the MSS from which today's LXX editions are made. The actual divergences, the role of Gen 2:24 in the OT, in Jewish and early Christian interpreta-

---

[113] There is as yet no master key for deciding whether 5:30 means that the whole context (i.e. Paul's teaching on marriage, education, masters and slaves) is meant to apply only to those human relationships in which all participants were Christians. An explicit exclusion of pagan couples is nowhere indicated. While the discussions of the master-slave relation in Philemon, perhaps also in the *Haustafeln* of Ephesians and Colossians, presuppose that both the masters and slaves believed in the Lord, I Cor 7:16 recalls the missionary opportunity offered in mixed marriages. Since Paul affirms (e.g. in Eph 1:10, 19–23; Col 1:15–20) that Christ's rule is extended far beyond the confines of the church, and since he appeals to the very creation of man and woman in 5:31, not to their conversion, he may have been willing to call this or that pagan husband of a pagan wife as much an imitator of God, as the authors of Genesis, Isaiah, and Job described Melchisedek, Cyrus, and Job as servants of God. Cf. J. Daniélou, *Holy Pagans of the Old Testament,* London: Longmans, 1957. Particularist Christological statements such as "Christ—the savior of his body" (vs. 23) do not invalidate universalistic utterances such as: "to comprehend under one head all things, those in heaven and upon earth" (1:10). Paul's teaching directed to "saints" (each one "of you," vs. 33) does not discount that the blessings and attitudes described in Eph 5 may be as real in mixed and pagan marriages as among Christians, or even more so. Since Paul's ethics share the international character of Wisdom literature (described in COMMENT X on 1:3–14 and made explicit in 5:15 ff.), the conclusion is inescapable that on the basis of his Christology he might have subscribed to I. Kant's "categorical imperative."

[114] The majority is constituted by the overwhelming number of the majuscule (uncial) and the Byzantine minuscule codices, the Latin and Syrian versions, most Greek and Latin fathers, and the Lectionaries. The minority which omits the reference to Christ's "flesh and bones," consists of Papyrus 46, the original script of Codex Sinaiticus, the Codices Alexandrinus and Vaticanus, and a few minuscules, the Ethiopian and some Coptic versions, the Latin edition of Origen, and the texts used by Methodius (third century), Euthalius (fifth century) and Ps.-Jerome (fifth century). Only the ninth-century Codex K reads, from his flesh and "his mouth"—an obvious error of a copyist.

[115] See Abbott's extensive argument. If the words contained in the variant readings had been authentic, it is unlikely that any copyist would ever have omitted them (Best, p. 178). But their addition has the effect that the actual quote from Gen 2:24 in Eph 5:31 is anticipated by a (less than exact) allusion to Gen 2:23 in Eph 5:30. Dibelius and Chavasse (p. 74) agree in stating that the addition is in harmony with the intent of the author of Ephesians. Schlier sees in it an early anti-Gnostic gloss directed against a teaching such as described by Irenaeus *adv. haer.* v 2:3.

[116] Compare, e.g. *dioti* ("for," "therefore": Rom 3:20); *menoun ge* ("rather," "on the contrary": Rom 10:18); *houtos gar* ("for this": Heb 7:1); *eti gar* ("for still": Heb 10:37).

[117] It is unlikely that Paul personally possessed and carried with him on his travels a scroll or codex of each OT book, though he may have owned some (II Tim 4:13). For study and for the composition of his letters, he probably attempted to use (if or as long as permitted) in diaspora synagogues and Jewish schools a Hebrew text, an Aramaic Targum, or a Greek version. He may have also possessed or used a typical collection of OT quotes resembling either the brief *Florilegium* found in Qumran Cave IV, or the Testimonia postulated by J. R. Harris, *Testimonies,* 2 vols., Cambridge University Press, 1916, 1920; cf. C. H. Dodd, *According to the Scriptures* (New York: Scribner's, 1953), pp. 28–60. Finally, he may have quoted from memory, drawing on what he had learned as a student, or on a liturgical version of a text used in the temple or in synagogues. Reasons for assuming that Paul meant to quote exactly will become apparent in the following NOTES.

tions, and the special sense which Paul discovered in this text or which is attributed to Paul's exegesis, will be discussed in COMMENT VI. Here we must
ask what is the logical referent of the conjunction "for this reason" (or "therefore," *anti toutou*). There are four possibilities:

a) Gen 2:24 itself refers back to the creation of Eve out of Adam, and to
Adam's joyous recognition of her as part of himself (Gen 2:21–23). Scholars
speak of an "aetiology" when a present name, situation, or custom is explained
by means of telling a primeval story. The introduction formula (in this case, the
conjunction "therefore," Heb. *al-kēn*) is a mark by which, in Gen 2 and elsewhere, an aetiology is recognized.[118] Since the quote from Gen 2:23 in Eph 5
appears not to belong to the original text of Ephesians, here the words "for this
reason" cannot have the same aetiological function which they had originally in
Gen 2:24. However, the insertion of elements from Gen 2:23 into Eph 5:30
may have been motivated by the attempt to maintain the original sense of the
introductory formula.

b) In Matt 19:5 and Mark 10:6–7 an allusion to Gen 1:27 ("he created them
male and female") precedes the quote from Gen 2:24. Thus in the Gospels the
words "for this reason"[119] receive a meaning which originally they did not
have. Their logical sense now is, man leaves his father and mother in order
to follow his wife, *because* God created them male and female.[120] In this
combination of the first with the second account of man's creation, according
to the Synoptics Jesus followed the same tendency toward harmonization which
can also be recognized in Philo and rabbinic writings, and later among Gnostic
writers—though what they said about the heavenly and earthly Adam, the
original bisexuality, the eventual separation or alienation, and the final reunion
of man is radically distinct from Jesus' interpretation. See COMMENTS VI B
and VII A for some examples. In Eph 5, however, no reference is made to the
first creation account. Here the words "for this reason" cannot point to the
creation of man as male and female after God's image.

c) In the prophetic books of the OT, *al-kēn* ("therefore," "for this reason")
is a regular element of "prophetic announcements of judgment" which follow
upon evil deeds previously spelled out. While aetiological passages, after the introduction "therefore," can have the verb in the past, present, or future tenses
without implying a strictly past, present, or futurist meaning, the prophets
speak often of a judgment that is to come. Yet Gen 2:24 did not originally
speak only of the future. Expositors of Eph 5:31 who press the future tenses
of the verbs "leave," "join," "become" (one flesh), and who see in this verse a
prediction of Christ's parousia and the future marriage of the lamb as is described in Rev 19:7–8; 21:2, 9, tacitly assume that the words "for this reason"
mean the same as in prophetic oracles and interpret Eph 5:31 as a futuristic

---

[118] E.g. "Therefore to this day the name of that place is called the Valley of Achor": Josh
7:26; "therefore to this day the Israelites do not eat the sinew of the hip": Gen 32:32; see also
Gen 10:9; 26:33. In many other aetiologies, e.g. Gen 3:14–19, "therefore" is not used. B. O. Long,
The Problem of Etiological Narrative in the Old Testament, BhZAW, 1968, discusses Gen 2:18–24
on pp. 53–54: not only the "name" woman, but the sexual attraction between man and woman is
explained by the aetiology.

[119] The Gospels and LXX have *heneken toutou*, not the synonym *anti toutou*. The latter is the
version of Heb. *al-kēn* given in Ephesians.

[120] Rather than, because Eve was taken from Adam. See also fn. 125.

announcement.[121] However, the context of this verse does not support them. The future tense of the three verbs mentioned is the so-called "gnomic" (i.e. proverbial) future which is solidly attested to in classical and NT Greek.[122]

d) The words "for this reason" in Eph 5 may be aetiological as in the original text of Genesis, but—whether or not the allusion to Gen 2:23 in Eph 5:30 var. lect. is considered authentic—they refer to the event which is described in the context of Ephesians: the Christological-soteriological origin of the church and its unifying effect, as described in 5:25–30. Presupposed in this case is the question: Why has it been written, "A man will leave . . . be joined . . . become one"? And the answer is given: Because in that great event in which the Messiah proved to be "savior of his body," the church (vs. 23), all that was said of Adam and Eve in Gen 2 was fulfilled! This, indeed, is most likely the meaning of the conjunction "for this reason" in 5:31, for in the very next verse Paul says explicitly that he interprets Gen 2:24 as referring to "Christ and the Church." Thus Paul combines the aetiological with the prophetic senses of *al-kēn, anti toutou,* and gives both a specific turn: instead of a present-day name or custom, they describe the sense and validity of a Scripture verse. Instead of referring to a purely future event of unification, Paul proclaims that "in the church and in the Messiah" the miracle predicted in Gen 2:24 is fulfilled; now God is praised as the one whose promise and "power" prove effective "in us" (Eph 3:20–21), and whose completed "work" is manifest to the ages (2:7, 10).

A man will leave his father and mother And be joined to his wife, And the two will become one flesh. In COMMENT VI A the various textual traditions of this quote will be compared. Here only a few philological and historical observations are necessary. Just like the LXX, which in Gen 2:24 and frequently elsewhere uses *anthrōpos* instead of the more precise *anēr* for rendering the Hebrew *īsh,* Paul uses *anthrōpos* in his quotation of Gen 2:24. But always and everywhere else in 5:22–33 when he speaks of husband and wife he employs the (correct) term *anēr.*[123] The shift from one term to the other probably has its cause in the conflation of Gen 1:26–27 with Gen 2:24.[124] Its consequences for the estimation of woman are far-reaching; they are reflected in a Pauline utterance such as; "A [male] man is the image and glory of God; but woman is the glory of man" (I Cor 11:7). However, in Eph 5 Paul does not invite such conclusions.[125] After faithfully quoting *anthrōpos* from the Greek version of

---

[121] Meyer, pp. 248–50 equates *father* and *mother* whom Christ *will leave,* with the seat of Christ at God's right hand in heaven. J. Jeremias, TWNTE, I, 143, 366, speaks of the pre-existent Messiah who *leaves* heaven. Muirhead, p. 184 (cf. 181, 183) uses the future tenses for forming the thesis, "It is only in the End that the Church becomes the Bride." According to Meyer, only at that moment will the Bride of Christ become his Wife. H. Grotius, Bengel, von Soden have spoken out against this type of interpretation. Others do not even mention it. If it were tenable it would support the futurist-eschatological substance of 1:14; 2:20; 4:13, 30.

[122] BDF, 349:1. See, e.g. Rom 3:20; 5:7; 7:3, cf. the gnomic aorist, BDF, 333:1.

[123] In the exposition of 4:13 it was shown that *anthrōpos* means "man" in general, whether male or female (cf. German *Mensch*), as distinct from animals, angels, and God, while *anēr* signifies an adult male as opposed to a child or a woman.

[124] See COMMENT VI B C.

[125] The opinion of J. Jeremias, TWNTE, I, 143, 366, that *anthrōpos* in Eph 5:31 means the pre-existent man and Messiah, would in the light of the history of religions mean that a bisexual (hermaphrodite) man was in mind; see COMMENTS VI B and VII A for references. But Paul follows as little as Jesus the mythological interpretations of Gen 1:26–27 and their combination with Gen 2:21–24.

Gen 2:24, he returns in vs. 33 to the proper term *anēr* ("husband"). The future tense of the verbs "leave," "join," and "become" does not have a future meaning here as shown in the preceding NOTE. Assuming, on the ground of vs. 32, that vs. 31 must be interpreted Christologically, and that the parousia of Christ cannot be meant—which present or past action of Christ does the author have in mind? Again, the incarnation, the crucifixion, and the sacraments of baptism and the eucharist have been suggested. In COMMENT VI more will be said about these alternatives. The verbs "leave" and "join" appear to pose a specific problem: following a suggestion made by J. J. Bachofen in his book on the Matriarchate (1861), interpreters of Gen 2:24 have mentioned the possibility that the formulation, "a man will leave his father and mother and be joined to his wife," may reflect the order of a matriarchal society. If Paul had been aware of this, Eph 5:31 would balance out a one-sided interpretation of his statement about man, the "head" (vs. 23), who is to be "feared" (vs. 33). But it is questionable whether the author of Gen 2–3 (the so-called Yahwist) had such an order in mind and whether Paul was aware of it or had any reason to allude to it. Hebrew *dabaq* ("to join," "to cleave," "to be close"; passive: "to be joined") and its Greek equivalents describe an intimate relation which can exist at most diverse stages of cultural and societal development. *Dabaq* denotes for example Shechem's love for Dinah (Gen 34:3); it means a voluntary, passionate, close relationship which involves a man's soul and body.[126] As regards the term "flesh," it was shown before that it could be a substitute for "body" or "self."[127] Does Gen 2:24[128] add a novel and perhaps unique meaning to the several senses of "flesh" that are presupposed elsewhere?[129] Nowhere else in the Bible does the formula "one flesh" occur. Just as the vss. 2:15, 16, 18 speak of two groups of persons that become "a single new man" in "one single body" through "one single Spirit," so the OT and Pauline formula "one flesh" describes the amazing result of the union of "two," even of a man and a woman, in "one." Certainly their sexual relationship is in mind, but not only this expression and means of union.[130] Their physical in-

---

[126] *Dabaq* is rendered in the LXX, the NT, and the Apostolic Fathers by *proskollaomai*. The Hebrew term is used more frequently in the book of Ruth than anywhere else in the OT, though not for her relationship to Boaz; see Ruth 1:14; 2:8, 21, 23. In describing romantic "attachments," LXX Gen 34:8 uses as synonyms *proeilato*; I Kings[I Sam] 18:1: *sunedethē*; Sir 25:1: *symperipheromenoi*. See Pedersen, *Israel*, I-II, 279–80, 288–92.

[127] See vss. 28–30, 33 and the NOTES to these verses.

[128] In its original OT setting and when it is quoted in I Cor 6:16; Eph 5:31; Matt 19:5; Mark 10:7–8.

[129] Bailey, p. 44, enumerates a total of eight meanings: (a) fleshly substance of the animal body as distinct from bones; (b) the body itself; (c) human being; (d) blood relatives; (e) mankind; (f) any mortal creature; (g) the whole creation; (h) the sexual organs. This catalogue cannot claim completeness since the typically Pauline (and Johannine) sense of "flesh" is omitted, that is, the evil intentionality and sphere in which man is hopelessly caught unless he is saved by the Spirit and grace; see esp. Bultmann, ThNT, I, 239–46; Schweizer, TWNTE, VII, 131–36.

[130] See Pedersen, *Israel*, I-II, 179, 267–68, 274–310, regarding the role of body, soul, gifts, touch, food, peace in a covenant relationship. Parallels of "one flesh" are: "one body": I Cor 6:16; cf. Eph 5:28; "one spirit": I Cor 6:17; "one new man": Eph 2:15; "one heart and one soul": Acts 4:32. Cf. "one person (*heis*) in Christ Jesus": Gal 3:28; "one Body in Christ": Rom 12:5; cf. I Cor 10:17. The myth told by a certain Aristophanes to the greater glory of Eros (see Plato *symp.* 189C–193D) does not speak of one body or one flesh though it affirms distinctly that man who is now male or female was created out of an original bisexual (hermaphrodite) human being and that the attraction between males and females aims at the restoration of the original (physical!) unity. The same is said of originally male-male and female-female persons: it serves to explain homosexual unions. According to Plato, Eros, the force (deity) operating in physical attraction and union, is the driving power of the most intimate spiritual and religious (not only sexual) relationship. In all realms of the psyche and society, of culture and nature, Plato distinguished the "heav-

tercourse and their life together is to be determined by their spiritual communion, according to I Cor 7:3–5, 10–16; cf. 26–39. A bond which is no more than
sexual, or "carnal," constitutes "one body"—but in a sense that is irreconcilable
with "belonging to Christ" (I Cor 6:16–17). According to Matt 19:6; Mark
10:9 the words "one flesh" mean that in their marital union a man and a
woman are "no longer two." Does this prevent them from remaining different
personalities?[131] Not according to Paul! For after speaking in 2:14–17 with
highest praise, even poetically, of the complete unification of Gentiles and Jews
in "a single new man," and while he called those unified "one body," "the body
of Christ" (1:22–23; 3:6; 4:4, etc.), he still speaks of "both [viz. the two] of us
who in one Spirit have free access to the Father." In Rom 2 and 11 he addresses baptized Jews and Gentiles specifically. Certainly he has advice for all
Christians in common, including husbands and wives (Eph 4:1–5:21). But he
knows that the personalities of husband and wife are different even in marriage:
special counsels are given to husbands and wives respectively. If he did not consider the church, the body of Christ (who is "one flesh" with Christ) "a whole in
herself, a person,"[132] he could never direct exhortations and reproaches to her
without presuming to correct or to blame Christ. Therefore "one flesh" cannot
mean a mystic or enthusiastic identification which wipes out personal distinction. Even when Christ dwells in the saints' heart (3:16; cf. Gal 2:20), or when
God dwells in the temple, there is no fusion.

32. *This [passage] has an eminent secret meaning.*[133] Lit. "this mystery
is great." Philologically, it is possible to translate, "The following mystery is
great"—as if Paul wanted to say, despite the greatness of this easily misunderstood mystery, I am now going to divulge the secret sense of Gen 2:24.[134] As
4:17 shows, the demonstrative pronoun *touto* ("this") can point forward.
But it is much more likely and almost commonly accepted that "this" refers
back to the Genesis text quoted in the preceding verse. In contrast to 1:9; 3:3,
4, 9; 6:19, here the translation of *mystērion* by "mystery" can express the
original sense. As shown in Comment XI on 1:3–14, the passages mentioned
spoke of only one secret, that is, the incorporation of the Gentiles into God's

enly" from the "common Eros"; see *symp.* 180D, 186A, 187–88, 205B–D, 208E. For this
philosopher, love for the absolutely beautiful and true, even for the world of ideas or ideals, stands
behind and above all love caused by, and shown to, lovable persons on earth, *symp.* 204B, 210A–
212A.
[131] While Batey, NTS 13 (1966), 270 ff. wants to translate "one flesh" by "one personality,"
Bailey, p. 110, may be nearer Paul's understanding of "one flesh" when he calls this term the "best
definite exemplification of union without confusion or loss of distinction." Von Allmen's (p. 29)
suggestion that the combination "of two different molecules which form a new chemical body" introduces a problematic analogy for it puts male and female on the level of soulless entities, overstresses
the physical meaning of "one flesh," and degrades the act of intercourse to a laboratory, or magical
process. The myth mentioned in the last fn. describes the result of the (re-)union of two persons
(whether they are hetero- or homosexual) as becoming "one [*hen*, neuter] out of two . . . instead of
two, one [*heis*, masculine] . . . out of two, one [*hets*, masc.]" (Plato *symp.* 191D; 192E). In the fulfillment of Eros' longing, that is in the beatific vision of the beautiful and good itself, there is no
place left for speaking of distinct personalities (210E; 211C–212A). The sobriety and this-worldliness
of Paul's description of love and its effect is distinct from such mystic or enthusiastic rapture. See
COMMENT IV B.
[132] See Best, p. 179. This author emphasizes that the church is not "the rump or trunk of which
Christ is the head . . . Headship implies here not organic unity but the power to rule."
[133] See Abbott, p. 174, for a collection of arguments suggesting such a translation. The works by
Zalotay, Colli, Dacquino, Salvia, Johnson listed in BIBLIOGRAPHY 21 could not be consulted but may
contain additional suggestions.
[134] Von Soden, p. 144.

people and house—a secret that was formerly hidden to all generations but is now revealed through Christ to the apostles and prophets, and has to be made known to the world. But Eph 5:32 speaks of one of several mysteries, perhaps one of those intimated in I Cor 4:1; 13:2; 14:2.[135] Their number is never specified nor are their titles or content fully disclosed; he would be pretentious who claimed to know all of them. This means that *mystērion* has a meaning in Eph 5:32 that is present elsewhere in the NT and also in other religious books,[136] but is exceptional in Ephesians and Colossians.[137] What can it mean? The following opinions are prominent:

a) *Mystērion* means "sacrament" in the technical-ecclesiastical sense of this term as defined by the Catholic Church in and since the Fourth Lateran Council (1215),[138] or as redefined by e.g. the Lutheran *Augsburg Confession* IX–XIII (1530) and the Calvinistic *Scottish Confession of Faith* XXI–XXIII (1560). In Eph 5:32 marriage is called a sacrament which "conveys the grace" earned by Christ's suffering and death, according to the Council of Trent (1563).

b) *Mystērion* is an equivalent of the English "mystery": it denotes the unfathomable and inexplicable core, the miraculous or mystical essence, the overwhelming presence or praiseworthy experience of a special relationship. In the history of interpretation, the following relationships have been suggested: (1) The special way in which one man and one woman are united in one flesh.[139] (2) The unique union of Christ with the church (as established in the incarnation, crucifixion, or eucharist; see, e.g. Bengel). (3) The ontic, logical and noetical relation between the unity of the divine pair (Christ-church), and

---

[135] Best, p. 179, goes too far when he assumes that the NT uses the term *mystērion* exclusively in the sense of "revealed secret."

[136] E.g. in Daniel, in Jewish apocalyptic writings, in Revelation, in Qumran literature, in the Apostolic Fathers; see COMMENT XI on 1:3–14.

[137] Abbott, pp. 174–75, Meuzelaar, *Der Leib des Messias*, pp. 47–48, and Batey, *Nuptial Imagery*, p. 31, n. 5, reject this conclusion. Batey stipulates that because *mystērion* meant "revealed secret" in all earlier Ephesian passages, it must have the same sense in 5:32. Robinson, p. 209, takes an even more radical position when he avers that only in Rev 1:20; 17:5, 7 is the same use made of *mystērion* as in Eph 5:32. In turn, Sampley, pp. 90–96, opposes the construction of alternatives; he believes that the concept "mystery of Christ" comprehends diverse elements that are not mutually exclusive.

[138] H. Denzinger-A. Schönmetzer, *Enchiridion Symbolorum*, 34th ed. (Freiburg: Herder, 1965), 794 and 1799–1801 (older editions, e.g. 18th–20th ed. [1932], 424, 969–71); cf. the *Decretum pro Armeniis* of the Council of Florence (1439), Denzinger-Schönmetzer, 1327 (old, 702). Since most Latin versions, including Vulg., have *sacramentum* in vs. 32, the definition and celebration of marriage as a "sacrament" was based (mainly, if not exclusively) on this one verse. For the exceptional translation of *mystērion* by *mysterium* or *ministerium* see Beuron, ed. *Vetus Latina*, 24/1, p. 259. The Protestant polemic against the (supposedly monolithic) Roman Catholic doctrine on marriage, in turn, was to some extent grounded in a reinterpretation of Eph 5:32—after a start for a reformed doctrine on marriage was made, e.g. in Luther's *Babylonian Captivity* (1520), WA, VI, 550–53; idem, *Sermon on the Mount*, on Matt 5:32, WA, XXXII, 376–81. The Eastern Orthodox churches celebrate marriage as a sacrament without being dependent on the Latin version of Eph 5:32. Jerome's Vulg. (and the earlier Latin versions, except those reading *mysterium*) have *sacramentum* also in Eph 1:9; 3:3, 9; Col 1:27; I Tim 3:16; Rev 1:20. Thus they reveal that they did not presuppose exclusively the "sacramental (ritual, legal, ecclesiastical)" sense of *sacramentum* which since Tertullian's time began to spread in the western church (see e.g. A. Kölping, *Sacramentum Tertullianeum*, Münster: Aschendorff, 1948, and H. von Soden, ZNW 12 (1911), 188–227). Cf. Calvin *Institutio* IV 19:36. Augustine and e.g. the Catholic scholars Erasmus, Cajetanus (quoted by Abbott, p. 175); Schlier, p. 263, n. 1; Mussner, pp. 147, 152, n. 359; H. Schnackenburg and J. Ratzinger in H. Greeven, et. al., *Theologie der Ehe*, pp. 28–29, 85–88), together with the Protestants von Allmen, pp. 28–30; Meuzelaar, *Der Leib des Messias*, pp. 46–47; H. Baltensweiler, pp. 230–34, uphold a rather "high" sacramental view of marriage, yet *without* presupposing that *mystērion* means *sacramentum* in 5:32.

[139] In Prov 30:18–19; "the way of a man with a maiden" ranks among the three or four things that are "too wonderful for me," RSV, NEB; "beyond my comprehension," JB.

of the human pair (husband-wife).[140] (4) The relation between creation and redemption.[141] The number of Catholic and Protestant scholars representing one or several of the last four interpretations is legion.[142]

(c) *Mysterion* indicates that the Scripture passage quoted in 5:31 is to be understood in an allegorical or typological way.[143] The interpretation given of Gen 2:24 in Eph 5:32 is strictly mystical (or allegorical, or pneumatical), but in 5:33 the apostle returns to the literal sense of the same text, according to Thomas Aquinas. This distinguishes Paul from the allegorists who have no room for the literal sense. In Eph 5[144] he no more denies the literal meaning of the OT texts quoted than does the author of the epistle to the Hebrews by his "typological" interpretation. But here and there a formerly hidden "secret meaning" is brought to light. The typological interpretation of 5:32 is older than its sacramental counterparts and at least as widely supported.[145]

While the three expositions of *mysterion* here sketched are not in all aspects mutually exclusive,[146] the third recommends itself by its simplicity, suitability to the context (vss. 21–30 and 33), and biblical and contemporary extra-

[140] The Scholastic technical term for this relation is *analogia relationis* or more specifically, *analogia proportionalitatis*.

[141] Or, the revelation that "in Adam the original man, the creation of God, the future Christ was hidden, but really present," and that therefore "in the creation is already hidden the redemption provided in Christ" (Schlier, p. 278; cf. K. Barth, III 1–4, esp. 1, 94–329). Similary Ratzinger (in Greeven, et al., *Theologie der Ehe*, p. 92) speaks of the ratification of the unity of creation and covenant, and of the representation and confirmation of God's faithfulness in man's faithfulness. "In its capability as order of the covenant," this truthfulness is also the "order of creation, and it enacts as order of the covenant the order of creation." This exposition of Eph 5 presupposes the "analogy of relation," but goes far beyond it; it is, indeed, "a great mystery" and cannot be easily understood. A specifically crude and insipid thought is found in W. Schubart, *Religion and Eros*, p. 244; he asserts that "a higher, super-polar unity" joins "the phallus and the cross, the holy symbols of creation and redemption."

[142] E.g. Jerome, Thomas Aquinas, *Summa Theol.* III suppl., qu. 42–68, esp. 42, art. 1; Haupt; Thornton, *The Common Life*, p. 225; Piper, n. 156; M. Meinertz; J. Huby (both in their commentaries on the Letters of Captivity); J. Schmid, *Der Epheserbrief der Apostles Paulus*. Biblische Studien XXII (Freiburg: Herder, 1928), 166 f.; K. Barth, III 1, 326; Dacquino; Johnson; Bieder, p. 62.

[143] At the time of Paul, Greek philologists had developed the art of finding a hidden "sub-sense" (*hyponoia*) in inspired writings of great men of old. An interpreter aware of the Muse who had inspired Homer and his like, would not be bound to the literal meaning of a text but could discover what was really meant. Philo and many rabbis used the allegorical method. In the NT it is employed in, e.g. Gal 3:16; 4:21–31; I Cor 9:9–10; Matt 13:1–23. The Apostolic Fathers and Apologists liked it, and the Alexandrians Clement and Origen, and Augustine later in the West, brought it to its full blossom. In medieval times, it was called "spiritual" or "mystical" interpretation. See R. M. Grant, *The Letter and the Spirit*, London: SPCK, 1951. A clear distinction between allegory and typology is suggested by R. P. C. Hanson, *Allegory and Event* (London: SCM, 1959), p. 7: allegory is ashamed of the concrete historical sense of a text and shows that only a timeless, spiritual, abstract truth is meant. Typology affirms both the original literal and the superior deeper sense(s); it treats the past as a precedent that is at the same time maintained and overcome with the new light of a novel interpretation or application.

[144] And in Gal 4:21–31; see esp. 4:29: "Just as then . . . so also now."

[145] Justin Martyr *dial.* 40, 44, appears to be the first post-biblical author who speaks explicitly of a Christological *mysterion* inherent in OT elements (that is, in the Paschal Lamb and Moses' Law). Eph 5:32 is explained in this sense by Chrysostom; Theodore of Mopsuestia; Theodoret; Jerome; Calvin; Bengel; Meyer; von Soden; Abbott; Robinson, pp. 125–26; Dibelius; G. Bornkamm, TWNTE, IV, 823; Best, p. 179; Piper; K. Barth, III 2, 316–17; III 4, 123, etc.; Mussner, pp. 147–52; Baltensweiler, pp. 230 ff.; Gaugler; Reicke, p. 30; and all of the two Catholic and two Protestant authors of the essays collected in Greeven, et. al., *Theologie der Ehe*, pp. 29, 78 f., 85 ff., 120.

[146] As illustrated by the occurrence of the same names in the several groups. Is, then, Origen's great vision true to the Bible? He assumed that the mystery of Christ's incarnation, the mystery of the church (the body of Christ), the mystery of the correlation of Spirit and letter in the Bible, and the mystery of Christ's presence in the eucharist are ultimately extensions or expressions of the same revealed truth (see esp. H. de Lubac, *Histoire et esprit* (Paris: Aubier, 1950), pp. 336–73; also M. Barth, *Conversation with the Bible* (New York: Holt, 1964), pp. 143–56. If so, then it can and must be stipulated that the *mysterion* of Eph 5:32 contains each one of the three senses mentioned, and more, at the same time. But the mysteries of Origen's theology are not necessarily the same as Paul's intention when he uses the noun *mysterion*.

biblical parallels. Reasons for this judgment will be offered in Comments VI and VII.

The predicate of *mystērion, megas* (lit. "great"), has most likely little or nothing to do with a specifically outstanding density, intensity, depth, or obscurity. The same adjective is attached to *mystērion* in I Tim 3:16.[147] In both cases the language is borrowed from "acclamation formulae," such as "Yahweh is great" (Ps 135:5); "Great is the Artemis of the Ephesians" (Acts 19:34); or "Babylon the Great" (Rev 17:5). In each case *megas* means important, eminent, glorious.[148]

I, for one, interpret it [as relating] to. The formula *lego eis,* "I say in relation to," is also found in Acts 2:25 and elsewhere.[149] Just as in the "antitheses" of Matt 5:22, 28, 32, etc., Jesus pronounced his own interpretation in opposition to other expositions of biblical texts, so here Paul ventures a personal exegesis. Here and there the words *egō de legō,* lit. "but I say," are exactly the same. Jesus turned against a legalistic, casuistic, pedantic (in part, Qumranite?)[150] exegesis. Which exposition is taken up in Eph 5:32? Several interpreters believe that the interpretation of Gen 2:24 to which Paul may allude must have been as allegorical as Paul's though it came to different results.[151] While there is hardly any evidence that Jewish prophets, Wisdom teachers, or the early rabbis saw in Gen 2 a foreshadowing of the Yahweh-Israel relationship,[152] the Phrygian Bishop Papias (ca. A.D. 140) and other second-century divines seem to have related the whole creation story to Christ and to the church.[153] Written primary evidence of such a tradition exists only in obscure, probably Gnostic, literature of the second century[154]—and in Eph 5. Certainly proto-Gnostic elements are contained in late Wisdom books, Philo, and among the Apostolic Fathers I Clement, Ignatius, and Hermas,[155] but other evidence is lacking. Therefore, it is more likely that those Gnosticizing second-century descriptions of Christ and the church which allude to Gen 1 and 2 are dependent upon Eph 5, than that Eph 5 (together with the Apostolic

---

[147] Philo *leg. all.* III 100, speaks of the "great mysteries" into which the more perfect and pure mind is initiated.

[148] Cf. "Alexander the Great," or "Charlemagne"; see also Peterson, *Heis Theos,* pp. 196 ff.; WBLex, 499, sect. 2b; Abbott; Robinson; C. Masson; Schlier; Best, p. 179.

[149] E.g. Herm. *Sim.* IX 26:6; Clement of Alexandria *Strom.* III 84 (549P; viz. 198 S 32).

[150] See C. V. Wolf "The Gospel to the Essenes," *Biblical Research* 3 (1958), 28 ff.; Braun, QuNT, I, 15–18.

[151] Dibelius, p. 95; Bornkamm, TWNTE, IV, 823; Schlier, p. 262; idem *Christus,* pp. 65–66; Sampley, pp. 52, 87–88, 102.

[152] See COMMENT VI B. However, the Song of Songs was explained this way not only by Rabbi Aquiba in the second century A.D., but probably by earlier rabbis; see Jeremias, TWNTE, IV, 1102, n. 28.

[153] The only evidence is found in E. Preuschen, *Antilegomena,* 2d ed. (Giessen: Töpelmann, 1905), pp. 96 and 100, where the following "Papias Fragments" are reconstructed from the ancient scholar Anastasius Sinaita's *hexaemeron* (I and II). According to Fragment 10, the doctrine of the millennium is taken "from Papias and Pantaenus, the Alexandrian priest, and the wise Ammonius—those exegetes who wrote [their books] before the [great] Synods of the Church and interpreted the whole six-days-work [of creation] as relating to Christ and the church." Fragment 11 confirms this: "The oldest ecclesiastical interpreters—I mean the philosophers Philo (the contemporary of the apostles), Papias and their followers gave a spiritual interpretation of the paradise story; they related it to the church of the Lord." These texts do not make clear which relationship was established.

[154] See COMMENTS VI B 3 and VII A.

[155] Schlier (pp. 268 ff.) discusses extensively e.g. II Clem. XIV; Ign. *Eph.* XVII 1; *Smyrn.* VIII 2; Polyc. *Phil.* v 1; Herm. *vis.* I 1:6; 3:4–5.

Fathers and the later Gnostic teachers) drew from a "pre-existent" Gnosticizing allegorical interpretation of Gen 1–2.[156] Only Philo's spiritual interpretation of the creation of the heavenly and the earthly men[157] antedates Ephesians; his allegory may have been known to Paul and attacked by the words; "But I interpret it as relating to. . . ." Yet Philo does not speak of "Christ and the church" and therefore cannot be drafted as originating the tradition mentioned by Papias. Actually, it cannot be stated with certainty whether or not the individuals or the school of interpretation from which Paul wanted to distinguish his own exposition of Gen 2:24 offered a literary interpretation of this verse.[158] Paul for his part does not deny that marriage can and must be explained on the ground of this text. However, he asserts that at its deepest level this key text speaks of "Christ and the church." Marriage does not exist in its own right. Therefore, it is not enough to describe and regulate it by calling it an institution belonging to creation—even if by creation an act of God's undeserved love and wise care is meant. Only Christ's love and the church's subordination to him are for Paul the key to understanding creation and marriage.

How much authority does Paul claim for his surprising exegesis? Greeven suggests that Paul gives "his personal opinion . . . without expecting that everybody would at once and unconditionally agree with him."[159] Indeed, Paul does not claim the position of Jesus Christ who can say "Amen" at the beginning of his own affirmations, who is in person the fulfillment and the realization of all promises of God,[160] and who will confirm the words spoken now by his final word at the Last Judgment.[161] In I Cor 7, a quasi-hierarchical distinction is made between the utterances introduced by "I would," "I think," "I say," "a concession," "my opinion," "I command," "a command of the Lord."[162] Still, whatever the emphasis upon the authority of a particular statement, in each case Paul is convinced "by the Lord's mercy to be trustworthy." For "I think that I, too, have the Spirit of God" (I Cor 7:25, 40). While he does not explicitly say that the truth of his opinion will speak for itself, he leaves it to the Spirit who works not only in him but also in his listeners and readers to prove

[156] Mussner, p. 151, n. 357. According to the subtle argument in his commentary which eliminates some of the methodological flaws present in his earlier book, *Christus*, pp. 60–75, Schlier does not wish to stipulate that Ephesians is dependent upon Gnostic teaching. Neither does he accept the proposition that the Gnosticizing and Gnostic doctrines are inspired by Ephesians. But he holds that Paul and the Gnostic groups have "a common background to which each reacts differently." Theirs is "a language common to both" (Schlier, p. 268). Schlier believes that Paul "takes up the questions posed by Hellenistic Judaistic Gnosticism," destroys its mythological presuppositions, and confronts it with the "mystery of marriage" (Schlier, pp. 275–76). See COMMENT VII C for an alternative.
[157] See COMMENT VI B.
[158] If the Jewish Gnosticizing pattern reconstructed by Schlier had existed and posed urgent questions and ethical problems, the other NT passages quoting Gen 2:24, i.e. I Cor 6; Matt 19; Mark 10, would have to show traces of it—either by accepting or by refuting at least some portions of it. But in those passages only the literal interpretation of Gen 2 is presupposed and used as an argument. Though I Cor 6:12–20, esp. vss. 16–17, and I Cor 7 with its careful discussion of sexual union, prepare the way for the interpretation of Gen 2 in Eph 5, Paul had at the time of writing I Corinthians not yet found a reason to unfold the "fuller sense" of Gen 2 which is proposed in Eph 5.
[159] *Theologie der Ehe*, pp. 78–79, n. 70.
[160] Matt 5:18; John 1:51, etc.; II Cor 1:20; see Schlier, TWNTE, I, 335–38.
[161] Matt 5:3–12, 18–20; 7:21–27; 25:14–30, 31–46, etc.
[162] *Thelō*: I Cor 7:7, 32; *nomizō*: vs. 26; *legō*: vss. 12, 35; *syggnomē*: vs. 6; *gnomē*: vss. 25, 40; *diatassomai*: vs. 17; *paraggellō*: I Thess 4:11; II Thess 3:4, 6, 10, 12; I Cor 11:17; *kyrios paraggellei, epitagē kyriou*: I Cor 7:10, 25; cf. 9:14. Cf. W. Schrage, *Die konkreten Einzelgebote in der paulinischen Paränese* (Gütersloh: Mohr, 1961), pp. 117–46, 241–50; Baltensweiler, p. 188.

the validity of his message, the authenticity of his ministry, and the authority of his person.[163] The gospel which he preaches is called by him nothing less than the "power of God for salvation"; it is the one gospel of Christ which must not be adulterated by additions, deletions, or changes; also it is the same as "announced beforehand . . . through the Law and the Prophets."[164] Always, except in I Thessalonians and Colossians, the proclamation of this gospel in writing includes arguments from the Scriptures; sometimes keen personal interpretations and even allegorizations are added. But Paul does not claim infallibility for himself. His bold interpretation of Gen 2:24 is introduced in a way which in Matt 5 means full divine authorization, "But I say unto you," but which in Eph 5:32 reveals some reticence and humility: "I, for one, interpret it as relating to . . ."

Christ and the church. All important MSS save one repeat *eis* before "the church" and require a literal translation such as "[as relating] to Christ and [as relating] to the church."[165] This does not mean that Paul wants to speak of two separate components of his spiritual interpretation[166] rather than one thing only: the interrelation of Christ and the church. The repetition of *eis* is probably a rhetorical device designed to indicate the one allegory—not two separate points from which separate applications (e.g. a creedal and a moral one) could be derived. In contrast to other allegorists,[167] Paul shows amazing restraint and discipline; he speaks only of "Christ and the church." In his allegorical exposition he does not spell out or give any details about the relation between this Bridegroom and Bride. Probably the statements made by Paul in 5:25–27 on "Christ and the church" motivated the apostle to desist from attributing a detailed allegorical meaning, e.g. to the "father," the "mother," the acts of "leaving," "joining," "becoming one flesh," as they are mentioned in Gen 2:24. If Paul had listed step by step the counterparts to all elements of Gen 2:24 in Christ's love of the church,[168] he would have created a series of statements competing with, and perhaps contradictory to, the hymn in Eph 5:25–27. There the mode, the instruments, the intention, and the result of Christ's love were described in sufficient detail. After the heavenly Bridegroom's love has been fully depicted as the origin and model of an earthly husband's love, Paul need not (and obviously will not) now make Christ a Husband who by entirely different means determines the conduct of the saints. In summary, Paul did not split up his Christological argument into two parts describing Christ's engagement (5:25–27) and marriage (5:296–332), and thereby become suspect for lack of clarity, perhaps even for arbitrariness because he switched from one to the other. On the contrary, the hermeneutics (methods of exact interpreta-

---

[163] See, e.g. Gal 3:2–5; I Cor 2:9–16; 9:2; II Cor 3:1–3. Paul can also point to the harmony of his teaching with the Jerusalem "pillars," Gal 2:1–10; to his sufferings and the strength provided by God's grace alone, II Cor 10–13; or, to the reflection and continuation of his mission in the churches' acts of thanksgiving and other fruits of the Spirit, Gal 1:24; 4:12–20; 5:22–24; II Cor 8–9, etc.

[164] Rom 1:1, 16–17; 3:21; Gal 1:6–9, etc.

[165] The Vatican Codex and Marcion, also the MSS of the Koine group, omit the second *eis*.

[166] Despite Meuzelaar's opinion to the contrary, *Der Leib des Messias*, p. 48, n. 1.

[167] E.g. the interpretation of the Parable of the Samaritan by Clement of Alexandria (*quis dives salvetur* 29, PG 9, 633–34), Origen (*hom. in Lucam* 34), and Augustine.

[168] Saying e.g. that the father means God, the mother Jerusalem, the joining incarnation, the unity in "one flesh," the eucharistic communion. Examples of detailed allegorizations will be given in COMMENT VI B.

tion) to be applied to the exposition of vss. 25–27 and 31–32 are not only complementary but identical and consistent. In the text describing the romance of Christ and the church it proved impossible to allegorize each feature of Christ's love and convert it into an exact mandate for the husband's behavior toward his wife. The source and character of true love were revealed in the hymnic epos of the unique love of the Bridegroom, but there was no casuistic prescription of the steps to be taken by a man over the years, days, and hours of courtship and marriage. In vss. 31–32 the same is true in reverse order: the details of a man's way with a woman are not blown up to yield detailed information about Christ's relationship to the church. In conclusion, there is neither a way nor a need to take sides in the struggle as to whether the parousia, the incarnation, the crucifixion, or the eucharist is the spiritual meaning of the words and the future tense in vs. 31, and of the term "one flesh." For the very quest for detail allegorization which is manifest in that struggle is immaterial, pointless, and opposed to the intent of the text. To repeat, Paul points out only the *henōsis* ("communion") of "Christ and the church." If anything specific in Christ's life has to be called the sum and apex of his love it would be just one deed and event: his self-delivery into death.[169] In 5:2 and 25 Paul himself affirms this: "The Messiah has loved us and [viz., that is] has given himself for us . . . He has loved the church and given himself for her." Compare the emphasis on his sacrifice in 1:7; 2:13–16.

33. *In any case, one by one, each one of you must love his wife as himself.* The Greek sentence begins with *plēn*. After a digression or enumeration, this conjunction can mean, "in sum,"[170] but it is more likely that here it signifies a contrast or exception.[171] Paul returns to the literal and commonly accepted meaning of Gen 2:24 and shows that he did not forget or deny it in disclosing his opinion on its "mysterious" sense.[172] The very strong imperative, "must love" (*agapatō*), the emphatic inclusion of every one of the saints, and finally the fact that here the husbands are addressed before the wives—these three features distinguish vs. 33 from vss. 22–25 where wives were exhorted first and burdened, as it seemed, with a heavier load. The relative harshness exhibited toward husbands in vs. 33a is complemented by the surprisingly soft manner with which Paul turns toward the wives in vs. 33b; see the next NOTE. Coming to the end of his argument, Paul apparently considered men much more recalcitrant about showing love for their wives, than wives about subordinating themselves. Since here the term "love" is a means of interpreting the verbs "leave," "be joint," "become one flesh," it clearly includes sexual love. In I Cor 7:2–5 Paul admonished both husband and wife not to deprive or defraud one

[169] The concentration upon one single point of comparison resembles the rigorous rule established by A. Jülicher, *Die Gleichnisreden Jesu*, 2 vols., 2d ed., Tübingen: Mohr, 1910. The limitation and concentration of the comparison offered by Paul in 5:25a and the allegory produced in 32b, also the fact that Paul concludes his argument in vs. 33 by returning to the literal sense of Gen 2:24, call for a revision of the widespread prejudice against Paul's allegories. Though he uses the term "allegorize" himself (in Gal 4:24), in Eph 5 he is engaged in parabolic, metaphoric, or typological exegesis rather than in allegory of a wilder sort. Cf. fn. 143.

[170] WBLex, 675: "breaking off a discussion and emphasizing what is important"; LSLex, 1419: "break off and pass to another subject." E.g. Calvin and the RSV interpret the word in this sense.

[171] Meyer: "but without excluding"; cf. von Soden. Abbott: "Howbeit—not to dwell on this matter of Christ and the Church, but to return . . ." BDF, 449:2: "only, in any case."

[172] Thomas Aquinas; von Soden, p. 145; Baltensweiler, pp. 232–33.

another. The right and need of the partner were declared the measure for beginning, continuing, or interrupting physical intercourse.[173] Certainly the harsh imperative "must love" is not a free pass for libido. A man following the example of Christ cannot and will not exploit his spouse. See COMMENT V A for a positive description of marital love and its difference from love of God, the neighbor, and self. The question whether the words "as himself" allude to the command (Lev 19:18) "Love your neighbor as yourself"[174] will be taken up in COMMENT V B.

and the wife . . . may she fear her husband. A complete change of tone has taken place. After the rigid instruction given each individual husband in imperative form, Paul speaks of "the wife"—hesitates, and continues with an *anacoluthon* (a broken sentence): "may she fear her husband" (*hina phobētai . . .*). In some cases such a *hina*-sentence replaces a (blunt) command or imperative,[175] but it does not in the two other instances in which it occurs in Pauline letters: in I Cor 7:29 Paul suggests that in the remaining short time (before the last woes and the parousia) "those who have wives live as though they had none (*hina . . . ōsin*). In II Cor 8:7 he utters his confidence that the Corinthians who abound in faith, proclamation, knowledge, zeal, and love, will also be abundant in contributing to the collection for Jerusalem (*hina . . . perisseuēte*). He adds, immediately and explicitly, "I say this not as a command" (II Cor 8:8). In consequence, that which is known of Pauline diction (or might be imitated by a disciple of Paul) prohibits the interpretation of Eph 5:33b as an imperative statement. Paul's sentence about the wife is so phrased as if he wanted to say, "I hope and trust she will be enabled to fear her husband; I expect it but I cannot command it." More briefly, "May she fear!"[176] However, the soft tone of "may" appears to be contradicted by the radicality of the verb "fear" which goes even farther than "subordinate" in vss. 21–22, 24. Despite the scarcity of dictionary and biblical evidence for the meanings "reverence" or "respect" of the Greek words *phobos* and *phobeomai*,[177] the modern versions quoted in fn. 175 and in other translations seek to make Paul less patriarchal and (vs. 33) more palatable to modern readers by substituting "respect" for "fear."[178] But elsewhere Paul does not consider it beneath a Christian's dignity to show "fear" at the right place and on proper occasions. All those addressed in the *Haustafeln,* both the seemingly superior and the allegedly inferior, are called to the "fear" of Christ (5:21). Such resumption of a motif from the beginning of a hymn or discourse has been called a ring-composition (see Introduction, section II) or an *inclusio* (cf. M. Dahood's frequent references in the

---

[173] See esp. Orr, pp. 6–11.   [174] Reicke, p. 32 affirms, Abbott denies this.
[175] According to BDF, 387:3; Schlier, p. 263. All the consulted English, French, German versions of Ephesians reckon with the applicability of this rule to the present text. Therefore they make vs. 33b sound as if it were a strict parallel of 33a. E.g. in NEB and NTTEV the husbands "must" love, the wife "must" (pay) respect. RSV and Phillips soften the command in both halves of vs. 33 and transform it into a counsel or good wish: "Let each one of you love . . . let the wife see that she respects." JB and C. Jordan's Cotton Patch Version make a slight distinction: "Must love . . . let respect," viz., "you all love . . . and let the woman have respect."
[176] Classical Greek writers would probably have used the optative (which is rarely employed in the NT) instead of the Pauline subjunctive. Cf. e.g. the exclamation, "O child, mayest thou become happier [*eutychesteros genoio*] than thy father" (Sophocles *Ajax* 550).
[177] See the last NOTE on 5:21.
[178] Von Soden, on the other hand, avoids the mollification: here as in 5:22, 23 "woman is placed in line with the slaves." This extreme view is not necessarily nearer the meaning of the original text than its opposites.

Anchor Bible to the occurrence of this pattern in the Psalms). If Paul had known the statement, "There is no fear in love, but perfect love casts out fear . . . He who fears is not perfected in love" (I John 4:18), he might have called for at least one exception: the love of Christ for the saints, and the love of the saints for Christ does not wipe out the fear and trembling with which they expect his coming.[179] When proselytes are called "God-fearers" (Acts 10:2; 13:16, etc.), there is no notion of undignified servility in this appellation. All depends on whom a person fears, on his reasons for fear, and on the corresponding special character of fear. To live in constant "fear of death" means to live in hopeless thralldom; from that fear men have been liberated through Christ's coming (Heb 2:15). Where there is nothing else but fear of men, a person is prone to neglect what the fear of God, the beginning of all wisdom, bestows and requires.[180] In the Bible and, e.g. in Sophocles' *Antigone,* fear of men is drastically cut to size, but this does not exempt men from a special fear of their fellow men which may be necessary or holy. A broad stream of OT, rabbinic, NT and extra-biblical traditions speaks of such fear.[181] In Rom 13: 3–5 evildoers (even among the Christians) are warned they must "fear" the political authorities and their wrath. At first sight, a similar thought seems to underlie Paul's exhortation to wives in Eph 5:33: the same evil impulse which can drive a man not to love his wife the way he "owes it" to God and her (5:28) may cause a wife to try to dominate her husband or to antagonize him and assume the role of a permanent revolutionary; see COMMENT II for evidence from Pauline churches. Just as a political revolutionary must "fear" the "wrath" of the authorities, wives appear to be enjoined to live in "fear" of (the wrath of) their husbands. But even in Rom 13:4–5 Paul places motivation by "conscience" higher than that by "fear." Certainly a wife's "fear" of her husband need not be a consequence either of a failure on her part or of a special risk she has taken to pursue a cause and tactics which she considers justified. She can have many *good* reasons to fear her husband, and can fear him in a way that does not degrade her in her own or in his eyes. When a husband loves his wife with a love inspired by Christ's love and (however feebly) resembling it, she would be a fool to prefer or seek autonomy apart from him, sufficiency in herself, or a dominant position over him (e.g. in applying to him a possessive or managerial motherly love, care, or anxiety). Instead of attempting to move him in the manner or by the tricks by which she may be able to move other men, she will be moved by him. Instead of shaping and changing him after her

[179] See COMMENT III for more extended arguments.
[180] Fear of men makes Pilate and visitors from Jerusalem in Antioch behave unwisely (John 19:8; Gal 2:12). Passages such as Pss 27:1; 118:6; Isa 41:13–14; 51:12; Acts 5:29; I Peter 2:17; Heb 13:6 show the limits of the fear of men.
[181] Robinson, p. 127, mentions the fear of parents, of Moses, of Joshua, of the king (Lev 19:3; Josh 4:14; Prov 24:21). In StB, I, 705–709 and III, 613, rabbinic references (e.g. from Bab. Kidd. 31a) are collected that show which kind of fear (Aramaic *kabōd;* German *Ehrfurcht*) was owed to the father and the husband. The classical Greeks recognized a special kind of healthy fear which certainly does not belong on the same level as those passions which, according to later Stoic teaching, are to be fought and subdued by a wise man. See e.g. Athene's recommendation in Aeschylus *Eumenides* 696 ff.

> Therefore, O citizens, I bid you bow
> In awe to this command, *Let no man live*
> *Uncurbed by Law nor curbed by Tyranny.*
> Nor banish ye the monarchy of Awe
> Beyond the walls; untouched by fear divine,
> No man does justice in the world of man.

heart's desire, she will feel thoroughly changed by him. Instead of bringing him under control, she will be overwhelmed by his love.[182] No less than the sunburned Shulammite from one occasion to another, she awaits her lover's coming and the ever-new experience of his love with fear and trembling.[183] A woman moved by *this* "fear" will by no means seek to make herself autonomous in relation to him who loves her[184] and she will receive him as one who in his own imperfect way reminds her of the true head of all the world, the church, her lover and herself: Jesus Christ, cf. 1:23; 4:15–16; 5:23, 29–30. She will be willing to be a companion to him as a very special "help," cf. Gen 2:18. There is nothing degrading in "fear" thus interpreted. The "fear" of which Paul speaks resembles that of the people who expect the Lord's coming "with uplifted heads," cf. Luke 21:28. Certainly Paul neither contemplated nor anticipated the emancipation of women occurring much later and still unfinished. But within the limits set by his contemporary world, he attempted to show that a woman is neither primarily passive, nor weaker than, nor inferior to man. He describes the union between husband and wife as a give and take, an exchange of offering and receiving, seeking and finding, tension and fulfillment. "Subordinate yourselves to one another!" Unless he and she are different there cannot be meaningful unity, but only boring sameness, stifling identity, abstract egalitarianism. Unless they demonstrate together to one another and all others what it means to be truly human, they do not live up to the creation of man in "God's image" as "male and female" (Gen 1:27). They are true mates and a convincing pair inasmuch as each one of them is active and passive, imaginative and yielding, preceding and following, in carrying out their special responsibilities for one another. According to Paul it is to be expected and it may and will happen that the husband's abounding love finds the response of the wife's admiring and festive fear. However, Paul does not prescribe or predict that even in the absence of love there must or can be a "fear (and trembling)" resembling that of the Bride expecting the Bridegroom's parousia.

[182] A beautiful illustration of this attitude is found in the lyrics and melodies of Mary Magdalene in A. L. Webber's and T. Rice's *Jesus Christ Superstar* (A Rock Opera, Decca Records, DX SA–7206, 1970). Mary Magdalene fears Jesus just because she loves him.

[183] Song of Songs 1:2–7; 2:3–17; 3:6–11; 5:2–16. In the Song of Songs, the love of two unequal partners is described: she is a country girl, he the king. While Paul does not presuppose an unequal social standing of wife and husband, there is yet a resemblance between Paul's "fear" of the wife and the "sickness with love" of which the Rose of Sharon speaks (in Song of Songs 2:5 and 5:8). Von Hattingberg, pp. 109, 248 speaks not of sickness but of fear, and throws some psychological light on the issue when he says, "From the view-point of reason it is paradoxical . . . [that a person desires what he fears]. In the sphere of love this ambivalence has been known for ages. It is felt in the frequent anxiety of the bride who impatiently yearns for the dreaded moment which will open her to love . . . 'Fear of . . .' may as well mean 'desire for . . .' " Since the *bridal* relation of the church to the Messiah is Paul's model of the wife's subordination to her husband, the attitude in which many a bride looks forward to the wedding night may well be included in the meaning of the verb "fear" in Eph 5:33. But an important difference between Paul's teaching and the quoted psychological observation should not be overlooked: Hattingberg speaks of a fear primarily related to a given event; Paul, however, speaks of the fear related to the person of the husband—without equating him with a *mysterium tremendum*.

[184] Von Allmen, p. 30.

COMMENTS I–VII on 5:21–33

1 Structure and Summary

Paul's exhortation to married people (5:21–33) forms the first of three parts of the social ethics that constitute the *Haustafel* (5:21 – 6:9).[185] The *Haustafel* is embedded among the general ethical admonitions to the whole Christian community and each of its members (4:17 – 5:20). All ethical statements are, in turn, part of the teaching on the public testimony of the church which begins with 3:1 and is grounded upon the proclamation of the foundation and formation of the church (1:3 – 2:22). After the union of Jews and Gentiles in the church was pointed out to be the great result of the Messiah's mission, death, and resurrection, Paul's proclamation is now put to a crucial test: does the Messiah Jesus whom the apostle preaches, and the community of the church whom he serves, in any way influence, change, and shape the life of men and women at its most intimate and perhaps most critical points?

It has been and still is widely believed that the author of Ephesians has stood this test in a uniquely competent way. If this were not the case uncounted marriage liturgies and manuals in the East and West would not contain key passages selected from Eph 5. Less enthusiastic is the reaction of modern exegetical scholars,[186] not to speak of feminists.[187] Attention is drawn to tensions and contradictions regarding marriage and woman that are found within the Pauline Epistles and appear to relativize the value of the extreme statements.[188] It is undisputed that in I Cor 7 and Eph 5 honorable attempts are made to reveal in terms of Paul's environment the relevance of faith in Christ for daily conduct. However, new times and situations seem to call not only for ever new interpretation of old canonical texts but also for new insights, counsels, and decisions. Church members in Hitler's Germany, such as D. Bonhoeffer, were forced by their faith in Christ to reject time-honored interpretations of Rom 13:1–7 which held this to be an unconditional command for total civic obedience; Rev 13 and other texts made them see the limitation of

---

[185] As earlier stated, the historical and literary problems of the *Haustafeln* will be discussed in the exposition of Col 3:18 ff.

[186] E.g. Preisker, pp. 27, 126, Delling, pp. 66 ff., and E. Stauffer, TWNTE, I, 652, confirm the widespread opinion that Paul's attitude to marriage is basically negative. A. Oepke, TWNTE, I, 785, finds in it "a tension . . . between a progressive and a Jewish reactionary tendency" (epitomized by the tension between Gal 3:28; I Cor 11:11–12; I Peter 3:7 on one, II Cor 11:3; I Cor 11:3, 7 on the other side). Stendahl, pp. 32–34, believes that equality of women *before God* is clearly proclaimed by Paul: "There is neither male nor female . . . in Christ Jesus" (Gal 3:28), but that in the early church the social inferences are not yet realized. Stauffer, TWNTE, I, 656, attempts to pass a kind judgment on Eph 5: "Sometimes the execution of . . . thought has been as artificial as its exegetical basis. But the enterprise is magnificent and bold. It is the only attempt of early Christianity to set marital duty definitely under the sign of the fact of Jesus." L. von Kirschbaum, K. Barth, von Allmen, Orr, Baltensweiler, Kähler and others elaborate mainly on the many traces of Paul's *positive* attitude to marriage and woman.

[187] The years in which this commentary is written are the era of the Women's Liberation Movement in the U.S., and of similar movements in other western countries. If Paul is mentioned in the pertinent literature at all, it is as an archenemy in whose name "submissiveness" is imposed upon and expected from all women.

[188] The arguments collected in I Cor 7 against marriage seem to conflict with the positive esteem for marriage in Eph 5. In turn, the subordination of wives postulated in Eph 5 appears to contradict the high praise which Paul gives to female cooperators, and equalitarian passages such as I Cor 7:2–5, 8–16, 26, 28, 32–34, 39. The expectation of the near parousia of the Lord dominates I Cor 7. Adaptation to environmental standards and the attempt to reconcile faith in Christ with *bourgeois* conduct have been found in Eph 5 – 6 and in other *Haustafeln*.

certain specific Pauline formulations. The question whether the change of time and culture permits or requires present-day Christians to reject the injunctions of I Cor 7 and Eph 5 cannot be treated in this commentary; only literal and historical problems can be taken up in the following—even those issues that may clarify Paul's orientation and the matters he wanted to point out to his readers. What elements are welded into a unit in Eph 5:21–33? How are they arranged? What intention is revealed?

The beginning, middle, and end of this passage contain exhortations in the form of direct imperatives or similar (stronger or weaker) verbal forms. All these exhortations, except the last pair, are supported by a single motivation: Christ.[189] Fear of Christ is the motive for mutual subordination (vs. 21); Christ's headship over the church is the standard of a wife's subordination to her husband (22–24); the Messiah's love is the ground and measure of the husband's love (25a); His unity with His Body and His care for the church are the reason why the husband who loves his wife loves himself (28–30). Since in *all* exhortations explicit references are made to Christ and the church, it seems that because of its naked imperative (they "must love") and warm wish ("may she fear"), vs. 33 falls out of the pattern. But the first impression is deceptive inasmuch as vs. 33 belongs to vss. 31–32, i.e. to the quote of the Gen 2 text which according to Paul is to be interpreted as a reference to "Christ and the church." Consequently, every "ought" contained in vss. 21–33 is supported by a Christological and ecclesiological "is."[190] Paul appears intent on saying nothing to the two partners in marriage unless he can show a Christological and ecclesiological reason. It is a trait typical of Paul to prefer this way of arguing to any other method: in vs. 32 he affirms explicitly that he is on his own: "I for one . . ." However, he does not proclaim only his private opinion; rather, the ethical topic at hand becomes for him an occasion to preach Jesus Christ himself.[191]

The genuinely Pauline hortatory and proclamatory elements are complemented by three groups of traditional materials. (1) There is a Christ-hymn (vss. 25–27) which earlier was called the "romance of Christ," composed (if not by Paul himself) probably in a Jewish-Christian environment. (2) There is a poetic Scripture quote from Genesis (vs. 31). (3) There are fragments of proverbial sayings of Jewish or pagan origin.[192] The denotation of the husband as "head of his wife" (vs. 23) cannot, as was shown in the NOTES on 5:23

---

[189] Cf. 4:17–32.

[190] Kähler, *Die Frau*, pp. 119–20, discusses the fact that *both* husband and wife are placed under Pauline indicatives *and* imperatives—so much so that neither of them can or must use Ephesians to make postulations of his own against his partner.

[191] According to Schlier, pp. 252–53, the "motivation" has actually gained the upper hand over the substance of the exhortation. A very careful attempt at describing (a) the traditional material in Eph 5:21–33, (b) the creative use made of it under Christological auspices, and (c) the structure and progress of thought, is made by Sampley, esp. pp. 103–8. A secular analogy to the introduction of Christ into the argument is found in, e.g. von Hattingberg's frequent references to "a higher third" which alone can unite the lovers and keep them together (pp. 179–81, 241, 262, 306, 334). Unlike von Hattingberg who cannot help but define this "third" in a confusing variety of ways—by God, by procreation, by a middle line between the two partners, by the coincidence of opposites, by reference to a sacrament—Paul's Christological argument is unambiguous, personal, warm, and free from abstract terms.

[192] Baltensweiler, p. 233, calls 5:22–23 a *Haustafel* into which "liturgical materials" were inserted in such fashion that their beginnings and ends are "fluid." But except in vs. 23b, quotation and conclusion formulae provide clear demarcations. Less clear, however, is the extension of the proverbial elements in vss. 28–29.

and 28, be identified as an axiomatic statement borrowed from Paul's or the Ephesians' environment. Most likely vss. 28b and 29a (the adage or adages about the relation of marital love to self-love) are, or allude to, popular proverbial sayings. The aetiological statement, borrowed from Gen 2 in vs. 31, proclaims a general truth.

All these elements are carefully selected and skillfully employed—as was the case with the traditional exhortations collected in 4:25 – 5:20. By using formulations other than his own Paul intends to establish a connection between his counsel and his readers' faith in Christ, the Scripture, and daily experience. All are drawn upon to support the apostle's ethical advice. All have an evangelical ring and add to the knowledge of Christ and the praise of God's glory: how great is the Messiah's love for the church, how close his unity with her! Each of the three elements might be considered sufficient for the point Paul wants to make, that is, the immediate relevance and indispensability of the Christ-church relationship for marriage.

Are the readers, however, confronted with three different, though intertwined arguments, motivations, reminders or illustrations—or are the three logically coherent and interdependent? In other words, do they form a threefold string in Paul's tapestry—or are three ropes tied together to keep the tent he erected upright?

Thomas Aquinas decided in favor of the first alternative. In his careful analysis he distinguished three separate arguments for a common purpose: (a) the example of Christ (vss. 25–27); (b) the nature of the husband, or the voice of reason (vss. 28–30); (c) the divine command, or the testimony of Scripture (vss. 31–32). While Thomas saw no problem in the complementary employment of these three supports, more recent interpreters have expressed (as will be shown in later COMMENTS) surprise at the appeal to self-love and at Paul's interpretation of Genesis. If the husband has to receive strength and direction from Christ's love at all—must that love be complemented by selfish love and strengthened by an argument from nature, as e.g. Calvin and Baltensweiler (p. 230) also assume? Can the Genesis text and the Christological argument be reconciled by as "forced" or "artificial" an interpretation of the OT as that proffered in vs. 32?

Others—as was observed in the NOTE on *mystērion* in vs. 32—have reacted with enthusiasm to the skillful combination of redemption and creation in Eph 5. Not even Lutheran scholars, who have grave reservations against the "legalism" emerging in the *Haustafeln,* condemn it as a mixture of gospel and law. A sizable group of interpreters discern basically only two arguments in 5:25–32, that is, the foundation of marriage ethics (a) in grace and (b) in nature. In order to make a distinction only between nature and grace (rather than between three or more motivations), the text from the creation story and the statements about self-love are treated as a unit. E.g. it is held that Gen 2:24 (in its literal meaning) was inserted by Paul only for the purpose of showing why a husband is so closely united with his wife that he cannot "hate his own flesh," but "loves himself" when he loves her.[193] However, vs. 32 reveals that Paul did not quote Gen 2 to strengthen a naturalistic element that might

[193] So, e.g. Mussner, p. 153, and Gaugler.

complement the Christological argument. For he does not interpret Gen 2 as a document outlining an abstract "order of creation" (*Schöpfungsordnung*), but as a prediction or description of Christ's love for the church.

Again, if the variant reading of vs. 30 is accepted as authentic, with its reference to the creation of Eve (the church) from the flesh and bones of Adam (Christ), four (rather than Thomas's three and his Catholic and Protestant imitators' two) arguments may be discovered in the core of 5:21-33: the "historic" origin of Eve (and/or the church) from Adam (viz. Christ) must then be added. Additional motivations for the conduct of husbands and wives may be found if the following are distinguished: (a) Christ's love; (b) self-love; (c) the commandment of Lev 19:18, "love your neighbor as yourself"; (d) the creation of Eve from the rib of Adam, or of the church from the open side of Christ (John 19:34) or in the Lord's Supper (I Cor 10:16-17); (e) the literal meaning of Gen 2:24; (f) the allegorical meaning of the same text. But these and other all too subtle distinctions may well reveal more of the analytical skill of Paul's interpreters, than of the apostle's intention and the comprehension of his first readers.

The connecting formulae, "In the same manner also" (vs. 28) and "For this reason" (vs. 31), show clearly that a continuous, climactic argument is unfolded in this passage.[194] It has the form of one single chain of thought, not a kaleidoscope. Paul begins by calling Christ the "head" and "savior" to whom it is an honor and joy to subordinate oneself (vss. 21-24). Then he breaks out in a song describing the Messiah as the Bridegroom who gives his life for the beloved and allows her to become what she could never be without him (vss. 25-27). Then he describes the effect of love: it forms a total unity and enriches the beloved and lover alike (vss. 28-30). Finally he ends with a Scripture quote and interpretation which confirm that God had nothing else in mind from the beginning of creation than such a unity as is now realized in Christ's relation to the church, and reflected in marriage. Explicit exhortations addressed to husbands and wives not only form the beginning and end of this proclamation of Christ, but occasionally also interrupt it. This part of Paul's ethics is so shaped that Christ is preached and the gospel proclaimed even in the discussion of a seemingly secular matter.

There are also simpler ways to describe the structure of 5:21-33. After an introduction which places men and women on an equal basis (vs. 21), the so-called "weaker" part (I Peter 3:7) is addressed first (vss. 22-24), then the husband (vss. 25-30), then both (vss. 31-33). Baltensweiler considers vss. 28b-33 an insertion by which the author wanted to make his main point: the testimony to The Great Mystery. Best, in turn, sees in vss. 22-27 a description of Christ's unique and complete love, in vss. 28-33 a witness to his continuous

---

[194] This is not to say that it would be strange for Paul to use diverse reasons in the service of one single exhortation. See e.g. the combination of scriptural, Christological, ecclesiological, liturgical, personal, common sense, emotional arguments in the Pauline pleas for the Jerusalem collection (II Cor 8-9). A similar barrage of reasons is given for a decent sustenance of a minister (I Cor 9:6-14), or for the proper appearance of women in public (I Cor 11:13-15); the reference to "nature" in vs. 14; cf. Rom 1:26, is specifically noteworthy. In Eph 6:1-4 at least four motivations underscore the obedience which children owe to their parents: (a) it corresponds to the being in the Lord (cf. it is "fitting for saints," 5:3); (b) it is right (even according to pagan and/or Jewish moral standards); (c) it is God's commandment; (d) it has a promise attached to it.

love; he calls the first group of verses a praise of Christ, the head, the second a praise of unity with Christ.[195]

Differing descriptions of the structure reveal whether the commentator attributes pre-eminence to the husband/wife topic or to the statements on Christ and the church. A decision between them need not be made. In this passage both topics are central, and both are ontologically and noetically so closely tied together that they cannot be unstrung—not even for the reconstruction of an original, supposedly Jewish or Greek *Haustafel*. The author moves from the subordination due to the head (vss. 21–24), through the description of the majesty of love (vss. 25–30), to the praise of its ground in the creator and redeemer God (vss. 31–33).

The dominant role of Christ in Paul's argument casts doubts upon the widespread theory that in this *Haustafel* Christ or some Christian formulae are placed in the service of a marriage concept inherited or recast by Paul from the views and customs of his environment. Actually, in his presentation the apostle does not ascend from marriage to Christ and the church.[196] Rather the problem of marriage gives him the occasion to praise Christ and to follow the procedure which determines the structure of Ephesians as a whole and each of its subsections: God, or the Messiah of God, whom Paul knows and praises, loves man in such a way that neither sin, nor death, nor former divisions, nor institutions, nor structures, and certainly not marriage, can escape the power and riches of grace.

The intention of Paul is to show that the "grace of our Lord Jesus Christ" gives husband and wife the basis, the strength, and the example which they need in order to live in that "peace to [or by] which God has called" them (I Cor 7:15). The "peace" between God and man, Jews and Gentiles, of which Paul spoke in Eph 2:14–16 shall be extended into every house and praised by the conduct of husband and wife.

The next COMMENT will discuss some elements of the situation which Paul's message addressed and by which he may have been influenced when he formulated his counsel.

II   The Position of Women and Marriage at Paul's Time

"We have courtesans (*hetairai*) for our pleasure, prostitutes (i.e. young female slaves) for daily physical use, wives to bring up legitimate children and to be faithful stewards in household matters."[197] Such a proud, possessive, or cynical statement may give frank expression to a classical Greek and Hellenistic male's feeling toward woman and marriage. According to rabbinic tradition,

[195] Baltensweiler, pp. 219–20; Best, p. 178.
[196] Muirhead, p. 186, "The thought moves from the Bridegroom and the Bride to the bridegroom and the bride, and not vice versa."
[197] Ps.-Demosthenes (ca. 340 B.C.) *adv. Neaeram* 122 (1386). Similar is the distinction of "wives, concubines and maidens" at Solomon's court which is made in Song of Songs 6:8–9; cf. 1:4; 8:12. Even the moralist Plutarch, who in his "Advice to Bride and Bridegroom" condemns the sowing of wild oats at one place, and recommends a wife who is in love with her husband for her faithfulness at another (*moralia* 145A; 768B), suggests in a third passage (*moralia* 140B; cf. 613A) that the noblesse of the Persian kings who engaged in licentiousness and debauchery with flutists, etc., only "after sending their wives away," i.e. behind their backs, be imitated.

R. Judah or R. Meir (both ca. A.D. 150) enjoined every Jewish man to say the following three blessings every morning: (I thank the Lord) "that he did not make me a Gentile, . . . a woman, . . . a boor."[198] Placing women on a level with pagans, slaves, or ignorant children, which is attested to in both pagan and Jewish sources, expresses less than the highest respect.

However, the Greek and Jewish texts just quoted (see fns. 12 and 35, *infra* the NOTES on 5:22, 23) present neither an exhaustive nor the most important characterization of the situation out of and into which Paul spoke. The position of married women in ancient Crete and Egypt was different from that in Greece and Rome, not to speak of Israel. In Greece, the freedom enjoyed by Spartan girls and the political responsibilities entrusted to their married sisters contrast with the imprisonment of Athenian women in a "monogamous harem." In Rome, from the time of Tiberius, both the ancient form of sacral marriage (*confarratio*) and the patriarchal contractual marriage, in which the wife came "under the hand" (*manus*) of her husband (that is, became his property), were on the way out. Instead, a mutual consensus guaranteed the rights of both partners in a third type of marriage: the wife spent at least three days a year in her parents' home in order to keep from coming into her husband's possession. Roman women of some social standing were free to pursue academic studies, to organize meetings, and to participate in worship ceremonies "for women only," as well as in street demonstrations. Lady Claudia, a contemporary of Caesar, not to speak of Cleopatra, used this liberty for other than innocent erotic and political adventures.[199]

While it was common for Greeks and Romans to speak of the "weaker" sex[200] and to treat unmarried and married women with a corresponding combination of courtesy and contempt, there was also a counter-movement which promoted equal rights for females. Not only philosophical, political, financial concerns, but also religious, poetic, and romantic forces were at work in most diverse cultural settings to change the position of women. The cultural trend of the last centuries before Paul and of his own age went toward the emancipation of women—in the case of marriage, toward loosening the unilateral bondage of wives.

The patron saint of the Egyptian women's movement was Isis. With the spread of the Isis cult and other Mystery Religions went the fact (and eventually, the right) that women gathered for worship without men. "Thou [Isis]

---

[198] Tos. Berakoth 7, 18; Bab. Menahoth 43b; cf. Jer. Berakoth 3, 3; 7, 2. Boucher, p. 53, follows the lead given by C. Taylor, *Sayings of the Jewish Fathers*, 2d ed. (Cambridge: University Press, 1897), pp. 137–40: when the rabbis formulated this prayer, they took over an originally Greek thought. E.g. Plutarch *vita C. Marii* 46, Diogenes Laertius I 33, and Lactantius *divinae institutiones* III 19, 17, affirm that Thales, Socrates, and Plato fostered this belief. "Acute Hellenization" of Jewish thought, rather than a genuinely Jewish or OT idea, is therefore expressed in the prayer quoted.

[199] As narrated with imagination by T. Wilder, *The Ides of March*, London: Longmans, 1948; repr. Harmondsworth: Penguin Modern Classics, 1961. Concise surveys of the general situation in East and West are given by H. Gressmann e.g. in RGG, 1st ed., II, 202–19; Oepke, TWNTE, I, 778–84, and in the articles on Marriage, Woman, Wedding, Divorce, etc., in EJ; RAC; Pauly-Wissowa; RGG; IDB; HDB, and other encyclopediae. Especially warm and passionate is J. Leipoldt's study, *Die Frau in der antiken Welt und im Urchristentum*, 3d ed., Leipzig: Koehler & Amelang, 1965. Some detailed questions regarding marriage in antiquity (such as the celibacy required of certain priestesses; the purity of virgins; the form of marriage ceremonies; the right to divorce, to remarry the same wife, to abandon unwanted children; the command of silence) will be mentioned in the following only in exceptional cases. Parallels and antitheses will be limited to those topics and aspects of marriage that are touched upon in Eph 5.

[200] See fn. 12 for examples.

gavest to women the same power as to men."[201] At a given period in Sparta women possessed two-thirds of the land. In Rome and Athens, and in some cases even among the Jews, they could obtain a divorce without losing the financial assets they had brought into marriage.[202] Among the Pythagoreans women enjoyed equal rights with men, and the Therapeutae described by Philo appear to have held women in similar esteem.[203] In Plato's *Republic* they bear political, educational, and military privileges and duties that are essentially equal to men's, though commensurate to the lesser physical strength of the female sex. Plato's argument for his revolutionary thought is the observation that a female dog is as useful to a shepherd as is her male counterpart. Therefore, women can and must belong to the "guardians" of the community.[204] Aristotle acknowledged that children can make a marriage stable, but he rejected the idea that the procreation of children is its sole purpose. Marriage was above all to be a community of love (*philiā*) in which the partners are helpers to one another, each contributing his particular gifts for the common welfare and joy.[205] This philosopher called it "barbarian" not to distinguish

[201] Papyrus Ox. 1380, 214–15 (ed. by B. P. Grenfell and A. S. Hant [London: Egyptian Exploration Fund, 1915], XI, 200).

[202] See esp. Bab. Kethuboth 77 and the other texts collected in StB, I, 318–20 for the conditions under which a Jewish woman could request a letter of divorce from her husband.

[203] Leipoldt, pp. 45, 59; Philo *vita contempl.* 2, 32, 68, 81. But in *apol. pro Jud.* (*hypothetica*) 380 (11:14–17) Philo says, "No Essene takes a wife, because a wife is a selfish creature . . . adept at beguiling the morals of her husband."

[204] Plato *resp.* v 451C–461D; 471D. Less convincing are his conclusions regarding communal possession of women and of all property, *resp.* v 458C–464D. Unlike the teaching proposed in *symp.* 191D, 192E (quoted in fn. 131) and in Eph 5:28–31. Plato's *Republic* does not know of one husband and one wife who become one (body). A third view of Plato's regarding women is represented by *Timaeus* 42A–C; 90C; 91A. According to these texts it is a divine punishment to be a woman, for a woman is halfway between a man and an animal. Cf. the similar opinion of the seventh century B.C. poet Semonides of Amorgos, quoted by Leipoldt, pp. 35, 167.

[205] *Eth. Nic.* VIII 12, 1162A. Aristotle's polemic is directed against the view that marriage had the primary function of procreation. The widespread ritual of a *hieros gamos* (a "holy wedding" or rather, a cultic copulation, e.g. of a king or priest with a selected female, representing a god and a goddess; see COMMENT VII A) was a fertility ritual, from which every married couple but also stables, trees, and fields of the land were to receive blessing (M. Eliade, *Cosmos and History*, Torchbook 50 [New York: Harper, 1959], pp. 25–27). The *gamoi hieroi* (ceremonies for sanctifying marriage) proposed by Plato (*resp.* v 458E; 460E) served the same purpose. (In turn, Ignatius, *Polyc.* v 1–2, appears to be the first Christian bishop who suggested an equivalent of an ecclesiastic marriage ceremony.) In *pol.* I 1552A; 1553B, Aristotle himself supported the view that marriage is above all the means for raising children. The Pseudo-Demosthenes dictum cited at the beginning of this COMMENT said the same. In Sparta bachelorhood was considered dishonorable because it deprived the state of future citizens and soldiers (Leipoldt, p. 27). The opinion that sexual intercourse is justified only when it aims at procreation became specifically influential under Stoic influence; to pursuers of wisdom all things passionate or pleasurable had become dubious. See, e.g. Musonius Rufus (ed. O. Hense, Leipzig: Teubner, 1905), 12, 63 ff.; Seneca *ep. ad Lucilium* 88:29: Tobit 8:6–7; *Test. Issachar* II 3; Philo *spec. leg.* III 36, 113; *praem.* 108; Josephus *c. Ap.* II 199, 202; *bell.* II 160–61; Clement of Alexandria *paed.* II 10, 92:2; Minucius Felix (an apologetic writer of the time of Tertullian) XXXI 5. See also fn. 27. OT passages such as Gen 1:28 ("be fruitful and multiply"; cf. Gen 3:16); Ps 127:2–3; Mal 2:15 speak of the promise or necessity of procreation, though without adding the Stoic discrimination against passion. The same is true of the possible allusion to Gen 1:28 in I Tim 2:15, and of the rabbinic doctrine saying that marriage and fecundity are divine commands; see, e.g. Yeb. 6, 6; P. Yeb. 6, 7, 13; T. Yeb. 8, 4; Kidd. 29b; Bab. Yeb. 63ab; Berakhoth 22a; Keth. 62b. As a biblical support, Exod 21:10 is quoted by the rabbis; see StB, II, 372–73; III, 368–71; Moore, *Judaism*, II, 119–20. Though, or because, only the husband was considered responsible for offspring, a woman's barrenness was declared a reason for divorce by some rabbis; by others, for taking a second wife; see StB, I, 317 for references, but also Philo's protest in *spec. leg.* III 35. In ancient Israel and even later, the necessity of procreation had its deepest motive in the promised birth of the Messiah. Thus a promise rather than a naked law was its ultimate ground. The endorsement of some elements of pagan asceticism by Christians who remained virgins even when married is in part explained by the conviction that the Messiah Jesus' birth from a woman made further marriage and procreation unnecessary—all the more since the parousia was expected in the immediate future; cf. I Cor 7 *passim;* 9:5; Mark 3:31–35; 10:29–30; Matt 19:12; Acts 8:26–39.

between a woman and a slave.[206] The second century B.C. Stoic philosopher Antipatros of Tarsus,[207] but even more beautifully Paul's contemporary Musonius Rufus, and finally Plutarch in about A.D. 100, wrote treatises on marriage which reveal a radical deviation from earlier Greek and Roman patriarchal concepts. The role of love, virtue, mutual help, and partnership in marriage is praised in the highest terms. Marriage is a bond tying together the two spouses so strongly that each of them is willing to give his life for the other.[208]

Long before enlightened philosophers championed the rights of women and the conception of marriage as partnership, Homer, the classic tragedians, Anacreon, and other poets had sung the praises not only of Hera and Athene but also of Nausicaa, Penelope, Andromache, Antigone, Cassandra, Iphigenia and other known and unknown, great and lovable women. There is also an unending stream of heroic and romantic literature, both in verse and in prose, that leads to the sensitive praises of Ovid and Horace. Testimony offered by letters, novels, tombstones, paintings, sculptures, and jewelry confirm this picture.

The examples mentioned suffice to show several things. In the ancient world a variety of concepts co-existed with or followed upon one another regarding the position of women and the order and purpose of marriage. Different periods and different geographical areas produced differing views. The same author, whether philosopher or poet, can apparently not only represent an opinion which conflicts with other authors, but also change his mind, contradict himself, depict various types of glorious single or married women, and recommend more than one meaningful model of marriage. Of course, there also existed an ample variety of patriarchal attitudes, as a special inquiry

[206] *Pol.* I 1252B. Yet later, in *pol.* I 1254A, he affirms that "the male is by nature superior, the female inferior"; in 1254B, that "equality of the two (viz. of soul and body as analogues of husband and wife) or the rule of the inferior is always hurtful"; in 1260A, that "silence is a woman's glory" (cf. Heliodor of Emesa *Aethiopica* I 21; third century A.D.); in 1259B that "the male is fitter to command than the female," while yet in a constitutional state (including the family) "the natures of the citizens are equal, and do not differ at all." Cf. the second NOTE on Eph 5:21 and fn. 12.

[207] His *Fragments* are found in J. von Arnim, *Stoicorum veterum fragmenta,* III (Leipzig: Teubner, 1903), 254 ff.

[208] Plutarch *moralia (conjug. praec.)* 142E; 143B; 145C admonishes the husband to "enter the feelings" of his wife, to be "kind to her by good will," to honor her as she honors him, to be a father, mother, brother, guide to her. In the same treatise he compares husband and wife to intertwined ropes. They are partners in possessing their property and having friends, relatives, and religion in common; their conversation and character make them "comrades"; though the woman has to "keep silence and stay at home" she is the husband's helpmeet. Certainly it is said, "All women are alike when the lights are out"; yet this is not true of a husband's wife. He has no greater respect for anybody than for her; if he mistreats her, how much worse will be his conduct to others. He is responsible for her intellectual advancement, and she is urged to "entertain high and splendid thoughts of her own"; Ulysses and Penelope rather than Paris and Helen are shining examples (*moralia* 140E–141A; 141D; 142D; 143DF; 145F–146A). Specifically warm is the attitude toward women also in such texts as Sir 26:1 ff.; Philo *de virt.* 110–12; Cicero *Tusc.* IV 32, 71–72; Stobaeus *eclogae* II 7, 11 ff.; Pliny the Younger *ep.* III 116; Seneca *ep.* 104:2; Diogenes Laertius VII 129. It appears that the farther west one went in the "civilized" ancient world, the freer the position of women at Paul's time. According to Leipoldt, p. 49, the Roman woman was, in contrast to her Greek contemporary, "her husband's comrade and cooperator." In East and West an alternative to this statute of woman and marriage is not only patriarchism, but also the total or temporary rejection of sexual intercourse and marriage. It is represented by rare OT instances Jer 16:2; Isa 56:1–8; by pagan priestly groups like the Vestals; by philosophers such as Epictetus (*diss.* III 22, 27) and some Neo-Platonists; also by the majority of the Essenes and by several Christian communities, including the monastic communities sanctioned by all churches except those of the Reformation. See Oepke, TWNTE, I, 779, and Baltensweiler, pp. 203–9, for a minimum of references. Among the pagan grounds for this attitude three are outstanding: the males' infinite superiority over females, the females' sacred marriage with a deity; the impurity of the sexual realm and of all human passions.

would reveal. Certainly the Ephesians knew of more than one custom-sanctioned or literally documented, traditional or revolutionary, attitude to women and marriage.

It can be questioned whether in writing 5:21–33 Paul was aware of this ongoing discussion with its fierce and often eloquent debates. The method he chose for making his points suggests a positive answer: just as philosophers spiced their diatribes on marriage with quotes from classical writers, and poets referred to the examples of great lovers rather than make use of abstract definitions, so Paul inserted quotes into his arguments. Christ's love, acclaimed in a Christ hymn, takes the place of the love affairs of Zeus, Paris, and so on; the obedient church replaces Hera, the guardian of morals, and Aphrodite, the protector of free love. Instead of Isis and Osiris, the divine pair, there is Christ and the church, a pair composed of a divine and a human partner. The book of Genesis is substituted for Homer's *Iliad* and *Odyssey* and similar epical accounts; carefully selected and reinterpreted proverbial sayings hold the position of sophisticated observations such as are exchanged among wise men, and crude scurrilities such as delight a stag party.[209]

However, another question is more crucial. Does the author of Eph 5 attempt to stem the rising tide of women's emancipation and the ongoing reinterpretation of marriage as a partnership of equals? More precisely, does he so confidently rely on late Jewish-patriarchal notions and other relics that he in effect does no more than adumbrate museum pieces with a Christological halo, and impose polished antiquities as a house rule upon the Christian community?

On the whole, modern scholars have answered the second question in the affirmative; see the examples in footnotes 3, 4, and 186. However, they do not belittle the author's noble intention to "Christianize" the tradition in which he had grown up. While the OT contains colorful stories of great women and covenant-like marriages,[210] it is easy to collect a florilegium of statements from Jewish sources that must look to egalitarians and feminists like a catalogue of vices. The passages quoted, e.g. in StB (see BIBLIOGRAPHY 21), by Oepke in the TWNTE, and by Leipoldt are so one-sided that they produce a disgusting picture, and not only for suffragettes.[211] However, the creation of

---

[209] In the preceding COMMENT and the pertinent NOTES, the several traditional materials in 5:23, 25–27, 28–29, 31, were discussed in detail.

[210] To mention only Sarah, Rebecca, Miriam, Deborah, Michal, Abigail, Hulda, Esther. The evil counter-example offered by Jezebel is not used to conclude that a man should never accept his wife's counsel. Num 27:8; 36:6, 8; Gen 24:39, 58 and the book of Ruth show that daughters could inherit land and give their consent to a betrothal.

[211] Men thank God for not being created as woman; women are enumerated together with (pagan) slaves and children or boors; they cannot fulfill certain specified functions in divine worship and are exempt from the keeping of some commandments; in the temple, the Court of Women lies outside the Court of Israelites (in orthodox synagogues to the present day women worship from veiled galleries); in certain cases women cannot be witnesses in court; a wife belongs to the husband's property; she must obey him, for this "is proper for a woman"; she can be unilaterally divorced for sometimes cheap reasons; polygamy is permitted; Eve's temptation and fall precedes Adam's and is typical of an inherent tendency in all women; a "woman is inferior to man in every respect"; etc. See e.g. Num 5; Eccles 7:26–29; Sir 25:24; *Test. Reuben* III 10; IV 1; VI 1–2; Philo *de ebrietate* 55; *op. mundi* 165, 167; *spec. leg.* II 24; Josephus *bell.* II 121; V 199; *ant.* III 5; *c. Ap.* II 201; Tos. Berakoth 7, 18; Sota 3, 4; Jer. Berak. 13b; Bab. Menachoth 43b; Kidd. 29b; Gittin 90; Kethuboth 27b; 72a ff.; Shabbath 152a. The distortion of Mal 2:14–16 by the interpretation that God hates the mutual divorce among pagan couples, but has privileged Israel by allowing a husband to divorce his wife (P. Kidd. I 58c, 16 and Gen. Rabba 18, 12c, quoted in StB, I, 213; II, 24), is ascribed to rabbis living about A.D. 300 and later, but cannot be traced back to Paul's time. The

this image is most likely one of the many effects of the traditional, popular, and scholarly anti-Semitism fostered in the Christian church. An unbiased study of the Jewish sources comes to a much more dialectical result. Many Jewish utterances speak of the obligation of husbands to their wives, of happy and model marriages, of wise and exemplary women.[212] All that they express regarding the equal status of husband and wife must not be neglected or counted as irrelevant. Paul cannot have followed "the Jewish tradition" for this tradition is neither uniform nor free of contradictions. Also, there is no single Jewish (Aramaic) equivalent for the Pauline "subordinate." Finally, in most Jewish sources (except Ps 45, the Song of Songs, and their literal or allegorical interpretations) a direct relationship between the order of marriage and the Messiah is not established or expounded. Though there are clear traces of some Jewish traditional elements in Paul's marriage counsels,[213] the substance of Eph 5:21-33 must be traced to another source.

In the Ephesian *Haustafel* and elsewhere Paul does not develop an ethical doctrine unrelated to specific problems of his times. He addresses himself to a specific situation with which he was acquainted through personal experience and hearsay. All Pauline epistles[214] are pastoral epistles which take up and answer specific problems, rather than tracts pronouncing timeless verities and abstract principles. What is known about the problems of married couples in congregations founded or addressed by Paul?

There is no reason to assume that the broad stream of women's emancipation running through the Hellenistic world had left untouched the Gentile and Jewish men and women who joined a Christian congregation. Since this stream was supported and found expression in the cults of specific deities and in the formation of religious communities,[215] it was unavoidable that the Christian community and its worship appeared to be a source of strength, offering a potentially powerful protection and an occasion to exercise and celebrate the emancipation of the "weak."[216] Here children were welcomed—on the basis of dominical sayings. Here a slave counted as much, if not more than, a master. For here The Child and Servant of God, Jesus Christ, was preached about and celebrated as the Lord of the world and the liberator of the op-

---

statement, "Non-Israelites have no divorce," was not meant to deny the fact of divorces among Gentiles, but excused Gentiles for remarrying the same woman who after her divorce had married another and then returned to her first. To Israel such a remarriage was forbidden: Deut 24:4 (also Rom 7:1-3?).

[212] See the injunction against divorce in Mal 2:14-16 as expounded in Gittin 90b; the command of monogamy based upon Gen 1:27; Deut 17:17 in CD IV 21 – v 2 (XIII 17?); Midr. Rabba Exod 14, 15: "Before God all are equal: women and slaves, poor and rich"; Tanna Elialm R. 9: "Whether Israelite or Gentile, man or woman, male or female slave—according to their works the Holy Spirit dwells also upon him." Cf. fns. 35 and 95. In her essay Boucher discusses additional rabbinic texts that reflect presumably old oral traditions. She wants to show that even at Paul's time some Jews pronounced the equality of women before God in such a way that a ground was laid for the equality in society, too. "It may be that the contrast between the Jews' subordination of women and the Christians' new interest in their equality has been too sharply drawn" (p. 55)—so she argues against Stendahl and others who hold that "glimpses" (Stendahl, p. 34) of religious and social equality occur first in the NT and indicate a deviation from traditional Judaism.

[213] This is most obvious in the argument for the (Jewish!) tradition of the appearance of women in public: I Cor 11:3-15. It holds true for Paul's appeal to the "Law" when he tells women not to disturb the service by endless questions (though they are permitted to pray and to prophesy): I Cor 11:5, 13; 14:26-36. It is also obvious in the deutero-Pauline passage: I Tim 2:11-15.

[214] Including Romans, as esp. the ethical chapters 12-15 reveal.

[215] Isis and other Mystery Cults, also Philo's Therapeutae, were mentioned earlier.

[216] See esp. Gal 3:28; I Cor 1:26-29; 7:23; Luke 6:20-21; James, *passim*.

pressed. At the places where rumors about the virgin birth of Christ began to circulate, the miraculous event could be understood as proof of female self-sufficiency and ultimate independence from the male.[217] Four things are certain:

a) As a cultural and religious center, Ephesus and its environment were open to all contemporary secular and religious currents and developments. The cult of the Great Mother and the Artemis temple stamped this city more than others as a bastion and bulwark of women's rights.

b) In Corinth women were among those church members to whom knowledge of Christ meant the sanction of a "wisdom" which "puffed them up" (I Cor 8:1, etc.) in their mutual relations. This vain wisdom led to the formation of religious parties and supposedly granted freedom to participate in idol festivals, and to engage in immoral conduct. In following this tendency of many Corinthian church members, some women of Corinth used the worship service for a display of the gained emancipation. Paul mentions that in a disturbing manner they liked to ask questions during the assemblies for worship rather than in the privacy of their homes (I Cor 14:33–35), and that they refused to wear that kerchief or veil which in Jewish and Jewish-Christian congregations signified a married woman's subordination to her husband (I Cor 11:5–10). While Paul gladly recognized and supported the appearance and activity of "praying and prophesying" women in worship, he was opposed to the introduction of precocious talk and the display of provocative attire in the assemblies of the saints.

c) Onesimus understood the freedom proclaimed by Paul[218] in a way which anticipated the peasants' understanding of Luther's message in the early Reformation period. Spiritual freedom had to include social liberty; if the master did not realize this, the servant felt all the more entitled to go ahead with its social, economical and political implementation.[219] What was good enough for a slave could equally be claimed as a right and duty of a baptized woman.[220]

d) Not only libertinistic but also ascetic tendencies developed in Pauline congregations. Total abstinence from sexual intercourse and marriage was

---

[217] K. Goldammer, RGG, III, 1016, speaks of the "combination of two ideal types of the female deity" in the ancient oriental cults of a "virginal mother-goddess," which included sacral prostitution. Several forms of the Isis cult, for example, illustrate the ambivalent religious and moral consequences of the worship of the Great Mother, ranging from castration to cultical and commercial prostitution, including among its options also matriarchism. See G. van der Leeuw, "Phenomenology of Religion," in *Religion in Essence*, vol. 1 (New York: Harper Torchbook 100), ch. 12:5; J. G. Frazer, *The Golden Bough*, abr. ed. (New York: Macmillan, 1960), pp. 416–17, 444–45; E. James, *The Cult of the Mother Goddess*, New York: Praeger, 1959; E. Neumann, *Die grosse Mutter* (Zurich: Rheinverlag, 1956), pp. 190–92, 209–11; tr., *The Great Mother*, Princeton University Press, 1963. On p. 256 (of the German edition) it is stated: "The feminine as the Great Mother is the Virgin—she who is the creation principle in its independence from the personal male." Neo-Platonic and other pagan notions regarding defilement by passions and intercourse gained the upperhand in Augustine's doctrine of original sin and in medieval Mariology; but originally they were not the only basis and criteria for explaining and praising the birth of Jesus from the Virgin Mary. Outside and inside the church, wherever a virgin is highly revered in the cult, sexual purity and abstention are not the only ways to celebrate the maiden or her miraculous offspring.

[218] E.g. in Gal 5:1–13; I Cor 7:21–23; Rom 6:18; Eph 3:12 var. lect.

[219] See the epistle to Philemon and I Cor 7:17–24, also the revolutionary tendency among the Christians in Rome who were called to order in Rom 13:1–7.

[220] Otherwise Paul would not have restrained women (as well as men) from unilateral separation or divorce and remarriage later (I Cor 7:10–16). Cf. the warning extended to women in I Tim 2:12: They must not seek authority "over the husband" (RSV errs in translating "over men").

promoted by a group in Corinth—but endorsed by Paul only with restrictions.[221]

These four facts contain a background or illustrate a *Sitz im Leben*, in which it is explicable why Paul starts and ends his marriage counsel with the admonition to "fear the Lord," to "subordinate oneself," and to "fear the [loving] husband."[222] He intended to assert the priority of Christ's rule over a revolution started for its own sake: "Because you fear Christ subordinate yourselves to one another" (5:21).

In the following COMMENTS some of the most important details of 5:21–33 are selected for further elucidation.

III   The Fear of Christ

Of all the NT *Haustafeln*, only in Eph 5:21 and 33 is reference made to "fear": "Because you fear Christ . . . may the wife fear her husband." In the NOTES to these verses it was shown that the substitution of words softer than "fear," e.g. "awe," "reverence" or "respect," contradicts philological evidence and must be rejected in favor of the literal translation.[223] Only the strong term "fear" corresponds to the Greek text. In using this term, Paul contradicts the enlightened religious, cultural, and social trends of his own time[224] probably as much as he alienates "modern man."[225] The apostle himself was

---

[221] While Paul decries fornication and homosexual intercourse in I Cor 6:12–20; Rom 1:26–27; Eph 4:19; 5:3, 5, he does not condemn the sexual drive and its satisfaction as such. But he proclaims the priority of the expectation of the parousia, of prayer, and of caring for the Lord, over the "passing" matters "of this world": I Cor 7:1–9, 25–40; cf. Titus 2:4–5.

[222] The problem he faced was apparently not essentially different from that mentioned in Gal 5:13: "Do not use your freedom as an opportunity for the flesh, but through love be servants of one another." Cf. I Peter 2:16: "Live as free men, yet without using your freedom as a pretext for evil." Either libertinistic indulgence in fleshly lust, or legalistic abstention from all that establishes the closest human tie, may be meant in these and other texts that warn of the misuse of freedom.

[223] While all attempts to make Ephesians understandable to modern man are to be hailed, historical and literal exactitude cannot be sacrificed to the endeavor to make Paul more palatable. Paul could and probably would have used *timē*, *timaō* (as earlier stated) or *aidōs*, *aideomai* (cf. Plato *leg.* I 646E–650D), instead of *phobos* and *phobeomai* if he wanted to call for an attitude different from fear. Plato was willing to permit a role to naked fear only in the education of orphans (*leg.* XI 927AB).

[224] While social and psychological tendencies were discussed in the preceding COMMENT, the religious trends cannot be summed up briefly. It must suffice to state (a) that the "fear of the Lord" proclaimed, e.g. in the Proverbs has hardly any parallels in the Egyptian and Babylonian materials incorporated into that book; (b) that Greeks and Romans did not like to consider themselves "servants" of their gods; (c) that "fear of the numinous" was being displaced by smoothly operated services in temples and synagogues; and (d) that the strong invasion of oriental Mystery Cults was resented by enlightened persons. Livy XXXVIII 8 ff. justifies a police action of the year 186 B.C. against a Mystery community by arguing that its imitators are bound so strongly to a deity that they can no longer be bound by a *sacramentum* ("religious oath") to their civic obligations. Official persecutions of the Christians were similarly motivated.

[225] In the wake of S. Kierkegaard's *Fear and Trembling* (Princeton University Press, 1941), and, *The Concept of Dread* (Princeton University Press, 1944), as reinterpreted for philosophers by M. Heidegger's, *Being and Time* (London: SCM, 1962) and for a broader public in psychotherapy and literary works, "dread" (or "anxiety"; in German *Angst*) has taken the place of "fear." The two are not the same. "Fear is removed when the specific external cause is removed. But anxiety is the general, the underlying common denominator of the person's capacity to experience threat, to experience his precarious situation. Anxiety, therefore, must be the generic term, and fear can only be understood as an objectified form of anxiety" (R. May, *Psychology and the Human Dilemma* [Princeton: Van Nostrand, 1966], p. 107). However, in the Bible "fear" is a relational concept which includes (a) the appearance and action of the person who is feared, (b) the immediate terrified reaction, and (c) a permanent attitude produced by the other person's power or authority, and the reaction to it. "Anxiety" in modern parlance means a state of the psyche (on the conscious or subconscious level) which may have for an object, e.g. Nothing(ness), something unknown or undefinable, or certain features of the technological age and its dubious achievements. Such anxiety resembles, in turn, the fear of demons, of nature, of the changing mood and unpredictability of the gods, which is attested in religions all over the world, for instance in Babylonian utterances

witness to a war against fear of otherworldly and this-worldly powers; it was waged by means and for the purpose of mental enlightenment, and of a reasonable technical, psychological, and sociological organization of human life. Only the literary and historical problem is to be treated here: What did the apostle mean by using the strong word "fear"? Did he perhaps contradict not only his contemporaries' feelings, but also what he himself had written about the supremacy of the love of God, Christ, and the neighbor? In, e.g. Rom 8:15, he had stated, "You received not the spirit of slavery to fall back into fear but . . . the love of Christ"!

The "fear of the husband" (vs. 33) is logically dependent upon the "fear of Christ" (vs. 21). This shows that according to Paul the "fear of the husband" is ontologically called into being by the "fear of Christ," and phenomenologically shaped and expressed after the pattern of man's relationship to the "savior of the body" (5:23). For this reason the meaning of "fear of Christ" must be clarified. Verse 22 states explicitly that the wife subordinates herself to the husband "as to the Lord." Variant readings of vs. 21 substitute "God" for "Christ"; they make clear that "Christ," "the Lord," even the divine Christ and Lord, is the object of fear, not a horrifying fellow man or human custom.[226] When the OT comes close to mentioning fear of the Messiah—it is the "Lord's Messiah" or the Lord himself, who is the object of fear among the tumultuous nations (Ps 2:7; cf. Isa 41:5).

Whenever the OT and NT, as well as intertestamental and later Jewish writings, speak of the "fear of God" or the "Lord," more is meant than awe, reverence, or respect. In the OT, the Elohist, Deuteronomy, the Deuteronomic redactors, the Prophets, the Psalms, and the Wisdom books frequently use the stem yr' ("fear") or one of its derivates and equivalents. The Priestly materials, including Song of Songs and Ezekiel (except, e.g. Ezek 12:18–20) speak rarely of fear. God is feared when he appears in an epiphany, dream or vision, and when he manifests himself in mighty deeds for his people, against his enemies, in nature or in the personal life of individuals. Then he is experienced as the numinous, the Holy One. The appropriate reaction is awe before his majesty, jubilation over his victory in the holy war, horror before

---

about Inini (Ishtar, the "deity of men, goddess of women") when she behaves like "an angry wild ox" (ANET, p. 384). Pertinent observations regarding the hermeneutical problem facing "modern man" in the biblical statements about fear, are made by H. R. Balz, "Furcht vor Gott?" EvTh 29 (1969), 626–44. See also S. Plath, *Furcht Gottes*, Arbeiten zur Theologie 2, Stuttgart: Calwer Verlag, 1963; J. Becker, "Gottesfurcht im Alten Testament," AnBib 25 (1965); and the articles on fear in theological wordbooks. Many arguments here reproduced are culled from Becker and Balz.

[226] The emphasis placed by Paul upon the dependence of the wife's subordination and fear upon the specific subordination and fear owed by all saints to the one Jesus Christ (rather than to undefined gods or moral principles, or a given definition of the common good) distinguishes Eph 5:21–33 radically from the appeal for good citizen- and partnership formulated, e.g. in Isocrates (orator, fifth–fourth centuries B.C.) *ep.* 2; Stobaeus *ecl.* III 32:1 ff.; IV 32:6 ff., etc. However, when Sophocles' Antigone trespasses against a city ordinance and gives her brother a minimal decent burial, she pleads her obligation to the deities of the family which in her case overrule the deities of the state. Equally in other Greek tragedies it is not fear in general, and certainly not fear of men, but awe of a specific deity that is depicted as a compelling force—like the fear of Christ in Paul; cf. the Aeschylus quote in fn. 181 above. Balz, EvTh 29 (1969) 635, 641, appears to have overlooked the dominant function of Eph 5:21 in the *Haustafel*: 5:21 – 6:9—or else he would not write, "In the *Haustafeln* . . . fear has been separated from its origin in the specific relationship [of man] to the dreadfully angry and infinitely loving God, and has been made a general, absolute attitude of behavior."

his irresistible power.[227] In Deuteronomy, fear of the Lord, the learning of his commandments, and love are used as synonyms. Here it is impossible to set the "love" of Yahweh against "fear," for neither is just an emotional attitude. Both mean to adhere to Yahweh faithfully, that is, to do his will according to his covenant and law. While Luther in his Smaller Catechism begins the interpretation of each of the Ten Commandments with the words, "We shall fear God and love Him . . . ," K. Barth suggests that fear of God is subsequent to the love for God. Probably the author of Deuteronomy would agree.[228] In Ephesians Paul speaks extensively of the love of God and Christ, and of brotherly love, before he mentions "fear" in 5:21, 33. Even in 5:25–33 love is dominant over fear, the covenant reality over sheer dependence. "Fear" may be called a "cultic" concept—if by cult is meant the total attitude of a covenant member to God and his neighbor, not just a form of lip service such as the classic prophets denounce. A similar cultic concept of "fear of God" is presupposed in the Psalms where either the worshiping assembly, or the whole chosen people, or pious individuals are called "God-fearers." To fear the Lord is to serve him faithfully, and vice versa.[229] In the Elohistic strands of the Pentateuch and in the Wisdom books, as well as occasionally in other passages, "fear of God" has primarily a moral sense which eventually can (but need not) lead to legalism, servility or calculation upon reward.[230]

In the NT the strongest exponents of a "theology of fear" are the Gospel of Mark and the apostle Paul. Fear and trembling seizes the disciples and crowds who see God's power at work in the miraculous deeds and words of Jesus of Nazareth—even before his resurrection. Fear is present even more after his

[227] Gen 3:10; Exod 3; Judg 5:4–5; Isa 6; Deut 33:2, etc. The personal character of God's appearance, the manifestation of his distinct will, and the missionary rather than the private character of such revelations of God distinguish them, despite some common features, from the experience of the *mysterium tremendum* described by R. Otto, *The Idea of the Holy*, London: Milford, 1923. Balz, EvTh 29 (1969), 638–39, describes the difference between the biblical and other religious statements on fear, by speaking of the absence in the Bible (a) of mythological orientation, (b) of the sheer dread of demons and natural powers which never permits a relationship of confidence, (c) of a power demonstration which aims at man's total dependence instead of freeing him for a personal response. Obviously, the Homeric god Phobos (the son of the war god, Ares) and his representation by horrid pictures of Gorgons and Medusae on the battle shields, but also the "fear (and pity)" raised (according to Aristotle *poet.* VI 1449B; *pol.* VIII 1343A) in the spectators of Greek tragedies by the incomprehensible fate of man, are met with an alternative. Fear is not replaced by the theory that no gods at all exist to be feared, or by the freedom from passions, emotions, affections, as preached by the Stoics. Rather the Bible proclaims that only the God of Israel who proves present and mighty in battles and afflictions is worthy to be feared. If he is honored with fear and trembling, then it is out of gratitude, joy and love—as esp. Deuteronomy and the Psalms show.

[228] See Becker, AnBib 25 (1965), 85–111; K. Baltzer, *Das Bundesformular*, WMANT 4 (1960), 44–47; and esp. W. L. Moran, "The Ancient Near Eastern Background of the Love of God in Deuteronomy," CBQ 25 (1963), 77–87. The passages Deut 4:10; 5:10, 29; 6:2, 5, 13, 24; 7:9; 8:6; 10:12, 20; 14:23; 17:19; 30:6, 16, and Josh 4:24; 24:14; I Sam 12:14, 24; I Kings 8:40, 43; II Kings 17:7, 25, 28, 32–39, 41 in the deuteronomistically edited books, are among the prime references. Bab. Sota 31a gives an account of a dispute over the question whether fear or love of God is more important? The decision falls in favor of love. Cf. K. Barth, II 1, 31–36.

[229] Pss 15:4; 22:23, 25; 25:14; 31:19; 34:9, 11; 103:13, 17; 111:5; 119:74, 79; 130:4, etc.; cf. I Kings 18:3, 12; II Kings 4:1; Jer 32:39–40; Isa 29:13; 63:17; Mal 3:16, 19[4:1]; Bar 3:7.

[230] Elohist: Gen 20:11; 22:12; 42:18; Exod 1:17, etc.; other texts: Ps 55:20; II Chron 19:7, 9; Neh 7:2; Mal 2:5; 3:5. Acts of obedience against distinct utterances of God's will are described as a result of "fear" in the Holiness Code: Lev 19:14, 32; 25:17, 36, 43, and in Neh 5:9, 15; prophetic directives are followed in "fear": Exod 9:20, 30; Jer 26:19; Hag 1:12. In the Wisdom books, Prov 1:7, 29; 2:5; 9:10; cf. Isa 11:2; 33:6 are specifically important examples: "Fear" is used as a parallel or synonym of "knowledge of God" or "wisdom." In other Wisdom texts "fear" approaches the meaning of prudence, carefulness, reckoning with the consequences, i.e. the good or bad remuneration from God's side. According to Becker, AnBib 25 (1965), 233–80, cf. 283, the latter use of fear opens the way to a nomistic attitude which gains the upper hand in the latest OT books and the LXX, but was still foreign to the Deuteronomist.

crucifixion and after the promise is made that he will appear again.[231] Just as in the Jewish nomenclature for proselytes, "God-fearers," so also in Mark fear is "an essential aspect of faith."[232] The same is true of Paul: "Fear and trembling"[233] are mentioned when the apostle is facing situations of extreme danger. The confrontations and the decisions to be made during his missionary activity are for the apostle transparent events; he always stands before God or Christ himself. Immediately after describing the judgment of the Messiah, in which all men will be requited according to the good or evil deeds they did during their lifetime, Paul speaks of the "fear of the Lord"; this fear motivates his actions, his sufferings, his hope for this life and the future (II Cor 5:10–11). In I Cor 10:22 he warns against "provoking the Lord to jealousy." In II Thess 1:5–10 he uses drastic apocalyptical language to describe the judgment of God to be held when the Lord Jesus "is revealed from heaven with his mighty angels in flaming fire." The connection of fear with judgment is most explicit in Eccles 12:13–14: "Fear God and keep his commandments. . . . For God will bring every deed into judgment." Eschatology can no more be eliminated from the undisputed Pauline letters than can the motive of fear be separated from Paul's message, exhortation, and personal conduct.

Five inferences can be drawn from this inquiry regarding the words "Because you fear Christ subordinate yourselves" (Eph 5:21).

a) Since there is no evidence that the exact words "because you fear Christ" (lit. "in the fear of Christ") were used anywhere in the OT, in Jewish intertestamental writings, in the temple, in synagogues, in heretical groups, or in the early church, they cannot be called "a traditional formula" or cliché, and treated as irrelevant to the context. Rather, whenever Paul speaks of "fear" he means what he says; the relative scarcity of statements about "fear" in his letters gives all the more weight to those which are found. The same holds true for a letter written or edited by a disciple of Paul, e.g. I Tim 5:20.

b) When the author speaks of the "fear" of Christ, he can have in mind either the numinous, the cultic, the moral, or the so-called nomistic notion of this term. Each of them occurs in the OT and those later Jewish writings that have strongly influenced Paul. While often in the OT several of these meanings are combined, in specific instances different shades of meaning can be discerned (see fn. 230). Since Paul, too, may have in mind either a combination of senses, or a special accentuation of one given sense, a one-sided decision cannot be made. Most likely none of the OT senses, not even the Wisdom

---

[231] Mark 4:41; 5:15, 33; 9:6; 16:8. Because the call, "Fear not," is taken up by Jesus in Mark 5:36; 6:50; 13:7; cf. John 6:20; 16:33. Balz, EvTh 29 (1969), 631–34, rejects the hypothesis that the original Gospel of Mark ended with 16:8.

[232] Balz, EvTh 29 (1969), 630 writes: "In his wrath and in his love God is great and terrible (. . . Deut. 7:21; Ps. 96:4; II Sam. 7:23, etc.). His deeds evoke fear, because they are marvelous, incomprehensible, powerful." But he is "not only experienced in threatening power which compels to flight, but as a holy and righteous power which requires submission and adoration, esp. from the Gentiles, Ps. 2:11; 9:20; 33:8 ff.; Ex. 14:31; Jer. 10:5 ff."; cf. TWNT, IX, 186–216. Balz wrote these words to sum up the OT evidence about fear; the same description also fits Mark's image of Jesus and Paul's proclamation of Christ. Sampley, pp. 114–21, esp. 121, may underplay the substance and function of "fear" when he assumes that it points to no more than "an initiative taken by God . . . or by Christ."

[233] Referring to the occurrence of this term in as widely different passages as Judg 7:3; Pss 2:11; 55:4–5; Ezek 12:18–20; I Cor 2:3; II Cor 7:15; Philip 2:12; Eph 6:5; Mark 5:33, JB calls this term "a biblical cliché" (note on I Cor 2:3). In II Cor 5:11; 7:11; Rom 11:20 "fear" alone is mentioned.

meaning of "fear," can be excluded. There is, however, no reason to assume that Paul wanted to find the ultimate motivation of ethics in a naked fear, unrelated to God and the special appearances, deeds, promises, and threats combined with God's name and the Messiah's coming. He certainly did not suggest that an absolute horror of the divine (panic, fright), fear of persecution by men, or calculation about the reward to be distributed by a blindfolded goddess Justitia, was to be the ground on which ethics would flourish. He speaks of the fear "of Christ" in order to distinguish this special fear from all other possible fears—including the ancient and modern existentialists' *Weltangst* which seems to be described by John 16:33 ("In the world you have tribulation") and is distinctly alluded to in Heb 2:15 where mankind is described as "those who through fear of death were subject to lifelong bondage."[234]

c) The eschatological overtone of the term "fear of Christ" is in harmony with the other distinctly eschatological elements in Ephesians.[235] It puts all ethical commands of the *Haustafel* under the sign of eschatological promise

[234] Following the lead given by Bultmann's understanding of the function of ancient myth as an expression of man's self-understanding, H. Jonas, *Gnostic Religion*, pp. 320–40, has attempted to demonstrate by the example of Gnosticism that ancient and modern man shared in basically the same *Angst* of fate, meaninglessness of existence, unpredictability of the future. Earlier it was mentioned that Sophocles in his *Antigone*, and Plato in *leg.* I 646E ff., recognized different types of fear. They pointed out that one of them can be more justified than the other.
However, does not I John 4:18 repudiate fear in all its forms and in principle? "There is not fear in love, but perfect love casts out fear!" Just as in I John not every kind of love—e.g. not the love for the world—but only the love of the Father, for the Father, and for brothers is recommended (2:10, 15; 4:7–10), so the "fear" which is "driven out by love" according to 4:17–21 may well be a very specific fear, determined by its object rather than only by its psychologic (subconscious or conscious, stimulating or laming) character. Fear of men, of the world, of death may be meant; but there is no reason to assume that I John, by speaking of "confidence for the day of judgment" (4:17), wanted to eradicate what the OT, Mark, and Paul describe as "fear of the Lord." Dodd, *The Johannine Epistles*, 3d ed. (London: Hodder and Stoughton, 1953), pp. 120–21 argues, "The more two persons love one another, the less they will be likely to be afraid of one another. It is true that each may have a very real fear of hurting the other (as we should fear to affront the love of God); but not because he is afraid of what the other may do to him. *A fortiori,* to live within the love of God is freedom from the ultimate fear." The radical contrast between "fear" and "love" in I John 4:18, which is as total as the contrast between "the world" and "the Father," or between "love of the world" and "of the Father," elucidates Eph 5:21 in at least one aspect: fear as such, without regard to its object, is not recommended by Paul as a "point of contact" for preaching the gospel or instructing in ethics (cf. Balz, EvTh 29 [1969], 641–42). Neither the threat of hell fire flowingly described in tent meetings, nor the glorification of "modern" man's anxiety, care, doubt or *Verfallenheit* can be meant by the "fear of Christ." In John 16:33 and the ca. 3000 occurrences of the phrase "Fear not!" in the Bible God, Jesus Christ, the gospel, faith are shown to be radically opposed to such fear, to overcome it, and to have no use for it whatsoever.
Again, is there, perhaps, a third kind of "fear" underlying a free man's ethical decision? Though Kierkegaard is called the father of modern existentialism, his two books on fear distinguish him radically from his twentieth-century admirers. The "possibility of the freedom" which is given to man, includes the "dread" of making a wrong decision, according to *The Concept of Dread*. Less psychological and more biblical is the argument proposed in *Fear and Trembling.* Here Kierkegaard points out an element that may be present not only in the story of Isaac's sacrifice on Mount Moriah: confronted with different, perhaps contradictory and mutually exclusive, moral obligations which appear to represent God's will, a man may not know what to do in a given situation. When Abraham was ready to sacrifice his son, he did it because he "feared God" (Gen 22:12). This "fear" made him free to suspend religious and moral principles and value judgments. It was much more than a powerful emotion in his soul or an anxious reflection on the consequences of disobedience. Here fear denotes the paradoxicality and the dialectic of faith and obedience: it exists only in relation to God and only as a characteristic of faith. It has nothing to do with crippling terror, cowardly timidity, calculated retaliation. Rather it is an act and produces acts of extreme courage; it makes man step boldly forward—however trembling his heart may be. Kierkegaard's keen exegesis of Gen 22 is in itself an act of such boldness. It is also exemplary for the understanding of the "fear of Christ" mentioned in Eph 5:21.
[235] See the references to Christ's parousia, 4:13; to the future of the church, 1:14; 2:20; 4:15–16; 5:27; to the last judgment, 6:8–9; to the present and coming days of tribulation, 3:13; 5:16; 6:13.

and hope, and calls for a conduct that heeds the crisis of the present, the last judgment, and the ultimate triumph of Christ.[236] Finally, it dispels the notion that here the poignant role of eschatology which is obvious in I Cor 7 has given way to a cheap or clever adaptation to environmental standards, to the quest for respectability in the world, and to securing for oneself no more than a long life on earth (cf. Eph 6:3).[237] According to Paul's earlier and later teachings, all marriage counseling among Christians is determined by the life, the presence, and the future coming of the Messiah.

d) The "fear of Christ," understood in the light of OT and NT references to "holy" fear, is occasioned by the good and glorious things achieved by Christ, and it anticipates more of the same in the future. Instead of doubt or distrust, its motives and characteristics are confidence and an uplifted heart. How could He be served otherwise than with fear and trembling, He who is so strong in healing, expelling evil spirits, teaching, leading, suffering? Most likely it is Paul's opinion in 5:21 that Jesus Christ is to be feared because his "love" is full of power and simply overwhelming (5:2, 25; cf. 2:4). This love overcomes all obstacles that might be found in mankind, in the powers of his environment, in the last judgment.[238]

If this be a good reason to "fear Christ," it becomes clear why and in which sense Paul can also hope that a wife would fear the husband who loves her (vs. 33): fear without love would be horrible. Just as God's love of man and man's responding love of God are the basis of the fear of God, so only the wife who is joined to her husband by love can fear her husband. Paul presupposes in vs. 33 that the wife loves her husband as much as, in vs. 21, he presupposes that the saints love Christ. In both cases, however, he mentions only "fear." His intention is to make sure that he who loves and that the act and attitude of loving do not neglect or override the freedom and dignity of the person of the beloved. True love esteems the person loved more highly than the self.[239] Therefore fear and subordination in love are the proper attitudes

[236] Not only in I, II Thessalonians are the coming of Christ and daily moral conduct indissolubly tied together. The ethics of early Christianity was informed by the coming of God's kingdom, as guaranteed by the advent of Jesus, the Messiah; see, e.g. Matt 5–7; 10:23, 25; A. Schweitzer, *The Quest of the Historical Jesus*, 3d ed. (London: Black, 1954), pp. 222–68, 328–401. More reliable than Schweitzer's theory of "radical eschatology" is A. Wilder, *Eschatology and Ethics*, 2d ed. New York: Harper, 1950. "Fear of the Lord," as mentioned in II Cor 5:11, means according to WBLex, 877 "fear of the judgment to come." The same is true of Eph 5:21.

[237] Explicit eschatological elements in the Corinthian chapter on marriage are the following: the references to the brevity of available time (before the parousia) and to the passing away of the form of this world: I Cor 7:29–31; the priority of "prayer" and "peace" and "pleasing" the Lord over pleasing a man or woman, and being engulfed in, and anxious about, worldly affairs: 7:5, 15, 29–34; the mention of world-wide and personal tribulation: 7:26, 28; the expectation that perhaps the spouse may be "saved" by the conduct of the partner: 7:16. The "Chicago School," represented by, e.g. S. J. Case and E. J. Goodspeed (see F. W. Beare, *The First Epistle of Peter* [Oxford: Blackwell, 1958], p. 195), questioned that there ever existed pre-NT *Haustafeln* and explained Col 3:18 ff.; Eph 22 ff. as a sign of the early Christians' "quest for respectability" in the Graeco-Roman environment.

[238] Cf. Mark 14:36–38; Heb 5:7–9; Rom 5:19; 8:31–39; Philip 2:6–8; 4:4–5; II Cor 5:10–21; II Tim 4:8.

[239] Balz, EvTh 29 (1969), 643–44 argues similarly regarding the relation between faith and fear. "He who renounces any mention of fear, would do as much as empty the concept of faith; faith without fear would have lost something essential, . . . [even] the total dependence upon a mightier one and the total claim imposed by a demanding will; faith without fear would be an enthusiastic celebration of man's own self-consciousness, and as such it would be unbelief . . . This is possible only upon the basis of NT faith . . . Always faith is totally exposed to the wrath and the love of God."

of a saint, according to the testimony of the whole Bible as summed up in Eph 5:21.

e) Neither a natural nor a fictional superiority of one part of mankind over the other,[240] but rather the authority of Christ, is the *Leitmotiv* of all that Paul will unfold in the *Haustafel*. The interpersonal relationships which are described in 5:22 – 6:9 and which are distinct for their historic, biological, and economic factuality, are treated here as problems that cannot be solved between human beings and according to human standards alone. Just as Paul showed in 2:11–12 that the intervention of the Messiah alone has unified the formerly hostile Jews and Gentiles, so he insists now that only a third party, and a conduct informed by the right and power of that party, brings light into darkness and order into chaos. The third party who cares equally for both the supposedly stronger and weaker groups is again Christ. Paul does not envision a solution to social-ethical problems without establishing an authority. But the authority he proclaims is not the authority of the husband, parents, masters, church, custom, resolution, or tradition (to say nothing of Paul himself) but solely Jesus Christ.[241]

These five observations make it imperative to turn to Paul's description of the unique and authoritative love of the Messiah himself.

IV   The Bridegroom and the Bride

In 5:25–32 Christ, the church, and their interrelationship are depicted by an imagery that—with one exception—is not found in the earlier parts of Ephesians. Many complementary terms have been used, among them most diverse metaphors: Christ was called the beloved Son; the church, the chosen people, God's children (1:4–6). He, the administrator; they, the heirs. He, the risen; they, those raised with and in him (1:20; 2:5–6). He, the savior; they, the saved (5:23; 2:5, 8). He, the head; they, his body and its members (1:22–23; 4:16). He, the bringer of peace; they, the people reconciled with God and one another (2:14–18). He, the priest and sacrifice; they, the people worshipping God the Father (2:13–18; 3:12; 4:11–12; 5:2). He, the keystone; they, the growing structure of God's temple (2:20–22). He, the inhabitant in human hearts; they, the men filled with strength, knowledge, and love (3:16–19). He, the giver of heavenly gifts; the church, his public agent entrusted with an exemplary service in the world (2:6–7; 3:10; 4:7–12). He, the approaching royal bridegroom; she, the festive bridal party going out to meet him (4:13).[242] Only the last-mentioned verse anticipates the Bridegroom-Bride imagery of 5:25–27. But each of the several metaphors made it unmistakably clear that ecclesiology (the doctrine of the church) depends on Christology, and that the two are inseparable, though by no means exchangeable.[243] In most of these texts the term "love" did occur and played a decisive

---

[240] As supposedly supported by biological, physical, psychological, historical evidence, not to speak of an unchangeable "creation order" that exists in God's plan apart from the function given to his Son. Eph 1:4–10 knows of only one "order" and leaves no room to play out creation against salvation. All powers are under *Christ's* feet (1:19–21).

[241] This is pointed out emphatically by, e.g. Thomas Aquinas, Calvin, Abbott, Dibelius.

[242] Schlier, pp. 278–79, offers a briefer resumé. According to him, in Eph 5:25 ff. specific emphasis falls upon the church as a personality of her own.

[243] In the Introduction, sections IV and VI, it was shown that this summary is contested by some scholars.

role. While it was missing in the hint regarding the meeting of bridegroom and bride in 4:13, this lack is amply made up for by the description of Christ and the church in the Bridegroom-Bride metaphors of 5:25 ff. Christ is The Loving Bridegroom; the church, The Beloved Bride. They are united in a covenant of love.[244] No one can speak of Christ or the church unless he speaks of this specific union of two free, though unequal partners.

In 5:25-27 this union is described in terms of a betrothal, in vss. 23-24 and 28-31 by allusion to marriage, as Schlier observes. The combination of the slightly variant images pertaining to engaged and married people respectively is more disturbing to modern readers than to Jews of Paul's time. For "betrothal was equivalent to marriage" in the OT,[245] and probably beyond the periods of history covered by the OT. Still, the bridal imagery in vss. 25-27 is in some important aspects distinct from the marital: its accent lies exclusively upon the *future* transformation and glory of the "bride," not on features related to the *present* status of a "wife." Some observations regarding the use of analogous imagery in the OT will bear this out.[246]

A   Precedents and Differences

In 5:25-27 there is no explicit quote from the OT,[247] but the passage bristles with allusions to the prophetic concept of Yahweh's covenant with Israel which includes bridal and marital imagery. From the time of Hosea to the days of Malachi, appropriate metaphors, comparisons, and stories were used to describe the passion, solidity, creativeness, rejection, jealousy, and renewal of Yahweh's love, to depict the shame of idolatry and prostitution, and/ or to enjoin the members of Israel to be faithful to their wives.[248] This is not the place to discuss the mythological (Canaanite or other) origin, background or counterparts of the belief in divine and human copulations ("syzygies," see COMMENT VII A), or to describe the re-enactment of the myth in cultic prostitution and other fertility rites. But it is necessary to mention that the prophets' thought and proclamation does not ascend from the observation of faithful marriages to the proclamation of Yahweh as the ideal husband. Rather

---

[244] See the NOTES on 1:4 ff. for the correlation of love and covenant in Deuteronomy and Moran's earlier mentioned essay in CBQ 25 (1963), 77-87. In COMMENT VII C references will be given for calling betrothal and marriage a "covenant." Muirhead's distinction between God's love for unrepenting sinners and Christ's love for responsive sinners, that is, between a love that does not care about the response of the beloved, and another love that does (ScotJT 5 (1952), 187), is not supported by OT or NT texts describing *agapē*.

[245] Oepke, TWNTE, I, 781 with reference to Gen 38:15 ff.; Exod 22:16-17; Num 5:11-31; Deut 22:23-24; see also StB, II, 393; Schlier, p. 280: "As his [Christ's] bride she [the church] is also his wife."

[246] It was mentioned earlier that Muirhead, ScotJT 5 (1952), attempts to point out the futurist rather than current status of the church as Christ's "wife." If the two are arbitrarily conflated, the distinct testimony of Rev 19 and 21 regarding the future marriage of the lamb with his Bride is contradicted; a perfectionist doctrine of the church ensues, saying that she is blameless (e.g. sinless and infallible) already at the present time. See also R. A. Batey, *Nuptial Imagery*, pp. 27-29, 65-69.

[247] See COMMENT VI for the quote of Gen 2:24 in Eph 5:31. Irenaeus *adv. haer.* IV 20:12 teaches that Moses' marriage with an "Ethiopian woman" (Exod 2:21) and Rahab of Jericho's attitude to the spies were antecedents of Christ's marriage to the "church from the Gentiles." Paul, however, seems not to have thought of these precedents. The church of which he speaks consists of Gentiles and Jews.

[248] See Hosea, *passim;* Jer 2:2; 3:1-16; 9:2; 31:1-3, 31-34; Ezek 16; 23; Isa 49:14-21; 50:1-2; 54:4-10; 60:15; 62:4-5; Mal 2:14-16. Sampley, pp. 30-61 presents a summary of the use made of some of the motifs mentioned, and esp. of Lev 19:18, Hosea, Jeremiah, Ezekiel, Song of Songs, Ps 45, and Jewish interpretations of Gen 2.

the prophets start from Yahweh's faithfulness and Israel's earlier response to God's love. What they know through revelation, faith, imagination, and reflection is what they apply to the chaotic situation created by Israel who prostituted herself. A sharp distinction between "whoring away from Yahweh" and unfaithfulness to earthly spouses or fornication was never made: Canaanite practices which threatened the worship of Yahweh gave a sacred halo to both;[249] one form of prostitution was conditioned by the other and identified with it.[250]

The existence of OT parallels to 5:25–27 and the similarity of the argument used by both make it unlikely that a "mystical relationship to the deity" is envisaged in Eph 5.[251] The strictly historical, intra-personal, and legal character of the OT covenant between Yahweh and his people is not converted by Paul into an impersonal experience of metaphysics within physics, transcendence within immanence, or of the coinherence of the divine and the human, of *agapē* and *erōs*.[252] In the OT and in Paul's interpretation, not even the term "one flesh" denotes the loss of individual personality of the two persons united; see last NOTE on 5:31 and COMMENT IV D.

But there are also essential differences between Eph 5:25–27 and its foreshadowings in OT prophetic books. All except one include essential distinctions from rabbinical and other descriptions of womanhood and marriage.

1) The OT speaks of the "Yahweh-Israel" covenant; Eph 5 describes the "Messiah's" covenant with a people composed of "Jews and Gentiles."[253]

2) The OT groom pays a price for acquiring a woman.[254] According to rabbinical teaching only by cash or an equivalent payment (in addition to a contract and cohabitation) does a woman become a man's wife and property.[255] In Eph 5 the Bridegroom pays, to use the terminology of I Peter 1: 18–19, "not with perishable things such as silver or gold, but with the precious blood" (cf. I Cor 7:23 and the hymnic line, "With his own blood he bought her"). OT servants of God offered themselves to God to redeem their people,

---

[249] Hosea 4:14; I Kings 14:24; 15:12; 22:46; II Kings 23:7 (without parallels in I, II Chronicles) mention prostitution in God's temple.

[250] In Hosea 4:10–14; 7:4–7; Jer 5:7–8; 13:26–27; 23:10–11, 14; Isa 57:3; Ezek 23:29–30, 37–38, 48–49 and elsewhere, the two meanings of whoring are indistinguishable, and sometimes a third is also present: political alliances with foreign powers. Temple prostitution is prohibited, e.g. in Deut 23: 17–18; the LXX version of the same verses (23:18–19) speaks of prostitution in general. For details see F. Hauck, TWNTE, IV, 730–32; VI, 580–90. In analogy, a "fornicator" is called an idolator in Eph 5:5; cf. Col 3:5; Rev 22:15.

[251] As Dibelius, p. 93 suggests—not without adding that the "sensual" element of Hellenistic mysticism is absent from this chapter.

[252] See COMMENT IV A on 3:14–21 for a discussion of the problem of mysticism in Ephesians.

[253] An exception to Jeremias' thesis (TWNTE, IV, 1099–1106) regarding the difference between the Messiah's and Yahweh's bridegroomship is found in the allegorical interpretations of Ps 45 and the Song of Songs in the Targum Ps 45:2 ff. (quoted in StB, III, 679–80) and Midr. Song of Sol. If not the OT writers themselves, then their rabbinical interpreters saw in the Messiah's (Son of David's) relationship to his beloved (queen or lady-love) an anticipation or guarantee of God's relationship to subjugated and converted Gentiles and/or to Israel. *God's* covenant has the form of his *Servant's* (Moses', Joshua's, the king's) covenant with the people in (Exod 14:31?) Deut 28:69[RSV 29:1]; Josh 24:25–27; II Kings 11:17; 23:3; Ezra 10:2–3; cf. H. W. Wolff, "Jahve als Bundesmittler," VT 6 (1956), 316–20; M. Noth, "Old Testament Covenant-making in the light of a Text from Mari," in *The Law in the Pentateuch and Other Studies* (Edinburgh/London: Oliver, 1966), pp. 108–31, esp. 114–18. If there was, e.g. in Ps 45, a reflection of a *hieros gamos* ritual in Israel at all, this would point in the same direction; see T. H. Gaster, "Psalm 45," JBL 74 (1955), 239–51; J. Becker, *Israel deutet seine Psalmen*, Stuttgarter Biblische Studien 18 (1966), 79–90.

[254] E.g. Gen 34:12; I Sam 18:20–27; Ruth 4:1–7, 10; Hosea 3:2; Isa 43:3–4.

[255] Bab. Kidd. 2a; 7a–9a; 11a–13b.

or risked their lives as intercessors.[256] Some kings of Israel suffered much, but even if they died in battles, they did not thereby unify Israel and Judah, or Israel and the nations. The Messiah described in Ephesians loved the church so much that he "gave himself for her" (5:25). "Greater love has no man than this, that a man lay down his life for his friends" (John 15:13; cf. 10:11–16; Eph 2:13–18; 5:2). Other lovers seek and enjoy the beloved women's surrender; this Bridegroom surrenders "himself" for his Bride. In many other cases a woman is—voluntarily or not—used and in one way or another victimized. This Bridegroom does not make his Bride pay for his love. What is "laid" down is the full price of love, paid by the Bridegroom himself, with "His blood" (1:7; 2:13).

3) Jeremiah (3:6–14) and Ezekiel (23) describe Yahweh in bold terms as bigamous: the two sisters Israel and Judah, viz. Oholah-Samaria and Oholibah-Jerusalem, are his wives. Or, two covenants are distinguished: one with David, another with the Levitical priests (Jer 34:19–26), viz. with Judah and with Levi (Mal 2:4 – 3:4). Second Isaiah (50:1) asks the survivors of Israel in exile, "Where is your mother's bill of divorce?" and admits no more than "your mother was put away." Ezekiel (23:18) says that Yahweh "turned in disgust from both sisters." But Jeremiah (3:8) goes so far as to speak of a "letter of divorce with which Yahweh sent Israel away," but not Judah. However, Ezekiel agrees with Jeremiah in stating that Judah, the Southern Kingdom, has not learned from the punishment inflicted upon her northern sister: Judah's sin is even worse (Ezek 23:11–14; Jer 3:11). All these prophets, including Hosea who may have been the first to use this language, crown their message with the promise of forgiveness and the invitation to the unfaithful to "return."[257] Malachi 2:16 sums up the prophets' proclamation by describing God's own attitude and its social-ethical implications with the words: "I hate divorce, says the Lord the God of Israel . . . So take heed to yourselves and do not be faithless." Eph 5:25–27 speaks of the one love of the Messiah for his one Bride. It is not denied that she still needs purification from disfiguring "wrinkles" and shameful "spots"; she is not yet "blameless" (5:26–27). But an indissoluble and monogamous relationship to a "resplendent" Bride is here in mind. No shadow of a cheated and disappointed husband's love falls upon the Bridegroom's love for his Bride; no dissonant chord destroys the envisaged harmony of the two. The mere thought of divorce—not to speak of its actual occurrence—is left far behind. If metaphors from the realm of marriage had been used here, they would have had to include references to such tensions, dangers, pitfalls as even Yahweh's "marriage" had to endure, according to the prophets. But the Bridegroom-Bride analogy in Ephesians "presupposes the renewed covenant with the chosen people."[258] On the basis of forgiveness granted (1:7) and enmity overcome (2:14–16), this relation is full of joy in the present, forgets what lies behind and points enthusiastically toward the future, that is, to the fulfillment of promises still outstanding regarding the union of Christ with the church; cf.

[256] E.g. Exod 32:30–32; Lev 16:11–19; only in Isa 53 is the actual death of the Servant mentioned.
[257] Hosea 2:16–23; Isa 49:14–21; 50:1–2; 54:7–8; 60:15; 62:4–5; Jer 31:2–34; cf. 33:19–26; Ezek 16:60–63. The only exception is Ezek 23.
[258] H. Greeven, in Dibelius, p. 93.

Rev 19:7; 21:2–27. As stated in the NOTES, Paul makes this love the basis and model of marital love, not a husband's love.[259]

4) In the OT the procreation of children is the primary purpose and supreme blessing of a couple.[260] In many rabbinical statements, also frequently in Christian and non-Christian custom and literature, the distinctive mark of femininity is seen in the capacity to bear children. Eve, Sarah, Leah, Rachel, Hannah, and millions of other women thanked God for it. For them the anxiety, pain, and enormous task of motherhood was more than repaid by the joy. "I have gotten a man with the help of the Lord" (Gen 4:1); "God has given me good reason to laugh" (Gen 21:6, NEB). Others are almost crushed under the burden. Technical and medical means to avoid impregnation and to escape the pain of bearing children were known in antiquity,[261] though not to the same extent as in the "modern" world. The *Haustafeln* do not declare it a woman's first duty to have babies—be it a minimum of children or as many as possible. Though in the *Haustafeln* there are specific sections that describe the parent-child relationship, the verses devoted to husband and wife do not mention offspring. After the coming of the Messiah who was "born from a woman" (Gal 4:4), the intimate relationship of love and subordination has become an end in itself—according to Eph 5:22–23 and the parallels—as long as it is an expression of a life in the "fear" of Christ, a form of public praise of "His love" for the church, and a demonstration of the voluntary subordination of the church to her Lord. Thus Paul liberates wives, and together with them all women, from the coercive notion that they are, above all, a soil receptive for implantation and therefore have to be ready at all times for reproduction.[262]

In summary, the OT contains precedents for Eph 5:25–27 that are indispensable tools for understanding this text. They prevent the expositor from relying exclusively on other, e.g. mythological and mystical, "parallels." See COMMENT VII A, B. But the OT precedents also require that the Ephesian passage be understood as a "new song" devoted to the reality of the renewed covenant: the covenant made by the Messiah which embraces Jews and Gentiles, men and women, masters and slaves under the banner of forgiveness, peace, and love.

B   The Vision of Love

Just like other love songs, Eph 5:25–27 paints the object of love in glowing colors. Though the terms "seeing," "knowing," or equivalent words expressing

---

[259] The "new beginning" made by the Messiah sent by God does not imply that Israel, Judah, or the Jews are at present divorced from God. The idea that God has divorced the Jews and entered a new marriage with another woman (the church) would attribute to God the "hardness of heart" chastised in Mark 10:9 par. It would make Him the model of a trespasser against the logion, "Whoever divorces his wife and marries another, commits adultery against her": Mark 10:11 par.; cf. I Cor 7:10–11. God's covenant and faithfulness stands and falls with his unshakable truthfulness to Israel. See also K. Barth, III 1, 322–24, regarding some differences between the OT and the NT utterances on marriage.

[260] Gen 1:28; I Sam 1; Mal 2:15; Ps 127:2–5. Rabbinical and Greek texts expressing the same thought were quoted in fn. 205. See also the second NOTE on Eph 5:3.

[261] Not only among prostitutes. According to the extended discussion in Bab. Yeb. 61a–66a, only the husband is responsible for procreation, not his wife; if he follows Onan's example (Gen 38:9) or neglects his wife, he acts as wickedly "as one who sheds blood."

[262] A further distinction between the Prophets and Eph 5 is suggested by Chavasse, p. 83: In the OT "the nuptial idea is only an allegory. For St. Paul it is the great reality." But H. Greeven, in Dibelius, p. 93, may be nearer the intention of the Prophets when he states: In Hosea a prophetic action accompanies the message as if to demonstrate that the bridal imagery is "not only a comparison."

the special vision and insight connected with love do not occur in this enco-
mium, the telic (futuristic) description of the Bride's perfection recalls a trait
found wherever true love is described.[263] Certainly, the cynic and the fool
say in their hearts, "Love is blind" or "I don't know what he sees in her." But a
person in love and a wise man will counter, "Love is a gift from above, an inspiration and enthusiasm which opens the eyes and makes seen the truth that
is hidden from persons ignorant of love." Where other people see only an "It,"
love has found the "Thou."[264]

This is not the place to compare the glorious works of painters, sculptors,
musicians, and poets with the actual merits of the objects of their love. Socrates,
the Virgin Mary, Héloise, and Beatrice have become for many later born mortals what visionary lovers have made of them. But the question must be asked:
What does Paul (or the unknown author of the love song in Eph 5:25–27) intend and achieve by describing *Christ's* relationship to the church after a pattern that is familiar not only to his own environment but also to many cultures
all over the world? Is he perhaps falling victim to the pagan pattern of idealiza-
tion, and does he attribute to Jesus Christ a vision of the church which may well
be called spirited, enthusiastic, idealistic but which is simply unrealistic? Certainly the letters to Galatia, Corinth, Rome, etc., and the exhortations found in
Eph 4–6, show that Paul knew the actual, less than ideal state of affairs in the
churches he founded, and his experiences with the Jerusalem and Judaean
churches were (despite their sometimes positive attitude to Paul, cf. Gal 1:22–
24) not so unambiguous as to encourage him to call any church "glorious" or
"free from spot and wrinkle." The OT also contains many visions concerning
things good or evil that are present or to come, but visions of a perfect bride
are found only in the Song of Solomon, perhaps in Ps 45, and in the allegorical
interpretation of these passages. In Eph 5:25–27 Paul seems to deviate from the
realistic character and meaning of the prophetic utterances on God's love and
covenant, and to replace them by a Platonic notion of an invisible, universal,
holy, and perfect church.

Still, it is far from certain that the apostle has an "idea" of the church in mind
or speaks of an "ideal church." Whenever he or another NT author make seemingly Platonizing references to a heavenly archetype of earthly matters,[265]
vital differences remain visible between their proclamation and Platonic philosophical tenets. God is proclaimed as the creator of heaven *and earth;* therefore, the material world is not in principle devalued in favor of an ideal, invisible, spiritual world. Instead of speaking of two spheres through which
(with the help of mediating agencies) the soul must ascend to see the perfect

---

[263] In the lyric poems of Sappho, Anacreon, Horace; in Alcibiades' "praise" of his companion
and teacher Socrates (Plato *symp.* 212–222B; in Demosthenes' "praise" of his young friend
Epicrates (Ps.-Demosthenes *eroticos*); in Dante's glorification of Beatrice (*Vita Nuova; Divina
Comedia,* esp. Song I of the *Paradiso*). Homosexual and heterosexual relationships have in non-
biblical literature produced the same kind of great paeans in verse and prose. Love between
brothers-in-arms (David, Jonathan, and Saul) is also highly praised in II Sam 1:19–27, esp. 23, 26;
cf. I Sam 18.

[264] See Bailey, pp. 13–16. A survey on the history of the "vision of love" (from Plato to
Goethe and up to recent times) is found in H. de Lubac's commentary on P. Teilhard de Chardin,
Hymnen an das Weibliche, German transl. by H. U. von Balthasar, Einsiedeln; Johannes-Verlag,
1968.

[265] E.g. in the distinction of a heavenly from an earthly Jerusalem or sanctuary (Gal 4:25–26;
Rev 21; Heb 8:5; 9:11; 10:1; 12:22–23; cf. also II Cor 12:2). Philo of Alexandria was the chief
contemporary exponent of the attempt to reconcile the OT with Platonic teachings.

(see Col 2:8–23; but also, e.g. II Cor 12:2; Rev 4:1), the NT speaks most frequently of two periods of time. The future stands over the present. One great event is announced by which heaven and earth are to become new. God has promised that one day he will descend from heaven with the fullness of his gifts and dwell among his creatures. The whole man is to be saved, not just his soul. The list of differences in the ontological, hermeneutical, and soteriological realms could be continued. But the examples given suggest that there may be similar distinctions between the Pauline (viz. hymnic, early Christian) vision of love described in Eph 5 and the romantic visions of lovers and poets who sang the praises of Ganymede, Aphrodite, the Shulammite, or Beatrice. Many Christians have praised the power and perfection of love in terms borrowed especially from Plato's *Symposium*. But Eph 5 is not necessarily an example of this procedure.

Among the various types of "visions of love," the following can be distinguished.

1) The beloved person is seen as a paragon of beauty, virtue, wisdom. In him or her is realized and incorporated what, at best, has been seen in a dream, hoped for in yearning, or anticipated in vague imagination. The experience of love then means that one specific person has become the culmination or end of the dream, the incarnation of the idea, the presence of the eternal or timeless, the peace and wholeness which seemed beyond reach.[266] Enthusiastic lovers claim to have found what nobody else can ever find—the one perfect incorporation of the ideal—and they encourage and inspire other people to find and enjoy other embodiments of the absolute. However, for the NT authors there is no other incarnation except in the Messiah Jesus. He is called the incarnate "Word" of God, not a realized idea or ideal (John 1:1–18). He is not the end of hope but is expected to come again in order to fulfill all promises and expectations. Highly developed post-NT reflection on the virgin mother of Jesus attributes similar qualifications to Mary; yet Paul's doctrine of the church is not developed on the basis of a Marian competition to his Christology.

2) In the man or woman who is loved, the lover finds much more than just a person—however ideal. The beloved can be the means or the guide by which the lover ascends to heavenly spheres. The mantic seer Diotima showed Socrates a mysterious way: after seeing one beautiful figure, a man (that is, his soul) can "quasi stepwise" proceed to see two, then all beautiful shapes; when the ascension continues he comes to perceive good morals and attitudes, even the virtues, and finally he arrives at the idea of beauty, i.e. beauty itself, the deity.[267] The concept of a "beatific vision" which is attained by this gradual ascent of the soul from fragments of beauty, goodness, and truth perceived on earth, and which ends with the transformation into an angel-like form of existence, has a rich history among Greeks, Jews, Christians. It is not limited to Gnostics and other Neo-Platonists, to the Mediterranean world, or to one period of history; it can be engendered by means other than the sight of a beau-

---

[266] The majority of romantic-lyric love poems probably belong in this category. When the fusion of the ideal, the beloved and the lover, is emphasized, a "mystical" union is expressed.

[267] Plato *symp.* 210E–212A. Earlier in the same treatise, Eros was described as a "great daimon" who mediates between the immortals and mortals by interpreting the gods and executing their will, but also by bringing human prayers and offering to the gods (202E–203A).

tiful and lovable person. But three examples can illustrate how this vision has been connected with a beloved woman: the medieval Mariology is summed up in the Benedictine formula: *Per Mariam ad Christum* ("Through Mary to Christ"); in the *Divina Comedia,* especially in the last four Songs of the *Purgatorio* and the first Songs of the *Paradiso,* Beatrice, the symbol of grace and of the pure church, leads Dante through repentance into the heavenly spheres; at the end of the second part of *Faust,* Goethe praises the feminine in general: *Das ewig Weibliche zieht uns hinan* ("The eternal feminine draws us upward"). Does Paul think along those lines in Eph 5? Indeed his thought moves from concern with a man's love for a woman, to the praise of Christ's love for the church. But if this looks like a logical ascent from lower to higher love and union, the development of his argument demonstrates just the opposite. (a) Human love does not by nature lead upward, but Christ's love is the cause and model of conjugal love. (b) Christ does not offer a convenient (and cheap) way *out* of the limitations and possible disappointments of interhuman love. Rather Christ's love is described as a way leading him deep *down* into involvement with a church composed of such Jews and Gentiles as were formerly dead in sin and are in temptation to relapse into their past. Basic and exemplary for the husband's love is the love of Christ which means engagement in great tasks, even on earth. (c) The beloved woman is not considered blameless in herself (whether in life or only after her death), but rather her Bridegroom gives his life for her in order to *make* her perfect by overcoming whatever traces of death in sins may still defile her. (d) The bride is not a welcome instrument or stepping stone for the lover to attain to higher worlds and finally to forget her after she has served her purpose. Full of joy, the Bridegroom knows nothing more lovable than she. The pleasure he seeks is her pleasure; he rejoices in sharing and bearing her suffering. Here is a happiness which deepens and grows as the two partners stay together.

3) To some authors the vision of love seems to be concentrated upon the meeting of a creative force with a receptive capacity. If Eros by birth is the child of father Plenty and mother Poverty, then the children to be procreated by those united in love are love's ultimate object and fulfillment. According to Plato's *Symposium,* "the communion of a husband and wife is procreation. For this is a divine matter, and even this, birth and conception are [something] immortal in the mortal, living being. . . . Generation is something eternal and immortal." Bodily offspring is but a poor symbol of far more beautiful, immortal children that can be begotten and born: when "the soul becomes pregnant . . . Wisdom and Virtue in general, . . . Temperance and Justice" will be born. In this way an (unmarried) teacher can have "children": great men who serve the state well are his offspring. Love's vision can be identified with the will to produce even such fruit.[268] The same can be phrased more simply: a man can love a woman because he trusts that he, and he alone, can be her teacher, guide, and educator, or can achieve something together with her for the benefit of others, which neither he nor she could ever perform alone. In this case love is informed by a strong will and hope: it is a means for serving a higher end. The accent placed upon communion and the absence of selfish interests distin-

[268] Plato *symp.* 203B; 206C–E; 209A–E.

guish this vision from those mentioned before. But is this version of the vision of love endorsed by Paul? The apostle has spoken of "children" and "offspring of light" (5:8–9). While in I Cor 4:15 Paul called himself the father of these children, he did not claim this honor in Ephesians where only God is called the "Father" loving, strong (1:2, 4–5; 3:14–15). In 5:31 and in all his statements on marriage Paul reveals his interest in a close communion of the spouses which excludes egotistic motivations or hopes on either side. Earlier a reference was made to the missionary character of a marriage between Christians, or a marriage in which at least one partner is a Christian (I Cor 7:12–16). However, in 5:25–27 there is no trace of an intention of Christ, the Bridegroom, to prove his creative teaching talents to the receptive church, and his love's ultimate motive is not located in the procreation of fine bodily or spiritual children. He does not use his love and his beloved as an instrument.

The vision of love described by Paul is *sui generis*. Though Christ's love includes features found in many a strong, wise and devoted man's love, there is something unique in his love: this lover has the will, the power, and the success to make his bride perfect. He loves his beloved only for her own sake. He seeks no other or higher reward than her alone. His love, incorporated in his bride, is an end in itself. The Messiah has set out and will not rest until she appears before himself glorious and free of any defect. He says and wants to say forever, "How lovely you are!"

The way in which the Messiah looks upon the church is not that of a girl-watcher, a Victorian chaperon, or a doctor, a judge, an artist after he has completed a piece of work. His "vision" consists of "seeing to it" that all becomes "very good," cf. Gen 1:31. He does not "look on a woman with a lustful eye" (Matt 5:28, NEB), but is the eminent example of what it means to be led by a "sound [lit. single] eye."[269] Thus, Eph 5:25–27 gives a testimony to the high esteem in which the church is held by God and Christ, and to the manner in which Christ makes this esteem distinct from a romantic illusion. In their own way these verses describe nothing else but what in another Pauline passage is called "justification of the ungodly" (Rom 4:5).

Some highlights from the history of interpretation illustrate this point.

A Jewish example of preaching Israel's justification by grace alone is found, e.g. in a midrash on Song of Sol 1:5. The Shulammite, the great King Solomon's lady-love, says of herself, "I am black, but I am beautiful" (cf. SegB). The rabbinical interpretation anticipates neither the advertisements for suntanned skin nor the slogan, "Black is beautiful." Rather it places greatest emphasis on the conjunction "but" and has this to say: "Israel is black every day of the week, but beautiful on the Sabbath; black she is every day of the year, but beautiful on the Day of Atonement; black she is in this world, but beautiful in the world to come."[270] It may be added that the girl herself, notwithstanding the pleasure she brings her lover, acknowledges her total dependence on his judgment, that is, on his way of looking at her: "I was in his eyes as one who brings [or finds] peace" (Song of Songs 8:10). Cf. Isa 43:4: "Because you are precious in my eyes and honored, I love you."

---

[269] *Test. Issachar* III 4; Luke 11:34; Matt 6:22–23. See C. Edlund, "Das Auge der Einfalt," ASNU 19 (1952), 51–122; H. J. Cadbury, "The Single Eye," HTR 47 (1954), 69–74.
[270] Midr. Song of Sol 87b; the exposition is attributed to Rabbi Chayyetha (ca. C.E. 350).

Among the Christian interpreters of the Bride's perfection, there is agreement that Eph 5:26–27 speaks of the glory of the church as a community, rather than only of the immaculate state of certain individuals.[271] However, the time and the mode of the church's entering into perfection are described in different ways.

Some speak only or primarily of the future perfection.[272] A total transformation will occur not only in individuals (as often stated in the NT), but in the church as a whole. The change will mean a glorification—but it will not be realized before the day of the general resurrection. The three final clauses beginning with *hina* ("in order to") and the futuristic subjunctives of the Greek verbs in vss. 25–27 are strong arguments for this interpretation. In this school of thought, Muirhead represents an extreme: "It is only at the end that the church becomes the bride. . . . Here and now her state can only be that of a school girl who wished she were married and out of this."[273] Gaugler avers that the eschatological state of the church is meant, not the present, but he does not go as far as Muirhead and deny that she is now already the bride.

A second group[274] relies on the testimony given in Ephesians[275] and elsewhere in the NT to "realized eschatology," even to the fulfillment of the great OT promises here and now. They hold that because of the creative power, will and word of Jesus Christ the present church is "holy," and that "holy" means either that she cannot sin at all, is infallible, is now in herself praiseworthy, or is totally clothed with the garment of forgiveness and able through repentance to restore its whiteness. The manifold futuristic elements in the Greek text of 5:25–27 are relegated almost entirely to oblivion, and the greater glory of the church is enhanced instead. Already now "the church . . . is the pillar and bulwark of the truth" (I Tim 3:15). She is looked at as if she were Christ's Wife rather than his Bride.

A third school distinguishes between the present and the future perfection of the church, but maintains that in 5:25–27 both the present status and the future are described in combination, and that one cannot be affirmed without the other. The strongest exponent of this school is Thomas Aquinas: "It would be highly improper for the immaculate bridegroom to be wed to a soiled bride. This is why he presents her to himself in an immaculate state, now through grace and in the future through glory." Different in details but in a similar vein

---

[271] Chavasse, pp. 66 ff., 110 ff., 158, has attempted to go back to the roots and follow up the development of the individualistic exposition of the Bridegroom-Bride imagery. He finds traces of individualism in e.g. Tertullian *de oratione* 22; *ad uxorem, passim;* Cyprian *de habit. virg.* 22; Augustine *serm.* 87, 7, and the full blossom of a private-mystical interpretation in Theodoret, Maximus Confessor, Bernhard of Clairvaux, Richard of St. Victor, Thomas Aquinas, St. John of the Cross. The latter called the soul (of each believer) the bride of Christ, though they did not deny that in Eph 5 the Bride is the community of believers. Chavasse does not wish to exclude the personal element from Eph 5: "Each of her [the church's] members, individually as well as corporately, participate in the bridal status and privileges." The same is true of local churches: "Each church is the Bride" (cf. II John 1; III John 1), though "there is but one Church, one Bride" (pp. 83–87).

[272] See esp. Augustine *homiliae in I Ioann.* III 5; *de continentia* 25; *tract. in Ioann.* CXXII 9. Among his arguments for the present imperfection of the church the parable of the net (with its mixed contents: Matt 13:47–50) ranks highly, as Chavasse, p. 143, points out.

[273] ScotJT 5 (1952), 184–185.

[274] Led by the united front of the Greek fathers and represented among more recent exegetes by, e.g. von Harless; von Hofmann; Haupt; Best, p. 175, n. 2. See also Augustine *hom. in Ps.* 44[45] 31. The ancient texts in which the church is called a "pure bride" are discussed by, e.g. F. J. Dölger, *Ichthys,* I (Rome: Herder, 1910), 97–105.

[275] E.g. in 2:6; 4:4–6; 5:8: "Now you are light."

run the expositions of Calvin, Bengel, Lightfoot,[276] Abbott, and Schlier. Indeed, just as elsewhere the adjective "holy," so the verb "to make holy" in 5:26 can have a cultic (sacramental) meaning implying forgiveness presently granted, and at the same time an ethical sense pointing to an external and internal transformation that is still to be realized. In that case, the sanctification that has begun now is still dependent upon its completion on the Last Day. The same can be the meaning of the verb *katharizō* ("to make clean") and the adjective *endoxos* ("glorious," "resplendent."). But if Paul had really intended to play on these or analogous double-meanings, he would probably have made them explicit—as he does, e.g. in Rom 3:26 (lit. "he is righteous and he makes righteous"). In I Cor 6:11 and elsewhere Paul speaks of completed purification, sanctification, justification—which do not exclude future glorification and transformation (I Cor 15). In Eph 5:25–27 only the love and death of Christ are dated in the past.

The first group of interpreters stays closest to the meaning of the Greek text. Paul speaks in Eph 5:26–27 of the church's "future" glory for which the Messiah prepares her at present, to which he will guide her, and in which he will receive her—despite the unholy "spots and wrinkles" which still mar her at the present time. If, then, marital love is an imitation of the Messiah's love that envisions and creates the great future of the beloved church, the love between a man and a woman requires the following elements: a fidelity that fills out the given time and makes it meaningful, imagination that transcends beyond the limits of reason or technology, and a strength that is able and willing to fight and overcome obstacles. A love that is determined by a "vision" like the Messiah's will always be a productive power and process.

The following sections will discuss in detail the intention of Christ and the means employed by him to make the church "blameless."

C The Glorification of the Bride

The intention and effect of the Messiah's love for the church are expressed in 5:27 by the words,

> To present to himself the church resplendent
> free from spot or wrinkle or any such thing
> so that she be holy and blameless.

While the overtones of "spot" and "wrinkle" and the sense of "holy" and "blameless" have been described in the NOTES, it is now necessary to discuss the background and implication of the term "present to himself" and of the predicate "resplendent." In the imaginative diction and surprising compactness of Eph 5:27 at least six important elements can be distinguished.

1) At a Jewish wedding the "presentation" of the bride to the bridegroom was entrusted to the "friend of the bride." The bride's best man had some of the functions which in American custom are fulfilled by the bride's father. In Judaea the bride's "friend" had his counterpart in the "friend of the bridegroom." These two indispensable assistants to a wedding were called *shōshbīnīn* (by a term derived perhaps from the verb *shābab*, "to be joined"). Their duties included matchmaking, communication between the homes of bridegroom and

bride for setting up and signing the marriage contract, preparation of the wedding feast, and supervision of the bridal chamber.[277] Because according to Gen 2:22 God had rendered this service to Eve when "He brought her to the man," the rabbis considered the Lord the originator of the office of the best man.[278] It was a sacred duty to perform this function with care and decorum. Though the rabbinical evidences are of a later time, the NT passages quoted in fn. 277 show that the custom was solidly established in the days of Jesus and Paul. Most likely the verb "to present" has the same "romantic" meaning in Eph 5:27 and II Cor 11:2.

But the love song of Eph 5:25–27 includes in its imagery two bold deviations from the custom to which it alludes: (a) instead of two separate matchmakers for the bridegroom and the bride, there is only one; (b) the best man is the bridegroom himself: "The Messiah . . . presents [the bride] to himself."[279] The combination of the two functions has a precedent in the passage from Ezekiel quoted earlier in which Yahweh was depicted as both the fatherly friend and the bridegroom of Jerusalem.[280] Paul does not claim such a prerogative for himself. According to II Cor 11:2 the apostle is only the friend of the bride, not her bridegroom; the bride in question is only a local church, not the church universal.[281]

2) While it is probable that the romantic song (vss. 25–27), and Paul in quoting this song, alluded to a Jewish wedding, it is by no means certain that the "Ephesians" realized the implication. Yet even if they were unable to do so, there were sufficient meanings in the term "to present" (*paristēmi*) which could make sense to them. In secular Greek, in the LXX, and in many NT instances, *paristēmi* means "to set before," "to introduce," "to place at someone's disposal." In addition, the meaning "to produce" may be viable for translating

[277] A "best man" occurs in the story of Samson's disastrous wedding; he ends up as the husband of the bride (Judg 14:20). The terms "friend of the bridegroom" and "sons of the bridal chamber" (*benē huppah*) occur in John 3:29 and Matt 9:15 par. The function of the bride's best man is mentioned in II Cor 11:2: "I betrothed you to Christ to present you as a pure bride to her one husband." A collection of pertinent statements from Talmud and Midrash is found in StB, I, 500–17.

[278] The picturesque elements of the Jewish tradition are composed into a charming unit by L. Ginzberg, *The Legends of the Jews*, I (Philadelphia: Jewish Publication Society, 1954), 68; cf. StB, I, 503–4.

[279] Bab. Kidd. 41a–46b states explicitly that a man can betroth a woman to himself, and that a father can give his daughter to a man without employing an intermediary. In the same tractate (58b–59a) the question is discussed whether the marriage is valid when the bridegroom's best man takes the girl for himself before the planned wedding? The answer is positive but the best man is called a "cheater." The Nestle-Aland edition of the NT and GNT do not reproduce a variant reading of Eph 5:27, to which Abbott alludes and which is fully documented in the Beuron edition of the *Vetus Latina*: instead of the better reading: literally "that he himself to himself [*autos heautō*] present the church . . . ," the variant reads: "that he present her, the church, to himself [*autēn heautō*]." The accumulation of offices in the Messiah's person is not denied by the variant, but less emphasized.

[280] Ezek 16:3–14. Perhaps the same conflation of functions underlies the cryptic verses I Cor 7:36–38: the contradictory explanations found in older and newer commentaries can be reconciled with one another if the roles of the father, the friend of the bride, and the as yet celibate husband are here not distributed over three persons, but treated as the total responsibility of one and the same member of the church. Similar accumulations of seemingly different offices can be observed elsewhere too. In descriptions of the judgment in Deutero-Isaiah, Yahweh sometimes is both judge and prosecutor; see E. von Waldow, *Der traditionsgeschichtliche Hintergrund der prophetischen Gerichtsreden*, BhZAW 85 (1963), 12–19. In allusions to the Holy War tradition God is both Lord of (all!) hosts *and* helper of Israel's army, *or* the director of the armies that fight and defeat Israel; compare, e.g. Exod 14–15; Judg 4–5, with Judg 2:14–15; I Sam 28:16; Isa 9:8–12; Deut 28:25; Jer 30:14; Lam 1:17; 2:5; Job 13:24; 19:11. The priestly, kingly, and prophetic offices of Jesus the Messiah are the most striking example of combined functions.

[281] As Best, p. 175, observes.

certain NT texts.[282] The person to whom the "presentation" is made may be a
king, a judge or a priest: appearing before a king, man hopes to find grace;
coming to court, he expects to be justified, that is, to receive a fair trial and just
verdict; standing before God or a priest, he depends on a word that assures him
of "peace." In the closest parallels to Eph 5:27 any one of these situations may
be in mind, but not a reference to a wedding.[283] The supplicant, applicant,
worshipper, plaintiff, or defendant does not bring unfailing perfection in and
with himself but hopes to receive a favorable judgment. Even the sacrificial
animals of the right age and without blemish do not guarantee that an offering
"presented" to God will be accepted: God's decision, whether announced directly or through an intermediary, is essential to the sacrifice.[284] At each occasion it is good for a man to appear before God and to present himself, his
case or his gift, not alone but with the aid of an interceding friend. Again, the
intermediary cannot make the applicant perfect; he has no creative power. But
he urges and works for perfection: "to present you as a pure bride" (II Cor
11:2); "that we may present every man perfect in Christ" (Col 1:28). "Do
your best to present yourself to God as . . . a man who has no cause to
be ashamed" (II Tim 2:15). "O Lord, who shall sojourn in thy tent? . . . He
who walks blamelessly. . . ." (Ps 15; cf. 24:3–6).

Jesus Christ, however, not only calls for perfection ("You shall be perfect as
your Father in heaven is perfect"—Matt 5:48), but according to Eph 2:15 he
"creates one new man," even the church, and in 4:24 he is himself called "the
new man" who clothes the saints with "true righteousness and piety." He does
not yearn or plead for perfection, nor analyze, criticize, or blindly assume it.
The power of his love is such that he will produce his partner's perfection. This
"immaculate bridegroom" sees to it himself that he will not be "wed to a soiled
bride" (cf. Thomas Aquinas). The "presentation" made to himself of a blameless bride is not "make-believe," an oriental overstatement, or a sheer illusion.[285] It is the completion of a "new creation;" compare Rev 21.

3) In contrast to the purist strictures imposed upon *agapē* (Christian love)
by Bishop A. Nygren, the Messiah's love includes the intention to do good not
only to the beloved Bride, but also to himself. "To himself" Christ will present
the blameless Bride; thus he "himself" will be pleased, enriched, satisfied by
this partner. There is not the slightest suspicion of a condescension that would
humiliate the Bride. All that pleases her also pleases him. According to 1:3–14

[282] The German play on the words *hinstellen-vorstellen-darstellen-zur Verfügung stellen-herstellen*,
which is used by Schlier for demonstrating all these shades of meaning, cannot be reproduced in
English.

[283] See Eph 1:4: "standing holy and blameless before him," and Col 1:22; "in order to present
you holy and blameless and irreproachable before him." In the Colossian passage the same verb
paristēmi is used as in Eph 5:27 (and II Cor 11:2).

[284] See e.g. G. von Rad, "Die Anrechnung des Glaubens zur Gerechtigkeit," TLZ 76 (1951),
129–32; Engl. tr. in *The Problem of the Hexateuch and other Essays* (New York: McGraw-Hill,
1966), pp. 125–30.

[285] At a Jewish wedding those following Rabbi Shammai's teaching talked about the greater
or the lesser beauty of the bride; they would not be caught in a lie. But R. Hillel taught his followers to sing the praises of the bride—whether she was lovely or ugly—with the words, "Beautiful, charming bride!" Around 320 c.e. another rabbi reported that in Palestine the wedding chant
was, "Not paint, not powder, not curling locks, but a charming chamois," see Bab. Kethubin 17a.
The actual transformation of the Messiah's bride from a girl marred by "spots" and "wrinkles" to a
"holy and blameless" woman makes this dissent among rabbis immaterial. When the Messiah's work
is completed, He and His Bride will be able to sing for their own pleasure and to the applause of all
the world for their mutual perfection, as exemplified by e.g. Song of Songs 4:7; 5:9–16; and 6:9.

the election, acquisition, and blessing by God of a people that was to "stand before him holy and blameless" (1:4) included an extension of God's glory and a gain in his power. God was not depicted as an immovable mover. So also the *agapē* of Christ reaps a rich harvest. What he does to the bride reflects his own glory and magnifies it. The warm rays of true love fall back upon the lover. Far from being impoverished or put to shame, by making the Bride "holy" and "resplendent" the Messiah "himself" is all the more sanctified and glorified.

So much for the term "present to himself." Three additional observations can explain the adjective "resplendent" (or "glorious"; Greek *endoxos*) which in the Pauline Epistles recurs only in I Cor 4:10, "You are held in honor [*endoxoi*], we in disrepute."

4) Among Greek writers who are not influenced by the Bible (the LXX and the NT) and its Jewish, Christian, and heretical interpreters, *dokeō* and the cognates and derivatives of this verb, especially the noun *doxa*, have a meaning which is nearer fiction than fact. *Dokeō* means to expect, think, have an opinion, pretend, seem, appear good. The sense of *doxa* is opinion, fancy, conjecture, repute. However, in its biblical and post-biblical use, this word has "lost part of its secular sense . . . and also taken on an alien and specifically religious meaning, shared by the verb *doxazō* ("to praise") rather than by *dokeō*."[286] What used to denote a possibly deceptive impression or opinion, was transformed to designate the "weighty," awe-inspiring, irresistible appearance of God in clouds of storm or in radiant light,[287] and his self-manifestation in mighty and wonderful acts[288] by which he proved himself the savior of men.[289] In some cases *doxa* means image or likeness.[290] There is no fiction or make-believe in such a manifestation. Rather human beings and all creatures, including heavenly bodies, as well as the sea and hills on earth, are forced to recognize God's majesty, his power to destroy and to save. All of them eventually must give glory to him. Just as the brilliant sky around the sun reveals the presence and power of the sun, radiates light, creates brightness, and invites admiration, so the glory of God creates glorification and calls for it. Applied to the term *endoxos* ("resplendent," "glorious") in Eph 5:27 this means: the splendor attributed to the Messiah's Bride is (a) a gift of God or the Messiah; (b) a transforming power, not just an imputation or a putative status;[291] (c) an event making the church "conformed to the image" and "inseparable from the love of Christ" (Rom 8:29, 35); and (d) a demonstration that is not limited to the Bride, but may be reflected on a wider public—just like Moses' shining face.[292]

[286] G. Kittel, TWNTE, II, 232; cf. the other contributions to the quoted article on *dokeō*, etc. by von Rad, W. Grundmann, TWNTE, II, 232–60; also von Rad, OTTh, pp. 239–41; L. H. Brockington, "The LXX Background of the New Testament use of *doxa*," in *Studies in the Gospels*, Fs R. H. Lightfoot, ed. D. E. Nineham (Oxford: Blackwell, 1955), pp. 1–8; C. Spicq, *Théologie morale*, I, 110, 126–33; H. U. von Balthasar, *Herrlichkeit*, III 2:1–2 (Einsiedeln: Johannes-Verlag, 1967, 1969).
[287] E.g. Deut 33:2; Ps 29; Acts 22:11; Rev 18:1. The reflection of God's light on a human face is mentioned in Exod 34:29–35.
[288] Exod 34:10; John 2:11; 11:4, 40.
[289] LXX Isa 40:5; Luke 3:4–6; Rom 6:4.
[290] Num 12:8; I Cor 11:7.
[291] Cf. "Now in Christ you are light" (5:8). These words do not mean, "You seem to be light," or "You live as though you were light." But they describe the beginning of the final transformation promised in 5:27. Cf. again Isa 43:4; "Because you are precious in my eyes and honored, I love you."
[292] Exod 34:29–35; cf. II Cor 3:12–18.

5) In Luke 7:25, the adjective *endoxos* occurs as a parallel term to "soft" and describes the quality of cloth worn "in royal courts." *Endoxos* may be specifically related to the dress of the Bride, for the Bridegroom described in Eph 5 appears to follow the precedent set by Yahweh: not only does he find the girl, choose her for himself, and promise her his troth, but he also washes and anoints her body and clothes her.[293] The details enumerated by Ezekiel (16:10–14) illustrate the meaning of the term "resplendent" in Eph 5:27. The fatherly friend and bridegroom bedecks the chosen girl with "embroidered cloth, leather, fine linen, silk." He adds "bracelets on the arms, a chain on the neck, a ring in the nose, earrings and a crown," all of "gold and silver." He does not forget to feed her with "fine flour, honey and oil." This way she becomes "exceedingly beautiful," attains "royal status,"[294] and is "perfect through the splendor bestowed upon her."[295] Ps 45:13–14 praises the gold-covered, many-colored robes of the princess, and Rev 19:7–8; 21:2 concentrates attention upon the dress which the Bride wears: Her "preparation" for the wedding consists essentially in the donning of this dress. If ever "clothes make a man," then above all they make a bride. Even the Shulammite whose charm is as little dependent on "paint and powder" (cf. fn. 285) or clothes as the grace is of "a mare of Pharaoh's chariots" or of "two fawns of a gazelle"[296] is wearing a "neck-string of jewels, and sandals." Her "flowing locks" cover her cheeks, and her "tresses are braided with ribbons." However, since she speaks of moments more intimate than a bridal procession or a wedding feast, she also says, "I had put off my garment, how could I put it on?"[297]

Why is so much emphasis set upon the outward appearance of the bride— especially when "outward adorning with braiding of hair, decoration of gold, and wearing of robes" can become an end in itself, a substitute for reverent and chaste behavior (I Peter 3:2–3), and a demonstration of vanity and pride?[298] The answer can be given by paraphrasing the exegesis of Thomas

[293] According to Jewish custom, women or girl friends of the bride would assist at the bridal bath and clothing before the wedding, not the bridegroom himself. Gifts of the bridegroom provided for dress and ornaments. The father of the bride was duty-bound to give his daughter a dowry corresponding to his means and social status. Gifts made by the friends of the bridal chamber had eventually to be matched by gifts of the bridegroom to them: Judg 14:10–19; cf. StB, I, 500 ff.; II, 384 ff. Since in the imagery of Eph 5:27 the Messiah is fatherly provider, friend, and bridegroom at the same time, he alone has to foot all the bills incurred. The payment made by the Messiah is explicitly mentioned in vs. 25: "He gave himself for her." He himself becomes her dowry, her wedding present, and her glorifying garment. In COMMENTS IV D, E, and F the several means employed for her "appropriation" will be described.

[294] The presence of enthronement symbols in wedding ceremonies was mentioned in the description of the ideal bridegroom: the "prince charming," in COMMENT VII on 4:1–16.

[295] Though the wording of Ezek 16:14 in today's LXX editions does not contain the adjective *endoxos*, the Hebrew text permits a translation which comes very near Eph 5:27. In Luke 13:17 *endoxos* means "famous" and describes the character of a deed rather than of a person. The "splendor" mentioned in Ezek 16:14 combines both elements. F. Mussner, p. 149, adds a third possible meaning of *endoxos*. He assumes that the term describes the bride's happy countenance: the bridegroom's effect upon her is to "make" her eyes, her whole face "radiant" (*strahlend machen*). The biblical texts quoted so far in this COMMENT do not mention the facial expression of the bride. But their authors would certainly not have denied that happiness shines from the eyes, the lips, the dimples of the beloved and lovely girl: "Then you shall see and be radiant, your heart throbbing and full," Isa 60:5 (RSV and JB combined).

[296] Song of Songs 1:9–17; 4:1–7; 7:1–9.

[297] Song of Songs 1:10; 4:4; 5:3; 7:1, 5, see esp. the NEB version.

[298] While these and other pieces of dress are jubilantly enumerated in Ezek 16:10–13, they are the occasion of scorn, ridicule, and condemnation in the case of the "daughters of Zion" who are denounced by the prophet Isaiah. A mockery of the Bride of Yahweh takes place when all the finery (including "anklets, headbands, crescents, scarves, perfume boxes, nose rings, handbags, girdles, sashes") are worn "haughtily with outstretched necks, wanton glances," when the girls

Aquinas quoted earlier: "It would be unfitting" for the king and bridegroom who "rides forth in majesty" (Ps 45:3–4; Rev 19:11–16) to have a queen and bride who lacks glory. Long enough have Jews and Gentiles been neglected, low, poor, ugly, dead in trespasses and sins;[299] now they are created anew and made a new person. They become the Messiah's bride through signs and gifts of love. This bride is made beautiful; riches are bestowed upon her; she is given royal status. In Eph 2:6 Paul had indeed stated that all the saints were raised up from death and put upon thrones; in 3:8 he had spoken of the "riches of Christ"; in 4:23–24 their total "renewal" through being clothed in a very special dress, the "New Man," was described; in 2:15 he called the making of the "New Man" (the bride) an act of creation. In Rom 8:30 "justification" and "glorification" are mentioned in one breath. Ephesians speaks only of glorification but understands it equally as the effect of sheer grace.

6) Finally, the term *endoxos* has a meaning which goes beyond the exclusive Bridegroom-Bride relationship described in (4) and (5). The wider sense may be called propagandistic, or in theological terminology, missionary. By the love which the Bridegroom shows his Bride and by the lavish manner in which he decks her out and lifts her up to himself, he reveals *urbi et orbi* (to his city and the whole world) what kind of man he is, of what grain he is made, of which attitude and action he is capable. He shows that he is free and yet willing to bind himself, and that he not only intends to do good but is able to carry out his decision. The royal Son introduces himself to his people by the partner he chooses to share his throne, and by the way in which he prepares and cele-brates the wedding.[300] When the Son of the "all-glorious Father" (1:17) de-cides to make his Bride "glorious" (or "resplendent") he reveals his full power in matters of glory. He is not only political ruler ("head over all powers"), bio-logical head (giving life and direction to the "body"), priestly mediator ("offer-ing himself," "making" and "pronouncing peace"), he also communicates glory. The majesty and mystery of the Holy are present and operative when he acts according to his love. This love is holy and therefore glorious, too.

In turn, the beloved and glorified Bride is not the sole end and destination of the Bridegroom's love and glory. Certainly she receives a unique boon and owes her lover a debt in which no one else can share. But she is also placed into the position of fulfilling a public service; in person she is the full demonstration of the life, care, devotion, power of the Bridegroom. She is the living proof of his faithfulness, patience, energy. "Through her" his majesty is publicized.[301]

"mince along as they go, tinkling with their feet," etc. (Isa 3:16–26). At a portal of the Strasbourg Cathedral, the lady representing the church and standing opposite a poor girl who signifies the synagogue, resembles not so much the Bride of Eph 5; Rev 19; 21, as those proud "daughters of Zion" whom "the Lord will smite with a scab," whose "secret parts he will lay bare," and "whose mighty lovers will fall in battle" (Isa 3:17, 25).

299 Ezek 16:1 ff.; Eph 2:1–3. Augustine *enarr. in Ps.* XLIV[XLV] 3 and 4, puts specific emphasis upon the fact that before her clothing with righteousness, etc., the bride was "ugly" and far from "white."

300 An adage such as, "Tell me which woman you love, and I will tell you who you are," may be truer to life than its better known French counterpart. Phillips' version of 5:27, ". . . to make her an altogether glorious church *in his eyes*," conveys one essential element of the text but hides the fact that more than the esteem in which the Messiah holds the church is meant. The term *endoxos* includes the high renown which the church will enjoy in public.

301 Cf. the formulation, "through the church" (3:10). The same missionary role is attributed to the church when her members are called "light" (5:8; Matt 5:14–15, etc.).

Even those who do not yet know him or who doubt his love and power will judge him according to his truthfulness and generosity toward his Chosen One.[302] In the interpretation of 2:7; 3:10 and of the term "body of Christ" (see COMMENT VI B 6 on 1:15–23) it was shown that the manifestation of Christ to the world is an essential element of the doctrine of the church unfolded in this epistle. The term *endoxos* in 5:27 sums up this teaching before it is reiterated for the last time in 6:18–20.

D Love and Death

The death of the Messiah has a place and function in his love for the church which is without parallel in the literary description of any lover's love, and is inimitable even by the most ardent human lover.[303] The cross of Christ is the ground on which the church stands, the source from which her life flows, the instrument by which her status as Christ's beloved is demonstrated.[304]

The relevance and uniqueness of Christ's death for his beloved becomes clear when it is compared with the occurrence of death or the death-motif in descriptions of the union of a man and a woman found outside Ephesians.[305]

1) Love can be called a sickness: "I am sick with love" (Song of Songs 2:5), and its "strength" can be experienced as equal to the power of "death" (Song of Songs 8:6). In turn, a "woman whose heart is snares and nets and whose hands are fetters" is "more bitter than death" (Eccles 7:26). But in Eph 5 Christ's death is much more than a point of comparison, and its cause has nothing to do with disease or bitterness.

2) Death can be mentioned as the limit of love on earth, as in the widespread marriage formula, " 'Til death do us part." Thus the superior power of death over life and love seems to be realistically acknowledged. A widower or a widow may remarry (I Cor 7:8–9); young widows are encouraged to do so (I Tim 5:14). However, Christ does not love his Bride just for the duration of his or her earthly life. His death stands at the beginning of his love for her; it knows no limit, but is a creative act by which the Bride receives a share in the same life which he was given in the resurrection from death.[306]

3) The death of a third party can be the price of love. Instead of paying for

---

[302] The Christological and ecclesiological teaching of Eph 5:27 has an anthropological parallel in I Cor 11:7. There Paul calls "the wife the glory of her husband," as if to say, She is in person his self-manifestation and represents him in public.

[303] A beautiful translation of Chrysostom's comment on Eph 5:25 is quoted by Abbott, p. 167, "Wouldst thou that thy wife should obey thee as the Church doth Christ? have care thyself for her, as Christ for the Church; and if it should be needful that thou shouldst give thy life for her, or be cut to pieces a thousand times, or endure anything whatever, refuse it not; yea, if thou hast suffered this thou hast not done what Christ did, for thou doest this for one with whom thou wert already united, but He for her who rejected Him and hated Him." Best, p. 174, mentions another difference: a husband may die for his wife, but he cannot cleanse her or present her as perfect; cf. Mussner, p. 149. Dibelius refers to the statement about the "savior of the body" in vs. 23: there and here a strict comparison between Christ and the husband is *not* intended. Schlier, however, believes that in marriage the husband cannot just imitate but *nachvollziehen* ("re-enact," "actualize") the love of the Bridegroom.

[304] Eph 2:16. Ignatius goes so far as to simply equate Christ's love and Christ's blood: "His blood . . . is incorruptible love (*agapē*)" (Rom. VII 3); "love . . . is the blood of Jesus Christ" (*Trall.* VIII 1).

[305] Comparisons from the animal realm—as the death of the male bee after he has inseminated the queen, or of the praying mantis who is decapitated by the female during their intercourse, and finally eaten—do not belong in this context.

[306] In COMMENTS IV on 1:15–23 and V–VI A on 2:11–22 an attempt was made to show how according to Ephesians the cross and the resurrection of Christ exert their power over Jews and Gentiles.

the bride in cash or equivalent gifts, the bridegroom is sometimes required to prove his worth by a heroic deed that threatens his own life but ends with the destruction of another. Only after slaying a monster does Perseus receive Andromeda; after killing two hundred Philistines, David is given the king's daughter (I Sam 18:20–27); the "victorious" king is the bridegroom in Ps 45 as well as in Rev 19.[307] In Goethe's Faust the hero has to kill Gretchen's brother in order to have his way with the beloved. In many cultures a dangerous rite de passage precedes marital union; only by avoiding or beating death does the bridegroom prove worthy for the wedding. According to Eph 5, Jesus Christ delivers himself unto death. No third party is sacrificed in order to make him attain the Bride. As mentioned earlier, no price is paid except his own blood.

4) Often the price of love is paid by the beloved girl or woman, rather than by the man. In surrendering herself to him, it is she who may lose her reputation, have to bear a child, and give birth to it. However great the risk and cost he shoulders in loving her and providing for her, her burden is the greater. In many cultures, the deflowering of the bride is considered a form of death; therefore marriage, funeral, and mystery rites can be intermixed and celebrated simultaneously. Even in an ideal case, such as Dante's Beatrice, it is only after her death that the beloved girl reaches the state of perfection in the man's eyes. The perfection attained in her death leads him into the perfect world! However, Jesus Christ surrenders himself for the beloved. Certainly he gains a bride whom he will present "to himself" as a perfect creature; he acts simultaneously for his name's sake and for her benefit. Yet he does not stake or take her life—on the contrary, he provides life for her forever by the gift of his life.

5) Lovemaking is a complement or an alternative to killing and dying, when soldiers use breaks between battles and the "right" of the victor for indiscriminate fornication and rape.[308] In turn, participation in a soldier's life and risks have often been used as an escape from unhappy love affairs. But for Jesus Christ love and death are not exchangeable alternatives, and neither of them is an escape from the other. His love is neither "saccharine" nor "insipid" nor "banal" because it is ennobled by "the tragic"—even the price of his own life.[309]

6) Love's fulfillment can be sought and found in death itself. Despair of the conditions and exigencies of life in the present world can become so extreme that death is voluntarily chosen or gladly endured. In various ways the myth of Tristan and Iseult,[310] the legend of Pyramus and Thisbe, the drama of Romeo and Juliet, and uncounted other moving stories praise love and decry the present life and world: this world is too poor a stage for ultimate love and unworthy of the greatest lovers; only in death can that union be found which no

---

[307] The motif of the conquering and victorious bridegroom is treated extensively by Chavasse, pp. 113 ff.

[308] According to R. May, pp. 105–9, the sex explosion following the invention of the atomic bomb can be explained as a "cover up for the fear of death"; Hemingway, whose novels depict life as worth living only when death might strike any moment, committed suicide at the moment he lost his potency, according to this psychologist.

[309] The terms quoted are May's (pp. 110, 120), although he is not speaking of Christ's love but presents his diagnosis and therapeutic for the erotic sickness of the present time.

[310] Whose influence upon western society is described by de Rougemont, passim. Cf. the chapter on "Death and Tragedy" in Schubart, pp. 161–72.

longer can be questioned, threatened, or broken.[311] Thus *Eros* can become a world-denying force. No longer are love and death just compared; rather they are experienced in combination and identification. No self-denying love appears as great as that which welcomes death for the beloved's sake or together with him. Again, Christ's attitude to death is different. He does not "work himself to death for the beloved,"[312] neither does he expect her to work toward such an end. Rather, he is the living proof that in this dark valley where men moan under the fear of death, there is life invincible, love enduring a solid meaning of existence, reason to rejoice in him, and to give hope to others. Instead of being otherworldly, his love is directed to life in this world. Instead of offering an escape, his love enables the beloved to take a stand here and now. Instead of the consolation of a myth, he gives the certainty of earth-shaking events: He has died, and behold he lives, and his beloved shall live also. His love is that of one who loves life; it is extended to people lest they despair in the anxieties of the present time.

The six preceding points suffice to show that the words, "The Messiah has loved the church and has given himself for her" (5:25) take up the association of love and death spoken of in romantic literature and poems, the symbolism of many rites, and the experience of many a man and woman. But they also demonstrate that the association of love with death is radically changed. Wherein lies the common core of the many individual differences that can be listed?

In proverbial sayings, legends, dramas, songs, mythical tales, age-old traditions, and ritual forms, the connection between love and death reveals that love (or eros) is raised to the level of a supreme and inescapable power. The magnitude of love and its tremendous mystery are acknowledged when the demon death is called in for comparison, provoked to show its teeth, or forced to admit its limits, abhorred or ridiculed, shunned or desired, treated as an escape hatch or embraced as ultimate fulfillment. Far from being annihilated through the confrontation with death, the great lovers of world literature became immortal even in their death. Loving, dying, being deified—these three events have become one. The same is expressed in affirmations, such as, in their sexual union man and woman are no longer simply human but are lifted upward to experience a heavenly union and ultimately become deified themselves, or voluntarily descend to find fulfillment in union with the depths of the earth or the powers of the underworld. In either case the world of reason and consciousness is dissolved or drowned in the much wider spheres of the unconscious.

Paul's message, however, has nothing to do with deification or demonization of the love between the sexes. Otherwise he would not quote the Genesis text in 5:31 saying that man and woman become "one *flesh*." How sobering, how destructive to a mythification of eros and sex, is this formulation! However, the basis of the demythologization carried out by Paul does not lie in this OT text (which itself perhaps contains some mythical features; see COMMENTS VI

---

[311] According to Plato's *symposium* 191A, the divided halves of the original man yearned so much for reunion with one another that they died in their mutual embrace. But thanks to Zeus' compassion they received eventually the capability to become fully one in this life, and to continue being one even in death (*symp.* 191B–192E).

[312] As some unloving husbands pretend to do—ignoring the fact that a dead husband is for a loving wife not replaceable by whatever treasures or merits he may have acquired for her.

B and VII A). The actual destruction of sex and eros mythology occurs in 5:25. By referring to the love of the incarnate Christ and his death on the cross, Paul offers an alternative to the tales about syzygies of heavenly or deified beings. By depicting Christ's death as the first step and means of Christ's love, Paul presents a substitute for the notion that love on earth must culminate or end in voluntary or tragic death. By showing that Christ crucified is alive and active to make the church holy and blameless, Paul excludes every shade of the dualistic world view in which death and life still struggle for victory. According to Paul love in the present world is not doomed; there is to be no need to seek an escape from life in time and space at any price.

In summary, Paul does not dodge the problem of death which will show its Medusan head wherever love is taken seriously. Rather in bearing testimony to the Messiah's love he shows that love will not finally be swallowed up by death, for death is overcome in the victory of Christ's love. Love is not ultimately delivered into the power of mythical glorifications; it is not a myth. For Jesus Christ proves its reality, actuality, and invincibility on earth, here and now.[313] Thus the apostle liberates both human lovers and beloved ones from the panicky fear that in their earthly love they are subjected and must pay tribute to the ambivalent, life-giving and life-taking, potential of a mythical power. All these "powers" are under Christ's feet (1:22; Rom 8:38–39). The lovers owe allegiance only to Christ (5:21); they are enabled and encouraged to follow *his* love.

Before the imitation of Christ's love can be discussed (in COMMENT V), two other elements of Eph 5:25–27 require elucidation. Mention is made not only of his death but also of a "word" and a "water-bath" by which he demonstrates his love and its creative power.

E   Sanctification by a Word

The history and the many shades of meaning of the concept *hagiazō* ("to sanctify," "to make holy") cannot be extensively presented here. Only those three senses have to be mentioned that may be reflected in the statement of Eph 5:26, "to make her [i.e. the church] holy by [his] word."

The oldest meaning is probably cultic: to set apart for God. Election, appropriation, and appointment for a service are pre-eminent in sanctification. "The proper subject of sanctification is not man but God. . . . Sanctification is not something that is worked up, but something that is rather sent down. . . . Holiness is not so much acquired as conceded."[314] In the OT, the objects of sanctification and the bearers of the attribute "holy" are not only persons but also things, including, e.g. Jerusalem and the Sabbath. The NT reserves the adjective "holy" almost exclusively, and the verb "to sanctify" without exception, for persons.[315] God, the Spirit of God, Jesus, angels, the believers are

---

[313] Cf. Batey, *Nuptial Imagery*, pp. 27–28.

[314] J. K. S. Read in his concise summary of the lexicographical evidence, in *A Theological Word Book of the Bible*, ed. A. Richardson (London: SCM, 1950), pp. 217–18. Additional references have been given in the NOTE on "Saints" (in 1:1) and in COMMENT VII on 1:3–14.

[315] Among the things called holy by the apostle Paul, are the Scriptures, the law, the worship, the brotherly kiss: Rom 1:2; 7:12; 12:1; 16:16. Cf. Matt 4:5; 24:15; 27:53; Luke 1:72, etc. In the Book of Acts, only those who oppose Christ and his witnesses insist upon the holiness of the Jerusalem temple: Acts 6:13; 21:28.

called holy; God makes holy his chosen ones and is, in turn, hallowed by them.[316] Among the instruments by which God sanctifies are declarative or legal statements, a touch, and above all, the blood of sacrifice. God uses these means in person, but he also entrusts them to the hands of chosen servants, that is, priests. When the author of Hebrews elaborates on the means by which God, Christ, or the Spirit sanctify men, he mentions the sacrifices which culminate and find their validation for good and all in the "blood of Christ."[317] The Pauline references to the "blood of Christ" serve the same purpose, see, e.g. Rom 3:25. The Gospel of John speaks of a "sanctification in truth" which is carried out by the "word" (*logos*) that "is the truth," i.e. by Jesus Christ himself who "sanctifies himself" in his death and thereby sanctifies those given to him by the Father (John 17:17, 19). The sanctifying "word" in John 17 is probably the same message as that which Paul calls "the word of the cross."[318] Just as an OT sacrifice was incomplete without the priest's declaratory statement, "Go in peace" (or the like), so the "peace made" by Christ is not effective without the "proclamation of peace" (Eph 2:14–17). By analogy the self-sacrifice of Christ (5:25) is declared valid by a spoken "word" (5:26).[319] So much for the cultic meaning of "sanctifying." If 5:25–27 were an allegory for the earthly husband's required steps before and in marriage, this cultic meaning would call for a cultic marriage ceremony. However, other senses of "sanctify" also require consideration.

A second meaning of "holy" and "sanctifying" is emphasized more by the classic OT prophets than by priests. The prophets intend to show that the people chosen by God cannot fulfill and exhaust their worship by ceremonial experiences and actions alone, but have to show in their social conduct that they are called to be holy as God is holy. A magical misinterpretation of "sanctification" was confronted and combatted with the elaboration upon the "ethical" character and demonstration of holiness. The election of Israel from the midst of its pagan neighbors included a commission which the members of Israel had to fulfill—among themselves and among the nations.[320] Since Eph 5:27 promises the liberation of the Bride from any spot and wrinkle, and since the presentation of the Bride in a glorious state includes her public appearance, the ethical and social meaning of *hagiazō* is not to be excluded from the interpretation of 5:26. The mention of purification and the reference to the instrumentality of a "word" in the same verse underline this exposition. In the OT puri-

---

[316] Cf. Lev 11:44–45; 19:2. In Matt 5:48 the term "perfect," in Luke 6:36 the adjective "merciful" is substituted for "holy." Matthew probably has the cultic sense of "holy" in mind (cf. COMMENT VII C on Eph 4:1–16); Luke unfolds its ethical meaning, in agreement with a tendency of the OT prophets.

[317] Heb 9:13–14; 10:10, 14, 29; 13:12.

[318] I Cor 1:18; cf. 1:23; 2:2.

[319] Bengel assumes that in 5:26 "sanctifying" must be explained by Heb 13:12: the death, the blood of Christ are its instruments. The means of "purification" are, according to Bengel, "baptism and the word." But in the NOTE on 5:26 it was shown that such a sharp distinction between sanctification and purification contradicts the style of poetic parallelism and the almost synonymous meaning of the two terms.

[320] The moral and missionary dimension of "holiness" is proclaimed not only in the books of Amos, Micah, Isaiah, Jeremiah, Ezekiel, but also in some priestly strands of the OT; see e.g. Lev 19:18, 34; 20:24–26; 21:4–8; Exod 19:5–6. Abbott and Greeven (in Dibelius, p. 94) have something essential in mind, but use questionable formulations when they affirm that sanctification "includes actual . . . infusion of holiness," or "equipment with revelatory power." Greeven certainly goes beyond the wording of Eph 5 when he assumes that "the church transmits in baptism the power of revelation." For according to vs. 26 the Messiah sanctifies, not the church.

fication ritual for a leper, the word spoken by the priest had a distinctly declaratory function, not a miraculous role: a person was pronounced clean *after* he had been healed from his disease, and thus was reintroduced into the circle of his family and town; but he was not "made" clean by the priest's word (Lev 14:9). To the word spoken by Jesus Christ is attributed a much greater power: "You are already made clean by the word which I have spoken to you" (John 15:3). According to Acts 15:9, "God cleanses the hearts of men by faith." Forgiveness of sins, as understood in OT cultic terms, is included in these statements—a forgiveness which implies the power and obligation to lead a new life, that is, in Luke's terms, to be "merciful as the Father in heaven is merciful" (Luke 6:36).[321]

A third meaning of "sanctifying" which may more specifically apply to the marriage context of Eph 5:26, was (in fn. 59) derived from the Babylonian tractate Kiddushin and a marriage formula used among Jews even at the present time. The biblical term for "to appropriate" and its equivalents are rendered by the verb "to sanctify." By "taking" a wife, a man "sanctifies" her as his own; thus he makes her "his wife."[322] This "sanctification" has, as the prophets made explicit,[323] its prototype in God's appropriation of Israel: "They shall be my people" and "I will be their God" (Jer 24:7; Lev. 26:12, etc.). According to Eph 5:23, a husband assumes in marriage a headship which obliges him to imitate the way in which "the Messiah is the head of the church." Just as God speaks specific words, e.g. the covenant formula quoted above, when he binds Israel to himself; just as Yahweh "plighted his troth" to the girl Jerusalem in order "to make her his" (Ezek 16:8)—so Eph 5:26 appears to refer to a specific word by which the Messiah makes the church his Bride. The tractate Kiddushin attributed grave importance to the exact words by which the girl would become bride and wife.[324] When at Jesus' baptism in the Jordan God declared his solidarity with him, a formula was used that was composed of elements from the Law, the Prophets, and the Writings, according to the Synoptic Gospels.[325] It is probable that the author of 5:26 has no less distinct a word in mind, when he speaks of "sanctification" (and purification) by a "word."

Which word? Even if the precise wording of the Bridegroom's declaration cannot be exactly traced or reconstructed, its contents can be plausibly summarized. The emphatic position given at the end of 5:26 to the formula, lit. "in a word," requires that its meaning and content be taken no less seriously than those of the term "in love" in 1:4.[326] To denote the "word" in question,

---

[321] In I Cor 7:14 married spouses are sanctified (probably by God) by their union when one of them is a saint. Jeremias speaks of a "missionary task in mixed marriages" ("Die missionarische Aufgabe in der Mischehe," in *Neutestamentliche Studien für R. Bultmann*, BhZNW 21 [1954], 255–60; cf. Baltensweiler, p. 193; Reicke, p. 29). However, H. Lietzmann (HbNT 8 [1933] on I Cor 7:16) opposes this interpretation though he declares it "linguistically possible."

[322] In fn. 90 to 5:28 some of the things were enumerated which, according to rabbinical teaching, a husband "owes" his wife.

[323] See COMMENT II.

[324] See the quotations in fn. 59.

[325] In the statement, "This is my beloved Son with whom I am well pleased," Matt 3:17 par., a "string of pearls" is woven out of Gen 22:2; Isa 42:1; Ps 2:7, as if to sum up all promises of the OT and to indicate their fulfillment at the present moment.

[326] The relevance of the formula, *en rhēmati* is probably minimized when it is not treated as a qualification of the whole verse but only as an explanation of the mysterious power of the "water-bath" (as e.g. in the interpretations of Augustine, Luther, and Calvin; see fn. 58). The mystery

Paul uses a Greek noun in 5:26 that is strange to his own diction: *rhēma*.[327] The fact that it is employed without an article fits well the assumed hymnic origin of 5:25–27, but contrasts strangely with the presence of the articles before "water" and "bath."[328] In consequence, Eph 5:26 may display a pre-Pauline meaning of *rhēma* which the apostle considered appropriate for the topic under discussion. Which meaning or meanings are viable?

In his commentary on Ephesians, Schlier briefly sums up the theories of other expositors. He rejects the idea that *rhēma* means "word" in general, "word" of institution (viz. of a sacrament, as, e.g. "In the night he was betrayed, the Lord Jesus . . ." I Cor 11:23–26), "word" of God, "word" of Christ, gospel, creed or confession of faith.[329] Instead, he follows an expository tradition saying that *rhēma* in Eph 5:26 means the "baptismal formula," i.e. "In the name of the Lord Jesus," or, "In the name of the Father, the Son, and the Holy Spirit. . . ."[330]

This drastic restriction of the meaning of *rhēma* is rejected by Abbott. It was certainly not in the mind of the Latin translators and interpreters of Ephesians who rendered the Greek noun by *verbum vitae* ("word of life").[331] While *rhēma* (unlike the more general term *logos*) sometimes signifies a specifically loaded word, a creative, oracular or revelatory utterance, there is no early Christian evidence at hand that would support the equation of *rhēma* with the liturgical formula, "In the name of . . ."[332] Even if it could be proven that the whole Christ hymn (Eph 5:25–27) was originally a liturgical piece composed and used for the service of baptism, it would be unlikely that such a (baptismal!) hymn would include a praise of another "baptismal" liturgical element.[333] Therefore it is doubtful whether *rhēma* means "the baptismal formula."

There is one alternative which much better suits the romantic context of 5:25–27 and the wider frame of the marriage counsel given in 5:21–33 than any of the interpretations mentioned so far. The "word" by which a man val-

---

of a "sacrament" would hardly have been explained in an aside, within the context of marriage counseling. On the other hand, the accent placed upon the "word" is neglected when, after the analogy of "greed" in 4:19 (lit. "in greed"), the "word" is interpreted as just one more element of the same kind as those mentioned before. E.g. Bengel simply juxtaposes "baptism and the word" as sources of purification, without observing that the "word" is also the means of sanctification.

[327] In Pauline writings, *rhēma* occurs only in or near LXX quotes, and once in an oxymoron that was certainly not coined by Paul, see Rom 10:8, 17–18; II Cor 13:1; Eph 6:17; II Cor 12:4. Among other NT books John's Gospel and the two works of Luke make frequent use of the term.

[328] See the next section of this COMMENT for an explanation of the articles, and the Introduction, section II, for the characteristics of hymns.

[329] One or several of these meanings are present or possible in Rom 10:8, 17; Eph 6:17; Heb 6:5; I Peter 1:25. They are valid for Eph 5:26, according to Augustine *tract. in Ioann.* LXXX; Jerome; G. Estius; Westcott, and others.

[330] See Acts 8:16, etc., and Matt 28:19. This tradition is represented, e.g. by Chrysostom; Theodoret; Erasmus; von Soden; Haupt; J. Huby; M. Meinertz, *Theologie des Neuen Testamentes*, II (Bonn: Hanstein, 1950), 149; Cerfaux, *Le Christ*, p. 267. Cf. Greeven in Dibelius; F. Hauck, TWNTE, III, 425, n. 79; Gaugler, p. 209. Robinson, pp. 125, 206–7, wavers between the opinions that *rhēma* means the formula spoken by the baptizer or the baptized, and that it denotes a *fuller* confession of faith or of the name that is imposed on the baptized person. Cf. G. Kittel, TWNTE, III, 117, n. 193.

[331] See Beuron, ed., *Vetus Latina*, 24:1, p. 243; Vulg.; Thomas Aquinas. It is probable that this Latin version originated from a conflation of Eph 5:26 with John 1:1–4.

[332] Herm. *vis.* III 3:5 and the other texts adduced by Schlier (i.e. I Cor 6:11; Acts 2:38; 10:44, 47–48; James 2:7; *Did.* IX 5; Herm. *vis.* III 7:3; *sim.* IX 14:5) contain no evidence whatsoever that *rhēma* is the name for a part of the baptismal liturgy.

[333] See the next section of this COMMENT for an extensive discussion of the relation of vs. 26 to baptism.

idly betrothes a woman to himself and makes her his wife can have many forms, as the rabbinical examples quoted in fn. 59 have shown. Adam recognized and greeted his spouse with the words, "This at last is bone of my bone and flesh of my flesh," according to Gen 2:23. Whatever be the specific form of the binding declaration made by a man—it has in all cultures and ages only one substance: "I love you." This pronouncement cannot be missing when more than mutual attraction is present and more than passing adventures and experiences are in the man's mind. The words "I love you" and their equivalents have more than descriptive and noetic character. They are creative and causative, an event in themselves, the opening of an avenue into a rich future. It is probable that vs. 26 describes the Messiah as the Bridegroom who says this decisive "word" to his Bride and thereby privately and publicly, decently and legally binds himself to her and her to him. As stated earlier, the covenant formula, "I will be your God, you shall be my people," is the closest parallel. Romantic literature abounds with references to similar formulations that are exchanged between lovers.

The transformation, union, and life created by this "word" are greater than the transubstantiation or transsignification which are attributed to the *forma sacramenti*, the right formula pronounced by an ecclesiastic at the right moment. Persons are changed and united through the word of love, not things. As the Genesis quotation in Eph 5:31 shows, Adam and Eve, all human beings, are created to participate in it—not only a select circle of initiates.

It was said before that the Messiah in person is the love which is described in I Cor 13. When he declares his love in words, he does more than offer an opinion: he gives his word to his chosen one, much as Yahweh "plighted his troth" to Jerusalem (Ezek 16:8). On the basis of this exposition of *rhēma* in Eph 5:26, it is appropriate to add in the English translation a possessive pronoun which is not found in the Greek original: the Messiah makes the church holy by "his" word.[334] The origin, weight, truth, and price of this word are described in 5:25: because the Messiah "has given himself" for the church, the "word" is valid by which he binds himself to her and her to him.

An astonishing accompaniment and effect of "his word" will be described in the next section.

F   Purification through a Bath

In the NOTE on 5:26 it was shown that *agiazō* and *katharizō* ("making holy" and "making clean") can be used as synonyms and can each describe a ritual act of appropriation. The person who is appropriated is selected from others, liberated from powers that held him or her captive, bound to the new owner, and given new life. Appropriation is for this reason a legal action with the

---

[334] Without losing its immediacy and creativeness, the word of the Messiah is pronounced also before Christ's coming and after his ascension, through the mouth of servants of Christ. "Christ speaks in me," affirms the apostle Paul in II Cor 13:3. "He who hears you hears me," Jesus said to his disciples; Luke 10:16. A friend of the Bridegroom (such as John the Baptist, John 3:29; cf. Matt 3:2; 4:17; 9:15) and a friend of the Bride (such as Paul, II Cor 11:2) have full power to speak in the Bridegroom's name and to play an indispensable role in the "matchmaking." The "word of Christ," whether pronounced by him or by them, is usually called the "gospel": Rom. 1:1, 16, etc. No one is permitted to exchange the "gospel of Christ," viz. the "revelation of Jesus Christ," for another message, or to adulterate it by omissions or additions: Gal 1:6-9; Rev 1:1-3; 22:18-19.

broadest dimensions: it can—as in the case of Ruth, Gomer, Jerusalem, Judah[335]—include election, redemption, forgiveness, entering a covenant, the gift of new existence and hope. None of these elements must be excluded or neglected when grasping the full meaning of the words, "to make her clean," in 5:26. All that in the last section was called the cultic, ethical, and legal senses of "making holy," is also essential to "making clean." A spoken "word" and its content described earlier belong to the act, whether it be described by only one of these verbs or by both.

However, it is astonishing that the verb "making clean" (or "purifying") is qualified by reference to a "water-bath" and that, unlike the "word" at the end of the Greek vs. 26, both the nouns "bath" and "water" have the definite article: literally, "*the* bath in *the* water." The occurrence of these articles in a hymn is contrary to hymnic style, but it need not mean that the phrase or line in which they are found has to be a gloss. Even the original hymn may have made allusion to a very specific washing in very special and well-known water. Certainly the translation of *tō loutrō tou hydatos* by "*a* water-bath" neglects an idiosyncrasy of this text. Since the Messiah is the subject of the sentence, the rendition of one or both of these articles by the possessive pronoun would be more literal: "*his* bath," in "*his* water." What do these words mean?

While a description of the use of water in sacred and profane purifications would lead too far afield,[336] some comments on the term *loutron* ("bath"; cf. Tit 3:5: "bath of regeneration") can contribute to the understanding of Eph 5:26. *Loutron* can mean the place, the means, or the action by which for hygienic or religious reasons—the two were not as sharply distinct in antiquity as in the post-enlightenment periods—sometimes also for pleasure, a washing is carried out. The possession or use of bathrooms was a privilege of the rich at the time of Paul. Swimming in a lake or in the sea was considered a pleasure by Greeks and Romans, not by Jews. Total immersion was a rare act whenever a bath was taken or given; it was certainly not a natural implication of the term "bath."

What then is the specific "water-bath" mentioned in Eph 5? Practically all interpreters in the East and West, in ancient, medieval, Reformation, and modern times, agree in explaining 5:26 as a reference to baptism.[337] The following will present some of the main arguments for this interpretation in systematic order, and point by point it will be shown why the "consensus of the fathers" is subject to question and further research if it is to be either confirmed or replaced by a more accurate exposition.

1) When Yahweh tells the people to prepare themselves for meeting him "on

---

[335] See section A of this COMMENT and the NOTE on "savior" in 5:23.

[336] Articles in encyclopedias, the indexes in works on the history of religions, and the special literature on baptism in the NT give access to the various, beneficial or fateful powers ascribed to water.

[337] See fn. 58 for a selection of ancient, medieval, and Reformation authors. To illustrate the diversity of authors who come to the same conclusion, only a few modern interpreters are listed: W. Heitmüller, *Im Namen Jesu* (Göttingen: Vandenhoeck, 1903), p. 328, n. 1; O. Casel, "Die Taufe als Brautbad für die Kirche," JbLW 5 (1925), 144–47; Dölger, *Ichthys*, pp. 87–112; Chavasse, pp. 81, 105; von Allmen, p. 29, n. 2; Best, p. 175, n. 1; Mussner, pp. 149–50; Kähler, *Die Frau*, pp. 112 ff.; Baltensweiler, p. 227; Kirby, pp. 151–52. See also the commentaries of, e.g. Abbott; Schlier; Beare; Gaugler. A bold summary of this school of thought is presented by Batey, *Nuptial Imagery*, p. 28: "Numerous individual baptisms are viewed as a single cleansing act for the whole church, just as a straight line may become a point by perspective."

the third day," the people's preparation and consecration includes the "washing of their garments" (Exod 19:10–11). Preparation by washing is even more pronounced in Ezek 16:4, 9: the girl Jerusalem, "not washed with water to cleanse her, nor rubbed with salt . . . on the day of her birth," is pitied by Yahweh, elected to be his bride, given God's word of troth, joined to him in a covenant, and thus becomes his. This election and covenant include a washing: I, says Yahweh, "bathed you with water and washed off your blood from you, and anointed you with oil." Most likely the Ezekiel text was known to the author of Eph 5:25–27: as Yahweh washes his Bride with water, so the Messiah washes the church. However, the Messiah's love appears even greater for he "gives himself for the church." And the metaphor of a water-bath appears to become palpable reality in the baptism administered "in the name of the Lord Jesus," or "of the Father, Son, and Holy Spirit."

This argument from Ezek 16 is beautiful and striking. But it fails to do justice to another Ezekiel text and its reflections in several NT passages. According to Ezek 36:25–27 the "clean water" which Yahweh will "sprinkle upon . . . the house of Israel" in order to "cleanse it from all uncleanliness," consists not of physical water but of the "new heart God will give," and the "new spirit he will put within Israel." The epistle to the Hebrews teaches that OT ablutions with water and purification with the blood of goats and bulls are replaced by "the blood of Christ, who through the eternal Spirit offered himself . . . to purify the conscience. A true heart in full assurance of faith . . . sprinkled clean from an evil conscience" and a body "washed with pure water," are characteristic of the worship proper to the New Covenant.[838] The Gospel of John states repeatedly that all the holy waters of OT history and tradition are now replaced through the Spirit given by the Messiah. "The water I shall give . . . will become a spring of water welling up to eternal life" (John 4:14). The term "rivers of living water" no longer designates a Palestinian spring, a holy well, or the Jordan, but "the Spirit which those who believed . . . were to receive" (John 7:38–39; cf. 3:5). If the hymn (Eph 5:25–27) referred to a saving physical water, e.g. to the use of water in the ritual of baptism,[839] it would relapse into the praise of cultic observances that are no longer appropriate to the Messianic period in which God is worshiped in "Spirit and in truth" (John 4:24).

2) A Jewish bride takes a bath before her wedding and crowns the bath by anointment with oil. There exists evidence in the Talmud of this or a similar custom, and it is attested not only among Muslims but also in cultures not exposed to Jewish influence.[840] Probably the bridal bath—if not because of a

---

[838] The "pure water" is obviously the blood of Christ and/or the Spirit; see Heb 6:2; 9:9–10, 12–14; 10:22.

[839] As indeed Herm. vis. III 3:5 does: ". . . the tower [the church] has been built upon the water. Your life was saved through water and will be saved [through it]." "Water saves" also according to Ps.-Clem. hom. VII 8; IX 24, 26; recogn. VI 9.

[840] Jewish references are collected, e.g. in StB, I, 506. Literature describing Jewish ritual baths was mentioned at the beginning of fn. 59. Leipoldt, p. 37, mentions the custom of bridal baths in Athens. It is possible that an intimation in Plutarch (amatoriae narrationes 772B) confirms the widespread use of this sacral ritual. J. Leipoldt, Die urchristliche Taufe im Lichte der Religionsgeschichte, Leipzig: Dörfling, 1928; C. M. Edsman, Le baptême de feu, ASNU 9, 1940; P. I. Lundberg, La typologie baptismale, ASNU 10, 1942; G. Wagner, Pauline Baptism and Pagan Mysteries, Edinburgh/London: Oliver, 1967, discuss analogies to Jewish and Christian baptisms in the pagan and Gnostic environment of the early church; cf. the context of fn. 359 to 1:3–14.

priestly prescription or a hallowed tradition, then for convenience and as proper preparation for the festival—was customary at Paul's time among Jews and non-Jews. The allusion to the purifying bath of the Messiah's Bride does not introduce a strange thought, and its application to the church's life seems natural: since water purifies in the bridal bath as well as in the church's baptism, the "water-bath" in 5:26 looks like a fitting metaphor for baptism. Even the unctions which here and there followed upon the use of water, appear to support the baptismal interpretation.[341] If Paul's reference to the "baptism" of Israel as a community in the Reed Sea (I Cor 10:1–2) is combined with, e.g. Hosea's and Jeremiah's utterances about the honeymoon of Yahweh and Israel in the wilderness (Hos 2; Jer 2), then the term "to baptize" in I Cor 10 can by implication denote Israel's bridal bath, and the equation of the communal bath with baptism seems fully demonstrated.

However, the actual attestation of the bridal bath is very scarce in rabbinical writings. Among other wedding preparations this bath receives only minor attention. Its importance was apparently so minute in rabbinical esteem that only by excessive exaggeration of its role could it be declared a prototype or antitype of the church's baptism. It may be asked whether an unimportant (though festive) private bath could suddenly have become the symbol of that baptism which, beginning with the earliest days of Christianity, was a required step for joining the church?[342] OT ceremonial prescriptions do not include the obligation of a bridal bath. Except for Ruth 3:3; Ezek 16:9; 23:40, OT romance and wedding stories do not refer to it; the NT marriage parables fail to mention it. In I Cor 10 Paul does not speak of the romance of Yahweh and Israel, and therefore not of a *bridal* bath. Robinson (pp. 125, 206–7) draws attention to the fact that, even in the ancient Jewish novel of Joseph and Aseneth, the bridal bath is not mentioned. Finally, and above all, all standards of decency would be crudely neglected, and the dramatic structure of Jewish and other wedding days would be broken to pieces, if Eph 5:26 asserted that the Bridegroom himself administered the pre-nuptial bath to his chosen one. When Yahweh fulfills a foster father's function in washing Jerusalem (Ezek 16:9), no objections can be raised. But the rabbis who describe Yahweh as the prototype of the "best man" never include among his praises the fact that He washed the bride. The theory that the Messiah (as Bridegroom, or as friend of the Bridegroom) performs the "bridal bath" with actual water not only goes beyond poetic license but is preposterous.[343] It suggests an "indecent exposure" which contradicts the chaste Bridegroom-Bride imagery of the context.

3) Doctors may prescribe water therapy; magicians sometimes apply it, too; Mystery Religions have initiation rituals, and even the Qumran Community

---

[341] One or several applications of oil, corresponding to the unction of an OT king or priest and other ancient rituals, belonged to the baptismal ritual by the end of the second century (Tertullian *de baptismo* 7, 8; see also Hippolytus' *Apostolic Tradition,* the *Syrian Didaskalia,* and the practice of several Gnostic groups mentioned by, e.g. C. A. Bouman, RGG, V, 1333). Passages such as II Cor 1:21–22 and I John 2:20, 27 do not suffice to prove that a ritual ointment belonged to baptism as early as in the first century, but may have contributed to the enrichment of the baptismal ritual.

[342] Notwithstanding the arguments to the contrary presented by E. Barnikol, "Das Fehlen der Taufe in den Quellenschriften der Apostelgeschichte . . . ," WZUH 6 (1956–57), 1–18.

[343] The doctrine that in every baptism not just the administering clergyman but Christ himself is the baptizer, can be supported on the grounds of texts other than 5:26.

practiced a daily bath in which water symbolized purification and/or new birth. Except in a Thracian mystery rite, the Greek terms *baptisma, baptizō,* or *baptō* ("baptism," "to baptize," "to dip") are not used to denote the ceremonial character of this act, but the NT uses *bapitzō* and *baptisma* as quasi-technical terms for baptism with water.[344] There are indisputable analogies among pagan, Jewish, and Christian water-rituals.[345] Just as a solemn baptism can be intended in non-Christian literature that describes "baths" even though the technical terminology of the NT does not occur, so in Eph 5:26 baptism could be meant. The absence of the terms *baptisma, baptizō* does not demonstrate against it. Among Gnostic groups, baptism was regarded as a saving event of supreme importance—but the term "baptism" is but one among many other designations of the sacrament. If it is supposed that Ephesians is an exponent of Gnosticizing Christianity or that it takes an anti-Gnostic stance,[346] two conclusions can be drawn: either 5:26 confirms Gnostic beliefs by averring that Christ himself performs baptism, or it refutes them by emphasizing that baptism is not primarily a gift to individuals confirming their private salvation, but is given to the community of the church as a whole.[347] In both cases, the baptismal interpretation would make good sense.

On the other hand, the study of earlier passages in Ephesians that supposedly required Gnosticizing or anti-Gnostic interpretation has shown that alternatives exist to the procedures of the pan-Gnostic school. OT, rabbinical, and also philosophical and other secular writings throw so much light upon many obscure passages in this epistle that there is no need to depend upon elements of second-century and later Gnosticism for their illumination. Other parallels from the history of religions are equally unsuitable: the description of the "water-bath" as an event experienced by the whole community radically distinguishes Eph 5:26 from medical, magical, and mystery practices in which individuals, one by one, received the healing treatment or initiation rite. It is unlikely that the author of the hymn 5:25–27 was so unwise as to suggest to Jewish- or pagan-born Christians that they were saved by a bath that resembled the water-cures and water-rituals which were prescribed and respected among them before their conversion. Finally, no text in the NT speaks about a water-baptism of the church as a whole which would parallel or support the baptismal interpretation of Eph 5:26. Baptism with water is always applied to individuals, however great their number. Only the description of Pentecost (Acts 2) and the narrative about the assembly in Cornelius' house in Caesarea (Acts 10–11) tell of a simultaneous communal "baptism" of the church or congregation. The "baptism" mentioned there is the "baptism with Spirit," not with water; personal water-baptism follows upon it as a minor event. Unless Eph 5:26 is a strange and isolated incident which, alone and in contradiction to all other NT

[344] These terms are also employed in a figurative (or rather in their original literal-metaphorical?) sense for denoting the abundant gift of the Spirit, destruction by fire, or death by drowning. See Mark 1:8 par.; I Cor 12:13; Acts 1:5; 10:38; 11:16; Luke 12:50. Cf. the examples of this use of *baptizō* in LSLex, 305. It can describe the sinking of a ship, the drunkenness of a man from wine, or the immersion in sleep, debts or grief.
[345] See the literature mentioned in fns. 59 and 340.
[346] Schlier, *Christus;* P. Pokorný, EuG, take these positions. See the Introduction, section III B, for details.
[347] H. Mentz, "Taufe und Kirche in ihrem ursprünglichen Zusammenhang," BEvTh 29, 1960, elaborates upon the communal character of the church's baptism.

baptismal texts, gives testimony to a communal water-baptism of the whole church, this verse does not speak of the ritual of baptism. As indicated in (1) and supported by the book of Acts, the gift of the Spirit may well be signified by the metaphor, "made clean by the bath in water."

4) An important sacramental argument requires reconsideration: the addition of *en rhēmati* (lit. "by a word") at the end of vs. 26 protects the church's ritual of water-baptism from magical or idolatrous misinterpretation. Since this verse is extremely useful for refuting a distorted sacramentalism or an overestimation of water alone, it must speak about baptism.[348]

Though this interpretation is striking, it is impossible to prove that it corresponds to Paul's intention, to the motivation of those who may have used the hymn before Paul, and to the comprehension of the first readers of Ephesians.

The doctrine of the sacraments developed by Augustine and his Catholic and Protestant followers presupposes the ontological and hermeneutical discussions of the neo-Platonic school. Confronted with the question, "How can there be a mediation between the primordial One (god) and the many forms of being in the material world, that is, between the ideal and the phenomenal realms?" several philosophers answered: by word and sign. The neo-Platonist Porphyrius, who took up intimations contained in Plotinus' teaching and who found a talented pupil in Jamblichus, made the study of divine oracles (the basic spiritual communication between the eternal and the temporal worlds) and of the divine signs supporting them, an object of scientific study in the West. Any figure, element, movement, or action can become a sign of eternal reality, though in themselves these things are but a part of the material, visible, and perishable world. By the addition of a word of interpretation the material element is made to participate in the illuminating and saving character of the divine word itself. This philosophical theory was developed in various forms after A.D. 200. It was ready to be endorsed by the Christians—only if combined with the mystery of the Logos' incarnation and the institution of the sacraments. In Origen's teaching the one incarnation of the eternal *Logos* in Jesus of Nazareth is surrounded, or continued, or expressed by additional incarnations or incorporations: in the Bible, in the eucharist, and in God's people (the body of Christ). While Origen did not add baptism to this list, nevertheless his doctrine of the sacraments was determined by the mediating function of the "word." Augustine's doctrine of word and signs is less Christocentric: the special relation of the Divine Word to man which is established in Christ's incarnation is not the basis and support of but a parallel to the general relation of uncreated reality to the creaturely world. The divine *res* is God, the Word, the Spirit; the created *res* is the sphere of visible and audible signs which is highlighted by the combination of word and element in the sacraments. In the context of Augustine's famous dictum, "When the word comes to the element, the sacrament comes into being, and so it is as much as a visible word," baptism is explicitly mentioned and Eph 5:26 quoted as evidence. Thus the adaptation of neo-Platonism and its incorporation into Christian doctrine were completed, and the course was laid out for later western teachers to elaborate

---

[348] See fn. 58 for references, esp. to Augustine's doctrine on the sacraments.

further on the sacraments.[349] However, there is no evidence that the same or similar ontological and hermeneutical problems as were faced by Plotinus, Porphyrius, Jamblichus, Origen, and Augustine between the third and the fifth centuries interested or troubled the author of the hymn Eph 5:25–27, Paul, and/or the Ephesians during the first century A.D. Though the reference to "water" and "word" in Eph 5:26 has made a significant contribution to sacramental debates of later ages, this fact cannot demonstrate that the verse was given its shape in anticipation of patristic and scholastic enquiries. As shown in the preceding section of this COMMENT, in its present context the "word" mentioned in 5:26 has a meaning that is distinct from the *causa formalis* with which it was identified in western sacramental teaching.

5) In the command formulated in Acts 22:16, "Be baptized and wash away your sins,"[350] in other NT passages, and in apocryphal and other second-century ecclesiastical literature, the verb (*apo-*)*louō* (to wash) and/or the noun *loutron* (bath) are almost technical terms for the description of baptism.[351] Since in Eph 5:26 "water" rather than blood or the Spirit is the means of purification, it is argued that baptism with water must be meant—without denying that "water" receives such power only through the word, the Spirit, and the blood of Christ. Therefore the pronouncement of the right formula, the effect of Christ's blood, and the gift of the Spirit must accompany the administration of water.

Again, it is remarkable that there is only one NT passage which unequivocally combines and identifies "baptism" and "washing": the text just quoted from Acts 22:16. The other NT passages that speak of "washing" or of a "bath"[352] are, except I Cor 6:11, usually dated as late as the book of Acts, that is, in the last decade of the first century, if not later. None of them contains the terms "baptism" or "baptize" which would compel the interpreter to understand them as statements on the church's baptism. The great majority of expositors, old and new, have explained them as baptismal texts by conjecture. While the conjecture may be justified in several cases, it is still not a foolproof demonstration that in early Christian congregations the metaphorical sense of "bath" and "washing" was always "baptism." There are passages which speak

---

[349] See Origen *fragm. in Matt.* 289AB; *hom. in Is.* I 5; *hom. in Jer.* XI 1; XXXIX; *philocalia* XV; *hom. in Lev.* I 1; and esp. H. de Lubac's interpretation of these passages in *Histoire et esprit*, pp. 336–73, esp. 363 ff. Augustine's general teaching on the relation between uncreated and created reality is developed in *de doctrina Christiana* (and here reproduced in an outline suggested in a letter of Prof. Martin A. Schmidt in Basel). The quote is from *tract. in Ioann.* LXXX 3. Among the studies on Augustine's relationship to neo-Platonism are W. Theiler, *Porphyrius und Augustin*, Schriften der Königsberger gelehrten Gesellschaft 10, Geisteswissenschaftliche Klasse 1, Halle: Niemeyer, 1933; A. Dahl, *Augustin und Plotin*, Lund: Lindstets, 1945; R. Jolivet, *Essai sur les rapports entre la pensée Grecque et la pensée Chrétienne*, Paris: Vrin, 1955. In the age of Scholasticism, additional philosophical elements—this time, e.g. from Aristotle's distinction between several "causes" and from his doctrine of "entelechy" (the operation and self-realization of the spiritual form in the world of matter)—contributed to the scholarly reflection on the essence of the sacraments.

[350] Or ". . . and be washed from your sins"—if the middle voice of the Greek verb is substituted for the passive.

[351] Oepke, TWNTE, IV, 303–7 observes, "As far as theological usage is concerned *louein* and *loutron* are baptismal terms." The references given by Oepke, and augmented by Schlier, p. 257, are Rev 1:5 var. lect.; Acts 22:16; I Cor 6:11; Heb 10:22; II Peter 2:22; John 13:10; Acts of John 84, 95; Acts of Thomas 25, 132, cf. 27; Acts of Paul and Thecla 34, 40; Acts of Paul 2:35; 3:6; 5:1–2; 7:20; Justin Martyr *apol.* I 61:3, 7, 10, 12–13, etc.; *dial.* 12:3; 13:1; 14:1; 18:2, etc.; Hippolytus *elenchos* V 7:9; 27:2–3; VII 42:1. Earlier mentioned were the second-century texts that attribute to (baptismal) water "saving" power, i.e. Ps.-Clem. *hom.* VII 8; XI 24, 26; *recogn.* VI 9; and Herm. *vis.* III 3:5.

[352] Titus 3:5; John 13:10; Heb 10:22; Rev 1:5 var. lect.

of washing, purification, sanctification, and which mention in the same breath the Spirit of God, the blood of Christ, the word of Christ, or faith. They do not intend to describe only or primarily baptism, though they do not exclude baptism as an illustration or application of their message.[353] But do not several texts distinctly identify baptism with purification or with its equivalent, the granting of forgiveness? An inquiry ends with a negative result.[354] In consequence, the significance of the words "make clean," "bath," "water" in Eph 5:26 may well be metaphorical. Most likely the "water" signifies the "Spirit" with whom only the coming Messiah can baptize, according to Mark 1:8 par.; and the "bath" (just as the references to "baptism" with the Spirit) points to the abundant outpouring of the Spirit—even on sons and daughters, with the effect of loud and public testimony to God, as Luke's Pentecost narrative indicates (Acts 2). The verb "make clean" can describe that renewed gift of the Spirit which is the essence of the "bath of [cosmic, rather than individual, see Matt 19:28] regeneration," according to Titus 3:5. Or, the "water" signifies the "blood of Christ" (viz. of the lamb) which in Heb 9–10 and Rev 7:14 is praised as the proper means of "washing" and "purification."[355]

6) An additional argument is the following: if the whole of Ephesians is an address to newly baptized people, and if in the context of 5:26 reference is made to the Eucharist ("the Messiah . . . provides and cares . . . for the

---

[353] See, e.g. II Cor 7:1; Heb 1:3; 9:14, 22–23; 10:2; I John 1:7, 9; Ps 51:2, 7–11; Ezek 36:25–27; cf. also the references given in fn. 59 and in the preceding section of this COMMENT.

[354] Schlier, pp. 256–57, who supports the baptismal interpretation of Eph 5:26, admits that "elsewhere in Paul and the NT *katharizein* ["to purify," "to make clean"] does not occur in explicit connection with baptism . . . Later *loutron* ["bath"] designates baptism relatively often." The terms "not . . . explicit," "later," and "relatively often" are well chosen and warn of a simplifying interpretation of the verse under review. Unlike the Synoptic Gospels, the Fourth Gospel does not contain a statement of John the Baptist regarding the relation between forgiveness and water-baptism. Only his disciples and/or Jewish theologians and ritualists felt the need to use John's baptism for entering into a dispute about "purification," see John 3:25. This dispute seems to have missed the point of John's water-baptism completely, i.e. the testimony to Him who was to come, and who (as the "Lamb of God") would "bear and take away [*airōn* has this double meaning] the sin of the world." In John's Gospel, the blood of Christ, not the water of baptism, is the means of forgiveness. The same is probably true of the Synoptic accounts: in his description of the Baptist's activity, Matthew does not even mention forgiveness. But in narrating the celebration of the Last Supper, he speaks of Christ's "blood poured out for forgiveness of sins" (26:28). Mark and Luke affirm that John's baptism was "for forgiveness of sins." What the ritual according to the Baptist's preaching expressed was "repentance" in the sense of an entreaty or application *for* forgiveness, not an actual washing (Mark 1:4–5; Luke 3:3). At any rate, the dirty Jordan water at John's baptismal place was an inept symbol for purification. At their own risk some people attributed to John's baptism the power to protect from God's wrath. John dispelled their notion with harsh words: "Brood of vipers, who advises you to escape . . . ?" (Matt 3:7; Luke 3:7). The testimony of the canonical Gospel texts is confirmed by 1QS III 4–12; *Sib. Or.* IV 162–74; Philo *de mutatione nominum* 124; *de plant.* 162; *quod Deus sit immutabilis* 8–9; *de cherubim* 95; Josephus *ant.* XVIII 5:2 (116–17). In short, in the immediate religious environment of John the Baptist the baptismal water-ritual was not considered to convey purity to the soul, but expressed confession of sin, yearning for purification, the resolution to lead a clean life. There was no general Jewish or Christian doctrine saying, Water purifies if only the right words accompany the ritual. Perhaps the disciples of John and the author of John's Gospel had a special connection with Ephesus—as several old traditions affirm. Even if this be true, there is no reason to assume that the "Ephesian" readers of Paul's epistle would, without hesitation, interpret the words "made clean through the bath by water in the word" (Eph 5:26) as a reference to baptism.

[355] Equally in some OT rituals, though water is used, it is sometimes not the water which makes clean. In one case the use of water attests to the previously regained purity (healing) from leprosy: Lev 14:6–9. Elsewhere, notoriously impure water (mixed with dust from the floor of the sanctuary) serves the vindication of a wife suspected of unfaithfulness (Num 5:11–31). Water mixed with the ashes of a red heifer is used "for the removal of sin" (Num 19:2–9). In the despised and dirty Jordan, Naaman the Syrian and the people coming to John the Baptist are to immerse themselves. All these waters show how great is the need for the "clean water" which was promised by Ezekiel and through which God himself would cleanse the heart—that *water* which is not a physical element but is identified with the *Spirit*, cf. Ezek 36:25–27; John 3:5.

church": see 5:29) and to the "sacrament" of marriage (as a widespread interpretation of 5:32 or 5:21–33 holds[356]), then it would be appropriate for the
sacrament of baptism to receive its due recognition as well. The sequence of vss.
26, 29, and 32 can show that baptism is the first among the sacraments offered
by Christ (through the church) to the faithful.

This way of reasoning is circular. The study of 1:14 and 4:22–24, 30 has
shown that the key passages used to demonstrate that Ephesians is a baptismal
homily do not necessarily confirm this theory, but call for a more accurate interpretation.[357] The fact that the readers of Ephesians were baptized, and the
possibility that Paul might allude to their baptism, do not yet demonstrate that
a church sacrament is directly mentioned, rather than that God and his Messiah prove to be present through the Spirit. If Eph 5:26 is not necessarily a reference to baptism with water, 5:29 is still less an indisputable hint of the bread
and wine provided at the Lord's Table.

7) Finally, it has been argued in edifying literature, rather than in scholarly
commentaries, that since baptism is called a cleansing bath that communicates (effects or confirms) forgiveness of sins, the reference in 5:26 to the Messiah who purifies the church urges husbands to show their love by forgiving
their wives' sins. No love without ever new granting of forgiveness! To forgive
is the way and essence of true love—this, then, is the practical moral application of 5:26. By forgiving his wife a husband proves to be her true "head," and
almost her "savior" (cf. 5:23).

But two objections must be raised: (a) It was shown earlier that the individual lines of the Christ hymn (5:25–27), as well as the line about the "savior" in
5:23, describe the unique sacrificial or sacramental love of Jesus Christ which
cannot be allegorized downward and taken as a step-by-step prescription of a
husband's behavior toward his wife. (b) It is highly improbable that in quoting
the hymn within the context of advice to married people, Paul intended to
place husbands in the place of the sinless Christ who mediates God's forgiveness (1:7), and only wives in the position of recipients, but never in the position
to grant forgiveness. Men need their wives' forbearance and pardon as wives
need to be forgiven by their husbands. "Forgive one another just as God has
forgiven you in Christ" (4:32). Of course, the bath given by the Messiah in his
very special "water" (the Spirit or the blood) means forgiveness and the baptism administered in the church bears testimony to this gift. But neither water-
baptism alone, nor forgiveness alone, and least of all a one-sided forgiveness
needed by women only, is the subject of the last line of 5:26.

The words, lit. "made clean through the bath in the water," are most likely a
praise of the new life given in common to all members of the church through
the death of Christ and the Spirit of God.

With this statement the interpretation of the hymn that sings the romance of
Christ and the church can be concluded. Some distinctive features of the Pauline application of the Christological and ecclesiological statements to married
couples can now be considered.

[356] See the first NOTE on 5:32.
[357] See COMMENTS XVI on 1:3–14 and V C 4:17–32.

V   Husband and Wife

The praise of Christ's love for his Bride is the ontology of love on earth, but cannot and will not substitute for a methodology of love, not to speak of its technology. The Messiah's love does not yield a casuistic regulation for the diverse steps which husband and wife take together, toward one another, and among outsiders. The following sections A and B will discuss the husband's attitude, section C the wife's response, and section D their common life in love.

A   Love Her, Love Her!

The many prose and poetic theological references in 5:21–33 to Christ's relation to the church are not made in order to avoid practical advice. Instead of being a lofty ideal, the love of the Messiah is concrete, historic, pragmatic: it pays no less than the price of death, cf. John 15:13. Therefore, this love can be the ground and model of the concrete, historic, and pragmatic attitude of the husband.

Yet was not the apostle a bachelor, who like many of his celibate priestly interpreters meant well in the advice he gave, who may also have studied thoroughly pertinent literature and learned from uncounted "cases" previously counselled—but who still lacked that personal experience and involvement which seems to be the privilege and burden of a married man? And was he not a typical representative of a conservative antiquated stance that is hardly understood and even less readily appreciated by modern readers?

The first question cannot be answered with a simple Yes or No. Several modern scholars have written on the issue of whether Paul was single throughout his life, or widowed following a separation from his wife during the first years after his conversion. The problem is as yet unsolved.[358] A partial answer to the second question was given in COMMENT II. Many seemingly archaic statements in Paul's counsel were probably provoked by wild features of a

---

[358] J. Jeremias, "War Paulus Witwer?" ZNW 25 (1926), 310–12; idem, "Nochmals: War Paulus Witwer?" ZNW 28 (1929), 321–23; E. Fascher, "Zur Witwerschaft des Paulus und der Auslegung von I Cor. 7," ZNW 28 (1929), 62–69; A. Oepke, "Probleme der vorchristlichen Zeit des Paulus," TSK 105 (1933), 406–10; Menoud, p. 23, n. 1; Orr, pp. 12–13. Cf. Clement of Alexandria strom. III 6:52–53 (192S); Eusebius HE III 30:1. Since there are only rare cases known of unmarried ancient rabbis (see, e.g. Moore, Judaism, II, 120), it is unlikely that Paul could have been educated in the way the teachers and practitioners of the law of his time as well as later ordained rabbis were trained, and yet have remained single (Jeremias). But a prophetic figure such as John the Baptist could follow one line of Qumran, viz. Essene, teaching and underscore his status as an outsider and his eschatological message by resisting the contemporary pressure that a good Jew be married and have children. In regard to Paul's own statements, the answer to the question depends on the interpretation of I Cor 7:8 and 9:5. Agamos in the first passage may mean widower as well as bachelor (LSLex, 5: "unmarried, single . . . man, whether bachelor or widower") and the parallel term, "widow" (gēra), in the same verse confirms the latter sense. From I Cor 9:5 some expositors derived the conclusion that Paul had a wife, but (unlike Peter) did not take her on his travels. If there was ever a "Mrs. Saul," it may well be that she did not follow her husband in his conversion. The apostle may have accepted her request for separation before she died—in agreement with his own advice to the Corinthians (I Cor 7:12–16) and with a Jewish practice. In StB, I, 318–19, some passages are collected from the several editions of the tractate Kethuboth that describe under which circumstances a Jewish wife can (through a court) request a letter of divorce from her husband. Mentioned are physical deformations, a disreputable professional occupation (such as that of a collector of dog excrements, or of ill-smelling liquids for tanning), the imposition of unseemly vows upon the wife. Certainly Paul does not make his competence to give advice dependent upon his personal experience. He calls himself a "father" or a "mother," and he speaks of "his children," without implying that he had produced physical offspring: I Thess 2:7, 11; Gal 4:19; I Cor 4:15, 17; II Tim 1:2; cf. I Tim 1:2; Titus 1:4; Philip 2:19–22.

women's liberation movement of his time and dealt only with its excesses, not with all of its causes and goals. As will be shown in COMMENT VII C, Paul's doctrine of marriage may best be described by the terms "partnership" or "covenant." However, an additional answer to the same question is now in order:

Paul not only asks the husband (1) to subordinate himself to his wife as she is to do to him (5:21), (2) to exert his responsibility as the "head" only after the fashion of the Messiah who laid down his life as a servant of those he loved (5:23, 25b), and (3) to heed the full meaning of Gen 2:24 (". . . the two will become one flesh"). Much more the sum and refrain of his special exhortation to the husbands is this: "Love your wives" (vs. 25a); "the husbands owe it [to God and man] to love their wives" (vs. 28); "each one of you must love his wife" (vs. 33). In short, the apostle tells the husbands in three statements to "love" her, love "her," "love her," and he has nothing to add beyond this. Paul refrains from prescribing a specific method or technique, but this reticence does not necessarily reflect incompetence or an attempt to dodge concrete issues. It may well be a sign of wisdom, and his insistence upon love is certainly in harmony with what a wife needs and seeks above all. The rabbis asserted (in the previously cited Bab. tractate Kiddushim, *passim*) that money, the contract, and intercourse make marriage. When they enumerated what else a man "owed" to his wife, they seldom mentioned love (but see, e.g. Bab. Yeb. 62b). Yet the Shulammite knew that legal terms alone, even if kept to the letter and beyond it, do not grasp and ensure the essential, the one thing needed when two shall be one: "If a man offered for [or instead of] love all the wealth of his house, it would be utterly scorned" (Song of Songs 8:7). The same can be said of a husband who gives his wife nothing more than great (though empty) words and gestures, including the demonstration of inexhaustible potency. I Cor 13 does not speak of marital but of brotherly love; still, the first three verses of this passage are eminently valid for husbands: resounding words, mastery of techniques, even the gift of one's body can be found lacking in "love." If this is the case, they are absolutely worthless, appearances to the contrary notwithstanding. Thus Paul—whether or not he knew from personal experience as much of *eros* as did Solomon's lady-love—agrees with the Shulammite on the essential point: it is love, and love alone, that makes a couple. Marriage is romance—or it is not marriage in the Pauline sense.[359] Certainly, there is nothing old-fashioned and outmoded in the monopoly attributed to love.[360] If only there is love, there will also be ways to express it with words, through gifts, and by physical contact. Paul would render a disservice to man-

---

[359] A merely tentative answer can be given to the question why Paul exhorts only husbands to love their wives, not the wives to love their husbands. (Only in Titus 2:5, in the context of a catalogue of the attitudes appropriate to a wife, does the term *philandros*, "husband-loving," occur.) It was hardly the apostle's opinion that wives needed no encouragement to love. But he may have been convinced that husbands more than wives are exposed to the temptation to offer cheap or costly gestures as a substitute. Baltensweiler, p. 229 suggests that more may be asked of the husbands than of the wives. But Eph 5 does not discuss different measures or standards.

[360] Instead of modern novels (by authors other than e.g. Ernest Hemingway and Henry Miller) and psychology and marriage books (among which the works of T. Bovet, P. Tournier, J. W. and L. F. Bird, R. May, H. von Hattingberg are outstanding), it is enough to quote a line from the musical *Camelot*. The question "How to handle a woman?" is simply and exhaustively answered by the words, "Love her, *love* her, love *her*." The different inflections of the formula unfold its immeasurable riches.

kind if he curtailed the imagination, inventiveness, and creativeness of love which are proven in time-honored and yet ever new ways.

This does not mean that he leaves it to every husband's fancy to define and express love the way he pleases—otherwise the attitude shown and actions performed by the husband might no longer be attitudes and actions of love. By incorporating the Christological hymn into his counsel, the apostle reveals that he considers elements such as the following constitutive for the substance of love between a man and a woman:

1) an act of election by which one person binds himself exclusively to one other person, and invites the other to do likewise, in a firm covenant of faithfulness;

2) a word of promise which makes explicit that the lover voluntarily surrenders himself and his possessions for the benefit and joy of the beloved;

3) a resolution and vision that within the bond created by election and promise the elect partner above all shall profit and come to perfection;

4) the full concentration upon the beloved person alone and the corresponding abstention from using the beloved for an ulterior purpose; the readiness to forget what lies behind and be oriented only to the future, as is the case between a loving bride and bridegroom;

5) the joy in being able to do good, to spend oneself, to effect changes from which not only the chosen partner but also a wider public can profit. Such love will be good not only for the beloved but also for the lover.

This analysis is derived from the description of the Messiah's love in 5:25–27.[361] Probably Paul would not take issue if someone claimed to have attained the same results without knowing or mentioning Christ.[362] More decisive for Paul than originality or an oral confession of Christ is the simple presence and rule of such love as resembles the love of Christ for the church.[363] For Paul there is no question that the Messiah Jesus did God's will in loving as he loved. The apostle's sole concern is that the same will be done also by married people, whatever their source of information. For him Christ is the reality, basis and model of all love, even of true love. He is convinced that God himself is the creator and protector of marriage and that even what has gone wrong in marriages is set right by God through Christ.[364] According to him, it is not only possible to praise God and Christ *in* married life, but under the auspices of the love revealed by God, faithful marital love will necessarily be a praise of the creator and redeemer.

This may explain why, in contrast to the prophets,[365] in 5:21–33 the Messiah's rather than God's love is called to mind. God's marital covenant with Israel was threatened and broken by Israel's harlotry. The renewal of the covenant was made through the Messiah. In Christ, God has proven that despite human faithlessness his own faithfulness is not nullified (Rom 3:3–4).

[361] In the preceding COMMENT (IV A–F) each of these elements was extensively illustrated.

[362] The same can be said of the hymn to brotherly or neighborly love in I Cor 13.

[363] It was earlier stated that, at least in I Cor 7, Paul also had in mind mixed marriages between believers and unbelievers.

[364] See his reference to Gen 2 in Eph 5:31; cf. the statement made about marriage in I Cor 7:15, "For God has called us in peace." The question whether Paul considered marriage a gift of the Spirit (*charisma*) (I Cor 7:4) comparable to gifts such as glossolalia or prophecy, probably has to be answered in the negative; see H. Lietzmann's commentary to I Corinthians (HbNT 8, 1933) and W. Michaelis' "Ehe und Charisma bei Paulus," ZST 5 (1928), 426–52.

[365] Though in agreement with Ps 45 and the Song of Songs.

The Messiah has demonstrated God's love in person. This love is not an abstraction or lofty ideal but took—after many precedents in Israel's history, e.g. in the life of King David—full and palpable form in the Messiah Jesus. He is the final institution and establishment of God's love.

Correspondingly, the love which Paul expects from every husband is not merely a certain disposition of the heart, mind, and will, a conviction that may find expression in patience and hope.[366] Rather this love will also create and maintain certain "constants," that is, elements and traits of a structural and institutional nature.

1) Marital love based upon and informed by the Messiah's love creates or upholds a monogamous marriage. Total love can be given to only one woman. Greatest intimacy requires the exclusion of any third person, not to speak of a harem of any size.[367]

2) In I Cor 7:10–15, Paul prohibits, by reference to a command of the Lord, both the separation of a believing wife from her husband, and the dismissal of a wife by a believing husband; only if the unbelieving partner insists shall the believer give his consent to a divorce.[368] Eph 5 contains no exception to the "equal rights and duties" attributed to husbands and wives in I Cor 7.[369] Equal, also, is the right of—and the warning about—remarriage (I Cor 7:8–9). However, Paul's distinct admonitions to husbands and wives show that he cannot be made a champion of indiscriminate "egalitarianism."

3) Finally, the love of Christ described by Paul as the ground and model of marital love excludes the assumption that only the will to beget a child or the unlimited procreation of children, or any other motive beyond the wholehearted concern for the wife's welfare, constitutes true marriage and the pre-

---

[366] As might be surmised when the statements about its substance are misunderstood as merely "spiritual" or abstract postulates.

[367] Throughout the OT Jewish and Christian tradition, "monandrism" (the institution that a woman has only one husband) is the indisputable complement to the worship of one God, Yahweh, the Father of Jesus Christ. Men and women who engage in promiscuous intercourse commit idolatry; see Hosea; I Kings 11:1–11; Eph 5:5; Rev 22:15, etc. Monogamy (strictly speaking: the marriage structure in which a man has only one wife) developed slowly in the course of Israel's history; see W. Plautz, "Monogamie und Polygamie im Alten Testament," ZAW 75 (1963), 3–27. Though the Yahwistic chapters Gen 2–3 presuppose monogamy, the patriarchs and King Solomon among others appear not to have known it. The prophets Jeremiah and Ezekiel depict Yahweh as bigamous—at least for a certain time, until the divided Northern and Southern kingdoms are reunited into one. Even the Shulammite who highly praises her lover's uniqueness and is praised for her incomparable perfection, knows the bite of jealousy: Song of Songs 5:9–16; 6:9; 8:6. She is aware of the competition of "sixty queens and eighty concubines, and maidens without number," or of "one thousand and two hundred" ladies, who have a share in her lover's attention: Song of Songs 1:4; 6:8, 9b; 8:12; cf. I Kings 10:8, 13; 11:3. In the NT, monogamy is explicitly prescribed only in I Tim 3:2, 12; Titus 1:6; and there solely for "bishops, deacons, presbyters." Yet it is clearly presupposed in the Gospel passages that speak of marriage, in all Haustafeln—and also in LXX Gen 2:24 where the word, "the two" (will be one flesh) is added to the Hebrew text, and in the Qumran document CD IV 20–v 2, VII 1–8 with reference to Gen 1:27; 7:9. The fact that Christ is the Lord of many churches (local congregations) cannot be used in defense of polygamy, for in Ephesians and Colossians (except Col 4:15–16) ekklēsiā ("church") means the church universal, the one people of God, not a local congregation.

[368] In Eph 5 Paul gives no indication whether he would have resisted and condemned divorce between members of the church under any circumstances. According to current traditio-historical criteria, the exception to the prohibition of divorce which is established by "adultery" (Matt 5:32; 19:9), is not part of the earliest "authentic" form of Jesus' logion on divorce; see Mark 10:11–17; Luke 16:18, and the arguments of Baltensweiler, pp. 87–102, and Greeven in Greeven, et al., Theologie der Ehe, pp. 57–77. In his essay, "Die Ehebruchsklausel bei Matthäus," TZ 15 (1959), 340–56, Baltensweiler argues that porneiā (usually translated by "adultery") can mean a marriage among relatives, and that the Matthean text commands (not, permits) the dissolution of such marriages. Still, the problem connected with the interpretation of Matthew cannot be tackled here.

[369] See esp. Kähler, Die Frau, pp. 22–27; Boucher, pp. 50–58; and the end of fn. 12, infra the NOTES on Eph 5:22.

requisite of meaningful physical intercourse. The apostle is far from asserting that only that couple is "blessed" (favored by God, a praise of God, and a blessing to others) which is given offspring. Under God and the Messiah, the creator and redeemer, marriage is an end in itself. The husband's love for his wife does not require justification by anything human except his relation to the person with whom he is united. He is not only permitted but told to love his wife for her own sake.[370] If he loved her ultimately only for Christ's or the offspring's sake, or out of compassion, or with calculation in mind, he would not truly love *her*. She has a claim upon his undivided attention. A man unwilling to find this treasure, pay this price and run this risk—which includes distraction from, or division of, his "care for the Lord"—had better not marry (I Cor 7:25–35). Still, marriage does not exclude a time for prayer. Even in marriage it can be demonstrated that God and Christ count more than worldly ways and ties (I Cor 7:5, 29; cf. Mark 10:29 var. lect.; Ezra 10:11 ff.).

The Pauline definition of Christ's love and its application to marital love cannot be used for legislation or casuistry of any kind. It is not a timeless principle or absolute truth, but a counsel given at a special time under special circumstances which can never be exactly the same again. Those Corinthians who at Paul's time were inflated by a worldly wisdom of their own[371] were not inclined to accept his message as a call to freedom, humility, mutual responsibility. But its liberating ring has not been muted throughout the life of the church, despite the misuse made of certain formulations in which his advice was expressed.

B   As Yourself

Among the realistic and pragmatic elements of Eph 5:21–33 which demonstrate the difference between this section of Ephesians and an idealistic, abstract or spiritualistic marriage counsel, is the reference to the "love of the self." In Lev 19:18, 34—within the context of a collection of generally very old laws, called the "Holiness Code"—all members of Israel are enjoined to "love as yourselves" both the "[consanguine] neighbor" and the "stranger." Paul appears to apply this directive to marriage: each husband "must love his wife as himself" (5:33). This blunt command at the end of his admonition is complemented and supported by the friendlier and more extensive arguments presented in vss. 28–31: the wife is the husband's "own body." By loving her he "loves himself." On the basis of the miracle and in following the example of Christ who loves and nurtures His body, the church, no husband can ever hate her who is his own flesh and "one flesh" with him. Since Paul does not explicitly quote Lev 19, it is not absolutely sure whether in Eph 5 he intended to offer an exposition of that OT text.[372] Still, Eph 5:28–31 appears to contain the only

---

[370] In fn. 205 (COMMENT II) and in COMMENT IV B, 3, the background and reasons were discussed for the omission of a reference to children in Eph 5:21–33. B. S. Childs, *Biblical Theology in Crisis* (Philadelphia: Westminster, 1970), pp. 173–74, shows that the "love for its own sake" which is described in the Song of Songs, is the opposite of a utilitarian or idolizing interpretation of love.

[371] See I Cor 1:21, 25; 2:6; 8:1; 13:2.

[372] If the question is answered in the affirmative (e.g. with Sampley, pp. 30–34, 139–44, 159), then Paul's interpretation contains the same combination of Christological foundation and practical application as the exposition of Gen 2:24 in Eph 5:32–33.

biblical elaboration on the words "as yourself."[373] What is known about the meaning of this formula?

1) Neither in the OT nor NT is there an analogy to the modern psychological theory that a person must first learn to accept himself before he can accept another person with love and care; and that finally, after relating to other persons, he may also accept God or learn what it is to be accepted by him. In the Holiness Code the manifestation of God's holiness, and the obligation by cult and conduct to respect his holiness and participate in it, are tied to the individual's life in the community of chosen people, including strangers, and accentuated by an energetic fight against the lack of purity and the presence of sin in man. The necessary battle *against* egotistic self-love is put into the service of holiness; love of self is an evil power. Only its *force* may be paralleled by the required love for the neighbor, but by no means may its *quality*.[374] By analogy, the logical structure of Eph 5:21–33 does not follow an ascending line from self-love to love of wife and finally to fear and love of the Messiah. Rather, on the basis of the "fear" and trembling with which the Messiah's love is experienced and his coming anticipated, Paul calls for mutual subordination and for love of the wife as the husband's own "body," "flesh," or "self." If "nature" and "grace" (in the sense of western theology) play a role in Paul's arguments at all, then Paul moves from grace to nature, not vice versa: marital love is a gift of Christ issuing in love of self, not an application of natural egotism upon a woman.[375] The way of love does not lead from ego-libido or egotism, through eros, to *agapē*. "Lovers of self" (*philautoi*) are in II Tim 3:2–4 mentioned in the company of "lovers of money, proud, arrogant, abusive, disobedient . . . ungrateful, unholy, inhuman [men] . . . lovers of pleasure rather than lovers of God." They are a plague of "the last days," rather than the model for husbands.

2) Since the husband is called the "head" of his wife, and the wife his "body" (vss. 23 and 28), the relation between husband and wife was considered by Thomas Aquinas and others an analogy to the soul-body relationship.[376] The Platonic, Aristotelian, and Stoic doctrine, saying that the noble

[373] Additional, though brief interpretory hints are given in the OT and NT texts mentioned in fns. 84, 85. The saying of Bab. Yeb. 62 ("a husband shall love his wife as himself"), may indicate that it was (or eventually became?) a rabbinical custom to use Lev 19 in marriage counselling.

[374] See F. Mass, "Die Selbstliebe nach Leviticus 19, 18," in Fs F. Baumgärtel, ed. L. Rost (Erlangen: Universitätsbund, 1959), pp. 109–13. Quite different is E. Fromm's attitude to self-love; see *The Art of Loving* (New York: Harper, 1956; also Bantam Books, 1957), ch. II 3d. Again different is the dialectical judgment of Aristotle (*eth. Nic.* IX 1166A–1169B), "The good man should be a lover of self . . . but the wicked man should not. . . . A man should be a lover of self; but in the sense in which most men are so, he ought not."

[375] See the NOTES on vss. 25a, 28–30, and COMMENTS I and III. The widespread contrasting interpretation of Eph 5:28 ff. which sees in these verses a reference to a law of "nature" (see, e.g. Thomas Aquinas; Calvin; Baltensweiler, p. 230), is justly called by Abbott and Best (pp. 177–78) "a degrading view of the wife," viz. "a most degrading conception of marriage." After, e.g. Delling, pp. 64 ff., saw no other way but to find Paul's attitude to marriage negative, such a Catholic as J. Ratzinger and a Protestant as H.-D. Wendland have come to the opposite conclusion; see their essays in Greeven, et al., *Theologie der Ehe*, pp. 81–115, 117–42. Augustine said in his *enarr. in Ps.* XLIV[XLV] 10; "Be displeased with yourself; be pleased with your Maker." Thus he did not consider nature, or natural self-love, so good that it ought to be endorsed as a way to God or to a woman.

[376] See fn. 34. Toward the end of COMMENT VI B on 1:15–23, it was shown that Paul himself called Christ the head because he exerts the function of the soul. He gives life to his body, directs the church, and manifests himself through her. However, the dominion of this "head" over the body is very different from that of a despot. Plutarch *moralia* (*conj. praec.*) 142E, was aware of the necessity that the husband's "strength" be shown in a way different from the control exerted by a despot over a piece of property. As quoted earlier, he admonished the husband to "enter into her [the wife's] feelings, and to be kind to her through good will."

soul can and must, with a strong hand and great wisdom, tame and direct the base body, was taken up by Christian interpreters and applied to marriage: A man who respects the superiority of the soul will not fall victim to the snares of his body or wife. If he loves his soul and accepts his responsibility, he will exert a sharp control over his lower nature. His self-love, that is, his concern for the soul, will be distinct from naked egotism. It strives for "salvation of the body" (vs. 23), viz. for the perfection of his wife, cf. vs. 27. Thus it includes an altruistic motive, though in an aristocratic form and not without an element of condescension. The sufferings inflicted upon girls, brides, and wives under the overt or hidden cover of the soul-body analogy are too great to be enumerated. It was not only in Gnostic circles that a man considered himself nearer the sun, heaven, strength, and perfection, and woman as a more earthly, weak, and inferior creature who was forever the temptress and potential seducer of Adam. This pattern prevailed in one or another form in many cultures, including the Christian East and West. Yet in Ephesians Paul does not mention the husband's love in order to support a theory and practice of the husband's superiority over his wife, for which the wife alone will have to pay. Instead of calling man the soul of his wife, he calls him "head" and defines the term "head" in a way that concentrates solely upon love for the wife. The Messiah's "vision" of His Bride which is Paul's model does not encourage the husband to aim above all at "the taming of the shrew"; rather it suggests that the husband do all and spend himself in order to make his wife perfect and radiant. See COMMENT IV B–C.

3) Some scholars see in the formula "as yourself" not only a concession to the factually present and seemingly insurmountable self-love, and certainly not a command to indulge in that love, but a limitation and injunction saying the love of self must be transcended.[377] These expositors do not deny the reality and power of self-love, but they refuse to believe that natural man's self-love is endorsed by the Bible as the presupposition of neighborly love. Rather they advise the sharp separation of *agapē* (or *charitas*) from *libido, eros,* even *philia* (the love of friends); only the measure of energy and passion, that is the *totality* of man's involvement in love of the baser kind, is acknowledged as a point of comparison between love of self and neighborly love. Ultimately they want to affirm that naked self-love must and will become the victim of true

[377] Barn. XIX 5 speaks of love above (*hyper*) one's own soul. Nygren, pp. 447–58, has collected Augustinian passages in which three forms of self-love are distinguished: (a) seeking one's own good; (b) seeking this good in oneself; (c) loving oneself and the neighbor in God. Only the highest of these three forms is expected of Christians. Bernhard of Clairvaux *de diligendo deo* VII–X (Nygren, pp. 646–48), elaborated on these distinctions. He separated fleshly love in which the self is loved for the self's sake, from the steps (*gradus*) of Christian love, that is, (a) love of God for one's own sake; (b) love of God for one's own *and* for God's sake; (c) love of God only for His own sake; (d) love of self for God's sake. Luther (*Divi Pauli apostoli ad Romanos Epistola,* in *Anfänge reformatorischer Bibelauslegung,* ed. J. Ficker, I, 4th ed. [Leipzig: Dieterich, 1930], *Scholien,* 219:8 ff., 336:5 ff.; cf. Nygren, pp. 709–16) was more radical: he taught that love of self is the root of all evil, and that to love means to hate oneself, notwithstanding the church fathers' opinion to the contrary. Man's chief sin and misery consist of his concentration upon himself (*incurvatus in se,* WA 18, 504:10 f; 491:1 ff.). But the love given by God seeketh not its own. In commenting on Gal 5:14 and Matt 22:39, Calvin (e.g. in CRCO 50, 251–52; 45, 612) states that love of self is not a command of God, that it creates all evils (though the Sophists and donkeys at the Sorbonne maintain the opposite!), and that it must be corrected. Calvin is convinced that love of self must be changed into love of others. Finally, K. Barth, I 2, 450–53 finds in Lev 19:18 and its NT parallels a limitation (not legitimization!) of self-love: "As the sinners that we are . . . we can offer ourselves only as sinners." By God's command, we are stamped *and* claimed even as such sinners.

love. The strength of this argument is incontestable. It must be seriously considered in the interpretation of the Gospels, of Galatians and Romans, and of other epistles that speak of *agapē*, but it does not fit Eph 5:28–33. For in this passage Christ's love of His Body, the church, is the basis and model of the husband's love of self. If there is nothing sinful and nothing to be "transcended" in the love of Christ for his so-called "other self," the church, then the same must be true of the love expected from the husband. Also it may be observed that no biblical passage speaks explicitly of the measure rather than the substance or quality of love when reference is made to Lev 19:18.

4) The research done by Pedersen and Freedman leads in a direction which has the advantage of being in full harmony with Eph 5.[378] In COMMENT IV B on 3:14–21 it was shown that in Ephesians, and probably also in the major part of the other biblical books, humanity has the basic structure of partnership. No one is human in the biblical sense unless he is related to another person. Ps 8 answers the question, "What is man?" by referring to God who thinks of man, creates man, cares for him, and gives him a task to fulfill. Other persons essential for the very existence of man are his parents, the leader and the members of his tribe, his neighbors, his children. God is the creator and has given himself and all these persons to man without asking his advice concerning the gift. May man choose to love, to obey, to treat his fellow men well and to fear God! But one partner is chosen by man's free election: his bride and wife.[379] In no case is any of these persons an "also-ran," a side-figure, a dispensable contribution to man's life. Rather in their own distinct ways God, this or that fellow man, and the marriage partner are necessary for and constitutive of a person's very life and self. Man does not and cannot live completely alone. His very life is human inasmuch as it is social. He has no self which he eventually can bring into relationship with God, a neighbor, or his chosen partner. Rather, if ever he becomes a conscious and mature self and gains awareness of his true being, it is because of the discovery and recognition of the partner or partners with whom he must, can, and will live. In electing Israel, God becomes the God (of Abraham, Isaac, Jacob, David, etc.) who is known and confessed in the future (Exod 3). In accepting God's choice, Israel becomes God's people and a nation (Josh 24). In binding himself to a woman, an adult male becomes a man. In returning a man's love, a girl becomes a woman. Among humans true selfhood (and an end to the nagging question, "Who am I?") is found only, if ever, in voluntarily entering a con-

---

[378] Y. Pedersen, *Israel*, I–II, 309, comments on Lev 19:18: "The life which the individual holds is not private property, but something common, which he shares with others, first and foremost with the family, and then the others with whom he has a covenant." D. N. Freedman, "The OT and the Ministry Today: An Exegetical Study of Leviticus 19:18b," *Pittsburgh Perspective* 5 (1964), 9–14, 30 confirms this: The self or soul of a person includes his family; therefore the intimate circle of the family is the model of love for the neighbor, the stranger, and even the enemy.

[379] I. A. Muirhead, ScotJT 5 (1952), 186, lays special emphasis on the difference between neighborly and marital love; he emphasizes that the latter is based upon a choice. Abbott, p. 177 stresses the distinction between rational or natural love (e.g. love of self) and the greater (marital) love that is informed by affection and emotion. R. May unfolds the indissoluble connection between true love and will. The fact that according to Gen 2:22–24 God gives and leads Eve to Adam, does not preclude Adam's joyful recognition and decision. The same can become true when parents arrange a marriage, though the absence of free choice can create obstacles to love—as in the case of Jacob and Leah. Rebecca is given the power to decide whether she will marry Isaac or not, though she has to make her decision without having seen her future husband (Gen 24). According to the book of Ruth, it was also possible that a girl took the initiative.

tractual, vocational, or marital bond.[380] A person can accept himself when he or she is accepted and has become able voluntarily to accept others—just as Christ became Messiah (in the full sense of the term) by God's acceptance of his offering in the resurrection (Rom 1:3–4) and as he proved to be the Messiah through the creation and sustenance of the people of God (Acts 2:32–36).

Thus, according to 5:28–33, there exists a necessary and legitimate acceptance and love of self. It has its Christological basis in the Messiah's love for the church. It is a gift of God handed out when man recognizes who is "bone of his bone" and "flesh of his flesh," and when he becomes "one flesh" with the God-given partner. As a woman is joined to a man in love, the man's love of her becomes love of his body and flesh, viz. love "of himself." The bounty of love spent falls back upon the lover. Even the Messiah does not only spend love, but receives by giving: He presents "to himself" a splendid bride. Thus the words "as yourself" in Lev 19:18, 34 and in Eph 5:33 do not indicate a comparison; rather they point to the reason and result of love.

In summary, man can only live as a human being when he voluntarily acknowledges that his very self, his own life, is constituted by the presence of a fellow person. This partner need not always be a woman; other people such as neighbors or foreigners fulfill the same indisputable function in Lev 19. But among all people who by nature or history constitute man as a truly human, i.e. social being, the freely chosen partner in marriage is outstanding, according to Eph 5.

The relationship between neighborly and marital love will be discussed in section D of this COMMENT, after the chosen woman's response to her husband has been studied in the next section.

C   Subordinate Yourself

Aristotle was convinced that "by nature the male is superior" to the female and "fitter to command." "The strength of man is shown in commanding, of woman in obeying."[381] Assuming that in Eph 5 the apostle Paul wanted to say practically the same, Thomas Aquinas wrote, "The relation of a husband to his wife is, in a certain way, like that of a master to his servant, insofar as the latter ought to be governed by the commands of his master." In the NOTE on the term "head" (of the wife) in vs. 23, in the exposition of the Christological basis of this title in vss. 23, 25–27, 29–30, and in section B 2 of this COMMENT, it was shown that Paul's concept of "head" was unique and radically different from that of Aristotle and Thomas Aquinas, who employed it to compare the husband-wife with the soul-body relationship. We ask now, has the description of the wife's attitude by the term "subordinate yourself" an equally unique and particular meaning?

The verb "subordinate" is by no means widespread or commonplace in Greek

---

[380] Subtle psychological observations regarding the discovery of oneself through the meeting with the other person are found in von Hattingberg, pp. 241, 245, 255–60, 313–14. See also R. May, *Man's Search for Himself*, New York: Norton, 1953.

[381] *Pol.* I 1254A; 1259B; 1260A. In the last of these passages a certain qualification of the *commands* is indicated which a husband can give his wife: he will rule in different ways over a slave, a female, and a child, respectively. If, as Batey (*Nuptial Imagery*, p. 22) assumes, in I Cor 11 Paul has described a "creation order" then indeed Paul, too, would proclaim nothing better than "the superiority of men over women."

literature dealing with marriage.[382] What did Paul mean (or perhaps a pre-Pauline Christian individual or community[383]) when he used the verb *hypotassō* first to describe the right attitude of all church members to one another, and then the wife's conduct toward her husband, and when he saw in the church's relationship to the Messiah the basis and model of both (vss. 21–24)?

In non-biblical literature *hypotassō* signifies "to place or arrange under, to assign to, to post in the shelter of, to subdue, to subject." The passive can mean "to be obedient"; its participle can denote a subordinate. The idea of an over-arching "order" can be present. Subordination happens not only between persons, but also between (abstract) things. There are "subordinates" in civic and military life; but Greek writers speak also of "subordinate" ideas or virtues. A military unit can be described by the same noun *taxis* that also denotes an abstract order. In both cases the act of subjection is called *hypotagē*. On occasion the rare noun *hypotaxis* is used to express one of the specific meanings of the verb *hypotassō*, that is, the taking of a position in a phalanx by a military unit.[384] In the latter case there is no thought of inferiority or servility among those who subordinate themselves.

In the Pauline Epistles, the verb "subordinate" occurs twenty-three times, the nouns *tagma* ("rank," "order," "status," etc.) and *diatagē* ("ordinance") once each, *taxis* ("order") two times, *hypotagē* ("subjection") four times.[385] The verb plays a much greater role in the NT than the several nouns. Two groups of statements can de discerned:

1) When the active of the verb "subordinate" is used (or the so-called *passivum divinum*), the power to subject is attributed to God alone—whether a person is subjected to God or another person, or whether a thing is subjected to a thing. "Not of their own will" are "principalities, powers" and "all things" subjected to the Messiah, and "the creation . . . to futility."[386] Sometimes reference is made to the hostility of the defeated or to their exposure to ridicule.[387] In all of these cases the act of subjugation and the fate of submission reveal the existence of a hierarchy, or establish the proper order of right and might. The weaker is put "in its place"; he has to obey and serve; law and order are thus established.[388] In describing the subjection of the "powers" and the

---

[382] According to his essay on the woman's subordination in the NT, Rengstorf succeeded in tracing the term "subordinate" only to Plutarch *moralia* 142E and Ps.-Callisthenes *hist. Alexandri Magni* I 22. Rengstorf believes for this and other reasons that the NT *Haustafeln* are not a "Christianized" edition of pagan prescription, but "a genuinely Christian product," see esp. pp. 132, 136, 139–40.

[383] Selwyn, *The First Epistle*, p. 423, cf. 101 ff., speaks of an early Christian "code of subordination" which antedates the insertion of the pertinent ethical passages into the NT epistles. Sampley believes that the author of Eph 5:21–33 provides no more than a slightly critical edition of such a code.

[384] See LSLex, 1897.

[385] Included in the total are three occurrences of the verb *hypotassō* and two of *hypotagē* in the Pastoral Epistles. I Clement (2:1 ff.) is outstanding among the Apostolic Fathers because of its love for the verb, to subordinate, and its cognates.

[386] I Cor 15:24–28 (with the synonyms "reign" and "abrogate," viz. "destroy," RSV); Rom 8:20; Philip 3:21; Eph 1:21–22; cf. Rom 13:1b (*tasso* instead of *hypotassō*); I Peter 3:22; Heb 2:8; Luke 10:17, 20.

[387] I Cor 15:26, 54–55; Col 2:15; cf. Rom 8:7.

[388] The terms used by Paul are *tagma* ("group" or "temporal order"?): I Cor 15:23; *taxis* ("order"; parallel to "decently"): I Cor 14:40; *diatagē* ("ordinance," "command," "disposition): Rom 13:2. Menoud, pp. 22–34; von Allmen, pp. 34–35; Rengstorf, pp. 138, 143; also K. Barth, III 4, 172–74; idem, *Community, State and Church*, Anchor Books A 221 (New York: Doubleday, 1960), pp. 133–39, cf. Baltensweiler, p. 221, place major emphasis on the fact that subordination contains the word "order" and/or means the occupation of the proper "place."

establishment of the right order, Paul never speaks of faith, hope, and love that was or is to be shown by those subordinated. Neither does he mention their heart, conscience or free will. Also he never addresses the gospel to those put in their place against their own will. For them he has no consolation or exhortation.[389]

2) His statements are entirely different when they concern the subordination of Christ, all members of the church, saints with prophetic gifts, or wives, children and slaves.[390] Then he uses middle or passive indicatives, participles or imperatives of the verb "subordinate," and describes a voluntary attitude of giving in, cooperating, assuming responsibility, and carrying a burden. He expects this kind of subordination only of Christ and of persons who are "in Christ," who possess what in I Peter 2:19 is called "consciousness of God,"[391] and who know how faith, hope, and love qualify the fear of the Lord. Such subordination can be offered with enthusiasm.[392] It is a demonstration of that "total humility, gentleness, mutual bearing, love, unity, peace" which in 4:1–3 were described as the constitutive works not of miserable slaves and bootlickers but of the free children of God, of persons in high standing, even of princes.[393]

[389] I Cor 15:54–55; Rom 8:20, 38–39; Col 2:15; cf. Eph 1:19–21.

[390] Esp. Bailey, pp. 129–36, but also Benoit; Cerfaux; Maurer, see BIBLIOGRAPHY 11 and the end of COMMENT V C on 1:15–23 for references; C. von Kirschbaum, p. 15; K. Barth, III 4, 172; and E. Kähler, passim, have elaborated on the difference between the treatment given e.g. the powers, and the expectation regarding the conduct of saints. The first are invalidated, ridiculed, swallowed up; Rev 20:14 foresees the end of their wickedness in the "pool of fire." The second are exhorted to accept subordination as it were inter pares ("among equals"). Bailey, passim, esp. pp. 66–67, 130, 135–36 argues the following way: what looks like a "relative position of superiority and inferiority" does not "affect essential equality . . . intrinsic worth and dignity of the individual"; only because of the intervening sin was the original sense of subordination (as indicated by Eve's creation out of Adam's rib, Gen 2:23–24) destroyed; subordination began to imply the distinction of a higher and a lower place; Adam was told to "rule" and his rule became hardly bearable through meeting with Eve's "desire" for her husband (Gen 3:16). But through Christ the original intention of the Creator was restored that there should be "equality and subordination" (viz. mutual yielding), as, e.g. the equalitarian description of the husband's and wife's responsibility in I Cor 7:3–5 demonstrates. These arguments may look like a myth of the rise, fall, and restoration of true subordination. They are nevertheless a forceful way to point out that "subordination" can be an attitude and action of free equal agents, not the breaking of will and the submission to shameful thralldom.

[391] References to the (good) "conscience" (syneidēsis) are also found in the context of "subordination" in I Peter 3:16, 21; Rom 13:5.

[392] Christ subordinates himself to God: I Cor 15:28 (Here the passive form hypotagēsetai probably has the sense of the middle, for Christ obeys God: Rom 5:19; Philip 2:6; according to Luke 2:51, Jesus "subordinates himself" to his parents). The spirit of the prophets is "subordinated" to prophets: I Cor 14:32. The "saints shall subordinate themselves" (a) to God: James 4:7; Heb 12:9; (b) to the civic authorities: Rom 13:1–7 (to avoid "fear" of them and the "wrath" of God; for the sake of the "conscience": vss. 3, 5); Titus 3:1; I Peter 2:13; (c) to outstanding church members: I Cor 16:16; I Peter 5:5; (d) to one another: Eph 5:21; I Peter 5:5. Wives belonging to the church shall show the same attitude toward their husbands: Eph 5:22–24 (synonym: "fear": vs. 33); Col 3:18; I Peter 3:1–6 (synonyms: "fear, obey, call Lord": vss. 2 and 6); Titus 2:4–5 (synonyms: "be sensible, loving their husbands, loving their children," etc.), and toward the "order" of "decent" worship: I Cor 15:34, 40; I Tim 2:11–12 ("in subordination"). Christian slaves shall subordinate themselves to their masters: Titus 2:9; I Peter 2:18 ("in fear"); cf. Eph 6:5–7; Col 3:22–23 ("obey with fear and trembling . . . wholeheartedly . . . from the bottom of your heart"). When Paul describes the "children's" relationship to their parents, he can put it under the heading of mutual subordination: Eph 5:21, but he never uses the term hypotassō to describe the specific respect they owe their parents alone. Instead, he speaks of "obeying" and "honoring": Eph 6:1–2; Col 3:20. References to the fear of the Lord, Christ or God, and to the Last Judgment are an essential element of the majority of the Pauline passages mentioning voluntary subordination, see COMMENT III. When there is nothing else but a "mind set upon the flesh," "subordination" to "God's law" is impossible: Rom 8:7. Paul is grieved because "Israel did not subordinate herself to God's righteousness": Rom 10:3.

[393] See COMMENTS II and III on 4:1–16. In that context it was shown that in Pauline diction even imperatives (and participles substituting for them) can have a totally evangelical ring. He appeals to the heart, the honor, the freedom of those raised with Christ and enthroned with him (2:6), when he exhorts them to walk as people "worthy of the vocation to which you were

As a community of responsible citizens or wedding guests who go out to meet the Perfect Man who approaches, Jesus Christ (4:13), they are well advised each to take his own proper position and fulfill his special function—otherwise the procession will turn into chaos and He who comes will be dishonored. Equally the necessity to fight onrushing inimical powers and to fulfill the church's mission (6:10–20) compels the saints to keep their ranks closed and proceed in order. It is probable that in Pauline *paraklēsis* ("exhortation") the term "subordinate" contains as much an allusion to a march- or battle-order as the verb *stoicheō* ("to move in line").[394] The eschatological expectation, the need to resist enemies in the present evil day, and the missionary responsibility explain why a military term of all things received a central place in Paul's marriage counselling.[395]

In addition to personal aspirations and contemporary cultural progress, the great hope, the grave struggle, and the enormous missionary task of the church and each of her members are at stake—even in the private spheres and the public appearance and conduct of marriage.[396] A woman thinking only of herself may resent her incorporation into a procession or phalanx, just as an egotistic husband will decline to be "head" of his wife after the example of "Christ the head." Paul, however, thinks better of husbands and wives. He is convinced that they possess the freedom and dignity to be a light in the world because they are no more "darkness but light in Christ" (5:8). Those women of Paul's time (especially in Corinth) who used the message of Christ for nothing better than a liberation movement and the enhancement of their own independence by a revolution for its own sake, fall out of that grace and freedom by and for which they were liberated. Neither a bride nor a wife can be glorious (or "resplendent") in her own light and right. What legitimate glory she receives and has comes from God and is shared with him who loves her.[397] Though wives are called the "weaker vessel," yet they are praised as "joint heirs of the grace of life" (I Peter 3:7).

The "order" a wife keeps when she subordinates herself is not "the order of marriage"—to which an "order" of slavery or child-rearing, political or ecclesi-

called": 4:1. In his penetrating treatment of Eph 5:21–33 Sampley omitted a study of the term "subordinate oneself." This omission appears to be the cause why he finds in Eph 5 and Gen 2:24 nothing more proclaimed than "a posture of passivity for the wife. . . . She is . . . the object. . . . The wives are constantly expected to be submissive" (pp. 112–13). K. C. Bushnell (pp. 292–99), however, elaborates on the substantial difference between (blind) obedience and (voluntary) subordination.

[394] See Gal 5:26; 6:16; Rom 4:12; Philip 3:16; cf. Acts 21:34. Though the verb *syzeugnymi* ("to put under one yoke") which Jesus used to describe a married couple's unity according to Matt 19:6; Mark 10:9 (cf. the "yokefellow" mentioned in Philip 4:3), has other than festival or military connotations, it may be a parallel to "subordinate." Certainly it illustrates beautifully what mutual subordination means in Eph 5:21.

[395] Probably the absence of this expectation and mission is the reason why, outside early Christian literature, the term "subordinate" is hardly ever used for the proper conduct of a community or of its individual members. Where there was no eschatology determined by the parousia, no special battle to be waged against the spiritual powers of this world, no missionary obligation for the proclamation and imitation of the Servant Messiah—there the military term "subordinate" made little or no sense. Concerning the military imagery of the Stoics and the thoroughly organized strategic order of the Qumran community, see COMMENT II on 6:10–20 at (3) and (4).

[396] The mission and conduct of the Christians among the outsiders and the missionary opportunity given to the wife receive special emphasis in I Peter 2:12; 3:1–2, 13–17. In addition, there is a reference to the "salvation" of a husband through his wife in I Cor 7:12–16. Titus 2:5 mentions the following motivation for the wife: "that the word of God may not be discredited."

[397] Gen 1:27; 2:23–24; I Cor 11:7; Eph 5:27.

astical life might correspond. Paul unfolds a "theology of orders" as little as
he knows of a theology of "vocations." Whatever he has to say in Ephesians regarding institutions and structures of creaturely life, he says in his references
to the subjugation to which only principalities and powers are exposed (1:21-
23).[398] In his appraisal of their present behavior he is not victim to any il-
lusions (6:10-15), but nowhere does he speak of a "marriage order" or "marriage principle" which has a claim upon husband and wife. The "order" which
he explicitly mentions outside Ephesians is that of the eschatological time (I Cor
15:24-28). He also speaks of an "order" valid in the service of God during the
church's worship (I Cor 14:40). Another arrangement or order of God which
he recognized is the Roman state (Rom 13:1-7). Yet he does not know of an
ideal or a pattern of "the Christian marriage" which is entered or ought to be
recognized by a man and a woman when they fall in love and marry. Theirs is
no obligation to a fixed model that can be exactly copied throughout all
generations; compare COMMENT VII C. Paul is not a man of abstractions. As
was shown earlier, the Bridegroom-Bride relationship between Christ and the
church is Paul's substitute for a law, a prescription, a fixed custom of conduct
in marriage. The spouses are responsible only to God's Messiah who "loved"
them and whom they "fear" (5:25, 21), to one another in their unique and
ever new bond of fidelity, and to the church's missionary task in its environment. Therefore, it is exclusively to the order of God's kingdom that the wife
subordinates herself in her subordination to her husband. She does it voluntarily, as a dignified and respected member of the elite chosen for the festival
procession and the struggle in which all of God's free children are engaged.

In conclusion, some of the specific elements shall be listed which distinguish
the exhortation to "subordination" in Eph 5 from analogous NT texts and
perhaps reveal a development of Paul's thought on marriage:

1) In all NT utterances on marriage the special and intimate relation between husband and wife has its basis, model, criterion—and limit—in the grace
of God and the Messiah. The exclusive union established by love, eros, and sex
does not separate a couple from God—as though they were condemned or
liberated to live in a realm that either substitutes for heaven or contradicts
it by nature. Marriage is neither so great a thing as to make God's blessing,
protection, and judgment superfluous—e.g. by deification of the loving couple,
or by dissolving all personal distinctions and problems—nor so base and secular
a matter as to be beyond the care of God and the beneficial use of the saints.
The subordination of the whole church to the Messiah is reflected in marriage.
To the wife, a husband's love can become transparent for Christ's infinitely
greater love. In her subordination to the husband, a wife can and shall serve
Christ himself. However, this does not mean that her subordination to the
husband ultimately bypasses the husband and uses him for nothing better than
a means of ecstatic union with Christ.[399] Just as Eph 5 intends the opposite
of a husbandly love that asserts: "Ultimately I love only Christ, not you, my
wife," so the same passage entitles the wife to turn to her husband "with all
her love." A woman's subordination to her husband "in everything" (5:24)

---

[398] See COMMENT V on 1:15-23.
[399] As in the case of a woman who in a given moment cried out, "Oh, Jesus, I am coming!" See
E. Cleaver, *Soul on Ice* (New York: Dell, 1968), p. 170.

need not compete with her devotion to Christ. It can and shall be "monandric," even "in Christ" and because she "fears Christ." If because of her "care for the Lord" and her desire to "please Him" she feels incapable of this subordination to a man, she shall not marry or remarry, according to I Cor 7:8–9, 25–40. But even in marriage she can ask for, and receive with her husband's consent, time for concentration on prayer (I Cor 7:5).

It is a distinctive mark of Eph 5 that here, unlike I Cor 7, impediments against marriage or limits of the wife's subordination are not mentioned. As previously shown, this omission is not caused by a neglect of the eschatological character of the present days, but by a different understanding and application of the needs of the present time: the chance and the task to stay together in the peace, unity and mission created by the Messiah.

2) Together with other *Haustafeln,* Eph 5 begins with the call for the wife's subordination and speaks of the husband's love only after addressing the wife. However, in 5:33, at the conclusion of Paul's argument, the order is reversed: here the wife's "fear" of her husband, a form of her subordination to him, is expected as a response to the husband's love. While Paul does not bluntly command this fear, he nevertheless warmly desires it. Only when a husband loves his wife in the way of Christ can a wife fear him in a manner which is distinct from the fear of the "wrath" of the authorities mentioned in Rom 13:4–5. Certainly a wife's fear of Christ (vs. 21) has precedence over her fear of the husband (vs. 33). This may well be the reason why Paul is so soft-spoken about the secondary fear: "May she fear her husband." In any case, the reversal of the sequence and the change of tone in vs. 33 are not incidental. As early as the Christological-ecclesiastical arguments of vss. 23–27, but also in vss. 30, 32 that frame the Gen 2 quotation, the priority of the Bridegroom's love over the Bride's response was clearly pointed out. He who is the "head" (and goes ahead) is the husband, whenever the Christological basis and model of marriage are maintained. Under the influence of the Christological-ecclesiological reasoning, Paul has given vs. 33 that surprising new form and character which distinguish it from vss. 22 and 24b. The subordination of the wife is now characterized as her response to the husband's love. It is a matter of the heart and the conscience—an attitude of self-giving, of radiating warmth, and above all an expression of insuperable love. How else can love be requited than by love? The wife's response to the husband's conquering love is her joyful and freely accepted subordination.[400] Therefore as repetitiously as Paul enjoins the husbands to love their wives, he also tells the wives to "subordinate" themselves. Unlike Titus 2:4–5 he does not present a catalogue of womanly virtues. Neither does he write a "constitution of marriage." According to modern sociological studies, three or more people living together require some sort of constitution; a couple, however, does not. Paul is convinced that love and subordination suffice to express and maintain a couple's unity. At the one instance in Eph 5 where he speaks of "fear" rather than "subordination" (vs. 33), he means a fear analogous to the "fear of Christ" mentioned in vs. 21. Bridal

---

[400] Since the exhortation calling for "spiritual" enthusiasm, "songs," and "thanksgiving" immediately precedes the utterances on subordination in 5:18–22, the act of voluntary yielding is best characterized as a "jubilant and singing subordination." Unlike I Cor 14:34; I Tim 2:11–12; I Peter 3:1, in Eph 5 wives are not explicitly constrained to be "silent!"

fear is not expelled by love, but caused and nurtured by it; see fn. 182, and COMMENT III.

3) In the teaching of Aristotle and his pagan and Christian followers, as also in I Peter 3:6, the subordination expected of the wife is called (or equated with) obedience. This is not the case in Eph 5. While for many authors, perhaps at times even for Paul, the verbs "subordinate oneself" and "obey" were synonyms, this cannot be demonstrated for the *Haustafel* in Eph 5–6. Only children and slaves are told to "obey" (6:1, 5). Certainly, obedience is—as much as love—to be interpreted as a form of the mutual "subordination" mentioned in 5:21, but Paul uses the verb "obey" neither for the attitude of the saints to the state (Rom 13:1–7) nor for the wives' conduct.[401] When, in the Corinthian congregation, a prophet or his interpreter gives another of its members the opportunity to speak[402]—equally when in the Capitol a senator "yields" to his fellow senator—then he does not "obey." Rather he uses the prerogative of a high-standing person to "recognize" his equal and give an opportunity to the immediate promotion of the common cause. The order (of worship, viz. of the Senate) which the prophet, his interpreter, or a senator respects, makes him free to subordinate himself without becoming an underling.[403] Jesus Christ demonstrates rather than loses his dignity by his subordination to the Father.[404] When a person is voluntarily amenable to another, gives way to him, and places himself at his service, he shows greater dignity and freedom than an individual who cannot bear to be a helper and partner to anyone but himself.[405] Ephesians 5 supports anything but blind obedience or the breaking of the wife's will. Rather, this chapter shows that in the realm of the crucified Servant-Messiah, the subjects respect an order of freedom and equality in which one person assists another—seemingly by renouncing rights possessed, actually in exercising the right to imitate the Messiah himself.[406] Even the utterances of Eph 5 on the subordination of wives have to be interpreted as statements praising an "order of freedom." A marriage which has its foundation "in Christ" is based on the freedom and dignity of both partners.[407]

4) In Matt 19:4 parts of the creation stories of Gen 1, 2 are quoted as essential to Jesus' teaching on marriage. Elements of certain Jewish teachings are reflected outside Ephesians in the Pauline references to Eve's creation and fall. There, together with Philo and some rabbis, Paul uses the sequence of the

---

[401] Bengel points out the difference between subordination and obedience; Bushnell, von Allmen, K. Barth, von Kirschbaum, Kähler, and a few other interpreters have followed the precedent set by him.

[402] I Cor 14:26–33, esp. vs. 30. Abbott, p. 164 follows G. G. Findlay's suggestion (in Expositor's Bible), when he offers this passage as a parallel of the mutual, as well as of the wives' specific subordination.

[403] The RSV translation of "subordinate yourself" by "be submissive" in Titus 2:5; 3:1; I Peter 3:1, 5 may have contributed to provoking the disdain of women conscious of their dignity. "Submission" is not the sense of "subordination" in the NT, except in the case of principalities and powers.

[404] I Cor 15:28; cf. Philip 2:6; Rom 5:19; 8:3; John 1:14.

[405] Baltensweiler, p. 219, n. 4 (cf. Schlier), suggests the German translation of *hypotassomai* ("to subordinate oneself") by *sich unterstellen* ("to place oneself at the disposition"). This interpretation is to the point.

[406] K. Barth, III 4, 174, concedes to F. D. E. Schleiermacher that, in her voluntarily accepted dependence, a woman can be a prototype even of man's true relationship to Christ. While in I Tim 2:12 only the wife is told not to "usurp authority" over her husband (*authenteō*), Paul tells all Christians to show humility to one another: Eph 4:2.

[407] K. Barth, III 4, 174; see Gal 3:28; 5:1, 13.

creation of Adam and Eve and the priority of Eve's fall as arguments against the revolutionary claims of women.[408] The request that wives wear a kerchief on their hair or a veil (I Cor 11:5–7) imposes a Jewish custom upon the women of Corinth.[409] But in Ephesians the discourse on marriage refers neither to the sequence of creation, nor to sin,[410] nor to specifically Jewish modes of attire. Instead, the reality of the New Covenant dominates the picture —totally, radically, radiantly. If ever there was a joyful affirmation of marriage, without any shadow and misgiving, then it is found in Eph 5. It is, therefore, altogether unlikely that either by defining the husband's headship or by demanding the wife's subordination Paul aimed at anything other than helping the couples in the congregation to live in joy and peace. A greater, wiser, and more positive description of marriage has not yet been found in Christian literaure.

The last question to be considered in this COMMENT concerns the relationship of the love described in Eph 5 to the attitude that elsewhere—inside and outside the Bible—is called love.

D Agape, Eros, and Sex

In the LXX and the NT, the same noun and verb, *agapē* and *agapaō*, denote the love of God and the Messiah for a chosen man or the elect people, and the love of God's children for God, Jesus Christ, the neighbor, a man, a woman, the self, or the world.[411] Occasionally *philiā, phileō*, and its derivatives are used as synonyms.[412] A strictly philological examination of the terminology used for "love" and "loving" outside and inside the Bible does not lead to the sharp distinctions among *agapē, philiā*, and *erōs* that have been made for the sake of systematic, ethical or moralistic clarification. Supposedly *agapē* always means an unselfish, self-giving attitude that is not influenced by the worth or any other qualities of the beloved; *philiā*, the friendly, reciprocal give and take between equals; *erōs*, the passionate or sophisticated desire to possess and/or use the other.[413]

[408] See I Cor 11:8–9; II Cor 11:3; I Tim 2:13–14. Von Allmen, p. 35, wants to exclude the fall of Eve, yet to retain her creation out of Adam, as a reason for the necessity of a wife's subordination.

[409] See StB, III, 435–37. The more a woman is considered her husband's property, the more the custom requires that she be covered by pieces of dress. Correspondingly, the bare breasts displayed by Cretan goddesses and noble ladies reveal the high and free status of women—perhaps a residue of a matriarchal or Amazon state; see Leipoldt, pp. 15–16. In I Cor 11:5–10 Paul speaks about a piece of cloth to be worn by women when they "pray and prophesy" in public worship. He makes no prescription regarding their appearance at home or on the street. In this as in other cases he expects that those "strong [in faith]" manifest their strength by giving due regard to the conscience of the "weak" (cf. Rom 14:1 – 15:6; I Cor 8:4–13).

[410] Paul does not undergird the husband's headship and the wife's subordination by quoting the post-lapsarian passage Gen 3:16: "Your desire shall be for your husband and he shall rule over you." Also it is not certain whether he thought of this verse (or of Gen 18:12–15, or of an "oral law") when in I Cor 14:34 he asserted that "the Law" commanded the wife's subordination.

[411] See the last NOTES on 1:4; 1:15; 4:2; the first NOTE on 5:2, and COMMENT III on 4:1–16 for references in the Bible and in exegetical literature. It was shown that "love" presupposes and includes the knowledge of the beloved person.

[412] E.g. Exod 33:11; John 11:11, 36; 15:13–15; 20:2; 21:15–17; I Cor 16:22; Titus 2:4; 3:15; Rev 3:19. The use of the verbs *eraō* and *stergō* ("to desire," and "to feel affection") is avoided as much as possible, though there are biblical stories describing passionate love between men and women. See fn. 48 for the few occurrences of derivatives from the stem *era*, and e.g. I Clem. 1:3; Polyc. *Phil.* IV 2 for the use of *stergō*.

[413] See, e.g. E. Stauffer, TWNTE, I, 35; Bailey, pp. 24–30; P. Tillich, *Systematic Theology*, I (University of Chicago Press, 1951), 279–82. Augustine *de civ. Dei* XIV 7, reports that some of his contemporaries considered *dilectio* or *caritas* a good thing, and *amor* a bad. However, he rejects this

It is unquestionable that there are great differences among the concepts of love that have become representative of "Jerusalem," "Athens," and a modern "love-in." But it is equally certain that in Ephesians the employment of the term "love" to describe the marital relation does not exclude from *agapē* all elements of mutual help, partnership between equals, passionate desire, and sexual fulfillment that have been attributed primarily to *philiā* and *erōs*. Modern interpreters who speak of "Eros rescued by Agape," or who affirm that "Agape fulfills Eros" and that "Eros is sanctified by the command of God," do more justice to the intention and effect of Eph 5:21–33 than the great classical philologist, U. von Wilamowitz-Moellendorff, according to whom "Paul knew nothing of Eros, Plato nothing of Agape." They also add the necessary corrective to A. Nygren's book on *Agape and Eros*.[414] While it is true that Plato's *Symposium* and *Phaedros* reveal expert knowledge about Eros, and Paul's letters about Agape—just as e.g. *Fanny Hill* and *Lady Chatterley* are distinguished exponents of the modern reaffirmation of sexual love—there is yet no reason to discriminate in favor of one school of love against the others, or to bear false witness against any of them.

The scope of Plato's *Symposium* surpasses in many respects that of his *Phaedros* and of the great books on love by other authors. Plato's teaching on Eros is so rich that it is impossible to speak of "the Greek," or "the Platonic concept of love" and on Paul's authority to relegate Eros *in toto* into limbo. No fewer than seven great discourses on Eros are reproduced in the *Symposium,* and each proffers new vistas on this inexhaustible theme. *Phaedros* glorifies Eros as the most glorious god who helps men find virtue and happiness (178A–180B). Pausanias distinguishes between the heavenly and the profane Eros; only the first transcends the realm of the body and helps the soul on the way to wisdom and virtue (180C–185C). Eryximachos demonstrates that not only men stand under Eros' power but also plants, animals, science, art, and religion (185D–189C). Aristophanes tells the fabulous myth of the double-beings (first created male-male, male-female, or female-female, then divided by Zeus because of their hybris) who yearn to be reunited and, through the aid of

---

distinction by pointing out that each of these terms also occur meaning the direct opposite. R. C. Trench, *Synonyms of the Bible*, 1880, repr. (Grand Rapids: Eerdmans, 1969), pp. 41–44, warns of discriminating value judgments; he indicates that, e.g. Plato and Philo (*vita contempl*. 2) sought to save *erōs* from its detractors.

[414] The first three quotes are from de Rougemont, pp. 320–24; Schlier, pp. 278–79; K. Barth, III 4, 220; cf. the defense of Eros against its Christian detractors in K. Barth, III 4, 126, 138, 222, 246, 250; IV 2, 337–51; see also Bieder, p. 62, n. 75; J. Ratzinger and H.-D. Wendland in Greeven, et al., *Theologie der Ehe*, pp. 101, 123–25; Bovet, ch. VIII. Similarly, the "Pastoral Constitution on the Church in the World" (*Gaudium et spes*, Vatican II), art. 49, affirms that God, through the gift of grace and love, heals, perfects and elevates "the eminently human love" including its physical expressions. Stimulated by Wilamowitz-Moellendorff whom he cites, Nygren wrote his famous work, *Agape and Eros*. In the summary of his studies in ancient literature, which Nygren himself presents on p. 210, he mentions the following arguments for his thesis that *Eros* and *Agape* must be seen in irreconcilable contrast: *Eros* is an acquisitive desire; *Agape*, sacrificial giving. *Eros* is an upward, *Agape* a downward movement. The first is man's way to *God;* the second, God's way to man. *Eros* is the effort for man's own salvation; *Agape* is the grace of God and salvation by divine love. *Eros* is egocentric, a sublime self-assertion; *Agape* is unselfish, self-giving love. *Eros* seeks to gain immortal life; *Agape* lives the life of God and is willing to lay down its life for the beloved. *Eros* depends on want and need, its aim is possession; *Agape* depends on wealth and is the freedom of giving. *Eros* is primarily human, but *Agape* is divine. *Eros* is determined by the quality of its object; *Agape* overflows spontaneously for the benefit of both the evil and the good. *Eros* discerns and utilizes the value of an object, *Agape* creates values in and for the beloved object. The quotes collected, e.g. in fn. 510 below, will contradict these differentiations.

Apollo and Hephaistos, learn to become one out of two (189C–193D). Agathon wishes to praise the god Eros in himself, rather than just the boons men receive from him; in poetic terms he extols Eros' youth, tenderness, tact, beauty, patience, kind rule, and sober-mindedness, all of which make him stronger than Ares and give him power to create life, peace, religion, and all good things (194E–197E). Socrates contributes what the seer Diotima has taught him. The mystery of initiation into love (209E) is intimated by the myth of the child of Abundance and Indigence who mediates between gods and men and leads the soul upward, from the world of phenomena to the realm of beauty itself (199C–212C). Finally Alcibiades crowns the discussion with his praise of Socrates, the very incorporation of Eros in one man and one life (212C–222B).

Though Apuleius' story of the romance between Eros and Psyche, for example, is interesting, charming, and rich in subtle psychological allusions,[415] there is yet nothing that equals in depth Plato's masterly attempt to look at love from all possible angles and to point to both its otherworldliness and its power on earth upon which all life, wisdom and joy depend. Plato describes and reveres Eros as a "god" or a half-divine, half-mortal "daimon." To Eros is attributed the "mediation" between gods and mortals who do not mix (178A, etc.; 202D–203A). In the same way that the Shulammite gave testimony to true love without ever referring to God the Father of Jesus Christ, Diotima, Socrates and/or Plato spoke of those aspects of love that need not be deprecated for the greater glory of Paul—or of Luther, as in Nygren's case. The zealotism and purism with which Christian writers have dug up flaws (e.g. hedonistic, egotistic, possessive, and haughty elements) in pagan descriptions of love, in order to advertise the unique character and contribution of their "Christian" religion, reveal not only a lack of that love which is supposedly being praised, but also a neglect of the wide reach of God's wisdom—and love. Two examples will suffice:

1) It is true that *erōs* can mean no more than carnal desire, its aspiration, and its fulfillment.[416] But if *agapē* is transformed into a theological and moralistic whip by which passionate lovers are chastised wherever they are found, it is no less deprived of its genuine sense. In the context of his exhortation that husbands love their wives, Paul approves of man's erotic impulse that makes him choose and follow a woman, and of their sexual union: "A man will leave his father and his mother and be joined to his wife, and the two will become one flesh" (Gen 2:24 in Eph 5:31). While the apostle denounces the "selfish lust" of the pagans who "do not know God," he knows and recommends the use of the

---

[415] See the new translation by A. Schaeffer and the psychological commentary by E. Neumann, *Apuleius, Amor and Psyche,* Zurich: Rascher, 1952.

[416] With arguments culled from post-Freudian psychology and P. Tillich's theology, May (*passim,* esp. pp. 38–39) attempts to rescue and restore true Eros from the clutches of and the confusion with sexual activities that are determined by no more than the most effective techniques for attaining orgasm. He argues that Eros is a daimon which does not permit a "purist" separation of man's soul from his body—as if love could ever be found in intercourse alone, without involving man's soul, will, and total self. Paul's counsel that there may but need not be temporary or total abstention from intercourse, perhaps even abstention from entering a marital bond (I Cor 7), and May's warning of the idolization of sex are parallels. When Paul follows the Prophetic tradition that identifies fornication and idolatry (Eph 5:5 etc.), and when he warns of those whose "god is their belly" and who "glory in their shame" (Philip 3:19), he fights the same fight in his time as the psychotherapist May does today in the realm of his competence. An agreement between the results of a careful study of NT marital texts and modern clinical psychology is also observed by, e.g. K. Barth, III 4, 138–39.

body (or of the wife? Paul uses the rabbinical term "vessel"; cf. 1 Peter 3:7) "in a holy and honorable way" (1 Thess 4:4–5, JB).

2) It is true that a love that will do no more than conquer, use, and gain the beloved—though perhaps for a higher purpose—borders on exploitation of the beloved. But even *agapē* does not leave the lover without gain. Paul has stated that the "loving" Father acquires a people for himself that becomes his "property" (1:11, 14), and that the risen Messiah presents "to himself" a glorious Bride (5:27), his body, the church (5:23, 30). With equal freedom Paul speaks of that which a husband gains through his love: a "body" whom he can "love" as his own true "self" (5:28–29). The appropriateness and relevance of Nygren's observations regarding the strictly altruistic, outgoing, self-giving character of *agapē* are obvious. But the love praised in the Bible is not ashamed of an earthly smell and a marvelous fragrance, as the Song of Songs shows. The *agapē* of which Paul speaks is no less deep and broad. If it existed only in a costly sacrifice or were no more than a gracious condescension, it could never really please the recipient, nor could it be a jubilant expression of the lover's joy. According to Paul, both the earthly lover and his beloved become changed, enriched, something new: even "one flesh" (5:31). If love were exhausted in a "religious" attitude or in a mere disposition of mind and emotion, and if it did not extend and reveal itself in physical acts, God's love shown in the incarnation and death of his Son could never have become the ground and model of marital love.[417]

For this reason Paul does not consider the physical, sexual realm too base for the *agapē* shown and commanded by God, if only love is the basis of sexual union between one man and one woman!

A final question regarding *agapē* can be answered on the ground of the preceding arguments: How is marital love related to love of the neighbor? It is obvious that both are called for and held together (a) by the command of the same Lord; (b) by the employment of the same word "love"; and (c) by the specification "as yourself." Equally clear are the differences constituted by the free choice of one marriage partner for life (which is unlike the "given-ness," the multiplicity, and exchangeability of neighbors), and by the intimate physical union of a couple which can be blessed with offspring.[418] But these historical, psychological, and physical elements do not exhaust the differences. If a bridegroom or husband loved his chosen one with only the love he has for all his neighbors, she would bitterly starve. If he showed her a minor or cheaper love than that for his neighbors (and enemies! Matt 5:44–48; cf. Rom 12:17–21), she could not live in peace with him. Does Eph 5 contain any intimations regarding the differences between marital and neighborly love?

Most likely the first is related to the second, as is God's particularism to the

---

[417] Calvin follows one of the Patristic traditions when he also considers the Lord's Supper the model of the physical element of marital love. According to him, in this meal "Christ effused himself into us." In the interpretation of vs. 29, the reasons for the eucharistic interpretation of the words, "he has given himself" (vs. 25) were mentioned—and criticized. See also COMMENT VI A, regarding the interpretation of the variant reading of vs. 30.

[418] As stated earlier, Paul does not suggest that the one bond of marriage, love, must be supplemented by the will to procreate. Still, the specific sexual union between a man and a woman which Paul mentions in 5:31 excludes the idea of homosexual marriages as much as the notion that human sexuality is either a playground to be used without obligations, or some piece of machinery whose use and perfection must be learned from technical experts and the methods and tools prescribed (or sold) by them.

universalistic character of his love. Abraham receives his blessing, but many nations are to be blessed in Abraham. The special election of Israel and the covenant that the Lord makes and renews only with this people do not prevent God from being the creator and sustainer of heaven and earth, and from also having a covenant with day and night.[419] The logos' incarnation in the Jew Jesus means also his incarnation in humankind. He who announces that "salvation is from the Jews," or who is called the "savior of the body" (i.e. the church), is also the "savior of the world" and "bears the world's sin." The Messiah who is the "head of the church" is also "head over all," and the one who "fills all things."[420] In each case the election of the first fruit is grounded in the right over all fruit, and the special treatment of the elected group demonstrates the power and will of God regarding all nations or things. The general does not invalidate the special. The particularistic action is a showpiece of the universal will of God; cf. I Tim 1:15–16; 2:4–7.

In Eph 5:21–33 the particular election of the church by the Messiah yields the pattern of marriage; but the special grace already experienced by the church does not exclude God's grace for those who are still to be reached by the mission of the apostle and through the service of the church.[421] By analogy, the special form of *agapē* between husband and wife flourishes within the framework of a general love for neighbors and enemies, is the school and test case of the latter, and publicizes its reality and power. The wife is the husband's primary and exemplary neighbor. Unless he demonstrates his humanity in his union with her, his membership in the congregation will be a fake; in vain will he claim to be truly human, a member of the human society as a whole. *Hic Rhodus—hic salta* ("here is the salient point")!

However, just as the election of ancient Israel included a demonstration of God's will for all nations, and as the present church of Jews and Gentiles is only a forerunner and signal of God's presence and the Messiah's gracious rule among all mankind and all creatures,[422] so the special bond of marriage also has its limitations. There are those given a special *charisma* who do not enter it, or do not remarry after death has dissolved their first marriage. Paul's personal counsel is to follow his own example and keep free from the entanglement in marital "sorrows," and free for undivided "care for the Lord" (I Cor 7:6, 25–40). According to a saying of Jesus some men are inept or unfit for marriage by birth, by the influence of fellow men, or by a choice made for the sake of the kingdom of heaven.[423] Another *logion* affirms—without denying that the sexual distinction will still be present—that men and women "in the resurrection neither marry nor are given in marriage, but are like angels" (Matt 22:30 par.). In Eph 5 Paul does not draw out the lines to such extremes, but elsewhere he, too, indicates a limitation of marital love: in I Cor 13:13 he means by "abiding" faith, hope, and love, the love of the saints for God and one another rather than marital love. As stated earlier, even in the highest and

---

[419] Gen 12:1–3; Jer 31:31–33; 33:20.
[420] John 1:29; 4:22, 42; Eph 1:22–23; 2:5, 8; 4:10; 5:23.
[421] Eph 2:7; 3:10; 5:8–9; 6:19–20.
[422] See Rom 8:21–25; James 1:18 ("first fruit of his creatures"); cf. Rev 21; also COMMENT VII on Eph 4:1–16.
[423] For the interpretation of the logion on the "eunuchs," see J. Blinzler, "Zur Auslegung von Matthäus 1912," ZNW 48 (1957), 254–70; Baltensweiler, pp. 103–9; Greeven, et. al., *Theologie der Ehe*, pp. 45–52.

deepest fulfillment of marriage, a man and a woman become "one flesh," not two divine and eternally interdependent spirits.

The last observation requires special study of the Genesis text cited in Eph 5:31 and of its interpretation by Paul.

VI   The Quotation from Genesis

Four times in Ephesians a Scripture text is more or less fully quoted and commented upon. A Prophetic text, speaking of "peace," is cited, explained, and applied to the readers' situation in 2:13–19. A passage from the Writings deals with the "gifts" of the enthroned Messiah, see 4:8–10. The third part of the OT canon, the Law (the Pentateuch) is twice represented: in 5:28–33 by a text from Gen 2, and in 6:2–3 by one of the Ten Commandments. The way and effect of union in "one flesh" and the attainment of "long life" are the contents of the latter two passages. Paul's interpretation of Gen 2:24 will now be discussed.

A   The Tradition of the Text

A formal and a material problem require attention before the characteristics of the Jewish and Pauline exposition of the Genesis text can be outlined: (1) How exact is the quotation of Gen 2:24 in Eph 5:31, that is, the reference to the man who leaves father and mother in order to become "one flesh" with a woman? (2) What are the reasons for and meanings of the allusion to Gen 2:23, viz. to the "flesh" and "bones," which is found in variant readings of Eph 5:30? While the first issue appears not to imply essential changes of interpretation, the second has an enormous potential relevance. The allusion to Gen 2:23 gives the flux of thought and development in 5:21–33 an unexpected twist which has grave consequences for the interpretation of the whole passage, perhaps even the whole epistle itself.

1) Paul appears intent on quoting literally from the Greek text of Gen 2. The reading of Gen 2:24 in Eph 5:31 agrees with the LXX in two instances where the LXX version differs from the Hebrew text: (a) *'Ish* which in Gen 2:24 means "mature man, bridegroom, husband," is (falsely!) rendered by *anthrōpos* ("man in general") rather than by the more precise *anēr*. The distinction is correctly made by Paul elsewhere in Ephesians.[424] (b) The numeral "the two" is added before the words "will become one flesh." While the Masoretic Hebrew text known today presupposes the monogamous and monandrous relationship between Adam and Eve without saying "the two,"[425] Paul follows (a pre-Masoretic Hebrew text? and) the Greek version and thereby gives specific and abundant emphasis to the binary bond that excludes additional

---

[424] See 2:15; 4:13, 22, 24; 5:22–25, 28, 33; cf. I Cor 11:3–12. In the second NOTE on 5:31 it was shown that the Greek translation of Hebrew *'ish* by *anthrōpos* expresses the idea that Adam (*anthrōpos*) alone, before Eve was created and without her company, was the carrier of God's image and glory; see Gen 1:27 and I Cor 11:7. Despite its endorsement by some rabbis and other Jews (see section B of this COMMENT) this interpretation of Gen 1:27 is highly questionable. For this verse speaks of *'ādām* (*anthrōpos*) not of *'ish* (*anēr*). According to W. Baumgartner, *Hebräisches und Aramäisches Lexikon zum Alten Testament*, I (Leiden: Brill, 1967), 14, *'ādām* means "mankind, people, humanity"—not an individual. See also Pedersen, *Israel*, I-II, 61; K. Barth, III I, 182–206; III 2, 323–24.

[425] However, the Samaritan, Syriac, and Targum Ps.-Jonathan texts of Gen 2:24 contain the numeral "the two," according to Leipoldt, p. 83.

members. Perhaps the LXX wished to stress even more than the Hebrew text the correspondence to the One God and his One People which is found in the exclusiveness of monogamy. Certainly Paul reveals this concern in 4:4–6 where the "oneness" of the Spirit, the church, the Lord, God, is pronounced in the tone of solemn confession. The Vulgate follows the LXX and Paul.

Yet there are also differences between the quote in Eph 5:31 and the LXX editions known today: (a) Paul does not use the possessive pronoun "of his" (*autou*) after "father" and "mother" which is present in (the Hebrew text and) the LXX.[426] (b) In the LXX and the majority of the Greek MSS of Ephesians, including Papyrus 46, the articles (*ton* and *tēn*) are found before "father" and "mother"; but a minority of the MSS seem to insist on the exact literal version of the Hebrew text and omit the articles.[427] (c) Instead of the LXX reading *heneken toutou* ("for this reason"), which recurs in the quote of Gen 2 in Mark 10:7 and is replaced in Matt 19:5 by the synonymous *heneka toutou*, Paul has *anti toutou*. It is most likely that here *anti toutou* is a synonym of *heneken toutou*, and must not be understood in the sense of "instead of this."[428] (d) Some MSS omit the middle statement in Eph 5:31: "and be joined to his wife."[429] The shortening of the (Hebrew and) LXX Genesis text may either be due to a simple oversight or "haplography" (omission by the copyist of one word or line of the text), or may express the wish to come to the main point as soon as possible, that is, to the term "one flesh," which explains and confirms the statements in 5:28–29 about the wife as the "body" or "flesh" of the husband. (e) A few MSS that are not even listed in GNT[430] agree with the Alexandrian Codex and a small number of other Codices of the LXX, Matt 19:5, and some variants of Mark 10:7, in reading *tē gynaiki* instead of *pros tēn gynaika*. In either case, the meaning is, "[will be joined] to his wife."

Except in the case of (d), Paul's deviations from the modern LXX editions do not demonstrate that he quoted inaccurately. As the other citations of Gen 2:24 in the NT show, several Greek texts were in use during the time of NT. At different stages of his life Paul himself may have used different Greek versions. At any rate, whether a longer or a shorter form of Gen 2 is considered more authentic, the sense of 5:31 does not differ.[431]

However, the same cannot be said of the addition to Eph 5:30 which is found in some MSS.

2) According to many textual traditions of this verse, the words "from his flesh and from his bones" form the end of 5:30;[432] they allude to Gen 2:23,

---

[426] Philo omits this pronoun, too; see *leg. all.* II 49.

[427] Codices Vaticanus, Claramontanus (original script), Boernerianus.

[428] See, e.g. Abbott's arguments against von Soden. The latter relates vs. 31 to vs. 29a: instead of "hating his own flesh, a man will . . ." This interpretation neglects the weight of vss. 29b, 30, the meaning of the Hebrew *al-kēn* ("therefore") before an aetiological statement (see the first NOTE on 5:31), and the fact that *anti* can be equivalent to *heneken* (WBLex, 72–73).

[429] Important MSS of Mark 10:7, also Marcion's (see Tertullian *c. Marc.* v 18; cf. III 5) and Origen's texts of Eph 5:31 (according to the *Catenae*, though not to *c. Cels.* IV 49 and *comm. in Matt.* XVII 34) omit the whole line; see Robinson, pp. 302–3.

[430] But see Papyrus 46, Codices Sinaiticus (first script), Alexandrinus, Claramontanus, Boernerianus; cf. Robinson, pp. 302–3, 430.

[431] Baltensweiler, p. 230.

[432] In a correction in Codex Sinaiticus; in the Codices Claramontanus, Boernerianus, Porfirianus (ninth century), psi (an eighth-ninth century codex located in the Athos monastery); in the majority of the codices of the Antiochian family, the Latin and Syriac versions, Irenaeus, Jerome, etc.; see GNT for a fuller listing. Minuscule 1985 has only: "from his bones." The ninth-century Codex K contains perhaps a scribal error: "from his mouth" (instead of "from his bones").

i.e. the welcome extended by Adam to the woman created by God out of his rib and brought to him. Arguments such as those collected by Abbott against the authenticity of these words are so strong that all modern critical editions of the Greek NT relegate the words mentioned to the apparatus. But their spurious origin does not invalidate their great role in the history of interpreting Ephesians, and the contribution which they can still make to a proper interpretation—or a fateful misunderstanding—of the context. The lack of textual authenticity need not preclude the truth of their content.

Three things are clear: (a) The sequence of "bone" and "flesh" in Gen 2:23 is reversed in Eph 5:30 var. lect., and the plural "bones" replaces "bone."[433] (b) The reference to flesh and bones can answer the question, "To which antecedent does *anti toutou* ('therefore,' 'for this reason') refer?"[434] The reason may be the same as in Gen 2:22–24: man and woman were one before their separation. In consequence, the union described by the formula "one flesh" is not a novel, unheard of event, but a *re*-union. What has been as much one as was Adam and his rib becomes "one again" in marriage. (c) The words in the variant reading can anticipate and augment the Christological interpretation of Gen 2 which Paul proposes in vs. 32: Eph 5 then proclaims not only the joining of Christ to his Bride, the church, but also the creation of the church out of Christ's side, viz. of his "flesh and bones."

A few examples reveal the diverse ways in which expositors have dealt with this issue. The sacramental and sacrificial interpretations were discussed previously, but several outstanding examples of an incarnational exposition must now be examined:

1) Chrysostom, Thomas Aquinas, and Calvin agree in affirming that the words "from his flesh and from his bones" speak of the "substantial" unity of the saints with Christ. The Son of God shares the same "nature" with them, and they are made to share in his, as the phrase "partakers of the divine nature" in II Peter 1:4 indicates.[435] Indeed, if in Eph 5 the saints were called "flesh from his flesh" or if Christ were designated here as partaking in man's flesh, a parallel might be drawn to the statements about the Logos' incarnation and its effect (e.g. John 1:14; Heb 2:16). But do the words, "from his flesh and bones" really mean that exchange in which Christ participates in human nature, and man in the divine? Certainly it is hard to find in Gen 2:22–24 and Eph 5:30–32 a clear indication that a participation in Christ's divine nature is proclaimed which would imply the saints' deification by the creation of the church.[436]

2) Augustine's elaboration on Irenaeus' recapitulation theory has exerted wide influence: Christ is the New Adam out of whom the church has been created, just as Eve was built from a rib of the Old Adam.[437] Indeed, in Rom 5

---

[433] Thomas Aquinas and Bengel are among the few who ventured to explain the first of these two changes: "flesh" and "bones" are here mentioned in a "mystical" (allegorical) sense. "Flesh" are those "weak [in faith] who are of the flesh," and "his bones" mean those "strong who are hard as bone," according to a suggestion of Thomas. Bengel affirms that, in the new creation, the flesh of Christ is given preference over the bones.

[434] This issue was discussed in the first NOTE on 5:31.

[435] Similarly, Baltensweiler, p. 230, speaks of the "equality in substance."

[436] Abbott ridicules these interpretations: "Surely [it is] a strange way of saying that our spiritual being is derived from Christ, to say that we are from his bones."

[437] *Tract. in Ioann.* CXX 2. Cf. Irenaeus *adv. haer.* III 22:2 ff., etc.; Tertullian *de jejunio* 3; *de anima* 43; also Chavasse, pp. 131–32; Daniélou, pp. 30–65.

and I Cor 15, also in Eph 4:22, 24; 5:31–32, the Old Adam-New Adam typology is unfolded. But does Eph 5:30 belong in their company? It is more likely that 5:30 var. lect. is an interpreter's or copyist's gloss which reveals his acquaintance with that typology, than that it is genuinely Pauline. Nowhere in his undisputed letters does Paul affirm that the creation of Eve is the prototype or antitype of the universal church's origin. Only John 19:34 may express this opinion. In II Cor 11:2–3 a local church is compared to Eve, but there is no reflection on her creation out of Adam. In turn, in I Cor 11:8–12 the creation of Eve out of Adam is repeatedly mentioned, but it is not explained as a prototype of the church's origin. At any rate, the depth and beauty of Augustine's thought is not dependent upon the authenticity of the variant reading of Eph 5:30.[438]

3) Other Augustinian elements have been taken up by, e.g. Chavasse, and extensively discussed and rebutted by Best.[439] The variant of vs. 30 is used as evidence of the doctrine of the "extended incarnation of Christ." Chavasse argues that just as "Eve was the continuation and projection of Adam's body . . . so the church, her antitype, is the continuation of Christ's incarnation." It was shown earlier that this theory has no support in the concepts "body" and "fullness" as they are used in Ephesians.[440]

4) Schlier, finally, sees in 5:30 var. lect. an inauthentic anti-Gnostic gloss: the allusion to Gen 2:23 serves the purpose of showing that the church is still "flesh," not yet purely spiritual.[441] However, Schlier does not discuss the possible positive relationship between the "gloss" and Gnosticism. In their expositions of 1:4, 10, 22–23; 2:14; 4:13, etc. the representatives of the Gnostic school affirm this positive relation of Ephesians to the Gnostic quest for truth, some important corrections notwithstanding. The same "mythical" pattern which was either created by Gnostic thinkers or taken over by them from a proto-Gnostic tradition is said to dominate Ephesians: the pre-existing church, viz. the souls of those to be saved, have once been cosubstantial with their divine originator; they were contained in the deity Aion or Man before falling out of this unity in the *katabolē* (creation, understood as "fall"). Finally they are reunited with him through the mission of the Redeemer who conveyed saving knowledge to them. Schlier's own interpretation of the "pre-existent" church (1:4), of the dividing "wall" (2:14), and of the "Perfect Man" (4:13) thrives upon the ground of the presupposed Valentinian, Manichaean and other Gnostic parallels. If it was good enough for Gnosticizing and Gnostic teachers to use Gen 2 to buttress their obscure doctrines, why should not the author of Ephesians have done the same for a more illustrious purpose?[442] The following syllogism appears convincing—though it has apparently not yet been discovered by the modern scholars who use the fully developed second- and third-century Gnosticism as a key to interpreting Ephesians:

---

[438] In Eph 2:15–16 the "creation" of the church was the subject matter. There "the cross" of Christ was denoted as the place, the time, the means of her creation, not the incarnation. See COMMENT V B on 2:11–22.

[439] Chavasse, p. 70; Best, pp. 194–97.

[440] See COMMENTS VI on 1:15–23, and V A, VI A on 2:11–22.

[441] Schlier, p. 261, n. 1. Cf. Irenaeus *adv. haer.* v 2:3; Tertullian *de anima* 11.

[442] The methods and judgments of Bultmann, the early Schlier, Jonas, Conzelmann, and the later Schlier's arguments contain important variations in details. See Introduction, section III B, and COMMENTS IV on 1:3–14; VI on 1:15–23; IV A on 2:11–22; VII C on 4:1–16 for a sketch of the Gnostic myth; pertinent modern literature is listed in BIBLIOGRAPHY 2.

a) Gen 2:22–24 describes the marital union as an event of recognition and reunion of a pre-existent oneness of two persons.

b) The "gloss" added to Eph 5:30 interprets these *three* verses in a Christological-ecclesiological way.

c) Therefore, the gloss affirms that the union of Christ with the church is the reunion of two originally cosubstantial beings.

This would mean that the church fills up what is wanting in the Prime Man, and contributes toward reconstituting him in his fullness in order to form the *totus Christus*. Indeed, Eph 5:30 var. lect. offers itself as indisputable evidence for Schlier's thesis. A Gnostic pattern (though drastically reinterpreted and reaccentuated) underlies the Christology and ecclesiology of Ephesians if only it is assumed that the "flesh and bones" mentioned here mean neither Jesus Christ's humanity or death, nor his human *and* divine natures, but solely the light-matter of the Primordial Man, in which the chosen spirits have always participated, and into which they are finally reintegrated. Indeed, Eph 5:30 var. lect. permits or supports the mentioned syllogism; this variant is actually the only instance in Ephesians that clearly can be claimed to buttress the Gnosticizing interpretation of this epistle.

But this fact does not invalidate another: for philological and literary reasons Eph 5:30 var. lect. must be considered a gloss added by a hand other than the author's. The interpretive line may have been inserted into the Pauline text quite innocently—perhaps with no other intention than to enrich the reference to Gen 2 which follows in 5:31. But it is also possible that the "interpretament" (to use a modern German expression) reveals a late attempt to convey a Gnosticizing character to Ephesians and to facilitate its Gnostic exploitation. In this case not only philological but also theological reasons speak in favor of the judgment that the gloss is spurious and must be bypassed in the final exposition of the context.

While it is clear that in Eph 5:21–33 Paul intended to give instruction on marriage in the light of the Messiah's love for the church, it is unlikely that he also wanted to present a novel teaching on the substance of the saints, that is, to proclaim the primordial substantial identity of the Redeemer and the redeemed.[443] The creation of the church out of two equally "sinful" human groups, the Jews and the Gentiles, was described in 2:1–22 and is not repudiated now. In totally un-Gnostic fashion, the "cross" was denoted there as the place, the means, and the moment of that "creation." Equally the reference to the Messiah "who has given himself for the church" (5:25) points only to the cross itself, not to another prior origin of the church.[444] It is sheer speculation, not an act of interpreting the better text of Eph 5, to assert that once upon a time the church was one with Christ (e.g. his rib and his flesh) long before he united himself and became one flesh with her in his crucifixion. Certainly in the sacraments (which are not explicitly mentioned in the context of marriage) the death of Christ is "proclaimed" and celebrated ("remembered"), according to I Cor 11:24–26. But there is no statement attributing to baptism

---

[443] Esp. Pokorný, EuG, p. 43 and *passim*, shows that Ephesians refutes this doctrine. Mussner, pp. 152–53 gives reasons against the assumption that this epistle teaches the pre-existence of the church.

[444] Kirby, EBP, p. 152, sums up the ecclesiastical message of Eph 5:21–33 by saying: "The marriage of Christ happens on the cross."

and the Lord's Supper that unique and creative force and function which are capable of producing the new creation. Paul's use of Gen 2 is more centripetal and specific than some of the copyists and interpreters of Ephesians have recognized.

In the next section, we will hear the voices of such expositors of Gen 2 who were nearer Paul's time and perhaps Paul's thought than some Christian commentators.

B Jewish and Gnostic Interpretations

A complete survey of the history and main characteristics of the interpretation of Gen 2, especially of the statements about the creation first of Adam, then of Eve, finally about their union in "one flesh," cannot be given here. Only a selection is to be presented from the many ponderous and facetious, imaginative and casuistic, romantic and pedantic allusions to Gen 2 that can be collected from the OT, the Jewish literature contemporary to the NT, later Jewish and some Gnostic sources. For comparison, Sampley's survey (pp. 51–61) may be consulted. Three special concerns can be mentioned that contribute to a proper assessment of Paul's use of Gen 2:24 in the light of his Jewish background and environment.

1) The basic question of anthropology which cries out for an answer is: What is man? Jewish teachers are convinced that the biblical creation stories, by describing the origin of man, also help to illustrate or explain his essence. Because God is the wise, loving, caring, omnipotent creator, man is what he is. No anthropology except that which is developed out of theology! Though Jews do not pronounce such dogmas, this is the intention and summary of the Jewish teaching in Paul's environment. For this reason they emphasize that God is man's creator, that man is created in God's image, that God blesses man and assigns him his tasks.

Most Jews do not see any contradiction between the creation accounts of Gen 1 and 2.[445] However, does not Gen 1:26–27; 5:2 speak of the *simultaneous* creation and Gen 2:7–24 of the *successive* formation of man and woman? This objection is met by Philo and several rabbis with the assertion that the "man" mentioned in Gen 1 was bisexual (androgynous), was then divided ("sawed") into two when man's rib or half of his chest was removed and Eve was built (Gen 2:22), and was finally rejoined into "one flesh" by God when he led the woman to the man (Gen 2:23–24). In consequence, "he who has no wife is no man," viz., ". . . is no complete man." The name "man" is originally given by God only to male and female in their original duality and communion (Gen 1:27; 5:2).[446] In its version of Gen 2:24 the LXX, however, employs the

---

[445] However, in *leg. all.* I 31–42, 53–55; II 4; cf. *op. mundi* 14–22, Philo distinguishes between the creation of the heavenly man in Gen 1, and of the earthly man in Gen 2. For the distinction of the First from the Second Adam in other Jewish or Jewish-influenced writings, see fn. 200 at COMMENT V on 4:17–32.

[446] Philo *leg. all.* II 13, 19–48; *op. mundi* 76, 134; *quis div. her.* 164; *qu. in. Gen.* I 25; Bab. Berakhoth 61a; Bab. Kethuboth 8a; Bab. Yeb. 63a Erub. 18a; GenR. 8a, 17 (6a, 11d); LevR. 14 (114a); Midr. Ps 139 5 (246b, 265a); Meg. 9a; Sepher Torah 1 9; Tanch. Shemoth 65a; see StB, I, 801–2, for a German translation of many rabbinical texts, and Ginzberg, *Legends of the Jews*, I (1909), 64–71; V (1925), 88–89, for an English summary of these texts. References to the androgynous first man are also found in, e.g. Irenaeus *adv. haer.* I 18:2. In WA, XLII, 53, Luther denounced the "fables" of an androgynous prime man which Nikolaus of Lyra had taken over from the medieval Jewish scholar Rashi.

For a discussion of the origin, variations, meanings, and applications of the notion of the androg-

noun man (*anthrōpos*) to designate the male alone. Equally the Jewish interpretation of Gen 1:27, which is reflected in I Cor 11:7 and holds that the male
alone is created in God's image, belongs to a school of thought which neglects
the fact that Hebrew *'ādām* means mankind as a social composite, and not a
mature male person, a bridegroom or husband alone.[447] On one occasion Philo
points out that the female Sense perception enters the solitary life of the male
Mind while that Mind is asleep.[448] More often he expresses the mood of Adam
on first sight of Eve and anticipates the rabbinic utterances on the joy, the
blessing, the goodness, the help that man is given through (re-)union with his
other half, woman. In short: "No wife—no joy!"[449] Thus the woman whom
God, the archetype of the "friend of the bridegroom," leads to man (Gen
2:22), is considered a gift of God,[450] just as in the teaching of Jesus, husband
and wife are joined together by God.[451] As mentioned earlier, the procreation

ynous first man, see e.g. R. Reitzenstein, "Zum Asclepius des Pseudo-Apuleius," ARW 7 (1904),
392–411, esp. 398–403; H. Windisch, KEKNT, on II Cor 11:2–3; Bousset, *Kyrios*, pp. 204–05; J.
Kroll, *Die Lehren des Hermes Trismegistos;* Beiträge zur Geschichte der Philosophie des Mit-
telalters XII:2–4 (Münster: Aschendorff, 1914), 51–54; D. Daube, *The New Testament and Rabbinic Judaism* (London: Athlone, 1956), pp. 71–83; idem, "Evangelisten und Rabbinen," ZNW 48
(1957), 119–26, esp. 125–26; P. Winter, "Sadoqite Fragment IV 20–21 and the Exegesis of Gen 1:27
in late Judaism," ZAW 68 (1956), 71–84, esp. 78–83; idem, "Gen 1:27 and Jesus' Saying on
Divorce," ZAW 70 (1958), 260–61; J. Jervell, *Imago Dei*, FRLANT 76, N.F. 58 (1960), 161–70;
R. A. Baer, *Philo's Use of the Categories Male and Female*, Arbeiten zur Literatur und Geschichte
des hellenistischen Judentums (Leiden: Brill, 1970), pp. 14–35, 83–84. Myths or folk tales that
speak of the original bisexuality of man are found not only in the western hemisphere, but also in
China, India, Iran, Babylonia, Egypt. See, e.g. A. Jeremias, *Das Alte Testament im Lichte des
Alten Orients*, 4th ed. (Leipzig: Hinrichs, 1930), p. 188; and C. H. Kraeling, *Anthropos and Son
of Man*, Columbia University Press, 1927. E. L. Dietrich, "Der Urmensch als androgyn," Zeitschrift
für Kirchengeschichte 58 (1934), 297–345, hails the restoration of the originally Orphic tradition of
the bisexual man by theological pioneers such as Jakob Boehme and Gottfried Arnold.
   The widespread notion of the perfect, complete, and undivided man corresponds to the observations of modern biologists who call sexuality an evolutionary process which so far has developed
from sexless beings to bisexual creatures and to the separation of the sexes. The Jewish writers of
Paul's and later times may have come to their interpretation of Gen 1:27 by the knowledge of
folklore, of scientific books, or of philosophical, belletristic, or historical literature such as Plato
symp. 189–93; Ovid *metamorph.* IV 285 ff.; Pliny the Elder *hist. nat.* VII 2–3.
   The notion of the androgynous original man has not yet been traced in the development of Jewish thought before the time of its close contact with the Hellenistic world. All Hebrew texts of
Gen 1:27 that are known and used today say: "God created man . . . he created him, male and
female he created them;" cf. Gen 5:2. The plural "them" contradicts the assumption that
only one person was created. As observed earlier, in Gen 1:27 "man" means mankind, not one
person. Whether Philo and the rabbis based their teaching on a text having "him" instead of
"them" at the end of the verse is not known. Perhaps their interpretation had two apologetic purposes: to harmonize Gen 1 and 2 (viz. the simultaneous and the successive creation of the first
pair), and to establish contact with a belief fostered in their environment. However, the primary
concern of the writers of Gen 1:26–27 and 2:18–24 was not apologetic but proclamatory. They
wanted to say that one person alone, male or female, does not possess or express the true and full
humanity which the Creator intended and established when he created man as a plurality, a community, a social being. While the rabbis maintain this doctrine, it vanishes in Philo's and in Jewish heretical teaching under the dictates of individualistic concerns; see (3) below in this section.
   [447] StB, III, mentions in its comments on I Cor 11:7 only NumR. 3 (140d) as evidence of the
Jewish teaching that "the glory of God arises from the [male!] men." In Mekh. Exod 12:14
(19a) and parallel texts quoted in StB, I, 801, explicit rabbinical polemics are found against the
(Greek Pentateuch) version made for King Ptolemy, i.e. against the LXX. But the objections raised
presuppose an LXX text other than is known today, and they do not impugn the use of *anthrōpos*
in Gen 2:24.
   [448] *Leg. all.* II 19–46; cf. *op. mundi* 53.
   [449] Gen 2:18, 23; 5:2; Deut 14:26; Ezek 24:25 are among the passages alluded to in Philo, *qu.
in Gen.* I 26, 28; cf. Bab. Yeb. 62a–63b.
   [450] Cf. COMMENT IV C.
   [451] See Matt 19:6 par. In Pesiq 11b, a story of Rabbi Jose ben Halaphta (ca. A.D. 150) is re-
counted which illustrates the evils which ensue when not God but, e.g. a matron arranges the pair-
ing of a thousand male and female slaves: after the wedding night, one man's head is split, another man's eye is torn out, a third man's foot is broken; and the new husbands say one after
another, I don't want her; cf. Sota 2a. StB, I, 803–4 gives more references.

of children is considered a blessing and a duty (Gen 1:28).[452] However, there are still other elements in the creation story upon which Jewish interpreters have focused their attention.

2) According to Philonic and rabbinical writings, Gen 2 contains indispensable hints regarding the decisive legal and moral aspects of marriage. This chapter not only describes man's nature and destiny; it is not only a source of *haggada* but also of *halacha,* i.e. legal-moral instruction. In fn. 59 *infra* NOTE on Eph 5:26 and in COMMENT IV E, it was shown how Adam's greeting was used ("This one at last! Bone of my bones and flesh of my flesh," Gen 2:23). The role of the right "word" was pointed out whereby a woman is appropriated, viz. "sanctified," by the man who loves her.[453] The validity of a betrothal and marriage depended to a large extent upon the use of the right formulation. The words of Gen 2:24: "a man . . . will leave his father and mother," are sometimes interpreted as referring to proselytes. If before his conversion to Judaism a proselyte was married to the sister or concubine of his father, to his own stepmother, to his mother's sister, or (after Oedipus' model) to his own mother, he "must dismiss" his wife and desist from living in incest.[454]

The phrase "joined to his wife" is even more emphatically understood in a sexual sense than the term "become one flesh!" According to some rabbis these phrases specify a natural mode of intercourse rather than unnatural practices; the exclusion of homosexual intercourse and of adultery; finally the prohibition of intercourse with animals.[455] Tobit 6:13–17 shows how through incense and prayer the "demon" which threatens marital intercourse can be put to flight.

Philo follows the main stream of contemporary Stoic thought in some of his positive statements on marriage. Since according to Gen 1 and 2 the woman is a part of man, her husband must care for her and she must share in his suffering, pleasure, and thought.[456] But even stronger is Plato's influence on Philo's interpretation of Gen 2. The Alexandrian philosopher observes that by "cleaving" to his wife, man dissolves himself into an inferior kind, even the "flesh," and "prefers love of passions to the love of God." The spiritual meaning of Gen 2:24 is this: Mind (*nous*) "forsakes" God, the "Father" of the universe, and Wisdom, the "Mother" of all, in order to be united to Sense percep-

[452] A more detailed study of the Jewish sources could show that the idea of "participation in God's own creative work" which is proclaimed in e.g. the "Pastoral Constitution of the Church in the World" (Vatican II), art. 50, takes up a Jewish thought. But compare e.g. Bab. Yeb. 63b, 64a, and fn. 205. Analogies to von Rad's interpretation of Gen 2:24 (*Genesis* [Philadelphia: Westminster, 1961], p. 82) saying that "one flesh" means the baby that is begotten appears not to exist in the Jewish tradition under review here.

[453] See esp. Bab. Kidd. *passim.* When, e.g. the bridegroom says, Be my rib, be my help, be my fortune, the engagement or marriage is valid.

[454] Midr. Gen 2:24; Sanh. 58a; StB, I, 802–3; III, 346. Rabbi Eleazar and Rabbi Aqiba (both ca. 100 C.E.) agreed on interpreting "father" in Gen 2:24 as meaning one of the father's marital or extramarital companions (enumerated in Lev 18:6–18). But they disagreed whether "father" and "mother" meant also the sisters of the two. Baltensweiler, TZ 15 (1959), 340–56; idem, *Die Ehe,* pp. 87–102; and J. B. Bauer, "Die matthäische Ehebruchsklausel," in *Bibel und Liturgie* 38 (1964–65), 101–6 (ref.), have built their novel interpretation of Matt 5:32 and 19:9 on passages such as these. However, the warning of Bab. Kidd. 6a is noteworthy: "He who is not an expert in matters related to divorce and marriage, must not occupy himself with them."

[455] Sanh. 58a Baraita; Bab. Sanh. 58b; GenR. 18 (12c); Pal. Kidd. I 58. Noahites (proselytes) are not punished for engaging in prohibited forms of intercourse before their conversion. The opinion of a certain Rabbi Eleazar and other teachers, saying that Adam tried to have intercourse with all animals before Eve was brought to him, is quoted in StB, III, 71. L. Ginzberg (*Legends of the Jews*) does not refer to it—perhaps because it is too preposterous to be taken seriously.

[456] *Op. mundi* 53; *qu. in Gen.* I 26, 28.

tion (aisthēsis). Instead of assimilating Sense to himself, Mind becomes one flesh, viz. "one passion," with Sense.[457] An exception to this abysmal fall of pure reason into the matriarchal or feministic clutches of sensuality is achieved by Levi: he disdains his earthly "father, mother, brothers, sons" (Deut 33:9); he forsakes even his metaphorical "father," Mind, and his "mother," the material body, and lets the Lord himself and alone be his portion. Thus he shows the true way of living up to Gen 2:24.[458] This imaginative interpretation practically belongs to the last group of Jewish exegetical concerns to be described.

3) The allegorization of the creation story of Gen 2 by ancient Jewish writers may or may not have been the background and stimulus of Paul's Christ-church allegory. Perhaps he was aware that his spiritual interpretation was in competition with one or several others.[459] Ginzberg is convinced that the allegorical interpretation of Gen 2:23–24 is not an "original" Jewish feat but a product of "enlightened" (Alexandrian) Jews.[460] Indeed, the sources are somewhat murky from which other scholars have reconstructed a full-blown allegorical "tradition" that is supposedly recognizable "behind" Eph 5, Pseudo-Philo, and the Gnostic doctrine of syzygies.[461] If Jewish Gnosticism had developed and spread early and wide enough to be of decisive influence upon the NT Haustafeln and especially upon Eph 5:31–33, then Paul's interpretation of Genesis could have been influenced by it, and/or directed against it. However,

---

[457] Before Philo, Plato (Phaedr. 82E) had spoken of the soul that is "joined" to the body. He meant by this term that the soul was fettered in the body and looked through it as through prison bars. However, in Sir 6:32–34 and 13:16 the term "be joined, cleave" appears in a neutral or good sense: a willing son shall "cleave" to wise men, and a loyal person "cleaves" to his king. Much later, Thomas Aquinas (in his commentary on Eph 5:31) also found a good meaning in this term: the union of a man and woman is called a fine thing which "delights the soul" (Sir 25:1–2). The act of "leaving" the higher for the sake of ministering to the lower and communicating with it, is described as a natural and moral process. Among men and animals the male's active and the female's passive capacities meet and complement one another; this happens when in the act of procreation they become one body. Thus, according to Thomas, the control of the soul over the body (which is the prototype of the husband's dominion over his wife) is not bought at the price of a catastrophic imprisonment of the noble soul in the lower sphere, the material and mortal body.

[458] Philo leg. all. II 49; cf. the context, esp. II 19–46, and de gig. 15. A positive evaluation of marriage, viz. of the marriage between Mind and Virtue (or of a marriage that produces virtues), is found elsewhere in Philo; see de Abr. 89–106; cherub. 40–49; de somn. I 200; II 185. Baer, Philo's Use, pp. 35–44, discusses the way in which Philo in op. mundi 136–70 describes the perfection of the first man and his later fate under the tension of mind and sensuality, as represented by man and woman respectively.

[459] See the first two NOTES on 5:32. Instead of mentioning anthropological, legal-moral, and spiritualizing Jewish interpretations, P. Winter (ZAW 68 [1956], 81) distinguishes between ethical, intellectual, and metaphysical Jewish expositions of the creation account.

[460] Ginzberg. Legends of the Jews, V, 88–89. Origen c. Cels. IV 38, is the only (solid?) witness to the Alexandrian tradition.

[461] Baltensweiler, pp. 231–32, speaks of a common interpretative tradition; cf. Schlier, p. 268, and fn. 153 infra the NOTES on 5:21–33. The sources drawn upon by these commentators are especially the book Baruch by Justin the Gnostic (see Batey, NTS 10 [1963], 121–27; idem, NTS 13 [1966], 270–81), and Ps.-Philo liber antiquitatum bibl.; see L. Cohn, "An Apocryphal Work Attributed to Philo of Alexandria," JQR 10 (1898), 277–332 (ref). The latter was recently made accessible again by G. Kirsch, The Text of Philo, Liber antiquitatum biblicarum, University of Notre Dame Press, 1949. A commentary on the Pseudo-Philonic work by P. Bogart is announced by J. Strugnell in JBL 89 (1970), 484. In the text reproduced by Kirsch (on pp. 111–270) nothing is said of Adam or the paradise which would justify mention of this book in the present context. Still the books of Justin and Ps.-Philo are said to contain elements contrary to the current opinion (as expressed by, e.g. Kirby, EBP, p. 152) that Jewish teachers never used the creation myth as an allegory for the Yahweh-Israel relationship. According to Justin, human nuptials symbolize the henōsis ("union") of the second and the third "principles," that is, of Elohim (God) and Eden. Other references to elements of "Gnosticizing Judaism or Jewish Gnosis which, however, always represent a break-away from Judaism," are collected by Schlier, pp. 274–75. The early Schlier's observation (Christus, p. 107) is still correct: in the OT itself, Gen 2:24 is never applied to Yahweh and the people. Mussner, p. 159 represents those scholars who consider the application of Gen 2 to Christ and the church an original creation of Paul.

both presuppositions are still debatable. At any rate, there are lines connecting Jewish Gnosticizing thought with the "mysteries of the syzygies" which appear to have been more often re-enacted in sexual orgies than by total abstinence from marriage and sexual intercourse.[462]

There is a common denominator to Philo's misgivings about the mingling of Mind and Sense and the endorsement of certain Gnostic teachers of "holy wedding" acts in the frame of the cultus. Common to these seeming opposites is the dualistic world view in which spirit and matter stand in tragic conflict. Marriage as described by Gen 2:24 meant to Philo that the heavenly matter was lost in the grip of the earthly; only in exceptional cases could a man save himself from perdition. Exhibitionist copulations as celebrated among some Gnostics sought to demonstrate the original unity, from which the lower part of the universe had fallen, and to enact and demonstrate in the physical realm the hoped-for metaphysical restoration of oneness.

Probably neither the licentiousness of some Gnostic groups nor the complementary legalistic asceticism of others can be ascribed to the specifically Jewish ingredients of second-century and later Gnosticism. Also, Paul's interpretation of the Genesis stories is so radically distinct from the Gnostic solutions to the tragic conflicts of the world and the individual that it is still safe to assume he was ignorant of them. As little as Rabbi Akiba's allegorical interpretation of the Song of Songs and the previously mentioned late rabbinical exposition of Ps 45 are explained by reference to Gnostic influence, can Paul's use of Gen 2:24 be attributed to Gnosticizing tenets—whether their origin be Jewish or pagan.

What, then, is the alternative Paul offered?

C   Paul's Exposition

In the preceding section ontological, legal-moral, and allegorical elements were distinguished that are found in Paul's environment and which he may have known. Though decisive traits of Paul's teaching on marriage reflect his Jewish upbringing and orientation,[463] his interpretation of Genesis differs radically

---

[462] R. M. Grant, *Gnosticism and Early Christianity*, Columbia University Press, 1959, rev. ed. 1966, has collected the evidence used in recent discussion to "explain Gnosticism as arising out of the debris of [Jewish] apocalyptic-eschatological hopes which resulted from the fall or falls of Jerusalem" (pp. viii; cf. 14, 24, 107, 128, etc.). Yet he does not wish to suggest that "everything" Gnostic must be traced to Jewish origins (pp. 36–39). Whether the ascetic sexual abstinence described or required, e.g. by *Acts of Thomas* 12:14–15; 88, etc.; *Acts of John* 113; *Acts of Paul and Thecla* 6 ff.; *Acts of Andrew* 5–6, has anything to do with Judaizing thinking, can be debated. But the obscene cultic practices of some Gnostic groups, among them the Valentinians, Ophites (Naassenes), and Marcosians, are more or less plainly related to specific interpretations of Gen 1–3. They assumed that the Yahweh-Eden or Christ-Achamoth (viz. Wisdom) copulation was attested in Genesis, and that it necessitated or permitted orgiastic celebrations of a *hieros gamos* ("holy wedding") in the cultic assembly of the true believers. Details are unknown but a combination of hints and allusions made chiefly to oppose the disreputable practices leave little choice for another picture. See II Clem. xiv; Irenaeus *adv. haer.* I 6:3–4 ("In every way they [the Valentinians] must always meditate the mystery of copulation [*syzygia*]"); I 21:3–4 ("They [the Marcosians] arrange a bridal chamber . . . which is quasi mystical . . . and call what is done by them in it, a 'spiritual wedding,' because it imitates the copulation of heavenly beings"); cf. I 4:1; 7:1–3; 11:1; 13:3; Clement of Alexandria *strom.* III 1:1; 5:1; 10:1; 27:5; Tertullian *adv. Valent.* 1; *de jejunio* 17; Hippolytus *el.* v 8:44–45; vi 19:5; 32:4; Epiphanius *haer.* 26:4; Eusebius HE iv 11. But not all "mysterious" interpretations of the Genesis stories found their applications in either an ascetic or a libertinistic attitude toward sex and marriage. See, e.g. the Papias Fragments quoted in fn. 153; II Clem. xiv 2; Clement of Alexandria *exc. ex Theod.* 21:2; 54:1; 55; Irenaeus *adv. haer.* I 18; 26:1–2; 28:1–2; 30; Ps.-Clem. *homilies* 16:12, 1 f.; Epiphanius *haer.* 30:3, 3 ff.; Hippolytus *el.* vii 33:1–2. All these texts are mentioned by Schlier, pp. 274–75 as potential parallels to Paul's Christ-church allegory.

[463] See COMMENT II and the rabbinical "parallels" to Eph 5:21–33 collected in the footnotes.

from those assumptions or conclusions which are represented by Philo, by earlier and later rabbis, and by Gnosticizing Jews and Christians. In addition, Paul's use of Gen 2:24 in Eph 5 reveals a change in emphasis over and against his teaching in I and II Corinthians. When Paul wrote Ephesians, he had apparently moved further away from certain speculative, legalistic, or fantastic lines and excesses found in Jewish exegesis. His mind and teaching had turned more radically toward the center of his message.[464]

In Eph 5 the position and function of Christ are much more vital than in those passages of the Corinthian correspondence that discuss the attitudes of women—not to speak of I Tim 2:15. In the Corinthian epistles, topics such as the following are discussed: marriage as a tie to the world; the kerchief or veil and the hair of women; the "law" that women keep silent during the assemblies for worship (except for prayer and prophetic speech). The last two of these topics reflect Jewish customs that are established by oral law (rabbinical teaching) rather than by the OT itself. Also the epistles to the Corinthians contain reminders that the husband is more directly God's image and glory than the wife, and that woman was deceived and fell into sin before man did. Finally there is a hint regarding holy children.[465] The following examples show both the change of Paul's teaching in Eph 5 from some features of Jewish teaching, and the development of his own thought.

1) In Ephesians there are no traces of the ontological Jewish statements about the bisexual prime man, about his division into two persons, and (except in the spurious variant reading of 5:30) about the reunion of the two halves in the marital embrace. Equally those Jewish teachings are not reiterated that affirmed (a) solely the male is God's image and glory, rather than both together, male *and* female; (b) the creation of Eve out of Adam and after Adam demonstrates her subordinate place; (c) the fact that Eve was deceived earlier than Adam and disobeyed God before Adam did proves her specific weakness and compels her to keep silent while her husband keeps her under his strict control; (d) a married woman must demonstrate her subordination by wearing a kerchief or veil in public. These manifold ontological teachings, including their aetiological reasonings and moral applications, are, in Ephesians, replaced by the reference to Christ's love and the church's subordination to him. There is only one ontic ground to the marital union in one flesh, and its historical and ethical implications: Jesus Christ's relation to the church (Eph 5:32).[466] Philo, the rabbis, Paul in writing I and II Corinthians, and the author

[464] An imitator of Paul would not only have marshalled enormous courage to deviate in Ephesians from the classical Pauline epistles, but he would also have run the risk of being easily unmasked as a falsifier. Or was he so outstanding a theologian as to outshine and overshadow Paul? No traces of such an unknown genius have been found so far in the period between circa A.D. 70–100 to which Ephesians is usually ascribed whenever it is considered deutero-Pauline.

[465] I Cor 9:5, 14, 31–33; 11:5–16; 14:33–36; II Cor 11:3. The deutero-Pauline passage I Tim 2:11–15 appears to be formed in a stream of tradition, and/or formulated by someone who (a) knew the Corinthian correspondence, (b) ignored or, perhaps, misunderstood its critical utterances against marriage (together with their foundation in eschatological expectation), and (c) was not influenced by the special teaching on marriage found in Eph 5, esp. its eschatological and Christological basis. Since I Timothy is directed to Ephesus (see I Tim 1:3) as much as is Ephesians (presupposing that the variant "in Ephesus" in Eph 1:1 and the biographical note 6:21–22 point out historical facts), the discrepancy between I Timothy and Ephesians is puzzling. The differences certainly do not suggest that the two epistles stem from the same "tradition," express the same ecclesiasticism and moralism, and must both be dated in the same "sub-apostolic" period. Cf. the Introduction, sections III D, IV–VII.

[466] See the NOTES for a discussion of the conjunction "for this reason" in Gen 2:24, and the new interpretation it is given in Eph 5:31 and its context.

of I Timothy—all attempted in their own ways to interpret the creation stories at the same time literally, historically, and morally, and to answer the puzzling question, "What mystery lies in and behind the act of 'becoming one flesh'?" Outside Ephesians, skillful use is made of details of the creation story, pointing out the nature of man. In Ephesians, however, Paul finds in these stories a prophecy of the "new" creation, even of the New Man and his Bride (2:15; 4:24; 5:25-27, 32). Elsewhere it is said that there was a perfect man in the dim past, and that the intervening division and fall determine the present status of man and woman, together with the rules of their mutual behavior. In Ephesians (unlike Rom 5; I Cor 15, etc.), Paul's interest lies not in the intrusion of sin and its consequences, but in the intervention of the Messiah who has raised those dead in sin, who cleanses his Bride, and will appear for the wedding (4:13). Resurrection, forgiveness, the happy meeting at the Bridegroom's parousia—these eschatological moments are decisive over the personal conduct of the saints—even when married.[467] On the other hand, there is one futuristic element in the Genesis statements on marriage that recurs in the Jewish teachings: children will be born to the pair (Gen 1:28) and this offspring will bruise the serpent's head (Gen 3:15). This genuinely futuristic and eschatological feature of the union of two in "one flesh" is bypassed with silence in Eph 5. The realization of eschatological hope in the coming of the Messiah has given Paul the freedom not to insist upon procreation and even to ignore it in this chapter.

Further differences are these: instead of calling each husband the image and glory of God, Ephesians calls only one person perfect: the Messiah (4:13). He alone is the image of God, according to Col 1:15; II Cor 4:6; Heb 1:3. His love makes him give and do everything to make his Bride "glorious"; such love is the basis and prototype of marital love. The basis of marriage is radically distinct from a nostalgic yearning for an ideal past. Marriage is not the cure for, or the repair of, the damaged creation.[468] Rather Christ's union with the church has effected an unprecedented situation: the new creation leaves no room for a dialectic tension or wavering between creation and redemption. Marriage is no longer explained as a "creation order," but as an expression of renewal of all things through Jesus Christ. Indeed, according to Paul, the supreme love and the first work and effect of Christ were announced, promised, and guaranteed as early as the creation story. But creation itself, viz. the creaturely existence which God gave to man in the beginning, was only an intimation of marriage, not its ontological and ethical ground. Only Jesus Christ's coming, his love, his death, his dominion are the final, solid basis and model.

2) To the change in ontology correspond the alternatives offered in Eph 5

---

[467] Stanley suggests that "Paul was the originator of the Christian interpretation of these Genesis narratives," and mentions as evidence the universalism, the apologetic purpose, the emphasis on sin which Paul finds in the Gen 1-3 stories (esp. pp. 251-52). However, Stanley bypasses the special accents in Paul's use of Gen 2 which are set in Eph 5:31-32.

[468] In Matt 19:4-8 par., the true order of marriage is described by a reference to the past: (a) to God's creation in Gen 1:27, and (b) to the union in "one flesh" promised to man and woman in Gen 2:24—*before* the fall, and before man's hardness of heart made Moses promulgate the law of Deut 24:1-4. In Jesus' argument the adage is reflected, the last things will be like the first, which is expressed, e.g. in the Prophets' references to the paradise, the patriarchal period or the time of the exodus.

to some of the legalistic and moralistic explications, as well as physical-technical applications, of Gen 2.[469] Why does Paul quote Genesis, which belongs to the "Law" in the Jewish canon, rather than a Prophetic or Psalm text? It is not sufficient to answer that this was customary, or that, after the many allusions to Prophetic statements and images in the hymn (5:25–27), an additional Prophetic reference would have looked redundant. Rather Paul intended to show—as he did also in Galatians and Romans by mentioning Abraham's faith in God's promise—that he respected the Torah (the Pentateuch) as the highest authority among all OT books, and that even such parts of the "Law" that had evoked legal, legalistic, and at times casuistic debates and interpretations (the so-called *halacha*) were in actuality Prophetic in nature: "A man will leave . . . will be joined . . . the two will become one . . ." The substance of this promise according to Paul is not only marital bliss: it is Christ's love for the church. Therefore what Gen 2:24 says about union in "one flesh" is for Paul a prophecy more than anything else. Marriage stands under the sign of God's promise; it is not at the mercy of human traditions, laws, and their interpretation.

Still, God's promise in Gen 2:24 includes a directive. In spelling out the implicit command Paul again goes his own way. The Jewish interpreters quoted earlier warned of the male mind's ensnarement in the trappings of female sensuality, and recommended a strict "rule" (cf. Gen 3:16) of the strong over the weak. Little else was left to wives but submissiveness. Paul, however, applies Gen 2:24 differently: only the husband is put under a blunt "must." That which he "must" do is "to love his wife," not to tame or dominate her, according to Eph 5:33a. The application for the woman is soft and friendly: "may she [be enabled to] fear her husband" (5:33b).

Philo, many rabbis, and Paul himself in I and II Corinthians, argued on the basis of the inferiority of woman, the later formed creature.[470] Neither did they forget the story of Eve's precedence in disobeying God, and her seduction of Adam as narrated in Gen 3. Paul uses only the ("supra-lapsarian") story of Gen 2 in Eph 5; he makes the Creator's grace and the Messiah's love the basis of marital advice and conduct—not the memory of the fall of Eve and Adam and their sin against God and one another. A further difference is the following:

When the rabbis used Gen 2:24 to declare marriage a Jew's sacred duty and to prescribe the right mode of sexual intercourse, they did not mention the Messiah and love. While they did not forget either in discussing marriage, their interest was concentrated upon other matters. In his allusions to the same Genesis text in I Cor 6–7, Paul mentions the Messiah, but not love. The saints' al-

---

[469] Paul is far from repudiating *all* features of Jewish interpretations: he takes no issue with teachings such as (a) that God joins the human pair (in 5:27 Jesus Christ himself fulfills the role attributed to God in Gen 2:23); (b) that the love for one woman excludes polygamy, adultery, and prostitution; (c) that a woman cannot be dismissed for any silly reason; (d) that a husband owes his wife affection, care, etc.

[470] They disregarded the fact that man is created *after* the animals, and that in the eschatological order of things he who comes later may be the greater, i.e. he is last but not least; see, e.g. Mal 3:1; 4:5–6; Matt 3:11 par.; John 1:15; I Cor 15:22, cf. 28. Bushnell, p. 346, assumes that Paul cannot possibly argue male superiority over the female on the grounds of his priority in creation; otherwise, cows would be superior to men, and the latter ought to be subordinated to them! As an alternative to the traditionally accepted, though paradoxical argument she suggests that I Tim 2:13–14 refers to the youth, immaturity, and lack of experience of Eve who was a "deceived person" while Adam was a "willful sinner" (p. 341).

legiance to the Messiah is shown to be the alternative to fornication and a caveat even against the union in "one flesh" that takes place in marriage. "Flesh"—in the sense of subjection to sin and hostility to the Spirit—triumphs in fornication and threatens even marriage. "One flesh" can become such "flesh"; the disdainful sexual liberty shown in immoral conduct throws its shadow over legitimate marriages. In I Cor 6:15–17 physical union with the prostitute is depicted as the opposite of spiritual union with the Lord; those who are "members of the Messiah," "joined to the Lord," and "one spirit" with him, cannot at the same time be "members of the whore" and "one body" or "one flesh" with her. And when Paul proceeds to discuss marriage in I Cor 7, he makes five points which show that his esteem for it is less than enthusiastic:

a) Marriage and regular physical intercourse between married people are for many Christians less evil than the damage done by desire and outright fornication. Marriage and marital intercourse may solve some problems, but pose others. Paul leaves it to the Corinthians to call physical contact with a woman "not good" (I Cor 7:1). But he does not call it "good" either (I Cor 7:8, 26).

b) The marital bond is a tie that binds man and woman to earthly care and obliges them to please one another rather than only the Lord. Thus marriage presupposes or entails a "division" of concerns: when the union in "one flesh" becomes the first concern, care for the Lord and for "holiness in body and spirit" can suffer; Satan can use the lack of self-control as a lever for his machinations; prayer can be neglected; the opportunities and requirements of the short present end-time are no longer recognized and met.

c) Provided that they are willing in their hearts and fairly convinced of their election by God for a special service, people who are not yet married had better remain single; married people shall abstain from intercourse "for a season" in order to be free for prayer. It would be better for widowers and widows not to remarry.

d) This advice does not include permission to married Christians to divorce their non-Christian spouses at random. The Lord's prohibition against divorce is maintained. Mixed marriages are to be considered a great missionary opportunity.

e) Finally, Paul acknowledges that not every saint has the *charisma* to remain single but that the "freedom" conveyed upon every "redeemed" and divinely appointed Christian is so great and deep that he can endure social freedom as well as the thralldom of slavery (and, by analogy, singleness as well as the "yoke" of marriage). The high "calling" of the Lord to eternal life is equally valid in both cases. "In the Lord" a woman is therefore "free" even to remarry after she has become a widow.[471]

In particular, the statements in I Cor 7 that speak of a "marrying . . . in the Lord" (vs. 39) and that declare God's "vocation" valid inside as much as outside earthly bondage (vss. 17–24) leave open and actually pave the way for the surprisingly positive statements on marriage in Ephesians.

In Eph 5, the Genesis text speaking of "one flesh" is quoted in a framework

[471] (a) I Cor 7:2–5, 9, 36; cf. I Thess 4:4–5; I Tim 5:14; (b) I Cor 7:5, 26, 29, 31–34; (c) 7:3–6, 35–40; (d) 7:10–16; (e) 7:7–8, 17–24, 39.

that magnifies both the Messiah and love. "The Messiah" and "love" are actually made the clues for the interpretation and application of the OT text. A decisive role is also played by the terms "head" and "body," "care" and "provision," "fear" and "subordination." The way these terms are juxtaposed and exchanged, combined and repeated, shows how Paul interprets "one flesh":

"One flesh" is an event, not a substance. It is a living phenomenon on earth, not a timeless mythical reality in heaven. It does not deify, but it demonstrates the peace between "the two" made by the Messiah (2:14–16). It is a transaction, a give and take between two, not an impersonal feeling or a private mood. It is a meeting of two, even peace between two different persons and attitudes, not the exclusion or prohibition of all distinctions. It is a social happening, not a purely intellectual state of mind or an exclusively physical combination. In short, as it takes at least two to form a unity and to have peace, so it also takes two to become and to be "one flesh." When in the exposition of the terms, "one new man" (2:15), "oneness" (4:3, 13), and "one" (4:4–6), the specific biblical and Pauline meanings of the word "one" were explained, it was shown that a dynamic force and manifestation is in the apostle's mind: the conversation and common life of at least two persons whose diversity is not simply extinguished but rather renewed and so shaped that it becomes a contrapuntal harmony. It is unlikely that Paul had forgotten this particular meaning of "one" when he quoted the formula "one flesh."

This, then, is Paul's interpretation of Gen 2:24, including the words "one flesh":

The "secret meaning" (5:32) of the verse in Genesis is the promise that Christ will elect the church to be his own. He will be united to her as the "head" to his "body." The challenge of his "love" will be answered by the church's "fear." To the work of his "care" she will gladly "subordinate" herself. The gift of his life for her will issue in her greater glory. Thus Christ and his chosen do not become "one cake" (ein Kuchen, as Luther once said), but form a pair with a rich common history. "One flesh" is therefore a miraculous, spiritual, physical, and social event that establishes the identity and glorifies the freedom of both participants with respect to one another, but does not dissolve them into an amorphous mass or an anonymous and impersonal mist.

The secret sense discovered in Gen 2:24 does not prevent Paul from also taking the literal meaning seriously and applying it to the ethical issue under discussion in Eph 5. He probably follows one of the intentions of the unknown original author of the Genesis text when he avers that the formula "one flesh" means the encounter, union, and cooperation of the husband's search, love, and care with the wife's voluntary subordination and joyful fear. Even this meeting and the peace realized in it are promised to husband and wife. The fulfillment of the promise of Gen 2:24 has its firm basis and shining model in the Christ-church relationship, the fruits of which the saints now enjoy. In the coming, the death, and the rule of Christ, the good will of God is revealed which reaches down from heaven to earth and is successful even in the world of space and time. In the Christ-event also the limits and criteria of marital bliss are set up. Above all, in this event it is guaranteed that even "in the Lord" (I Cor 7:39), "because they fear Christ" and "subordinate themselves to him" (Eph 5:21,

24a), spouses can with good conscience enjoy the meeting of mutual love and subordination; of male and female gifts and needs; of "his" and "her" individual character traits, inclinations, and passions. The ever new encounter and partnership of these two constitute marriage and "one flesh."

The meeting and mating of the two persons can be legislated and manipulated as little as the union and cooperation of head and body. The union is a gift of God and his Messiah who is the Creator and Redeemer at the same time. The blessing which is indispensable, unless the encounter and mutual "knowledge" is to become a lifelong battle, cannot be secured by attaining clerical permission for marriage or by a church wedding, as stipulated, e.g. by Ignatius (*Polyc.* v 1–2). Rather Paul's reference to the Genesis passage shows that he considered a man's spouse to be a special gift of God. It may be concluded that he considered it right and meet to seek God's blessing and to render thanks for this gift not only in private. Finally, the realization of full union in "one flesh" is not a monopoly held by Christians only. While Paul affirms that the Messiah's coming and love are grounds for the marital unity and oneness he nowhere intimates that the promise of Gen 2:24 is exclusively valid for those baptized. He reads in Genesis that even the (unbaptized) Adam and Eve had become "one flesh"; God's promise reaches further than the walls of the church.

Thus in Paul's teaching on marriage, all casuistry is replaced by gratitude for the gift of total communion between two people. Their union is depicted as a sign of the "peace" given "those far" and "those near" and as a training in and witness to the *agapē* to be shown to many neighbors.[472]

3) Finally, Paul's interpretation and use of Gen 2:24 presents an alternative to those allegorizations of Gen 1 and 2 that were produced by a few Hellenistic Jews, such as Philo and Justin the Gnostic, to either deprecate or exalt the value of the female created by God, of sexual intercourse, and of marriage. Though Paul's theology is not bare of all dualistic traits, he does not show the same proclivity to a strictly dualistic ontology which can be observed among Platonizing Jews.[473] Also missing is an ambiguity or vacillation between the goodness and evil of sexuality and its social expression. Paul's clear "No" to fornication (5:3, 5) and his equally clear "Yes" to marital union (5:21–33) replace the disdain of sex as well as its elevation to divine rank. To the historical character of Christ's romance corresponds the concrete, specific character of its ethical implications. While a narrative and moral allegorization is present in both the Gnosticizing and the Pauline interpretations of Gen 2, the restraint

---

[472] See the end of COMMENT V D; J. W. and L. F. Bird, *passim;* von Hattingberg, pp. 171–72, 180, 213, 247, 281–82. Bovet, chs. I–V, XIV, esp. pp. 72 ff., describes marriage as a "great drama" in which (because of God's love) through the communication of the two partners a new person comes into being: the so-called "marriage-person . . . a new dimension of existence."

[473] Some of the dualistic elements and methods that are reflected in Paul have been described in COMMENTS II and III on 2:1–10 and VIII on 4:17–32. The effect of a strong Platonizing influence on or interpretation of the creation story is exemplified by, e.g. the exposition and application of Gen 1:27 ("God created them male and female") in II Clem. XIV (a pseudonymous document, perhaps from Alexandria, Egypt, between A.D. 120 and 170). Here Christ and the church are depicted as a pre-existent pair "created before the sun and the moon." The eternal spiritual body of Christ (the church) is "manifested in the flesh of Christ" in order "to save us." "He who guards her in the flesh, without corruption, will receive her back again in the Holy Spirit." The application of this almost incomprehensible teaching consists in II Clem. XV 1 of the recommendation of "self-control" (*egkrateia*). "Flesh" is here understood in two senses: as a revelatory substance, *and* as the evil material form of existence. Schlier (pp. 268–69) has attempted to explain these "confusing, . . . clumsy and difficult utterances" of II Clement and to sue them as evidence for his mythological interpretation of Eph 5; see COMMENT VII A 4.

and precision of Paul's method and results are essentially different from the wild adventures of Gnostic speculations and cultic re-enactments.

The salient point in the three distinctions just described is the same in each case. Unlike Philo, the rabbis, and the Hellenistic Jews mentioned earlier who did their best to describe the mysteries of Gen 2:24 and its key term "one flesh" without ever mentioning a Messiah, Paul understood the verse as testimony to Jesus the Messiah who had come, had died, had elected Jews and Gentiles, and had joined them together to be God's people: the church. While in I Cor 6–7 Paul's reference to the Messiah and Lord issued in warnings against the catastrophes and dangers of the union in "one flesh," in Eph 5 the mention of the Messiah culminates in the praise of His and of marital "love." Here, together with the Genesis text, all affairs related to marriage are explained on a Christological basis and under the auspices of love.

Still, this observation does not solve all major puzzles of Paul's interpretation of Genesis. The term "one flesh" in 5:31 especially has stimulated earlier and more recent expositors to ask the question, "Where and how did or does the Messiah become 'one flesh' with the church?"

Among the answers given, the four outstanding ones have already been mentioned in passing: by his incarnation (John 1:14, etc.);[474] by the reconciliation effected on the cross (2:13–18);[475] through baptism;[476] through the Lord's Supper.[477] It was shown that not one of such detailed allegorizations of Eph 5:31 is supported by the context. For only "Christ and the church," that is Christ's love for the church, is in Paul's mind, as he says explicitly in 5:32. The details of Christ's love and care, including especially his death on the cross, are enumerated in the hymn (5:25–27) and must not be culled by allegorizing every word of the Genesis text. Even when Paul spiritualizes he keeps the literal meaning of the text quoted in mind.

In summary, Paul attributes to the term "one flesh" the following specific meanings:

1) "One flesh" is the sexual union that is undergirded by spiritual and psychic unity, especially by a love that rejoices in doing good to the other whatever the price; a fear that expresses gratitude, expectation of the best, and confidence; a mutual subordination that is eminently exemplified by the wife's acceptance of the "yoke" (Matt 19:6) of a common mission and task.

2) "One flesh" is the meeting and uniting of two persons in a "new social unit"[478] which stands separate from other units such as the house of father and

---

[474] Irenaeus (in his statements on recapitulation; see the NOTE on "Comprehended under one head" in 1:10), Augustine (enarr. in Ps. XLIV[XLV] 12), Jerome, and Thomas Aquinas (in their commentaries on Ephesians) went most daringly into detail. In his incarnation, Christ forsook God the Father and the synagogue his Mother; by his unprecedented relationship to the church, he caused her to endure an inescapably bad relationship with her mother-in-law, the synagogue, according to Augustine. Jerome substituted the heavenly Jerusalem for the synagogue in the role of the Mother left behind. Thomas followed Augustine's detailed allegorization, yet without mentioning the in-law problem. He quoted John 16:28 for Christ's leaving the Father, Jer 12:7 for his leaving the Mother, Matt 28:20 for his perpetual clinging to his wife, the church. When Bengel suggested (the paradox) that "we are spiritually procreated out of the humanity of Christ who had flesh and bones," he may have thought either of the incarnation or of the Lord's Supper.
[475] H. Grotius.
[476] Theodoret, Oecumenius, Ambrosiaster; among modern interpreters, e.g. Mussner, pp. 151–52.
[477] Irenaeus adv. haer. v 5:2–3; von Harless; H. Olshausen; Calvin. The latter's description in quasi-sexual terms of the Lord's Supper was already quoted in fn. 417: "Christus . . . se quodammodo in nos transfundit."
[478] Bailey, p. 43, uses this term in his attempt to define the original meaning of "one flesh" in Gen 2:24.

mother, the tribe, even the church. This nuclear social group owes its existence to a voluntary act of recognition or mutual knowledge.[479] It transcends natural, historical, psychological differences and overcomes discord. It expresses and fulfills the Creator's will that humanity be fellow humanity (or "humanity by partnership"[480]), but does not wipe out the personal idiosyncrasy, responsibility, and accountability of each partner.[481]

3) "One flesh" is an organic process which is both a hidden metabolism and a public phenomenon. It depends equally on the unique encounter of the given moment and the stretch of time required to reveal fidelity. It relishes the present because of an even more glorious future (rather than because of sweet memories).

4) "One flesh" is a this-worldly, time-bound event which does not pretend to effect the partners' transferral out of time and space, their deification or spiritualization. It proves that more can be said and is true of "flesh" than that its "ways have been corrupted" (Gen 6:12; Rom 8, etc.). It belongs to the good creation of God. It is redeemed and "shall see the glory of the Lord" (Isa 40:5; Luke 3:6). Life "in the flesh" can be a life in God's service and to his honor (Gal 2:20; II Cor 10:3).

However this list might be expanded, one element must *not* be added: the statement that according to Paul "one flesh" is "also" a symbol of Christ's union with the church (as in Augustine's and the Roman Catholic teaching on the "goods" of marriage). The Christ-church union is not one feature among others which give the marital union its ground, validity, form, purpose, and blessing: in Eph 5, it is the sole basis upon which all statements on marriage are founded. Standing on this ground, a marriage counselor such as Paul is free to talk in completely secular terms about the constituent features of marriage.

In the course of the western interpretation of Eph 5, various answers have been given to the question, what is the one essential condition for a valid marriage? At different periods in different cultures different answers were given, and a variety of marriage models were tried out. Sexual union, mutual consent, love, fidelity, benefits such as friendship, rescue from sexual pressure and misery, and the raising of children, have been proposed as the indispensable basis and essential bond of marriage.[482] While Paul's exegesis of Gen 2:24 does not pretend to solve all problems, it still speaks as a contribution to facing the vital problems of society as a whole and of individual couples, even at the present time. Paul avers that salvation through the Messiah and a love like his are the one basis and bond of the union between husband and wife.

[479] See Piper, pp. 52–67, for an extensive discussion of the sexual meaning of the verb "to know" in Gen 4:1, etc.

[480] See COMMENTS VI A on 2:11–22 and IV B on 3:14–21.

[481] When (in seeming contradiction to Matt 19:6) Pelagius affirms, *Duo sunt in carne una* ("they are two in one flesh") he does justice to Paul's distinct admonitions to husband and wife. The concept "corporate personality" which since H. W. Robinson is often used to describe the unity of several persons, sometimes even of the trinity, poses rather than solves the problem at hand.

[482] The Roman lawyer Ulpian's dictum, *Nuptias non concubitus sed consensus fecit* ("consent, not intercourse makes a marriage"; quoted by Bailey, p. 45) was taken by Thomas Aquinas (*Summa Theol.* III supp. 45:1, 2 resp., 4 resp.; cf. III 29:2 resp.). Petrus Lombardus (*sententiae* IV dist. 27:5–6) emphasized the engagement; N. Berdyaev (*The Destiny of Man* [London: Bless, 1937], pp. 103–7), love; E. Brunner (*The Divine Imperative* [Philadelphia: Westminster, 1947], pp. 340–83), fidelity. Earlier mentioned were the opinions that marriage is primarily a hospital for healing untempered sexual drives, a nest for breeding children, or a companionship for mutual help. Bainton gives a useful survey on the types of marriage that followed one upon another in the western hemisphere.

It has been argued that Paul's "exegetical basis" and the "execution of the whole thought . . . are artificial."[483] Value judgments on the work of biblical authors are not among the tasks of a commentator. However, it must be stated that Paul's exegesis and counsel in Ephesians are sober and clear—especially if they are compared with the Jewish alternatives offered at about his time, and with his own statements earlier in I and II Corinthians. He was convinced that Christ himself is as much the key to a secret meaning enclosed in a Scripture text (5:32) as he is the savior of the church (5:23) and the model of personal and communal conduct (5:25, 29–30).

The next question to be answered is this: does Paul's reliance upon Christ, the protector, illuminator, and guide of marriage, bring the apostle into a specifically close relationship with his Gentile-born readers?

VII   Myth, Sacrament, or Covenant?

A serious problem is posed by the passage 5:21–33: as shown in the preceding COMMENT, in the years after he had written to the Corinthians Paul moved farther away than before from some of the contemporary Jewish elaborations, regulations, and speculations related to the Genesis texts on man and woman, and to marriage in general. Did the apostle to the Gentiles, therefore, throw himself into the arms of, or fall victim to, pagan notions of the origin and order of marriage—though he intended no more than to preach Christ alone? Dependent on this issue is the question: Is it Paul's goal to "sacralize" marriage and, despite all evidence to the contrary, in actuality to subordinate it to the legal and ceremonial control of the church? Or, are there any traces of a concept of marriage that may be called "secular"? Three opinions vie for recognition:

(a) The thesis that pagan-mythological views regarding a metaphysical foundation of marriage heavily contributed to the teaching of Eph 5:21–33, has found its main supporter in Schlier. (b) The tradition that says, "Marriage is a sacral matter," is expressed in the Roman Catholic (also in the Eastern Orthodox, and the occasional Protestant) designation of marriage as a sacrament.[484] (c) Luther's dictum, "Marriage belongs to city hall," has become a shibboleth in the majority of Protestant circles.[485] Consequently, in God's name or not, marriage has also been explained as a civic and secular rather than a religious matter. These three views will be examined in three separate sections.

A   Marriage in Myths

This is not the place to discuss the many meanings of the term "myth" in the ancient world and in modern discussion. Also, it is impossible to base the following arguments on only one definition of myth. It may suffice to state that prominent scholars use this term in the modern interpretation of Eph 5:21–33, and

---

[483] E. Stauffer, TWNTE, I, 656.
[484] Before and after his conversion to Roman Catholicism (in *Christus* and *Brief an die Epheser*), Schlier explained Eph 5 from the background of parallels in the history of religions. In his later work he defends a (qualified) sacramental understanding of marriage (see sections A and B below). This scholar demonstrates in person that pagan mythological arguments need not contradict ecclesiastic sacramentalism but can be used to support it. It was stated earlier that several Protestant scholars have followed in Schlier's tracks.
[485] References to Luther's writings have been given in fn. 138.

that they employ it in more than one sense. Among the elements called "mythological" are the following:

1) Eph 5 presents a renewal, or rather, a Messianic transformation, of the prophetic marriage imagery used in the OT to describe the covenant between Yahweh and Israel. If Canaanite religion had not contained myths describing in marriage terminology the heaven-earth, deity-land, or Baal-Astarte relationship and the rituals celebrating it, prophets such as Hosea might not have used their keen marriage metaphors. Did they, therefore, mythologize Israel's faith by speaking of a wedding with Yahweh? When they spoke of God as Israel's husband they certainly did not intend to Canaanize the faith in Yahweh and the cult offered to him. Rather their emphatic statements about the love and the freedom of God, their references to specific moments in the history of God and his people, and their requests for conversion, social justice, and spiritual worship can be called acts of radical demythologization.[486] However, the question may be raised whether Paul failed where the prophets felt they must succeed.

2) The Genesis passage quoted in Eph 5:31 is a part of the stories that are sometimes called the biblical "creation myths." In actuality, Gen 1 may better fit the *Gattung* of priestly, primitive scientific (catalogical) Wisdom writings, and the Yahwist's work in Gen 2–3 can be attributed to the *genre* of legend. Whichever classification and nomenclature is most appropriate, the Priestly and the Yahwistic accounts appear to have originated in the face of pagan myths that sought to explain the present world in terms of its origin. While they intended to counter Canaanite or Babylonian myths, they had no guarantee against being victimized by them. Equally, Paul's daring allegorical interpretation of one part of the creation story, the earthy Gen 2:24, may look like a mythification.[487]

3) The notion of the primordial androgynous man need not be attributed solely to pre-scientific, scientific, folkloristic, artistic, or fantastic attempts to explain the mutual attraction of males and females; see fn. 446 for bibliographical references. This notion can also be a myth or part of a myth that seeks to comprehend all dimensions of human thought and existence.[488] Whether or not the Genesis stories were intentionally or coincidentally mythologized in the Philonic and rabbinical passages mentioned in COMMENT VI B is open to debate; the result depends upon the definition of myth. What remains unequivocal, however, is the mythological combination carried out in a pagan

---

[486] Cf. von Rad, OTTh, II, 140–47, cf. 364–66; H. W. Wolff, *Hosea*, Biblischer Kommentar 14 (Neukirchen: Neukirchener Verlag, 1961), xviii–xix, 13–16, 45–80, etc.

[487] Some modern interpreters (e.g. H. Wikenhauser, *Die Kirche als der mystische Leib*, 2d ed. [Münster: Aschendorff, 1940], p. 203; Cerfaux, *Théologie de l'église*, pp. 291–93; J. A. T. Robinson, *The Body*, SBT 5 [1952], 52, 82, n. 1; Hanson, *Unity*, 139) affirm that the OT foundation of Paul's thought excludes by definition the consideration of mythical influence upon him. But the mere allusion to, or quotation of, OT texts in Eph 5 does not yet sufficiently demonstrate the absence of all mythological elements.

[488] In Plato's rendition (*symp.* 189–193), this myth has the following content: the original bisexual (also the male-male, female-female) creatures are so exceedingly mobile and strong that they fall victim to hybris and threaten the gods. Should they be annihilated? Rather than destroy those who can offer worship and sacrifices, Zeus decides to split them and thus double the number of potential sacrifices! In a first operation the creatures are divided into two halves, but prove unable to live; a second surgery puts the sex organs of the divided halves at their proper place. Hephaistos gives instruction in the technique of love and Eros can have his way: to make one out of two, in both life and death. The sum of the matter is the urgent invitation to show pious reverence to the gods, and above all to praise Eros for his essence, the power to reunite what was split.

document, composed perhaps in Alexandria during the first post-Christian centuries. In the "Poimandres," a part of the *Corpus Hermeticum*, elements of Babylonian astrology, Greek philosophy, Iranian mythology, and the biblical creation stories are interwoven.[489] Mythology is also present in those Gnostic statements that describe the Perfect Man as androgynous and tell of his division and reunion.[490] If the allusion to Gen 2:23 in the variant reading of Eph 4:30 is genuine, the following mythological argument can be found by analogy in Eph 5: just as Christ is reunited with the partner who always was a part of him, even the church, so the marital, especially the sexual union of a man and a woman restores an original state of oneness.

4) More than anything else the Gnostic notion of syzygies (the copulation of heavenly beings that can be imitated in the intercourse between males and females on earth) lies behind Eph 5, according to Schlier and those who anticipated and followed his interpretation.[491] In his commentary on Ephesians Schlier emphasizes that he has in mind neither a direct dependence of this letter on the post-Pauline Gnostic sources, nor the dependence of the Gnostics upon Paul—though according to e.g. Irenaeus I 8:4–5 the Gnostics did use quotes from Ephesians. Schlier affirms only that Ephesians and the Gnostics have "a common background . . . a common language"; Paul "took up the questions" raised by a "Gnosticism connected with Hellenized Judaism" and offered his own answers as an alternative to the Gnostic solutions; "in destroying their myth" he established his own doctrine of "the mystery of marriage" (pp. 267–68, 275–76). The myth is in this case conceived as an expression of the legitimate human questions about man's existence; it is assumed that Paul takes up its language and concern without endorsing its message. As stated elsewhere by Schlier, the Christian answer is distinguished by its concentration upon the crucified Jesus rather than a timeless Redeemer, and upon an ethical dualism of decision rather than a metaphysical dualism with its ascetic or libertine applications in the cultic and moral realms. Still, Schlier assumes that in one decisive issue there is no difference between the mystery of the syzygies and the mystery of marriage as preached by Paul: here and there a

---

[489] The god Man sees his own reflection in the water beneath him. He falls in love with this reflection (his female partner). Out of their union arise seven herm-aphrodites (bisexual, androgynous creatures), who then are separated from god and one another. They become males and females, increase, and multiply in carnal desire (*erōs*). Their intercourse is the result of the fall of the Heavenly Man. Compare e.g. the Gospel of Thomas' teaching (16, 22, 49, 75, 114; viz. 84:4; 85:20–26; 89:28; 94:12; 99:22–24) according to which the perfect man is bisexual and, therefore, in no need of sex. See Hippolytus v 7 and Schenke, GMG, for references from the *Corpus Hermeticum* and for a discussion of the components and the formation of the (later!) Gnostic Redeemer Myth.

[490] See COMMENT VII C on 4:1–16.

[491] W. Bousset, *Hauptprobleme der Gnosis* (Göttingen: Vandenhoeck, 1907), pp. 315 ff.: idem, *Kyrios*, pp. 204–5; R. Reitzenstein, HMyRel, pp. 34 ff., 245 ff.; Bultmann, ThNT, I, 134–35, 151–52; Schlier, *Christus*, pp. 60–75, esp. 70–71, n. 2; idem, *Religionsgeschichtliche Untersuchungen zu den Ignatiusbriefen*, BhZNW 8, 91; idem, *Epheser*, pp. 268–76; E. Käsemann, *Leib und Leib Christi* (Tübingen: Mohr, 1933), pp. 84–140; Batey, NTS 10 (1963), 121–27; NTS 13 (1966), 270–81; Baltensweiler, pp. 227–33. Further literature on Gnosticism is listed in BIBLIOGRAPHY 2. Quotes from Irenaeus and other Patristic references for the Gnostic doctrine and practice of the "mystery of syzygy" were given in fn. 462 at the preceding COMMENT. The combinations made by Gnostics between their "syzygy" and the creation stories of Genesis are illustrated esp. by II Clem. XIV; Irenaeus *adv. haer.* I 18; Clement of Alexandria *exc. ex Theod.* 21:1; 54:1; 55; Ps.-Clem. *hom.* XVI 12, 1–2; Epiphanius *haer.* 30:3, 3 ff., according to Schlier, p. 275. Cf. Grant, *Gnosticism and Early Christianity*, pp. 60, 85, 114, 149. It appears that the majority of Anglo-Saxon commentators on Ephesians agree with that minority of German language expositors (as e.g. Maurer, EvTh 11 [1951], 170; Gaugler, p. 211; Mussner, p. 149; cf. K. G. Kuhn, NTS 7 [1960–61], 346, regarding Qumran), who consider Schlier's Gnosticizing interpretation too forced, historically unfounded, and lacking in clarity to deserve general acceptance.

Nachvollzug (reenactment, actualization, representation) takes place. What makes marriage, including physical intercourse, a "mystery" (pp. 263–76)? The imitation, presentation, application, realization of the heavenly event in concrete, temporal, cultical and/or existential terms! Thus the model of the relationship between heaven and earth, its general validity and daily renewal, is considered the same in Gnosticism and in Paul. When religion is related to sex as heavenly order or ideal is to earthly realization, then Ephesians reproduces exactly the same myth-ritual pattern which seems to prevail whenever myths or holy stories are told and a *hieros logos* (word of institution and/or explanation) justifies an earthly undertaking in a cultic frame.

5) The monopoly of the Gnosticizing interpretation of Eph 5 can be broken and its limitations transcended when the alleged parallel to Eph 5, the Gnostic myth and practice of syzygy, is complemented or replaced by the *hieros gamos* ("holy wedding"; a ritual found in various forms in many cultural settings). The rite consists of an exemplary copulation between a high-ranking personality (usually a king or priest) and a female representative of the earth, a city, or a land. In the sacred act of union the vicar of the deity ensures the cooperation of heaven and earth, an ever-new creation or integration of life and order, and the fertility upon which depend peace, another year of toil, and the hope of rich and poor.[492] Since in Ephesians the holy relationship between Christ and the church is the cause and model by which human marriage is sacralized, it may seem that the mythological-cultical pattern of the *hieros gamos* offers the best way to understand this chapter.

The sum of each of these mythological explanations is this: the Hellenistic Jew Paul reproduced in Eph 5 one or several ancient mythological models; he alluded to popular and/or sophisticated Hellenistic beliefs and practices; he used Hellenistic ways of hermeneutics in order to fulfill his missionary task and pastoral duty to Gentile-born Christians. Many critical interpreters—but not Schlier—believe that the radical Hellenization of the doctrine of marriage in Ephesians, and its divergence from the contents of I Cor 7, reveal the hand of an author who belongs to the post-apostolic age. Still, the skill and imagination they invested in collecting mythical elements and in using them to interpret Eph 5 are not yet sufficient to prove that the "parallels" from the history of religions are exact. Beginning with the last of the arguments presented so far and working backwards, the following observations are necessary:

1) Unlike Jesus Christ's death, the *hieros gamos* is not an event that has taken place once and for all; it must be repeated at certain intervals in order to

---

[492] The Babylonian New Year Festivals in which the king fulfilled Marduk's role, and the Dionysos Mysteries of Eleusia are among the best known dramatic forms of the *hieros gamos*. Plato (*resp.* v 458E) uses the term in the plural. For further information see e.g. A. M. Blackman, in S. H. Hooke, *Myth and Ritual* (London: Oxford University Press, 1933), pp. 9, 19, 34–39, etc.; A. Klinz, in Pauly-Wissowa, suppl. VI, 107–13. The evidence is summed up by M. Eliade (*Cosmos and History*, pp. 23–25) in the following way: "Every human union has its model and justification in the *hieros gamos*." Schlier, pp. 264–67, gives many examples of the spread of *hieros gamos* sanctuaries and rites in the Hellenistic world. He prefers an explanation of Eph 5 upon the background of this rite, to references to the Yahweh-Israel metaphors of the OT prophets, but negates "a direct relationship of the Pauline utterances in Eph 5 to the notions . . . of Hellenistic-Jewish circles." Actually he places less emphasis on the *hieros gamos* parallels to Eph 5 than on those found in the Gnostic system of the *syzygies;* cf. Batey, *Nuptial Imagery*, pp. 64–76, cf. 26, 36–37. Baltensweiler believes that in Eph 5 the *hieros gamos* idea is taken up—"but probably in a negative sense." Dibelius, p. 95, however, bluntly asserts that in Eph 5 "the rules for married people are derived from the *hieros gamos*."

be effective. Eph 5:25 mentions Christ's unique death, not an ever continued ritual. His death is by no means similar to a sexual act, nor is it described as analogous to one. The *hieros gamos* aims at fertility and guarantees it. In Eph 5:21-33 there is not the slightest reference to children procreated by Christ and the church or by earthly pairs.

2) The elaborate Gnostic (especially the Valentinian) system of syzygies by which the deity unfolds itself in thirty aeons, and in which the elect join in order to enter the divine fullness,[493] is completely foreign to Eph 5. The formation of that system took place about a century after the writing of this letter, and clear evidence has not yet been found that Ephesians, the Valentinians, the Naassenes, and the Markosians were dependent on one common tradition or source. In Ephesians, the advent, death, and continuous work of Christ in history determines the argument, not a timeless tale about origins, tensions, and reunions. The myth-ritual syndrome is not in mind.[494] The spirit-matter, mind-flesh, heaven-earth dualism expressed in the Gnostic syzygy system has no analogies whatever in Eph 5. The Christ-church pair does not fit this pattern; the terms "body" and "flesh" are used in a positive sense. A flight of the soul out of this world is not suggested. There is no mystery of the bridal chamber to be celebrated in sexual orgies or to be respected by radical asceticism. These and other differences between Eph 5 and the Gnostic syzygy systems are so radical and complete that it is amazing they could ever be ignored or minimized.

3) Eph 5 describes neither the union between Christ and the church nor the union of husband and wife as a reunion. Neither is it stated that the right order between husband and wife will be found in a paradisaical state. Unlike the Gospel passage in which Jesus harkens back to what God did in creation and to a state preceding the hardening of man's heart (Matt 19:4-8), Eph 5 presents the love of Jesus Christ as the basis and model of the husband-wife relationship. His love is presented as the scope of the Genesis story; his death is praised as the event by which all stains are washed away from his chosen. His engagement to the church, with its prospects for a glorious future, determines the way of a man with a woman, not the doctrine that things will be all right if only the last things are like the first. The myth of the original androgynous perfection of man seeks to counterbalance or stem the intrusion of evil, separation, enmity. But the memory of Christ's death, attention to his word, and the experience of the Spirit's work rely upon overcoming sin and trust in the promise of a new creation.

4) As shown earlier, a strictly allegorical interpretation of Gen 2:24 converts the concrete and historical terms of this verse into a timeless verity, describing Christ's eternal coexistence with Wisdom or with a spiritual church. In the same vein, this verse has been used to warn against the ever-threatening submission of Mind to Sensuality. On the other hand, the literal sense of Gen 2:24 has one element in common with a mythical tale or its moral application: it bespeaks what always has happened, does occur, and will be repeated. How-

---

[493] See the sketch of the system in COMMENT VI C on 1:15-23, and Schlier's excursus, pp. 264-76.

[494] Except in the improbable case that *mystērion* in 5:32 does not mean "secret meaning," but is used in the sense of the Mystery Religions and Gnosticism. See the first NOTE on 5:32.

ever, unlike some myths, neither its literal sense nor Paul's allegorical interpretation point to a story in which only gods are the agents, or to a tension between the abstract powers to which men are exposed. The actual way of a man with a woman, and the history of Christ and the church—these are what Paul mentions, not information about gods, virtues, vices, and rituals. Since, in the context, the church is not a deity but rather the church of Jews and Gentiles which still has tangible spots and wrinkles, and since the woman mentioned in the same verses is not a paragon of weakness or vice, it is impossible to speak of a mythological-dualistic Scripture interpretation in 5:30–33. "Typological interpretation" is a more fitting term, for biblical typology combines history (of the present or future) with history (of the past) or vice versa.[495]

5) When Paul describes the crucified and risen Messiah's love for the church in terms that resemble the Prophetic portrayals of Yahweh's love for Israel, he avoids a possible misinterpretation of the Prophetic imagery. Prophetic references to the invisible God's love, passion, jealousy, and anger sound so anthropomorphic that they resemble mythical traits. Paul's references to the love shown on the cross and in ever new gifts after the resurrection need not be bare of legendary and imaginative traits, but they speak unmistakably of a historical person and historical events. Many myths project onto heaven what happens on earth, or vice versa. They intend to demonstrate the heavenly protection and guarantee for earthly enterprises. They seek to show that and how some earthly things can be divine and can deify man, as Greek and Roman myths sanctify marital and extramarital sexual unions by referring to the example given by the gods. More sophisticated Greek thought such as Plato's declares that Eros himself is a god. Paul, however, demythologizes love and sex: *agapē* is not a power that tears man out of this world and lets him find refuge in the beyond. Rather it is brought by Christ into the world in order to flourish among people. It is not so other-worldly that it can be found only in death; neither is it so this-worldly that Christ can have nothing to do with it. A warning against the assumption that sexual union of itself is an ultimate, a god, a way to heaven, is contained in the description of the Messiah as a Bridegroom rather than a husband. In His love for the church there is no equivalent to sexual union and the procreation of children. Sex is called neither divine nor deifying nor immortalizing.[496] Male and female, including the result of their union, are only "flesh." But even the "one flesh" created in the union of a man and a woman is under the protection and guidance of the unique and exemplary *agapē* of Christ. Through the Messiah God liberates man from his enslavement to a mythical god Eros or Sex. He gives him "The Freedom of Sexual Love."[497]

If the "myths" of sex, love, and marriage are squarely faced anywhere, then it is in Eph 5. Paul could not have lived and traveled in Asia Minor and

[495] According to von Rad (OTTh, II, 356–87), the same is true of the OT prophets; faith in Yahweh is not built upon the "mythological thought of analogy" but expressed in terms of "historical-eschatological typology."

[496] Jesus' statement that there is no marriage in the resurrection (Matt 22:30) points in the same direction.

[497] As the well-chosen title of J. W. and L. F. Bird's book suggests. See also von Balthasar, *Herrlichkeit*, III 2:2 (1969), 452–53.

Greece, and he could not have stayed in Rome, without learning of diverse myths about the union between a man and a woman. Eph 5 reveals his acquaintance with contemporary religious movements, including their social expression. Therefore it is impossible to explain this chapter without discovering points of contact between the Pauline and the mythological viewpoints. The apostle does not simply overlook the beauty and the ugliness, the heights and the depths, the parallels and the contradictions found in mythological teachings and practices. But it is an arbitrary procedure to select from the many mythological tangents only second- and third-century Gnostic syzygy elements, and to declare that Paul's teaching on marriage is dependent on the same mythological conceptions as those exotic doctrines and cultic-ethical "actualizations." In choosing that way, Schlier made Eph 5 the final and supposedly unconquerable bastion of a Gnosticizing interpretation of Ephesians as a whole. The site chosen for that bastion and its fate have more resemblance to Custer's last stand than to the solid foundation of Zion.

Still, there is yet another way to support the idea that Paul's thinking moves on mythical—and if not on mythical, then on mystical—lines:[498]

B   Marriage—a Sacrament?

The question whether the nature of marriage in Eph 5 is correctly interpreted with the ecclesiastical term "sacrament" depends on the definition and usefulness of this term. In the preceding NOTES and COMMENTS four reasons for calling marriage a sacrament on the ground of Eph 5 have been subject to grave doubts. They will now be recapitulated and expanded.

1) It is impossible to demonstrate that *mystērion* in 5:32 means "sacrament" in any of the ecclesiastical senses of the term occurring in western theology, or that it signifies "mystery" as this word is understood in the definition of rituals by the Eastern Orthodox churches.[499]

2) Only if it could be proven beyond any reasonable doubt that Eph 5:21–33 bristles with allusions to the church's sacraments, i.e. to baptism in 5:26 and the Lord's Supper in 5:29, might the conclusion be appropriate that marriage is also depicted as a "great sacrament."[500] But the presupposition can be questioned; and even if proved solid, a conclusion drawn "by analogy" is not compelling.

3) It is most likely and almost certain that marriage must be understood as a sacrament (corresponding e.g. to the initiation and celebration rites of the Mystery Religions)—*if* the Christ-church relationship is meant to serve as the mythological ground of marriage. For what is true of e.g. the Marduk myth which is reenacted in the Babylonian Akitu Festival, is true of many a myth: the undated, timeless story of the divine persons makes necessary a concrete ap-

---

[498] Dibelius, p. 95, does not elaborate on the connection, but calls e.g. the *hieros gamos* idea a "mythical-mystical notion"; on p. 93 he speaks of "a mystical foundation of the husband-wife relationship."

[499] See the first NOTE on 5:32, esp. fn. 138, and COMMENT XI on 1:3–14.

[500] In commenting upon Eph 5:32, Thomas Aquinas calls four sacraments "great": baptism because of its effect: the forgiveness of sin and the opening of paradise; confirmation because of its administrator: the bishop; the eucharist because of its substance: the whole Christ; marriage because of its signification: the union of Christ and the church. In the NOTES on 5:26, 29, 30 and esp. in COMMENTS IV F and VI A it was shown that an allusion to baptism and the Lord's Supper has been discovered or upheld by most diverse expositors.

plication, demonstration, representation or actualization in a sacred rite. Often, though not always in the history of religion, a ritual is the complement of a myth, and vice versa. However, when a historical event is presupposed which has a date, a place, eyewitnesses, and other signs of original tangibility and concreteness, then "reenactment" (*Nachvollzug* in Schlier's terminology[501]) is not the appropriate name for the celebration. The accounts of the institution of the Passover and the Lord's Supper, which are both related to specific and unique historic (not mythical) events, employ the term "remembrance" or "memory."[502] As equivalents Paul uses once the verb "to proclaim" and on another occasion the concept "communion."[503] Though elements, movements, and gestures may remind the celebrating assembly of individual traits of the original event, the uniqueness of the great deed which is "remembered" and "proclaimed" is far too much respected to permit or suggest a "reenactment." Only when the original lacks flesh and bones—as do the mythical deities and tales—does the ritual itself have a magical and mediating function. Then it makes the spiritual material, the timeless timely, the impersonal personal, the essential existential. Since Paul does not conceive of Christ's love for the church as an undatable, abstract, unrelated event, but calls the cross its culmination and demonstration, he has no need to call for reenactments or actualizations. What is real requires no "realization" through a ritual. What proves powerful at the present and what determines the future time by its energy is not dependent on "representations." Indeed, the Gnostics had a curious way of "meditating" on the "mystery" of the syzygy: they reenacted the heavenly copulations in their "sacrament of the bridal chamber."[504] Obviously Schlier has derived the strange concept of *Nachvollzug* from this Gnostic pattern; he calls marriage a "sacrament" and a "mystery," because he believes that a *Nachvollzug* similar to the Gnostic reenactment takes place within it![505] Paul, however, never explains baptism or communion as a *Nachvollzug*. Least of all does he proclaim in Eph 5 that the unique deed accomplished by Christ the "Savior" in his death (i.e. the creation of the perfect Bride, 2:15; 5:23, 25–27) can or must be actualized or reenacted by husbands.

4) Among the characteristics or criteria of a sacrament collected in the western churches are the following: (a) the institution by Christ, (b) the use of the proper formula, (c) the saving power of a "visible word," (d) the benefit to believers only. The first of these conditions is only fulfilled in Eph 5 if e.g. Bonaventura's somewhat strained distinction of three sorts of sacraments and their institution is accepted.[506] The second condition, according to Augus-

---

[501] The pages on which he untiringly repeats this term in his commentary were mentioned in fn. 26 *infra* third NOTE on 5:23.

[502] Exod 12:14; 13:3; I Cor 11:24–25; Luke 22:19. In the NOTES on Eph 1:16 and 2:11 it was shown that "to remember" is much more than to recollect intellectually. It means to celebrate and to act on the basis of a given event.

[503] I Cor 11:26; 10:16.

[504] Irenaeus *adv. haer.* I 6:3–4; 7:1–3; see fn. 462 for more references.

[505] Pp. 262–63, n. 1, 276.

[506] According to the summary given by Ratzinger (in Greeven, et. al., *Theologie der Ehe*, pp. 88–91) Bonaventura distinguished (in IV *sententiarum* d 23 a 1, qu. 2d): (a) two sacraments of the old *and new* covenants, established by the law of nature and confirmed by Christ, that is, marriage and penitence; (b) three sacraments outlined for Israel under the old covenant but in reality belonging to the new covenant and instituted by Christ for the church: baptism, eucharist, and ordination; (c) two sacraments belonging solely to the new covenant, supported by Christ, but instituted only by the Spirit in the church: confirmation and extreme unction.

tine and his followers, is met by the reference to a "word" in 5:26.[507] The third speaks to a question that was not posed at Paul's time.[508] Finally the restriction of the marital blessing solely to believing couples may be derived from 5:30, 33 (the reference to "members" of Christ's body and their special privilege and responsibility) but is contradicted by the admonition given to members of mixed marriages in I Cor 7:12–16 and I Peter 3:1–2.

The relative weakness of the arguments listed so far is not so obvious and incontestable as to exclude completely each and every sacramental concept of marriage. Some scholars have retained the term "sacrament of marriage" in full awareness of several or all the deficiencies in the time-honored defenses erected for it. They suggest stronger arguments for their thesis:

Whether Augustine really wanted to call marriage a sacrament is not sure. Certainly he did not anticipate the definitions and casuistry of the Florentine, the Fourth Lateran, and the Tridentine Councils.[509] In his diction, *sacramentum* meant above all the history and the time of salvation. Ratzinger uses this concept of "sacrament" to state that Christ himself is the proper sacrament between God and man, and that what the church calls sacraments is strictly tied to one mystery only, Christ's. According to the same author the joining of husband and wife is in Paul's teaching neither a neutral nor a secular thing outside the Christ-mystery, but their union is "taken up" into the order of the (new) covenant. "In marriage, sex and eros are accepted inside the covenant."[510] Among the ways to express the sacramental mystery of marriage in theological terms, to describe its relationship to Christ or the new covenant, and to proclaim what it means for the existence of man, are the following: marriage typifies the coinherence of creation and redemption;[511] it is "quasi an epiphany of the covenant between Christ and the church. The communion of Christ with the church is in operation;"[512] it is "a sign effective *ex opere operato;*"[513] it is a part of the mystery of Christ for it not only symbolizes but recreates the union of Christ with the church, the union of God and man which is realized in Christ's body is reenacted and continued in marriage;[514] it "conveys grace" and "augments the saving grace."[515] When marriage is called a sacrament in the context of such statements, "sacrament" is meant to denote a matter of im-

[507] This word (*rhēma*) which is usually interpreted as meaning the baptismal formula, probably means the declaration of love that crowns an engagement or the marriage vows; see COMMENT IV E.
[508] See the discussion of the neo-Platonic influences upon Origen and Augustine in COMMENT IV F 4.
[509] Or the intricacies of Pius' XI encyclical *Casti conubii*, 1930. See H. Denzinger-A. Schönmetzer, *Enchiridion Symbolorum*, 34th ed. (Freiburg: Herder, 1967), 794, 1797–1816, 3700–3724. The index in Denzinger-Schönmetzer, J 9a–d (pp. 907–9), gives ready access to other official Roman Catholic statements on marriage.
[510] Ratzinger, in Greeven, et al., *Theologie der Ehe*, pp. 88–93. Bieder (p. 62, n. 75) argues similarly: the essence of the "mystery" of marriage is the "incomprehensible unity of *eros* and *agape* in the Lord's service." Von Balthasar, *Herrlichkeit*, III 2:2, 452, speaks of the imprint of the form of *agape* upon *eros*, and distinguishes it from the misconception that *agape* is "eschatologically sublimated *eros.*" W. Stählin, *Mysterium* (Kassel: Stauda, 1971), pp. 194–96, declares it wrong to speak of a transformation of *eros* into *agape*, and to consider marriage a sacrament, but he insists upon calling marriage a mystery "in, with and under" which the great "mystery of God . . . will occur and take shape."
[511] See, e.g. the references given in fn. 141.
[512] H. Schmauch, *Katholische Dogmatik*, IV:1, 3d and 4th eds. (Munich: Hueber, 1952), 622.
[513] M. J. Scheeben, *Handbuch der Katholischen Dogmatik*, IV (Freiburg: Herder, 1903), 769 ff.
[514] L. Johnson, "The Mystery of Marriage," Scripture 11 (Edinburgh, 1959), 1–6 (ref.), appears to be influenced esp. by Schlier.
[515] Council of Trent, *Canones de sacramento matrimonii* 1, 1563; Pius XI, encyclical *Casti conubii*, 1930 (Denzinger-Schönmetzer, 1801, 3714). However, in the main body of *Casti conubii* less emphasis is placed on grace and sacrament than on natural law.

mense depth and relevance which goes beyond explanation by natural law, experience, ecclesiastical definitions, and canonical manipulation. It indicates participation in ultimate reality, the operation of grace in an effective sign, the permanence received in sacredness.[516] The connection established in Eph 5 between Christ's saving love and marital love (and in Matt 19:6 between the work of the creator and the order of marriage) is the main exegetical reason for this description of marriage.

However, Christian interpreters of the Bible do not possess a monopoly on the term sacrament and its application to marriage; e.g. Buber calls the I-Thou relationship, especially the dialogue-relation, a sacrament. And on the basis of the philosophy of A. N. Whitehead and P. Tillich, the psychotherapist May argues: "All reality . . . has the ontological character of negative-positive polarity"; this character can be called "male-female." "A process of dynamic movement between polarities" or a "polar rhythm" is experienced directly and intimately in sexual intercourse. May concludes: "In sex we thus enact the sacrament of intimacy and withdrawal, union and distance" in "eternally repeated participation in each other."[517]

These "sacramental" conceptions of marriage and sex are more spiritual than the descriptions of marital intercourse which speak only or primarily of procreation and of a cure against fleshly desire.[518] The Christians who support the equation of marriage with a sacrament intend to say that marriage is a means of grace by which man and woman participate in the mystery of creation, incarnation, redemption, reconciliation, perfection. Marriage is then a gift, a sign, and a means of a spiritual reality, and the Christ-church analogy of Eph 5 demonstrates that this spiritual foundation and orientation of marriage is indispensable. Opinion may be divided on issues such as the following: Does the sacrament of marriage so conceived necessarily entail ecclesiastical jurisdiction over all legal and moral aspects of marriage? Are the church ceremony of the wedding, or the consent expressed in the betrothal, or the intercourse, or the mutual help of the partners, alone or in combination the decisive and necessary sacramental acts? Is only a marriage between Christians valid and sure to receive God's blessing? Whatever the answer to these questions, the sacramental character of marriage can be upheld, but only if it is defined in broad, deep, spiritual terms. "Sacramental," then, has essentially the same meaning as "mystical." In this case the specific contribution of Eph 5 to the biblical doctrine of marriage is to demonstrate the Mystique of Marriage.[519]

[516] Despite his sympathy with the companionate conception of marriage (as it was developed by radical Protestant sects, the Quakers, the English Puritans), Bainton (p. 107) calls for more stress on the sacramental aspect of marriage. This way he hopes marriage will find a way out of the present confusion and toward greater solidity.

[517] Pp. 112–13. See also von Hattingberg, (pp. 100, 140 ff., 239 ff., 327) who describes love and marriage as a "grace and sacrament" without burdening these terms with their particular ecclesiastical or theological meanings.

[518] The tradition epitomized by Augustine's de bono conjug. (PL 40, 373–96) was sketched in fn. 27. Augustine himself defined "the good" of marriage not only by (a) proles and (b) fides (productivity and faithful mutual service) but also by (c) sacramentum (i.e. the indivisibility guaranteed by the union of Christ with the church); see de bono conjug. 394D; de gen. ad lit. IX 7 12 (PL 34, 397D). His teaching was canonized in the Council of Florence's Decretum pro Armeniis, 1430 (Denzinger-Schönmetzer, 1326).

[519] An alternative or a complement to mystification by sacramentalism is legalization. Since medieval times, Canon lawyers have used the concept of "marriage, a sacrament" for establishing

But some critical remarks about the sacralization of marriage must now be added on the basis of the exegetical NOTES and COMMENTS previously made:

1) The sacramental doctrine of marriage makes every marriage between Christians equivalent to a *hieros gamos*. A democratization takes place which not only attributes to each couple's union what on pagan festival days has been the privilege of the king or priest, but also neglects the singularity of Christ's betrothal to the church as described in 5:25–27, 32. If marriage is a sacrament after the model of the *hieros gamos*, the union and peace between God and man established by Christ is enacted and achieved again and again by each couple in their common life. However, Paul leaves no doubt about the uniqueness and completeness of the Christ-church communion. The marriage of which he speaks is an earthly consequence, not a semiheavenly repetition of Christ's romance. It is this-worldly rather than a mediation between heaven and earth.

2) The thesis that marriage is a sacrament amounts to a sacralization or mystification of a structure or institution in human society. Yet it is questionable whether Paul really intends to subject married individuals to the requirements and laws of a given institution. He fails to provide materials by which the institution of marriage can be "Christianized" to the extent that the ideal of a "Christian marriage" emerges. If his concept of marriage were sacramental, he would contradict his strictures against justification by (works of) law, and would establish a "law and order" of marriage to which men have to bow if they want to serve God. Thralldom to angelic or demonic powers and institutions would only be replaced by the yoke of a new law. The freedom Paul preached elsewhere would thus be belied. But when the apostle affirms that Christ's very specific and personal love for the church, and the church's voluntary and joyful subordination to her Savior, are the ground and prototype of the husband-wife relationship, he does not proclaim a law; neither does he establish a new principality or power between God and man. Rather he intends to say: What is and has become for many the heavy yoke of bondage, even the societal institution of marriage, is now replaced by a union created out of the dynamic of self-giving love and voluntary subordination, or fear. The apostle means neither the love for an institution, nor the subordination to "law and order," nor the fear of structures of societal life. He speaks only of love and fear between the partners in marriage. Mutual submission of both partners to one another is the sum of his message; the vocabulary of his letters does not contain the term "marriage."[520]

3) The sacramental interpretation of Eph 5 continues that pagan doctrine and practice of Eros in which the partners use one another in order to attain a good that lies far beyond the partner and his well-being. In *de doctrina Christiana*, Augustine made the distinction between uncreated matter (*res increata,*

---

ecclesiastical jurisdiction. The encyclical *Casti conubii* (1930) begins by affirming this connection. Another consequence was the permission given for clandestine marriages and the conflict of western churches with modern states over the question of valid wedding ceremonies and eventual divorce proceedings. However, the legal, social, political consequences of the sacramentalization of marriage cannot be discussed here.

[520] Only in Heb 13:4 is *gamos* used in the institutional sense. Elsewhere in the NT (e.g. nine times in Matthew) it means the celebration of a "wedding."

that is, God) which is to be "enjoyed" (*frui*) and created matter (*res creata*, including the signs) which is to be "used" (*uti*). Plato's Eros made use of lovable fellow men in order to let the soul ascend to the intuition of the perfect. Dante's beloved and blameless Beatrice became his guide to the whole world of perfection. If "the good" of marriage consists primarily in the benefits to be attained by each individual partner—a good which in concert and by mutual help they may more easily attain than by remaining single—then marriage must indeed be called a sacrament, a means of grace, an effective sign, a way to salvation. It is then a way to escape from the world while living in it. Paul, however, speaks of the husband's love for his wife which resembles Christ's unselfish and sacrificial love, and of the wife's subordination to or fear of her husband which is free from selfish calculation. According to Paul, two married people do everything for one another; they accept and enjoy one another as a gift of God given here and now. Because they fear Christ, their interrelation is characterized by care for each other. Marriage is the confluence of love and the acceptance of love. It is strictly personal, just as Christ's love for the church and the church's response to it do not seek a higher, impersonal good, but only concrete, specific unity—unashamed of the earthiness of the cross and of the present church. A fellow person will not be truly loved if he or she is used to resolve ontological tensions or to achieve a private heavenly bliss. Jesus Christ's love for Jews and Gentiles gives man the freedom to love his fellow man for his own sake. His love does not justify a secret individual egotism.

In summary, the sacramental interpretation of marriage is most intimately related to pagan, mythological, dualistic, and individualistic concepts and aspirations. The sacralization of marriage in sacramental terms means in effect a mythification of Christ's relationship to the church, or of the joint life of a man and a woman, or both. But Paul speaks of the Messiah crucified in history, and of marriage as a purely historical event. Pagan myth-ritual patterns do not help to explain the NT testimony about Jesus the Messiah and the responsible worship of God by the saints. While marriage has been glorified and celebrated as a sacrament out of noble intentions, the employment of the term "sacrament" and many concomitant speculations and practices contradict the message and exhortation of Eph 5. Among those who have most violently condemned the equation of marriage with a sacrament is Calvin. He considered the late medieval Roman Catholic interpretation of Eph 5 equivalent to a "mixture of heaven and earth," and the transformation of marriage into a sacrament "a den of abominations."[521]

Is there any viable alternative to the mythological explanation and its sister, the sacramental application of Eph 5?

C   Marriage as a Covenant

Natural law; unwritten age-old magical and tribal tradition; laws and customs established by tyrannical, aristocratic, or democratic governments; exceptions, innovations, revolutions, and experiments introduced by groups and individuals—these and other factors are quoted in support of various sociological types and structures of marriage. Neither Gen 2 nor Eph 5 contains the materials for a legalistic casuistry which by definition would exclude a variety of marriage types as they have developed in the past and may still emerge in different cultural settings. Paul and the Gen 2 passage leave the door open for necessary changes, eventual progress, and the enactment of change and progress by reformations or courageous new experiments—if only the grace of God and the gift of freedom and responsibility remain fundamental—so that the solidity of marriage and the joy of those married shall not be exposed to neglect and contempt. God himself protects the freedom and steadfastness of love.

However, according to the books of Exodus and Deuteronomy, Israel's way out of slavery also included the protection and direction of God's people by the Ten Commandments. Similarly, the essence of that marriage to which Gen 2 and Eph 5 point is not without certain principles of a quasi-institutional character. While, according to the OT and NT, God's blessing and life eternal cannot be gained, bought, or earned through human acts of obedience, at least one thing will be avoided as long as God's directives are respected: the transformation of God's promised blessing into curse, that is, the loss of the life already given by God. Five principles can now be recognized in Eph 5. Like the majority of the Ten Commandments, they reveal by their negative form that they describe and warn against pitfalls rather than give detailed prescriptions:

1) Polygamy in all its public and private forms is practically excluded. But there is no explicit injunction in the NT to dissolve polygamous ties entered into before the baptism of husbands and/or wives.

2) Neither a patriarchal nor a matriarchal order of marriage is prescribed.

3) Marriage is not meant to be first and above all for the purpose of breeding offspring.

4) Their mutual love and devotion does not excuse married people from the responsibility to love God and his Anointed One above all, and to love their neighbors and subordinate themselves to them.

5) Both the mythological and the mystical (viz. sacral or sacramental) determinations of marriage have no place among God's people.

Still, the texts quoted leave the choice open among types and expressions of marriage which are more or less hedonistic, romantic, idealistic, materialistic, companionate, or status and work orientated. Paul's vagueness on many issues for which a secular or canon lawyer and every traditional or revolutionary man would prefer to have quotable ordinances, prevents the misuse of Eph 5 as a straitjacket.[522] Paul's arguments and exhortations provide counsel, not dictates. Just as each period in church history, each part of the church, and each married pair were given the liberty to find out by experience what the will of God is (cf. 5:10), and to interpret the apostle's counsel to the best of their abilities, so each modern man and woman, congregation and church is freed rather than constrained by Paul's advice to use their reason, emotion, experience, and judgment to find the way to which Eph 5 directs them. If the love of Christ for the church finds its response in the proper fear of Christ, and if men and

---

[522] Cf. H. D. Wendland, in Greeven, et al., *Theologie der Ehe*, p. 120.

women are not ashamed to imitate His love in their love, and the church's voluntary obedience in their subordination—then "everything is permitted" (or "all things are lawful," I Cor 6:12; 10:23).

Love, subordination, and fear are in each case an event, not institutions. They cannot be defined, enforced, or caught in social, legal, economic, and physical terms. Their original sacrificial demonstration by Christ and their ethical imitation by individual couples defy institutionalization or transformation into principles, a set of timeless values, or a catalogue of virtues. Both the confluence of love, subordination, and fear, and the correlation between Christ-church and husband-wife are miracles that have happened and will happen through God's grace. But just as Christ and the church are a couple unlike any other, and just as the union of one man with one woman is a unique event, so the specific form and expression of love meeting fear differ from one couple's engagement and marriage to those of another. Those loving couples are right who claim to experience love in a unique and unprecedented way. As stated earlier, the openness of Paul to the vision of love, and his awareness of the cost and the freedom of love, defy every typology of "the Christian marriage." Even as an instructor in ethics Paul is an "apostle of liberty."[523]

In both the OT and the NT, the true and free love of God unites the Lover and the Beloved in the firm structure of covenant. God manifests his love and his freedom by electing Israel, and by binding her to himself and himself to her. His covenant is a one-sided matter inasmuch as it is based upon his will and initiative, his word of promise, the blessing he alone can bestow, the requests only he can make. But it also has bilateral features: by the promise which underlies the making and keeping of the covenant, God will make Israel free so that she can serve him voluntarily, with the response of a truthfulness, faithfulness, and righteousness that reflect God's own freedom and love. In the OT the accent is placed at different points: either on the free promise of the divine partner, or upon the mutual obligation of both partners, or upon the obligation of the human partner alone.[524] But in each case the binding of the two partners by a word, for a common history, and toward a given end, does not mean the loss of freedom for either of them. Rather it demonstrates God's freedom, effects man's freedom, and guarantees and glorifies the freedom of both. The NT, especially Paul in Galatians, adds nothing new to the inherited concept of covenant that brings freedom. But it confirms the solidity, finality, and universality of the covenant, and glorifies its renewal through the covenant-mediator, Jesus Christ. What Paul says in 2:11–22 about the union of Jews and Gentiles who are joined in one covenant so as to have "free" access to God, is also reflected in the contents of 5:21–33; both passages are "strikingly similar" (Sampley, p. 161).

While Paul, in elaborating on the analogy of the Christ-church relationship to husband and wife, does not use the abstract term "covenant" (*diathēkē*) to

[523] See R. N. Longenecker, *Paul, Apostle of Liberty*, New York: Harper, 1964.
[524] See esp. E. Eichrodt, *Theology of the Old Testament*, I–III, Philadelphia: Westminster, 1961; J. Begrich, "Berit," in *Gesammelte Studien zum Alten Testament* (Munich: Kaiser, 1964), pp. 3–15; D. N. Freedman, "Divine Commitment and Human Obligation," *Interpretation* 18 (1964), 419–34; D. J. McCarthy, "Treaty and Covenant," AnBib 18, 1963. A study by S. O. Hills is in preparation, which will offer a radical alternative to the treatment of the covenant topic by G. Mendenhall, *Law and Covenant*, Pittsburgh: Biblical Colloquium, 1955.

denote marriage, some Prophets explicitly or implicitly have described marriage with the same term *berith* that they also use for Yahweh's covenant with Israel.[525] Passages that designate the wife as her husband's property, as e.g. Ezek 16:8 (". . . and you became mine"), do not contradict the covenantal relationship. For if the specific covenant of Yahweh with Israel includes, and is expressed by, the declaration of a change in property rights: "I will be your God, and you will be my people" (Lev 26:12, etc.), then it is not strange that the antitypical marriage covenant presupposes an analogous transaction. "I am thine and you mine"—this classic line from a medieval song does not fit each and every covenant, but it suitably describes the covenant of love, marriage.[526]

The total involvement and obligation of each partner excludes the notion that their covenant is either only a sacral or a purely secular matter.[527] On "the earth" which "is the Lord's," including "all that fills it" (Ps 24:1), the distinction between sacred and profane makes little sense. Paul agrees with rabbinical teaching when he speaks of the "sanctification" of the partner in marriage.[528] In God's people all things must be said and done in the name or to the glory of the Lord, cf. Col 3:17. Since God who made a covenant with Abraham and the people he had elected is the creator of man and woman, the "friend" who joins them, the judge of their union, the source of blessing without which it cannot flourish, it makes sense to use the biblical term "covenant" (despite its quaintness and legal associations) as the most fitting description of the structure of marriage, as proclaimed by Eph 5.

But it is also possible to do justice to both Eph 5 and the Gen 2 passage quoted by Paul by describing marriage with the more secular terms "partnership" or "companionship." In Mal 2:14 and Prov 2:17 "companion" is the title of the partner in marriage; according to Gen 2:18 it was God's will to create for man a "helper fit for him"; in Sir 36:24 a wife is called man's "best possession" because she is "a helper fit for him and a pillar of support."[529] Without this help, without the partner of the other sex, man's humanity would not be complete. He would not be the image of God (Gen 1:27). Because he is given this help, he is free to be human in the true and full sense of this term, that is:

---

[525] Betrothal by the "plighting" of "troth" is equated with "entering a covenant": Ezek 16:8, cf. 59–62; the term "covenant of peace" sums up the description of the husbandly care of Yahweh for Israel, Isa 54:1–10; a full catalogue of the covenant terms "righteousness, justice, steadfast love, mercy, faithfulness" appears in the description of Yahweh's eternal betrothal to Israel which is exemplary for, and to be expressed by, Hosea's relationship to his (unfaithful) wife, Hos 1–3; esp. 2:19–20; Israel has "broken the covenant" with her "husband" Yahweh, Jer 31:32. Yahweh is "witness to the covenant between you and the wife of your youth, to whom you have been faithless though she is your companion and your wife by covenant," Mal 2:14. Cf. Prov 2:17: "A loose woman . . . forsakes the companion of her youth and forgets the covenant of her God."

[529] A transfer of personal property also characterizes the closeness of the "covenant" between Jonathan and David: I Sam 18:1, 3–4. See also Ruth 1:16.

[527] The discussion of the equation of marriage with sacrament in COMMENT VII B has shown that Eph 5 does not support sacralization in terms of church control. Luther, however, attributed to "city hall," "lawyers," and "reason" the administration of marriage and all legal questions related to it, and declared that marriage is "a secular and external matter." He and Calvin (see fn. 521) may have overreacted in choosing their language against medieval sacramentalism. A "secularization" in the modern sense of the word was certainly not in the Reformers' mind. Otherwise, e.g. Luther would not have described marriage as a school of conduct in obedience to Christ.

[528] See I Cor 7:14; Eph 5:26 and the rabbinical references in fn. 59.

[529] In fn. 208 corresponding passages have been quoted from Greek and Latin writers.

co-human, a social being.[530] Earlier (see COMMENT IV on 3:14–21) it was shown that the mystical notion of the individual's capacity to be human in and by himself is displaced in Ephesians by the concept of "humanity by partnership." In Eph 3:16–17 Jesus Christ appears in God's name as the one great partner who redeems every man from proud or intolerable loneliness. In Gen 2 and Eph 5 a man and a woman are the human partners given by God to one another for the same purpose. Certainly they cannot redeem one another, but they can rejoice as "coheirs of the grace of life" (I Peter 3:7).

In the western church, the "companionate" concept of marriage[531] was developed first among some radical groups of the Reformation, then by Dutch Calvinists, finally by British and American Puritans.[532] For a long time arguments for, and experiments with, this concept were rejected by traditional church circles. But the lack of understanding found among scribes and lawyers, celibates and patriarchalists does not demonstrate that this concept is an improper conclusion to be drawn from the message and exhortation of Eph 5. On the contrary, this chapter belongs among the outstanding literary documents that provide a charter of liberty and responsibility to both partners in marriage, based upon the dignity, peace, and unity given to them by God through Jesus Christ. Eph 5 intends to help all men, especially all couples, to live together in peace. It frees them from enslavement to powers, traditions, ideals, patterns, and above all from the temptation to seek a solution to their problems in a dualistic ontology, a tyrannic hierarchy, or an equalitarian competition.[533] It liberates them to experience the triumph of unselfish love and voluntary mutual help.

It is not by chance that the discussion of marriage stands at the beginning of the *Haustafel* and of Paul's special ethical instructions. For the epitome of social life and the gravest of all social problems are located in marriage. The contribution which Paul makes can be summed up this way: he shows that there is no solution to problems and no peace except in the encounter of love with subordination in love, and in the meeting of gracious and faithful election with joyful fear. The partnership of one man with one woman is the prime occasion and form of this interaction and cooperation, for the human marriage covenant has a solid ground and shining example in the Lord's covenant with his people.

[530] See Calvin on Gen 2:21, CRCO XXIII 49; K. Barth, III 1, 183–206, 324 etc. Cf. Bab. Yeb. 63a. In their own way, the pagan and the Jewish tales of the original androgynous man intended to say the same. But in contrast to pagan and Christian-Gnostic thought (see, e.g. the end of the *Gospel of Thomas*) neither Gen 1–2, nor Eph 5, nor any other biblical text predicts that at the end man's social structure of existence, as expressed by the different sexes, will be overcome by a type of humanity in which a single person possesses all perfection. In Paul's teaching the oneness of "male and female in Christ" (Gal 3:28) means their union and peace, not their intermixture and amalgamation.

[531] Bailey, pp. 62, 106, raises some objections against the "partnership" nomenclature, because it can obfuscate the special I-Thou relationship that is established in the marital *henōsis* ("unity").

[532] See de Rougement, and Bainton.

[533] Which appear to be viable options for modern men and women.

PART TWO   *Parents and Children*   6:1–4

6   1 Children, obey your parents because of the Lord; for this is right.
2 "Honor your father and mother"
—this is a basic commandment and contains a promise—
3 "in order that it shall be well with you
    and you may live long in the land."
4 And fathers, do not provoke the wrath of your children, but bring
them up the way the Lord disciplines and corrects [you].

PART THREE   *Masters and Slaves*   6:5–9

5 Slaves, obey your earthly lords with fear and trembling, as whole-
heartedly as [you obey] the Messiah. 6 Do not imitate people who
seek to please men by putting on a show, but do God's will from the
bottom of your heart, as slaves of Christ. 7 Render your service with
fervor—as [a service] to the Lord, not to men. 8 Be aware that the
same good which a man performs—be he slave or free—this he will
receive from the Lord. 9 And lords, act the same way toward them.
Stop using threats. Be aware that in heaven the same Lord is [ruling]
over them and over you: he who fosters no favoritism.

GLOSSES

Instead of supplying extended NOTES and COMMENTS as has been done with
earlier sections of Ephesians, at this point we add only a few GLOSSES to the
text of 6:1–9. The preceding intensive discussion of the husband-wife passage
certainly calls for an equally thorough study of the sociological and cultural
background, the Christological and eschatological orientation, and the traditional as well as the unique elements of the exhortations directed to parents and
children, masters and slaves. But spatial limitations do not permit us to present
all the problems of translation, the ambiguous terminology, the details, the
sweeping lines, the highlights, and the cultural and social implications of 6:1–9.
Paul's utterances on the parent-child relationship will be scrutinized in the commentary on Colossians and Philemon, AB, vol. 34B, especially in the exposition
of Col 3:20–21; Paul's counsel to masters and slaves will be intensively discussed in the exegesis of Philemon. At present some general remarks about the
content of Eph 6:1–9 must suffice.

1) Paul's selection of special ethical topics follows the pattern of *Haustafeln,*

and the selection appears to be very narrow. Why in addition to marriage are only the parent-child and master-slave relationships chosen for discussion, while the realms of private personal existence and the vast range of man's responsible involvement in social, political, cultural, economic matters are by-passed in silence? It looks as if a "domestication" has taken place and reached catastrophic dimensions. The very name *Haustafeln* reveals that modern interpreters found no more in Paul's special ethics than a reduction of the scope of a Christian's responsibility to the four walls of his abode. Even if these walls included the fields, manufacturing premises, and offices in which parents, children, and slaves work, they form narrow confines—so it appears.

However, the name *Haustafel* ("tablet of household rules") is probably a misnomer. The Ten Commandments, Aristotle in his *politeia*, Stoics in their diatribes and treatises, and rabbis in their halachic instruction, also give special attention to the husband-wife, parent-children, master-slave relationships and treat them in combination. The selection and concatenation of these three pairs is in no case meant to excuse man from personal self-discipline and from wide and public responsibilities. Rather the three relationships are considered as basic to each person's own life, to his membership in a community or state, and to his participation in the cultural and economic conditions and processes of his time. To be specific:

a) Man is a *sexual* being in the totality of his relationships. Therefore the discussion of the man-woman relation stands at the head of all other discussions.

b) Man is a *historical* being, tied to a past, struggling through the present, confronted with future time, and trying to bridge the gap with education. His historicity is epitomized by the fact that he was born from parents he did not choose (and who might not have chosen him), and that he produces children whose character and ways he cannot determine.

c) Man is a *material* being and has for better or worse a place in an economic framework where he possesses and produces much, little, or nothing, and where he also lives as a consumer. The wide realm of entanglement in economic exigencies is in focus when the master-slave relation is discussed.

In short, the so-called *Haustafeln* are misinterpreted when they are supposed to express no more than narrow and petty moral rules. In actuality they reveal that man can only live as a social being, that the problems of his soul, his peace, his survival, his conduct, his destiny are among the relationships and possible tensions into which he is placed by his sex, his history, and his dependence upon production and consumption. Paul intends to show that none of these realms is too far from Christ, too base, too confused, too malignant, too rotten to be the theater of an obedient, peaceful, and enjoyable life.

2) The arguments chosen by Paul to exhort children and parents, slaves and masters, are surprising for their richness. In fn. 194 to Eph 5:21–33, four Pauline motivations were listed for the obedience of "children": (a) they are "in the Lord"; (b) they are expected to do what is "right"; (c) they have a "commandment" of God; and (d) they are given a "promise" (6:1–3). "Fathers" are urged to heed the discipline which the "Lord" himself exerts (6:4). "Slaves" are reminded that they are slaves of Christ and work for him; God's will can-

not be done by them except voluntarily and wholeheartedly; they will receive good from the "Lord"; they are equal to free men in their dependence upon the Lord's reward. These manifold Christological, psychological, and soteriological reasons crown the exhortation to "fear" their masters and avoid the cheap tricks of sycophants. Finally, "masters" are reminded of their Master in heaven and the equal treatment he gives to high and low. The following points are outstanding in the way these motivations are combined:

a) The Christological argument has the strongest and the determinative position. It implies that both the supposedly high and the supposedly low are subordinated to the same highest authority. Therefore, before the Lord *and* before one another, parents and children, masters and slaves occupy the same position: all must obey (6:1, 4–7, 9). In this they are equals: none is nearer or dearer to God and the Messiah than the other, cf. Gal 3:28. The emancipation of those suppressed and exploited, and their access to a moral and legal status of equality, are the necessary consequences of Paul's Christological argument.

b) To the Christological basis of the exhortation belongs its eschatological foundation. This is most explicit in the references to the reward and the impartiality of the Lord in 6:8–9: in both verses allusion is made to the last judgment. Sweating slaves and threatening masters alike are to live now as people determined by the future. Though the mention of what is "right," of a "long life" on earth, and of the possible "wrath" of children seems to express only this-worldly motivations, the formula "because of the Lord" (lit. "in the Lord"), the reference to the "promise" given by God, finally the model of the Lord's on-going and unfinished "discipline and correction," show that the eschatological perspective is kept in mind. Parenthood and slave ownership are not eternal establishments that are by definition in the right. The same is true of the younger generation's resentment of the older, and of the worker's temptation to cheat his master or to seek revenge in sabotage and strikes. The coming Lord alone decides on the right or wrong done by old and young, rich and poor.

c) The theological arguments are complemented by pragmatic reasons. Paul expects children to behave in the way that is considered "right" outside as well as inside the church. He assumes they want to grow up and live long just as their fathers wish to avoid angry scenes and the dreadful grapes of wrath. He knows of the temptation to rebel against all authority, to seek conformity with people who get by with pseudo-pleasantness and compliance, or to humiliate subordinates by using strong words and threats. He is aware that good work can only be produced when the laborer's heart is in it. Thus high theology is not the only thing on the apostle's mind; on the basis of his Christology and soteriology he emphasizes the practicability of his advice and wishes to help his readers to find a good way of living. A hedonistic element is present among the motivations—just as in the commandment to honor one's parents and in other commandments contained in the book of Deuteronomy. But Paul does not promote egotistic and superficial hedonism: only what is "right" (6:1) and "good" (6:8) for the benefit of the community of old and young, male and female, rich and poor, corresponds to the inspired "singing," "thankful" behavior and mutual "subordination" which were described in 5:18–21.

So much for the motivations.

3) At first sight the substance and sum of Paul's exhortations seem to burden the weak and support the more powerful. In three verses he commands children to obey, whereas only one verse is addressed to their fathers. Four verses tell slaves to obey in fear and to do good work; one verse suffices for a warning directed toward their masters. In substance, fathers (or, parents? See LSLex, 1368, art. *patēr* VII 2) are encouraged to be wise and humble educators; masters are told to rule well; children and slaves are exhorted to obey all the more willingly. But children are reminded to have confidence in a "promise" (which includes outliving their parents); and slaves are made conscious that they work for the Lord and will be fully rewarded by him. While this promise and vision of noble employment can serve to console and perhaps make more tolerable the position of children and slaves, still it appears to include nothing that will stop injustice or change a humiliating situation. In summary, all that Paul says in regard to the generation gap and economic problems appears to be as time-bound, conservative, and suppressive as his utterances on marriage often are in the eyes of those who champion women's emancipation.

Again, an exact comparison of Paul's arguments with the progressive and reactionary pagan and Jewish voices of his environment leads to a qualification and correction of superficial impressions. Particularly outstanding are the following elements:

a) Unlike many Greek, Latin, and rabbinical teachers of ethics, Paul does not only or primarily address the free male members of the human society. He makes wives, children, and slaves as responsible for a good social order as those who wield, or presume to possess, superior power (cf. Rom 13:1–7). The vision of "participation" by all members of society in the common good includes the establishment of a common and shared responsibility. When Paul places major emphasis on the contribution of the supposedly "weaker" members, in actuality he takes a revolutionary step. *They* above all shall and will be the carriers of responsibility, changes, and progress! Yet instead of the dream of a perfect society, it is the knowledge of the crucified Lord's authority which gives Paul the courage to trust in the "power" that "is made perfect in weakness" (II Cor 12:9).

b) When Paul speaks to the slaves, he speaks not only of "fear and trembling," "obedience," and "service." He also appeals to their "wholeheartedness" (lit. "singleness of hearts," 6:5, corresponding to the single or sound eye in Luke 11:34, etc.), to the "bottom of their hearts" (lit. "the soul," 6:6), to their "fervor" (lit. "good will, favor," 6:7), and to their knowledge of the Lord's fairness (6:8; cf. the role of the "conscience" in Rom 13:5; I Peter 2:19). He shows them their dignity as laborers in the Lord's employment, which cannot be questioned or abrogated even by cruel or pagan masters, and which must not be belied by doing poor work and offering cheap lip service. Again, it is only on the basis and after the model of the Servant-Messiah that Paul expects the enthusiastic acceptance of subordinate positions (Philip 2:3–11). The kind of service he suggests is unimaginable except rendered "in the Lord," "to the

Lord," and in confidence in the Lord's judgment. It is an expression of the freedom of those who, just like Paul, are "prisoners" (3:1; 4:1) of the Messiah Jesus and engaged in His service.

c) The goal which Paul holds up to his readers bristles with seeming paradoxes. Instead of condoning short-ranged impulses and decisions, Paul directs children toward a conduct that endures and outlives haphazard whims and obstacles. Instead of permitting parents some outbursts of indignant wrath, Paul makes them responsible for avoiding anger: they must prevent the growth of an angry generation. Educators have first of all to accept the education they need themselves. Enthusiasm for work substitutes for the despair found in drudgery and is the clever means to make it bearable. The good a person does is in the last resort no longer something he produces but a gift received from the Lord. Masters are foreseen who treat their slaves as equal colleagues rather than underlings. In each case the paradox would be absurd and the expectation of its realization utopian—if Paul assumed that parents and children, masters and slaves had to resolve their problems by their own resources. But he has a firm ground for his exhortations and hope; he knows that Jews and Gentiles have become one people through the intervention of a third party: the Messiah Jesus. He is convinced that the sociological groups enumerated in the *Hausta-feln* can find peace when they "subordinate themselves to one another because they fear Christ" (5:21).

The content of the *Haustafel* (5:21 – 6:9) is thoroughly permeated by references to the Lord. Step by step it is totally dependent upon the reality and validity of Christ's work and his presence. For this reason it is impossible to reconstruct from it supposedly "original" Jewish or Greek tables of moral advice, and to assume that their "Christianization" took place by adding a series of glosses. No pagan ideology or social pattern can be Christianized by sugar-coating. The ethics of Ephesians is in the so-called *Haustafeln* as much as in its other main parts an original witness of faith, and an invitation for a genuine public testimony to Jesus Christ who created "one new man" (2:15) out of divided people.

XII THE SUPERIOR POWER
(6:10–20)

6 10 For the remaining time become strong in the Lord, that is, by the strength of his power. 11 Put on God's [splendid] armor in order to be able to stand firm against the schemes of the devil. 12 For we are wrestling not with blood and flesh, but with the governments, with the authorities, with the overlords of this dark world, with the spiritual hosts of evil in the heavens. 13 Therefore take up God's [splendid] armor so that you are able to put up resistance on the darkest day, to carry out everything, and to stand firm.
14 Stand firm now
   "Girded with truth around your waist,
   clad with righteousness for a cuirass,"
15 steadfast because the gospel of peace is strapped under your feet.
16 With all [this equipment] take up faith as the shield with which you will be able to quench the fire-missiles of the evil one. 17 Take salvation as your helmet and the sword provided by the Spirit, that is, the word of God.
18 In the Spirit pray at all times through every kind of prayer and petition. To this end stay awake in persevering intercession for all the saints, 19 especially for me [. Pray] that the word may be given to me to open my lips and in high spirits to make the secret known [by proclaiming] the gospel. 20 For this cause I am an ambassador in chains [. Pray] that I may become frank and bold in my proclamation. For this I must be.

NOTES

6:10. *For the remaining time.* Paul has a limited period of time in mind.[1] Its beginning is probably the making of peace between Jews and Gentiles through the cross and the resurrection, and the revelation of God's secret;[2] it will be terminated on the day when the Bridegroom meets the Bride and the

[1] The special literature cited only by authors' names in the following NOTES and COMMENTS on 6:10–20 is listed in BIBLIOGRAPHY 22. A. M. Woodruff, my academic assistant during the winter 1969/70, has collected much source and secondary material related to spiritual warfare and made important suggestions for its interpretation.
[2] Eph 2:11–22; 1:19–21; viz. 1:9; 3:5.

Lord holds judgment over all. Then the strife described in the following verses will be over and God's people will be liberated.[3] A variant reading obfuscates the "interim" character of both the available time and the struggle to be faced.[4] The better MSS and exact philology require that the introduction of 16:10–20 be translated in a way that not only announces a conclusion to be drawn but also expresses a limitation of time.[5] Some MSS read after *loipon*, "[my] brothers," but the better texts omit this address. In all undisputed letters Paul frequently uses this warm phrase.[6] His lack of personal acquaintance with the readers of Ephesians may have caused him to omit it, and its use in analogous passages in other Pauline letters and at the end of this epistle may have led some copyists to add it. In Eph 6:21 Tychicus is called Paul's beloved "brother," and all the saints are denoted as "brethren" in 6:23.

become strong. As the parallel "be fortified with power" (3:16; cf. Col 1:11) shows, a power which comes to man from outside is meant, rather than an increase in strength flowing from internal resources. "I can do all things in him [the Lord] who strengthens me" (Philip 4:13).[7] "My power is made perfect in weakness" (II Cor 12:9).

in the Lord, that is, by the strength of his power. Lit. "in the Lord and in the strength . . ." In emphasizing that no strength other than God's own can fortify the saints, Paul follows a trend of the LXX.[8] Certainly his words imply a psychological appeal to man's will and a call to courage. But when he speaks of the Lord and his "strength" rather than saying, become strong "in your souls," or "in the right spirit," he shows why and by what means the saints receive a very specific strength that is even stronger than self-discipline. They are "citizens . . . in the kingdom of the Messiah and God" (2:19; 5:5); they live from the incomparable power that was demonstrated in the past through the resurrection of Christ and the subjugation of all other powers (1:19–21), and that will now and from day to day strengthen the heart of each individual (3:16–19). The strength available to them is the resurrection power; more

---

[3] The most outspoken futurist-eschatological passages in Ephesians are 1:14; 4:13, 30; 6:9.

[4] The texts of the Koine-group, the Codices Claramontanus (sixth century) and Boernerianus (ninth century), also the majority of extant MSS (but neither Papyrus 46 nor the first script of Sinaiticus, nor the Vatican and Alexandrian Codices) have the absolute accusative *to loipon*, instead of the genitive *tou loipou*. With and without the article, *loipon* in Pauline diction usually means "finally," in both a logical and rhetorical sense; see I Thess 4:1; II Thess 3:1; II Cor 13:11; Philip 3:1; 4:8. However, in I Cor 7:29 *to loipon* occurs immediately after a reference to the brevity of the time available.

[5] BDF, 160, Abbott, Schlier and Gaugler translate, "for the future." WBLex, 481 wants to uphold "finally," though against the evidence adduced from non-biblical literature.

[6] I Thess 2:14, 17; 3:7; 4:1, 10; 5:1, 4, 12, 14, 25, etc. E. Schweizer, "Zur Echtheit des Kolosser und Epheserbriefes," in *Neotestamentica* (Zürich: Zwingli, 1963), p. 249, considers the absence of this formula as evidence against the letter's authenticity.

[7] The active of the verb *(en)dynamoō* occurs also in I Tim 1:12; II Tim 4:17, the passive in Rom 4:20; Heb 11:34; II Tim 2:1; Acts 9:22. *Endynamousthe* in Eph 6:10 has the meaning of the passive ("be strengthened by God") rather than the middle ("pull yourselves together") according to Abbott, pp. 180–81.

[8] The Hebrew OT speaks not only of the strength of God and the strength given by God, e.g. in Isa 8:11, but uses the hithpael of verbs such as *hazaq* to denote "strengthening oneself," "showing oneself strong," "having courage." In I Kings[I Sam] 30:6; II Kings[II Sam] 10:12, perhaps also in I Kings[I Sam] 4:9; III Kings 21[I Kings 20]:22 and elsewhere, the LXX renders these reflexive forms by the passive of *krataioō* ("strengthen"); see the Hebrew Concordance of G. Lisowski, p. 475, and the LXX Concordance of Hatch-Redpath, pp. 782–83 for further references, and Pedersen, III–IV, 15–18, for a discussion of the underlying psychology of warfare in Israel. While Pedersen concludes that "weapons are very far from deciding alone the issue in war" and sets the possession of "the proper psychic force" in opposition to them (p. 18), Paul takes a positive view of the proper weaponry—even the "armor of God."

briefly, God is their power in person. They can and shall rely on it, that is, on Him.[9] According to Gaugler, the saints "go into battle as victors." Indeed, the strength of God and from God means salvation for his people, e.g. in Isa 35:4; 41:10, but the context describes the peace gained rather than the victory won, cf. Eph 6:15. The distinct meanings of the several terms used to denote "strength" and "power" have been mentioned in fn. 39 to the NOTES on 1:19. Abbott emphasizes that the "strength of God's power" is not a simple hendiadys. In the OT and Jewish apocryphal literature the superiority of God's power is also expressed by titles such as King of kings.[10] Thomas Aquinas interprets the double term used in Eph 6:10 by "God's virtuous power"; he defines virtue as "the perfection of power."[11]

11. *Put on God's [splendid] armor.* Lit. ". . . the whole armor of God." The etymological sense and the classical use of *panoplia* are the same: often the term means the full and complete equipment of a soldier with weapons of offense and defense. The word is found at the introduction of lists of weapons or as a substitute for their enumeration.[12] It can also serve as a summary description of all the apparel with which a woman "dresses up" to show herself in public.[13] OT and Qumran Hebrew has no equivalent general term; instead of the abstract "total armor," usually the *kēlim* or *keēlē milḥāmāh*, i.e. the instruments of war, are mentioned.[14] When (mainly in the translation of the latest books of the OT) the LXX uses the term *panoplia*, then it denotes— with the possible exception of Wisd Sol 5:17—the harness or shield rather than the complete weaponry.[15] But because of the special references to the "cuirass" and the "shield" in Eph 6:14–16, *panoplia* cannot mean one piece of weaponry only in 6:11 and 13. COMMENT III A will explain why the translation "splendid armor" is more appropriate here than the version "whole armor."

in order to be able to stand firm. In the great majority of its occurrences in the NT, the verb *dynamai*, here translated "to be able,"[16] denotes some-

[9] Schlier, p. 289. Gaugler says the same of Christ. A decision whether "Lord" in 6:10 means God or the Messiah, cannot be made. 6:9 (cf. II Cor 5:10) suggests that "the Lord" is Christ, but 6:11 and 13 speak of "God's" armor. In Exod 15:3; cf. Jer 20:11, God (the Lord) is called a man of war, in Isa 11:4–5 the equipment of the Messiah is described. Eph 1:19 ff. distinctly glorifies God's power, but 1:10 and 3:16–17 show that all power is given to the Messiah and enters into human hearts through him.

[10] E.g. Isa 40:26; I Enoch 1:4; see W. Grundmann, *Der Begriff der Kraft in der neutestamentlichen Gedankenwelt*, Stuttgart: Kohlhammer, 1932 (ref.); idem, TWNTE, III, 402; Percy, pp. 195–96.

[11] Cf. Bengel on 1:19. The LXX shows a certain reticence in using the Greek term *kratos* ("strength"), at least in the rendition of the prophetic and early historical books, though not of the Psalms. Perhaps the implication of a contest against an opponent contradicted the monotheistic concern of the LXX translators.

[12] Thucydides III 114; Isocrates XVI 29; Polybius VI 23.

[13] Herodotus I 160; cf. IV 180; Plato *leg.* VII 796B.

[14] Deut 1:41; Judg 9:54; 18:11; I Sam 8:12; 14:1, 6; II Kings 7:15; Jer 21:4, etc.; 1QpHab VI 4; 1QM VIII 8; XVI 6–7; 1QH II 26; VI 31. Oepke, pp. 293, 296.

[15] II Kings[II Sam] 2:21: dress or spoil. Job 39:20: (unlike MT) the war horse is clothed with a *panoplia*, i.e. perhaps with the terror created by his snort, his hooves (cf. II Macc 3:25), his courage. Since in Wisd Sol 5:17 God's "zeal" is called the *panoplia* of God and since other pieces of his armor are equally identified, this *panoplia* stands beside rather than above the various other weapons. In Sir 46:5–6 only "hailstones" are mentioned as God's *panoplia*; in I Macc 13:29 *panopliai* are put upon pillars surrounding a tomb; in II Macc 3:25; 11:8 a "golden" *panoplia* is worn by supernatural riders coming to rescue Israel from dreadful enemies; in 15:28 the enemy is found dead in "full armor"; in 10:30 *panopliai* function as shields. In I Kings[I Sam] 10:17; Ps 5:12; II Chron 23:9; Aquila II Sam 8:7; Aquila and Symm. Ps 90[91]:4; Symm. II Kings 11:10 Hebrew terms for "shield" are translated by *panoplia*.

[16] With WBLex, 206, JB, RSV. But compare the other sense in, e.g. Matt 26:9; Acts 26:32.

thing other than a possibility (or probability) distinct from reality (or actuality). *Dynamai* signifies (in a pragmatic, almost mechanical sense) the presence and exercise of sufficient power. In the LXX this verb is preferred for the translation of *yakōl*, "to be able, to hold, to endure, to stand, to have it in one's power, to prevail." Just as the English language knows the concept of an "able man" in a physical, legal, or military sense, so in the LXX the adjective *dynatos* sometimes translates the Hebrew *gibbōr* or *gibbōr ḥayil* which means "manly, vigorous," viz. warrior, hero.[17] Correspondingly, the noun *dynamis* can mean "army," "armed forces," or "garrison."[18] The phrase, "Put on . . . armor *in order to be* able," indicates, therefore, that just as clothes make the man[19] so arms make the soldier. The saints are "able"-bodied men not by nature, nor by one act of ordination in the past (e.g. by their baptism), but only inasmuch as again and again they take up the special armor given to them.[20] "Whoever renders service, [shall do it] as one who renders it by the strength which God supplies" (I Peter 4:11). In Eph 4:23-24; Col 3:10, the armor or strength that is "put on" is equated with the "New Man" who in Rom 13:12, 14 and Gal 3:27 is identified with Christ. The verb "stand firm" (*istēmi*) occurs again in Eph 6:13-14. It "belongs to the language of war" (Gaugler) and either means "to take over," "to hold a watch post" (Hab 2:1) or "to stand and hold out in a critical position on a battlefield."[21] Sometimes the LXX translates the Hebrew *'āmad* ("stand") by *antistēmi* ("withstand").[22] Both verbs, "stand" and "withstand," are also found in Eph 6:13, "stand" alone again in 6:14. What makes this term worthy of such repetition? A specific biblical meaning of "stand" has been elaborated upon by von Rad: he explains Exod 14:13 ("Fear not, stand firm and see the salvation of the Lord which he will work for you today") by referring to passages that seem to suggest human "passivity" in which men simply watch the miracle performed by Yahweh in his "Holy War."[23] Indeed, without God's help and victory neither Israel nor the church can "stand." But in Eph 6, and also in the literature of Qumran, passivity is certainly not the aim and result of the power communicated by God. Again, a different interpretation is given by some scholars to the word "stand" in vs. 13. The formula "standing before God" was discussed in the last NOTE on 1:4.[24] Since it plays

---

[17] See LXX Josh 6:2; 8:3; 10:7; Judg 5:23; 6:12; 11:1; I Kings[I Sam] 2:4; 14:52, etc., also esp. I, II Chronicles and Psalms. In I Macc 3:38, 58; 4:3, 30; 10:19 *dynatos* means "soldier," in 9:21 "military leader," in Judith 16:6[7] "king."

[18] E.g. LXX I Macc 3:13; 10:6; II Esd 12:9; 13:34[Neh 2:9; 4:2].

[19] See COMMENT V B–C on Eph 4:17-32.

[20] Similarly Aaron, Levi, Joshua receive their ministry by being properly "invested." This investment had to be repeated on each day of worship, see Exod 28:3 ff.; 29:5 ff.; 40:12-13; Lev 8:5-13; 16:4; Zech 3:3-5; *Test. Levi* VIII 2-10. The terms "putting on strength, honor, majesty, righteousness, salvation, beauty, glory, shame," etc. allude to the same thought pattern; see e.g. Isa 49:18; 50:3; 51:9; 52:1; 61:10; Pss 93:1; 104:1; 132:9, 16; Prov 23:21; 31:25; Job 8:22; 29:14; 40:10. A proverb quoted by King Ahab warns of a magical misunderstanding: "Let not him that girds on his armor boast himself as he that puts it off," I Kings 20:11.

[21] Thucydides V 104; Xenophon *anabasis* I 10:1; Polybius IV 61; Exod 14:13; LXX Nahum 2:9[2:8]; Matt 12:25. Outside the Bible it can even have the transitive sense of "bringing to a standstill," "staying," "checking"; see LSLex, 841. Its antonym is "to flee," according to Abbott, or "to fall"; Rom 11:20; I Cor 7:37; 10:12. In Plato's *symposium* (217C; 219-221B) Socrates' accomplishments in the gymnasium, in battle, and elsewhere are described. They include not only the capacity to drink any amount of liquor without getting drunk, but also a miraculous power to "stand" for hours and hours in meditation (*symp.*, 220A, C, D).

[22] Josh 21:44; 23:9; Judg 2:14; Esther 9:2; Ps 75[76]:7; Obad 1:11; Isa 50:8; Daniel (four times).

[23] Isa 22:11; 31:1-2; II Chron 20:17, as opposed to, e.g. Isa 5:12. See von Rad, pp. 10, 46, 56-61.

[24] Also in COMMENT VII on 1:3-14.

a certain role in Philo and other so-called proto-Gnostic writings, Dibelius and Schlier interpret "standing" in 6:13–14 in a Gnostic sense.[25] They do not dispute that in 6:11 "stand firm" has a military significance. However, unless the contents of 6:11b and 12 present unequivocal evidence to the contrary, it is unlikely that the meaning of the verb is changed in vss. 13 and 14. At the end of COMMENTS II and IV the question of Gnostic influence upon Eph 6 will be discussed.

the schemes of the devil. The term "scheme" (*methodeia*) has occurred in 4:14 and was explained in the last NOTE on that verse. Cognate words also have a derogatory sense outside Ephesians.[26] The name "devil" (instead of "Satan") indicates perhaps that here—just as in 4:27—an element of traditional material is used. 1QH IV 12–13 speaks of the "wiles of Belial" (*zimmōt beliyaʿal*).[27] Presumably under the influence of Rev 12, Thomas Aquinas saw the viciousness of the Devil in the fact that he does not attack "God in himself," but "in his members." In the hymn, "A Mighty Fortress," Luther describes the cunning of the arch-enemy. Rev 12, together with other apocalyptic passages and some Qumran texts, speaks of a war between God and the Devil; see COMMENT II. Still, Paul does not speak of a "Holy War" of God, and in Ephesians (unlike I Tim 6:12?) he does not suggest that he understands the saints as crusaders.[28] He probably wanted to avoid supporting a dualistic, mythological, and chauvinistic attitude.

12. *we are wrestling not with blood and flesh.* Lit. "Our struggle is not . . ." A rather impressive textual tradition has, "your" struggle.[29] It is more likely that the unexpected pronoun "our" was changed to "your" by mistake or for the purpose of uniformity with the context than that an original "your" was converted into "our" (Abbott). While it is clear that *palē* ("struggle" or "wrestling") is used in a spiritual sense, the metaphor has been explained in various ways. A hand-to-hand fight is designated by the Greek word, not struggle or conflict in general (as in the English adage, "life is a struggle"). If a sport contest is in mind, then the form and rules of the ancient *pagkration* may apply; this was an "'all-in' contest in boxing and wrestling."[30] But if hand-to-hand fighting "in battle" is meant, no means of inflicting wounds, pain, and death are excluded. No doubt Eph 6 describes a "spiritual war" and "spiritual weapons"; but rather than use the term "war" (*polemos*) Paul chooses a concept that originally denotes the activity of an athlete.[31] The

---

[25] Schlier, p. 293, refers to I Enoch 62:8; 1QS IV 21, etc., and considers "vanishing and perishing" (I Enoch 69:29) its opposite.

[26] Robinson, p. 185, refers to LXX II Kings[II Sam] 19:27; Polybius XXXVIII 4, 10; Plutarch *moralia*, 176A, etc.

[27] In 1QM XV 9 the enemies of the elect flock are called the "congregation of vice" whose works are done in darkness. "Spirits of deceit" are mentioned in *Test. Asher* VI 2. The "angel of darkness" or "spirit of evil" who does his work by "malice and lie, pride and arrogance of heart, denial, cheating and hypocrisy" is described in 1QS III 20–24; VI 9–14.

[28] The incomplete lines 1QM XV 16–18 appear to speak of God's own war against Beliar. 1QM LX 15 (cf. XI 2; XIX 3 ff.) calls the war in which the elect are engaged, a "war of God" (*milḥemet ʾēl*), perhaps an allusion to the "wars of Yahweh": I Sam 18:17; 25:28; Num 21:14. Not earlier than at Emperor Constantine's time, Christian writers such as Firmicus Maternus began to support the notion of a holy war fought with arms in which the church was to participate; see von Harnack, pp. 18–46.

[29] Papyrus 46, Vaticanus, Claramontanus (first script); Boernerianus, the old Italic versions, and others.

[30] See LSLex, 1284, 1291; Robinson, p. 213.

[31] *Palaistra* is a cognate of *palē*. A *palaistra*, as mentioned in II Macc 4:14, is a wrestling school or ground, perhaps a sort of gymnasium (I Macc 1:14; II Macc 4:9, 12), not a military barrack or training ground.

emphasis placed on "peace" in 2:14–16; 4:3 and 6:15 may have prevented Paul from speaking in this epistle of an ongoing war.[32] Just as, e.g. Plato and Philo mixed metaphors of sport and of war, so Paul appears to have conflated them.[33] Again, the effect of Paul's choice is an antidote against a tragic-dualistic world view. Life is not by definition a battle, war is not the father of all things. But the attacks extended against the Christians require that they stand their ground as "good sports" and soldiers. While in the Pauline description of the Christians' internal battle in Galatians, Romans, and II Corinthians the "flesh" is the opponent, and in I Peter 2:11 and James 4:1–2 the "desires" are the adversaries, Eph 6:12 describes another fight: a struggle "not with blood and flesh."[34] "The contrast . . . between human and superhuman powers" is meant (Abbott). A reason why the formula "flesh and blood" (meaning humanity in its frail and perishing aspect, or in rare cases, the outstanding sacrificial elements)[35] is reversed here has not yet been found, as Dibelius observes; see also Heb 2:14; John 1:13. Perhaps "blood" substitutes for "soul" or "life"; for "the life of the flesh is in the blood," according to Lev 17:11. In this case "blood and flesh" is a synonym of "soul and body."

with the governments, with the authorities, with the overlords of this dark world, with the spiritual hosts of evil in the heavens. The first two of these four terms resume the diction found in 1:21 and 3:10. The other two contribute information about the nature and history of all evil powers. As in 2:2 where the air or "atmosphere" was the location of the Devil's reign, now "the heavens" are mentioned as the seat of all powers, i.e. one region of heaven which is to be clearly distinguished from others. See COMMENT IV for details and variant interpretations.

13. *take up God's [splendid] armor so that you are able to put up resistance . . . and to stand firm.* The translation "[splendid] armor" is explained in COMMENT III A, and the version, "that you are able," in the second NOTE on vs. 11. In that NOTE evidence was given for the military sense of the terms "stand" and "resist." Because Dibelius and Schlier found in 6:12 an allusion to the soul's journey into heaven and the resistance to be overcome along the way, they attributed to "stand" in vs. 13 a different meaning than in vs. 11: to stand (perfect) before God. But if vs. 12 does not speak of the soul's ascent,[36] "stand" has here, and in vs. 14, the same sense as in vs. 11: to hold the post, to resist in the battle of the present time. "Resistance" against the Devil is to be

---

[32] The diction chosen in Gal 5:17; Rom 6–8; II Cor 10:3–5, in the Pastoral Epistles and in Revelation does not show the same restraint.

[33] E.g. Plato *leg.* III 404A; IV Macc 3:4–5; Philo *Abr.* 243–44; Ignatius *Polyc.* VI 1–2. For a discussion see Pfitzner, esp. pp. 42–43, 158–59, 193; also Schlier, p. 290. Incidentally, Paul's use of the term *palē* dispels the idea that a Christian can engage in battle against evil as if from the safe distance of a B52 bomber. Rather he stands in a hand-to-hand combat and bears the corresponding risks.

[34] Jerome, Thomas Aquinas, and others fail to notice this particularity of Eph 6. They think of the "desires" of the "flesh" that stand opposed to the Spirit (Gal 5:17), and they explain the spiritual war (in a Stoicizing way) as a battle against the passions. Bond produces the same interpretation by referring to the "desires" mentioned in Rom 13:14. Thomas Aquinas adds to the text the word "only" in order to uphold the same exegesis: "Our wrestling is not *only* against flesh and blood." Schlier and Gaugler, however, agree in stating that in Eph 6 neither the self nor fellow man, but spirits are the adversaries. Calvin warns against underestimating this enemy.

[35] See e.g. Sir 14:18; I Enoch 15:4; Gal 1:16; I Cor 15:50; John 6:51–56; also the rabbinical passages quoted in StB, I, 730–31; and J. Behm, TWNTE, I, 172–73; H. Lietzmann on Rom 8, HbNT, 8, 4th ed. (1933), 80–83.

[36] As will be shown at the end of COMMENT IV.

offered here on earth, also according to James 4:7; I Peter 5:9. The imperative "take up" recurs in vs. 16. While the more civilian synonym "put on"
expresses the ostentatious, demonstrative, ornamental, assuring act and effect
of dressing oneself,[87] "taking up" is sometimes a technical military term.[88] It
describes the last preparation and final step necessary before the actual battle
begins. "The spiritualizing description of the arms . . . does not exclude
that a most real battle is in mind.[39]

on the darkest day. Lit. "on the evil day." This formula was anticipated by
"the evil days" mentioned in 5:16. In the Wisdom literature of the OT especially, references are found to good and evil days that occur during the normal
life span of a person. Each in his own time experiences evil days; lest he be destroyed by them he asks God for his saving interference; he trusts that God
who sent them will also terminate them; he is sure that evil-doers will be caught
by them.[40] Death, anticipated by the threat or fear of death, is both the agent
and the substance of "evil." Therefore the day of a man's death, viz. the hour
of his dying (Luther: *das Stündlein*), can be meant by "the evil day." However, the historic and prophetic books of the OT also speak of one "Day" or of
"Those Days" in a sense which far overshadows the relevance of the recurrent
days of an individual's misery, punishment, or death. In the light of those utterances, the reference to "the darkest day" here may indicate that even now is
the last time. See COMMENT V.

to carry out everything. Do these words speak of the preparation for battle,
or of the actual battle and victory? The Greek original is ambiguous, since
"everything" (lit. "all") is not defined, and the verb used here can have different, perhaps contradictory, meanings:

a) *Katergazomai* may mean "to carry to victory," "to defeat," "to finish
a job."[41] If in 6:13 Paul uses the verb in its military sense, then no less than
four commands may be in his mind: Take up arms! Form the battle line! Attack and defeat the enemy as arranged! Occupy and hold the field![42] Not exactly the same but analogous actions are registered in the books of the
Maccabees and in the War Scroll of Qumran. However, does Paul really have
in mind a "victory" to be gained for God the King,[43] perhaps by means of a
powerful invasion into or through the heavenly realms occupied by malicious
guardians which results in the "taking of the kingdom of heaven by violence"?[44]

---

[87] In I Thess 5:8; Rom 13:12; Eph 6:11 passages such as Isa 51:9; 59:17 are reflected, indirectly
also the texts mentioned earlier describing the "investment" of the high priest or the king.

[88] See, e.g. Herodotus III 78; IV 53; IX 46; Josephus *ant.* IV 88; XX 110, 121.

[39] Dibelius, p. 97.

[40] See, e.g. Pss 22; 37:13; 41:1[LXX 40:2]; 49:5; 102:3, 11; 139:16; Job 3:3–6; 5:14; Prov 16:4
[LXX 16:9]; 24:10; Eccles 7:14; cf. 8:8; 9:12; 11:8. In some of these passages no more may be
meant than what in English is called "a rainy day."

[41] In a military sense in, e.g. Herodotus I 123; VI 2; Thucydides VI 11:1; Josephus *ant.* II 44;
LXX Ezek 34:4; Lev 25:39 var. lect.; I Esd 4:4 (for other senses see, e.g. Exod 15:17; 35:33).
Chrysostom, von Hofmann, von Soden, Schlier, WBLex, 423, favor this interpretation.

[42] Or, if "stand" should be used here in a sense different from 6:11: Present yourselves to the
commander after the victory!

[43] Cf. the term "winning a most glorious victory" (*hypernikaō*) in Rom 8:37, the prominent role
of the term "overcome" (*nikaō*) in the book of Revelation *passim*, where legal and military meanings
are combined, and in the prayerful slogan, "We shall overcome."

[44] The language used in Matt 11:12; Luke 16:16 may be borrowed from the Zealots—though a
new interpretation of the Lukan text has recently been offered by Ph.-M. Menoud, "Le sens du
verbe *biazetai* dans Lc 16,16" in *Mélanges Bibliques*, Fs B. Rigaux (Gembloux: Duculot, 1970),
pp. 207–12. He argues that an "urgent invitation by means of the gospel" is meant.

If this be the case, then at the end of his life Paul has returned to elements of his zealot past;[45] then he finally did endorse the idea of a "holy war," perhaps in dependence on, certainly in analogy to, the militant theology and ethics of Qumran.

b) But serious objections have been raised: neither in the Pauline letters nor elsewhere in the NT does *katergazomai* ever have the sense "to conquer," "to subdue."[46] It either means to "prepare" (II Cor 5:5)[47] or "to accomplish" (Rom 7:15–20), that is, "to work out, to bring about, to effect" (II Cor 9:11; Philip 2:12, etc.). Robinson and Abbott decide in favor of "accomplishing, doing all that [your] duty requires"; the Vulg. and Thomas Aquinas translate by "perfect in all things."[48] Since it is unlikely that in vs. 13 Paul speaks of the result of the combat and then in vs. 14 returns to discuss the necessary stance during the fight ("stand firm") and the proper preparation ("be girded . . . and ready . . . take up these pieces," vss. 14–17), the words *hapanta katergasamenoi* ("carry out everything") probably summarize the preparation for battle; see, e.g. Bengel and Gaugler.[49] In Eph 6 far more emphasis is placed on readiness and firmness in the struggle than upon any actual human accomplishment during the battle. The good works which the saints will do according to 2:10 are "prepared by God" long beforehand. "The good which a man performs . . . this he will receive from the Lord" (6:8). This may well be the reason why 6:10 ff. speaks of no more than the "taking up" of armor. After this is "carried out," the saints can let the good works, viz. the several pieces of armor, have their way; cf. Philip 2:12–13; 3:12–14. The victory is God's, not theirs.

14. *Girded . . . around your waist.* A girdle is used for many purposes.[50] While sashes were made of cloth and other wide girdles served as pockets, the tight belts worn by workers and warriors in the ancient world were made of leather. A person girded himself for activities, such as departing, walking long distances, working, officiating, e.g. as a priest or judge, or fighting in an arena or in war.[51] The girdle was taken off for rest.[52] One of at least three different girdles worn by soldiers can be meant in Eph 6:14: (a) The breech-like leather apron worn by Roman soldiers to protect the lower abdomen;[53]

---

[45] In Gal 1:14 and Acts 22:3 Paul uses the term "Zealot" of himself. In the Pastoral Epistles, esp. in II Timothy (2:5 and 4:7; these passages are nearer to Paul's own diction than I Timothy and Titus), military images and the consciousness of impending victory are prominent. A recent book on Paul by T. Caldwell is entitled *Great Lion of God*, New York: Doubleday, 1970.

[46] That this fact "makes no difference" (*hat Nichts auf sich*) is stipulated, yet fails to be demonstrated, by von Hofmann, p. 253.

[47] Also in, e.g. Herodotus VII 6:1; Xenophon *memorabilia Socratis* II 3:11. Dibelius prefers the translation "preparing" to "conquering."

[48] Thomas Aquinas uses the occasion to make an excursus on three sorts of perfection.

[49] Jerome chooses a translation which takes no position among the alternatives. His vague version *universa operati* corresponds to the translation offered here. G. Bertram, TWNTE, III, 634–35 feels unable to decide for either "conquer" or "prepare."

[50] To cover man's nakedness and shame: Gen 3:7; as an adornment, e.g. of women: Isa 3:24; 32:11, or of a king: Ps 45:3; as a sign of cultic, civil, or military rank: Exod 28:4; I Sam 18:4; Isa 11:5; 22:21; Rev 1:13; 15:6; as a prophetic symbol (against the soft city life?): II Kings 1:8; Matt 3:4; as a sign of readiness for a debate: Job 38:3; 40:7; etc.

[51] See the collection of examples from inside and outside the Bible by Oepke, TWNTE, II, 302–308 and in LSLex, 759.

[52] Herodotus VIII 120. A loosened girdle could be a sign of exhaustion: Isa 5:27, but also of the loss of virginity: Homer *Odyssey* XI 245; cf. Herm. *sim.* IX 2:4.

[53] Oepke, pp. 303, 307. According to Wevers, p. 825, this apron also served for tying down the breastplate. This specific interpretation of "girding" suggests (or presupposes) that Paul follows in

(b) the sword-belt which was buckled on together with the sword (and dagger, in the case of an officer), as the decisive (usually last) step in the process of preparing oneself for battle;[54] (c) the special belt or sash (Latin, *cingulum*) designating an officer or high official.[55] The last meaning is probably best suited for interpreting Eph 6:14, for a clear allusion is made to Isa 11:5: "Righteousness shall be the girdle of his waist, and faithfulness the girdle of his loins." In Isaiah this girdle is a distinctive sign of the high office held by the "Branch," i.e. the Messiah, but according to Paul it is given to all the saints.[56] They form an army in which each one bears the insignia of supreme dignity; no room is left to distinguish between officers and enlisted men, or between noblemen and commoners.[57] At the same time, the "girding" of all Christians excludes a distinction between weak and strong soldiers, military clerks in the rear and heroic fighters in the front line. For the strength of God's power is promised to each of them, and the expression "gird one's loins" (in our translation, "girded around your waist") is synonymous with the idiom, "gird with strength."[58] The opposite is to be girded by someone else and to be led away involuntarily (John 21:18; Acts 21:11), or to be girded with a rope or with sackcloth (Isa 3:24, etc.).

with truth. Lit. "in truth." It is unlikely that the term "truth" is introduced here in order to distinguish real girding or real fighting from false readiness or mere skirmishing. Also it is doubtful whether "truth" means only or primarily the (Greek, Persian, Stoic, etc.) virtue of "veracity," as opposed to the lack of conviction and honesty.[59] How should a human virtue suffice for "standing" in

---

14–17 the normal sequence of putting on or taking up one piece of equipment after another. Thomas Aquinas assumes that first three pieces of clothing, then two for protecting oneself, then one for attack are listed. But Schlier, p. 294, doubts whether a specific order can be recognized.

[54] David girds on the sword *over* the armor and can no longer walk freely: I Sam 17:39. "Girded with a sword" is a synonym for the ability to fight or readiness for battle: I Sam 25:13; Exod 32:27; Neh 4:18; cf. Isa 5:27. Since in the list of Eph 6:14–17 "the sword" is mentioned last, and since vs. 17 speaks of "taking" rather than of drawing the sword, it is unlikely that vs. 14 speaks of the sword-belt.

[55] See the references in fn. 50. Calvin and Bengel assume that the "girding" served an ornamental purpose. Like clothing in general (see COMMENT V B on 4:17–32), "girding" in particular could be the means and sign of the conveyance of power. In turn, according to Josh 4:13; 6:7, 9, 13; Num 32:21, 27, 29, 32, the special power exhibited by "armed [viz. girded] men" has its proper place in cultic appearance before the ark, viz. before Yahweh.

[56] Oepke, p. 307.

[57] Cf. COMMENT VI on 4:1–16, in which it was shown that Ephesians excludes the distinction between priesthood and laity. However, I Clem. 37 points out that in the "army" constituted by the Christians "not all are prefects, nor tribunes, nor centurions, nor in charge of fifty men."

[58] In Rom 14:1–15:13 a so-called "weak" group of Christians is distinguished from a "strong" one. But in II Cor 10–13 all Christians, including Christ and Paul, belong to the "weak" who are "made strong" only by the "power of God." While the "loins" can be a metaphor of "strength" even without reference to a belt, "girding oneself" is a symbol for displaying power and courage, and for going to work; see, e.g. Pss 18:32; 65:6; 93:1; Isa 45:5; Job 38:3; 40:7; Prov 31:17; Nahum 2:1; Luke 12:35, 37; 17:8; John 13:4, 5. In second-century Christian literature, being "decently girded" is used as a symbol of chastity and continence; see Herm. *sim.* IX 2:4; 9:5 and the passages in Clement of Alexandria quoted in TWNTE, V, 308. Thomas Aquinas follows this trend when he explains the belt of Eph 6:14 as a protection against "carnal desires."

[59] In German: *Wahrhaftigkeit*, i.e. the sincerity, honesty, reliability, credibility of a man who thinks straight and speaks the truth. Calvin, Grotius, Abbott choose this interpretation, but von Hofmann, Schlier, Conzelmann, Gaugler and others reject it. Indeed, the first virtue of a Persian catalogue of virtues, mentioned by Kamlah, pp. 94, 116–17, is "[speaking] the truth" (*kushta*). But it is questionable whether through the channel of Qumran (1QS III 13 – IV 26, esp. III 18–19, 24; IV 6, 17, 19, 23–35) this typically Persian meaning of truth became decisive for Ephesians, and whether it excludes or relegates to secondary rank any other meaning of truth. For even in the Qumran texts the opposite of truth is not only lie and fraud, but also avarice, laziness, malice, pride, conceit, foolishness, fornication, blasphemy, etc., see e.g. 1QS IV 9–14.

the eschatological battle? It might be a sign of the strength required, but hardly the source of it. See COMMENT III B for an interpretation of "truth" in the context of "righteousness," "faith," "peace," etc. There it will be shown that the OT background and particularly the connection which Isaiah establishes between these terms and the Messiah are the key to the exegesis of Eph 6:14–17. By making allusion to Isa 11:5 and 59:17, the text of Eph 6 practically forces the reader to use that key.[60] However, since in Eph 4:25 special emphasis is placed on speaking the truth, veracity cannot be totally excluded from 6:14. Though among the saints honesty and sincerity cannot be idolized as "absolute" virtues, they are indispensable for the testimony to the salvation of sinners by grace, even to the "true word" that "saves" and to every "constructive" talk (1:13; 4:29). The fact that "truth," rather than "righteousness" or "faithfulness" (as in Isa 11:5) is attached to the metaphor "girding," shows that Paul's formulations are not slavishly dependent upon the OT or any other firm tradition.[61] The varying allegorizations found inside and outside Pauline literature show a certain playfulness. Metaphorical language and allegorizations are an art form in which details cannot be pressed and exploited.[62]

clad with . . . a cuirass. Cf. "cuirasse" in SegB. When the Greek noun thorax denotes a piece of armor, it can mean everything that was worn at different periods to protect the body between the shoulders and loins. Originally it was a sleeveless jacket made of many layers of linen or leather that was tied and worn like a corset or bodice.[63] Eventually, at different times and places, this doublet was studded with pieces of metal, then reinforced by a breastplate (sometimes also a backplate), fastened under or over the leather. An even more developed form consisted of metal plates hanging on broad shoulder straps that

---

[60] Oepke, p. 314 (cf. 302, 307, 310) emphasizes that "not just the subjective attitude is meant, but an objective, divinely given reality." Gaugler calls "truth" "a divine being." The Hebrew text of Ps 91:4 f. ("His faithfulness is a shield and buckler") is rendered by LXX Ps 90:4: "His [God's] truth will cover you all around as [lit. with] a weapon." Truth and faithfulness are used as synonyms and described as actions and gifts of God. D. N. Freedman (by letter) has drawn my attention to the fact that these or other "virtues" are sometimes portrayed in the Psalms as attendants of God, who precede and follow him when he appears in his glory. Perhaps they are Israelite equivalents of, or Israel's polemic response to, the gods who wait on El in the divine assembly, according to Canaanite mythology. They can be called personified attributes of God, or demythologized deities. Cf. Pss 36:5–7; 89:5–8, 24. In Ps 89:14 four such attributes are listed: "righteousness and justice" constitute the pedestal of the divine throne; "steadfast love and faithfulness" proceed in front of the deity. Canaanite mythology is also reflected in e.g. Hab 3:5.

[61] E.g. in calling righteousness a "cuirass," he perhaps follows Wisd Sol 5:18 which in turn follows Isa 59:17. When I Thess 5:8 and Eph 6:17 speak of the "helmet of salvation" they allude to the same verse from Isaiah. However, in Wisd Sol 5:18 the helmet is identified with "impartial justice." Isa 59:17 mentions "garments of vengeance"; Exod 28:15–30; 39:8–21 speak of a gloriously adorned "breastpiece of judgment" worn by the high priest. In I Thess 5:8 the cuirass consists of "faith and love." Rom 13:12 refers in abbreviated fashion to the "weapons of light," and Rom 6:13 to "weapons of righteousness." Regarding the "shield" see the NOTE on 6:16. In the army of the Qumran community, "Truth of God, Righteousness of God, Glory of God, Judgment of God," is written on the standards when the troops move out for battle, other slogans when the battle begins, others again after victory.

[62] Attempts such as Oepke's to explain Isa 11:4–5 by saying David's house "will be closely bound up" with righteousness and faithfulness, seem to correspond to the homiletics used by Isaiah, but may well put too much strain on the prophet's imagery. Calvin calls it a "frivolous curiosity" to ask for the specific connection in Ephesians between the girdle (rather than the cuirass) and righteousness; Paul's intention is merely to show that truth and righteousness are useful weapons. Abbott warns against "pressing too minutely" the attributes attached to each piece of equipment.

[63] In French, the term cuirasse is a derivative from cuir ("leather"). Snodgrass has collected pictures showing the development of the cuirass, see plates 9, 17, 21, 37, 42–45. On pp. 92–93 he uses the old term cors(e)let to describe it. Cf. Wevers, p. 825.

were connected with wire and tied down with pieces of leather.[64] At later stages scale mails, then chain mails (first used by archers and charioteers), eventually also solid armors were developed for foot soldiers; but only the rich could afford them.[65] The development always went from light to heavier to all too heavy—and sometimes back to light, forming an endless cycle.[66] The high priest's "breastpiece of judgment" (Exod 28:15 ff.; 39:8 ff.) resembled a *thōrax*.[67] The diction of Eph 6:14 does not permit us to decide which material, form or weight of the *thōrax* Paul has in mind. However, since the context probably describes the equipment of a Roman infantryman of Paul's time,[68] translators and commentators usually assume that the apostle was thinking of the frontal metal piece, which is mentioned by Polybius, appears on contemporary images, reliefs and statues of soldiers, and is properly translated by "breastplate."[69] Indeed this part of a soldier's equipment was useful—but it was only the second-best protection of a man's chest. Whoever could afford it used the very best available: a scale or chain mail that covered chest and hips. Since elsewhere Paul has depicted the saints as rich heirs and noblemen,[70] he would be negligent and self-contradictory if at this point he insinuated that God provides them with no more than a breastplate, rather than with a mail as worn by the rich and by officers. The translation of the ambiguous *thōrax* by "cuirass" permits the reader to think of the best protection rather than only of armor mediocre in quality and effectiveness.

"Righteousness" belongs to the terminology of God's covenant with his people; e.g. Isa 11:4–5 demonstrates that it is an attribute and action of the Messiah. As little as truth could be defined merely by reference to the virtue of veracity, can "righteousness" be restricted to the moral sense of this term.[71] COMMENT VI will discuss whether the occurrence of "righteousness" in the ethical context of Eph 6 excludes the interpretation in the sense of "God's righteousness" which is unfolded in Rom 1:16–17; 3:21–31, etc. The same COMMENT will describe the dignity and responsibility which are imparted to the man who is chosen to be girded with truth and clothed with the breastcover of righteousness: he is made nothing less than a judge. The soldiers of Eph 6:10–20 fight their battle not only on fields but also in courtrooms. The fact that according to this exposition Eph 6:14 mixes war imagery with judgment sym-

---

[64] This type of harness left some vital spots unprotected, as in, e.g. King Ahab's case: I Kings 22:34.

[65] Polybius VI 23; Yadin, *Art of Warfare*, I, 84–85.

[66] The weight of Goliath's coat of scale or chain mail (not counting his bronze helmet and sheaves, and his spear) is given as 60 kilograms (ca. 130 pounds) I Sam [I Kings] 17:5. But even Saul's armor which may have ranged between 17 and 24 kilograms, was too heavy for David: I Sam 17:38–39.

[67] Philo (*spec. leg.* I 86) calls the woven and pearl-embroidered breastpiece *thōrakoeidēs*.

[68] Omitting, as will be shown in COMMENT III A, the greaves, the lighter and heavier spears mentioned in Polybius VI 23, and the camping and assault equipment listed in Josephus *bell.* II 93 ff.

[69] See the plates in J. Kromayer-G. Veith, after p. 448 for the Roman armor, after p. 80 for the Greek. Rev 9:9 mentions in the description of locusts "scales like iron breastplates."

[70] 1:18; 2:6; 3:6, 8, 12; 4:1; COMMENT II on 4:1–16. See also the ornamental and official meaning of the "girdle" which was earlier described.

[71] In Plato's philosophy, righteousness is the basic structure of the state: *resp.* I – IV, and of the human soul: *resp.* IV 443C, etc. According to Aristotle *eth. Nic.* V 3, 1129B, it is the first among the social virtues. Thomas Aquinas defines the "breastplate of righteousness" as the protection against desire for the neighbor's property. Calvin rules out the *justitia imputativa* and suggests *vitae innocentia*. P. Stuhlmacher, "Gerechtigkeit Gottes bei Paulus," FRLANT 87 (1965), 216, believes that in Eph 6:14 (as much as in 4:24; 5:9) "righteousness" is—in contrast to Paul's concept—completely "ethicized." Abbott speaks of the "uprightness of character." Haupt and Gaugler have come to similar conclusions: they propose that righteousness is "the quality of man that pleases God."

bolism is not strange. The same conflation occurs also in the OT, in Qumran and apocalyptic literature.[72]

15. *steadfast because the gospel of peace is strapped under your feet.* Lit. "having your feet strapped in readiness of the gospel . . ." A great puzzle in this line is the formula *en etoimasiā*. The noun *etoimasiā*, which is usually rendered by "readiness" or "preparation," never recurs in the NT, and its meaning in Eph 6:15 is obscure. Solutions have been proposed which emphasize either the equipment given, or the preparation carried out, or the preparedness achieved, or the mental disposition required.[73] However, the traditional interpretations appear to disregard (a) the special meaning which *etoimasiā* has in the LXX, (b) the special function of a soldier's footwear, (c) the absence in Eph 6 of any reference to the "beautiful feet" mentioned in Isa 52:7 and Rom 10:15.[74] Phillips and the authors of NEB have apparently taken these facts into consideration and translate *en etoimasiā* by "firmly," viz. "to give you a firm footing." Their version is supported by a thin chain of expositors that seems to begin with Chrysostom, is continued by A. Bynaeus in his monograph on "The Shoes of the Hebrews," and has never been completely broken off.[75] In COMMENT III C it will be argued that *etoimasiā* must be translated by a concept expressing solidity, firmness, solid foundation.[76]

The mention of the "gospel of peace" in the context of military imagery has been called by A. Harnack "a lofty paradox."[77] An OT example of the sudden transition from war to peace, or of a reference to a war that will bring peace, is found in Isa 11:4–9: the Messiah "smites the earth with the rod of his mouth and slays the wicked" with the breath of his lips in order to restore the para-

---

[72] God's victories are God's *sedaqot* (acts of gracious judgment) in, e.g. Judg 5:11; I Sam 12:7; Isa 56:1; Ps 7:6–13. At the time of judgment the sword of God is drawn: 1QH vi 27–34, esp. 29. The combination of might and right is praised in *Ps Sol* 17:42[37], the so-called Marseillaise of militant Judaism. The rider on the white horse, called Faithful and True, "judges and makes war in righteousness" (Rev 19:11). "War will be overcome by war" in the Last Judgment for "the basic theme in both the war and the judgment is the same," according to O. Bauernfeind, TWNTE, VI, 513. In western theology, the problematic concept of a "just war" seems to combine judgment and war in a similar way. But Eph 6 calls for a reexamination of this term because here Paul affirms neither that a cause can be so just as to justify a war with all available weapons, nor that the outcome of certain battles, as e.g. Oliver Cromwell seemed to believe, proves the righteousness of a cause or of its militant defenders; see R. Paul, *The Lord Protector*, repr. Grand Rapids: Eerdmans, 1964. A very subtle discussion of the so-called "just war" is found in, e.g. J. H. Yoder, *Karl Barth and the Problem of War*, Nashville: Abingdon, 1970. In Ephesians the promotion of righteousness (in the biblical sense, i.e. of faithfulness, salvation and peace for the poor and needy) is in itself the war to be waged by the saints.

[73] See fn. 214 to COMMENT III C for examples.

[74] (a) In the Nestle and GNT Greek text of the NT, the words *en etoimasiā* are printed in bold type and JB uses special print in order to mark them as a quote from the OT. However, no equivalent to these two words is found in Isa 52:7 to which Eph 6:15 obviously alludes. Which text, then, is cited—if the two words are a quote at all? Not only the modern editors of the Greek text but the author of Eph 6:15 himself may have thought of the LXX passages: II Esd[Ezra] 2:68; 3:3; Pss 9:38[10:17]; 64:10[65:9]; 88:15[89:14]; Wisd Sol 13:12; Nahum 2:4; Zech 5:11, that is, of the only occurrences of *etoimasiā* in the LXX. Or they may have had in mind one of the over a hundred LXX texts in which cognates of this noun are used, i.e. the verb *etoimazō* and the adjective *etoimos*. (b) Since the strapping of something under one's feet figures among other acts of arming oneself, boots rather than sandals may be meant. (c) The feet of the messenger who runs over the mountains are obviously free of any footwear—see COMMENT III C 3. "The boot of the tramping warrior in the tumult" (Isa 9:15) is one thing, "the [bare] feet of a [welcome] herald" (Isa 52:7) or of a Greek or Roman athlete another.

[75] See Bengel; Buscarlet; E. Hatch, *Essays in Biblical Greek* (Oxford: Clarendon, 1889), pp. 51–55; cf. E. H. Blakeney, ET 55 (1943), 138; J. A. F. Gregg, ET 56 (1944), 54.

[76] Cf. Philip 1:28; "Not frightened in anything by your opponents." The exhortation to be men and stand solid is found in I Cor 16:13; II Cor 1:24; Philip 1:27, etc.

[77] *Eine erhabene Paradoxie*, p. 13; cf. Dibelius. Abbott speaks of an oxymoron, and Chrysostom expressed the coincidence of opposites by stating, "When we make war with the devil we have peace with God."

disiacal peace between wolf and lamb. According to Zech 9:10; 12:6–14, he who cuts off "the chariot," the "war horse," the "battle bow," "shall command peace to the nations"; Judah will be like a "blazing pot" among the "peoples round about"; "on that day the feeblest" in Jerusalem "shall be like David," and then a "spirit of compassion and supplication" will be "poured out." In the same context in which Paul speaks of the "meekness and gentleness of the Messiah," he also mentions "weapons of warfare" with which arguments and obstacles are destroyed (II Cor 10:1–6). The "peace" and the "gospel" to which Eph 6:15 refers can only be the "peace made" and "proclaimed" by the Messiah which was described in 2:13–18. It is not a victory of men inside God's kingdom over men outside it that makes the saints stand "steadfast." Rather the Messianic "peace" which has united and will further draw together "those far" and "those near" gives the strength to resist non-human, demonic attacks however spiritual their origin.

16. *With all* [*this equipment*]. The reading *en pāsin*, lit. "in all," is replaced by *epi pāsin* in a great number of MSS.[78] Both variants probably have the same sense: "in addition to all," rather than "above all," or "at all times."[79] There is no indication that the shield is more necessary, or necessary for a more extended period, than the other pieces of equipment.

take up faith as the shield. Lit. "having taken up the shield of faith." In fn. 38 references were given to show that "take up" is a technical military term. The translation of Greek participles (such as, lit. "having strapped," vs. 15, and "having taken up," vs. 16) by imperatives was discussed in fn. 23 to 3:14–21. The Greek term *thyreos* is derived from *thyra* ("door") and describes the large, door-shaped or vaulted "shield," in contrast to the small, round, convex shield, *aspis* (also *pelta*).[80] Originally the small shield consisted of wickerwork covered with hide, and the large shield was made of wood and leather.[81] Later the frame and the boss(es), and in some cases the whole shield, were fabricated of metal, bronze, iron, or even gold.[82] People of high rank used the services of a shield bearer.[83] The Roman legionary's *scutum*, to which Paul alludes, had an iron frame and sometimes a metal boss at the center of the front. This shield served well even against incendiary missiles when its several layers of

---

[78] The same variant readings occur in Luke 16:26.

[79] The arguments proffered by e.g. Robinson, p. 215, Abbott, p. 186, Dibelius, pp. 98–99, Oepke, p. 313, n. 8, discourage translations such as given in RSV; JB; NTTEV. Cf. Luke 3:20: "He [Herod] added this to them all" (*epi pāsin*). Conzelmann, pp. 90–91, appears to believe that the "shield of faith" was added by the author of Ephesians to the traditional OT elements used before and after vs. 16: "The concept . . . of faith . . . holds all other concepts together."

[80] The Hebrew equivalent for the first is *māgēn*, for the second, *sinnāh* or *šelet*. In the LXX, the terms for the large and the small shield are often confused, or one of them is translated by "weapon" (*oplon*); see e.g. LXX Ps 34[35]:2; MT Ps 46[MT 46]:3, 9. Snodgrass, *passim* (see "shield" in the Index and esp. pp. 104, 123) shows that occasionally *thyreos* means not only the large figure eight-shaped, rectangular or tower shield, but also a smaller, e.g. oval, protective weapon. In Polybius II 30:3; VI 23:2 the diverse Roman shields are described.

[81] Thucydides II 72. Therefore fire could burn a shield: Ezek 39:9 (LXX Ps 45:10[MT Ps 46:9] has "chariots" instead of "shields"). Unless special measures were taken, such a shield was useless against burning arrows and javelins.

[82] II Sam 8:7; I Kings 10:16; 14:26–27; II Chron 9:16; 12:9–11; I Macc 6:2, 39; 14:24; 15:18; *Test. Levi* VI 1. The possession of golden shields indicated wealth, the gift of an especially heavy shield of gold sealed a treaty. Such shields, properly arranged and displayed, were considered beautiful: Ezek 27:10–11; cf. Song of Songs 4:4. Pride and might were expressed by shields: Ps 3:3; Nahum 2:3; Job 41:15. The bronze shields of the Qumran army were polished like a mirror and loaded with ornaments of gold, silver, bronze, precious stones, according to 1QM V 4–6.

[83] As in the case of Goliath, Saul, and Jonathan: I Sam 14:1–17; 17:7; 31:4–6.

leather were soaked in water before the battle.[84] Under Emperor Constantine, the heavy *scutum* was abandoned in favor of the lighter oval *clipeus* or round *parma*.

It is clear that a shield of any form served for protection and could therefore be considered a merely defensive weapon.[85] Yet men advancing behind their huge shields, even the *thyreoi*, were as threatening in the ancient world as soldiers riding in an armored car are today; and closely formed units, advancing shield by shield and with a compact cover of shields above their heads, were as much instruments of attack as modern tanks.[86] While in Greek literature outside the Bible (also in Ignatius *Polyc.* VI 2) "shield" is not used in a figurative sense, and while it occurs nowhere else in the NT, the canonical Psalms describe God as a "shield" with surprising frequency, and other OT books use the same image.[87] According to Zech 12:8, the effect of God's shielding is that "the feeblest" is like David, and the "house of David" like God. Other results are described, e.g. in Ps 18.[88] It is most likely that OT imagery was in Paul's mind when he compared faith with a "shield"; just as e.g. in Ps 7:10, 13 the divine "shield" and the "fiery shafts" of the godless are mentioned in the same context, so Paul describes the "shield of faith" as a protection against the "fiery missiles" of the evil one. While in I Thess 5:8 "faith and love" are the essence of the "cuirass," in Eph 6:16 the large "shield" consists of "faith"; in turn, Wisd Sol 5:19 identifies the small shield with "invincible holiness."

What is meant by faith in Eph 6:16? In the Psalm texts mentioned in fn. 87, not only God, that is, Yahweh himself, but also his "favor" and "salvation" are called a "shield"; sometimes the terms "strength," "help," "sun," and "king" are parallels of "shield."[89] The Messiah may be called "shield" in Ps 84:9. These OT utterances make it unlikely that only man's faith is meant in a text as drenched in OT thought pattern as is Eph 6. Certainly human faith is not excluded, for "He [God] is a shield to those taking refuge in Him" (Prov 30:5, etc.): the exhortation to have faith and to "fear not" may have one of its *Sitze*

---

[84] See, e.g. Josephus *bell.* III 173, for a corresponding use of rawhides (from recently flayed oxen) on palisades. The attribution of a fire-extinguishing quality to the shield has puzzled many interpreters of Eph 6:16, among them Calvin, Dibelius, Oepke. But it is not paradoxical: (wet) leather would serve the purpose: see Thucydides II 75. However, if a shield was not properly prepared against fiery missiles it would have to be thrown away.

[85] Abbott and others.

[86] The terror produced by shields is reflected in, e.g. Isa 22:6; 37:33; Jer 46[LXX 26]:3, 9; Job 15:26; II Kings 19:32; see also Yadin, *Art of Warfare*, pp. 13 ff., 83 ff.; 155, 196 f. Compact units of warriors holding their large shields side-by-side before and above themselves, were (first?) used by the Assyrians for approaching the gates and walls of a besieged city. The Romans called this formation a *testudo*. Josephus *bell.* III 270–71 describes how it operated; eventually, burning oil thrown from the city wall could frustrate even such an attack. An allusion to a *testudo* may occur in Ezek 26:8. See Kromayer-Veith, plate 51, for a picture.

[87] Gen 15:1; II Sam 22:3, 31, 36; Ps 3:3 (but see Dahood's reading: *māgōn* instead of *magēn*, "suzerain" instead of "shield," *Psalms I* (AB, vol. 16, 16–18, 45, etc.); Pss 5:12; 18:2, 30; 28:7; 33:20; 47:10; 59:11; 84:9, 11; 89:18; 115:10; 144:2; Prov 2:7; 30:5. Perhaps the LXX translators make a concession to Greek thought and diction when they consistently avoid the use of the noun "shield" for God or for his help. In most cases they substitute a verb: God "shields" or "protects." Sometimes they also use for their translation a noun with verbal sense such as *antilēmpsis* ("defense"): Ps 88:19[MT 89:18], or *hyperaspistēs* ("protector"): Ps 17:3, 31[MT 18:2, 30]. Cf. *Test. Benjamin* III 4; IV 3; *Ps. Sol.* 7:6[7]; *Sib. Or.* III 705–6.

[88] Images related to the meaning of "shield" are "rock," "refuge," "fortress"; see e.g. Ps 31:1–4. In Ps 144:1–2 the terms, "He who trains my hands for war, my rock, my fortress, my stronghold, my deliverer, my shield, and he in whom I take refuge, who subdues the people under him" are used as synonyms. In this text, even "refuge" and "fortress" include the meaning of aggression and victory.

[89] Pss 5:12; 7:10; 28:7; 33:20; 115:10; 84:11; 89:18.

im Leben in the Holy War.[90] But above the absence of fear among the people, and higher than their own trust and faith, stands the faithfulness of God himself, and the faithful service of the one who is anointed by God.[91] The "good fight of the faith" could not be fought by any man (cf. I Tim 6:12) if man had to rely on his own faith: "I believe; help my unbelief!" (Mark 9:24). The "faith" to which "victory over the world" is given is as much "born from God" (I John 5:4) as the brotherly love among men is founded upon and preceded by the love of God for men (I John 4:10, 19). The same "shield" which Yahweh is asked to take up in Ps 35:2 is to be seized by all the saints, according to Eph 6:16.

to quench the fire-missiles of the evil one. In fn. 84 it was stated that in the ancient world wet leather was used to extinguish burning missiles. Eph 6:16 speaks only of "missiles," not of burning oil poured down from a city wall. Among the "fiery missiles" most frequently used were arrows or spears tipped with tow and dipped in pitch.[92] Arrow-throwing machines had the effect of mitrailleuses; much heavier loads of burning materials were launched from catapults. When Paul calls the shield an effective defense, he is probably thinking only of the lighter ammunition—though the location of the inimical hosts "in the heavens" (vs. 12) does not totally exclude the idea of artillery shooting its lightning-like rounds at the saints from afar, with deafening noise.[93] In Eph 6 only the *enemies* of God and of the saints make use of fire. This is consistent with the fact that here Yahweh's particular offensive weapons in the Holy War are not included among the weapons given to the saints.[94] But it differs from those OT and apocalyptic utterances that speak of God's appearance in fire and of the use of fiery missiles or torrents by God and his angels.[95] In Eph 6 the saints themselves do not spew fire at the principalities

[90] Exod 14:13–14; Deut 20:3; Josh 8:1, etc.; cf. the discharge of all who are afraid in Josh 7:3. Von Rad, pp. 11–12.

[91] In the exposition of the words "[saved] through faith" (see the first NOTE on 2:8) the distinctiveness and the reciprocal character of the faithfulness of God, of the Messiah, and of the saints were discussed, and references were given that force the interpreter to speak of both a triple and a single meaning of "faith." Thomas Aquinas leads the host of those expositors who call "faith" a (theological) and moral "virtue" that is presupposed by all other virtues and serves to extinguish the "fiery missiles" of the burning desires. Gaugler goes far beyond this interpretation; according to him faith is not only reliance upon God's power but is itself a protective power. Even more radical is K. Barth's interpretation ("Des Christen Wehr und Waffen," *Eine Schweizer Stimme*, pp. 125–26) saying that God himself is the armor of the Christians. The congruence of the terms "putting on the armor of God," "putting on the new man," "putting on Christ" in the Pauline exhortation (I Thess 5:8; Gal 3:28; Rom 13:12, 14; Eph 4:24; 6:11–17, etc.), suggests that Christ and *his* faith can be meant by the "shield of faith." The allusion to Isa 11:4–5 in Eph 6:14 has clearly shown that a weapon of the Messiah is given to the saints; the allusions to Isa 59:17 and Wisd Sol 5:17–20 reveal that divine attributes are in mind.

[92] Herodotus VIII 52. The term *belos*, in our translation rendered by "missile," means "arrow," according to WBLex, 138. Actually any sort of missile or weapon could be meant, including trees, rocks, axes, thunderbolts, etc.; see J. J. Wettstein, *Novum Testamentum Graece*, II, Amsterdam: Donner, 1752, on Eph 6:16.

[93] See Diels-Schramm, for a discussion of Philo the Mechanic's *belopoeica* (esp. LXXXII 2; LXXXVII 10) in which defensive and offensive tactics for an effective use of catapults are described or proposed.

[94] See COMMENTS I–III.

[95] Yahweh appears "with flaming fire at his right hand": Deut 33:2 (if this translation is correct, the imagery resembles that of Babylonian and Assyrian war-gods, including Marduk and Assur, who hold lightning or arrows or other weapons in their hand). God appears in fire at the bush, on Mount Sinai, in the wilderness, in battle: Exod 3:2–3; 19:16–19; 13:21–22; 40:38; Isa 66:15–16, etc. "Our God is a consuming fire": Heb 12:29; cf. 12:18–19. "He has prepared his deadly weapons making his arrows fiery shafts": Pss 7:13; cf. 21:9. The "spirit of judgment" is a "spirit of burning"; for by fire God executes his judgment: Isa 4:4; 66:15–16, etc. This is illustrated by the destruction of rebels: Num 16:35; of servants of the king and enemies of Elijah: II Kings 1:10–14;

and powers. Instead of flame-throwers and napalm-canisters by which the opponents and their strongholds might be burned, they are given shields which "enable them to quench" (only) the fire thrown at them. The fiery attacks endured now are unlike the fire of the last judgment of God to which all men and all the creation will be exposed (II Thess 1:8; II Peter 3:12, etc.). The character and effect of the Devil's missiles are distinctly penultimate. But just as in many apocalyptic and NT texts, the saints are warned: fire can belong to hell and can be a manifestation of the realm of the Devil.[96] Especially in the Thanksgiving Psalms of Qumran, reference is made to "arrows of the Pit," "flames of the spear like [lit. in] fire that consumes trees," the "torrents of Belial" that devour forests and the very foundations of the mountains.[97] The term "fire-missiles of the evil one"[98] confirms the impression that parallel imagery is used in the NT and Qumran,[99] but does not demonstrate the literary dependence of Paul's letter upon the Thanksgiving Psalms. In fn. 95 evidence was given of that OT and apocalyptic tradition from which both Qumran and Ephesians probably derived their specific formulations.[100] In particular, one application of the weapons-imagery is common to Qumran and Ephesians: Unlike Isa 57:5 and I Cor 7:9,[101] the metaphor "fiery," is not applied to the way in which evil desire, lust, and temptation "burn" in man. Rather, external threats to the saints are meant as caused by persecution or assimilation imposed upon them by religious, cultural, political forces in their environment. Just as the outstanding men of faith, i.e. "Gideon, Barak, Samson, Jephtha, David, Samuel and the Prophets . . . through faith . . . quenched raging fire" (Heb 11:32–34), so all the saints "will be able" to resist the seemingly superior weaponry of the evil spirits that possess cosmic (not only psychic or carnal) power. The same protection against fire which in Dan 3:22–28 is attributed on the one hand to a man whose "appearance is like a son of the gods," and on the other to the "trust" of "Shadrach, Meshach and Abednego in God," is in Eph 6 provided by the "shield of faith."

---

[96] Sir 48:3; of all enemies on the Day of the Lord: Mal 4:1; cf. LXX Esther 8:18x; 1QH vi 17–18; 1QpHab x 13; II Peter 3:7; Rev 9:18; 20:9, etc. According to Matt 3:11 John the Baptist spoke of a judgment-baptism by "Spirit and fire." Num 21:30, etc. shows that the Israelites could serve as instruments of God's judgment: by fire they destroy the Moabites. "Like a blazing pot in the midst of wood, they devour the nations" around them: Zech 12:6. Jewish apocryphal literature affirms that the Man from the Sea (the Messiah) overcomes his enemies by the "fiery stream . . . flaming breath . . . storm of sparks" issuing from his mouth: IV Ezra 13:10. East of Eden, the cherubim used a flaming sword: Gen 3:24, and God's heavenly hosts shall use fiery weapons: II (Slavonic) Enoch 29:1–3 (also 1QM xi 10?); II Bar 27:9; 48:8; Sib. Or. iii 54, 72–73, 287, 672–73, 810, etc.; 1QH xiv 1; 1QH viii 12. According to some of these texts, God uses Beliar to execute his judgment.

[96] Matt 3:10–12; 5:22; 18:8–9; 25:41; Jude 7; II Peter 3:7; Rev 21:8, etc.; I Enoch 54:1; 90:24–27; 100:9, cf. 100:7; Test. Judah xxv 3, etc.; also 1QS iv 13.

[97] 1QH ii 26; iii 16, 27–31 (viii 20?); xvii 13; cf. Kuhn, p. 300.

[98] That is, of the devil. The term "the evil one" may go back to the language of Jesus himself; it is certainly widespread in the NT and expresses an early tradition; see II Thess 3:3; Matt 6:13; 13:19, 38; John 17:15; I John 2:13–14; 5:18–19; cf. Dibelius, p. 99.

[99] For example, the idea of testing by fire is found in 1QM xvii 1; I Cor 3:13, 15; II Peter 3:7 (also Mark 9:49?).

[100] Burrows, Dead Sea Scrolls, p. 337, refers to one of the 1QH texts (ii 26?) that speaks of "lances flashing in the sun" (not of flaming darts) and therefore uses imagery that differs from Eph 6. But the parallel passages in 1QH do not support this view, and Braun, QuNT, I, 223, points out that the difference between Qumran and Ephesians consists rather in the notion of an imminent Holy War, promoted by Qumran, and the stress which is laid in Ephesians upon putting on the armor and a conduct appropriate to the spiritual weapons.

[101] See also IV Macc 3:17; Thomas Aquinas' and Abbott's exposition of Eph 6:16, and T. S. Eliot's "Fire Sermon" in The Waste Land.

17. *Take salvation as your helmet.* Lit. ". . . the helmet of the saving [person, thing, or event]."[102] A helmet was made of leather, bronze, iron, or, in special cases, gold. What was originally no more than a protective cap developed—especially by the addition of crests—into a heavy, decorative, and expensive item. An inside lining of felt or sponge made the weight bearable. Nothing short of an ax or hammer could pierce a heavy helmet, and in some cases a hinged visor added frontal protection. Roman soldiers wore a bronze helmet equipped with cheek pieces.[103] Other, sometimes very decorative, helmets were worn by officers at official occasions.

According to a Jewish Midrash, the "helmet of salvation" mentioned in Isa 59:17 is a crown which belongs, together with other "garments of glory," to the Messiah's adornment when he will stand on a mountain and announce to Israel that salvation is nigh.[104] Sometimes in Hebrew the nouns "salvation" and "peace" (*teši'āh, šālōm*, etc.) mean "victory."[105] Since the Greeks did not use the word "helmet" in a figurative sense, the formula "helmet of salvation" must be interpreted in the light of its biblical background, that is, of Isa 59:17 and the parallel term "helmet of the hope of salvation" (I Thess 5:8). Most likely, a "helmet of victory" is in mind which is more ornate than a battle helmet and demonstrates that the battle has been won: the saints are to "take" this helmet as a gift from God.[106] They go into battle and stand the heat of the day in full confidence of the outcome, with no uncertainty in their minds;[107] for they wear the same battle-proven helmet which God straps on his head (according to the original meaning of Isa 59:17) and which is defined by "impartial justice" in Wisd Sol 5:18.[108] At the same time an act of democratization and of knighting takes place. God's victory is passed down to all of the saints, and the saints are treated as people worthy to be elevated to God and to share in his victory. Is a future or a present "salvation" denoted by the term *sōtērios*?[109]

---

[102] In non-biblical Greek, the adjective *sōtērios* means "saving, bringing safety." The adjective is also used as a substantive: the masculine singular can mean as much as "savior" (*sōtēr*), the neuter plural: "deliverance," also "thanks-offerings for deliverance," or "[a physician's] fee," see LSLex, 1751. In the LXX several Hebrew terms denoting help, salvation, peace, are rendered by the singular *sōtērion* (with and without article), often in a context speaking of sacrifices for deliverance. *Sōtērion* in the sense of "salvation" occurs in the NT only when the immediate dependence upon the LXX is obvious: Luke 2:30; 3:6; Acts 28:28 (Robinson). But the word is used in its original, adjectival sense in Titus 2:11. Theodoret and Bengel give a strictly Christological interpretation: they hold that the masculine of the adjective *sōtērios* is used in Eph 6:17 and that Jesus Christ himself is "The Saving One."

[103] See Oepke, p. 314; Yadin, *Art of Warfare*, pp. 85–86; Wevers, p. 825.

[104] Beth ha-Midr. III 73:17; quoted in StB, III, 618.

[105] E.g. Zeph 3:17; Ps 118:15; Prov 21:31. Also Isa 59:17?

[106] Only in connection with the "helmet" is the verb *dechomai* ("*receive*") used; but this does not indicate that the other pieces of armor which are "put on" or "taken up" are gifts to any lesser degree than the "helmet." *Dechomai* is omitted in some MSS and the Italic versions. E.g. in Luke 2:28; 16:6–7; 22:17 it means the same as *lambanō*, "to take." In LXX Isa 59:17 and Wisd Sol 5:18 a more technical term is used: "he strapped on" (*peritithēmi*).

[107] Analogies to, and differences from, the Qumranite and Stoic conviction of ultimate victory will be mentioned in COMMENT II.

[108] For reasons unknown the text of Wisd Sol 5 uses for "helmet" the word *korys*, rather than *kephaleia* which is found in Isa 59; I Thess 5:8 and Eph 6. This difference indicates that Paul is more directly dependent on Isa 59 than on Wisd Sol 5. Ignatius *Polyc.* VI 2 follows the choice of Isaiah and Paul, but declares "faith" as the metaphorical meaning of the helmet. In turn, Ps 18:35 speaks of the "shield of salvation." Thus the interchangeability of the metaphors and their allegorical interpretation is richly documented, see also fn 61.

[109] In the last NOTE on 2:5 the futuristic and other meanings of the terms "save," "salvation" have been discussed. E.g. Calvin and Schlier emphasize that 6:17 points primarily to the hope for (future) salvation. Oepke, p. 315, however, does not exclude the trust in that salvation which is already given. The use of the perfect tense of the verb "to save" in 2:5, 8 supports his interpretation.

I Thess 5:8 speaks of the "hope of salvation," and in Pauline passages such as Rom 5:9–10 "salvation" does not come before the day of the Last Judgment. In the exposition of Eph 6:17, a decision for either a futuristic or a present concept of salvation cannot be made. The "darkest day" on which the described battle takes place (6:13) is a penultimate day in which the same grace that is given to the present aeon manifests itself as eternal grace (cf. 6:24).

the sword provided by the Spirit, that is, the word of God. Lit. "the sword of the Spirit, which is . . ." The Greek term used for "sword" (machaira) denotes a short sword which is a more handy defensive and aggressive weapon than the long sword (rhomphaiā) mentioned in Luke 2:35 and Rev 1:16; 2:12; 19:15, etc. Machaira is also the name of a knife used for sacrifice or for carving meat (see Heb 4:12) and of a dagger or a curved saber. But in the context of the Roman legionary's weaponry from which Paul selects his metaphors in Eph 6, it can only signify the short, straight sword of the Roman soldiers. This machaira was not only a symbol of jurisdiction over life and death (Rom 13:4), but also of persecution and senseless bloodshed (Rom 8:35; Rev 6:4). Grammatical reasons and the context permit the following interpretation of vs. 17b: the metaphor "sword" means the Spirit,[110] the "Spirit" in turn is identified with "God's word." However, in Greek, the words "that is" (ho estin) do not always refer to the immediately preceding word, and the neuter gender of the relative pronoun does not necessarily point to the preceding neuter noun. Either the whole preceding sentence can be the referent, or any name or noun of masculine, feminine, or neuter gender that is used in the context either in the singular or the plural form.[111] A double interpretation of the "sword" (a) by "Spirit" and (b) by "word of God" would not be in line with the context which gives only one meaning to each weapon. Also, the simple equation of "Spirit" and "word" which would inhere in the double interpretation poses almost insuperable problems.[112] Therefore, the Greek genitive tou pneumatos ("of the Spirit") either substitutes for the adjective "spiritual" which occurs in terms such as spiritual blessing, spiritual gifts, spiritual hymns (1:3; I Cor 14:1; Eph 5:19)—in this case Paul speaks of a spiritual (or allegorical?) sword—or tou pneumatos may be the genitive of origin or authorship, in which case "the sword given by this Spirit" or "the sword provided by the Spirit" is the proper

---

[110] In the Greek text of vss. 14–17a, after the naming of a weapon, the terms "righteousness, gospel, faith, salvation" were always used with the article and the genitive form. BDF, 167, speaks of an "appositive genitive" which describes the contents or substance of the preceding word; cf. "house of the tent," "earnest of the Spirit," "sign of the circumcision," "wall of the fence," in II Cor 5:1, 5; Rom 4:11; Eph 2:14. But BDF does not mention Eph 6:17 as an example of this kind of genitive, and Abbott, p. 187, denies the presence of a "genitive of apposition" at this place; he suggests for 6:17 the translation, "word of God is given by the Spirit."

[111] NT examples of the comprehensive meaning of "that is" are: Eph 5:5; Col 1:24; Matt 1:23; 12:4; Mark 12:42; Acts 2:32; 11:30; Gal 2:10; Heb 7:2, etc. Variant readings of e.g. John 19:17; Col 2:17; 3:14 show that not all copyists were willing to endorse the neglect of the preceding noun's gender or the omission of the attraction of the relative pronoun to the gender of the following predicate.

[112] A poetic parallelism, such as "smite with the rod of his mouth" and "slay with the breath of his lips" (Isa 11:4) appears to support the identification of word and Spirit. Cf. I Cor 2:4, JB: "The word I spoke, the gospel I proclaimed . . . carried conviction by spiritual power"; John 6:63: "The words that I have spoken to you are spirit and life"; see also II Cor 3:17. Conzelmann, p. 91, affirms that the three nouns "sword," "Spirit," and "word" are equated. But Schlier rejects this interpretation: the wording of Eph 6:17 does not bear out the synonymous character of Spirit and the word of God. In Eph 1:13; 2:17–18 and elsewhere in the NT where "the word" and "the Spirit" are mentioned in one breath, the two are never used as synonymous or interchangeable terms.

translation of the Greek text, as Abbott suggests. The widespread and emphatic Pauline utterances that attribute the Christians' faith and testimony to the gift and work of the Holy Spirit are then the closest parallels.[113] The term *rhēma* which here and in 5:26 denotes "word" means in Pauline diction a specifically weighty, be it creative, revelatory, prophetic, or otherwise binding pronouncement.[114] Because of the parenthetic context, especially 4:25, 29; 5:13, 18–19, a reference to prophetic speech, to the singing of spiritual hymns, and to prayer (see vs. 18) cannot be excluded. In addition, *rhēma* can mean words of God that are found in the OT,[115] or words of the Lord that are quoted by Paul[116] (and later gathered in the Gospels). Whether a traditional or a freshly inspired "word of God" is in mind, this "word" can be called the cutting edge of the Spirit—but it must be maintained that the word itself, not the Spirit, is the sword. "He made my mouth like a sharp sword" (Isa 49:2). Cf. Heb 4:12: "The word of God is living and active, sharper than any two-edged sword." Just like the Messiah in Isa 11, so all the saints in Ephesus can wield the sword of the word only because they are inspired.[117]

Paul's reference to the "sword" of the "word" is at first sight too obscure to determine which of the various "words" he may have had in mind. But where the study of OT precedents fails to give an answer, the context is not mute. In 2:17 and 6:15 Paul has spoken of "proclaiming peace," cf. 6:19. In the very next verse Paul will speak simply and with great emphasis of "prayer." Therefore it is probable that the "word of God," which he calls a "sword," has to do most directly with the preaching of the gospel and with prayer, or is identified with them. The OT pre-history of the allegorization of the sword, the use of speeches, prayers, and yells in battles, and the alternatives which are thereby offered to the interpretation of Eph 6, will be briefly sketched at the end of COMMENT III D.

18. *In the Spirit pray.* The connection of these and the following words with the preceding enumeration and interpretation of the six parts of the armor is very close. In the Greek text the present participle of the verbs "pray" and "stay awake" (or "watch") may refer to putting on the whole armor, or to taking up the sword alone. In consequence, persistent "prayer" can be the essence and modality of the whole process of arming oneself, or only of the seizing of the sword. However, in ethical contexts the participles can also substitute for imperatives[118] and introduce a new thought, as the weighty formula "in the Spirit" (in Greek, at the end of this verse) suggests. The relationship of the Holy "Spirit" to prayer, and the question whether vs. 18 is a combination or an interpretation of the weapons listed in vss. 14–17, will be discussed in COMMENT I. Often prayer has been interpreted as the seventh piece of armor, but some exegetes assert that it expresses the metaphorical sense of all arms mentioned and of their use in daily life; see also COMMENT VI.

---

[113] I Cor 2:1–16; 7:40; 12:3; 14, *passim;* Gal 3:1–5; Eph 3:5; cf. Matt 10:19–20; John 3:34; 14:26; 20:22–23; Acts 2:4, 17–18; 4:8; 10:44–46; 15:28, etc.

[114] See the second half of COMMENT IV E on Eph 5:21–33.

[115] Gaugler gives an example: the way in which Jesus, according to Matt 4 par., uses words from Deuteronomy as weapons against the devil's temptations.

[116] I Thess 4:15; I Cor 7:10, etc.; cf. Acts 20:35.

[117] The continued inspiration of all Christians which is presupposed in Ephesians was discussed in COMMENT III on 1:15–23. Cf. 5:18–19.

[118] Cf. Dibelius, and the discussion of the participles in the exposition of 3:17 and 4:2.

at all times through every kind of prayer and petition. . . . in persevering intercession for all the saints. Lit. "at all times through all prayer and petition . . . in all perseverance and petition for all the saints." Abbott suggests the translation "prayer of every form." The word "all" is repeated no fewer than four times in the Greek text. In each case it expresses a manifold universal concern: (a) for man's whole lifetime, in all its years, days, hours and minutes; (b) for the whole range and all forms of public and private prayer, including the desperate cry, "Help!"; (c) for the whole mental, emotional, and physical range of personal existence, and the energies present or to be received and used in the head, the heart, and the limbs; (d) for the whole community of the church, particularly its weakest members. Nothing less is suggested than that the life and strife of the saints be one great prayer to God, that this prayer be offered in ever new forms however good or bad the circumstances, and that this prayer not be self-centered but express the need and hope of all the saints. Because the formula "to pray a prayer" is idiomatic[119] (just as "dreaming a dream" or "loving with love"), the words (lit.) "through all prayer and petition" belong to the verb "pray" rather than to the remote verb "stand" at the beginning of vs. 14, Abbott's opinion to the contrary notwithstanding.

Here, as in other passages, the apostle composes a list of different terms denoting prayer.[120] The several forms of prayer can be as little separated from one another and used selectively as any of the divine weapons mentioned in vss. 14–17. Although a sharp definition of each one cannot be given, all probably have specific meanings and functions. In addition, one term (*deēsis*) occurs twice in 6:18—each time with a different meaning.[121] Theodoret and Grotius explained "prayer" (*proseuchē*) as an entreaty "to obtain good" (*precatio*), and sharply distinguished it from a "petition" (*deēsis*) which they interpreted as a request to God "to avert evil" (*deprecatio*).[122] But according to Trench "this distinction is altogether arbitrary." A differentiation based on the use of the two nouns may be important: *proseuchē* and the cognate verb always mean calling on God, whereas *deēsis* can also signify a petition addressed to man. In many NT occurrences the first is more general and comprehensive, the second more specific (Calvin, Bengel). But the two can also be used interchangeably; a difference in grades of fervor, or between inwardness and outwardness, is not inherent in them. It is probable that at the beginning of Eph 6:18 both terms together form a hendiadys[123] and describe adoration, while the second noun (*deēsis*) means "intercession" when used alone toward the end of the verse (Dibelius). *Proskarterēsis* (perseverance) occurs only here in the NT and is very rare in pre-NT Greek. Much more widespread is the verb *proskartereō*, "to persist obstinately," "to adhere fiercely," "to devote oneself to something."[124] In the NT, it usually means adherence (with unshakable tenacity)

[119] See Philip 1:4; James 5:17.
[120] Eph 1:15–16; Rom 1:8–10, 15–16; Philip 1:3–4; 4:6; Col 4:2–3; cf. I Tim 2:1, etc.
[121] For the following see esp. R. C. Trench, *Synonyms of the New Testament* (repr. Grand Rapids: Eerdmans, 1969), pp. 188–92, and H. Greeven, TWNTE, II, 40–42; idem and J. Herrman, TWNTE, II, 775–808.
[122] The verb *deō* from which *deēsis* is derived, means originally "to lack, to miss, to stand in need." Cf. the use of *deēsis* in the sense of "need" by Aristotle *rhet.* II 1385A.
[123] Cf. LXX Jer 11:14; III Kings[I Kings] 8:45; II Chron 6:19; Acts 1:14 var. lect.; Ignatius *Magn.* VII 1.
[124] Six times in Acts, also in Rom 12:12; 13:6; Col 4:2; Mark 3:9; cf. Ignatius *Phila.* VIII 1.

to prayer, but it can also denote the firm attachment to, e.g. a person or a doctrine. In each case an ever new decision and passionate fidelity is in mind, not a mechanical attachment as if by glue or magnetic force.[125]

To this end stay awake. The purpose of staying awake is "praying," rather than putting on arms. The term *agrypneō,* which is used here, originally has a different sense from the verb *grēgoreō* which occurs more frequently in the NT, especially in the exhortation to "watch and pray." *Grēgoreō* is found in the parallel Col 4:2 and means, "to watch, to be vigilant"; it describes e.g. a servant's *or* a soldier's duty.[126] *Agrypneō,* however, means literally, "to lie sleepless, to pass a sleepless night, to suffer from insomnia," and is used in the NT for a servant's attitude, without implying that his service is of military character.[127] Still, in the NT and in later literature both verbs are used as synonyms. The choice made in Eph 6:18 for the more civilian *agrypneō* instead of the more military *grēgoreō* indicates that the author did not intend to call prayer and watchfulness for prayer a part of the saints' military equipment. See COMMENT I. In COMMENT VI a study will be made of the literal and metaphorical, the historical and eschatological meanings of the term "watch and pray."

19. *especially for me.* The translation of *kai hyper emou* by "and [pray also] for me"[128] fails to do justice to the shade of meaning which the conjunction *kai* ("and, also, even") has at this point. In the Greek text the preposition "for" (*peri*) before "the saints" in vs. 18 is less precise than the analogous preposition *hyper* before "me" in vs. 19.[129] The combination of *kai* with the more pointed *hyper* makes it most likely that (just as in 5:18) "*kai* introduces a special case" (Abbott). The reason why Paul puts himself so much in the foreground will be outlined in COMMENT VII.

[. *Pray*] *that the word may be given to me to open my lips.* Lit. ". . . in the opening of my mouth." Probably under the influence of the parallel statement in Col 4:3, RSV, "that God may open to us a door for the word," some expositors see in Eph 6:19 a reference to an "opportunity for the gospel."[130] Indeed, the metaphors *topos* (in e.g. 4:27) and *thyrā* ("door") can have this meaning.[131] In particular, either an "opening" to the doors of Paul's prison, or an opening of the "door of faith" (Acts 14:27) to Paul's prosecutors, judges and a wider public, or the coincidence of both "openings" may be considered the one

[125] Notably absent from the terms Paul uses to decribe prayer in Eph 6, are the terms *euchē, eucharistiā* and *enteuxis* and the cognate verbs, see, e.g. James 5:15-16; II Cor 13:7, 9; I Thess 3:10; Rom 1:8; Col 2:7; 4:2; I Tim 2:1; 4:5; Rom 8:27, 34. The first may be avoided by the apostle because it could mean "vow," as in Acts 18:18; 21:23; cf. Greeven, TWNTE, II, 808. The second, "thanksgiving," has been given a prominent place in Eph 5:4; cf. 1:16, and is brought into the foreground in Colossians more than anywhere else. The third noun means "intercession" as well as "prayer" in general: I Tim 2:1; 4:5; in Paul's time it did not possess the exclusive meaning which English "intercession" has. However, in Rom 8:26-27, 34; 11:2; cf. Heb 7:25; Acts 25:24, the verb (*hyper-*)*entygchanō* means distinctly, "to intercede." Eph 1:16, etc. and 6:18 show that Paul could use other terms as well for describing this form of prayer.
[126] I Thess 5:6-10; I Peter 5:8; Mark 14:34-38; Matt 24:42-43, etc.; Luke 12:37, 39. Ignatius *Polyc.* i 3; *Did.* xvi 1. See COMMENT II.
[127] Mark 13:33; Luke 21:36; Heb 13:17; cf. Barn. xx 2; xxi 7; *Did.* v 2.
[128] See RSV, NEB, JB, NTTEV for variant interpretations suggesting that the request for intercession on his behalf is an afterthought by the author.
[129] Paul does not specify what the "Ephesians" shall ask for in their intercession for "all the saints"; but he is very specific regarding their prayers for him, as the next words show.
[130] E.g. Thomas Aquinas and Haupt.
[131] While JB uses the term "opportunity" in its version of 6:19, scholars such as Dibelius, Schlier, Gaugler reject this interpretation.

great opportunity which Paul needs.[132] However, the text of Eph 6:19 speaks only of the "opening of the mouth." May the right "word" open Paul's mouth! For this the saints are to pray. The apostle makes clear from whence this "word" comes: within the context of prayer, the passive form, "may be given," is a reference to God.[133] From Him alone Paul can receive what he must say. Combined with the somewhat pathetic formula, "opening the mouth," the "giving of the word" equals a traditional biblical idiom which denotes "inspiration." "O Lord, open thou my lips, and my mouth shall show forth thy praise" (Ps 51:15). "The Lord put forth his hand and touched my mouth . . . Behold I have put my words in your mouth" (Jer 1:9). "When I speak to you, I will open your mouth, and you shall say to them, Thus says the Lord God" (Ezek 3:27).[134] Paul does not compose a message to the world himself but rather passes on what has been entrusted to him. The gospel he preaches is the unchangeable "gospel of Christ" (Gal 1:6–9; Eph 2:17), however personal and variable his formulations and accentuations. In II Cor 5:19 Paul called it "the word of reconciliation," in Eph 6:17, cf. Acts 13:46, the "word of God." This interpretation of "giving the word" and "opening the mouth" does not exclude some less important elements. E.g. for his proclamation of "God's word" Paul needs the "right word" at the right time (Schlier; Gaugler), that is, the clarity, intelligibility, power which are prerequisites of communication. Unless he receives the proper thought, language, and diction from God, charges such as that Paul lacks "plausible words of wisdom" (I Cor 2:4); "his speech is of no account" (II Cor 10:10, RSV);[135] or, "Paul, you are mad" (Acts 26:24) will hinder the acceptance of the gospel. At the end of his life (unlike Gal 1:6–9; I Cor 1–3; and II Cor 10–13) Paul may have been aware of some insufficiency on his part. Still, a concern for polished or persuasive speech, or for appropriate repartee in debate, seems to be absent from Eph 6:19–20. Paul is anxious only about one substantial and one formal element of the "word" he has to preach:

[132] See I Cor 16:9; II Cor 2:12; Acts 14:27; Rev 3:8, 20. Heb 12:17 speaks of a *"chance"* (*topos*) to repent.

[133] The so-called *passivum divinum* is frequently used by Jewish authors. It facilitates the avoidance of mentioning God's name "in vain": Exod 20:7. In Eph 1:18 (lit. "being illuminated") and 3:16 ("be fortified"), God is the logical subject. However, in more classical Greek, *logon didōmi* ("to give a word") means "to give account," or "to make a speech"; see Rom 14:12; I Cor 14:9; cf. Luke 16:2 (*apodidōmi logon*).

[134] Cf. Ezek 29:21. According to Abbott, p. 189, the phrase "opening the mouth" occurs only when grave utterances are in question. As much as a stricken or a dumb person is in dire need of an "opening of his mouth," so are the men chosen to utter prophetic and apostolic messages. God, or Jesus Christ, or the Spirit (of Wisdom) alone can give the gift of the right speech: Wisd Sol 10:21; Mark 7:34–35; Matt 10:19–20; 16:17; Acts 2:4; 4:8; etc.; cf. Robinson, p. 136. The character, power, and contents of inspiration are described in most picturesque detail in the story of the Aramaean (Syrian) seer Balaam, in Num 22–24; esp. 22:12–22, 38; 23:12, 20, 26; 24:4, 13, 16. In Ps 51, but occasionally also in pre-exilic prophetic books (such as Micah 3:8; Hosea 9:7; Isa 11:2–4), and most frequently in post-exilic literature (e.g. Isa 42:1; 59:21; 61:1; Zech 7:12; Num 11:29; Neh 9:30; *Ps Sol* 17:42[37]; I Enoch 62:2) prayer, prophecy, and/or the passing of right judgment are attributed to the gift of the Spirit; see also I Cor 2:9–16. However, among the Sadducees, and in a lesser degree among Pharisees and rabbinical teachers (though not in Qumran), the prophetic words inspired by the Spirit were of inferior authority to the words of the Lord entrusted to Moses and codified in the Pentateuch. Despite Eph 6:17, where the (sword of) "the word" is described as a gift of the Spirit, the omission of any explicit reference to the Holy Spirit in Eph 6:19–20 may reflect the rabbinic distinction: Paul hopes to speak "the word" with no less authority than Moses, cf. II Cor 3:4–18. The absence of the article before "word" in the Greek text of Eph 6:19 may indicate that Paul uses a traditional (hymnic?) formulation; it need not demonstrate that speech of minor authority is in mind.

[135] JB renders this verse: "He is no preacher at all"; NEB: "As a speaker he is below contempt"; cf. II Cor 11:6.

its substance must be the "gospel," and the form of his speech must be "frank and bold" (vss. 19–20).

and in high spirits to make the secret known [by proclaiming] the gospel. Lit. "in boldness to make known the secret of the gospel." Arguments for the origin of the term *parrhēsiā* and for its translation by "high spirits" were presented in the second NOTE on 3:12. Since the opening of Paul's mouth is done by God and his "word" rather than by Paul, the term *en parrhēsiā* belongs to the verb, to "make known," not to the preceding words.[136] Especially in Acts, this noun describes the manner in which the apostles give their testimony.[137] An earlier observation is now confirmed: Paul does not ask for release from prison and for external freedom, but only for the right spirit to carry on his work, be it then "in chains."[138] In COMMENT XI on 1:3–14 it was explained why in Ephesians and Colossians (unlike Daniel, apocalyptic, and Qumran literature) *mystērion* means "secret" rather than mystery. The attribute, lit. "of the gospel," is not found in some MSS.[139] The mention of the gospel probably belongs to the original text. But the Greek genitive, "of the gospel," is a genitive of quality or substance rather than an indication that the gospel is a secret in whole or in part. Through the gospel God manifests the formerly hidden truth: in eternity God was and is determined to draw the Gentiles into his house, and he has now carried out his decision through Jesus Christ (1:10). The gospel is the means by which this is made known publicly. According to Thomas Aquinas, "Paul praises the duty of preaching for its prominence and grandeur."[140] Again, the centrality of verbal proclamation in mission work does not exclude other (non-verbal) forms of witnessing to Jesus Christ and his united people.[141] If in vs. 18 the terms "staying awake" and "pray" do not carry only one narrow meaning (see COMMENT VI), then it is unlikely that the references to the "gospel" and its "proclamation" in vss. 19–20 point exclusively to the preaching, teaching, and counseling activity of the apostle. The next words make this explicit.

20. *For this cause I am an ambassador in chains.* Instead of rattling his chains, attempting to break them, or cursing God or himself for the miserable social, psychic, physical situation into which his service to Jesus Christ has brought him,[142] Paul demonstrates that he has accepted his captivity without bitterness and bears it with good humor. He denotes his ministry with the political-legal term "ambassador" which includes the full power to represent a

---

[136] Nestle, GNT, ZB; Phillips, NEB decide for this syntactical connection, Luther and KJ for the opposite, RSV and JB choose translations which leave the issue open, as indeed on philological grounds alone no decision can be made. Cf. the term "in love" in 1:4.

[137] I Thess 2:2; Acts 2:29; 4:29, 31; in the Codex Bezae Cantabrigiensis also Acts 6:10; 16:4.

[138] Calvin; Abbott and others. But in II Thess 3:2 Paul asks for "deliverance from wicked and evil men."

[139] Vaticanus, Boernerianus, and some western commentators.

[140] In 2:20 and 4:11 the foundation of the church upon the apostolic and prophetic proclamation was emphasized and, beginning with 1:13, the role of the preached "word" was stressed repeatedly.

[141] The several forms of the apostle's witness were described in COMMENT III A–D on 3:1–13. The many ways in which the church is to let the same light shine that also has transformed herself, form the substance of each of Paul's utterances on church order and ethics in chapters 4–6.

[142] Unlike the literature collected under the name of Jeremiah, the epistles known under the name of Paul contain no accusations and lamentations. Although Rom 7 is somewhat reminiscent of an "Individual Lamentation Psalm" and certainly does make use of its style, yet it is free of all overtones of complaint or rebellion.

potentate or a government.[143] In II Cor 5:20 the same title describes Paul as God's spokesman: he speaks "for Christ" or "on behalf of Christ" (*hyper Christou*). In Eph 6:20, the "gospel" or the revelation of the "secret" is the "cause" Paul represents.[144] Unlike II Cor 5, Eph 6 makes a pun with the term, "I am an ambassador": Paul coins an oxymoron when he calls himself an "ambassador in chains." Three elements can be discerned in this paradox: (a) The term "chain" (*alysis*) signifies among other things the (golden) adornment(s) worn around the neck and wrists by rich ladies or high ranking men.[145] On festive occasions ambassadors wear such chains in order to reveal the riches, power, and dignity of the government they represent. Because Paul serves Christ crucified, he considers the painful iron prison chains as most appropriate insignia for the representation of his Lord. "The world has more splendid ambassadors" (Bengel), but this does not bother Paul. (b) Under normal circumstances, the ambassador of a foreign power can be snubbed or expelled, but not imprisoned by the government to which he is delegated. "Chains" were a metaphor used in Greek for imprisonment.[146] By describing himself as an incarcerated delegate, Paul reminded his readers of the wrong he was suffering. It is all the more noteworthy that instead of complaining or urging for his release, he only hopes for the support and increase of his *parrhēsiā* ("frankness, boldness").[147] (c) When a delegate is imprisoned his mission appears to be not only in jeopardy, but at an end. In his epistle to the Philippians[148] Paul discusses this issue at length. He begins, climaxes, and concludes his argument by stating that his imprisonment, as well as other forms of seeming impediment, humiliation, hostility, death threat, bodily harm and psychic anguish, have proven useful for spreading the gospel, are necessary for a servant of Christ, and offer a model rather than a warning for all those who believe in Christ.[149]

[. *Pray*] *that I may become frank and bold in my proclamation. For this I must be.* Lit. "that in it I have joyful boldness as it is necessary for me to speak." For the sake of clarity, three deviations have been made from the

[143] See the exposition of 4:11 in which it was shown why Paul preferred non-religious nomenclature. Some literature on the term apostle and its legal implications was listed in fn. 2 to 1:1–2. However, in Gnostic writings of the second and later centuries, the one or the many "messengers" of the highest deity held a distinctly religious office.

[144] See the next NOTE, part (b) for an explication of the rendition of *hyper hou* (lit. "for which") by the weighty formula "for this cause." In II Corinthians, Ephesians and all other Pauline letters, the person (of Christ) and the cause (of the gospel) represented by Paul are inseparable. The gospel preached by Paul is the "gospel of God," Rom 1:1; cf. 1:16–17, or "of Christ," Gal 1:17; II Cor 11:4; etc. Always the proclamation and representation of the gospel involves man's total existence—the whole life of the missionary himself, and that of the Jews and Gentiles who are addressed. It has its origin and center in "hearing," "speaking," and "believing" (cf. Eph 1:13) but also includes obedient conduct and joy in suffering. Among the undisputed letters of Paul, II Cor 5:17–21 anticipates the particular message of Ephesians (and Colossians) more explicitly than other passages, for there and here the renewal of the whole "world" by "reconciliation" (or "peace") between God and man, and between man and his fellow man, is more emphasized than "peace of mind" or other benefits experienced by the individual.

[145] In the Colossian parallel to Eph 6:20, i.e. in 4:18, *desmos* ("fetter") is used, not *alysis;* cf. the term *desmios* ("prisoner") in Eph 3:1; 4:1; Philem 1, 9; II Tim 1:8. However, in Eph 6, a term is chosen which can imply more than imprisonment—just as in the description of the "[splendid] armor" more than military usefulness is in mind, see COMMENT III A.

[146] LSLex, 74. In all NT occurrences of *alysis*, except the present, only chain or imprisonment is meant; see esp. Acts 12:6–7; 21:33; 28:20; II Tim 1:16.

[147] Theophylact; Bengel; Abbott; Schlier.

[148] Which was probably written sometime (two years?) before Ephesians from a prison in Rome.

[149] Philip 1:12–30; 2:19–30; 3:10–21. Cf. Rom 8:17–39; Col 1:24, etc.

Greek text: (a) The verb "pray" which occurred in vs. 18 has been repeated lest it be forgotten that in each of vss. 18, 19, 20 Paul asks for the intercession of the saints.[150] Like each of them he has continually to receive and "put on" the "strength" called "God's armor" (6:10–17). Paul, too, is dependent upon an ever new supply of power and the gift of courage.[151] (b) The Greek words *en autō* (lit. "in it") resume the formula *hyper hou* (lit. "for which") at the beginning of this verse and refer to the proclamation of "the gospel."[152] In our translation both formulae are treated as a hendiadys and rendered by the single term, "for this cause," rather than by a repetition which in English would sound redundant. (c) In Greek, the one word meaning "to be frank and bold" (*parrhēsiazomai*)[153] is somewhat separated from the verb *laleō* (lit. "to speak" or "to speak up") at the end of vs. 20. *Parrhēsiazomai* means originally (etymologically) a boldness shown only in speech, but eventually it also denotes a frank and bold behavior in all ways. Both meanings must be expressed in an accurate English version. Therefore, frankness and boldness are first associated with speaking (that is, with "proclamation") in our translation, whereas a reference to the total attitude follows at the end of the verse. Two things are affirmed in vs. 20: what he is, Paul has to show in his speech, but his mode of speaking also demonstrates his total freedom, and such a man he "must be." He who is a bold speaker also "must be" a frank and courageous man, or else his manner of speech would be refuted by his life.[154] The opposite would be, "to be ashamed of the gospel" or "to be put to shame by God."[155] The brief clause, "For this I must be" (lit. "as it is necessary for me to speak"), signals the transition from the petition for intercession to the giving of personal information. In I Cor 9:16–18 Paul called his evangelistic commission a task laid upon him by "necessity" (*anagkē*), against which rebellion could never succeed.[156] Joy and gratitude regarding the institution of the apostolic and prophetic ministry were expressed in Eph 2:20; 3:5; 4:11. This is repeated in 6:20: there is no other way to be a witness for Christ than by the courageous testimony of a man who is free—even in chains.[157] Ministers who fulfill their duty "sadly" rather than joyfully are of "no advantage" to those whom they serve, according to Heb 13:17. If Christ were proclaimed only as crucified, there would be little reason for joy. But the same God who raised Christ from the dead and with him raised all the saints, is also the source of confidence and courage. No separation can be made between the substance and the form of the gospel which Paul will preach. The congregation is asked to support his ministry by intercession on his behalf before God.

[150] According to e.g. II Cor 7:5–6, Paul was far from being a heroic figure or superman: he was "afflicted at every turn" by "conflicts from without and fears from within," and he depended completely on "God who comforts the downcast."

[151] Cf. John 3:27: "No one can receive anything except when it is given him from heaven."

[152] As Bengel; Abbott; Gaugler point out.

[153] The cognate noun in the preceding verse was translated by "high spirits"; its meaning was discussed in the second NOTE on 3:12.

[154] In the parallel Col 4:13, however, the accent appears to lie only on Paul's performance as a preacher.

[155] Rom 1:16; cf. Philip 1:20; II Cor 10:8; I Peter 4:16; I John 2:28; cf. Matt 10:32; Luke 12:8.

[156] The first prediction of the suffering of the Son of Man in the Synoptic Gospels speaks of a similar "must" to which Jesus subjects himself, see Matt 16:21 par. God's revelation rather than a blind fate creates this necessity, see e.g. Luke 24:7, 26, 44, 46.

[157] According to Plato's *apologia* and *Crito*, Socrates accepted his imprisonment with a similar serenity. The Stoics saw in this attitude the exemplary behavior of a wise man.

COMMENTS I–VII on 6:10–20

I Structure and Summary

Eph 6:10–20 consists of three main parts: vss. 11–13, vss. 14–17, and vss. 18–20. The whole section is properly introduced by a first verse that identifies the topic at hand.

According to vs. 10, the saints know God's superior power. They are not left to their own resources, but shall confidently let God work in them and through them. What does it mean to be "strong in the Lord"?

Part I (vss. 11–13) compares God's power to an imposing armor which is God's own, and is now placed at the disposition of the saints for use in an imminent battle. They need nothing less; for the leader, the character, the location, the tactics of the opposing forces are superhuman, and dark are the place and the day of the battle. But where people left to themselves would falter and succumb, the armor of God provides the power to resist and hold out.

Part II (vss. 14–17) lists the six arms that form this armor. The catalogue appears to follow the several steps which a Roman soldier of Paul's time would take in preparation for battle. The majority of the arms mentioned are defensive rather than aggressive. The metaphorical meaning of each weapon is spelled out. The saints shall take up truth, righteousness, and solid footing in the gospel; against faith, hope in the present and future salvation, and the word of God, the inimical powers cannot prevail. The allusions made to OT passages show that all these weapons are used and tested by God himself, and that they are first entrusted to one person on earth: the Messiah. Isa 11:2–5 avers that through the Spirit, or together with the Spirit, a special armament is given to God's Anointed One: the (sword of) the word and the girdle of righteousness. Eph 6 goes beyond the OT: through the mediation of the Messiah and the Spirit, God's weapons are now transferred to all the saints.[158] The logic of the argument is this: if these arms are spiritual, and if they are sufficient for God and Jesus Christ—they will certainly be good enough for the saints.

Part III (vss. 18–20) exhorts the saints to be vigilant in prayer and proclamation. The saints are and remain dependent on God's help and blessing; thus they constitute a community of prayer and intercession. The church is co-responsible for Paul's mission among unbelievers and participates in it by her intercession. While the saints are no more than beggars and while Paul's imprisonment looks like a tremendous setback, all members of the congregation are urged to ask for God's help and sustenance—both for themselves and for Paul. In the congregation no one is "a lone, lorn creature," no one a self-made hero. The weakest members, as well as he who is considered strong, are equally dependent upon the intercession of their fellow saints.

Within Ephesians, the letter that describes the gospel as a gospel of peace,

---

[158] Probably for this reason, the same metaphor recurs in the formulae "putting on Christ"; "putting on the New Man"; "putting on compassion, kindness, lowliness, meekness"; "putting on the glorious armor," viz. "the weapons of light"; "putting on the imperishable" and "immortality"; I Thess 5:8; Gal 3:27; I Cor 15:53–54; II Cor 5:3; Rom 13:12, 14; Col 3:10, 12; Eph 4:24; 6:11, 14. See COMMENT VI for a more detailed demonstration of the Christocentric basis of the transfer of God's weapons to man.

military images and the call to take a soldier's stand come as a surprise. It seems paradoxical that the Messiah's peace should issue in war. Yet while according to Matt 10:34 and Luke 12:51 Jesus came to bring a sword, not peace, and while he used aggressive tactics against e.g. the strong one (the devil) and the demons (Matt 12:22–30 par.), Ephesians speaks only about a war imposed upon the saints by inimical powers. The Christians can be compared to Daniel in the lions' den; as little as Daniel are they told to twist the lions' tails. When fiery missiles are shot at them they are not to respond in kind. They are not depicted as crusaders, their warfare is not called a holy war. But they are enabled to hold their ground. By the attitude with which he suffers his imprisonment, Paul illustrates that even seeming defeats can be borne with good humor. Eph 6:10–20 discourages a dualistic world view finding solace in the eternal struggle of light against darkness, as well as lamentations about the tragic predicament of God's children. Ruled out also are the reliance upon a strength immanent in man, and the claim that ultimately the church will be victorious over the world. No one except God will be victorious in the strife described here.

A specific problem is posed by the relationship of the second part of 6:10–20 to the third. Is prayer in 6:18 implicitly denoted as the seventh weapon with which God equips the saints? At least four reasons speak in favor of this assumption: (a) The formula "in the Spirit" corresponds to the formula "in Christ."[159] The same Spirit which gives the right "word" according to 6:17 (cf. 6:19) is also the source and the ground, the sphere and the instrument of prayer. In allusion to the Messiah's girdle (as described in Isa 11:5), the girdle given to the saints is mentioned in Eph 6:14. It is possible that now, in 6:18, the gift of the Spirit to the Messiah (Isa 11:2) is the background of the reference to the Spirit in which the saints are to pray. Prayer would then be another gift from God added to the various pieces of equipment mentioned in Eph 6:14–17 (Schlier). (b) When in Isa 11:2 an attempt is made to specify all attributes of the Spirit, seven features are enumerated in succession.[160] Lists of all kinds show a preference for the number seven.[161] If the weaponry of Eph 6 was meant to be complete in number and sufficient in quality, then seven arms were a better symbol than only six. (c) In the OT and in later Jewish literature, prayer is depicted as a battle, or it is offered before, in, or after bat-

---

[159] Dibelius, p. 99; cf. COMMENT I on 1:1–2. The passages Gal 4:6; Rom 8:15, 26; Jude 20 (also Rev 1:10; 4:2) may explain why the Spirit rather than God or Christ is called the source and ground of prayer. According to Chrysostom, the opposite of "prayer in the Spirit" is *battologiā*, a stammering and stuttering form of speech. The verb *battologeō* which in Matt 6:7 caricaturizes the prayers of the Gentiles, can mean babbling (WBLex, 137) or heaping up empty phrases (RSV). However, the reference to the Spirit in Eph 6:18 points to more than poor rhetoric.

[160] I.e. Spirit "of the Lord, of wisdom, of understanding, of counsel, of might, of knowledge, of fear of the Lord." Seven good and seven evil spirits are mentioned in *Test. Reuben* 2–3. The "seven" spirits mentioned in Rev 1:4; 4:5; 5:6 may mean "seven angels," cf. Rev 8:12; 15:1, etc., but they can also signify one Spirit in all dimensions of his essence and activity. However, among the Persians, six good spirits (*amesha spentas*) are enumerated who are at the same time gods and virtues, and can be described in cosmological, psychological, or theological terms, see Kamlah, pp. 59 ff.

[161] According to some commentaries, the beatitudes collected in Matt 5:3–10 contained originally seven similarly phrased sayings (not eight). In scholastic teaching seven virtues and seven vices express the sum total of ethical instruction. The Bible begins with an account of the creation in seven days and ends with a book in which units of seven form the structure of the eschatological events.

tle.[162] Therefore, prayer appears not only to fit well the military imagery chosen by Paul in Eph 6, but to be part of it. (d) The term *agrypneō*, "to stay awake," which is used in vs. 19, seems to allude to a military watch and therefore to demonstrate that Paul continues on the line of military metaphors. It is a mark of an invincible army that "none is weary, none stumbles, none slumbers or sleeps" (Isa 5:27).

But arguments to the contrary are even stronger. (a) Unlike his diction in Eph 6:14–17, in 6:18 Paul does not mention by name any specific piece of armor. (b) In the closest parallel to 6:18, 20 (i.e. Col 4:2–4) and in other epistles, Paul speaks of prayer without ever calling it a weapon or a fight.[163] (c) The term used for "stay awake" in Eph 6:18 is not a military term and therefore does not necessarily suggest that the Christians are assigned to strategic watchposts.[164]

Certainly the OT and NT do not prohibit the homiletical description of prayer as a "weapon given by God"[165] or as a struggle for God's grace. Yet, Eph 6 does not use such terminology; on the contrary, military metaphors are limited to 6:11–17.[166] What then is the function of vss. 18–20 in relation to the two preceding parts of this passage? The most likely reason why metaphors of war do not occur here is that these verses offer in direct discourse the author's interpretation of the previously used military images. According to his own explication and application, the military metaphors must not be misused to support the idea of crusades. Works of peace are in Paul's mind, not a secret glorification of war, or even of so-called "just wars." The armed struggle of the Christians consists only of their prayer and their participation in spreading the gospel of peace. Examples of this exposition are those monastic communities, e.g. the Benedictines and Jesuits, who submit themselves each in their own way to a quasi-military discipline in order to lead a life of prayer and service, viz. to spread by all means the truth in the way they were given to grasp it. In the last centuries before the destruction of Jerusalem in A.D. 70 a similar discipline, combined with the will to engage in physical battles, is found in the Qumran Community. Eph 6:10–20 does not intend to separate a special group of disciplined fighters from the mass of the saints. Rather the life of the whole church and of each of its members is depicted here as an uninterrupted stance of prayer and total involvement in the spreading of the gospel. According to this passage,

[162] Jacob struggles at the Jabbok, Gen 32:22–30. While Moses continues to pray, Israel is given victory over the Amalekites, Exod 17:11–12. He used "prayer and petition by incense" as the "shield of his ministry" in the dispute with Pharaoh, Wisd Sol 18:21. He "girded his loins with prayer" after Israel had made the golden calf, according to the rabbinical interpretation in NumR. 2 (158a). Prayer is Joseph's weapon against the spirit of Beliar working in the shameless Egyptian woman, *Test. Joseph* VII 4; VIII 1. In II Macc 15:27 a battle is described in which victory is won by men "fighting with their hands and praying to God in their hearts." *Ps Sol* XV 3–6[2–4] avers that a man is strong, powerful, safe from hurt by the flame of fire only "in giving thanks to God's name." The Greek verb *synagōnizomai* ("to fight along with") used in a reference to prayer in Rom 15:30 ("strive together with me in your prayers to God," RSV; "be my allies in the fight; pray to God." NEB) may allude to a military battle, not just to a sportive contest. Calvin explains Eph 6:18 in the sense of "fighting by prayers," and Gaugler, p. 228 affirms that prayer belongs to the spiritual armor. Bond (ch. 10) calls prayer the Christians' line of communication with their base of supplies.
[163] Rom 1:8–10, etc.; I Thess 5:17–18, 25; I Cor 7:5; Philip 1:3–4, 19; 4:6; Philem 22; cf. I Tim 2:1; Eph 1:15 ff.; 3:14 ff. Pfitzner, p. 117, shows why Rom 15:30 must not be used as a proof text for the equation of prayer with a fight.
[164] See the last NOTES on 6:18, esp. the references given in fns. 126 and 127.
[165] Schlier: *eine Gotteswaffe*.
[166] Dibelius; Schlier; Pfitzner. The term "subordinate" as used in 5:21–24 probably also belongs to these metaphors.

faith, resistance against evil, worship and mission are the inseparable marks of the living church.[167]

II Military Metaphors in Paul's Environment

Wherever he went, the apostle Paul could not help seeing Roman soldiers and hearing about their exploits. But Eph 6:11–17 lacks any evidence that Paul possessed a first-hand knowledge of weapons and the art of war. His metaphorical use of military terms appears to be dictated by a literary tradition rather than by personal experiences.[168] At least three such traditions contain precedents and analogies to Paul's thought and diction in Eph 6.

First, the description of Yahweh as "a man of war" is represented in pre- and post-exilic strands of the OT,[169] and in the corresponding notions of ancient Near Eastern, Greek, and Roman gods of war. Often the features of a warrior were attributed to the highest deity.[170]

Second, the OT speaks about a war, or wars, of Yahweh. Recent scholarship calls this the Holy War. At least once this war implies that God's people "have only to be still" and "see [watch] . . . the Lord fighting for them" with his very special weaponry.[171] Among other nations and in other cultures, the wars waged by a deity or among groups of gods, and the human wars in which they participate, are sometimes described with the intention of showing that a lifelong battle or occasional crusade is the inescapable human predicament.[172]

---

[167] Other characteristics of the church that are specifically emphasized in Ephesians have been described in COMMENTS III and XIV on 1:3–14; III and VI B on 1:15–23; IV–V on 2:1–10; VI–VII on 2:11–22; IV on 3:1–13; II–III, VI–VIII on 4:1–16; VI on 4:17–32; III on 5:1–20; IV on 5:21–33. Harnack describes the development of the discussion about spiritual warfare in the early church, and Welzig supplements Harnack by a brief survey on the history of the same motif in the medieval church, the Reformation period (esp. Erasmus), and later centuries.

[168] Schlier, pp. 298–99. The author of I Clement, however, was so totally immersed in military thought that in ch. 37 he simply transferred the distinction between officers and privates to the structure and organization of the church.

[169] Exod 15:3; Isa 42:13; 52:10, etc.; see Hempel, pp. 33–45; C. Westermann, Das Buch Jesaja, Das Alte Testament Deutsch 19 (Göttingen: Vandenhoeck, 1966), 278–79; W. Kessler, Gott geht es ums Ganze, Die Botschaft des Alten Testament 19 (Stuttgart: Calwer Verlag, 1960), 44–51; H. Odeberg, Trito-Isaiah, Universitets Arsskrift, Teologi 1 (Uppsala, 1931), 189–97.

[170] E.g. to Marduk, Assur, Adad, Neith, Anat, Baal. See, e.g. Gressmann, plates 91, 98, 103, 113, 128; Pritchard, ANET 66; idem, The Ancient Near East in Pictures (Princeton University Press, 1954), plates 26–40, 490, 494, 496, 500, 525–26, 531–32, 789; Tallquist, pp. 92–111. Similar materials from Persia and China are accessible through, e.g. C. Colpe, Die religionsgeschichtliche Schule, I, FRLANT 78 (1961), 83, 94–95; E. Waldschmidt-W. Lentz, Die Stellung Jesu im Manichäismus, Abhandlungen der preussischen Akademie der Wissenschaften 1926, philologisch-historische Klasse 4, 125.

[171] Exod 14:13–14. Wars of Yahweh are mentioned in I Sam 18:17; 25:28; Num 21:14. The special weapons used by Yahweh to subdue his and his people's enemies are thunder, lightning, fire, hornets, hailstones, earthquake and the resulting confusion; see esp. Judg 4–5. According to Wisd Sol 5:17, 20, "He makes creation his weapon . . . creation will join him to fight the madmen." See von Rad, esp. pp. 6–14, and the summary of von Rad's study given by Bauernfeind in TWNTE, VI, 507–9. According to Buber, p. 144; Pedersen, III–IV, 21; Cross, p. 17, the concept "Holy War" applied only to the events between Israel's exodus from Egypt and the conquest of the promised land. Cross also attempts to show, esp. by an exegesis of Ps 24, that the historical and mythological themes of the early tradition were "wedded" to the kingship motives and found their expression in cultic festivals, which in turn provided material for the late Prophetic eschatology. Smend has further elaborated on the "War(s) of Yahweh." He considers the Yahweh was not an exponent of the cultus of a closed federation, its priests and its sanctuary (the amphictyony of the Twelve Tribes, Shiloh, and the Ark), but the presupposition and nucleus of the specific relationship between Yahweh and the whole of Israel. According to Smend the tradition of charismatic leaders such as Moses contains many more historic elements than has been accepted under the influence of M. Noth's work.

[172] Examples are: the conflict of Greek deities over Troy, or of the patron deities siding with Creon or with Antigone, respectively; the identification of the oriental kings' wars with wars of their gods against other gods, kings, lands; finally, the philosophic (mostly Stoic) equation of life with continuous warfare.

Finally the OT and the tradition of other nations, cultures, and religions contain tales about the construction, possession, and use of miracle weapons by privileged men, and the description of virtues as symbolic weapons.[173]

Elements of these three groups are frequently interchanged. Also, other groups or numbers of motifs have been suggested as a means to interpret Eph 6.[174] However the background and environment of Paul's military metaphors are depicted, the apostle did not simply appropriate one of the existing forms; neither did he endorse all of them nor offer a mixture of his own. A brief list of the motifs that appear to be reflected in Eph 6 and a sketch of their distinctive features will show some of the original traits and accents in Paul's discourse on the spiritual weapons.

1) Neither the Babylonian myth of Marduk's fight with Tiamat, nor its parallels in e.g. the Assyrian descriptions of the god Assur or of special war gods, exerted any direct influence upon Paul. Rather, the formulations chosen in Ephesians show that Paul made use of concepts and terms that were more than just an example or reflection of ancient Near Eastern notions of a warrior god. The apostle quoted from OT texts which, at the time of their composition, had already drastically modified and challenged prevailing patterns, and had sought to point out the unique character and way of Yahweh.[175] To be specific: The myth, the portrayal and the annual festival of Marduk point to a struggle between several deities whereby Marduk's rule is threatened. His ordeal is connected with the cycles of nature, i.e. with the seasons and with fertility. The victorious Marduk is worshiped as the guarantor of the Babylonian king and of his national and international politics. The heavenly guarantee of the king's rule must be ever renewed in the Akitu festival. The earthly king and warrior is lifted upon the throne of the victorious deity. Yet the texts quoted by Paul do not speak of the deification of man, of politics, of natural processes. Isa 11 praises the free choice of Yahweh who elects and equips the Messiah to do justice to the poor, and Isa 59 celebrates the gracious and unique intervention of Yahweh in favor of his helpless people.[176]

---

[173] Special qualities are ascribed to e.g. the sword of Goliath, I Sam 21:9. Reitzenstein, pp. 192–215, has drawn attention to Persian lists of virtues that use military imagery. Kamlah, pp. 189–96, assumes that Ephesians shows the influence of Persian thought-patterns.

[174] In the second edition of his commentary, Dibelius mentions two types of imagery; in the third (edited by H. Greeven) three are listed; Gaugler also counts three, but Conzelmann speaks of four. The mythological concept of a war deity is one thing, the religious and philosophical idea that the life of a good man is service and warfare under the auspices of a deity is another. Maccabean, Zealotic, and Qumranite militarism has its counterpart in the strife for virtue as expressed in the Persian tradition as well as in the cults of Isis and of Mithras, whose worshipers call themselves "soldiers" of their deity.

[175] Paul does not allude to the classic OT chapters that describe the war of Yahweh with e.g. Egypt, Amalek, Jericho, the Canaanites, the Midianites: Exod 14–15; 17; Josh 6; Judg 4–5. Therefore, there is no reason to transfer the alleged OT concept of a Holy War to the exposition of Eph 6. Although Paul uses no quotation formula, he does quote Isa 11:4–5 and 59:17 in Eph 6:14 and 17, and he alludes distinctly to Isa 52:7 in Eph 6:15. In I Thess 5:8 only Isa 59:17 is quoted. Wisd Sol 5:17–20 shows as many traces of Isa 11 and 59 as are found in Eph 6, but Paul does not appear directly dependent on this text; see Robinson, pp. 212–26. However, J. Geyer, The Wisdom of Solomon (London: SCM, 1963), p. 75 asserts that the author of Eph 6 "must surely have drawn" on Wisd Sol 5. Less directly, perhaps unconsciously, Paul seems to be influenced by passages such as Pss 7:6, 10, 12; 18:2, 30–35; 35:1–6; Isa 51:9–23, and by descriptions of the Day of Yahweh as found in, e.g. Isa 22:5–8; Jer 46:3–12; Joel 3:9–21; Nahum 1:15; 2:1–13; Zech 2:6, 8; Job 29:14.

[176] Buber, pp. 142–45, describes a vital difference between God and a war god: Yahweh only fights his own wars; Exod 15:3 does not say, He is a man of war, but, He becomes one if necessary.

2) Kamlah has emphatically asserted that, although Paul used OT materials in his undisputed letters, OT sources are not sufficient to explain Eph 6; rather he sees in this chapter traces of Iranian doctrines that describe the myth of the Prime Man (*Ur-Mensch*).[177] As was shown in COMMENT VII on 4:17–32, exhortation in the form of a catalogue of virtues, if found in a dualistic cosmological framework, can indeed demonstrate Iranian influence. Since Eph 6 contains a catalogue of weapons which is also a catalogue of "virtues," an Iranian mark on this chapter appears indisputable.[178] It is possible that either by way of Qumran or of the Mithras cult[179] Paul had become acquainted with ideas and formulations such as the following: (a) the equation of virtues with "weapons"; (b) the designation of these arms as "weapons of light" or "weapons of righteousness"; (c) the distinction between "worldly weapons," serving a "worldly" behavior, and weapons that are useful for the good fight and the conduct directed by the "Spirit"; (d) the reference to "sons of light" and the description of the whole life as a military service (*strateuomai*) or contest (*agōnizomai*).[180]

But the impression of Paul's direct or indirect dependence upon Iranian teachings and images is probably deceptive. If there are essential differences between Eph 6 and Persian catalogues of virtues, then the theory cannot be upheld that the substance of Eph 6 was determined by such a tradition—whether it was oral, written, or cultic.[181]

The following observations may be important: (a) In Iranian anthropology, the soul is the weaponry of the Prime Man;[182] in Eph 6 there is no reference to the soul—and if there were, it would probably be described with Jer 17:9 as "deceitful above all things and desperately corrupt." God's armor must protect spirit, soul, and body; it is not found in any better part of man, e.g. a light substance residing in man by nature. (b) The cosmological dualism underlying

---

[177] Kamlah, pp. 36–37, 202–7. The same author follows Schlier (pp. 289–300) when on pp. 59–62, 76, 85–96 he speaks of a combination of Babylonian and Iranian mythological elements. Reitzenstein, pp. 192–215, appears to have been the first scholar of the history-of-religion school who pointed in that direction. Certainly Mani (who flourished shortly before A.D. 300) is the classical exponent of the amalgamation of Babylonian, Iranian, and Christian materials. However, if the theory of Reitzenstein, Schlier, and Kamlah is correct, then the author of Ephesians (or Philo, see fn. 182) deserves first credit for this attempt.

[178] According to one Persian source (*Dīnā-i Moinōg-ī*, Khirad 43, quoted by Oepke, TWNTE, V, 298) Ahuramazda and heaven are won, and Ahriman and hell are avoided, "if one makes the spirit of wisdom one's rearguard and carries the spirit of content with life as a weapon . . . and takes the spirit of truth as a shield, the spirit of gratitude as a club, the spirit of full vigilance as a bow, the spirit of generosity as an arrow; and if one takes the spirit of moderation as a spear, the spirit of steadfastness as a gauntlet and the spirit of [belief in] destiny as armor."

[179] The Qumran material will be treated separately in (4), below. Early evidence for the thought and diction of the members of the Mithras cult and of similar features of the Isis cult is found in e.g. Livy XXXIX 15:13; Tertullian *de corona* 15; Apuleius *metamorph.* XI 14–15.

[180] Gal 5:16–23; Rom 6:13; 13:12; 15:30; II Cor 6:7; 10:3–4; Eph 5:8; cf. I Tim 1:18; II Tim 2:3–4; I Cor 9:7.

[181] E.g. F. Cumont, *Oriental Religions in Roman Paganism* (London: Open Court, 1911), xviii–xxi, denies that the imagery used in the early church (i.e. by Paul and in I Clement) is dependent on Mithraism. Only on the third level of the hierarchy among the Mithras worshipers was a man called a soldier (*miles*). Paul attributes to all the saints the same weapons and the same rank.

[182] Kamlah, p. 92. This idea is probably reflected in Philo's teaching, according to which the *logos* ("rational speech" or "reason") is the weapon given by God, *somn.* I 103; cf. 108. According to other statements of the same philosopher, the virtues constitute the armor of reason (*Abr.* 243), and Moses is the captain and leader in the "war to the death for true religion" (*sacr. Abelis et Caini* 130). Evil spirits (*kēres*), reminiscent of the evil spirits of the Iranian religion, fight against the *logos*, according to *somn.* I 105. The fact that Philo may well have been influenced by Persian thought and that the Qumran and apocalyptic writings show a similar openness to it, does not demonstrate that Eph 6 can only be explained upon the same supposition.

the Iranian dualistic anthropology is perhaps reflected in the terms "overlords of this dark world" and "spiritual hosts of evil" (6:12). Yet it cannot be overlooked that the creed presupposed and proclaimed in Ephesians is monotheistic (4:4–6) and that no traces are present of a tragic world view. (c) In the Iranian religion, gods, good spirits, and virtues were virtually identified. Thus quasi-metaphysical status was given to the virtues, and the paragon of virtue, the Prime Man, was a mythological figure. Eph 6, however, does not equate the weapons with virtues. If the author had wanted to do this, the "gospel of peace," "salvation," and the "word of God"—all of which are something other than virtues—would not figure among the allegorical meanings of specific weapons.[183] (d) In the Iranian religion the way is prepared for the Gnostic teaching that a mystical identity exists between the pious and the Messenger of Light (the Prime-Anthropos Redeemer). Indeed, Ephesians speaks of union with Christ: Christ is the head of the church, and he fills the community of the saints (1:22–23, etc.); according to 3:16–17 he dwells through faith in the hearts of the saints. However, the allusions to Isa 11:4–5 in Eph 6:14–17 do not indicate a mystical identification of the saints with Jesus Christ. What is said to them is based upon the coming, the death, the resurrection and the second advent of Christ. It does not in any way obscure or erase the difference between the Savior and the saved.

3) Representatives of later Stoicism called life a "military service" because they considered it an uninterrupted struggle between reason and passion.[184] Their euphemistic use of war imagery has at least two roots in classical Greek thought. (a) Homer and Hesiod had made a distinction between two types of war: while Ares fights for war's sake, Athene fights noble battles for good ends.[185] (b) According to Plato, Socrates knew that he had to maintain faithfully the station (*phrourā*) on which the gods had placed him.[186] Through the older Stoics (Zeno and Chrysippus) and the middle Stoics (Panaitios and Posidonius), the idea of the militant wise man was mediated to the younger Stoics, among them Seneca and Epictetus. Socrates is their paragon of virtue because he holds his post, demonstrates his responsibility to the gods and his freedom within the clutches of fate, shows how to bear tribulations, despise danger

[183] According to Kamlah, pp. 191–95, the weapons do not consist of "virtues" in the undisputed Pauline letters. There, "putting on the weapons" means to "put on Christ" (Rom 13:12, 14); the armor is "an image for the new being in Christ [that is oriented] toward the new life of those baptized"; and when there is a catalogue presented, it "describes the new being created by God" and has the function of "a baptismal exhortation." In Ephesians, however, which Kamlah considers not authentic, "faith is the most important virtue." The author of Ephesians supposedly selected those passages from Isa 59 and 52 which "combined weapons and similar things with virtues." However, when Wisd Sol 18:14–19 describes the *logos* as jumping from heaven in full battle-dress and waging the war of God with the weapon of God's command, and when in Wisd Sol 18:20–25 Aaron is depicted as the divine warrior, clothed with the weapons of his ministry, i.e. prayer and sacrifice, the moralizing equation of weapons with virtues has not yet taken place. The same is true of Isa 59:17: the arms there mentioned are not virtues, but "the weapons of the divine war are concepts which anticipate the outcome of the battle" (Westermann, pp. 278–79). The same must probably be said of Eph 6.
[184] Seneca *ep.* 97; Epictetus *diss.* III 24:21–37, etc.; see Emonds for an intensive study of spiritual warfare in Stoicism and for additional references.
[185] Homer *Iliad* v 388, 761, 851 ff., 896; *Od.* VIII 267 ff.; Hesiod *theogonia* 922, 926; *opera et dies* 17–24, 145 f. Heraclitus' statement, "War is the father of all things," includes the observation that not only evil issues from war; see Bauernfeind, TWNTE, V, 1504.
[186] *Phaedr.* 62B; cf. *apol.* 28D; see Emonds for a discussion of the dialectical meaning of *phrourā* which can mean watch post as well as prison. In *leg.* I 626E, Plato speaks of man's struggle against his baser "self" which can lead to "the first and best victory of all."

and death, fight fatigue, avoid laziness, etc.[187] Since occasionally also in the OT life is described as a "warfare" (ṣābā) or as a "service" (ᶜabōdāh) in the domestic, cultic, or military sense of the term,[188] and since Stoicism clearly developed toward a monotheistic idea of the deity, the Jewish philosopher, Philo, felt free to interpret the Bible in Stoic terms.[189] There are obvious analogies between the Stoic and Philonic teaching and imagery on one side, and Eph 6 on the other: Paul makes no reference to weapons that can be associated with passions, e.g. to the "garments of vindication" (nāqām) or the "zeal and stern wrath" of God which are mentioned in Isa 59:17 and Wisd Sol 5:17, 20. A quiet, sober, and dispassionate certainty prevails. It resembles the Stoic's trust in the victory of reason. But at least four elements distinguish Pauline from Stoic thought:[190] (a) Weaponry for the spiritual warfare is given by God who is revealed through the Messiah Jesus; it is not provided by reason which governs the universe, nor identified with man's higher self. (b) The conflict is much more serious than that between spirit and matter, reason and passion, or order and chaos. In Pauline teaching, the "desires" of the "flesh" (Rom 13:14, etc.) represent a "spiritual" antagonist of God and man, even "another law" that makes war against the "law of God." The "law of sin and death" is a power that man cannot overcome by sheer good will and energetic strife. Rather, man is "held captive" in that law and cannot free himself by innate forces. He is liberated only through the grace of God shown in Jesus Christ and through the "law of the Spirit of life" which has superseded the former condemnation and misery.[191] (c) In the struggle of which Paul speaks, all powers of the present evil aeon are confronted with the superior power of the new. Paul does not distinguish different levels of being, nor capitalize on the existence of a higher and a lower self. Not the attainment of individual perfection, but rather the dawn of a new time and a new history is proclaimed. The stage of the drama depicted by Paul is the court of God; the time is the final period of the present aeon. (d) In consequence, the war now waged with spiritual weapons is a war in which the whole community of the people of God is engaged. This people fights in closed ranks. If Paul is a special case in the fellowship of all the saints, it is because of his great commission (Eph 6:18–20). But Ephesians does not envisage the saints as lonely heroes who fight the battle and win victory independent of the support of a community.

4) In Jewish apocalyptic and in Qumran literature, there are more "paral-

---

[187] Ps.-Aristotle *de mundo*, belongs to the middle Stoicism. He lists signals of alarm, shield, cuirass, greaves, girdle, helmet, the war horse, the chariot, the battle cries by which the wise man is encouraged to follow one commander and one (holy) will. References to the detailed explications and applications of Socrates' example by Seneca and Epictetus are given in Emonds, pp. 30–48.

[188] Isa 40:2; Job 7:1; 10:17; 14:14; cf. Dan 10:1.

[189] Philo calls God "our Defender, a weapon" and mentions spiritual weapons in *somn.* I 173, 255. The *logos* is a weapon, *leg. all.* III 155; *somn.* I 103. Polytheism is the root of wars in the soul and in the world; a war against war is necessary; inner peace is the presupposition of political peace. God is the only one who can help in this fight; however, man must not be an idle spectator, but fight the wild beast that is in himself, *conf. ling.* 41–59. While Philo does not use the term soldier (*stratiōtēs*) to describe a pious man, he does call life a warfare (*strateuomai*) against desires, and depicts Moses and every virtuous person as men waging war (*strateusamenos strateiān*) for virtue, *leg. all.* III 14; *de ebr.* 75–76. Thus Moses, on other occasions Abraham, takes the place held by Socrates among the Stoics.

[190] For the following, cf. Pfitzner, p. 162, etc.

[191] Rom 7:22–25; 8:1–11.

lels" to Eph 6 than in any group of non-biblical materials mentioned so far.[192] Among the common traits that are strongly influenced by OT events, promises, exhortations and prayers, the following are outstanding: descriptions of the coming war and of the armor given by God are accompanied by the appeal to the saints for action and bold use of their special weapons. The coming war is unlike any other: it is eschatological. While anointed leaders (be it an individual or a group) or the help of the angels of God are indispensable, only the community of the chosen together can carry out the assigned task. Unheard-of tribulations have to be faced; prayer is necessary, for the victory is in God's hands.[193] A stream of tradition similar to the one reflected in Qumran literature and in apocalyptical books, can be traced not only in Eph 6 but in all Pauline and other NT statements on the final conflict. However, it cannot be demonstrated that Eph 6 is more dependent on a written exponent of that tradition than is any other page of the NT. The War Scroll of Qumran contains elements that are without any parallels in Eph 6, and, in turn, Eph 6 adds several special points to the common motifs. (a) Instead of triumphant joy in the destruction of their human enemies, Ephesians has only one concern: that the peace made by Jesus Christ be proclaimed and enjoyed despite the attack of demonic forces. (b) Instead of calling for the battle of a closed community against the outside world, Ephesians speaks of the church that represents the inclusion of the Gentiles in the people of God; this church is *for* the world, not against it. (c) Instead of adding man-made arms to their moral armament, emblazoned with brilliant ornaments and symbolic inscriptions, the saints of the NT community take up only the spiritual arms of truth, righteousness, etc. (d) The Qumranite concern with proper ranks and tactics is replaced by the confidence that God will give his weapons to each one of the saints and that this ar-

---

[192] Omitted at this place is a comparison between Eph 6:10–20 and the ideology and conduct of the Zealots, members of a religious and political Jewish movement that emulated the Maccabees. By violent acts designed to protect the holiness of the temple, guerrilla attacks upon the Roman occupation troops, and open warfare, the Zealots sought to hasten the coming of God's kingdom. The movement perished heroically with the fall of the fortress Masada in 73 C.E. While in the apocalyptic and Qumranite circles both physical and spiritual arms play a decisive role, the Zealots appear to have limited themselves to the use of tangible weapons. Although the attacks and battles of the Zealots were as spiritually motivated and as much identified with God's own holy war as was the case in Qumran, clear evidence is still lacking which would show that they attributed to their weapons the same spiritual quality as recorded in the War Scroll of Qumran (1QM). See W. R. Farmer, *Maccabees, Zealots and Josephus*, Columbia University Press, 1965; M. Hengel, *Die Zeloten*, Leiden: Brill, 1961; Y. Yadin, *Masada*, New York: Random House, 1966.

The apostle Paul must have been aware of the existence and activity of the Zealotic movement. In Gal 1:14 and Acts 22:3 he describes his own past as that of a "zealot" for the law. But his teaching in Eph 6 is as different from the religious and political ideology of the Zealots as is the message and the conduct of Jesus, according to the Gospels. The attempts made by S. G. F. Brandon in *The Fall of Jerusalem*, London: SPCK, 1957; *Jesus and the Zealots*, Manchester University Press, 1967; and *The Trial of Jesus of Nazareth*, London: Bradford, 1968, to demonstrate that the historical Jesus (though not the domesticated Jesus of the Gospels) sympathized with the Zealots and used some of their methods, has been countered by strong arguments; see M. Hengel's review of Brandon's "Jesus and the Zealots." JSS 14 (1969), 231–40; *Evangelische Kommentare* 2 (Stuttgart: Kohlhammer, 1969), 694–96; H. R. Balz, TLZ 95 (1970), 30–32; O. Cullmann, *Jesus and the Revolutionaries*, New York: Harper, 1970.

[193] See 1QS I 16–18; IV 23; 1QSb V 25; 1QH II; III 24–39; V 22; VI 28–35; 1QpHab VI 4–12; 4Qtest 23–30; CD VII 20–21 (IX 9–10); 1QM, *passim*. For literature about the "war of God" described in the Qumran Scrolls, see BIBLIOGRAPHY 22. Among the references in the apocalyptic books (a part of which has also been found in the Qumran caves) are *Test. Simeon* V 5; *Test. Dan* V 10–11; *Test. Asher* VII 3; I Enoch 8:1; 9:6; 10:4–8; 13:1; 54:5, etc.; 88:2; 91:12; 94:7–10; 99:16; 100:1–5; IV Ezra 12:33; 13:1–13; II Bar 40:2, *Ass. Mos.* 10:7; 12:8; 16; *Ps. Sol.* 17:21–25[23–24]; *Sib. Or.* III 171–74; 202–4, 235–36, etc., esp. III 652–64 and V 381–85. Just as in Judg 5:11; I Sam 12:7; Micah 6:5, the victory of God is called a deed of righteousness (seḏāqāh), so in the apocalyptic books the final battle is connected with the Last Judgment.

mor will suffice for all their needs. (e) Finally, Paul interprets his literal and metaphorical references to arms and warfare as a call to prayer for the undaunted continuation of his mission work. The "gospel of peace" for the world is totally different from the interpretation and application of the Law by the people of Qumran. These antitheses are so pointed that it must be assumed that Paul had knowledge of the war ideology of Qumran and of the militant spirit and tactics of the Zealots. Instead of imitating either group, he went back to one of the sources of the tradition represented by Qumran (and probably neglected by the Zealots): the book (viz. books) passed on under the name of Isaiah. When he spoke of "God's armor" he did not think in terms of a Holy War.

5) The theory that Gnostic elements, especially the myth of the soul's journey into heaven, is reflected in Eph 6 needs only to be mentioned by name. It does not have any support in the text.[194]

III   The Splendid Armor

Four terms used in Eph 6 to describe the "armor of God" require special consideration. As stated previously, many translations render *panopliā* in Eph 6:11 and 13 by "whole armor" or an equivalent expression denoting completeness. The question to be raised now is this: Do these translations correspond to the meaning of *panopliā* in the present context? Further, it must be asked whether the term *dikaiosynē* ("righteousness"), which in Eph 6:14–17 occurs in the company of "truth," "steadfastness," "faith," and "salvation," also includes or signifies the "righteousness of God," as indeed it does in the undisputed Pauline letters? Many commentators hold that here it carries merely an ethical connotation. Next, the reference in 6:15 to shoes being "strapped" on by the saints contains the noun *etoimasiā* ("preparedness, readiness"). What sense does this term have in this context? Finally, the comparison of the "word of God" with a "sword" has an OT history which can elucidate the meaning of vs. 17. These four issues will be discussed separately:

A   The Panoply

The proposal to be made here is that in Eph 6 the use of the term *panopliā* (rather than *opla*, "weapons") emphasizes the quality of the weapons rather than their complete number. Five arguments speak against the seemingly literal translation of *panopliā* by "whole armor."

1) The version "whole armor" is redundant (Robinson) and is replaced in JB, NEB, and especially NTTEV with a translation which indicates that only those special weapons are meant which are given by God to man.

2) The armor used by God in the so-called Holy War includes the terror inflicted upon the enemies by water, hailstones, darkness, thunder, confusion and

---

[194] This theory was suggested tentatively by Bousset, pp. 143–45; reinforced by Reitzenstein's arguments, endorsed by Schlier (*Christus*), and apparently abandoned again by the same author in his commentary on Ephesians. Dibelius, Abbott, and Greeven, TWNTE, V, 721, reject the Gnosticizing interpretation. Even Conzelmann, who at other occasions follows Schlier's lead, comments on 6:12 by saying: "Unlike Gnosticism, there is no flight from and abandonment of the world, but a struggle for the world by which it is reclaimed for [subjection to] the rule of its creator" (p. 89). Texts such as Ginza (left) I 26–27; II 45 are too late to serve as a key for the interpretation of Ephesians. See also the end of COMMENT IV.

the ensuing mutual slaughter.[195] Wisd Sol 5:17, cf. 20, describes the arsenal and tactics of God with the words: "He will put on from head to foot the armor of his wrath, and make all creation his weapon."[196] In Hab 3:4–15 "rays flashing" from God's hands, God's "horses" with their "trampling" hooves, and God's "chariot of victory" are enumerated. Eph 6, however, mentions neither the wrath of God nor the outspokenly aggressive weapons of God, nor the tactics associated with them. Not only Yahweh but also the Near Eastern deities had at their disposal a greater variety of arms than are listed in Eph 6.[197]

3) The term *panoplia* cannot have been chosen with the intention to introduce a complete list of the man-made arms that were used in the wars between nations.[198] The Egyptian, Babylonian, Assyrian, Canaanite, Israelite, Greek, and Roman armies consisted not only of heavily armed infantrymen, but sometimes also of light troops armed with bow and arrow, and cavalry and chariots. In Amos 2:13–16 no less than seven classes or groups of warriors are described. In biblical and non-biblical documents, artillery in the form of stone and arrow throwers and battering rams also play a decisive role. In II Cor 10:3–4 Paul shows that he was acquainted with the tools and tactics for besieging a city. In Eph 6:14–17 only infantry weapons are enumerated. Among the weapons of infantrymen worn at different periods, in this passage the battle-ax, the mace, the sling, the bow and arrows, the heavy and light spears, the dagger, also greaves are missing—not to speak of a Roman soldier's additional equipment.[199] No mention seems to be made of the special gear, or at least of the insignia, of officers; forgotten are trumpets, tubas, bugles, horns; there are no standards or flags; no strategy, no scheme involving the cooperation of other units, and no intimidating parades before and victory demonstrations after the battle. In fact, Eph 6 presents no more than a selection of weapons and instructions for their use, not a complete inventory of an arsenal; neither does this chapter resemble a tactical and strategic handbook.[200] Why then does Paul speak of a *panoplia*? In the latest OT occurrences of this noun, *panoplia* does not mean "complete armor" (see fn. 15) but has a special sense which will be discussed in (5).

4) The function of weapons is not restricted to their use in combat, that is, to the protection of the warrior who wears them and to the destruction of his foe. They also increase self-assurance; they impress friends and terrify enemies; they can become spoils that seal the opponents' defeat and demonstrate the victors' success. As gifts they serve to confirm a friendship or treaty. They can be worn as a sign of rank, and can be stockpiled in a temple to demonstrate or secure one's wealth and power. They also have ornamental value;

[195] Exod 14–15; 23:27; Deut 7:23; Josh 10:10–11; 24:7; Judg 4:15; 7:22; I Sam 7:10; 14:15, 20; see von Rad, pp. 7–12.
[196] The translation of NEB is to be preferred to that of RSV and JB.
[197] See, e.g. tablet IV of the *Enumah Elish* in ANET, and the reliefs of Marduk and Assur mentioned in fn. 170.
[198] These arms are enumerated in, e.g. Homer *Iliad* VII 207; Polybius VI 22–23; 1QM v 4–14; VI 15; Josephus *bell.* III 93–95, 98–102, 127, 145; Ignatius *Polyc.* VI 1–2; I Sam 17:5–7, 38–40; 18:4; Jer 46:3–4; Ezek 38:4; 39:9; I Chron 5:18; II Chron 26:14–15; Neh 4:16[10].
[199] Josephus says in *bell.* IV 95 that "an infantryman is almost as heavily laden as a pack-mule" when he carries (on the march, not in battle) a saw, a basket, a pick, an ax, a strap, a bill-hook, a chain and three days' provisions.
[200] The same is true of the closest biblical parallels, i.e. Isa 59:17; Wisd Sol 5:17–20; I Thess 5:8; II Cor 6:7; 10:3–5; Rom 6:13; 13:12.

sometimes they are exponents of vanity.[201] Thus there exists not only a technical or military, but also a moral or psychological function of arms. Since Eph 6 explicitly mentions only one function of one specific piece of armor—the quenching of fiery arrows with the shield[202]—and since a major accent is placed upon the "taking up" of arms (not wielding them), the moral or psychological function of the armament given by God is emphasized more than its completeness or its usefulness for killing. The equation of the several arms with "truth," "righteousness," "gospel," "faith," "salvation" and the "word of God" confirms this impression. The ease with which weapons and military imagery were allegorized among different nations and in different cultures, reflects the ultra-military function of armor.[203] The decent, quiet, peaceful life of a civilian can be described in military terms and called a spiritual militia. A NT example of this is offered by the epistles to Timothy.[204]

5) There are texts in and outside the Bible which explicitly establish a connection between arms and a splendid public display of beauty, honor, radiant light, fire, or terror.[205] In Eph 6:11–17 the term *panopliā* and the several arms listed take up this tradition rather than a form used by those who administrate arsenals. Therefore, *panopliā* is more accurately rendered here by "[splendid] armor" than by "whole armor."[206]

B Righteousness

In the discussion of the Persian and Stoic parallels to Eph 6 collected above, it was stated that "truth," "righteousness," "faith" may mean something other than "virtues." "Peace," "salvation," "Spirit," "word of God" certainly cannot be given this summary title. If half of the metaphorical weapons are thus different from virtues, then the whole list of weapons and interpretatory nouns must not be equated with a "catalogue of virtues." But if these terms are not held together by their strictly ethical character, what does connect them and explain their appearance in list form?

[201] Biblical examples are I Sam 17–18; 31:9–10; Isa 22:8b (MT, not LXX); I Kings 10:17; 14:26; II Kings 11:8, 10; II Chron 9:16; 11:12; 12:9–11; 23:7–10; I Macc 4:57; 6:2; 15:17–18. Adornment, (*kata-*)*kosmeō*, by a *panopliā* is mentioned in Polybius III 62:5; Plato *leg.* v 796C; the "girdle" is a decoration and sign of rank in Isa 22:21; Exod 28:4; 29:5; 39:21; I Sam 2:18; Dan 10:5; Rev 1:13; 15:6, etc.; a special "helmet" can be worn and a special "shield" can be carried on victory parades; see Oepke, pp. 303–7, 313–15.
[202] See the Notes on vs. 16 for an explanation.
[203] See the preceding Comment for examples.
[204] I Tim 1:18; II Tim 2:3–4.
[205] Marduk's armor is an "armor of terror," the turban on his head is a halo, *Enumah Elish* IV, line 57, etc.; see Pritchard, ANET, p. 66. The god Assur like Marduk is adorned with attributes of the sun deity: the radiant light emanating from his weapons and from his crown demonstrates power and courage, and it instills terror, see Tallquist, pp. 40–49, 107–9. Yahweh, "clothed in vindication" and "wrapped in fury" makes his name and glory feared, Isa 59:17–19; cf. Sir 46:6. Women are adorned by weapons according to Herodotus I 60; IV 180; Plato *leg.* VIII 796C; the Shulammite's neck is like a tower of David on which a thousand shields are hanging, Song of Songs 4:4. Cf. the musical instruments and "many weapons" of a wedding party mentioned in Ezek 27:10–12. Shields, mail, helmets reflecting the sun make the hills upon which the army advances "ablaze and gleaming like flaming torches"; the noise of armor is frightening, I Macc 6:35, 39, 41. Judas Maccabeus "extends the glory of his people" when he puts on his weapons, I Macc 3:3–4. Golden is the armor of the terrifying rider who suddenly appears to defeat Israel's enemy, II Macc 3:25; 11:8. Even in peace time the garments of war donned by youths can be called "the glories," I Macc 14:9. In the same breath, Yahweh is called "a shield about me" and "my glory," Ps 3:3. The preservation of the conquered enemy's arms serves the purpose of manifesting the "wonderful deeds of the Mighty One," II Bar 63:8. The several functions of the golden shields in the temple (I Kings 10:16–17) were mentioned before.
[206] The arguments of Calvin, Abbott, and other scholars notwithstanding. In Luke 11:22, however, the traditional translation cannot be questioned.

The OT provides an answer, and with it certain apocalyptic, Qumranite, NT and later rabbinical books which each in their own way seek to interpret the OT. Terms such as "truth," "righteousness," "steadfastness," "faith," "peace," "salvation," "the Spirit," and "the word of God," occur when the ground and effect of God's attitude and action is described in relation to the people with whom he has made a *covenant*. All these terms denote a social relationship, i.e. the covenant which is at the same time personal and political, saving and ethical.[207] It was mentioned earlier that God's covenant called for reciprocation, and that the promised Messiah represents both God's "promise" and man's "Amen" (II Cor 1:20). He realizes in person both God's faithfulness and man's faith, the power of God's Spirit and the right spirit of confidence and obedience. Almost half of the Psalms were attributed to God's Anointed, David—probably because the pious in Israel wanted to pray with his words and in his spirit, and hoped to experience salvation as he did.

The occurrence of "righteousness" in Eph 6:14, within an allusion to the Messianic promise (Isa 11:1–9), is of specific importance. In the context of the book of Isaiah, "righteousness" means help, salvation, and peace for the downtrodden. No one except the Messiah can and will establish it among his people and the nations. It is a gift of God.[208] The author of Ephesians was aware of the character and mediation of the righteousness mentioned by Isaiah. Indeed, the proclamation of "peace" and the "salvation" in vss. 15 and 17 belong in the same category as does "righteousness"; each is a piece of armor taken up by the saints, and each is a gift of God. In consequence, in Eph 6 the term "righteousness" does not have a meaning that contradicts its sense in the undisputed Pauline letters. The "righteousness of God" is meant through which man is justified by grace alone (Rom 3:21–31).[209] In his undisputed letters Paul also speaks of "weapons of righteousness" that have to be put on and used. Thus he follows those passages of the Law, the Prophets, and the Psalms which call upon Israel and any of its members to respond to God's grace and to keep the covenant by doing what is right.[210] The promise and proclamation

---

[207] The nouns occur in various combinations; some of them are used as synonyms in e.g. Hosea 2:19; Isa 32:17; Ps 85:7–13; Rom 3:2–5; see also G. Quell-R. Bultmann, TWNTE, I, 232–51; G. Schrenk, TWNTE, II, 192–210; N. H. Snaith, *The Distinctive Ideas of the Old Testament* 5th ed. (London: Epworth, 1953), pp. 50–142. The indexes in e.g. R. H. Charles, *Apocrypha and Pseudepigrapha*, Oxford: Clarendon, 1913; Moore, *Judaism;* and the *Qumran Concordance* of K. G. Kuhn, Göttingen: Vandenhoeck, 1960, give access to the apocalyptic, rabbinic, and Qumranite books.

[208] See esp. Isa 9:2–7; 33:17–22; 42:1–9; 61:1–3.

[209] See also Gal 2:15–21; 3:6–21; II Cor 5:21; Rom 1:17; 3–6; 9:30–33; 10:1–8; Philip 3:9. J. Eadie and Oepke affirm the harmony between Eph 6:14 and Romans or Galatians, but Schlier is somewhat obscure when he writes, "Of course, at this place [in Eph 6:14] *dikaiosynē* is not the forensic righteousness [of God, preached in Galatians, Romans, Philippians] which is accounted to man, but the righteousness of God which permits him to be righteous who enters into its realm. Such is man's righteousness by faith [*Glaubensgerechtigkeit*], i.e. God's righteousness seized by faith: it is righteousness in life [*Lebensgerechtigkeit*], i.e. righteousness that is acted out in life, one of the four later so-called cardinal virtues."

[210] II Cor 6:7 and Rom 6:13; cf. 13:12. Not only in Eph 4:24; 5:9; 6:1 do "righteousness" and the adjective "righteous" include or underscore the attitude and act of obedience. Paul speaks of the "service" and "servants of righteousness"; he attempts for himself and expects all the saints to concentrate on that which is "right," II Cor 3:9; 11–15; Philip 1:7; 4:8. The fact that in certain letters and passages the ethical implications of "righteousness" receive special emphasis does not demonstrate their deutero-Pauline origin. Rather it means that Paul and John the Baptist and Jesus (according to Matt 3:15; 5:6, 10, 20; 21:32) have an analogous understanding of "righteousness": it is both God's gracious gift and man's new life—though, on different occasions, the accent may be placed more on the one or on the other.

("word") of God's gracious, miraculous, and saving attitude and action shall "not return empty" to God, but "accomplish" the purpose of God and flourish (Isa 55:11a).

The righteousness of God which is a gift includes the high calling of those who are saved by it. Paul never speaks of a faith that is quietistic in regard to ethics, and passive in situations that demand decision and action.[211] "Obedience of faith" is the purpose of Paul's mission, according to Rom 1:5. God's perfect righteousness shows its power in its effect: the response of man manifested by an attitude taken and acts done in the "service of righteousness" (II Cor 3:9).[212]

This leads to still another aspect of the "righteousness" mentioned in Eph 6:14. In the OT, righteousness is not always compared with a weapon, but there are passages saying that it is "put on" and "worn" as an ornamental or official belt, a breastpiece, a robe or a turban.[213] In all cases, great dignity and responsibility is conveyed to the man who "dons" righteousness. When he is clothed with God's righteousness he becomes a righteous judge. His is now the high office of a king, a priest, or an elder in the gate. He has to see to it that righteousness be established for all who hunger and thirst for their right and for peace. This meaning of being "clothed with righteousness" cannot be excluded from the interpretation of Eph 6. It confirms the suggestion made earlier that all the soldiers described here hold the rank of officers, since they are provided with the sort of cuirass reserved for the rich and the powerful, the high and mighty. The "girding with righteousness" means, therefore, that a great honor and heavy duty is entrusted to each of the saints. In the struggle assigned to them, they are to be wise, righteous, and merciful judges—just as were those OT kings, priests, and elders who carried out God's will.

C   Steadfastness

In most modern versions and commentaries, the words *en etoimasiā* in Eph 6:15 are rendered in a way that points to a "preparation" or its result, the "preparedness."[214] There are, however, reasons for another translation which

---

[211] The statement "To one who does not work but trusts him who justifies the ungodly, his faith is reckoned for righteousness" (Rom 4:5) is no exception. Only work in the sense of speculating upon reward is meant, not acts of obedience done in gratitude for God's promise and gift; see e.g. Rom 4:20-21, and the passages quoted in COMMENT VI on 2:1-10.

[212] Qumran attests to the same awareness of justification by the righteousness and grace of God alone, *and* of ethical obligation that bind the community and each of its members. By their repentance, their cult, their discipline, their warfare, the members of this group intended nothing other than praise of God's righteousness. See esp. 1QS x 11-13, 25-26; xi 2-20; cf. 1QH, *passim;* 1QpHab vii 15 – viii 3.

[213] Isa 11:4-5; Exod 28:15 ff.; Job 29:14; Sir 27:8; Bar 4:20.

[214] RSV owes its version "with the equipment" probably to LSLex, 703, and WBLex, 316; but these dictionaries stipulate that it is *only* in Eph 6:15 that *etoimasiā* means equipment! In all other secular and biblical occurrences of the term, either the act or the result of preparation is meant. NTTEV translates by "readiness [to announce]" and thus stays closer to the common Greek meaning of the noun, also to parallel NT texts such as Titus 3:1; II Tim 2:21; I Peter 3:15 that speak of preparation for doing good works, viz. for defending the Christians' hope against detractors. Compare "the good works provided [lit. prepared] by God," Eph 2:10, and the preparing or guiding (*euthynō*) of "our feet on the way of peace," Luke 1:79. The interpretation of Eph 6:15 by the Vulg.; Beza; Erasmus; Calvin; Coccejus; Robinson, pp. 135, 215; Abbott; W. Grundmann, TWNTE, II, 706; Oepke, TWNTE, V, 612; Gaugler follows this line. But Calvin and Abbott add a qualification: the first speaks of readiness for service which is established by the gospel (rather than oriented toward a mission *for* the gospel); the second believes that "preparation to preach the Gospel" is not every saint's business, since not all Christians are preachers. JB translates by "eagerness [to preach]" and SegB by "zeal [which the gospel gives]." Thus, the prep-

emphasizes solidity and stability. Arguments for the version "steadfast" are the following:

1) Most frequently in the LXX, words derived from the Greek stem *etoim* translate the Hebrew verb *kūn* or its cognates. This verb means, "to be [or to stand] firm," "taut," "well founded" or "established"; the corresponding noun *mākōn* signifies "established place" or "foundation." Certainly the authors of the LXX were aware of the meaning of *kūn* and *mākōn;* according to them, words derived from the Greek stem *etoim* denoted the act or result of "standing firm."[215]

2) In the Orient, ordinary people walked barefoot or in sandals, and most ancient wars seem to have been fought by unshod infantry, cavalry, charioteers, and artillerymen. However, ancient sculptures and descriptions show that shoes were a part of the Assyrian and the Roman soldier's regular outfit. The heavy, nailed boot of the Assyrians reached up to the calf and was tied with laces—if they broke, it was a sign of defeat (Isa 5:27). According to Isa 9:5; Zech 10:5, this boot could be used for "trampling" down enemies. Paul, however, does not speak of foes lying in the mud at the saints' feet. Rather there is agreement among the commentators that he has in mind the *caliga* ("half-boot") of the Roman legionary which was made of leather, left the toes free, had heavy studded soles, and was tied to the ankles and shins with more or less ornamental straps.[216] Among the Egyptians, the post-classical Greeks, and the Romans of the imperial period, high shoes, worn in different colors, were a sign of a civilian's riches, rank or vanity. In Jesus' parable, the prodigal son receives together with a festival robe and a ring, "shoes on his feet" as an (extravagant) sign of the restoration of his honor and dignity (Luke 15:22). But the Roman soldier's boots served primarily other purposes: they equipped him for long marches and for a solid stance while he threw his (heavy or light) spear, used his sword, and shielded himself against arrows, lances, and stones.[217] While they did not impede his mobility, they prevented his foot from sliding, just like the studded shoes of today's soccer players. At the same time, they were not designed to facilitate running, e.g. in flight from the enemy.

3) When someone wanted to be quick and run fast he went without sandals

---

aration or readiness is located in the psyche of man, esp. his mental, emotional, and volitional disposition. Thomas Aquinas embellishes this type of exposition with vivid imagination: the soles of the sandals "signify . . . the raising of the mind from earthly matters . . ."; the sandals "are open above, in which an eagerness for divine wisdom is signified."

[215] See L. Koehler-W. Baumgartner, *Lexicon in Veteris Testamenti Libros,* Leiden: Brill, 1953; Hatch-Redpath, *Concordance to the LXX,* Oxford: Clarendon, 1893. Interpreters such as Robinson and Abbott show awareness of the special meaning of the derivation from the stem *etoim* in the LXX, but unlike Bynaeus and his followers they do not conclude that in Eph 6 Paul used *etoimasiā* in the LXX sense. The peculiar Septuagintal meaning may have been surprising (or unknown) to the readers of Ephesians, but it was current among Hebrew-Christians, as Matt 25:34 (also 41?); I Cor 2:9; Heb 11:16; perhaps also Eph 2:10, show. In any case, the preposition *en* ("in") before *etoimasiā* does not represent the instrumental sense of the Hebrew *bᵉ*. Instead of introducing the means or piece of equipment *by* which the saints are shod, it probably refers to the ground *upon* which they stand, or to the (well-established) realm with*in* which they live. Compare the COMMENT on the formula "in Christ" (I on 1:1–2) and the meaning of the phrase "in the Spirit" in 6:18.

[216] See Kromayer-Veith, plates 34–38, 40. Emperor Caligula owed his (nick)name to this boot.

[217] While in Mark 6:9 Jesus commands that his apostles wear sandals (*sandalia*), in Matt 10:10; Luke 10:4; cf. 22:35 he prohibited them to use any kind of footwear (*hypodēmata*). Bynaeus, p. 92, tries to solve the contradiction by having Jesus forbid a spare pair of sandals. Other harmonizers teach (probably erroneously) that sandals are permitted but shoes excluded. It may be that a different function of the footgear worn in Rome and in Palestine accounts for the different traditions of the logion in Mark and Matthew, respectively. See Oepke, p. 311.

or shoes.[218] "Quick to shed blood" are the "feet" of the evildoers, not their shoes or sandals (Isa 59:7; Rom 3:15).[219] The men having these fast feet do not know the way of peace (Rom 3:17). In turn "the feet" are admired rather than the footwear of the victory-messenger who comes running over the mountains (Isa 52:7).[220]

In summary, despite the allusion to Isa 52:7 with the words "gospel of peace," Eph 6:15 belongs to the same pattern of military metaphors as is found in vss. 14, 16–17. This verse does not use the messenger imagery of Rom 10: 14–18; rather, Paul speaks here of the equipment provided by God which makes Christians able to "stand" and "resist." They can say, "We shall not be moved." Cf. Ps 121:3: "He will not let your foot be moved."[221]

D   The Sword of the Word

The metaphorical usage of the noun "sword" and of the verbs describing its use and effect has a long history in the OT:

1) Some texts speak of the sword of Yahweh which is "sent out" against his enemies and is "whetted" and "drunk with blood."[222] This sword can work salvation for Israel, as in the battle of Gideon,[223] or in the case of the king who is girded with righteousness and wears his sword to help the poor (Isa 11:4; Ps 45:3–5). It is a warning to Israel when put into the hand of her enemy (Ezek 30:24–25). Sometimes Babylonians, Assyrians, and Egyptians speak of the sword of their gods, but a basic distinction exists between the OT and e.g. the Assyrian political theology: the Assyrian army is called "the iron sword of the god Assur" and is at the same time the "army of the king of the gods."[224] Since the earthly king fully represents the god Assur, there is no need for the latter to be immediately involved in the heat of the battlefield. Yahweh, however, often participates in person in Israel's battles, using his own arms. If the "Lord of hosts" chooses troops to carry out his will, he is not dependent upon the recruits and swords of Israel, but wins the victory with his holy angels.[225] He also can win with a ridiculously small number of men (Judg 7) or

---

[218] Bynaeus, p. 66, quotes Musonius (from Stobaeus' *eclogae*): "Sandals are quasi fetters and impediments of the feet"; in Sparta they were prohibited; athletes took them off.

[219] When in Ps 18:29, 33 the Lord is praised for "making my feet like hind's feet" so that "I can leap over a wall," and for "setting me secure on the heights," then his very special grace is extolled. Usually a man's feet do not possess the quality of the hind's hooves which enable the animal not only to run fast and jump high, but also to stand firm in the tiniest foothold offered by a cliff.

[220] The suggestion of Cross, pp. 29–30, that this verse introduces the theophany of "the divine warrior" described in Isa 10–12, is worth mentioning, but does not immediately affect the issue discussed here.

[221] Kamlah, p. 191, n. 2, suggests the translation of 6:15 by "The feet shod with the kind [of shoe] created by the gospel of peace."

[222] Amos 9:4; Isa 31:8; 34:5–6; Deut 32:41–42; Jer 25:29; 47:6; Ezek 21:3, 14–16, 28–32; 32:10; Zeph 2:12; Zech 13:7; Ps 7:12.

[223] The battle cry, "A sword for the Lord and Gideon" (Judg 7:20) probably means that God's sword was equated with Gideon's and vice versa.

[224] See Tallquist, pp. 96–99.

[225] Josh 5:13–15; II Sam 5:24; Deut 9:3, etc. Only in exceptional cases does the OT speak of armies constituted by (several of) the twelve tribes that "come to the help of the Lord," Judg 5:23. Reference can be made to a nation that is "the rod of his anger," Isa 10:5. But it may be important that Ephraim is called his helmet, Judah his scepter, Ps 108:8, not his sword. A rabbinical passage sets the accent on the peaceful intention of the Lord, even when he comes with his hosts. "Rabbi Simeon used to say: Note how different from the ways of God are the ways of men. When a human king goes to war, he goes with multitudes and legions, but when he goes on a peaceful mission he goes alone. Not so the Holy One, blessed be he. When He goes on a mission of peace, He goes forth with multitudes and legions," NumR. 10–11 (157a–164a).

by means of a pebble flung from a sling (I Sam 17). According to Exod 14:13–14; cf. Ps 17:13–15; 35:1 ff., etc., Israel or individual members of this people simply watch him win. Though sometimes, e.g. in Exod 17; I Sam 15, they are called to execute God's will against his enemies, they cannot erect monuments to celebrate victory as their own achievement.[226] When Saul does this, he seals his own downfall (I Sam 15:12).

2) Several OT texts combine the sword with the "word." Either Yahweh himself "slays" people—even his beloved Ephraim—"by the words of his mouth" (Hosea 6:5); "his all-powerful word leaps from heaven . . . a stern warrior carrying the sharp sword of thy authentic command" (Wisd Sol 18:15–16); or "he makes the mouth of a prophet like a sharp sword" (Isa 49:2); or "the teeth" of the godless are called "spears and arrows," and "their tongues sharp swords" (Ps 57:4; cf. 64:3). In the NT, words with the power to kill are symbolized by the "sword" issuing from the Messiah's mouth.[227] The opposite of such use is to command peace, or to bring peace.[228] In Eph 6:17 the sword is the last weapon which is to be taken up. The saints are enjoined to proceed aggressively against the evil spirits. The peace given to them and kept by them is an expanding and conquering power, not a mood fostered in the seclusion of a self-contained in-group.

3) Words and sounds can play a decisive role in battles, not only in the OT but in the whole ancient world, to say nothing of later periods. Oracles are sought to secure a fortunate outcome; curses are pronounced upon the enemy; encouraging speeches are delivered to the troops; last-minute prayers are spoken before the battle; crisp commands are shouted and acknowledged; yells and obscenities accompany the charge. However, in Ephesians the "word" used in the confrontation of the saints with the world is the "gospel of peace" which was first proclaimed by the Messiah himself (2:17; 6:15; cf. Heb 2:3–4). According to Eph 6:18–20, the particular mode of wielding the "sword of the word" is the prayer of the saints to God and the announcement of good news in prisons, before courts, in the world's capital, Rome, and thus virtually to all the world, cf. Acts 28:30–31. It is clear that the mere quotation of Bible texts does not in itself exhaust the use of the "word of God" which the saints are to make. Ever new prayers, meditations, and forms of proclamation are indispensable for their mission.

IV   The Host of Opponents

Earlier in this commentary the meaning of the terms "governments" and "authorities" was discussed. The same two nouns are used in 6:12 and enriched by the additional titles of "overlords of this dark world" and "spiritual hosts of evil."[229] At least three observations are important for interpreting the present section of Ephesians:

a) The "principalities and powers" are at the same time intangible spiritual entities and concrete historical, social, or psychic structures or institutions of all

---

[226] See von Rad, pp. 7–13 for a collection of pertinent passages.
[227] Rev 1:16; 19:15. According to a legend recorded in Acts 5:1–11, a lying couple dies immediately after the pronouncement of judgment. The sword is a symbol of legal power over life and death in Rom 13:4.
[228] See, e.g. Zech 9:10; Matt 10:13; Eph 2:17.
[229] See COMMENTS V on 1:15–23 and II on 2:1–10.

created things and all created life. They represent a certain order in God's creation—though their idolization by man has often resulted in chaotic conditions. It was stated that on exegetical grounds it is as yet impossible to identify exactly the several groups mentioned by Paul or to sketch the hierarchy among them. Their many names indicate their diversity, and listing them sometimes expresses the desire either to secure their help or to ward off their interference.

b) Because of the death and the resurrection of the Messiah Jesus, these powers are already subject to God and Christ,[230] and they face an even more total subjugation in the future (I Cor 15:25–27). In the meantime, some of them deserve the saints' loyal cooperation (Rom 13:1–7; Eph 6:5–9, etc.). They are "servants of God for the good" of man, but none of them must be idolized or worshiped.[231] Their location "in the heavens"[232] does not guarantee that all of them follow the example of those who serve for the best of a "quiet and peaceable" life (I Tim 2:2) or for the "salvation" of the elect people (Heb 1: 14). On the contrary, even Satan can operate from heaven (Job 1–2). According to Ephesians, the devil rules from one (limited!) region of the heavens: he is called "ruler of the atmosphere." In Gnostic teaching this place separates man from God, and the earth from heaven. Therefore it is called a wall (*oros*).[233] Paul emphasizes in Rom 8:38–39 that no "power" is able finally to "separate" the saints from "the love of God."

c) Although the powers mentioned include "death" and can eventually deserve the name of "enemies," not all of them are evil. Life, angels, high points of human existence or destiny are among them (Rom 8:38–39). Whether they be good or evil, they all face total subjection to the Messiah and to God at the end of the present aeon (I Cor 15:25–27). While in Eph 1:21, perhaps also in 2:7; 3:10, good and evil forces are listed, 6:12 speaks only of evil powers. The attributes "of this dark world" (lit. "of this darkness"[234]), and "of evil" may either belong to the third and fourth group only, or qualify the first two ("governments" and "authorities") as well. Certainly the last two of the four titles would be redundant if the first pair implied their evil character by definition.[235] Against the corrupted structures and institutions the saints have to "wrestle"; those powers must be "resisted" (6:12–13).

It may be asked whether the powers mentioned in Eph 6 are the same as the demons which according to the Gospels threaten, dominate, and seek to destroy the life of individuals. An affirmative answer is suggested by the following ob-

---

[230] Col. 2:15; Eph 1:20–21; I Peter 3:22; Heb 1:4–13; 2:7–8.

[231] Col 2:18, 23; Rev 13; 22:8–9, etc.

[232] From the "heavens" comes God's full blessing, Eph 1:3, and "in the heavens" the saints are already "enthroned," 2:6. Calvin insists that the accent in Eph 6:12 is not on the location in the air, but on the general superiority of the Satanic realm over man; Schlier, p. 291 speaks of the "unperspicuous, unseizable" position held by these powers.

[233] The "dividing wall" mentioned in Eph 2:14 anticipates second-century and later Gnostic imagery. According to Eph 2 this wall also separates man from man.

[234] A strong group of variant readings has: "of the darkness of this aeon"—perhaps because "this darkness" is a rare expression (Abbott). According to Conzelmann, the perversion of this world into darkness shows that the world is not a neutral place. 1QS III 20–21 speaks of an "angel of darkness, the evil spirit which nevertheless was created by God. See the literature on "light" listed in COMMENT IV on Eph 5:1–20, fn. 171.

[235] As e.g. H. Schlier assumes in his book, *Principalities and Powers*, New York: Herder, 1961. Thomas Aquinas, however, distinguishes three classes of angels: (a) cherubim, seraphim, archangels who are always good; (b) principalities and powers that are good or bad; (c) the devil and the demons.

servations: just like the powers in Eph 6, so the demons mentioned in the Gospels are not of "blood and flesh"; both are specifically dangerous because of their "spiritual," seemingly intangible, unalterable and invincible character. The distinction between the demons and powers, however, appears to be that the demons affect the individual incidentally, whereas the powers threaten all men at all times. Admittedly the two kinds of threats cannot be fully explained apart from one another. According to the insights of C. G. Jung a collective unconscious is essential to the structure of the individual psyche. Individual suffering may therefore be the result of pressures experienced by the whole human community. The following arguments support an interpretation of Eph 6 which emphasizes the social tensions and pressures.[236]

1) The special concern in Ephesians is to present the gospel as a message related to man's social essence and existence. In this letter the exclusion of the Gentiles from God's kingdom and the mutual enmity between outsiders and insiders express the past human condition which is now radically changed by the revelation of the Gentiles' inclusion and the making of peace between Jews and Gentiles. The "social gospel" of Ephesians does not minimize or exclude the fact that psychic forces determine, uphold, or seek to destroy man's individual existence and "peace of mind." But just as in Romans the personal chapters 6–8 are imbedded in chapters 1–5 and 9–16 which deal with all mankind, so in Eph 3:16–17; 4:22–24 references to the personal and psychic realms are embraced by the message of social peace. It is not impossible, but rather unlikely, that Paul would concentrate his attention solely or primarily on man's private existence and struggles at a point so near the end of his letter.

2) The "fiery missiles" to which the saints are exposed (6:16) are not the pangs of carnal desire or the signs of very special personal afflictions and conflicts, but they are to be identified as the influences, temptations, tests, persecutions, and sufferings that come from outside upon the community of the saints.[237] In the NOTES it was shown that the expression "blood and flesh" (6:12) includes the internal conflicts of man. Even these psychic and moral conflicts are explicitly excluded from consideration when Paul asserts that the "powers" of which he speaks here do *not* consist of "blood and flesh."[238]

3) The third and fourth titles of the opponents show clearly that cosmic, political, social, and similar powers are meant: the word *kosmokratores,* here translated by "overlords," originally means planets, and in magical texts (inferior) gods. Rabbis use equivalent terms to describe Great Kings such as Nebuchadnezzar, Evilmerodach, Belshazzar; Jewish apocalyptic and sectarian writ-

---

[236] Perhaps the powers named in 6:12 can be compared to today's USA, UN, or Common Market, or to the intangible substance of what is called the establishment, the government, Wall Street, the Military-Industrial Complex, the Peace Movement, the University, White Supremacy, Black Power, the good life, hunger, etc. These examples show that the diverse powers do not necessarily form a united front, and the battles raging among them can threaten to quash the saints. Neither an "established" nor a "gathered church"—whether dominated by its clergy or its laity, or by both—can claim to be essentially different from the powers in its environment. Rather, because of its purported connection with heaven, it can be as dangerous to true believers as any outside enemy—as indeed is shown by the fate of Jesus among his own people, portrayed in the Gospels, in Acts, and e.g. in Dostoevski's story of the Grand Inquisitor (in *The Brothers Karamazov*) or by the experience of many a "saint" or reformer in the course of two thousand years of church history.

[237] See the end of the last NOTE on 6:16.

[238] Cf. Whiteley, and G. H. C. Macgregor, "Principalities and Powers: the Cosmic Background of Paul's Thought," NTS 1 (1954), 17–28, esp. 19.

ings describe the demons Mastema, Azazel, Sammael, or the arch-enemy Beliar (or Belial) by corresponding attributes. "Ruler of the world" is a title of Satan in the Fourth Gospel and among Valentinian Gnostics. However, in the LXX a similarly universalistic title (such as "king" or "lord of the world") is attributed to God himself, and even at the present time Jewish prayers maintain this custom.[239] When Eph 6 was written, *kosmokratōr* had not yet assumed the bad sense it received in Gnosticism—otherwise the attached reference to the realm of darkness would be superfluous. But, while the plural "overlords" dispels a dualistic (Manichean) notion of one good and one bad *kosmokratōr,* it yet points out the enormous power of the many evil opponents of God and the saints.

4) The adjective *ta pneumatica* (lit. "the spirituals"), rendered by "the spiritual hosts," corresponds to the designation of the devil as a "spirit" in 2:2 and the demons as "spirits" in Mark 1:23, 26, etc. While the "unclean spirits" prefer to reside in men and can be exorcised by the word and the gesture of a person authorized by God or prepared to treat them, the "spiritual hosts" who make their attacks from "the heavens" must be combated with additional and even stronger arms. According to Rev 12:7-17 Michael and his angels evict the devil and his hosts from the heavens. Eph 6 far from avers that the saints can take that action. Earth-bound as they still are, they are protected by God's own truth, righteousness, peace. They need not die in fear and terror; also, they have no time for self-pity and no reason to worship or placate the attacking powers. They are equipped to face them squarely.

However, Chrysostom, Theodoret, Oecomenius, and other ancient interpreters as well as some modern scholars believe that the struggle of the saints takes place in "the heavens." According to them, the soul has to overcome demonic obstacles before it can penetrate into full union with God.[240] This view attributes to the inimical spiritual powers the function which in Gen 3 is fulfilled by the Cherubim with the flaming sword. But Eph 6 does not state, "Our wrestling takes place in heaven," and, therefore, does not speak of a "war in heaven," cf. Rev 12:7. Also, the interpretation of the words "stand," "resist," and "carry out everything" in the NOTE on 6:11, 13-14 has shown that the idea of storming the kingdom of heaven is not present. Unlike the author of Revelation, Paul uses a minimum of terms and concepts that have a distinctly legendary or mythological character.

Still, Paul's abstention from dabbling in pagan mythologies does not prevent him from describing the struggle of the saints with the powers as an event that belongs to the end-time of the world and is characterized by eschatological traits. The next COMMENT will demonstrate this even more clearly.

---

[239] See e.g. Jamblichus *de mysteriis* II 3; IX 10; Irenaeus I 5:4 (cf. 1:1) and the *Book of Archontes* found in Chenoboskion; Jub 10:7; II Macc 7:9; 13:14; John 12:31; 14:30; 16:11; for further references see, e.g. LSLex, 984; Abbott; Schlier. In the LXX, except in Job (sixteen times) and Zech 11:4, *pantokratōr* is the translation of "[Yahweh] Zebaoth."

[240] In fn. 194 were mentioned names of recent interpreters who suggest that 6:12 reproduces the Gnostic belief in the "journey of the soul to heaven"—a journey which leads past angelic or demonic powers that attempt to block the way. Schlier, *Christus,* pp. 7-18, considers I Peter 3:19-22 and Eph 4:8-10 the closest parallels to 6:12-13. More recently, in his commentary (p. 291), he speaks of "formal and linguistic analogies from the Gnostic realm," and he explains the "heavens" by "the atmosphere of existence."

V   The Darkest Day

The historical and prophetic books of the OT as well as apocalyptic writings speak of "the Day" or "Those Days" that have come or will dawn either within the foreseeable future or at the end of time and history.[241] At that moment, God will manifest himself in an irresistible and glorious way by demonstrating his presence and power through one great act of judgment and salvation. Some prophets warned their contemporaries: Even those who await the Day as a day of light will experience it as "darkness" (Amos 5:18; Zeph 1:14–18). The means by which Yahweh triumphs over his enemies inside and outside Israel are often (e.g. in Ezek 38–39) described in military terminology; as stated in e.g. Exod 15:3; cf. 14:25, God proves himself a "man of war." The narrators and prophets do not speak of a war, armies, or arms as made and used by men, but of the war of God fought (sometimes by the hosts appointed by him against his antagonists) with the weaponry which he alone controls.[242] In Jewish sectarian and apocalyptic books,[243] also in the Little Apocalypse of Mark 13 par., and in the Book of Revelation, the description of the last Day(s) is closely linked with the prediction not just of conventional wars, but also of an unprecedented battle: the final demonstration and victory of God's power in which not only the angels have a share, but in which the chosen people participate as soldiers, onlookers, or fugitives.

While Mark 13 and the book of Revelation stress the endurance of the saints and can be interpreted as recommendations for resistance by patience, perhaps even by a quietistic attitude, Eph 6, together with the Qumran literature, urges the saints to most active resistance on that Day. Since the aggressive miracle weapons of God are not mentioned here, ample room is left for the active engagement of the saints in battle and for the use of the weapons given them. This does not preclude the eschatological character of the struggle. The references to the "darkness" and the "hosts" of evil, and to the "strength of God's power" which is to be manifested now, require that Eph 6:10–20 in general, and the Day mentioned in 6:13 specifically, be interpreted in an eschatological-apocalyptical sense.[244] The translation "the darkest day" was chosen in order to make this point.

However, the day of the struggle does not dawn only in the remote future.[245] As much as Ephesians expresses a "realized eschatology of salvation," it also speaks of the experience of eschatological tribulations at the present time. The struggle against the spiritual hosts of evil is necessary now, just be-

[241] Josh 4:14; 7:25; 10:13–14; Judg 4:14; Isa 2:12; 13:6, 9; 22:5; 34:8; Amos 5:18–20; Hosea 6:2?; Jer 46:10; Lam 2:22; Ezek 7:10; 13:5; 30:3; 34:12; Obad 15; Zeph 1:7–8, 14–18; Zech 14:13; Joel 2:1–11. In its description of the future, e.g. Isa 9:4 points back to "the day of Midian," that is, the victory gained under Gideon over the Midianites (Judg 7).

[242] According to von Rad, pp. 56–67, esp. p. 61, the prophetic statements on the Day or Days to come renew the tradition of "the Holy War." A sketch of the development of the prophecies regarding the Day or the last time is also found in von Rad, TWNTE, II, 943–47; idem, OTTh II (1965), 119–25. If the term "eschatological" is applied to the message of the classical prophets of Israel, it does not refer to events outside time, but means visitation of Yahweh in the past, present, or future course of history, and the "inauguration of a new era" (TWNTE, II, 946).

[243] E.g. CD viii 2–3; 1QM xv 1, 12; xvi 1 ff.; Test. Dan v 10; Ass. Mos. i 18; Ps Sol xv 6–8[4–6].

[244] Schlier and Gaugler speak of the last struggle(s) before the parousia; Dibelius finds a parallel in II Thess 2:3 (the great defection at the end of the world). Cf. also I Thess 5:6–8.

[245] G. Delling's statement, "Nowhere is there any suggestion that this day . . . is already present or even reaches into the present" (TWNTE, II 952–53), is not convincing; the reference to Eph 6:13 made in the context disproves the proposition.

cause it anticipates, and participates in, the final opposition of God to all evil—
and God's victory over it. "The darkest day" immediately precedes the day of
liberation; it announces its proximity. Even in the penultimate time, the saints
have to deal with the ultimate.

VI   Watch and Pray

What is meant by the command to "stay awake" (6:18), viz. to "be watch-
ful" (Col 4:2)?[246] This terminology is used in its literal sense in the story of
Jesus in Gethsemane,[247] where even the three closest disciples fall asleep. The
meaning is literal also in the parables of the servants who have to stay awake
and be ready for the coming of a thief or the return of the master, as well as in
the story of the virgins who go out to meet the bridegroom. The vigils held
in monasteries and convents, or on special days of prayer, are an attempt to
obey fully the command to "watch and pray." Not only the angels but also
the people assembled around God's throne pray day and night (Rev 4:8, 10;
7:15). What the seer perceives in a vision has its earthly counterpart: Paul
speaks of his "unceasing" prayer for the congregation;[248] he expects a good
widow to pray day and night. John of Patmos exhorts the churches of Asia
Minor to be vigilant.[249] This is not to say that men on earth can be like the
angels who always worship, or like God who "neither sleeps nor slumbers" (Ps
121:4). Yet on the unique night in Gethsemane Jesus asks his disciples to stay
awake and watch with him. In visions and parables, watches and vigils imply
deprivation of physical sleep.

However, in the explication and application of visions and parables, the term
"to watch" becomes a metaphor and denotes spiritual alertness. Whether the
disciples and saints in the several congregations are asleep or awake—"at all
times" they are to be ready. By the time the NT was put into writing, and perhaps even earlier, the words "watch and pray" had become "typical eschatological exhortations" (Conzelmann). Essential was "not a physical state of being awake but the eschatological being awake for [meeting] the eschatological
temptation."[250] The so-called "darkest day" (Eph 6:13) immediately precedes
the day on which the Bridegroom-King arrives and the final liberation is gained
(1:14; 4:13, 30). Only a metaphorical interpretation of "staying awake"
(6:18) corresponds to the reason why the saints cannot afford to be drowsy,
lazy, or concerned with their own comfort and desires.

"Staying awake" means to be totally oriented toward that which comes and
to respond readily to Him who comes. Physical sleep can be resisted, avoided,
or overcome through willpower and discipline, a fakir's training, or by use of
drugs. Abstinence from physical sleep is in itself neither a remedy against
temptation nor a demonstration of preparedness for the Messiah's final advent.

---

[246] The original difference between *agrypneō* and *grēgoreō* was discussed in the NOTES on Eph 6:18.
See also Barn. XXI 7; *Did.* v 2; XVI 1; Ignatius *Polyc.* I 3.
[247] Jesus "passes the night in prayer to God" also in Luke 6:12.
[248] The passages are collected in fn. 74 *infra* COMMENT II on 1:15-23.
[249] I Tim 5:5; Rev 3:2-3; 16:15; cf. I Thess 5:17-18.
[250] Dibelius, "Das historische Problem der Leidensgeschichte," in *Botschaft und Geschichte*, I
(Tübingen: Mohr, 1953), 254. In his commentary on Col 4:2 (HbNT 12 [1953], 50), the same
author refers to Rom 13:11 and I Thess 5:6 and speaks of "prayer as the best kind of religious
watchfulness."

It is not automatically a service rendered to God. Even when pious men succeed in most rigorous self-discipline, they may fall under the judgment pronounced by Jesus against ostentatious forms of prayer and fasting (Matt 6:5–6, 16–18). Eph 6:18 speaks of constant resistance against temptations, especially the one great final temptation, and of the unfading hope for the coming of the Lord. This watch and this hope determine the measure and manner of the fight against laziness, fatigue, and despair.

Since the charge to "stay awake" is a metaphor calling for the total vigilance just described, the parallel charge to "pray . . . with all prayers" is not likely to point exclusively to formalized prayers offered in community or in solitude. Rather, the saints are encouraged to offer their whole life and being as a prayer to God—whether they be active or passive, speaking or silent, whether they render a palpable service to Christ and their fellow man or share in the suffering of Christ and the world by bearing pain and misery in loneliness.[251] In Eph 6:18, life is characterized as one uninterrupted address and response to God, a cry for help from the depth, an expression of memory and hope based on God's great deeds, an attempt to do justice to the fact that only from Him, with Him, and for Him can man exist from day to day and pass through the final tribulation.

The climax of 6:18 consists of the call for intercession on behalf of all the saints. Here it is acknowledged that neither in spiritual nor in material matters do the saints belong to the rich and secure of the present "dark world." Rather, the church is gathered from the poor, consists of those poor, and stands at the side of the poor whenever she is true to her head, Jesus Christ, who "though he was rich . . . for your sake he became poor so that through his poverty you might become rich" (II Cor 8:9). The saints still live in an earthly "tent" (II Cor 5:1–10); indeed, they "possess forgiveness" and are heirs to immeasurable riches (Eph 1:7–8; 3:8). But they are still far from being perfect (4:13; 5:26–27). The community of the saints has a mission to fulfill which requires that God equip it continuously with strength, wisdom, courage, humor—and with the bread necessary for each day.

However, the church prays not only for herself and her members. In 6:19–20 Paul speaks of his mission to unbelievers. As will be shown in the next COMMENT, all the saints are involved in the testimony which he must give. Therefore, the prayer of the saints includes and expresses above all their care for others. They live, act, suffer, and speak before God as representatives and examples[252] of the persons, conditions, needs, and hopes of their brothers in faith and of those "afar" who do not yet know that they are joined to the community of the "near," cf. 2:13–17. The personal and the social, the devotional and the missionary dimensions of life are inseparable, according to Eph 6:18–20.

---

[251] W. Stringfellow, *A New Birthday*, Garden City, New York: Doubleday, 1970, gives a personal and moving account of his attempt to live life as a continual act of worship. A more formal type of prayer is by no means excluded by this widening of the concept of prayer. See, e.g. K. H. Miskotte, *Der Weg des Gebetes*, Munich: Kaiser, 1964.

[252] In Pauline diction: as types (*typoi*), I Thess 1:7; II Thess 3:9; I Cor 10:6; cf. I Tim 1:16; 4:12; Titus 2:7.

VII   The Mission of Paul and the Community

In Eph 3:1–14 and 4:1, Paul made it plain that he considered himself more than a fellow traveler among the saints. He is an exceptional figure deserving of special attention.[253] In some of his epistles, Paul gives his readers reason to raise their eyebrows at a self-consciousness that appears inflated beyond limits.[254] Still, he never withholds information showing why he is a special case. The following can be gathered from Eph 3:1–13; 4:1; 6:19–20:

a) He considers himself not the best or highest, but "less than the least of the saints" (3:8); cf. the self-designations, "the least of the apostles" "unfit to be called an apostle" (I Cor 15:9), and "the foremost of sinners" (I Tim 1:15). The weaker a member of the body (the church), the more honor is due to him (I Cor 12:22–23).[255] The saying, "The poor are the pearls of the church," is beautifully illustrated by Paul.

b) Paul has been entrusted by God with a special "gift of grace" which is identified with a particular commission. To him the "secret" of the Gentiles' inclusion in God's people was "revealed," and he was destined to announce it to them (3:2–9). In Eph 6:19–20 he avers that nothing except the gift and commission conveyed to him by God, even his ministry, require the special intercession of the saints on his behalf.

c) Paul is in prison while he writes this epistle (3:1; 4:1; 6:20). According to the earlier passages of Ephesians he has accepted suffering and tribulation as a necessary part of his ministry (3:13); in the same spirit he does now abstain from requesting the saints to ask God for special favors on his behalf.[256] Instead of mentioning patience, strength of character, alleviation of his fate, or the quickest possible release from prison, the apostle speaks only of the right word and the right spirit which he needs to be given in order to carry on. Since the "chains" are no obstacle to his mission, God need not be entreated to unloose them. Paul is so totally preoccupied with his missionary ministry that he has no time for self-pity. He asks for special intercession only because his task cannot be fulfilled unless he lives from grace to grace.[257]

Thus the armed stance of the saints in the dark and evil world is identified with their personal involvement and participation in the clear and courageous propagation of the gospel, both in the existing congregations and in the whole world. Not all the saints are given the same chance and the same special task as the apostle. They are not in his prison, need not stand his trial, cannot give testimony in exactly the same way he does. But by their intercession they can

---

[253] In Galatians and Philippians, passim; in I Cor 9; II Cor 1–4; 10–13; Rom 1:1–17; 9:1–3; 11:1, this is even more pronounced.

[254] In II Cor 3 he compares himself with Moses. In Gal 1:6–9 he comes close to declaring his teaching canonical. In II Cor 10–13 Paul not only quotes critical remarks made about him but ironically adds fuel to the charge that he boasts about himself. In I Tim 1:16 he is called a "prototype" (hypotypōsis) of (all) those who are to become believers.

[255] In I Cor 10:16–17; 11:20–34; II Cor 8:9; 13:3–5 and Philip 2:5–11, Christological reasons are proffered to support the same proposition.

[256] Cf. esp. II Corinthians and Philippians, also COMMENT III C on 3:1–13.

[257] Calvin emphasizes two other points. (a) Nobody is so richly endowed with gifts of God that he no longer needs the intercession of others. (b) Intercessions are to be made for the living, not for the dead. Though these or similar thoughts are true enough, they are typical of the relative blindness of Augustine, the Scholastics and the Reformers to the missionary orientation of Paul's theology. Essential to the understanding of Eph 6:17–20 is the immediate connection between the "word of God," "prayer," and "proclamation."

declare before God and men their solidarity with him and with his commission. On the other hand, Paul cannot and will not fight the good fight of faith in splendid isolation. God alone can and must equip him with all he needs for his ministry. By leading a life of intercession on Paul's behalf, the saints help and assist him. Their intercession is more than a merely emotional, verbal, or moral support; it manifests that an "apostolic" mission is theirs, too (3:7–10; cf. 2:7; 5:8–14; 6:15).

The uniqueness of the apostle Paul and of his message in Ephesians is that the grace given to him creates a community that fulfills an evangelizing and missionary function in its environment and beyond.[258]

---

[258] The same is true of the concepts of discipleship and of the church that are expressed in Matt 5:13–16; 28:19–20; Luke 10:1–16; 24:47–48; Acts 1:8; John 17:18; I Peter 2:9.

XIII CONCLUSION
(6:21–24)

6 21 In order that you, too, may have knowledge about me and the state of my affairs . . . Tychicus, our dear brother and faithful servant in the Lord, will make known to you all [matters of this kind]. 22 For this very purpose I have sent him to you, that you may know of our situation and that he reassure your hearts.

23 Peace to the brothers, love, and, above all, faith from God the Father and the Lord Jesus Christ. 24 Grace with all who love our Lord Jesus Christ, in eternity.

NOTES

21. *In order that you, too, may have knowledge about me and the state of my affairs.* The occurrence of "too" (*kai*) between the words "you" and "have knowledge" has been explained in different ways: (a) Not only the Colossians to whom Paul (supposedly) had written first, and to whom Tychicus was also sent (see Col 4:7–8), but "also the Ephesians" shall have personal information (Meyer). (b) Paul has received news about or from the Ephesians (1:15; 4:20–21); now they "in turn" are entitled to receive a communication from him (Gaugler). (c) Although Paul does not know them personally as he does know the saints in many other cities, they, too, shall receive an account of his fate (Abbott).[1] The first of these interpretations is supported neither by Colossians nor Ephesians. Nowhere is it stated that Colossians was written first, Ephesians later. To use the word *kai* in Eph 6:21 as evidence is a *petitio principii*. A combination of the second and third exposition seems, for the time being, the safest procedure. The words *ti prassō* (here translated by "and the state of my affairs") literally mean "what I do." According to Abbott their sense is "how I do," not "what I am doing." This short clause is not found in the parallel Col 4:7. The terms "affairs," and "matters of this kind" were chosen for our translation because the vague Greek original seems to refer to the state of Paul's trial at the emperor's court, rather than to dramas taking place in his soul, or strictly personal experiences with friends or foes.[2]

21–22. *Tychicus . . . will make known to you all [matters of this kind]. . . . For this very purpose I have sent him to you.* The Greek sentence is as broken as the English version given here. It is possible that Paul originally intended to

---

[1] Dibelius excludes the first two interpretations without deciding for the last. He suspects that *kai* may not be in the right place.
[2] As mentioned in, e.g. Rom 7; II Cor 1–4; 10–13; Philip 4:10–12.

write down (or dictate) some personal communications, and then decided that the great number of necessary or desirable details would lead too far and had better be left to Tychicus' oral report. Or, perhaps Paul suddenly remembered how foolish and boastful an enumeration of each of his sufferings and achievements might sound, cf. II Cor 11:16 – 12:12. The syntactically defective sentence, "In order that you . . . all Tychicus will make known to you," certainly looks more original and genuinely Pauline than its abbreviated and polished counterpart in Col 4:7: "All that concerns me, Tychicus will make known to you." It is much more likely that Paul or one of his secretaries used Eph 6:21 in writing to the Colossians and excised what looked improper or superfluous, than that the correct diction of Col 4:7 was truncated by a pseudonymous author of Ephesians.[3]

An account of the translation and history of exposition of the rest of vss. 21 and 22, as well as a discussion of the person and mission of Tychicus,[4] of the complimentary way in which he is described, and of the success of his visit for which Paul hopes, will be presented in the exposition of Col 4:7-8 in AB, vol. 34B. Here it must suffice to restate that Paul does not worry about the chains that tie him, or about his own comfort, but only about the Ephesians lest they be left without reassurance and consolation (Thomas Aquinas). Since he is unable to leave his present location, he sends them more than good words: he dispatches his intimate friend and companion to visit them. In Rom 9:3, Paul has shown his willingness to stake and forgo his own salvation (viz. "to be accursed") if only he can save his brothers.

23. *Peace to the brothers, love, and, above all, faith.* Lit. ". . . love with faith." The benediction formula, "Peace to the brethren," cf. "grace with all who love" (vs. 24, i.e. including women), is unprecedented and without parallels in the NT epistles. The general or specific meaning of the term "peace," and reasons for the deviation from the usual formula, Grace and/or peace (be) with *you,* will be discussed in the COMMENT. In vs. 23 "love" (*agapē*) probably means love between man and man, especially between the saints. This love was described not only in I Cor 13, but also several times in Ephesians.[5] A poorly documented variant reading of Eph 6:23 has "mercy" (*eleos*) instead of love; because mercy cannot be shown by men toward God, this variant confirms the interpretation of "love" by "brotherly love." Since the very next verse refers explicitly to the love of men for "the Lord," it is unlikely that 6:23 is a mere duplication and also speaks of the love for God or Christ. The mention of "love" after "peace" reveals the same connection between "love" and "peace" as was indicated in 4:2-3: only on the basis of the "peace" created by God through the Messiah for "those far" and "those near" (2:13-17) can there be "love." I John speaks of God who "has loved us first," and Romans of the "love poured out through the Holy Spirit into the hearts" of men.[6] Brotherly

---

[3] Mitton, EE, pp. 58–99, asserts the opposite: in 6:21–22 the writer of Ephesians "reproduced exactly" (from the original, from a copy, or from memory) twenty-nine consecutive words that Paul had written to the Colossians, omitting only the two words *kai syndoulos* ("and fellow slave") after "faithful servant." Seven consecutive words are exactly the same in the formalized introduction, Eph 1:1–2||Col 1:1–2, and in Eph 3:2||Col 1:25; Eph 3:9||Col 1:26, five words in Eph 1:7||Col 1:14 and Eph 4:16||Col 2:19.

[4] The same name also appears in II Tim 4:12; Titus 3:12; Acts 20:4.

[5] 1:15; 3:17; 4:2, 15–16; 5:2, 25, 28, 33; however 2:4; 3:19; 5:2, 25 speak of the love of God or Christ for man, and 1:4 (3:17?; 4:15–16?) of man's love for God.

[6] I John 4:10–11, 20–21; 5:1–2; Rom 5:5; cf. Gal 5:22.

love is a gift of God, not an achievement over which man exercises control. Through God's blessing it has been granted and still will be given.[7] If the sequence of the members of the triad "peace-love-faith" is considered important, it indicates that the peace which God has created brings forth two things, "love" for the neighbor and "faith" in God. But the syntax chosen in Greek for connecting "peace" and "love" with "faith" supports another interpretation which assigns priority to faith over the two others (or perhaps only over the second, "love").[8] The translation of *meta pisteos* (lit. "with faith") by "and above all, faith" recommends itself for several reasons:

a) In the undisputed Pauline epistles, "faith" is much more than an accompaniment of love. Though love is called "greater" (I Cor 13:13), it can also be described as the effect or instrument of faith, as the formula, "faith working through love," indicates (Gal 5:6). Man is justified or saved by faith (Eph 2:8; Gal 2:16, etc.), rather than by love. In the better MSS of Eph 1:15, "faith" alone (without the addition of "and love") describes the total life of the congregation for which Paul gives thanks to God.

b) In many passages the person going "with" (*meta*) is either equal or inferior in rank to the one he accompanies. The same is true of things.[9] In Eph 6:23 "faith" is probably related to both peace and love,[10] and its position at the end of the enumeration suggests—in analogy to that of love in I Cor 13:13—that here it holds the highest rank.

c) It has been remarked repeatedly that in Ephesians much less is said about "faith" than, e.g. in Galatians, Romans, Philippians. But while in this letter Paul indeed emphasizes the social above the personal dimension of the gospel, he has not forgotten faith. As he began with a reference to those "faithful" (1:1, 15) and mentioned the "faith" of God, the Messiah, or the saints again at important moments,[11] so now he concludes the epistle by averring that no other "peace" and "love" are meant than those that create and sustain "faith" and are, in turn, received and confessed by it.

from God the Father and the Lord Jesus Christ. In COMMENT II on 1:1–2 the terms "Father" and "Lord" were discussed, and it was shown that the mention of "God the Father" and the "Lord Jesus Christ" in one breath does not imply any polytheistic notions; cf. 5:5.[12] At the end of Ephesians, Paul al-

---

[7] Eph 1:3–4; 2:10; cf. 6:8.

[8] By analogy, in I Cor 13:13 the composition of the triad "faith-hope-love" ends with the special praise of its last member: "The greatest of these is love." Yet in I Thess 1:3; 5:8; Col 1:4–5 the same triad occurs as in I Cor 13 without indicating a special rank for one of its members. Equally the six metaphorical weapons of Eph 6:14–17 were not so grouped as to reveal the priority of one above the others.

[9] By eating "with" tax-collectors, Jesus incurs the charge of fraternizing with them, Mark 2:16; Luke 15:2; the communion of a believer "with" an unbeliever is denounced in II Cor 6:15; rejoicing "with" those rejoicing is commanded in Rom 12:15. By calling the disciples to be *with* him, Jesus makes them his followers, Mark 3:14. When Paul goes "with" Barnabas to Jerusalem, taking Titus along, then Barnabas is the first in rank, Paul the second, and Titus in the lowest position, Gal 2:1. When abstract nouns introduced by the preposition "with" are connected with other nouns or verbs, they describe the attitude which must *control* behavior, not only accompany it. According to e.g. Philip 1:4; 4:6, a person makes a petition "with" joy and holds an expectation "with" joy or "with" thanksgiving. Philip 2:12 speaks of working out the salvation "with" fear and trembling, cf. Eph 4:2; 6:5, 7, etc. However, in phrases such as "God is with us" (Matt 1:23), or "peace be with you" (I Peter 5:14), God and peace are the dominant members.

[10] As Gaugler observes, in contrast to, e.g. Robinson who suggests that paraphrase, "love accompanied by faith."

[11] Eph 2:8; 3:12, 17; 4:5, 13; 6:16.

[12] See also COMMENT III A on 3:14–21 for additional information on the title "Father."

ludes to the widespread early Christian liturgical blessing that belonged to the beginning of the liturgy and appears within the first verses of the majority of the NT letters. Just as in those blessings, "grace and peace" from any source other than "God the Father" and the "Lord Jesus Christ" are not solid and reliable enough to form the substance of a benediction. The separation of "peace" in vs. 23 from "grace" in vs. 24 and other differences characterizing the shift of the substance of the opening blessing to the conclusion of Ephesians, will be considered in the COMMENT.

24. *Grace with all who love our Lord Jesus Christ.* The phrase, those "who love the Lord," is a traditional formula describing the people who fear God, serve him, and keep his commandments.[13] Use of this phrase demonstrates that by speaking of the "subordination" of the church to the Messiah and of her "fear" of him in 5:21, 24,[14] Paul by no means excluded or minimized her "love." Neither in degree, quality, nor effect; neither in originality, creativity, nor as a "power of salvation" (Rom 1:16; Eph 2:5, 8; 5:23) does the love of man for God and the Messiah reach the love of God and the Messiah for the church. And yet Paul declared the latter to be the basis and model of a husband's love for his wife, and described the wife's love as "fear of her husband" (5:33) corresponding to the "fear of Christ" (5:21) that characterizes the church's love for him. While the Gospel of Mark does not report any response of the children who are welcomed in Jesus' company and blessed by him, those children of the heavenly Father who "have heard the gospel and believed" it, were "sealed" with the Spirit, and were equipped with his gifts (1:13–14; 4:7), are in Eph 6:24 called people who "love the Lord." As was made clear in 4:1–3, 13, 17–32, etc., the response of the saints to the love of Christ is still far from perfect. The saints are warned lest God's love turn into wrath and they lose their inheritance (5:3–5; cf. Rev 3:11). Yet, at the end of Ephesians, it is not their weakness that is called to mind, but God's strong grace, not impending defection and betrayal, but the attachment to the Lord by a "love" however imperfect. If the saints are scrutinized as individuals or as community, they are found wanting in every regard (4:17 – 5:14). However, in the light of the power of God's "grace" and the Messiah's "love" for the church, it is not the lack of worthy motivations, intentions and achievements that counts. The imperfect and time-bound character of the reciprocal love of the saints is irrelevant as long as they "love" the Messiah-Bridegroom with yearning, hope, and fear. Judged and engulfed by God's grace as the saints are, they are not only exposed to God's eternal judgment, but also protected by his eternal love and given a permanent share in this love. The last two words of Ephesians make this explicit:

in eternity.[15] The literal meaning of *aphtharsiā* is "incorruption," "incor-

---

[13] See esp. Exod 20:6; Deut 5:10; also the Hebrew and Greek texts of Ps 97[96]:10. The book of Deuteronomy is untiring in its call for love of God, see 6:5; 10:12; 11:1, 13, 22, etc. Paul speaks of those who love "God" in I Cor 2:9 (in the frame of a quotation from an unknown source); also in I Cor 8:3; Rom 8:28; cf. James 1:12; 2:5. In the Johannine writings, more emphasis is placed upon the love for "Jesus" than in any other part of the NT, see John 8:42; 14:15, 21, etc.; 21:15–17; I John 4:20–21; 5:1–2. Love for the "Lord [Jesus Christ]" is mentioned in I Cor 16:22 and I Peter 1:8. In no case is this love an alternative either to "fear" (see COMMENT III on Eph 5:21–33) or to the "keeping of the commandments" (see, e.g. John 14:15).

[14] Equally by mentioning nothing else than the wife's subordination to her husband, 5:22, 24.

[15] A great number of Greek MSS (though none among those considered the oldest and least revised) and the old Latin and Syriac versions add "Amen" after "in eternity." Thus they in-

ruptibility," or "immortality"; it can describe a quality of God, man, or things.[16]
Three puzzles are posed by the use of *aphtharsiā* in Eph 6:24: (a) Has Paul in
mind only the absence of corruption and mortality, or has the term acquired
before his time or under his pen a positive meaning?[17] (b) Is the noun used in
its moral or its temporal sense (incorruption, viz. perfection; or immortality,
viz. eternity), or have these two originally distinct meanings been blended into
one?[18] (c) Which part of 6:24 is qualified by the concluding words, *en aphtharsiā*? Does this verse speak (1) of the immaculate and/or abiding "grace"
which protects the saints, or (2) of the spotless and/or never-ending "love" of
the saints for the "Lord," or (3) of the glory and/or eternity of the "Lord" himself? The last group of questions can be avoided if the preposition *en* ("in")

---

clude in the apostolic letter the response given by a Jewish or early Christian congregation to a
sermon or prayer—as indeed Paul himself has done in e.g. Gal 1:5; 6:18; Rom 1:25; 11:36; cf.
Rev 1:6, etc. While the "Amen" in Eph 6:24 var. lect. need not necessarily be inauthentic, the
MS evidence speaks against this reading. A postscript is found in the MSS of the Koine Group
which reads: "Written from Rome through Tychicus." This addition is (like the similar postscripts
to other NT letters) certainly not authentic. However, its contents may be accurate. See the Introduction, sections V and VII.

[16] LSLex, 289; WBLex, 124–25. The word does not occur in classical Greek writings; it belongs
to the sophisticated style of the Hellenistic period. The cognate adjective *aphthartos* has the same
three different meanings as the noun: (a) "[factually] uncorrupted, not decaying"; (b) "[potentially]
incorruptible"; (c) "[quantitatively and qualitatively] eternal." The cognate noun and the adjective
aphthoriā and *aphthoros* are used less frequently and only in a narrower sense; they express in-cor-
ruption, soundness, purity, i.e. a high moral status, not the impossibility of corruption, nor the possession of immortality or eternity. *Aphtharsiā* and *aphthartos* describe a deity, see Diogenes Laertius
X 123; Rom 1:23; I Tim 1:17, or a manifestation of God, Wisd Sol 12:1; 18:4; cf. I Peter 1:23, or a
heavenly gift to man, Wisd Sol 2:23; 6:17–20; 8:13, 17; 18:4; IV Macc 9:22; I Cor 9:25; 15:42, 50,
52–54; Rom 2:7; II Tim 1:10; I Peter 1:3–4; 3:4. *Aphthoriā* and *aphthoros* are used to characterize
men or things, e.g. virgins: Esther 2:2, or sound doctrine: Titus 2:7. See Robinson, pp. 137–38, 217–
20; R. C. Trench, *Synonyms of the New Testament* (repr. Grand Rapids: Eerdmans, 1969), pp. 253–
54. Philo wrote a tract on the *Aphtharsiā* (in Latin *aeternitas*) of the world, in which he discusses
the treatment of this subject by Plato, Aristotle, the Stoics, the Epicureans, and in the book of
Genesis.

[17] The etymology (*in*-corruption, *in*-corruptibility, *im*-mortality) seems to suggest that Paul
treads on the path of the so-called *via negativa* of philosophy and theology which was chosen by
mystics as well as scholastics as an approach to the deepest mysteries. Yet this procedure is not
rooted in the classical Hebrew OT description of God, and has but feeble support in the Pauline
letters (not to speak of the Gospels), except perhaps in the Pastoral Epistles. Because in other
doxologies Paul uses the positive term for "eternity" which the Jewish and Christian communities
had taken over from the OT, that is, "into the ages [of ages]," Gal 1:5; Rom 1:25; 9:5; 11:36;
16:27, etc.; cf. Matt 6:13 var. lect., *aphtharsiā* may well have a positive meaning in Eph 6:24.
The adjectives *aïdios* and *aiōnios*, which describe God's "eternal" power, "eternal" life, "eternal"
glory, etc. in Rom 1:20; 2:7; II Cor 4:17; I Peter 5:10; II Peter 1:11; Rev 14:6, point in the same
direction.

[18] When Philo speaks of the *aphtharsiā* of the world, he does not deny the corruption and
mortality of man but asserts only the "eternity" of the world. In turn, when in Wisd Sol 2:23;
6:17, 20; 8:13, 17; 12:1; 18:4, the "spirit," the "light of the Law," the "image of God" im-
printed upon man, or the "life" attained by the followers of Wisdom have this attribute, not
only infinite "temporal" extension is meant, but also "moral" impeccability and perfection. In
I Cor 15:53–54 Paul speaks in poetic parallel lines of *aphtharsiā* and *athanasiā* (lit. "immortality"). Probably he did not consider them exact synonyms but wanted to say that on the
last day both perfection *and* eternity will be "put on" by all creatures that are now "corruptible" and
"mortal." The two *present* deficiencies and the two *future* gifts of God are apparently distinguishable
but not separable. Perhaps under the influence of these verses Origen interpreted *aphtharsiā* in Eph
6:24 merely by reference to sin. He emphasized that not only "virginity" but also the absence of
non-sexual sins was meant. In Ignatius' letters, *aphtharsiā* and *aphthartos* are used in the sense of
absence of both physical destruction and moral corruption; it is applied to the bodies of individual
persons as well as to the church as a whole, see Ignatius *Eph.* XVII 1; *Magn.* VI 2; *Phila.* IX 2; *Polyc.*
II 3; *Trall.* XI 2; *Rom.* VII 3; Robinson, pp. 217–20. After the second century, the commentators
showed a tendency to combine purity of conduct with indestructibility of eternal life. Later Greek
writers put more emphasis on the incorruption of life, while (under the influence of Titus 2:7?) the
Latins preferred to speak of the soundness of doctrine. Abbott explains *aphtharsiā* in Rom 2:7;
II Tim 1:10, etc. as meaning "incorruptibility of future immortality," but holds that in Eph 6:24 the
moral sense prevails over the temporal—yet without totally excluding the latter; thus it means "more
than sincerity," that is, "imperishableness, incorruptibility."

before *aphtharsiā* is considered a substitute for either "with" or "and."[19] In this case *aphtharsiā* does not characterize any particular single word in 6:24, but is, in company with "peace," "love," "faith," "grace," a fifth description of the substance of God's blessing. "Grace together with blessed immortality"—this paraphrase of Robinson is then the best interpretation.[20]

A simple solution to the problem, perhaps choosing one or two among the philologically justifiable interpretations, would be arbitrary.[21] Careful exegetes have come to mutually exclusive results, or have admitted that several interpretations may be true to the text. In our translation, "eternity" was preferred to the more literal renditions for three reasons: (a) The use of *aphtharsiā* in the book of Wisdom (see fns. 16 and 18) makes it likely that Paul had in mind a positive attribute of God or of one of his gifts. (b) Many NT benedictions and doxologies end with a reference to "eternity" rather than to moral perfection. Therefore it is probable that in the hymnic letter to the Ephesians, the final benediction also ends with praise of the "eternal." (c) The imposition of a condition upon the saints[22] would spoil the tone of this letter, for it would have Ephesians conclude with an expression of the author's doubt as to the readers' election and good faith. Since he does not question that they love God, he need not add, "but you must love him eternally."

Because there is no compelling philological reason why the words "in eternity" should be connected with only one part of 6:24, in our version they are separated by a comma from the other elements of this sentence. Even in the position of an afterthought or appendix, they pertain to the whole verse and each of its parts: just as in other doxologies, so here "eternity" is mentioned in order to praise the Lord himself, together with his manifestation and gift, and with the inclusion of the saints in his glory.

"Eternity" fits the end of Ephesians particularly because this epistle emphasizes—without excluding the future advent of the Messiah, the Last Judgment, and the glorification of God's own people[23]—the eternal election of the saints which is now effective in their vocation. Now they participate in the fulfillment of the eternal promises, and now they exemplify to the world the validity of the eternal gospel of peace.[24] The eternal grace is with the saints forever. Their life in time and space, in imperfection and expectation, is embedded in God's eternity. Their "love of the Lord" demonstrates their awareness of their salvation and their gratitude for the good life given them.

[19] Precedents for this use of Hebrew *bᵉ* in the Qumran scrolls, and eventually of Greek *en* in Ephesians, were mentioned earlier.

[20] Robinson, p. 200, does not explicitly say that *en* can mean "and" or "together with." He believes that *aphtharsiā* is connected with "love" and defines it by "that endless and unbroken life in which love has triumphed over death and dissolution." Schlier admits that the syntactical connection is debatable, but avers that "the sense of the statement is clear . . . Grace completes itself in imperishableness." The translations "including imperishableness" and "for imperishableness" are suggested by him as equally viable.

[21] Agreeing with Origen, Calvin, Bengel, also Abbott's first choice, LSLex, 289, recommends for Eph 6:24 the moral sense "sincerity, integrity." This suggests that Ephesians ends with a warning signal aimed at hypocrites. Overlooked is the fact that in the LXX and in Paul, God himself, his manifestation, and his gift to man are characterized by *aphtharsiā*. WBLex, 125, and Dibelius leave it open which is meant: immortal life in which those loving the Lord already partake, or the reign of the Lord in immortal glory. But Abbott allows and Gaugler affirms that *aphtharsiā* is connected with "grace," not with "the Lord."

[22] Saying e.g. only when you truly, really, and perfectly love God are the contents of the whole epistle and the blessing with "grace" and "peace" valid for you.

[23] 1:14; 4:13; 6:9, 13, etc.

[24] 1:4-13; 2:6-7, 17; 3:10; 4:1; 6:15, 19-20.

COMMENT on 6:21–24

The Final Blessing

Several features distinguish the concluding words of Ephesians from the ending of other epistles.[25]

1) Secular Greek epistles[26] end with a good wish phrased in the second person: "Be healthy," "farewell," "good luck," etc. The majority of the NT epistles[27] retain the form of a concluding direct address to the recipients that includes the use of the second person pronouns "you" and "your"; but they replace the trivial Greek wish for well-being with a blessing pronounced in God's name: "The grace of our Lord Jesus Christ [be] with your spirit. Amen" (Gal 6:18). "Grace [be] with all of you" (Heb 13:25). "Peace to all of you" (I Peter 5:14). "Grace . . . love . . . and communion of the Holy Spirit with you all" (II Cor 13:14), etc.[28] Eph 6:23–24 does not conform to the pattern, because it uses the third person to denote those blessed: "Peace to the brothers . . . ," "grace with all who love." This form of blessing reveals a slightly greater distance between the apostle and his readers than is noticeable in the other letters. The distance is not to be exaggerated, for those blessed are still called "brothers" and people who "love the Lord."[29] But a small amount of aloofness remains; it is without parallel even in those letters where Paul dealt most harshly with the saints, i.e. in Galatians and II Corinthians. Robinson assumes that the encyclical character of Ephesians explains the difference. But Galatians, I Peter, and Colossians (see 4:16, 18) are encyclicals and yet do not use the third person in their blessings. The lack of personal acquaintance between Paul and the "Ephesians" (1:15; 3:2; 4:20–21) may account for the change. It is also possible that, once again, a fixed (though as yet undocumented) liturgical formula is used, or that Paul, in dictating this epistle (perhaps to the Tychicus recommended in 6:21–22)[30] said to his scribe: "Convey peace to the brothers . . . grace to those who love the Lord," etc. In this case, the scribe considered 6:21–22 an improper ending to the epistle (as in-

---

[25] Compare the elements listed by Abbott.

[26] As collected by A. S. Hunt and C. C. Edgar, *Select Papyri*, I, Loeb Classical Library (Harvard University Press, 1952), 268–395.

[27] A minority reproduces other Greek epistolary customs: II and III John end with greetings, James and I John with admonitions. An innovation over against the contemporary model is the conscious structure of an epistle after the pattern of a liturgy of adoration which ends with a doxology (Jude and II Peter), or with a promise of Christ (see the seven letters in Rev 2–3).

[28] At the end of several Pauline epistles, only "grace" is pronounced upon the saints. Is, therefore, the omission of a reference to other attitudes, acts and gifts of God a mark of an authentically Pauline letter? II Thess 3:17–18; cf. Gal 6:11, 18 have sometimes been interpreted in this sense. The Pastoral Epistles, which in their present form are hardly genuine, speak of "grace" alone and may have imitated an alleged trademark of Paul; cf. also Heb 13:25. But in Rom 15:13, 33 (though not in 16:20); I Cor 16:23–24; II Cor 13:14, Paul shows that he did not consider himself bound to a single formula.

[29] Among Jews the address, "Brothers," was originally reserved for fellow Jews: Acts 2:29, 37; 3:17; 7:2; 9:17. But in the early church this address became a sign of the Gentiles' incorporation into Israel as citizens of equal right, I Thess 1:4; 2:1, 9, 14, 17, etc.; cf. Eph 6:10 var. lect. The term "grace" in its particular Pauline usage denoted the cause of this incorporation, see Robinson, pp. 221–28. As earlier stated, the term "to love the Lord" is in Deuteronomy a synonym of "to fear the Lord." Since at Paul's time "God-fearers" was a technical term denoting proselytes who had not yet fully joined the community of Israel, Paul may have preferred to describe the Gentile-Christians in Ephesus by another title, i.e. as those "who love the Lord." This term signifies their full participation in the covenant and worship of God.

[30] See the postscript to 6:24 mentioned in fn. 15.

deed the parallel recommendation Col 4:7-9 does not form the end of Colossians), and he reproduced Paul's exact last words, omitting "convey."

2) Most Pauline letters conclude with a blessing formulated in one brief statement.[31] In Ephesians the final benediction consists of two sentences, each of which seemingly might stand alone and suffice to bring the epistle to a ringing conclusion.[32] Combined as they now are, they appear to contain repetitious elements. The title "brothers" alone, and the formula "all who love the Lord" alone, are each for itself sufficient to describe the members of the church; but the combination of both makes the diction ponderous. It *is* meaningful, but at first sight it is also somewhat strange that those "who love the Lord" are in turn blessed not only with "peace" and "faith," but also with "love." Perhaps the author wants to say that love is poured out upon love (as is "grace upon grace," according to John 1:16); or he intends to point back to that indivisible and coinherent divine and human love which was mentioned in the interpretation of the words "in love" at the end of Eph 1:4. In any case, 6:23-24 may well be another example of the redundancy observed earlier in the epistle.[33] Here as elsewhere elements borrowed from some early Christian tradition are combined with formulations expressing typically Pauline concerns in Pauline fashion. This way the whole of Ephesians is summed up in two brisk statements about the gift of "peace" and "grace," joined with "faith" and "love." The surprising term "in eternity" is reminiscent of the many elements of both "realized" and futuristic eschatology that are contained in this document. Certainly, the fact that 6:23-24 is a hymnic summary of Ephesians (which in turn is a hymnic summary of the whole of Paul's teaching!) does not disprove the authenticity of the epistle as a whole or of its ending. On the contrary, since inauthentic epistles were circulated as early as Paul's time,[34] an imitator of Paul would probably have terminated Ephesians with the typically Pauline benediction formula, "Grace [be] with you." No one was as free as Paul himself to deviate from supposedly fixed Pauline patterns and to confess his faith in original formulations.[35]

3) In vs. 23 "peace" is mentioned in association with "love" and "faith," yet in vs. 24 "grace" stands in majestic solitude. Why is the normal sequence of "grace and peace" reversed in Ephesians?[36] The following issue is decisive:

[31] A notable exception is the Epistle to the Romans which contains no fewer than four concluding formulae, a part of which was added in perhaps ever new postscripts: a blessing (a) with "joy and peace" from the "God of hope," 15:13; (b) by the presence of the "God of peace," 15:33; (c) with the "grace of our Lord Jesus," 16:20; (d) by a doxology phrased in distinctly un-Pauline language, 16:25-27. Another exception is I Cor 16:22-24 where Paul adds to the early Christian call, *Maranā thā* ("our Lord, come"), and to the blessing, "The grace of our Lord Jesus [be] with you," the warm personal assurance, "My love [is] with you all in the Messiah Jesus."

[32] In Gal 6:18, etc., only "grace," in I Peter 5:14 only "peace" is the substance of blessing.

[33] Cf. Rom 8:38-39; 11:33-36; II Cor 13:13.

[34] As II Thess 2:2; 3:17, perhaps also Gal 6:11, demonstrate.

[35] The points of difference between Eph 6:23-24 and final benedictions of other Pauline letters "speak for the genuineness of the Epistle, and against the hypothesis of an imitator," according to Abbott, p. 190. However, since both similarity and dissimilarity can be used as arguments for or against authenticity of a document, neither is a fail-safe criterion. Therefore the ending of Ephesians is certainly not a compelling reason for declaring this epistle either authentic or inauthentic. But every court has to decide *in dubio pro reo* (in doubtful cases in favor of the defendant).

[36] Thomas Aquinas does not ask this question but explains the reversed order with some general remarks: "Although the bestowal of grace precedes peace and the mutual love of men among themselves and with God . . . nevertheless in its own way peace does precede the putting of grace into action and the preservation of truth and charity. . . . Peace and charity contribute greatly to the preservation of grace—they could not be had without it."

Does "peace" have here the specific sense unfolded in 2:11–22, called to mind in 4:3, and presupposed again in the formula, "gospel of peace" (6:15)? Or does it mean something less specific than, or different from, the "reconciliation" of Jews and Gentiles with one another and with God?[37] It is most unlikely that the writer who concludes Ephesians with the blessing of 6:23–24 has forgotten or intends to neglect or contradict the core of the message communicated earlier. The "love" mentioned in vs. 23 is probably brotherly love, and vs. 24 speaks of those "loving the Lord." The same distinction, sequence, and expression of indissoluble unity between man's attitude to fellow man and his relationship to God was also essential in the description of the "peace made" by the "Messiah" in 2:13–17. By the removal of the enmity between men the hostility between men and God was also abolished; peace and love displaced contempt, hatred, and divisiveness. Therefore, the distinction *and* the connection of love for men and love for God in vss. 23–24 reveal that here the same "peace" is meant as elsewhere in Ephesians.

Here as before the author of this epistle does not mean that there can be "peace, love, and faith" before God reveals his "grace" through the Messiah and the Spirit. Rather, he reaffirms in 6:23–24, following the sequence chosen in 2:13–16, that the gift of "grace" consists of the creation of a new community and is, therefore, a social and public event; cf. 2:5–8; 3:7–10.

"Grace" as an attribute of God is as eternal as his decision to unite Jews and Gentiles in Jesus Christ and to reveal his secret at the proper time (1:6–10). Grace as a manifestation of God calls and saves those who had been dead in sin and unites them with Christ and one another (1:15; 2:5–8). Grace as a "gift" of God equips men to be witnesses to his mighty deeds before all the world (3:2, 7–8; 4:7–12, 29). Grace as the abiding "power" of God conveys to mortal men a share in eternal life (6:24). Thus the end of Ephesians points back to the source of "peace." Those given peace and proclaiming it participate in the very "life of God" (4:18), from here to eternity.

---

[37] Whenever *šālōm* is mentioned in the OT, and *eirēnē* ("peace") in the LXX and the NT, it is a weighty matter—even when used as the ordinary Semitic greeting. Since in the Bible the infinitely rich and comprehensive Hebrew term stands behind *eirēnē*, the latter signifies much more than the absence of war or presence of "peace of the soul," see COMMENT II on 1:1–2. When "peace" is the substance or a substantial element of a final benediction, it is never only the object of a good wish; rather peace is pronounced (according to Schlier, "imposed") in the name of God and Christ, with all the implications that the term "Messianic peace" (cf. John 14:27; 16:33) and "God of peace" might possess. See II Thess 3:16; II Cor 13:11; Rom 15:33; I Peter 5:14; III John 15; cf. I Thess 5:23; Rom 16:20. But only in Ephesians do the joining of Jews and Gentiles together in "one" new man, and the reconciliation of this "new man" with God (2:13–17) take the central place which "justification" and "faith" have in other Pauline epistles. In this epistle more than anywhere else an individualistic and psychological misunderstanding is ruled out. Only here is "peace" not just one element of preaching among others, but *the* substance of the gospel, 2:17; 6:15. Bengel and Schlier e.g. affirm that Eph 6:23 must be interpreted as a reference to 2:13–17, but Dibelius and Gaugler deny this; they assume that 6:23 is no more than an imitation of the initial and final blessing of other epistles.

BIBLIOGRAPHIES

I COMMENTARIES AND SPECIAL STUDIES

Note: The works listed in this bibliography are cited by abbreviations —see individual entries—throughout both volumes, 34 and 34A.

Abbott, T. K. *The Epistles to the Ephesians and to the Colossians.* ICC. 5th ed. London: Clark, 1946. *Cited as* Abbott.

Ambrosiaster. *Commentaria in epistolam B. Pauli ad Ephesios.* PL 16, 371–404. *Cited as* Ambrosiaster.

Beare, F. W. *The Epistle to the Ephesians.* IB, X, 597–749. *Cited as* IB, X.

Bengel, J. A. *Gnomon Novi Testamenti.* Tübingen: Schramm, 1742. *Cited as* Bengel.

Benoit, P. *Les Épîtres de saint Paul aux Philippiens, à Philémon, aux Colossiens, aux Éphésiens.* 2d ed. Paris: Du Cerf, 1953. *Cited as* Benoit.

Calvin, J. *Commentarius in epistolam ad Ephesios.* CRCO 15, 1895. Columns 141–240. *Cited as* Calvin.

Catenae. See below, Cramer, J. A.

Chrysostom. *Homiliae in epistolam ad Ephesios.* PG 62, 7–176. *Cited as* Chrysostom.

Conzelmann, H. *Der Brief an die Epheser.* NTD 8, 1965. *Cited as* Conzelmann.

Cramer, J. A., ed. *Catenae Graecorum Patrum in Novum Testamentum,* 6. Oxford: Typographia Academica, 1834. Pages 100–225. Cited as *Catenae.*

Cross, F. L., ed. *Studies in Ephesians.* London: Mowbray, 1956. *Cited as* Cross.

Dahl, N. A. *Das Volk Gottes.* SNVA 2, 1941; reprinted 1962. *Cited as* Dahl.

Dibelius, M. and Greeven, H. *An die Kolosser, Epheser, an Philemon.* HbNT 12. 3d ed. Tübingen: Mohr, 1953. *Cited as* Dibelius.

Eadie, J. *A Commentary on the Greek Text of the Epistle of Paul to the Ephesians.* 2d ed. New York: Carter, 1861. *Cited as* Eadie.

Ephraim the Syrian. *Commentarii in Epistolas D. Pauli.* Venice: Typographia Sancti Lazari, 1893. Pages 140–56. *Cited as* Ephraem.

Erasmus of Rotterdam. *In Novum Testamentum Annotationes.* Basel: Froben, 1519. Pages 413 ff. Reprinted 1540. Pages 591 ff. Etc. *Cited as* Erasmus.

Gaugler, E. *Der Epheserbrief.* ANS 6, 1966. *Cited as* Gaugler.

Goodspeed, E. J. *The Meaning of Ephesians.* University of Chicago Press, 1933. *Cited as* Goodspeed.

Grotius, Hugo. *Annotationes in Novum Testamentum,* II. 1646. Reprinted Leipzig: Tetzscher, 1757. *Cited as* Grotius.

Hanson, S. *The Unity of the Church in the New Testament, Colossians and Ephesians.* ASNU 14. Uppsala: Almquist, 1946. Cited as *Unity.*

von Harless, G. C. A. *Commentar über den Brief Pauli an die Epheser.* 2d ed. Erlangen: Heider, 1834. *Cited as* von Harless.

Haupt, E. *Der Brief an die Epheser.* KEKNT 8. 7th rev. ed. 1902. *Cited as* Haupt.

von Hofmann, J. C. K. *Der Brief Pauli an die Epheser.* HSNT 6: 1, 1870. *Cited as* von Hofmann.

Holtzmann, H. J. *Kritik der Epheser- und Kolosserbriefe.* Leipzig: Engelmann, 1872. *Cited as* Holtzmann.

Jerome. *Commentaria in epistolam ad Ephesios.* PL 26, 459–554. *Cited as* Jerome.

Kirby, J. C. *Ephesians, Baptism and Pentecost.* McGill University Press, and London: SPCK, 1968. *Cited as* EBP.

Lueken, W. "Der Brief an die Epheser," in SNT 2. 2d ed. 1908. Pages 348–72. *Cited as* Lueken.

Mackay, J. A. *God's Order.* New York: Macmillan, 1953. *Cited as* Mackay.

Masson, C. *L'épître de S. Paul aux Éphésiens.* CNT 9. Neuchâtel: Delachaux, 1953. *Cited as* Masson.

Meyer, H. A. W. *Critical and Exegetical Handbook to the Epistle to the Ephesians.* New York: Funk and Wagnalls, 1884. KEKNT 9, 1859. 3d German ed. *Cited as* Meyer from the German edition.

Mitton, C. L. *The Epistle to the Ephesians: Its Authorship, Origin and Purpose.* Oxford: Clarendon Press, 1951. *Cited as* EE.

Oecumenius. *Pauli apostoli ad Ephesios epistola.* PG 118, 1170–1266. *Cited as* Oecumenius.

Pelagius. See below, Souter, A.

Percy, E. *Die Probleme der Kolosser- und Epheserbriefe.* Lund: Gleerup, 1946. *Cited as* Percy.

Pokorný, P. *Der Epheserbrief und die Gnosis.* Berlin: Evangelische Verlagsanstalt, 1965. *Cited as* EuG.

Robinson, J. A. *St. Paul's Epistle to the Ephesians.* 2d ed. London: Clark, 1922. *Cited as* Robinson.

Schlier, H. *Der Brief an die Epheser.* 2d ed. Düsseldorf: Patmos, 1958. *Cited as* Schlier.

—— *Christus und die Kirche im Epheserbrief.* BHTh 6, 1930, repr. 1966. Cited as *Christus.*

Scott, E. F. *The Epistles of Paul to the Colossians, to Philemon, and to the Ephesians.* MNTC 11, 1930. *Cited as* Scott.

von Soden, H. *Der Brief an die Epheser.* HCNT 3, 1891. Pages 79–153. *Cited as* von Soden.

Souter, A., ed. *Pelagius' Exposition of the Thirteen Epistles of St. Paul.* Cambridge University Press, 1922. Pages 344–80. *Cited as* Pelagius.

Synge, F. C. *St. Paul's Epistle to the Ephesians.* London: SPCK, 1954. *Cited as* Synge.

Theodore of Mopsuestia. *In Epistolas B. Pauli Commentarii.* H. B. Swete, ed. Cambridge University Press, 1880. I, 112–96. *Cited as* Theodore of Mopsuestia.

Theodoret. *Interpretatio epistolae ad Ephesios.* PG 82, 508–58. *Cited as* Theodoret.

Theophylact. *Commentarius in epistolam ad Ephesios.* PG 124, 1031–1138. *Cited as* Theophylact.

Thomas Aquinas. *Commentary on Saint Paul's Epistle to the Ephesians.* M. L. Lamb, trans. Albany: Magi Books, 1966. *Cited as* Thomas Aquinas.

Westcott, B. F. *St. Paul's Epistle to the Ephesians.* London: Macmillan, 1906. Reprinted Grand Rapids: Eerdmans, n.d. *Cited as* Westcott.

de Wette, W. M. L. *Kurze Erklärung der Briefe an die Kolosser, an Philemon, an die Epheser und Philipper.* Kurzgefasstes exegetisches Handbuch zum Neuen Testament, II 4. Leipzig: Weidmann, 1847. *Cited as* de Wette.

II SECTIONAL BIBLIOGRAPHIES

BIBLIOGRAPHY 17

Note: The works listed in this and succeeding sectional bibliographies are cited by abbreviation, sometimes the author's name only, in the section specified parenthetically in the subheading.

(COMMENT II on 4:1–16)

Basis and Structure of Pauline Ethics

Bultmann, R. "Das Problem der Ethik bei Paulus," ZNW 23 (1924), 123–40. Trans., "The Problem of Ethics in the Writings of Paul," in *The Old and the New Man.* Richmond: Knox, 1956. Pages 7–32.

——— *Theology of the New Testament,* I. New York: Harper, 1951. Pages 323–33. *Cited as* ThNT, I.

Dodd, C. H. *The Apostolic Preaching and its Development.* London: Hodder, 1936.

——— *Gospel and Law.* Columbia University Press, 1951.

Furnish, V. P. *Theology and Ethics in Paul.* Nashville: Abingdon, 1968.

Kuss, O. *Der Römerbrief,* II. 2d ed. Regensburg: Pustet, 1963. Pages 396–432.

Merk, O. *Handeln aus Glauben: Die Motivierungen der paulinischen Ethik.* Marburg: Elwert, 1968.

Oepke, A. *Der Brief des Paulus an die Galater,* Theologischer Handkommer zum Neuen Testament 9. 2d ed. Berlin: Evangelische Verlagsanstalt, 1957. Pages 144–45.

Schenke, H.-M. *Das Verhältnis von Indikativ und Imperativ bei Paulus.* Diss. Berlin, 1957 (ref.).

Schlier, H. "Vom Wesen der apostolischen Ermahnung," in *Die Zeit der Kirche.* Freiburg: Herder, 1956. Pages 74–89.

——— *Der Brief an die Galater.* KEKNT 7. 13th ed., 1965. Pages 264–67.

Schrage, W. *Die konkreten Einzelgebote in der paulinischen Paränese.* Gütersloh: Mohn, 1961.

Windisch, H. "Das Problem des Paulinischen Imperativs," ZNW 23 (1924), 265–81.

BIBLIOGRAPHY 18

(COMMENT V on 4:17–32)

Old and New Man

Barrett, C. K. *From First Adam to Last.* New York: Scribner's, 1962. Especially pages 98–99, 110–12.

Barth, K. *Christ and Adam.* New York: Harper, 1957. Repr. New York: Collier Books. 1967.

Brandenburger, E. *Adam and Christus.* WMANT 7, 1962.

Cullmann, O. *Christology of the New Testament.* Philadelphia: Westminster, 1959. Pages 137–92.

Davies, W. D. *Paul and Rabbinic Judaism.* London: SPCK, 1955. Pages 31–57, 86–146; cf. pages 268, 274, 304, 357. *Cited as* PRJ.

Murmelstein, B. "Adam, ein Beitrag zur Messiaslehre," WZKM 35 (1928), 242–72; 36 (1929), 51–86.

Ray, B. "L'homme nouveau selon S. Paul," RSPR 48 (1964), 603–29, esp. 615 ff.; 49 (1965), 161–95, esp. 173–84.

Schmithals, W. *Gnosis in Korinth.* Göttingen: Vandenhoeck, 1964. Pages 104–10. Rev. English ed., *Gnosticism in Corinth.* Nashville: Abingdon, 1971. Especially pages 71–76.

Schoeps, H. J. *Theologie und Geschichte des Judenchristentums.* Tübingen: Mohr, 1949. Pages 98–108.

Scroggs, R. *The Last Adam.* Philadelphia: Fortress, 1966.

Tannehill, R. C. *Dying and Rising with Christ.* Berlin: Töpelmann, 1967. Pages 24–30.

BIBLIOGRAPHY 19

(COMMENT VIII on 4:17–32)

Ethical Catalogues and Haustafeln

Carrington, P. *The Primitive Christian Catechism.* Cambridge University Press, 1940.

Daube, D. *The New Testament and Rabbinic Judaism.* London: Athlone Press, 1956. Pages 90–105.

Dibelius, M. *An die Kolosser, Epheser, an Philemon.* 3d ed. HbNT 12 (1953), 48–50.

Easton, B. S. "New Testament Ethical Lists," JBL 5 (1932), 1–12.

Gnilka, J. "Paränetische Traditionen im Epheserbrief," in *Mélanges bibliques,* Fs B. Rigaux, ed. A. Descamps and A. de Halleux. Gembloux: Duculot, 1970. Pages 397–410, especially 407–10.

Hunter, A. M. *Paul and his Predecessors.* Philadelphia: Westminster, 1961. Pages 52–57.

Kamlah, E. *Die Form der katalogischen Paränese im Neuen Testament.* WUNT 7, 1964. *Cited as* DFKP.

Klein, G. *Der älteste christliche Katechismus und die jüdische Propagandaliteratur.* Berlin: Reimer, 1909.

Schrage, W. *Die konkreten Einzelgebote in der paulinischen Paränese.* Gütersloh: Mohr, 1961.

Selwyn, E. *The First Epistle of St. Peter.* London: Macmillan, 1947. Pages 363–439.

Vögtle, A. *Die Tugend- und Lasterkataloge im Neuen Testament.* NTAbh 16:4–5, 1936.

Weidinger, H. *Die Haustafeln.* Leipzig: Hinrichs, 1928.

Wibbing, S. *Die Tugend- und Lasterkataloge im Neuen Testament.* BhZNW 25, 1959.

BIBLIOGRAPHY 20

(COMMENT II on 5:1–20)

Imitation of God

Auerbach, E. *Mimesis.* Berne: Francke, 1946. Rev. ed., 1959. Trans. *Mimesis,* Anchor Book 107. Garden City: Doubleday, 1957.

Betz, H. D. *Nachfolge und Nachahmung Jesu Christi im Neuen Testament.* BHTh 37, 1967.

Buber, M. "Imitatio Dei," in *Israel and the World.* New York: Schocken, 1948. Pages 66–77.

DeBoer, W. P. *The Imitation of Paul.* Kampen: Kok, 1962 (ref.).

Eliade, M. *Le mythe de l'éternal retour.* Paris: Gallimard, 1949. Trans. *Cosmos and History.* Harper Torchbook 50. New York, 1959.

Gulin, E. G. *Die Nachfolge Gottes.* Studia Orientalia 1 (Helsingfors, 1925), 34–50.

Marmorstein, A. "The Imitation of God (*Imitatio Dei*) in the Haggadah," in *Studies in Jewish Theology.* Oxford University Press, 1950. Pages 106–21.

Nielen, J. M. "Die Kultsprache der Nachfolge und Nachahmung Gottes," in *Heilige Überlieferungen,* Fs J. Herwegen. Münster: Aschendorff, 1938. Pages 59–85.

Schoeps, H. J. *Aus frühchristlicher Zeit.* Tübingen: Mohr, 1950. Pages 286–301.

Schulz, A. *Nachfolgen und Nachahmen.* Munich: Kösel, 1962. Especially pages 226–42.

——— *Unter dem Anspruch Gottes: Das Neutestamentliche Zeugnis von der Nachahmung.* Studien zum Alten und Neuen Testamentes 6. Munich: Kösel, 1967.

Schweizer, E. *Lordship and Discipleship.* SBT 28, 1960.
688–744, especially 701–6.
Spicq, C. *Théologie morale du Nouveau Testament.* Paris: Gabalda, 1965. II,

BIBLIOGRAPHY 21
(NOTES and COMMENTS on 5:21–33)

Husband and Wife

von Allmen, J. J. *Maris et femmes d'après saint Paul.* CTh 29, 1951. Trans. *The Pauline Teaching on Marriage.* New York: Harper, 1952.
Bachofen, J. J. *Mutterrecht.* Stuttgart: Kries, 1861. Trans. *Myth, Religion and Mother Right.* London: Routledge, 1967.
Bailey, D. S. *The Mystery of Love and Marriage.* New York: Harper, 1952.
Bainton, R. *What Christianity Says About Sex, Love, and Marriage.* New York: Association Press, 1953.
Baltensweiler, H. *Die Ehe im Neuen Testament.* ATANT 52, 1967.
Barth, K. *Church Dogmatics.* Edinburgh: Clark, 1958–1961. III, 1 (1958), 176–206, 288–329; 2 (1960), 222–324; 4 (1961) 116–240. IV, 2 (1958), 727–840.
Batey, R. A. "Jewish Gnosticism and the Hieros Gamos of Eph. 5:21–33," NTS 10 (1963), 121–27.
——— "Paul's Bride Image," *Interpretation* 7 (1963), 176–82.
——— *New Testament Nuptial Imagery.* Leiden: Brill, 1971. Cited as *Nuptial Imagery.*
Best, E. *One Body in Christ.* London: SPCK, 1955.
Bieder, W. *Das Mysterium Christi und der Messias.* Zürich: EVZ, 1964.
Bird, J. W. and L. F. *The Freedom of Sexual Love.* Garden City: Doubleday, 1967.
Boucher, M. "Some Unexplored Parallels to I Cor. 11:11–12 and Gal. 3:28," CBQ 31 (1969), 50–58.
Bovet, T. *Kompendium der Ehekunde.* Tübingen: Katzmann, 1969.
Bushnell, K. C. *God's Word to Women.* 4th ed. Piedmont, California, 1930. Published by author.
Chavasse, C. *The Bride of Christ.* London: Faber, 1940.
Colli, P. *La pericopa Paolina ad Ephesios v.32 nella interpretazione dei SS. Padri e del concilio di Trento.* Diss. Parma, 1951 (ref.).
Dacquino, P. "Note su Ef. 5, 22–31," *Scuola Cattolica* 86 (Milan, 1958), 221–33 (ref.).
Daniélou, J. *From Shadow to Reality.* Westminster, Maryland: Newman, 1960. Pages 30–65.
Delling, G. *Paulus Stellung zu Frau und Ehe.* BWANT IV 5, 1931.
Greeven, H. "Zu den Aussagen des Neuen Testaments über die Ehe," ZEE 1 (1957), 109–25.
———, Schnackenburg, R., Ratzinger, J., and Wendland, H.-D. *Theologie der Ehe.* Regensburg: Pustet, 1969.

von Hattingberg, H. *Ueber die Liebe.* Munich: Kinder Taschenbücherei, Geist und Leben 2022–23, n.d.

Johnson, L. "The Mystery of Marriage," *Scripture* 11 (Edinburgh, 1959), 1–6 (ref.).

Kähler, E. "Zur Unterordnung der Frau im Neuen Testament," ZEE 3 (1959), 1–13.

——— *Die Frau in den Paulinischen Briefen.* Zurich/Frankfurt: Gotthelf, 1960. Cited as *Die Frau.*

von Kirschbaum, C. *Die wirkliche Frau.* Zurich: EVZ, 1949.

Kramer, S. N. *The Sacred Marriage Rite.* Indiana University Press, 1969.

Leipoldt, J. *Die Frau in der antiken Welt und im Urchristentum.* 3d ed. Leipzig: Koehler & Amelang, 1965.

May, R. *Love and Will.* New York: Norton, 1969.

Menoud, P.-M. "Marriage et célibat selon saint Paul," *Revue de théologie et de philosophie* 39 (Geneva, 1951), 22–34.

Messenger, E. C. *Two in One Flesh.* 3 vols. London: Sands, 1948–49.

Moore, G. F. *Judaism,* II. 7th ed. Harvard University Press, 1954. Pages 119–31.

Muirhead, I. A. "The Bride of Christ," ScotJT 5 (1952), 175–87.

Mussner, F. *Christus, das All und die Kirche.* Trier: Paulus-Verlag, 1955. Pages 147–60.

Neumann, E. *The Great Mother.* 2d ed. Bollingen Series 47. New York: Pantheon, 1963.

Nygren, A. *Agape and Eros.* 3 vols. London: SPCK, 1932, 1938, 1939. Quoted from reprint, Philadelphia: Westminster, 1953.

Orr, W. "Paul's Treatment of Marriage in I Cor. 7," *Pittsburgh Perspective* 8, no. 3, (1967), 5–22.

Piper, O. R. *The Christian Interpretation of Sex.* New York: Scribner's, 1941.

Preisker, H. *Christentum und Ehe in den ersten drei Jahrhunderten.* Berlin: Töpelmann, 1927.

Reicke, B. "Neuzeitliche und neutestamentliche Auffasung von Liebe und Ehe," NovT 1 (1956), 21–34.

Rengstorf, K. H. "Die neutestamentlichen Mahnungen an die Frau, sich dem Manne unterzuordnen," in *Verbum Dei manet in aeternum,* Fs O. Schmitz. Witten: Luther Verlag, 1953. Pages 131–45.

Salvia, B. *Magnum Sacramentum.* Diss. Pontifical Gregorian University, Rome, 1959 (ref.).

Sampley, J. P. *And the Two Shall Become One Flesh.* NTS monograph series 16, 1971.

Schlier, H. *Christus und die Kirche im Epheserbrief.* BHTh 6, 1930, reprinted 1966. Pages 50–75.

Schubart, W. *Religion und Eros.* Munich: Beck, 1944.

von Soden, H. *"Mysterion und sacramentum in den ersten zwei Jahrhunderten der Kirche," ZNW 12 (1911), 188–227, especially 206–24.

Stanley, D. M. "Paul's Interest in the Early Chapters of Genesis," AnBib 17–18 I, 1963.

Stendahl, K. *The Bible and the Role of Women.* Philadelphia: Fortress, 1966.

Strack, H. L.-Billerbeck, P. *Kommentar zum Neuen Testament aus Talmud und Midrash.* 6 vols. Munich: Beck, 1922–61. I, 303–21, 500–18, 801–7; II, 23–24, 372–99; III, 367–77, 435–43, 610–14; IV, 754–55. *Cited as* StB.

Weidinger, H. *Die Haustafeln.* Leipzig: Hinrichs, 1928.

Zalotay, J. *Sacramentum hoc magnum est (Eph. 5,32).* Diss. Vienna, 1934 (ref.).

BIBLIOGRAPHY 22

(NOTES and COMMENTS on 6:10–20)

Spiritual Armor

Bardtke, H. "Der gegenwärtige Stand der Erforschung der in Palästina gefundenen hebräischen Handschriften, 29, Die Kriegsrolle von Qumran übersetzt," TLZ 80 (1955), 401–20.

Barth, K. "Des Christen Wehr und Waffen," in *Eine Schweizer Stimme,* 2d ed. Zürich: EVZ, 1948. Pages 123–46, especially 123–32.

Bauernfeind, O. TWNTE, VI, 502–15; VII, 701–13.

Bond, C. L. *Winning with God.* Washington: Review, 1940.

Bousset, W. "Die Himmelsreise der Seele," ARW 4 (1901), 136–69, 229–73.

Braun, H. *Qumran und das Neue Testament,* I. Tübingen: Mohr, 1966. Pages 222–25. *Cited as* QuNT.

Bruce, F. F. "Qumran and Early Christianity," NTS 2 (1956), 176–90, especially 188–90.

Buber, M. *Kingship of God.* 3d ed. New York: Harper, 1967. Especially pages 142–48.

Burrows, M. *The Dead Sea Scrolls.* New York: Viking, 1955. Especially pages 336–37.

——— *More Light on the Dead Sea Scrolls.* New York: Viking, 1958. Especially pages 346–52.

Buscarlet, A. F. "The Preparation of the Gospel of Peace," ET 9 (1897), 38–40.

Bynaeus, A. *De calceis Hebraeorum.* Dordrecht: Goris, 1695. Especially pages 61–76.

Cross, F. M. "The Divine Warrior in Israel's Early Cult," in *Biblical Motifs,* ed. A. Altman. Harvard University Press, 1966. Pages 11–31.

Diels, H., and Schramm, E. *Exzerpte aus Philos Mechanik.* Abhandlungen der preussische Akademie der Wissenschaften, philologisch-historische. Klasse XII, Berlin, 1920.

Emonds, H. "Geistlicher Kriegsdienst," in *Heilige Überlieferung,* Fs I. Herwegen, ed. O. Casel. Münster: Aschendorff, 1938. Pages 21–50.

Erasmus von Rotterdam, Ausgewählte Schriften I (epistula ad Paulum Volzium; enchiridion militis Christiani), ed. W. Welzig. Darmstadt: Wissenschaftliche Buchgesellschaft, 1968. Pages xiii–xxv.

Gressmann, H. *Altorientalische Texte und Bilder zum Alten Testament.* Tübingen: Mohr, 1909.

von Harnack, A. *Militia Christi.* Tübingen: Mohr, 1905.

Hempel, J. *Gott und Mensch im Alten Testament.* 2d ed. BWANT III 2, 1936. Pages 33–45.

Jeremias, J. "Qumran et la théologie," NRT 85 (1963), 674–90.

Kamlah, E. *Die Form der katalogischen Paränese im Neuen Testament.* WUNT 7, 1964. Especially pages 189–96.

Kromayer, J., and Veith, G. *Heerwesen und Kriegführung der Griechen und Römer.* Munich: Beck, 1928, reprinted 1963.

Kuhn, K. G. "New Light on Temptation, Sin and Flesh in the New Testament," in SaNT. Pages 94–113.

———— TWNTE, V, 298–300.

Molin, G. *Die Söhne des Lichts.* Vienna/Munich: Herald, 1954. Pages 104–7.

Oepke, A. TWNTE, V, 292–315.

Pedersen, J. *Israel, Its Life and Its Culture.* 2d ed. 4 vols in 2. Oxford University Press, 1946. Especially III–IV, 1–32.

Pfitzner, V. C. *Paul and the Agon Motif.* NovT Supplement 16. Leiden: Brill, 1967.

Pritchard, J., ed. *Ancient Near Eastern Texts Relating to the Old Testament.* 2d ed. Princeton University Press, 1954. *Cited as* ANET.

———— *The Ancient Near East in Pictures.* Princeton University Press, 1954.

———— *The Ancient Near East, Supplementary Texts and Pictures.* Princeton University Press, 1969.

von Rad, G. *Der Heilige Krieg.* Munich: Kaiser, 1957.

Reitzenstein, R. *Hellenistische Mysterienreligionen.* 3d ed. Leipzig: Teubner, 1927. Pages 192–215.

Schlier, H. *Christus und die Kirche.* Tübingen: Mohr, 1930. Pages 7–8.

Schrader, E., ed. *Keilinschriftliche Bibliothek,* II. Berlin: Reuther, 1890.

Smend, R. *Yahweh War and Tribal Federation.* Nashville: Abingdon, 1970.

Snodgrass, A. M. *Arms and Armor of the Greeks.* Cornell University Press, 1967.

Tallquist, K. *Der assyrische Gott.* Societas Orientalis Fennica, Studia Orientalia IV:3, Helsingfors, 1932.

Welzig, W. See *Erasmus.*

Wevers, J. W. *Interpreter's Dictionary of the Bible,* IV. Pages 820–25.

Whiteley, D. E. H. "Expository Problems in Eph. 6:12—Evil Powers," ET 68 (1957), 100–103.

Yadin, Y. *The War of the Sons of Light.* Jerusalem: Bialik, 1955 (ref.).

———— *The Scroll of the War.* Oxford University Press, 1962.

———— *The Art of Warfare in Biblical Lands.* 2 vols. New York: McGraw-Hill, 1963.

INDEXES

NAMES

Aalen, S. 414
Abbott, T. K. 22, 25, 38, 73, 124, 136, 152,
206, 212, 233, 254, 257, 259, 260, 262, 264,
265, 266, 272, 274, 295, 297, 317, 328, 329,
331, 333, 335, 338, 340, 342, 345, 346, 349,
364, 370, 371, 372, 374, 380, 390, 396, 397,
431, 444, 445, 446, 449, 458, 463, 470, 471,
472, 488, 490, 491, 493, 499, 500, 503, 505,
508, 509, 510, 513, 514, 515, 516, 519, 521,
529, 534, 537, 557, 558, 561, 562, 563, 564,
566, 567, 570, 573, 580, 582, 583, 587, 605,
608, 612, 615, 616, 619, 626, 629, 630, 633–
34, 636, 637, 641, 642, 643, 644, 647, 648,
668, 678, 679, 684, 688, 690, 692, 705, 707,
714, 721, 722, 760, 761, 762, 763, 766, 767,
768, 769, 770, 771, 772, 774, 776, 777, 778,
779, 780, 781, 782, 783, 793, 795, 797, 798,
801, 803, 809, 813, 814, 815, 816, 821
Abelsen, S. 419
Acts, apocryphal. *See* specific persons
Aeschylus 616, 649
Aland, K. 59, 679
Albertz, M. 13, 38, 407
Albright, W. F. 458, 473
Allan, A. 38, 69, 407, 409
Allegro, J. M. 317
von Allmen, J.-J. 611, 615, 629, 641, 642,
650, 651, 692, 709, 714, 715, 826
Almquist, H. 490
ab Alpe, A. 411
Althaus, P. 110
Ambrose 468
Ambrosiaster 90, 272, 285, 297, 315, 348,
375, 380, 395, 401, 433, 577, 736, 841
Ammonius 644
Amstutz, J. 387, 419
Anacreon 658, 673
Anastasius Sinaita 644
Andrew, Acts of 396, 729
Andrew, martyrology of 396
Andrew, M. E. 512
Anselm of Canterbury 328, 428
Antiochus IV Epiphanes 279
Antipatros of Tarsus 658
Antoninus Liberalis 578
Antoninus Pius 255, 277
Aphraates 318, 557
Apostles' (Apostolic) Creed 96, 270–71,
463, 469
Apuleius 543, 601, 717, 789
Aquinas. *See* Thomas Aquinas
Archontes, Essence of 171
Aristias, Letter of 284, 526, 556, 589
Aristophanes 627
Aristotle 85, 187, 188, 194, 209, 224, 449,
455, 492, 513, 521, 560, 562, 570, 578, 581,
589, 590, 609, 618, 621, 631, 657, 664, 705,
708, 714, 755, 769, 778, 813
Aristotle, Pseudo- 337, 551, 791
von Arnim, J. 185, 658
Arnold, G. 726
Arvedson, T. 345, 410
Asting, R. 38, 113, 147, 407, 479
Athanasius 368, 589
Attila 524

Auerbach, E. 589, 825
Augsburg Confession 642
Augsten, R. J. 545
Augustine 46, 48, 74, 206, 212, 225, 230,
231, 238, 241, 248, 280, 296, 309, 318, 342,
396, 495, 557, 593, 615, 625, 642, 643, 646,
677, 683, 689, 690, 696, 697, 705, 706, 715–
16, 722–23, 736, 745–46, 747, 748–49, 807
Aulen, G. 173, 413, 432

Babbitt, F. C. 618
Bachofen, J. J. 640, 826
Bacon, B. 25
Baeck, L. 419
Baer, R. A. 726, 728
Bailey, D. S. 608, 630, 640, 641, 673, 710,
715, 736, 737, 753, 826
Bailey, R. E. 575
Bainton, R. 737, 747, 753, 826
Baltensweiler, A. 561, 608, 609, 611, 612,
613, 615, 616, 618, 622, 635, 642, 643, 645,
647, 651, 652, 653, 654, 655, 658, 689, 692,
701, 703, 705, 709, 714, 719, 721, 722, 727,
728, 740, 741, 826
von Balthasar, H. U. 203, 673, 681, 743,
746
Baltzer, K. 664
Balz, H. R. 663, 664, 665, 666, 792
Bammel, E. 218
Barclay, W. 86
Bardtke, H. 828
Barnabas, Epistle of (Barn.) 30, 36, 82,
136, 213, 215, 274, 294, 321, 370, 433, 476,
527, 560, 565, 609, 706, 779, 805
Barnikol, E. 135, 694
Barr, J. 128
Barr, R. R. 230, 411
Barrett, C. K. 418, 465, 538, 824
Bartels, K. H. 147
Barth, C. 108, 233, 411
Barth, G. 492
Barth, K. 102, 105, 108, 112, 135, 198, 206,
238, 241, 345, 351, 363, 368, 387, 412, 413,
414, 418, 446, 495, 527, 543, 604, 605, 608,
612, 614, 615, 629, 630, 632, 643, 651, 664,
672, 706, 709, 710, 714, 716, 717, 720, 753,
773, 824, 826, 828
Barth, M. 35, 43, 47, 48, 65, 135, 168, 174,
194, 225, 235, 241, 296, 299, 412, 431, 434,
451, 526, 558, 643
Bartsch, H.-W. 124, 404
Baruch (Bar) 20, 111, 245, 285, 462, 538,
774, 792, 795
Basilides 13, 37, 196, 202
Basilius (the Great) of Caesarea 68, 380
Batey, R. A. 68, 198, 641, 642, 669, 687,
692, 708, 728, 740, 741, 826
Bauer, J. B. 727
Bauer, W. (WBLex) 68, 72, 78, 79, 88, 136,
142, 158, 216, 222, 227, 257, 287, 330,
367, 368, 378, 429, 444, 448, 449, 464, 479,
485, 501, 561, 567, 570, 573, 576, 604, 608,
613, 614, 644, 647, 667, 721, 760, 761, 765,
773, 785, 797, 813, 814
Bauernfeind, O. 770, 787, 790, 828

TOPICS

Aeon. *See* Time, aeon
Aliens. *See* Strangers
Angels. *See* Principalities and Powers
Anthropology 126, 186–92, 175f., 198, 252, 357, 369–71, 384–94, 508f., 518, 523, 528, 540f., 546, 640, 707f., 725–27, 789, 791. *Cf.* God, image of; Husband and Wife; Humanity; Man, "inner man," etc.
Anthropomorphism and Theomorphism 118, 474, 559, 569, 588
Anti-Semitism 43, 217, 328, 502, 660
Apologetics 30, 166, 179, 526
Apostle 65, 141, 145, 163, 314–17, 331–32, 335, 356–63, 453
Aristocracy. *See* Elite
Asceticism 15, 17, 41, 634, 661f., 728, 742
Astrology 601
Atheism 260
Author of Ephesians. *See* Ephesians, author
Authority 164, 362–63, 383, 395, 426, 430, 452, 499, 605, 645f., 668, 677, 780

Baptism 45, 124, 132, 135–43, 149f., 205, 234, 305, 385, 466–70, 481f., 521, 532, 543f., 574, 624f., 635, 690–99, 736. *Cf.* Eucharist; Sacraments
Beauty, aesthetics, art 226, 674f., 682, 795
Blessing 22n., 71–79, 101–3, 110, 118, 243, 726, 735, 810–17
Body. *See* Jesus Christ, and the church: head and body
Bridegroom and bride. *See* Jesus Christ, and the church: bridegroom and bride
Building 22, 34, 44, 270–74, 314f., 375f., 440, 450f. *Cf.* Temple

Canaanite elements 148, 169n., 353, 380n., 473f., 528, 739, 768
Canon 29, 37, 362, 575
Casuistry 525, 550, 593, 605, 647, 700
Catalogues 177, 224, 427, 454, 458, 521, 550–52, 590, 789, 795f.
Catechism 532, 551
Catholicism, early 35, 46, 596
Celibacy 700. *Cf.* Marriage
Charisma 32, 43, 101f., 340, 430, 435, 439, 449f., 598, 719, 733
Charity 517f. *Cf.* Ethics
Children 441f., 491f., 555, 582, 660. *Cf.* Procreation
Christology. *See* Jesus Christ
Church; Ecclesiology 17–18, 33, 35, 56, 91–92, 126, 153, 206, 209, 243, 275–76, 296, 304, 307–25, 347, 363–66, 375–76, 384, 386, 596, 620, 627, 646f., 668f.
  body of Christ, head and body. *See* Jesus Christ, and the church
  bride of Christ. *See* Jesus Christ, and the church: bridegroom and bride
  clergy and laity 136, 147, 290, 306, 339, 311–13, 359, 430, 435, 477–84, 520, 727
  community 183, 191, 207, 219, 269, 276, 309–11, 358, 388–95, 493f., 537f., 807f.
  constitution 435, 451, 477f., 483f.
  discipline 560, 572, 585, 592–98, 756

hierarchy, bishops, papacy 158, 437–39, 481f. *Cf.* Church, clergy and laity
holiness. *See* Church, saints; Sanctification
house of God. *See* Temple
infallibility 164, 530, 677. *Cf.* Authority
intercession 58f., 108, 145–210, 322, 348, 368–74, 377, 482, 584f., 778f., 782–84, 806–8. *Cf.* Jesus Christ, intecession
and Israel. *See* Israel
Jews and Gentiles. *See* Jews, and Gentiles
limits 471, 495–503. *Cf.* Church, unity; Church, and world
migrating people of God 25, 485–87, 493, 495f.
militant and triumphant 382, 444f., 479
mission. *See* Church, and world
pre-existence 111f., 724f., 735n.
priestly function 482–85. *Cf.* Church, intercession; Ministry
saints 66, 99, 147, 151, 157, 160, 162–64, 177, 233f., 238, 269f., 313, 322, 335, 340, 395, 449, 451, 454f., 459, 477–84, 510, 604, 649, 687–91, 762, 778, 784, 800, 814
second Christ 158f., 193, 197, 296, 494, 619f., 641, 707
servant. *See* Church, and world; Servant
tertium genus 303, 310
unity, oneness. *See* Unity
universal and local 451f.
and world 119, 135, 198f., 206, 209, 242, 281f., 321, 322–66, 376, 388, 444f., 462, 479–81, 596, 711–13, 800, 806–8
Circumcision 32, 136, 247, 254–58, 279–82
Clothing 138, 505f., 532, 539–45, 681f., 714f., 761f., 765, 766f., 797, 798. *Cf.* Conversion; Renewal
Confession; Creeds 6, 96, 105, 112, 153f., 179, 189, 269n., 303, 331f., 429, 444, 462–72, 488, 505, 533, 557
Conscience 606, 693, 757
Conversion 132, 234, 597. *Cf.* Renewal
Cosmology. *See* Cosmos, all things
Cosmos, all things 89, 91f., 109f., 156f., 175–79, 381, 429, 434, 471, 589
Covenant 74f., 133, 197–99, 208, 218f., 225, 239, 258, 279f., 334, 455, 556, 568, 668–72, 689, 693, 746, 749–53
Creation. *See* God, creator
Creativity 691
Crusades 763, 785–87
Cultus. *See* Worship

Death 169, 171, 182, 211–13, 232–36, 307
Decency 560, 561f., 631f.
Deification 387, 556, 686f., 722
Determinism 87f., 105–9, 171, 346f., 552, 602f. *Cf.* Faith, activity and passivity; God, will
Demons. *See* Devil; Principalities and powers
Devil; Satan; Belial; Beliar 171, 214, 228–32, 252, 488, 514f., 538, 546f., 763–65, 772–74, 801. *Cf.* Principalities and powers
Didache 54, 426. *Cf.* Teachers
Divorce 657, 671, 703, 733

846   INDEX

Hedonism 756
Hell 433f., 595, 774
Hellenistic elements 26, 166f., 172, 193f.,
    230, 265, 292, 340, 387n., 390, 499,
    588–91, 655–62, 726n., 740f.
Heresy, opponents of Paul 442f., 565f. Cf.
    Ephesians, addressees
Hermeneutics 54, 288f., 382, 472–77, 641–
    47, 696f., 741. Cf. Old Testament;
    Sensus plenior; Typology
Hierarchy. See Church, hierarchy
Hieros Gamos 197, 740–42, 748. Cf.
    Marriage; Sexuality
History 98f., 102, 106, 128, 345, 387f., 534f.,
    741–43, 755
Holiness. See Sanctification
Hope 116, 129, 150f., 259, 322–25, 429,
    484–96, 806. Cf. Eschatology;
    Inheritance
Humanity 358, 388–94, 719, 737, 752f.
Humility 339f., 379, 427, 458
Humor 360, 537, 781
Husband and wife 607–753. Cf. Marriage
Hymns 6–10, 21, 54, 96, 99f., 114, 116n.,
    137, 153f., 217f., 261, 267, 268, 315,
    360, 429, 435, 473, 484, 524, 557, 574f.,
    582–86, 616, 622f., 627f., 690, 702

Idealism 700
Idolatry 526f., 561, 563, 801
Imagery 238f., 268, 270f., 272f., 282–87,
    307, 337, 371, 373, 434, 440, 445, 486,
    531f., 539–43, 567f., 575, 761–77, 787–
    93
Imitation 555f., 588–92. Cf. God, image of
Immortality 686, 813
Indicative and imperative 53, 426, 453–57,
    522, 620
Individualism 119, 168, 176, 262, 273, 278,
    310, 384f., 389, 427f., 446, 493f., 519,
    677, 705
Infallibility. See Church, infallibility
Inheritance 19, 80f., 93, 96f., 117, 151, 337,
    564
Initiation. See Baptism; Circumcision
Inspiration 148, 162–64, 315, 362f., 585f.,
    592, 608, 780
Institutions and structures 144, 174f., 180f.,
    703. Cf. Sociology
Intercession. See Church, intercession; Jesus
    Christ, intercession
Interpolation 484, 505
Israel 66, 73, 108, 109, 115, 132f., 151, 207f.,
    233, 235f., 245–47, 255–58, 268f., 270,
    315, 485–87, 526f., 669–72, 693f. Cf.
    Jews
    land of 257

Jerusalem 12, 270, 320f., 357. Cf. Zion
Jesus Christ
    and Adam 537–40, 544, 552, 654, 722f.,
    726
    administrator 86–88, 108, 127–29, 273, 328
    blood, cross, sacrifice 9, 25, 83, 109, 281f.,
    291–305, 312f., 525, 557–60, 591, 671,
    684–88, 698f.
    and the church: bridegroom and bride 34,
    111, 295f., 392, 485–96, 623–29, 668–700
    and the church: head and body 32, 90–92,
    153f., 156–59, 185f., 192–99, 209, 268,
    337, 440, 443–47, 448–50, 512f., 546,
    614f., 617, 620, 635–37, 639

and the church, keystone 271, 314–20,
    323, 445, 668
cosmic rule 22, 25, 33, 42, 91f., 103, 109f.,
    153f., 156f., 165, 168, 170f., 175f., 182,
    380, 434
creator 295f.
descent and ascent 237, 431–34, 472–77
divinity. See Jesus Christ, son of God
earthly ministry 85, 353, 535–36
faith of 68, 224f., 489
"in Christ" 28, 56, 68–71, 82f., 107–9,
    132, 195, 213, 222, 250, 268, 272f., 295,
    296, 347, 385, 426, 557, 710, 714, 760f.
"in us" 370f., 388–92
incarnation 193, 197, 230, 298, 302–5,
    320, 434, 533–35, 696, 722f.
intercession, mediation 25, 58f., 300f.,
    344, 363, 680, 746–49, 784, 796. Cf.
    Church, intercession; Prayer
logos 112, 200, 302, 534f., 590, 674, 696f.
Lord 72f., 486, 497, 499, 611f.
messiah 30, 66, 74f., 92, 108, 126, 132,
    178f., 207, 220, 256, 258, 299, 302f.,
    306, 321f., 440, 679, 768, 771, 772, 775,
    777, 784, 788, 796
parousia 35, 116, 319, 349, 484–96, 638,
    731, 805f.
pre-existence 25, 109–12, 256, 293n., 347,
    533. Cf. Pre-existence
presence 209, 433, 434
priest 266–68, 298–305, 312f., 558. Cf.
    Jesus Christ, intercession
resurrection 23, 43f., 143, 152f., 164–70
son of God 82f., 88, 110, 488f., 533f., 564f.
son of man 207, 333f.
"totus Christus" 494n., 724
two natures. See Jesus Christ, incarnation
"with Christ" 220, 385, 544
Jews 43, 132f., 216f., 245, 248, 254f., 592f.,
    656n., 693f., 725–29. Cf. Anti-Semitism;
    Israel; Jews, and Gentiles
    and Gentiles 30, 33f., 42f., 47f., 92, 127,
    130–33, 144, 165, 207, 220, 225, 235f.,
    239f., 291–307, 337, 354f., 378, 382–84,
    394f., 502, 526f., 670, 802
Joy 81, 140f., 307, 313f., 360, 531, 548f.,
    562f., 671f., 702, 713n., 715, 726, 783. Cf.
    Praise; Singing
"Judaizers" 43, 244–48, 310
Judgment; Last judgment; Lawsuit 238–42,
    249, 592–98, 665–67, 756, 774. Cf. Wrath
Justification 34, 36, 45–48, 221, 244, 248–50,
    266, 542, 546, 553, 559, 577, 676. Cf.
    Righteousness

Kerygma. See Gospel
Kneeling 377–79
Knowledge 14, 20, 84f., 119–28, 135,
    148f., 163, 187, 330f., 333f., 345, 356,
    363f., 372f., 375, 393–95, 397, 579f.,
    599, 604–6. Cf. Gnosticism

Labor 515–18
Laity. See Church, clergy and laity
Law 42, 83, 110, 119, 130, 181, 227, 239,
    241, 244–48, 284f., 287–91, 390, 453–
    57, 459, 475f., 527, 593n., 631, 720, 732,
    791
    abolished 264f., 306
    antinomianism 42, 244, 286, 306, 661
    canon law 468, 596
    curse 289f.
    legalism 244–48, 550–53, 572, 585, 597,
    631, 701, 704, 727, 732, 738, 749f.

KEY TO THE TEXT